# 2014-2015
# EVANGELICAL SUNDAY SCHOOL LESSON COMMENTARY

**SIXTY-THIRD ANNUAL VOLUME**
Based on the
Pentecostal-Charismatic Bible Lesson Series

### Editorial Staff
Lance Colkmire—Editor
Tammy Hatfield—Editorial Assistant
Terry Hart—General Director of Publications

### Lesson Exposition Writers

| | |
|---|---|
| Lance Colkmire | Homer G. Rhea |
| Jerald Daffe | Joshua F. Rice |
| Thomas Doolittle | Richard Keith Whitt |
| Lee Roy Martin | Sabord Woods |

Published by

**PATHWAY PRESS**          Cleveland, Tennessee

*To place an order, call 1-800-553-8506.
*To contact the editor, call 423-478-7597 or
email at *Lance_Colkmire@pathwaypress.org*.

Lesson treatments in the *Evangelical Sunday School Lesson Commentary* for 2014-2015 are based on the outlines of the Pentecostal-Charismatic Bible Lesson Series prepared by the Pentecostal-Charismatic Curriculum Commission.

Copyright 2014

PATHWAY PRESS, Cleveland, Tennessee

ISBN: 978-1-59684-810-8 Hardbound
ISBN: 978-1-59684-811-5 Large Print

ISSN: 1555-5801

Printed in the United States of America

## TABLE OF CONTENTS

Introduction to the 2013-2014 Commentary . . . . . . . . . . . . . . . . . . . . . . . 7
Using the 2014-2015 Commentary . . . . . . . . . . . . . . . . . . . . . . . . . . . . . 8
Scripture Texts Used in Lesson Exposition . . . . . . . . . . . . . . . . . . . . . . 9
Scripture Texts Used in Golden Text Challenge . . . . . . . . . . . . . . . . . . 11
Acknowledgments . . . . . . . . . . . . . . . . . . . . . . . . . . . . . . . . . . . . . . . . 13
Lesson Series (2013-2020) . . . . . . . . . . . . . . . . . . . . . . . . . . . . . . . . . 15

### FALL QUARTER LESSONS
Introduction to Fall Quarter Lessons . . . . . . . . . . . . . . . . . . . . . . . . . . . 16

#### UNIT ONE THEME—GREAT EVENTS IN GENESIS
1. September 7, Joseph the Dreamer . . . . . . . . . . . . . . . . . . . . . . . . . . 17
2. September 14, Joseph the Prince . . . . . . . . . . . . . . . . . . . . . . . . . . 28
3. September 21, Caleb the Brave . . . . . . . . . . . . . . . . . . . . . . . . . . . 39
4. September 28, Abigail the Wise . . . . . . . . . . . . . . . . . . . . . . . . . . . 51
5. October 5, Elisha the Prophet . . . . . . . . . . . . . . . . . . . . . . . . . . . . . 62
6. October 12, John the Baptist . . . . . . . . . . . . . . . . . . . . . . . . . . . . . 73
7. October 19, Philip the Evangelist . . . . . . . . . . . . . . . . . . . . . . . . . . 85

#### UNIT TWO THEME—PARABLES OF JESUS (Stories Jesus Told)
8. October 26, Story About Forgiveness . . . . . . . . . . . . . . . . . . . . . . . 96
9. November 2, Stories About the Kingdom . . . . . . . . . . . . . . . . . . . . 106
10. November 9, Stories About Prayer . . . . . . . . . . . . . . . . . . . . . . . . 116
11. November 16, Stories About Stewardship . . . . . . . . . . . . . . . . . . . 126
12. November 23, Stories About Finding the Lost . . . . . . . . . . . . . . . 135
13. November 30, Stories About Responding to Christ . . . . . . . . . . . 146

### WINTER QUARTER LESSONS
Introduction to Winter Quarter Lessons . . . . . . . . . . . . . . . . . . . . . . . . 156

#### UNIT ONE THEME—LAW AND GRACE IN THE NEW TESTAMENT
1. December 7, Why Do We Need Grace? . . . . . . . . . . . . . . . . . . . . . 157
2. December 14, Saved by Grace . . . . . . . . . . . . . . . . . . . . . . . . . . . 166
3. December 21, The Savior Is Born (Christmas) . . . . . . . . . . . . . . . . 175
4. December 28, Grace Demands Righteous Living . . . . . . . . . . . . . 185
5. January 4, Dead, Yielded, and Free . . . . . . . . . . . . . . . . . . . . . . . 194
6. January 11, What Does God's Grace Promise? . . . . . . . . . . . . . . 204

#### UNIT TWO THEME—GOD'S MORAL LAW (Genesis-Deuteronomy)
7. January 18, Hold Human Life Sacred . . . . . . . . . . . . . . . . . . . . . . 213
8. January 25, Worship Only the Lord God . . . . . . . . . . . . . . . . . . . . 223
9. February 1, Honor God's Name . . . . . . . . . . . . . . . . . . . . . . . . . . 233
10. February 8, Justice for All . . . . . . . . . . . . . . . . . . . . . . . . . . . . . . 243
11. February 15, Be Sexually Pure . . . . . . . . . . . . . . . . . . . . . . . . . . 253
12. February 22, How Should We Treat Others? . . . . . . . . . . . . . . . . 263

**SPRING QUARTER LESSONS**
  Introduction to Spring Quarter Lessons .......................... 272

  UNIT ONE THEME—LIFE OF SAMUEL
    1. March 1, God Calls Young Samuel ........................... 273
    2. March 8, Samuel's Ministry Established ...................... 282
    3. March 15, Israel Demands a King ............................ 291
    4. March 22, Samuel, Example of Integrity ...................... 301
    5. March 29, Disobedience to God Brings Judgment .............. 311
    6. April 5, Empty Tomb; Living Savior (Easter) .................. 321
    7. April 12, Samuel Anoints David King ......................... 330

  UNIT TWO THEME—THE EARLY CHURCH (Acts, Part I)
    8. April 19, Life in the Early Church ............................ 339
    9. April 26, Preaching, Power, and Perseverance ................ 347
    10. May 3, Living and Dying for Christ .......................... 355
    11. May 10, From Persecutor to Preacher ....................... 364
    12. May 17, Including the Excluded ............................. 372
    13. May 24, Baptism in the Holy Spirit (Pentecost) ............... 380
    14. May 31, The Church Prevails ............................... 389

**SUMMER QUARTER LESSONS**
  Introduction to Summer Quarter Lessons ......................... 397

  UNIT ONE THEME—DIFFERENT TYPES OF PSALMS
    1. June 7, Psalms of Lament ................................... 398
    2. June 14, Psalms of Thanksgiving ............................ 408
    3. June 21, Psalms of Praise .................................. 418
    4. June 28, Wisdom Psalms ................................... 427
    5. July 5, Covenant Psalms .................................... 436
    6. July 12, Psalms of Ascent ................................... 445
    7. July 19, Psalms of Divine Justice ............................ 454
    8. July 26, Messianic Psalms .................................. 463

  UNIT TWO THEME—PRACTICAL CHRISTIANITY (James)
    9. August 2, Encouragement for Dealing With Trials .............. 468
    10. August 9, Christian Faith in Action .......................... 482
    11. August 16, Tame Your Tongue .............................. 491
    12. August 23, Do Not Live Worldly ............................. 500
    13. August 30, Cultivate Right Attitudes ......................... 509

## INTRODUCTION TO THE 2014-2015 COMMENTARY

The *Evangelical Sunday School Lesson Commentary* contains in a single volume a full study of the Sunday school lessons for the months beginning with September 2014 and running through August 2015. The twelve months of lessons draw from both the Old Testament and the New Testament in an effort to provide balance and establish relationship between these distinct but inspired writings. The lessons in this 2014-2015 volume are drawn from the second year of a seven-year series, which will be completed in August 2020. (The series is printed in full on page 15 of this volume.)

The lessons for the *Evangelical Commentary* are based on the Pentecostal-Charismatic Bible Lesson Series Outlines, prepared by the Pentecostal-Charismatic Curriculum Commission. (The Pentecostal-Charismatic Curriculum Commission is a member of the National Association of Evangelicals.) The lessons in this volume, taken together with the other annual volumes of lessons in the cycle, provide a valuable commentary on a wide range of biblical subjects. Each quarter is divided into two or more units of study.

The 2014-2015 commentary is the work of a team of Christian scholars and writers who have developed the volume under the supervision of Pathway Press. All the major writers represent a team of ministers committed to a strictly evangelical interpretation of the Scriptures. The guiding theological principles of this commentary are expressed in the following statement of faith:

1. WE BELIEVE the Bible to be the inspired, the only infallible, authoritative Word of God.

2. WE BELIEVE that there is one God, eternally existing in three persons: Father, Son, and Holy Spirit.

3. WE BELIEVE in the deity of our Lord Jesus Christ, in His virgin birth, in His sinless life, in His miracles, in His vicarious and atoning death through His shed blood, in His bodily resurrection, in His ascension to the right hand of the Father, and in His personal return in power and glory.

4. WE BELIEVE that for the salvation of lost and sinful men, personal reception of the Lord Jesus Christ and regeneration by the Holy Spirit are absolutely essential.

5. WE BELIEVE in the present ministry of the Holy Spirit by whose cleansing and indwelling the Christian is enabled to live a godly life.

6. WE BELIEVE in the personal return of the Lord Jesus Christ.

7. WE BELIEVE in the resurrection of both the saved and the lost—they that are saved, unto the resurrection of life; and they that are lost, unto the resurrection of damnation.

8. WE BELIEVE in the spiritual unity of believers in our Lord Jesus Christ.

## USING THE 2014-2015 COMMENTARY

The *Evangelical Sunday School Lesson Commentary* for 2014-2015 is presented to the reader with the hope that it will become his or her weekly companion through the months ahead.

Quarterly unit themes for the 2014-2015 volume are as follows:
- Fall Quarter—Unit One: "Great Stories of the Bible"; Unit Two: "Parables of Jesus (Stories Jesus Told)"
- Winter Quarter—Unit One: "Law and Grace in the New Testament"; Unit Two: "God's Moral Law (Genesis-Deuteronomy)"
- Spring Quarter—Unit One: "Life of Samuel"; Unit Two: "The Early Church (Acts, Part I)"
- Summer Quarter—Unit One: "Different Types of Psalms"; Unit Two: "Practical Christianity (James)"

The lesson sequence used in this volume is prepared by the Pentecostal-Charismatic Curriculum Commission. The specific material used in developing each lesson is written and edited under the guidance of the editorial staff of Pathway Press.

INTRODUCTION: The opening of each week's lesson features a one-page introduction. It provides background information that sets the stage for the lesson.

CONTEXT: A time and place is given for most lessons. Where there is a wide range of ideas regarding the exact time or place, we favor the majority opinion of conservative scholars.

PRINTED TEXT: The printed text is the body of Scripture designated each week for verse-by-verse study in the classroom. Drawing on the study text the teacher delves into this printed text, exploring its content with the students.

CENTRAL TRUTH and FOCUS: The central truth states the single unifying principle that the expositors attempted to clarify in each lesson. The focus describes the overall lesson goal.

EXPOSITION and LESSON OUTLINE: The heart of this commentary—and probably the heart of the teacher's instruction each week—is the exposition of the printed text. This exposition material is organized in outline form, which indicates how the material is to be divided for study.

QUOTATIONS and ILLUSTRATIONS: Each section of every lesson contains illustrations and sayings the teacher can use in connecting the lesson to daily living.

QUESTIONS are printed throughout the lesson to help students explore the Scripture text and how it speaks to believers today.

CONCLUSION: Each lesson ends with a brief conclusion that makes a summarizing statement.

The GOLDEN TEXT CHALLENGE for each week is a brief reflection on that single verse. The word *challenge* is used because its purpose is to help students apply this key verse to their life.

DAILY DEVOTIONS: Daily Bible readings are included for the teacher to use in his or her own devotions throughout the week, as well as to share with members of their class.

## SCRIPTURE TEXTS USED IN LESSON EXPOSITION

**Genesis**
| | |
|---|---|
| 2:18, 23-24 | February 15 |
| 9:5-6 | January 18 |
| 37:3-11, 23-33 | September 7 |
| 39:1-10, 19-23 | September 14 |
| 41:14-16, 28-31, 38-40 | September 14 |

**Exodus**
| | |
|---|---|
| 18:25-26 | February 8 |
| 20:2-6 | January 25 |
| 20:7 | February 1 |
| 20:13 | January 18 |
| 20:14 | February 15 |
| 20:15 | February 22 |
| 22:1, 25 | February 22 |
| 22:28 | February 1 |

**Leviticus**
| | |
|---|---|
| 6:2, 4-5 | February 22 |
| 18:3, 24-25, 30 | February 15 |
| 19:12 | February 1 |
| 19:15 | February 8 |
| 19:16 | January 18 |
| 20:1-3, 9-10, 22 | January 18 |
| 20:22 | January 18 |
| 20:23-24, 26 | January 18 |
| 20:26 | January 18 |
| 24:16 | February 1 |

**Numbers**
| | |
|---|---|
| 13:17-20, 27-33 | September 21 |
| 14:6-9, 20-24 | September 21 |
| 15:30-31 | February 1 |
| 35:31, 33 | February 18 |

**Deuteronomy**
| | |
|---|---|
| 4:15-16, 23-24, 29, 31-32, 35, 39 | January 25 |
| 15:7-8 | February 22 |
| 16:18-20 | February 8 |
| 17:8-9 | February 8 |
| 19:2-3, 10 | January 18 |
| 19:13 | January 18 |
| 19:15-16, 19 | February 8 |
| 21:7, 9 | January 18 |
| 24:5 | February 15 |
| 24:15, 19 | February 22 |
| 25:1 | February 8 |
| 25:15 | February 22 |

**Joshua**
| | |
|---|---|
| 14:9-13 | September 21 |

**1 Samuel**
| | |
|---|---|
| 7:1-17 | March 8 |
| 8:1-11, 19-20 | March 15 |
| 9:15-17 | March 15 |
| 10:1, 9-10, 20-24 | March 15 |
| 11:12-15 | March 22 |
| 12:7, 13-25 | March 22 |
| 13:6-14 | March 29 |
| 15:2-3, 9-11, 17-22 | March 29 |
| 15:34-35 | April 12 |
| 16:1-23 | April 12 |
| 25:4-5, 10-18, 32-39 | September 28 |

**2 Samuel**
| | |
|---|---|
| 12:14 | February 1 |

**1 Kings**
| | |
|---|---|
| 19:19-21 | October 5 |

**2 Kings**
| | |
|---|---|
| 2:13-15, 21-22 | October 5 |
| 4:38-41 | October 5 |
| 13:18-21 | October 5 |

**Psalms**
| | |
|---|---|
| 1:1-6 | June 28 |
| 2:2-4, 6-9, 12 | July 26 |
| 4:1, 6-8 | June 7 |
| 17:1-3, 7-9, 15 | June 7 |
| 22:1-2, 14-18 | July 26 |
| 32:1-2, 7, 10-11 | June 14 |
| 33:1, 6-9, 11, 14-15 | June 21 |
| 35:1-4, 10 | July 19 |
| 36:1-12 | June 28 |
| 66:1-5, 8-9, 20 | June 21 |
| 78:1-6 | July 5 |
| 80:1-7 | June 7 |
| 81:8-13 | July 5 |
| 89:1-7 | July 5 |
| 103:1-5, 22 | June 21 |
| 109:1-3, 26-27 | July 19 |
| 110:1-4 | July 26 |
| 116:1-5, 17-19 | June 14 |
| 118:1-7, 28-29 | June 14 |
| 121:1-8 | July 12 |

## Psalms (cont.)
| | |
|---|---|
| 122:1-9 | July 12 |
| 127:1, 3-5 | June 28 |
| 128:1-4 | June 28 |
| 130:5-8 | July 12 |
| 131:1-3 | July 12 |
| 140:1-7, 12-13 | July 19 |

## Proverbs
| | |
|---|---|
| 5:3-5, 8, 11, 18-19, 21 | February 15 |
| 14:31 | February 1 |

## Matthew
| | |
|---|---|
| 3:4-11 | October 12 |
| 5:34, 37 | February 1 |
| 13:24-25, 36-43 | November 2 |
| 14:1-9 | October 12 |
| 18:21-35 | October 26 |
| 20:1-16 | November 30 |
| 21:28-32 | November 2 |

## Mark
| | |
|---|---|
| 4:26-32 | November 2 |

## Luke
| | |
|---|---|
| 1:62-64, 76-80 | October 12 |
| 2:1, 4-12, 22, 25-32 | December 21 |
| 7:28 | October 12 |
| 11:5-13 | November 9 |
| 12:16-21 | November 16 |
| 15:4-13, 17-19, 21-24 | November 23 |
| 16:1-13 | November 16 |
| 17:3-4 | October 26 |
| 18:1-14 | November 9 |

## John
| | |
|---|---|
| 1:14, 17 | December 7 |
| 14:15-24 | November 30 |
| 20:1-2, 6-9, 11-16, 19-21 | April 5 |

## Acts
| | |
|---|---|
| 1:4-5 | May 24 |
| 2:1-8, 12-18, 39 | May 24 |
| 2:42-47 | April 19 |
| 3:12-13, 19 | April 26 |
| 4:23-24, 29-31 | April 19 |
| 5:1-5 | April 26 |
| 5:12-16 | April 19 |
| 5:18-21, 40-41 | April 26 |
| 6:1-3 | May 3 |
| 6:3, 5 | October 19 |

## Acts (cont.)
| | |
|---|---|
| 6:5-6 | May 3 |
| 6:7 | October 19 |
| 6:8-10, 12-13 | May 3 |
| 7:54-57, 59-60 | May 3 |
| 8:5-7, 12-13, 26-31, 35-39 | October 19 |
| 9:3-7, 10-11, 15-18, 20-22 | May 10 |
| 10:3-5, 11-14, 19-20, 34-35, 39-40, 42-45 | May 17 |
| 12:1-3, 5, 7, 9, 11-14, 16-17, 21, 23-24 | May 31 |
| 21:8-9 | October 19 |

## Romans
| | |
|---|---|
| 2:23-24 | February 1 |
| 3:19-24 | December 14 |
| 4:13-14, 16, 23-25 | January 11 |
| 5:1-2 | December 7 |
| 5:12-21 | December 28 |
| 6:1-4 | December 28 |
| 6:5-18, 20-23 | January 4 |
| 7:9-11 | December 14 |
| 8:2-3 | December 14 |

## 2 Corinthians
| | |
|---|---|
| 9:12-13 | February 1 |

## Galatians
| | |
|---|---|
| 2:20-21 | December 14 |
| 3:19, 21-22, 24, 26, 29 | January 11 |
| 4:4-7 | January 11 |
| 5:1-6 | December 7 |

## Ephesians
| | |
|---|---|
| 1:3, 5, 7, 10 | December 7 |
| 2:5, 8-9 | December 7 |

## 1 Timothy
| | |
|---|---|
| 1:15-16 | December 14 |

## James
| | |
|---|---|
| 1:2-6, 12-17, 19-25 | August 2 |
| 2:1-17, 26 | August 9 |
| 3:1-18 | August 16 |
| 4:1-17 | August 23 |
| 5:1-7, 9-11, 13-16, 19-20 | August 30 |

## SCRIPTURE TEXTS USED IN GOLDEN TEXT CHALLENGE

**Genesis**
9:6 — January 18

**Exodus**
20:7 — February 1

**Deuteronomy**
4:39 — January 25

**Joshua**
14:8 — September 21

**1 Samuel**
3:10 — March 1
3:20 — March 8
8:7 — March 15
12:23 — March 22
15:22 — January 30
16:13 — April 12
25:3 — September 28

**Psalms**
2:7 — July 26
17:1 — June 7
37:5 — September 7
66:8 — June 21
78:5 — July 5
118:1 — June 14
122:1 — July 12
128:1 — June 28
140:12 — July 19

**Proverbs**
12:18 — August 16
16:9 — September 14

**Micah**
6:8 — February 8

**Matthew**
6:14-15 — October 26

**Mark**
16:6 — April 5

**Luke**
2:11 — December 21
6:31 — February 22
7:27 — October 12
15:10 — November 23

**John**
3:3 — November 2

**Acts**
2:39 — May 24
2:42 — April 19
5:32 — April 26
6:8 — May 3
8:6 — October 19
9:15 — May 10
10:34-35 — May 17
12:24 — May 31

**Romans**
6:4 — December 28
6:11 — January 4

**1 Corinthians**
4:2 — November 16
7:2 — February 15

**Galatians**
4:7 — January 11

**Ephesians**
2:4-5 — December 7

**1 Timothy**
1:15 — December 14

**2 Timothy**
1:9 — October 5

**James**
1:12 — August 2
2:8 — August 9
4:7 — August 23
5:8 — August 30

**1 John**
5:14-15 — November 9

**Revelation**
3:20 — November 30

## ACKNOWLEDGMENTS

Many books and Web sites have been used in the research that has gone into the 2014-2015 *Evangelical Commentary*. The major books that have been used are listed below.

### Bibles
*English Standard Version* (*ESV*), Good News Publishers, Wheaton, Illinois
*King James Version*, Oxford University Press, Oxford, England
*Life Application Study Bible*, Zondervan Publishing House, Grand Rapids
*New American Standard Bible* (*NASB*), The Lockman Foundation, La Habra, California
*New English Translation*, bible.org
*New International Version* (*NIV*), Zondervan Publishing House, Grand Rapids
*New King James Version* (*NKJV*), Thomas Nelson Publishers, Nashville
*New Living Translation* (*NLT*), Tyndale House Publishers, Carol Stream, Illinois
*New Spirit-Filled Life Bible*, Thomas Nelson Publishers, Nashville
*The Amplified Bible* (*Amp.*), The Lockman Foundation, La Habra, California
*The Message* (*TM*), NavPress, Colorado Springs
*The Nelson Study Bible*, Thomas Nelson Publishers, Nashville
*Word in Life Study Bible*, Thomas Nelson Publishers, Nashville

### Commentaries
*Adam Clarke's Commentary*, Abingdon-Cokesbury, Nashville
*Barnes' Notes*, BibleSoft.com
*Commentaries on the Old Testament* (Keil & Delitzsch), Eerdmans Publishing Co., Grand Rapids
*Ellicott's Bible Commentary*, Zondervan Publishing House, Grand Rapids
*Genesis: Beginning and Blessing*, R. Kent Hughes, Crossway Books, Memphis, Tennessee
*Jamieson, Fausset and Brown Commentary*, BibleSoft.com
*Life Application Commentary*, Tyndale House, Carol Stream, Illinois
*Matthew Henry's Commentary*, BibleSoft.com
*The Bible Exposition Commentary: New Testament*, Warren Wiersbe, Victor Books, Colorado Springs
*The Bible Knowledge Commentary*, David C. Cook, Colorado Springs
*The Epistle to the Romans*, John Murray, Eerdmans Publishing Co., Grand Rapids
*The Expositor's Bible Commentary*, Zondervan Publishing House, Grand Rapids
*The Greatest Letter Ever Written*, French L. Arrington, Pathway Press, Cleveland, Tennessee
*The Pulpit Commentary*, Eerdmans Publishing Co., Grand Rapids
*The Wesleyan Commentary*, Eerdmans Publishing Co., Grand Rapids
*The Wycliffe Bible Commentary*, Moody Press, Chicago
*Tyndale Old Testament Commentaries*, Nashville, Tyndale House
*Zondervan NIV Bible Commentary*, Zondervan Publishing House, Grand Rapids

### Illustrations
*Quotable Quotations*, Scripture Press Publications, Wheaton, Illinois

*The Encyclopedia of Religious Quotations*, Fleming H. Revell Co., Old Tappan, New Jersey
*The Face of God*, *The Hands of God*, and *The Heart of God*, Woodrow Kroll, Elm Hill Books, Nashville
*Who Said That?*, George Sweeting, Moody Press, Chicago

**Reference Books**
*A Greek-English Lexicon of the New Testament*, Joseph Henry Thayer, Hendrickson Publishers, Peabody, Massachusetts
*Biblical Characters From the Old and New Testament*, Alexander Whyte, Kregel Publications, Grand Rapids
*Pronouncing Bible Names*, Broadman & Holman Publishers, Nashville
*The Complete Word Study Old Testament*, AMG Publishers, Chattanooga, Tennessee
*The Interpreter's Dictionary of the Bible*, Abingdon Press, Nashville
*The Moody Handbook of Theology*, Paul Enns, Moody Press, Chicago
*Vincent's Word Studies in the New Testament*, W. E. Vincent, Hendrickson Publishers, Peabody, Massachusetts
*Vine's Complete Expository Dictionary of Old and New Testament Words*, W. E. Vine, Thomas Nelson, Nashville
Wuest's Word Studies From the Greek New Testament, Kenneth Wuest, Eerdman's Publishing Co., Grand Rapids

# Pentecostal-Charismatic Bible Lesson Series (2013-2020)

| Fall Quarter<br>September, October, November | Winter Quarter<br>December, January, February | Spring Quarter<br>March, April, May | Summer Quarter<br>June, July, August |
|---|---|---|---|
| **Fall 2013**<br>1 • Great Events in Genesis<br>2 • Discourses in Matthew | **Winter 2013-14**<br>1 • Songs and Hymns in the New Testament<br>2 • Wisdom From Ecclesiastes & Proverbs | **Spring 2014**<br>1 • Hope in the Book of Isaiah<br>2 • Principles for Christian Living (1, 2, 3 John) | **Summer 2014**<br>1 • The Exodus<br>2 • The Doctrine of Salvation |
| **Fall 2014**<br>1 • Great Stories of the Bible<br>2 • Parables of Jesus (Stories Jesus Told) | **Winter 2014-15**<br>1 • Law and Grace in the New Testament<br>2 • Universal Moral Law (Genesis–Deuteronomy) | **Spring 2015**<br>1 • Life of Samuel<br>2 • The Early Church (Acts, Part 1) | **Summer 2015**<br>1 • Different Types of Psalms<br>2 • Practical Christianity (James) |
| **Fall 2015**<br>1 • The Book of Joshua<br>2 • Mark (Jesus in Action) | **Winter 2015-16**<br>1 • Messianic Prophecies<br>2 • Normal Christian Living (Ephesians) | **Spring 2016**<br>1 • Jeremiah and Lamentations<br>2 • Lessons From 1 Corinthians | **Summer 2016**<br>1 • David & Solomon<br>2 • Life's Transitions (Adult Life Stages) |
| **Fall 2016**<br>1 • More Great Stories of the Bible<br>2 • 1 & 2 Peter, Jude | **Winter 2016-17**<br>1 • Minor Prophets (Part 1)<br>2 • Letter to the Romans | **Spring 2017**<br>1 • The Era of the Judges<br>2 • Paul's Journeys (Acts, Part 2) | **Summer 2017**<br>1 • Good Lessons From Bad Examples<br>2 • Good Lessons From Good Examples |
| **Fall 2017**<br>1 • Luke (The Compassion of Jesus)<br>2 • The Holy Trinity | **Winter 2017-18**<br>1 • Kings of Judah<br>2 • The Christian Family | **Spring 2018**<br>1 • Ezekiel<br>2 • 2 Corinthians | **Summer 2018**<br>1 • Ezra & Nehemiah<br>2 • Philippians & Colossians (Philemon) |
| **Fall 2018**<br>1 • Abraham, Isaac, & Jacob<br>2 • Pastoral Letters | **Winter 2018-19**<br>1 • Minor Prophets (Part 2)<br>2 • Miracles of Jesus | **Spring 2019**<br>1 • Women of Faith<br>2 • Fruits & Gifts of the Spirit | **Summer 2019**<br>1 • Best-Known Psalms<br>2 • Hebrews |
| **Fall 2019**<br>1 • Job: A Life of Integrity<br>2 • John (The Son of God) | **Winter 2019-20**<br>1 • Major Christian Beliefs<br>2 • 1 & 2 Thessalonians | **Spring 2020**<br>1 • Daniel<br>2 • Galatians | **Summer 2020**<br>1 • The Bible's Influence in Society<br>2 • Revelation |

# Introduction to Fall Quarter

"Great Stories of the Bible" (lessons 1-7) include narratives from the lives of Joseph, Caleb, Abigail, Elisha, John the Baptist, and Philip the evangelist.

Dr. Sabord Woods, longtime professor of English at Lee University, who now lives in Jesup, Georgia, wrote the expositions. He holds B.A. and M.A. degrees from Georgia Southern College; M.A., Church of God Theological Seminary; Ph.D., University of Tennessee.

---

The second unit, "Parables of Jesus (Stories Jesus Told)," covers teachings on forgiveness, the kingdom of God, prayer, stewardship, evangelism, and salvation (lessons 8-13).

This unit was written by Dr. Homer G. Rhea (L.H.D.), who has served the church in many capacities, including editor in chief of Church of God Publications, pastor, district overseer, and chairman of the Ministerial Internship Program (Mississippi). An ordained minister since 1966, Dr. Rhea is the author of three books, has contributed to other books, and has written numerous magazine articles.

September 7, 2014 (Lesson 1)

# Joseph the Dreamer

**Genesis 37:1-36**

**Unit Theme:**
Great Stories of the Bible

**Central Truth:**
God has a purpose for every person's life.

**Focus:**
Affirm that God knows our future and maintain trust in Him.

**Context:**
Around 1820-1800 BC in grazing lands around Shechem

**Golden Text:**
"Commit thy way unto the Lord; trust also in him; and he shall bring it to pass" (Ps. 37:5).

**Study Outline:**
I. Prophetic Dreams
   (Gen. 37:1-11)
II. An Evil Plot
   (Gen. 37:12-28)
III. A Brokenhearted Father
   (Gen. 37:29-36)

## INTRODUCTION

The Book of Genesis contains *overarching divine purposes* in process of accomplishment from chapters 1 to 50. After man's fall into sin, God began a process of *restoration* of humankind to the full position occupied before Adam sinned. In Genesis the emphasis is on the *land* and the *blessing*, and always in the background is *divine providence*—God working within human circumstance to bring to fruition His irrevocable promises.

God ordained that the land of Canaan come into the possession of Abraham's descendants because of an overarching divine purpose that would benefit all humankind. The *land* (the habitable earth) in the beginning of time had been prepared by God as a habitat for human beings walking in fellowship with Him. Adam's fall into sin, rather than ending God's efforts on humanity's behalf, set in motion His time clock for restoration.

At an early stage in this process of restoration, a particular allotment of land, Canaan, was divinely selected as the heritage of Abraham's posterity—God's chosen people, ordained for the achievement of universally beneficial purposes. This promised territory was their everlasting possession (Gen. 13:14-17) with clearly defined boundaries (15:18-21). During the Millennium, it will be the center of Christ's kingdom on earth (see Zech. 14).

God's overarching purposes, with few exceptions, are worked out through the lives of sinful men and women who, because of selfish or even downright evil motives, may have limited or no awareness of God's intentions and no interest in furthering those intentions. Nonetheless, although human immaturity or outright evil can shape or hinder the ongoing movement through time of God's plan, it cannot ultimately thwart it.

One reason Jacob and his family were sent into Egypt was that the heinous behavior of current inhabitants of Canaan had not yet reached that ultimate stage which would signal God's retribution (Gen. 15:16). Thus, the nation of Israel could not yet inhabit their promised land.

In 12:1-3, God gave to Abram seven promises. Among them was *divine blessing*. God would bless him and make his name great, and he would be a blessing. God would bless everyone who blessed him and curse everyone who cursed him. In Abram, moreover, "all families of the earth" would be blessed. From this point forward, the divine blessing was passed from Abraham to Isaac to Jacob to selected sons of Jacob—not always to the expected heir, but nonetheless an unbroken, divinely ordained line of blessing, intended to ultimately benefit all humankind.

The story of Joseph must be viewed in relation to the foregoing divine purposes. Through the providence of God, he was abased in order to be exalted and preserve his family—God's chosen people, who (as an ethnic group) would, with inevitable flaws and imperfections, survive to be God's light to the nations. One member of that family, Judah, would carry the lineage of the coming Messiah.

## I. PROPHETIC DREAMS (Gen. 37:1-11)

### A. Jacob's Lineage (vv. 1-2)

**¹ And Jacob dwelt in the land wherein his father was a stranger, in the land of Canaan. ² These are the generations of Jacob. Joseph, being seventeen years old, was feeding the flock with his brethren; and the lad was with the sons of Bilhah, and with the sons of Zilpah, his father's wives: and Joseph brought unto his father their evil report.**

The nine sections of the Book of Genesis are marked by summary statements like that comprising 37:2: "These are the records of the generations of Jacob" (Derek Kidner, *Genesis: An Introduction and Commentary*). Prior to the current section, Jacob's long period of internal conflict and external struggle with Esau (his brother) and Laban (his uncle) had ensued, comprising chapters 30 to 33. Jacob had won a hard-fought battle with himself that found its climax in 32:24-32, when he wrestled with a "Man" identifiable as divine and would not desist until this mysterious figure had blessed him and renamed him *Israel*, meaning "he who strives with God."

Jacob would later summarize his life in his greeting of Pharaoh: "The years of my sojourning are one hundred and thirty; few and unpleasant have been the years of my life, nor have they attained the years that my fathers lived during the days of their sojourning" (47:9 NASB). After dealing with willful, often evil behavior from his ten older sons and apparently losing his favored son Joseph to death, Jacob had lived through two difficult years of severe famine. He would finally enjoy seventeen years of reunion with Joseph before dying at age 147.

The Book of Genesis records the unbroken succession of patriarchs and its conclusion with two events: (1) Jacob's inspired blessing of his twelve sons and burial with great dignity in the traditional family space in the cave of Machpelah near Mamre in Canaan (49:1—50:14) and (2) the planned preservation of Joseph's embalmed remains so they could be taken to Canaan for burial in the family plot at the conclusion of Israel's long sojourn in Egypt (50:22-26).

Joseph, Rachel's eldest son and Jacob's eleventh, was a youthful seventeen when he entered Scripture while serving his father as a shepherd along with his brothers Dan, Naphtali, Gad, and Asher. Joseph, perhaps unwisely from a natural perspective, gave his father a "bad report" concerning these brothers (37:2 NKJV). Their character and performance likely merited his report, but Joseph thereby placed himself in a difficult position for continuing work with siblings whom he had "bad-mouthed" to their father.

---

- What do you suppose was the content of Joseph's "evil report"?

> "I would by my will have tale-bearers and tale-hearers punished—the one hanging by the tongue, the other by the ears."—Plautus

---

B. Joseph's Relationship With His Brothers (vv. 3-4)

**³ Now Israel loved Joseph more than all his children, because he was the son of his old age: and he made him a coat of many colours. ⁴ And when his brethren saw that their father loved him more than all his brethren, they hated him, and could not speak peaceably unto him.**

Joseph was the first son of Jacob's beloved Rachel, who had died in childbirth when Jacob's youngest son, Benjamin, was born. Jacob's twelve sons and one daughter were born to four different wives—Leah (six sons and a daughter), her handmaid Zilpah (two sons), Rachel (two sons), and her handmaid Bilhah (two sons). This domestic arrangement was "tailor-made" for jealousy and strife. It was apparent to all that Rachel had been favored by Jacob, and it became equally apparent that Rachel's son Joseph was his father's preferred son. (Although Jacob favored Rachel over Leah, one should not therefore think that *God* favored Rachel over Leah. In fact, the Messiah would come from the lineage of Judah, one of Leah's sons.)

Scripture implies that Jacob was a doting aging parent who bestowed on his favorite son *eldest son status*, despite Joseph's next-to-youngest position among his brothers. R. Kent Hughes states that the "coat of many colors" was "a sleeved coat that reached to the wrists and ankles, thus setting Joseph apart as the one who would receive the double portion of the inheritance" (*Genesis: Beginning and Blessing*).

It was inevitable that older brothers from three different mothers would not only vie with each other constantly for position and favor, but would resent deeply a younger half-brother who was so obviously preferred by their father. Their resentment of Joseph became ever worse until it finally descended to outright hatred. Jacob could not perceive the depth of antagonism held toward Joseph since, as head of a patriarchal family, Jacob himself would receive great deference from his sons while they were in his presence, and since the older brothers would conceal from their father their hatred of Joseph.

---

1. Why did Jacob love Joseph more?
2. How much did Joseph's brothers hate him?

> "Hating people is like burning down your own house to get rid of a rat."—H. E. Forscick

---

### C. Joseph's Disquieting Dreams (vv. 5-10)

**5 And Joseph dreamed a dream, and he told it his brethren: and they hated him yet the more. 6 And he said unto them, Hear, I pray you, this dream which I have dreamed: 7 For, behold, we were binding sheaves in the field, and, lo, my sheaf arose, and also stood upright; and, behold, your sheaves stood round about, and made obeisance to my sheaf. 8 And his brethren said to him, Shalt thou indeed reign over us? or shalt thou indeed have dominion over us? And they hated him yet the more for his dreams, and for his words. 9 And he dreamed yet another dream, and told it his brethren, and said, Behold, I have dreamed a dream more; and, behold, the sun and the moon and the eleven stars made obeisance to me. 10 And he told it to his father, and to his brethren: and his father rebuked him, and said unto him, What is this dream that thou hast dreamed? Shall I and thy mother and thy brethren indeed come to bow down ourselves to thee to the earth?**

The young Joseph had two dreams that, upon being told, further complicated his relationship with his older brothers. We now know that divine providence was behind these dreams. Bible scholars, moreover, assure us that in ancient Hebrew culture the doubling of the dreams meant their fulfillment was certain. In the first dream, Joseph and his brothers were harvesting grain. Joseph's sheaf arose and stood upright; and those of his brothers also arose, stood upright, and "made obeisance" to Joseph's sheaf.

When Joseph related the dream to his brothers, they hated him more than ever, and their reply seethed with resentment: "Will you indeed reign over us, or have dominion over us?" (see v. 8). The brothers assumed that Joseph cherished ideas of rule over them and, as a result, had experienced the dreams as wish fulfillment. The hated coat and the preferment of Joseph by Jacob would have naturally implanted such thoughts in the brothers.

The young and highly pampered Joseph had no idea of the ill effect the telling of his dreams to his brothers would have, and he surely did not even begin to imagine what such familial hatred could cause. A person with Joseph's benevolent spirit (as it would later prove to be) could not even conceive of actions such as those his brothers would plan and carry out. From the beginning, Joseph's character was far superior to that of his brothers, but spiritual insight, totally absent in Joseph's brothers, was still in process of formation in Joseph. Certainly, from any natural perspective, sharing such a dream with his brothers was naïve and foolish; nonetheless, divine providence was operating within Joseph's supposedly ill-advised action.

In Joseph's second dream, the sun, moon, and eleven stars "made obeisance" to him. The detail of this dream had reference to Jacob, his surviving wife Leah, and Joseph's eleven brothers. When Joseph related this dream to his father, Jacob rebuked him ("addressed harshly, scolded, reproved," according to *The Complete Word Study Old Testament*). The dreams in themselves, despite Jacob's disturbance because of them, were not worthy of blame, even if they had not later proved prophetic, since one could hardly help what he dreamed. Nonetheless, the response of natural wisdom would be that Joseph would have kept the dreams to himself. But then if he had, God's providential plan for preservation of Jacob's family could not have unfolded. (Can we conclude that God sometimes works through behavior perceived at the time as unwise?)

---

1. Why did Joseph tell his brothers his dreams? How did it affect them?
2. What questions did his brothers ask regarding his dreams?

> "God gives us hopes and dreams for certain things to happen in our lives, but He doesn't always allow us to see the exact timing of His plan."—Joyce Meyer

---

D. The Aftermath of the Dreams (v. 11)

**11 And his brethren envied him; but his father observed the saying.**

Joseph's brothers were envious and jealous. Maybe they feared that Joseph's dreams were indeed worthy of being taken seriously (after all, he was wearing the hated special coat given him by their father). If they had not harbored such fear, they would have been merely contemptuous of Joseph, certainly not envious and maybe not even jealous. In any case, plans to ensure that such dreams could never prove true began to form in their malicious minds.

Joseph's father, despite his immediate response of rebuke of Joseph, did not dismiss his second dream; instead, he "observed the saying." Because of his own past spiritual experience, Jacob knew that God sometimes spoke through dreams; therefore, he took Joseph's dream seriously and continued to reflect on it. Jacob, however, could not even begin to imagine what his sons would concoct and perpetrate against their brother, although his brother Esau had nursed murderous thoughts against him.

---

- Explain the different responses of Joseph's dad and his brothers.

## II. AN EVIL PLOT (Gen. 37:12-28)

### A. Jacob's Mission for Joseph (vv. 12-17)

(Genesis 37:12-17 is not included in the printed text.)

Jacob must have had wide grazing rights within Canaan, or else open grazing was customary. Although the family tents were located long-term at Hebron, about twenty miles west of the Dead Sea, Jacob's older sons had taken the flocks to Shechem, about fifty miles north of Hebron. They apparently had been out of contact with their father for some time, so Jacob decided to send Joseph to determine the "welfare" of his brothers and of the flocks. Joseph's reply was "Here am I"—the response of a compliant and obedient spirit (and perhaps also a response that reveals satisfaction at representing his father to his brothers).

When Joseph reached the vicinity of Shechem, a man found him wandering in a field and asked him what he was searching for. The man quickly discerned whom Joseph was seeking and informed him he had overheard the men say they were headed fifteen miles farther north to Dothan. Joseph went to Dothan and found his brothers there. Neither Jacob nor Joseph had any idea of the state the older brothers had reached regarding Joseph and what most of them were devising.

---

- How well did Joseph follow his father's instructions?

> "Siblings [have] mutuality of parentage. Sisterhood and brotherhood is a condition people have to work at."—Mary Angelou

---

### B. The Evil Plot Against Joseph (vv. 18-24)

(Genesis 37:18-22 is not included in the printed text.)

**23 And it came to pass, when Joseph was come unto his brethren, that they stript Joseph out of his coat, his coat of many colours that was on him; 24 And they took him, and cast him into a pit: and the pit was empty, there was no water in it.**

Any fraternal restraints regarding Joseph were long since absent from the minds of most of his older brothers. When they saw Joseph approaching at a distance wearing the hated coat, nine of them conspired to murder him, contemptuously calling him "that master-dreamer" (v. 19 TLB) and revealing thereby that they had distanced themselves from him emotionally and divested themselves of all humane considerations. Their plan was to kill him, throw him into a pit, and claim to their father that a wild beast had devoured him.

Reuben, the oldest brother, attending to some duty apart from the group, was not in on the plan. When he returned, he suggested that they not kill Joseph, just throw him into a pit. His plan was to rescue Joseph later and restore him to their father. Even though Reuben was reluctant to participate in fratricide, he was not able to exercise any degree of effective leadership or restraint over these men. They merely delayed the planned murder when Reuben interceded. They stripped Joseph of the hated coat and threw him into a waterless pit.

1. What did Joseph's brothers call him, and why (v. 19)? What do you suppose was the tone in their voice?
2. Describe Joseph's brothers' conspiracy (v. 20).
3. How did Reuben differ from his brothers (vv. 21-22)?
4. How significant a role did Joseph's coat play in this story?

> "Sometimes God makes use of instruments for good to His people, who designed nothing but evil and mischief to them. Thus, Joseph's brethren were instrumental to his advancement in that very thing in which they designed his ruin."—John Flavel

---

C. The Selling of Joseph (vv. 25-28)

**25 And they sat down to eat bread: and they lifted up their eyes and looked, and, behold, a company of Ishmeelites came from Gilead with their camels bearing spicery and balm and myrrh, going to carry it down to Egypt. 26 And Judah said unto his brethren, What profit is it if we slay our brother, and conceal his blood? 27 Come, and let us sell him to the Ishmeelites, and let not our hand be upon him; for he is our brother and our flesh. And his brethren were content. 28 Then there passed by Midianites merchantmen; and they drew and lifted up Joseph out of the pit, and sold Joseph to the Ishmeelites for twenty pieces of silver: and they brought Joseph into Egypt.**

The chilling heartlessness of the men is suggested by their sitting down to eat a meal while their brother, hungry and perhaps even bruised by the fall, pleaded with them to take him out of the pit. As the brothers were finishing their meal, they looked up and saw travelers in the distance. A caravan of Ishmeelites was coming south from Gilead bearing expensive wares to trade in Egypt. These traders are also called Midianites. Derek Kidner points out that "the alternation of the names . . . would suggest that they were synonymous or overlapping terms, even if no other evidence confirmed it. It is in fact settled by Judges 8:24, which says of the Midianites 'they had golden earrings, because they were Ishmaelites'" (*Genesis: An Introduction and Commentary*).

The brothers still were intent on murdering Joseph, and there is no evidence that Reuben's rescue plan would have succeeded. Judah, beginning to displace Reuben in leadership, dissuaded them by appealing to their greed (greed, in this case, outweighing murderous hatred). Judah's plan, while not murder, was scarcely less heartless. The brothers sold Joseph to the Ishmeelites for twenty shekels of silver.

---

1. Would you call this caravan's appearance a coincidence or providence? Why?
2. To what did Judah appeal to change his brothers' minds (vv. 26-27)?

3. In the scene described in verse 28, why do you suppose no dialogue is recorded?

> "In any trial, in any bitter situation, you are not alone, you are not helpless, you are not a victim. You have a tree, a cross, shown to you by the Sovereign God of Calvary. Whatever the trial or temptation, it is not more than you can bear. It is bearable. It can be handled."—Kay Arthur

---

## III. A BROKENHEARTED FATHER (Gen. 37:29-36)

### A. Reuben's Distress (vv. 29-30)

**29 And Reuben returned unto the pit; and, behold, Joseph was not in the pit; and he rent his clothes. 30 And he returned unto his brethren, and said, The child is not; and I, whither shall I go?**

Reuben, absent during the transaction with the Ishmaelites, was distraught when he returned and found his brother Joseph absent from the pit. He "tore his clothes" (NKJV), "an ancient Semitic demonstration of grief, anger, or repentance" (*New Spirit-Filled Life Bible*)—in this case, most likely anger, frustration, and worry about his father's reaction. He felt he could not face his father with the news that Joseph was missing. Reuben seems to have had no knowledge of or part in the selling of Joseph, and perhaps did not share his brothers' degree of malice toward Joseph. However, as the eldest son, Reuben revealed a surprising lack of influence over his brothers—perhaps because of his earlier defiance of patriarchal authority by violating or seducing Bilhah, one of his father's wives (35:22).

---

- What is the meaning of Reuben's question (v. 30)?

---

### B. The Deception of Jacob (vv. 31-35)

**31 And they took Joseph's coat, and killed a kid of the goats, and dipped the coat in the blood; 32 And they sent the coat of many colours, and they brought it to their father; and said, This have we found: know now whether it be thy son's coat or no. 33 And he knew it, and said, It is my son's coat; an evil beast hath devoured him; Joseph is without doubt rent in pieces. 34 And Jacob rent his clothes, and put sackcloth upon his loins, and mourned for his son many days. 35 And all his sons and all his daughters rose up to comfort him; but he refused to be comforted; and he said, For I will go down into the grave unto my son mourning. Thus his father wept for him.**

To pacify Reuben and to conceal their dastardly deed from their father, who they knew would be devastated by the loss of his beloved Joseph, the brothers took the hated coat (symbol of all they despised about Joseph), killed a young goat, dipped the coat in the blood, and took it to their father. Jacob, recognizing the coat, *concluded* ("knew," the text says ironically) that Joseph had been torn to pieces and devoured by some wild animal. Did Jacob suspect foul play in the death of Joseph or, after reflection, come to suspect it? Genesis 42:38 contains evidence of Jacob's possible suspicion.

Any discerning reader can see how the dynamics of Jacob's family would have produced deep resentment and even malice toward the favored son—multiple wives, half-brothers with four different mothers, special treatment of a younger half-brother, adult males having their behavior evaluated by the younger favored son and reported to their father, and all this exacerbated by their hearing Joseph's dreams. But even given all such possible motivation, the planned murder of Joseph and the selling of him into slavery could only come from heinously evil hearts.

Jacob manifested all the ancient Semitic signs of mourning—rending his garments, donning sackcloth (a rough, burlap-like, loose covering), and weeping for many days. We can imagine the fake external signs of mourning and sympathy with their father's grief on the part of the guilty brothers, their responses too extreme or contrived to be truly believable if observed closely.

---

1. What tone of voice did the brothers likely use in their statement to Jacob (v. 32)?
2. What was Jacob's conclusion?
3. How far were the brothers willing to go to comfort their father?

> "To maintain perpetual wrath is akin to the practice and temper of devils; but to prevent and suppress rising resentment is wise and glorious, is manly and divine."—Isaac Watts

---

C. Joseph, a Slave in Egypt (v. 36)

**36 And the Midianites sold him into Egypt unto Potiphar, an officer of Pharaoh's, and captain of the guard.**

Joseph, most likely in chains, was carried to Egypt by the Midianite traders and sold on the auction block—evaluated physically like an animal (stripped to the buff and punched, pulled, and jerked about), then selected on the basis of his handsome features and intelligent aspect as a house slave by Potiphar, captain of Pharaoh's bodyguard. This favored son, pampered by his father and groomed for family leadership, must now bow to every whim of a powerful military officer accustomed to having his every wish obeyed as a command. What normal, pampered seventeen-year-old would survive well under such circumstances, and what will we discover in Joseph that will cause him to exceed any realistic expectations?

---

- What was Joseph's fate?

### Daniel and Joseph

In 605 BC, King Nebuchadnezzar invaded Judah and took captive a number of young men of royal or aristocratic background. These young men were deprived suddenly of their privileged Jewish status, even their names, and thrust into a totally strange culture, where they became steeped in Babylonian literature and learning. Among these young Jewish captives were Daniel, Hananiah, Mishael, and Azariah. Most of the privileged young Jews likely blended passively into Babylonian culture. These young men, however, highly intelligent and totally committed to the faith of their fathers, retained their unwavering spiritual commitment despite strong pressures and allurements.

Daniel offers an instructive comparison with Joseph. He would rise to the zenith of governmental responsibility and power as did Joseph, although the circumstances attending Daniel's elevation varied markedly from those propelling Joseph to power.

### CONCLUSION

Jacob was favored by his mother (Rebekah), and Esau was the favorite of his father (Isaac). This favoritism produced drastic consequences for the two brothers. Although Jacob (through trickery) received his father's blessing, he must flee to Syria to escape his brother's wrath. While Jacob learned valuable lessons during his twenty-year exile, he did not develop the psychological wisdom that would have prevented the repetition of the family tragedy during the next generation. Instead, he showed favoritism toward Rachel and her eldest son and thereby perpetuated a multigenerational family problem. Nonetheless, divine providence worked within this human cauldron of resentment and malice to produce long-term blessing for humankind.

### GOLDEN TEXT CHALLENGE

"COMMIT THY WAY UNTO THE LORD; TRUST ALSO IN HIM; AND HE SHALL BRING IT TO PASS" (Ps. 37:5).

Psalm 37 begins by encouraging the righteous not to be overly concerned and fret over those who are unrighteous and unbelievers, for they will soon be cut down like the grass. Rather, they should trust in the Lord and delight themselves in Him. The focus of life should be on the positive instead of on the negative. There is a promise that in doing these things, God will give them the desires of their hearts.

Verse 5 has three important parts: (1) the need to commit to the Lord; (2) to trust in Him; and (3) to enjoy the fulfillment of a committed lifestyle. This verse encourages the righteous to commit their "way" to the Lord. The word *way* is used fifty-three times in the Psalms and implies a lifestyle or way of life. The word *commit* means "to place in charge, to entrust, or to consign."

The righteous are to give themselves unreservedly to God, and then rest in the assurance that He will direct aright the committed life. After committing themselves to God, there must be complete trust in Him and in His ability to do all that they have faith to commit to Him. Then He will bring His promise to pass.

**Daily Devotions:**
- M. Jacob's Dream
  Genesis 28:10-17
- T. Solomon's Dream
  1 Kings 3:5-15
- W. Nebuchadnezzar's Dream
  Daniel 4:19-27
- T. Joseph's Dream
  Matthew 1:18-25
- F. Peter's Vision
  Acts 10:9-20
- S. Paul's Vision
  Acts 16:6-10

September 14, 2014 (Lesson 2)
# Joseph the Prince
### Genesis 39:1-23; 41:1-52

**Unit Theme:**
Great Stories of the Bible

**Central Truth:**
In everything, God is working for good.

**Focus:**
Confess and submit to God's sovereignty in the lows and highs of life.

**Context:**
In Egypt, probably between 1800 and 1775 BC

**Golden Text:**
"A man's heart deviseth his way: but the Lord directeth his steps" (Prov. 16:9).

**Study Outline:**
I. Temptation, Accusation, and Imprisonment
   (Gen. 39:1-23)
II. Pharaoh's Dreams Interpreted
   (Gen. 41:1-32)
III. God Exalts and Blesses Joseph
   (Gen. 41:33-52)

## INTRODUCTION

The Bible contains many truly miraculous occurrences—for example, the birth of Isaac, the burning bush, and Israel's crossing of the Red Sea on dry land. These events are interruptions of the normal course of events that some would call *violations* of natural law. Since God created the universe and upholds it by the word of His power, nothing He does can credibly be called a "violation." Perhaps "suspension" is better. But *law* itself may be a misnomer, since the term usually carries the connotation of enactment by some body and involves *keeping* or *breaking*. Certainly, miracles involve the suspension of rule, or regularity, whether properly law or not.

In any case, our triune God governs the universe as He sees fit; and, contrary to the ideas of the eighteenth-century Deists and the strict rationalists of other ages, He is in no sense limited by the operational regularity which He set in motion and causes to function in accordance with His omniscience and omnipotence. Evangelical believers know that God can and does work authentic miracles today as He did throughout the several thousand years of Bible history, although today's miracles may differ in kind from some of those in the Bible.

The term *miracle* is thrown around quite loosely. The birth of a child is a wonderful event, but it isn't a miracle; it is, rather, an entirely natural event that engages and refreshes us by presenting us with awe-inspiring innocence in a world filled with ugliness and tragedy. When, through time-lapse photography, we watch a plant sprout from a seed, grow to maturity, and produce a lovely flower, we are tempted to use the word *miracle* to describe the process. Nonetheless, although this series of events touches us emotionally and might indeed amaze us at the moment, it, again, is merely a sped-up and highlighted example of a natural process that constantly occurs all around us, although usually without attracting our attention.

Some might call the unexpected changes in the life of Joseph miraculous. Beyond doubt, they are happenings that are out of the ordinary, and they are ultimately ordered by the Lord. They are, in fact, unexpected changes deeply rooted in the character of the individuals involved. Rather than viewing them as miracles, we should see in them the behind-the-scenes working of divine providence—God's sovereignty manifested within the normal flow of events, however unexpected and life-altering. They are of crucial importance to the history of Israel and salvation history. They should also remind us that God is working in our lives today—even in the mundane, everyday events—to bring about His will for us in time and eternity.

I. TEMPTATION, ACCUSATION, AND IMPRISONMENT (Gen. 39:1-23)

A. Enslaved but Favored (vv. 1-6)

**¹ And Joseph was brought down to Egypt; and Potiphar, an officer of Pharaoh, captain of the guard, an Egyptian, bought him of the hands of the Ishmeelites, which had brought him down thither. ² And the Lord was with Joseph, and he was a prosperous man; and he was in the house of his master the Egyptian. ³ And his master saw that the Lord was with him, and that the Lord made all that he did to prosper in his hand. ⁴ And Joseph found grace in his sight, and he served him: and he made him overseer over his house, and all that he had he put into his hand. ⁵ And it came to pass from the time that he had made him overseer in his house, and over all that he had, that the Lord blessed the Egyptian's house for Joseph's sake; and the blessing of the Lord was upon all that he had in the house, and in the field. ⁶ And he left all that he had in Joseph's hand; and he knew not ought he had, save the bread which he did eat. And Joseph was a goodly person, and well favoured.**

Joseph was taken from the slave market by his new master, Potiphar, and most likely put under the direct supervision of a house steward who answered immediately to Potiphar's wife and finally to Potiphar himself. Being much closer to his father than were his brothers, Joseph had learned, and/or absorbed, deep personal integrity from Jacob, who had gleaned this lesson from long, painful experience. Moreover, Joseph had exceptional natural abilities—both intelligence and talent (already recognized and rewarded by his admittedly doting and partial father). Too, as Joseph's dream-visions had predicted would happen, God was at work behind the flow of events, orchestrating the ups and downs of the life of this young adult for His immediate, intermediate, and long-term purposes.

Joseph became "a successful man" (v. 2 NKJV). Four good indicators of eventual success are personal integrity, a strong work ethic, at least normal capability, and good interpersonal skills. Added to these four might be proper training for one's vocation if the situation calls for special training. But, even given these strong indicators, various unpredictable barriers may prevent or limit human success.

Joseph manifested the first three immediately (as his earlier life in Canaan had indicated he would). Moreover, he quickly mastered the fourth and would have picked up quickly any necessary training; plus, he enjoyed God's unfailing grace. Therefore, in God's own time, success, as defined by Scripture, would be his.

External success for Joseph in this situation meant favor from his superiors, but, in his own mind, it would mean satisfaction in excellent performance in the sight of God and man. Potiphar soon observed in Joseph's demeanor and behavior the presence of the indicators of success named above.

Potiphar would not have understood the divine source ultimately behind Joseph's success since, as an Egyptian aristocrat, he would have been a worshiper of Egyptian deities and would therefore not have understood the nature and expectations of the God of revelation. He would instead have observed the external indications of what Moses, the inspired writer of Genesis, knew to be God's behind-the-scenes activity in and through Joseph. God had created and conditioned Joseph for the role He needed him to fill in Potiphar's house in Egypt.

Potiphar was favorably impressed by Joseph and eventually promoted him to the position of overseer of his house, or, better for current readers, estate, since all his possessions were under Joseph's authority. God brought prosperity to Potiphar for Joseph's sake, whether in the house or in the field. Eventually, Potiphar didn't even bother to supervise Joseph because he did his work so well, acted with such integrity, and brought such prosperity to his master.

---

1. How was Joseph the slave "prosperous" (vv. 2-3)?
2. Describe Potiphar's confidence in Joseph (vv. 4-6).

> "The man who has an easy way through life, will be spiritually weak, flabby, and impoverished. He won't be able to do all that God wants him to do. But the one who has gone through trials and testing successfully, will be strong and capable of doing all the will of God."—Zac Zoonen

---

B. Temptation (vv. 7-12)

   (Genesis 39:11-12 is not included in the printed text.)

⁷ And it came to pass after these things, that his master's wife cast her eyes upon Joseph; and she said, Lie with me. ⁸ But he refused, and said unto his master's wife, Behold, my master wotteth not what is with me in the house, and he hath committed all that he hath to my hand; ⁹ There is none greater in this house than I; neither hath he kept back any thing from me but thee, because thou art his wife: how then can I do this great wickedness, and sin against God? ¹⁰ And it came to pass, as she spake to Joseph day by day, that he hearkened not unto her, to lie by her, or to be with her.

The deep integrity of Joseph became fully operative when Potiphar's wife cast lustful eyes on him. Joseph was attractive in appearance and personality. Likely, the mistress of the house was bored and accustomed to having her way with subordinates in the household. So she gave Joseph an invitation to improper intimacy. The deep integrity of Joseph became fully operative when Potiphar's wife cast lustful eyes on him. Joseph was attractive in appearance and personality. Likely, the mistress of the house was bored and accustomed to having her way with subordinates in the household. So she gave Joseph an invitation to improper intimacy.

This likely was not her first such departure from propriety, but most likely the first refusal. After all, household slaves enjoyed privileges other servants would not experience, and all were quite aware of the power the mistress of the house could exercise over them. Who would risk losing such privileges and angering so powerful a superior, particularly when her anger and any resulting false accusation could result in their imprisonment or execution? Joseph was a virile young man in a dangerous and alluring situation. Faced with a sexual temptation, King David, a choice servant of God and a ruler of great power, succumbed and brought upon himself and others great sorrow and loss (2 Sam. 11—12). Joseph's temptation was genuine and powerful. It was also a supreme test of his character.

Despite allurements and the danger of refusal, Joseph did not yield. He first cited the trust his master had placed in him (Gen. 39:8). The King James Version employs the archaic verb *wotteth* ("knows," NKJV) to express the idea that Potiphar didn't bother to acquaint himself with any of the details of Joseph's oversight because he trusted him so completely. That trust had been well earned and had resulted in promotion to chief steward over Potiphar's entire estate.

Joseph reminded his master's wife that only she had been withheld from him. Then he called this invitation to adultery exactly what it was in the sight of Joseph's God, the true God of biblical revelation—"this great wickedness" (v. 9). The appeal of Joseph to his integrity before God would be totally lost on Potiphar's wife, since she did not think on such a high level. But he must make this appeal for the woman to hear the full account of why he had made what would appear to her a strange and insulting refusal.

She persisted in her temptation of Joseph, and he persisted in his refusal. In fact, he was careful not to place himself in any compromising situation. Over time, the lust of Potiphar's wife shifted to anger, then to malice. She might have been a beautiful, intelligent woman (she had to be to attract such a highly placed husband), but she was lacking in character; hence, she did not hesitate to resort to spiteful recriminations. Joseph had to be indoors to attend to his assigned duties; therefore, he couldn't entirely avoid Potiphar's wife. So she had a means of executing her vengeful plan.

She caught him by his outer garment, saying, "Lie with me" (v. 12). By then she didn't expect compliance, although she would have welcomed it. Instead, she was now beginning to work her malicious plot. Joseph responded by fleeing the house—the precisely appropriate moral response.

---

1. What would be a "great evil," and why (v. 9 NASB)?
2. How frequently did Potiphar's wife tempt Joseph, and how did he protect himself (v. 10)?
3. Why didn't Joseph just tell Potiphar about his wife's actions?
4. What does verse 12 say about battling temptation?

> "Integrity characterizes the entire person, not just part of him. He is righteous and honest through and through. He is not only that inside, but also in outer action."—R. Kent Hughes

---

C. Accusation (vv. 13-19)

(Genesis 39:13-18 is not included in the printed text.)

**¹⁹ And it came to pass, when his master heard the words of his wife, which she spake unto him, saying, After this manner did thy servant to me; that his wrath was kindled.**

Potiphar's wife now showed Joseph's garment (which he left in her hands) to other men in the house and accused him of attempted rape, telling them the lie that she had cried out loudly upon being accosted. She referred to Joseph as "this Hebrew" (v. 14 NIV) and suggested he was expressing contempt and total disregard for the privileges afforded him by her husband. If Joseph had been attempting rape, he would have been more calculating, making sure to carry away the evidence, his outer garment. He was, in fact, fleeing for his life—morally, spiritually, and (potentially) physically.

Potiphar's wife kept her "evidence" to show to Potiphar when he came home. She told him her tale regarding Joseph, arousing (as she had planned) her husband's anger. Potiphar could easily have had Joseph executed had he wished; after all, Joseph was a slave totally at the disposal of his master. I suspect, however, that Potiphar was aware of his wife's predilections and therefore did not accept without reservations her tale about Joseph (see R. Kent Hughes, *Genesis: Beginning and Blessing*). It did not fit what Potiphar had observed already regarding the young man. In fact, Potiphar's anger might have been toward his wife as well as Joseph (if not instead of Joseph). But Potiphar had no concrete contrary evidence other than Joseph's own story, and Scripture does not indicate whether he even heard Joseph's account. In any case, under God's providential care, Joseph was preserved for the next stage in God's plan for him.

1. Why did Potiphar's wife first accuse Joseph before his fellow servants (vv. 14-15)?
2. How strong was the evidence against Joseph?

> "Even doubtful accusations leave a stain behind them."—Thomas Fuller

### D. Imprisonment (vv. 20-23)

**20 And Joseph's master took him, and put him into the prison, a place where the king's prisoners were bound: and he was there in the prison. 21 But the Lord was with Joseph, and shewed him mercy, and gave him favour in the sight of the keeper of the prison. 22 And the keeper of the prison committed to Joseph's hand all the prisoners that were in the prison; and whatsoever they did there, he was the doer of it. 23 The keeper of the prison looked not to any thing that was under his hand; because the Lord was with him, and that which he did, the Lord made it to prosper.**

Potiphar put Joseph in the prison over which he himself had final oversight (39:1; 40:3), though he himself was not directly in charge. (It is important to note this in relation to the events that follow.) God continued to work within the circumstances surrounding Joseph. God's presence attended him, His mercy was upon him, and He gave him favor with the keeper of the prison.

The keeper soon observed Joseph's intelligence, leadership acumen, and pleasing personality. These qualities are not named *per se*, but are plausible observable traits that would cause the keeper of the prison to place Joseph in charge of all prisoners in that institution.

We should observe that if Potiphar had wished, he could have prevented Joseph's preferment since he was in authority over the keeper (see Derek Kidner, *Genesis*). Interestingly, the keeper of the prison behaved just as Potiphar did when Joseph was in his household. He left Joseph totally in charge without even checking up on him. Behind the scenes, God was ordering the succession of events necessary to Joseph's eventually being placed precisely in position for the preservation of his family and the population of Egypt.

1. What three ways did the Lord minister to Joseph in prison (v. 21)?
2. How was Joseph's position in prison similar to his former position in Potiphar's house?

> "God uses prisons to train people for future roles of leadership or martyrdom."—Charles Colson

## II. PHARAOH'S DREAMS INTERPRETED (Gen. 41:1-32)

According to chapter 40, Pharaoh's prisoners were incarcerated in the prison which Joseph managed under the keeper who answered to Potiphar. Pharaoh's cupbearer and baker, thrown into this prison for unstated reasons, each had a dream that troubled him. The cupbearer dreamed of a vine with three branches that budded and produced grapes. The cupbearer pressed the grapes into Pharaoh's cup and placed it in his hand. The baker dreamed he had three white baskets on his head filled with baked goods for Pharaoh, which were devoured by birds.

When the cupbearer and the baker related their dreams to Joseph, he asserted that the power to interpret dreams belonged to God; nonetheless, he interpreted their dreams—that the cupbearer would be restored to his position, while the baker would be hanged. Joseph's interpretations, as any Bible reader would expect by now, proved accurate. Joseph asked the cupbearer to remember him to Pharaoh once he was restored to his position, but the cupbearer quickly forgot—a lapse of memory ordered by God because it was not yet time for Joseph's elevation.

A. Pharaoh's Dreams and the Cupbearer's Recollection (vv. 1-14)

(Genesis 41:1-13 is not included in the printed text.)
**14 Then Pharaoh sent and called Joseph, and they brought him hastily out of the dungeon: and he shaved himself, and changed his raiment, and came in unto Pharaoh.**

Two years later, Pharaoh himself had two dreams. In the first dream, seven wholesome cows came out of the Nile River and fed in the meadow. Then seven lean, ugly cows came from the Nile, stood by the other cows, and quickly devoured them (vv. 2-4). In the second dream, seven heads of grain appeared on a single stalk, "plump and good" (v. 5 NKJV), followed by seven blighted heads, which sprang up after the good heads and quickly devoured them (vv. 6-7). Pharaoh was troubled by his dreams and summoned his magicians and wise men, who, unsurprisingly, could not interpret them (v. 8).

The cupbearer now remembered Joseph's ability to provide accurate interpretations of his and the baker's dreams and informed Pharaoh, who quickly called for Joseph. Joseph shaved and dressed and appeared before Pharaoh with the expected Egyptian appearance and attire. We have observed Joseph as he rose to great trust because of his ability and integrity, sank to the bottom of observable reputation because of false accusation, began to be restored to trust and responsibility within prison walls, and now stood before Pharaoh, poised to rise to the zenith of greatness.

---

1. How did God speak to Pharaoh (vv. 1-7)?
2. Who could not help Pharaoh, and why not (v. 8)?
3. What happened "quickly" (v. 14 NIV)?

> "God will prove to you how good and acceptable and perfect His will is when He's got His hands on the steering wheel of your life."—Stuart and Jill Briscoe

B. Pharaoh's Request of Joseph (vv. 15-24)

(Genesis 41:17-24 is not included in the printed text.)

**¹⁵ And Pharaoh said unto Joseph, I have dreamed a dream, and there is none that can interpret it: and I have heard say of thee, that thou canst understand a dream to interpret it. ¹⁶ And Joseph answered Pharaoh, saying, It is not in me: God shall give Pharaoh an answer of peace.**

Pharaoh, without delay, presented his request to Joseph, asserting that no one had been able to interpret his dreams. He also relayed to Joseph the information conveyed by the cupbearer regarding his interpretive skill. Joseph's response to Pharaoh revealed once again his settled convictions regarding his relationship with God and God's entire trustworthiness—God would act consonant with His powerful yet benevolent nature. Joseph, at this moment, had no idea what would happen after this occasion; however, he had developed trust in the God of his fathers and therefore believed He would be true to that nature already revealed to his ancestors and observable in his own spiritual history.

---

- What had Pharaoh heard about Joseph (v. 15), and how did Joseph correct it (v. 16)?

---

C. Joseph's Interpretation of Pharaoh's Dreams (vv. 25-32)

(Genesis 41:25-27, 32 is not included in the printed text.)

**²⁸ This is the thing which I have spoken unto Pharaoh: What God is about to do he sheweth unto Pharaoh. ²⁹ Behold, there come seven years of great plenty throughout all the land of Egypt: ³⁰ And there shall arise after them seven years of famine; and all the plenty shall be forgotten in the land of Egypt; and the famine shall consume the land; ³¹ And the plenty shall not be known in the land by reason of that famine following; for it shall be very grievous.**

When Pharaoh conveyed to Joseph the content of his two dreams, Joseph asserted that God had revealed to him what He was about to accomplish throughout his domain of rule. The images of the two dreams had identical meaning. God would send seven years of great prosperity, followed by seven years of severe famine that would deplete all the resources of Egypt. It is not revealed in this immediate context how wide the extent of that famine would be, but we are told elsewhere it would reach far beyond the borders of Egypt itself (Gen. 41:57; 47:13).

When God sends severe circumstances, such hardship is not without meaning or purpose. He would reveal something of His nature to Pharaoh, regardless of his response, and He would preserve from starvation both the Egyptian populace and the family of Israel. Moreover, although this was yet unknown to Joseph, He would use him as His primary human instrument (see 45:7-8).

The doubling of Pharaoh's dream, according to Joseph, meant that God's intention was set and the predicted events would happen without delay. In the words of R. Kent Hughes, "The interpretation that Joseph gave here announced to Pharaoh and to all of Egypt that the one true God controlled their existence" (*Genesis*).

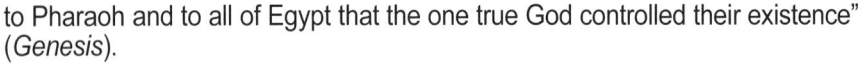

• Why was the dream "repeated to Pharaoh twice" (v. 32 NKJV)?

> **Daniel's Interpretations**
> The statesman-prophet Daniel, in some ways parallel to Joseph, recounted to King Nebuchadnezzar a dream he could not recall in which God foretold the progress and demise of four great empires. Daniel was elevated to high administrative positions which he held during the reigns of several kings. A second dream of Nebuchadnezzar interpreted by Daniel was followed by the king's spending seven years in the grip of animal-like insanity because of his enormous arrogance. Nebuchadnezzar afterward acknowledged the God of biblical revelation. Like Joseph, Daniel was greatly valuable to God at a crucial time in human history.

III. GOD EXALTS AND BLESSES JOSEPH (Gen. 41:33-52)

A. Joseph's Advice to Pharaoh (vv. 33-36)

(Genesis 41:33-36 is not included in the printed text.)

Joseph not only revealed to Pharaoh the years of prosperity and famine just ahead; he gave him a detailed plan for the nation's survival. This sensible plan would only have intensified Pharaoh's trust in the reliability of Joseph's interpretation of his dreams. Joseph advised that Pharaoh place a "discerning and wise man" (v. 33 NKJV) over the land of Egypt. He was to appoint overseers under him to collect one-fifth of all produce during the years of prosperity, and place that food in cities throughout the country to serve as a reserve for the years of famine to follow, so that no citizen of Egypt should perish. Joseph harbored no personal schemes, expectations of reward, or self-serving intentions; he merely relayed the message given him by God.

• Explain Joseph's plan.

B. Pharaoh's Elevation of Joseph (vv. 37-46, 50-52)

(Genesis 41:37, 41-46, 50-52 is not included in the printed text.)

**38 And Pharaoh said unto his servants, Can we find such a one as this is, a man in whom the Spirit of God is? 39 And Pharaoh said unto Joseph, Forasmuch as God hath shewed thee all this, there is none so discreet and wise as thou art: 40 Thou shalt be over my house, and according unto**

**thy word shall all my people be ruled: only in the throne will I be greater than thou.**

After Pharaoh and his servants heard Joseph's interpretation of Pharaoh's dreams and his wise plan of action, they concurred that his advice was trustworthy. Pharaoh then decided that Joseph himself was the ideal viceroy for this time of crisis. This pagan ruler recognized God's presence in Joseph's life, although he could not comprehend the full implications of that acknowledgment.

Joseph would be directly under Pharaoh himself, he would have charge over Pharaoh's own house, and he would have full authority over all Egypt. Pharaoh's signet ring would be the seal of Joseph's strong, even dictatorial authority. Joseph was now dressed in regal garments with a gold chain about his neck and driven around in a chariot second only to that of Pharaoh himself, while all individuals in view were compelled to bow the knee.

Pharaoh changed Joseph's name to *Zaphnath-Paaneah*, which likely means "God speaks and He lives" (*New Spirit-Filled Life Bible*)—an Egyptian name suitable to his commanding role (v. 45). He also gave him a wife suitable to his elevated position, and she soon bore Joseph two sons—*Manasseh*, meaning "making forgetful," and *Ephraim*, meaning "fruitfulness" (vv. 50-52). Joseph, now thirty, had been in Egypt for thirteen years, a period of dizzying ups-and-downs, and now was elevated to the pinnacle of political rule.

---

1. What did Pharaoh recognize about Joseph (v. 38)?
2. List the symbols of Joseph's position (vv. 42-43).
3. Explain the significance of the naming of two sons (vv. 50-52).

> "A providence is shaping our ends; a plan is developing in our lives; a supreme and loving Being is making all things work together for good."—F. B. Meyer

---

C. Joseph's Administration of Egypt (vv. 47 49)

(Genesis 41:47-49 is not included in the printed text.)

Joseph put into place the measures he had recommended to Pharaoh during his initial interview with him. During the seven years of unparalleled prosperity, he stored in the cities, close to the productive fields, the enormous quantity of surplus grain. Afterward, the worldwide famine began, but, because of Joseph's shrewd application of intelligence, Egypt did not lack for bread. The storehouses were opened, and the numerous applicants for food bought grain.

## CONCLUSION

With Joseph's plan in place, suppliants from Egypt and surrounding countries purchased grain. This included Joseph's brothers, who began a process of moral growth as they, for their own good, were subjected to a series of tests of character imposed by Joseph. Finally, he revealed his identity to his startled brothers, and his entire family came to reside in Egypt during the period of great famine.

In Genesis 50:19-20, Joseph said to his brothers, "Do not be afraid, for am I in the place of God? But as for you, you meant evil against me; but God meant it for good, in order to bring it about as it is this day, to save many people alive."

## GOLDEN TEXT CHALLENGE

"A MAN'S HEART DEVISETH HIS WAY: BUT THE LORD DIRECTETH HIS STEPS" (Prov. 16:9).

As a *reasonable creature*: Man has the faculty of contriving for himself. His heart devises his way, designs an end, and projects ways and means leading to that end. The more shame for him if he does not devise the way how to please God and provide for his everlasting state.

As *depending creatures*, subject to the direction and dominion of their Maker: If men devise their way, so as to make God's glory their end and His will their rule, they may expect that He will direct their steps by His Spirit and grace, so that they shall not miss their way nor come short of their end. . . . The design of this is to teach us to say, "If the Lord will, we shall live, and do this, or that" (James 4:14-15), and to have our eye to God, not only in the great turns of our lives, but in every step we take (1 Thess. 3:11).—*Matthew Henry's Commentary*

**Daily Devotions:**

M. Trust in God's Righteousness
   Psalm 4:1-8
T. Trust in God's Justice
   Psalm 7:1-10
W. Trust in God's Salvation
   Psalm 25:1-11
T. Trust in God's Faithfulness
   Mark 10:23-31
F. Trust in God's Deliverance
   2 Corinthians 1:3-11
S. Trust in the Living God
   1 Timothy 6:17-19

September 21, 2014 (Lesson 3)
# Caleb the Brave

**Numbers 13:17 through 14:24; Joshua 14:1-15**

---

**Unit Theme:**
Great Stories of the Bible

**Central Truth:**
Faith in God produces extraordinary courage.

**Focus:**
Boldly believe and bravely act on the promises of God.

**Context:**
Israel fails to enter the Promised Land (around 1448-1441 BC), but finally does so some forty years later.

**Golden Text:**
"My brethren that went up with me made the heart of the people melt: but I [Caleb] wholly followed the Lord my God" (Josh. 14:8).

**Study Outline:**
I. Conflicting Reports
   (Num. 13:17-33)
II. Speaking Boldly for God
   (Num. 14:1-10, 20-24)
III. Receiving the Inheritance
   (Josh 14:6-14)

## INTRODUCTION

According to well-known early records, ancient cultures such as Greece (*The Iliad, The Odyssey*) and Rome (*The Aeneid*) passed through an age of heroes when mythical figures produced great military feats and interacted with gods and goddesses that often were less admirable in character than the human figures they assisted. When compared with accounts of other ancient cultures, the history of ancient Israel is not at all typical.

The Old Testament records the life of a people in covenant with the Lord from the days of Abraham (ca. 1900 BC) forward. That covenant was renewed and elaborated at Mount Sinai, where God revealed Himself through terrifying visible signs and thunderous words to Moses and his fellow Israelites, whom He had recently rescued from Egypt and delivered from Pharaoh. When Israel had to fight military battles, they almost always fought in direct obedience to God, and they very often experienced victories over superior forces through supernatural interventions.

Israel was a spiritually immature, fearful people—called to greatness, but perennially lacking in discipline and determination. They did not fight battles because they were warlike and itching for a fight; rather, they were pressed into service at the behest of leaders who had encountered God and who proved heroic because they led with courage and usually with integrity. Moreover, among these ancient Israelites, there were great people of valor who responded to the call of these divinely appointed leaders.

When we apply the word *hero* to men and women of Scripture, we need to tweak the usual definition by *Merriam-Webster's Collegiate Dictionary* as "an illustrious warrior" or "a man admired for his achievements and noble qualities." In the Bible, the achievement was either in the spiritual or moral realm, or else a victory by a political and/or military leader who acted under orders from the Lord and with great consequences for God's covenant people. These heroes were more often men, but certainly not always, since women of strong character such as Miriam, Deborah, and Abigail proved invaluable in the service of God.

Among the heroes considered in our current lesson series are *Joseph* (a moral and spiritual giant whose leadership resulted in the preservation of God's covenant people and of a great foreign nation), *Caleb* (a mighty military hero strong in character), and *Abigail* (a woman of wisdom whose discernment offset her husband's folly). Often a Bible hero, as in Caleb's case, must oppose the popular will in order to support the wisdom and will of God. In the current lesson, Moses, under divine direction, stood poised to lead the Israelites into battle to conquer Canaan, according to God's covenant with Abraham made several generations earlier (see Gen. 15:13-16). The bold hero central to our present study, Caleb, was one of twelve men selected for pre-battle reconnaissance.

The heroes of my childhood were the spiritual leaders in our rural church community. John Graham, pastor of Spring Grove Free Will Baptist Church, was a simple gospel preacher, but renowned for his holiness of character. Sunday school teachers such as Eula Stewart, Aletha Anderson, and B. C. Brown were steeped in Scripture and exuded sweetness of spirit. W. J. Cothern, the pastor of the Jesup Church of God during my adolescence, moved in the realm of the Spirit. He thereby helped me understand, to the extent such could be absorbed at that point in my spiritual experience, the working of the Holy Spirit in my own life, and he ingrained in me and our entire congregation a deep faith in the miraculous and an abiding respect for the Word of God. Such true spiritual heroes prove their mettle as they battle in the realm of the Spirit (Eph. 6:10-19).

I. CONFLICTING REPORTS (Num. 13:17-33)

Deuteronomy 1:22-23 states that the people of Israel requested Moses to select men to "search . . . out the land" of Canaan, and thereby determine the route to take and the cities to invade. In Numbers 13:2, the Lord instructed Moses to send a leader from each tribe to "spy out the land" (NKJV). When we compare these texts of Scripture, we discern that, upon the request of the people, the Lord acquiesced in their will and so commanded Moses. This reconnaissance was a wise choice, or else the Lord would not have approved it. But the request of the people might in itself have indicated anxiety born of spiritual doubt (see Ps. 95:7-11; Heb.3:7-12).

Numbers 1:3-16 lists a leader from each tribe to stand with Moses when the nation must "go forth to war." The list of spies in chapter 13 is different from the earlier group, perhaps younger, but doubtless equally skilled physically and militarily and, in each case, also a leader of his tribe. Several sources point to a shortened form of *Yahweh* as a prefix, or of *Elohim* as a suffix, in the names of several of these men (e.g., *Gaddiel*, v. 10). Moreover, even when the divine name is not explicit, it is usually implied. For instance, the name of *Gaddi* (v. 11) means "fortune," but "my fortune is in God" is clearly to be inferred (*The Expositor's Bible Commentary*). These names point to the noble spiritual heritage of the men. Over all, the men selected for reconnaissance have a commonly occurring yet nonetheless deeply meaningful name to live up to.

Caleb's name differs from the others. One source states that *Caleb* means "dog" in Hebrew, while another source suggests "bold" as its derivation. *Dog*, on the surface, seems totally inconsistent with Caleb's character. But Caleb's name, in this case, would likely point to fidelity and reliability—age-old characteristics of intelligent, well-bred canines. Caleb, moreover, proved himself the personification of responsible boldness.

The name of Caleb's companion, *Joshua*, originally had been *Hoshea* ("deliverance"), but Moses changed the name of his gifted assistant to *Joshua* ("the Lord is deliverance"), identical in Hebrew to that of *Jesus*, our Messiah and Lord.

A. Mission Planned and Executed (vv. 17-25)

(Numbers 13:21-25 is not included in the printed text.)

**17 And Moses sent them to spy out the land of Canaan, and said unto them, Get you up this way southward, and go up into the mountains; 18 And see the land, what it is; and the people that dwelleth therein, whether they be strong or weak, few or many; 19 And what the land is that they dwell in, whether it be good or bad; and what cities they be that they dwell in, whether in tents, or in strong holds; 20 And what the land is, whether it be fat or lean, whether there be wood therein, or not. And be ye of good courage, and bring of the fruit of the land. Now the time was the time of the firstripe grapes.**

Moses gave the twelve spies a specific commission. They were to inspect thoroughly the mountainous areas of southern Canaan before going all the way to the edge of what is now Lebanon. They were to observe carefully both the land itself and its inhabitants: Was the land of Canaan populous or scarcely peopled? Were its ethnic groups strong or weak militarily? Did the people live primarily in cities or in the countryside? Were their homes temporary dwellings or well-built houses protected by walls and towers? What was the topography of the land—was it well forested or desert, well suited to agriculture and grazing or rocky and barren? Finally, Moses directed that the spies perform their task courageously and return to camp with samples of produce.

Verses 21-25 state that the twelve men traveled throughout Canaan from the Wilderness of Zin (just above Kadesh-Barnea, where Israel was encamped) to Rehob, a city "at the northern end of the valley of the Jordan" near Mount Hermon (*Hasting's Dictionary of the Bible*). Hebron was the ancient location where Abraham had dwelt during much of his sojourn in Canaan four centuries earlier. There the spies saw extremely tall men who had descended from Anak, an ancient ethnic group that inhabited a sizeable area in south Canaan (see the detailed description in Josh. 11:21). The majority of the spies cowered in fear even at the thought of these men.

On their return trip through the south of Canaan, the twelve visited the Valley of Eshcol, where they cut off a branch of a grapevine containing a huge cluster of grapes. Two of the men bore this remarkable sample of fruit between them, while others carried luscious pomegranates and figs.

One valuable lesson that current Christians can learn from this divinely ordered reconnaissance is how essential it is for God's people, whatever the mission, *to plan thoroughly with guidance from the Holy Spirit.* The Acts of the Apostles includes such examples of Holy Spirit-guided planning: the appointment of the seven deacons (6:1-7), the selection and commissioning of Barnabas and Saul (13:1-3), and the council at Jerusalem (15:1-31). Whether the need at hand was generally spiritual, specifically doctrinal, or primarily material, the early church sought spiritual counsel and proceeded wisely.

---

1. Describe the mission Moses gave to the spies (vv. 17-20).
2. How well was the mission carried out (vv. 21-25)?

> "We have ample evidence that the Lord is able to guide. The promises cover every imaginable situation. All we need to do is to take the hand He stretches out."—Elisabeth Elliot

---

B. Majority Report and Caleb's Rebuttal (vv. 26-33)

²⁶ And they went and came to Moses, and to Aaron, and to all the congregation of the children of Israel, unto the wilderness of Paran, to Kadesh; and brought back word unto them, and unto all the congregation, and shewed them the fruit of the land. ²⁷ And they told him, and said, We came unto the land whither thou sentest us, and surely it floweth with milk and honey; and this is the fruit of it. ²⁸ Nevertheless the people be strong that dwell in the land, and the cities are walled, and very great: and moreover we saw the children of Anak there. ²⁹ The Amalekites dwell in the land of the south: and the Hittites, and the Jebusites, and the Amorites, dwell in the mountains: and the Canaanites dwell by the sea, and by the coast of Jordan. ³⁰ And Caleb stilled the people before Moses, and said, Let us go up at once, and possess it; for we are well able to overcome it. ³¹ But the men that went up with him said, We be not able to go up against the people; for they are stronger than we. ³² And they brought up an evil report of the land which they had searched unto the children of Israel, saying, The land, through which we have gone to search it, is a land that eateth up the inhabitants thereof; and all the people that we saw in it are men of a great stature. ³³ And there we saw the giants, the sons of Anak, which come of the giants: and we were in our own sight as grasshoppers, and so we were in their sight.

When the twelve spies returned to Kadesh-Barnea in the Wilderness of Paran, they gave their report simultaneously to Moses and Aaron, the chief leaders, and the congregation at large. The men had accomplished their mission and now were ready to describe the land and its inhabitants. The spies assured their fellow Israelites that the land of Canaan "flowed with milk and honey," a term first used in Scripture by the Lord himself when He commissioned Moses to lead Israel out of Egypt (Ex. 3:8). The visual evidence inevitably supported the divine characterization.

The returned spies displayed their samples of fruit seen in Canaan. Then, to indicate a transition in their report, the ten-man majority employed a conjunctive adverb signaling contrast—"nevertheless" (Num. 13:28)—as they moved to a specific description of the cities and inhabitants of the land. They thereby indicated the negative report to follow.

The spies characterized the cities they had visited as "walled," or well fortified, and as "very great." The inhabitants were described as "strong," and, as a further clue to the majority's negative overall point of view, they cited the "descendants of Anak" first (v. 28 NKJV). Fear dominated this majority report. It specified by geographical location the ethnic groups inhabiting Canaan—Amalekites in the south; Hittites, Jebusites, and Amorites in the mountains; and Canaanites by the sea and near the Jordan River—formidable foes who struck fear in the hearts of others.

The Amalekites proved to be implacable enemies of Israel until their eventual total annihilation (1 Chron. 4:42-43). The Hittites' very existence in Canaan was denied by archaeologists until the discovery of artifacts proved otherwise (*The Apologetics Study Bible*); however, the Bible records the Hittites' existence in Canaan as early as Abraham's time (Gen. 15:20). The Jebusites were finally ejected from Jerusalem and its central fortress long after the general overthrow of most original inhabitants of Canaan and then only by David, Israel's greatest king (2 Sam. 5:6-10). Finally, the Philistines (among the Canaanites) were a thorn in Israel's side for many generations after the monarchy was established.

The total removal of these foes of Israel from Canaan was delayed because of the perennial spiritual disobedience of God's people (see Judg. 2:1-6). The enemies of Israel (and therefore of God) would fall only before spiritual might, not military superiority.

Caleb interrupted a majority report that was becoming ever more fear-laden and negative and, for a moment, "quieted the people" (Num. 13:30 NKJV). His strong rebuttal was concise, bold, and courageous. "Let us go up at once, and possess it; for we are well able to overcome it." Caleb evidently took into consideration events immediately previous to the occasion— supernatural deliverance from Egypt, visible protection by the Lord, a supernatural supply of food, and a divine display of authority and power at Sinai. To conquer Canaan was God's will, and He had already proved Himself awesome in might and totally reliable.

Caleb, by his demeanor—communicated through decisive rhetoric—demonstrated confidence and boldness. In his rapid-fire, positive, one-sentence rebuttal, Caleb asserted that Israel was "well able" to overcome its opponents; he used a Hebrew word that denoted "having the capacity to prevail or succeed" (*New Spirit-Filled Life Bible*).

Joshua at this juncture remained silent, perhaps because as Moses' assistant, he would have been presumed by skeptics to support Israel's leader rather than to speak independently. Later, he would give Caleb strong support. The majority of ten, contradicting Caleb, insisted that their foes were too formidable, the land of Canaan "devours its inhabitants" (v. 32 NKJV), and all its occupants were of larger-than-normal stature. They had seen giants, descendants of Anak, and, in comparison with them, felt like grasshoppers. They also believed they had been viewed by the giants as grasshoppers (v. 33).

The fear in the hearts of the majority, created by unbelief, sparked in them a negative imaginative response, distorting their collective memory and altering their recollection of the actual land and people witnessed in Canaan. The stature of the giants seemed to grow and the perception of Israel's strength seemed to diminish with the passing hours.

---

1. How did the spies describe the land's produce (vv. 26-27)?
2. How did they describe the land's inhabitants and cities (vv. 28-29, 31-33)?
3. Contrast Caleb's advice with the majority report (v. 30).

> "How very little can be done under the spirit of fear."—Florence Nightingale

---

II. SPEAKING BOLDLY FOR GOD (Num. 14:1-10, 20-24)

A. Dispirited People, Humbled Leadership (vv. 1-5)

(Numbers 14:1-5 is not included in the printed text.)

Upon hearing the dispiriting majority report, the congregation of Israel wept like distraught infants throughout the night and (in the morning) complained bitterly against their divinely appointed leaders (vv. 1-3). In fact, they were rejecting the leadership of the Lord himself. They decided that slavery in Egypt was better than the bleak prospect they imagined as before them in Canaan, and they were determined to appoint a leader for their rebellion and return to the land of captivity (v. 4).

Moses and Aaron prostrated themselves before the faithless, rebellious assembly (v. 5). This posture of Israel's leadership indicated their sense of complete helplessness in the face of such an affront to God and so total a rejection of divinely sanctioned leadership. Israel's leaders appeared to be throwing themselves on the mercies of God in abject, spontaneous abandonment of all prerogatives because of sheer alarm at their people's rash behavior and perhaps from dread of the Lord's possible wrathful response to the people.

---

1. How did the people respond to the majority report (vv. 1-4)?
2. What did Moses and Aaron do, and why (v. 5)?

---

B. Caleb and Joshua's Positive Report (vv. 6-10)

(Numbers 14:10 is not included in the printed text.)

**⁶ And Joshua the son of Nun, and Caleb the son of Jephunneh, which were of them that searched the land, rent their clothes: ⁷ And they spake unto all the company of the children of Israel, saying, The land, which we passed through to search it, is an exceeding good land. ⁸ If the Lord delight in us, then he will bring us into this land, and give it us; a land which floweth with milk and honey. ⁹ Only rebel not ye against the Lord, neither fear ye the people of the land; for they are bread for us: their defence is departed from them, and the Lord is with us: fear them not.**

Caleb and Joshua tore their clothes, a traditional Hebrew expression of dismay. Then they asserted to the rebellious congregation that the land of Canaan which they had surveyed was "exceedingly good" (v. 7 NKJV). They next communicated an immediately relevant but ominous conditional truth—"if the Lord delight[s] in us" (v. 8). Evidently, God would take no delight in the entirely foolish and emotionally immature response of the congregation of Israel at this moment. Israel was dependent on divine favor for success and now was on the verge of relinquishing it. A study of Numbers and Joshua shows that constant direct divine intervention led to the eventual military success of Israel a generation later. Without God, Israel was helpless.

Joshua and Caleb emphasized that if the Lord was pleased with Israel He would reward them with His bountiful land of promise, flowing with "milk and honey" (v. 8). But the faithful spies also warned the nation against rebellion, even as they assured them that they need not cower in fear before Canaan's inhabitants (v. 9). It appears that at this point, despite Israel's initial expression of cowardice and rebellion, they might yet have redeemed themselves in God's sight and moved forward into Canaan. At least this seems to have been the hope of Caleb and Joshua. These stalwart defenders of truth said of Israel's potential foes, "They are our bread" (NKJV). The ten-man majority had said that Canaan *devoured* its people; Joshua and Caleb retorted that under God, Israel's enemies would be defeated as easily as eating bread.

Finally, the two courageous men referred to a bedrock, divinely produced reality—the *protection* of Israel's enemies had deserted them. In Genesis 15:16, God had promised Abraham regarding his descendants, "In the fourth generation they shall return here, for the iniquity of the Amorites is not yet complete" (NKJV). The *New Spirit-Filled Life Bible* asserts that the Amorites "represent all the inhabitants of Canaan" and that "God's judgment must await its perfect timing." Caleb and Joshua were asserting that God's shade of "protection from the heat" had departed from the inhabitants of Canaan (see *The Complete Word Study of the Old Testament*). This expression asserts the complete vulnerability of Canaan's armies to obedient, trusting people under God's leadership since the iniquity of Canaan was now ripe for judgment.

The response of the congregation of Israel to Caleb and Joshua was nonetheless rejection to the point of homicidal violence—they insisted that these men of God be stoned (Num. 14:10). For the Lord of covenant, this was the final insult. His glory appeared visibly in the Tabernacle in the sight of all Israel, intervening to remind the rebels of His omnipotence and to circumvent the dastardly stoning of His faithful servants.

---

1. What did Joshua and Caleb believe (vv. 6-8)?

2. What did Joshua and Caleb declare about the land's inhabitants (v. 9)?
3. How were Joshua and Caleb's lives saved (v. 10)?

> "Whenever you make up your mind to refuse to go where God wants you to go and to do what God wants you to do, you must make up your mind at the same time to renounce the friendship of God. You cannot walk with Him and at the same time be in rebellion against Him. God has no possible way of entering into fellowship with the soul that is disobedient to His will. Believe me, it is absolutely useless, it is mere mockery, to say 'Lord, Lord' and then refuse to do the things that He commands you to do."—Clovis G. Chappell

---

C. Dire Repercussions (vv. 20-24)

(Numbers 14:20-23 is not included in the printed text.)

**²⁴ But my servant Caleb, because he had another spirit with him, and hath followed me fully, him will I bring into the land whereinto he went; and his seed shall possess it.**

God threatened to strike the rebellious congregation of Israel with a pestilence, disinherit them, and create out of Moses' descendants a greater nation than Israel (vv. 11-12). Moses, in one of the most remarkable passages of Old Testament Scripture, interceded for Israel on the basis of the nature and reputation of God himself (vv. 13-19). Moses said that if God abandoned Israel, His enemies would claim that He was not able to bring His people into Canaan. Moses appealed to the Lord's *chesed* (a Hebrew word of pivotal importance, meaning "covenant love and mercy"). Moses rehearsed before the Lord words He himself had revealed to Moses in Exodus 34:6-9 regarding His immutable character.

God heard Moses and pardoned Israel (v. 20), but His pardon did not mean their terrible sin of rebellion would go unpunished. Rather, every adult Hebrew male twenty years old or older, and therefore eligible for military service, would perish in the wilderness during the next thirty-eight years (vv. 22-23). The exceptions were Caleb and Joshua (v. 30). Caleb had "a different spirit in him" and "followed [God] fully" (v. 24 NKJV).

Joshua, as Moses' assistant, however brave and admirable, would have been expected by the people to stand with his superior and, moreover, would in the next generation ascend to top leadership. Caleb, meanwhile, singularly bold and courageous and with no reasonable expectation of reward, stood against the tide solely because of his stalwart faith and character.

---

1. Describe the solemn oath made by the Lord (vv. 22-23).
2. What did the Lord declare about Caleb (v. 24)?

> "We must not lose sight of the fact that God's wrath is very real and very justified. We have all sinned incessantly against a holy,

righteous God. We have rebelled willfully against His commands, defied His moral law, and acted in total defiance of His known will for us. Because of these actions we're justly objects of His wrath."—Jerry Bridges

## III. RECEIVING THE INHERITANCE (Josh. 14:6-14)

### A. Caleb's Request (vv. 6-9)

⁶ Then the children of Judah came unto Joshua in Gilgal: and Caleb the son of Jephunneh the Kenezite said unto him, Thou knowest the thing that the Lord said unto Moses the man of God concerning me and thee in Kadeshbarnea. ⁷ Forty years old was I when Moses the servant of the Lord sent me from Kadeshbarnea to espy out the land; and I brought him word again as it was in mine heart. ⁸ Nevertheless my brethren that went up with me made the heart of the people melt: but I wholly followed the Lord my God. ⁹ And Moses sware on that day, saying, Surely the land whereon thy feet have trodden shall be thine inheritance, and thy children's for ever, because thou hast wholly followed the Lord my God.

The Lord had made an irrevocable promise of inheritance to Caleb at the very meeting where his cowardly fellow spies met their death in a plague sent by God (Num. 14:24, 36-37). Forty-five years later, when Canaan was being conquered and apportioned, only Caleb and Joshua remained from their entire generation of adult Israelite males. Caleb and his brethren from the tribe of Judah came before Joshua to request his promised apportionment. Caleb, with his entire tribe supporting him, reminded Joshua how he had followed the Lord "wholeheartedly" (Josh. 14:9 NIV).

- What promise of the Lord does Caleb recall?

"Courage comes to those who seek the Lord and trust Him completely."—Woodrow Kroll

### B. Caleb's Character and Physical Prowess (vv. 10-12)

¹⁰ And now, behold, the Lord hath kept me alive, as he said, these forty and five years, even since the Lord spake this word unto Moses, while the children of Israel wandered in the wilderness: and now, lo, I am this day fourscore and five years old. ¹¹ As yet I am as strong this day as I was in the day that Moses sent me: as my strength was then, even so is my strength now, for war, both to go out, and to come in. ¹² Now therefore give me this mountain, whereof the Lord spake in that day; for thou heardest in that day how the Anakims were there, and that the cities were great and

**fenced: if so be the Lord will be with me, then I shall be able to drive them out, as the Lord said.**

Interpreting God's promise to refer specifically to the mountain on which Hebron and its surrounding lands stood, Caleb said, "Give me this mountain" (v. 12). Though, over all, Canaan had now been conquered, there were still pockets of strong resistance, and among the unconquered were those giants before whom Israel had cowered and who still controlled Hebron. Caleb, at eighty-five, was ready to claim his promised possession.

Caleb attributed his condition at eighty-five to preservation by the Lord. He had retained health of mind and body while his contemporaries withered and died in the wilderness. Moreover, he had participated in several years of battle as Joshua and the younger generation had fought for Canaan, but he was still strong, fit to engage and to finish his final battle. The inhabitants of the vicinity of Hebron were formidable, descendants of the larger-than-life-size foes who had intimidated the former generation of Israelites. But Caleb was not intimidated, and his strength had not weakened.

Caleb's blessing from God was extraordinary, the direct result of his faithfulness when others faltered. But God is unremittingly faithful to His covenant people, whether under the old covenant or the new. The apostle Paul reminded the church at Corinth, "God is faithful, by whom you were called into the fellowship of His Son, Jesus Christ our Lord" (1 Cor. 1:9 NKJV). Therefore, He would provide believers at Corinth and throughout Christian history with every spiritual gift needed and "confirm [them] unto the end" so that they might be "blameless in the day of our Lord Jesus Christ" (v. 8). Our spiritual journey might be extended in time, as was Caleb's life in the wilderness, or it might quickly reach its temporal conclusion. Whatever the case, we will experience the abiding presence of the Holy Spirit and the completely sufficient gifts of God's grace.

---

1. How does Caleb describe himself (vv. 10-11)?
2. What was Caleb anxious to do (v. 12)?

> "Faith is not only necessary to salvation, it is also necessary to live a life pleasing to God. Faith enables us to claim the promises of God, but it also enables us to obey the commands of God. Faith enables us to obey when obedience is costly or seems unreasonable to the natural mind."—Jerry Bridges

---

C. Caleb's Request Granted (vv. 13-14)

**[13] And Joshua blessed him, and gave unto Caleb the son of Jephunneh Hebron for an inheritance. [14] Hebron therefore became the inheritance of Caleb the son of Jephunneh the Kenezite unto this day, because that he wholly followed the Lord God of Israel.**

One quality of a great leader is *reliability*. Without fail, he or she follows through on commitments, carrying out promises. Joshua had assumed the mantle of leadership upon the death of his great mentor, Moses, and proved both capable and stalwart in character. Joshua, moreover, was a skilled military commander who executed precisely the commands of the Lord and therefore led his people to great victories. He fulfilled his commitments, and God's promise to Joshua's early companion Caleb was not the least of these. Joshua *blessed* Caleb and awarded him the opportunity to claim his inheritance.

- What does it mean to "wholly follow" the Lord?

"Faith is to believe what you do not see; the reward of this faith is to see what you believe."—Augustine

## CONCLUSION

Caleb's boldness was born out of sterling character and a deeply ingrained trust in the Lord of Israel. He had witnessed the supernatural actions of God on behalf of his recently liberated fellow Israelites, and he had come to an unshakeable faith that enabled him to stand in the face of Israel's enemies—whether from within or without. This trust, shared by Joshua, preserved both men when their fellow spies for Israel met their death at the hand of the Lord and also kept them strong for a generation while their contemporaries died around them.

In the new generation, Joshua assumed the mantle of supreme leadership under the Lord. Once Israel had conquered most of Canaan, Caleb was permitted, through a great final courageous feat, to achieve his temporal reward. He yet stands as an excellent Old Testament example of boldness and courage. We, too, can persevere against the odds and be exemplars of Christian faithfulness in our generation.

## GOLDEN TEXT CHALLENGE

"MY BRETHREN THAT WENT UP WITH ME MADE THE HEART OF THE PEOPLE MELT: BUT I [CALEB] WHOLLY FOLLOWED THE LORD MY GOD" (Josh. 14:8).

Caleb's statement of fact concerning his having "followed the Lord" is not to be taken as boasting. It is rather a simple declaration of the truth that he had done his duty in bringing back the report he did. In that incident, as well as in all others, he had sought only to honor God. He was faithful to the trust placed in him by sending him into Canaan. His words about having fully followed the Lord are not his words, but those of the Lord himself.

It was God's will that the Israelites advance and take Canaan, and Caleb had done his best to induce them to do so. Unfortunately, the report of ten of his companions had only added to the terror of the faithless people. It adds much to the praise of following God, if we do so when others desert Him. Caleb honestly felt he had sought God's glory on that occasion. Like the apostle Paul, he could look back across the years with confidence that he had been faithful (2 Tim. 4:7).

**Daily Devotions:**
- M. Courage During Transition
  Deuteronomy 31:1-8
- T. Courage to Confront Evil
  2 Chronicles 15:1-9
- W. Courage to Wait
  Psalm 37:1-7
- T. Courageous Request
  Mark 15:42-47
- F. Courageous Testimony
  Acts 4:5-13
- S. Praying for Greater Courage
  Acts 4:23-31

September 28, 2014 (Lesson 4)
# Abigail the Wise
### I Samuel 25:1-42

**Unit Theme:**
Great Stories of the Bible

**Central Truth:**
A wise person makes thoughtful decisions.

**Focus:**
Esteem wisdom over rashness and make prudent choices.

**Context:**
Around 1050 BC near Carmel in the mountain country of Judah

**Golden Text:**
"She [Abigail] was a woman of good understanding, and of a beautiful countenance: but the man [Nabal] was churlish and evil in his doings" (1 Sam. 25:3).

**Study Outline:**
I. Harsh and Worthless Nabal
   (1 Sam. 25:2-17)
II. Intelligent and Discerning Abigail
   (1 Sam. 25:18-35)
III. Nabal's Demise; Abigail's Ascent
   (1 Sam. 25:36-42)

## INTRODUCTION

Abigail, the admirable lady central to this lesson, exhibited wisdom and strength of character under great pressure. As a result, she has served as an example to both genders and to all age groups for three millennia. It is of great spiritual value to study the women of Scripture—from the Old Testament (Eve, Sarah, Rahab, Miriam, Ruth, Hannah, Abigail, and Esther) to the New Testament (Elizabeth, mother of John the Baptist; Mary, the mother of Jesus; the widow of Nain; Mary Magdalene; Mary and Martha, sisters of Lazarus; Lydia, the seller of purple; and Lois and Eunice, the grandmother and mother of Timothy). These fascinating and inspiring women vary greatly in qualities of character and personality. Some, moreover, were thrust from obscurity into the limelight because of faithful obedience, while others remained unheralded, yet exercised strong influence behind the scenes.

The wife, mother, or sister of a male biblical leader at times exercised strong influence on that leader. Sarah, Abraham's beautiful, persuasive wife, led him into a bad decision crucial to subsequent world history—the birth of Ishmael—but she was nonetheless a woman of faith who bore with deserved distinction her divinely altered name, which in Hebrew means "princess." Miriam, Moses' sister, was instrumental in her younger brother's receiving care as an infant by his own mother, when, having been placed in an ark of bulrushes to preserve his life, he was discovered by Pharaoh's daughter, and Miriam (close by) recommended their mother Jochebed as his nurse. Miriam also exhibited contagious joy in celebratory worship after Israel's victory at the Red Sea. But she also rebelled against divinely mandated leadership and suffered punishment and disgrace as a result.

Hannah, a godly wife unable to conceive, persisted in prayer until Eli the priest assured her that her prayer would be answered. After her son Samuel was born, she dedicated his life totally to the service of God, and he later became an outstanding prophet and judge of Israel.

One Old Testament woman who figured significantly in political leadership was Jezebel, wicked queen of King Ahab. She influenced her spineless and faithless husband toward idolatry and heinous evil. In contrast, Esther, elevated providentially to the position of queen of Persia, was instrumental in the deliverance of her fellow Jews from destruction instigated by the evil Haman.

In the New Testament, Elizabeth (a righteous woman) was (with her husband, Zachariah) divinely chosen to parent John the Baptist, forerunner of Jesus. Her cousin Mary, mother of Jesus, was entrusted with a unique mission—to conceive (through the agency of the Holy Spirit) and to bear Jesus, the incarnate Son of God, then to serve (with Joseph) as His parent and guardian during His infancy and childhood.

Abigail, heroine of our current lesson, proved to be strong, perceptive, courageous, and worthy of divine trust in a crucial situation. She contravened the hateful action of her evil husband and circumvented a misguided act of revenge by David.

## I. HARSH AND WORTHLESS NABAL (1 Sam. 25:2-17)

Though destined to be king of Israel, David was still hiding and fleeing from the divinely rejected, tormented Saul, who pursued him relentlessly with superior military force. David and his men hid among the rocky crags and fastnesses of the Wilderness of Paran, far south of Saul's headquarters in Gibeah. David, along with six hundred trusted followers, protected the shepherds of a prominent descendant of Caleb named Nabal, apparently with his knowledge and acquiescence.

### A. Nabal—Churlish Man of Wealth (vv. 2-3)

**² And there was a man in Maon, whose possessions were in Carmel; and the man was very great, and he had three thousand sheep, and a thousand goats: and he was shearing his sheep in Carmel. ³ Now the name of the man was Nabal; and the name of his wife Abigail: and she was a woman of good understanding, and of a beautiful countenance: but the man was churlish and evil in his doings; and he was of the house of Caleb.**

Nabal was a landholder at Carmel in the area of Maon, near the Wilderness of Paran. He owned three thousand sheep and one thousand goats, enough to make him very wealthy. Nabal's name, likely a homonym for *fool* in the Hebrew tongue, was eventually taken to *be* "fool," or else it was an appellation given Nabal after the fact because of his harshness and evil dealing, his original name being erased from memory over time. The word *fool* in the Old Testament denotes a godless person, one devoid of moral and spiritual insight (Ps. 14:1; Prov. 12:15-16), or one who is wicked and vile, sometimes called a *son of Belial*. Nabal's folly was not intellectual in origin (i.e., he was not a philosophical skeptic or an atheist on allegedly rational grounds); rather, it was moral and spiritual. In fact, Nabal, a true biblical fool, was a vile sinner, guilty before God.

Nabal's wife, Abigail, the complete opposite of her husband, was wise and beautiful. She probably had little, if anything, to do with her marriage to this contemptible man but, instead, entered upon an arranged marriage. Her parents probably thought it a great honor to have their daughter married to a man of substance, not realizing or considering his moral and spiritual qualities.

---

- Contrast Nabal with Abigail.

> "The wise man considers what he wants, and the fool what he abounds in."—Lancelot Addison

---

B. David's Request and Nabal's Response (4-11)

(1 Samuel 25:6-9 is not included in the printed text.)

**4 And David heard in the wilderness that Nabal did shear his sheep. 5 And David sent out ten young men, and David said unto the young men, Get you up to Carmel, and go to Nabal, and greet him in my name.**

**10 And Nabal answered David's servants, and said, Who is David? And who is the son of Jesse? There be many servants now a days that break away every man from his master. 11 Shall I then take my bread, and my water, and my flesh that I have killed for my shearers, and give it unto men, whom I know not whence they be?**

Sheep-shearing was a festive occasion when the landowners' servants were given generous portions of food and drink. On the occasion of Nabal's sheep-shearing, David sent ten young followers to Carmel to greet Nabal and to request a contribution of food in exchange for the protection Nabal's shepherds had received from David and his men, who were encamped near Nabal's grazing lands. The young men greeted Nabal warmly and relayed David's request for a contribution, reminding Nabal that they had protected his shepherds and ensured that no sheep went missing. Though this may sound like unsolicited protection in return for reward with an implied threat upon refusal, most Bible interpreters see it in more benign terms, assuming that Nabal had solicited protection or else had knowledge of it, acquiesced in it, and gladly benefitted from it.

David's men waited for Nabal's response, which proved to be neither acceptance of the request nor polite refusal, but, rather, outright vilification of their leader. Nabal sarcastically questioned David's origins and termed him a breakaway servant of Saul unworthy of assistance. In reality, Nabal knew well who David was, but chose to benefit from his presence close by without appropriate acknowledgment. For pragmatic reasons—he did not want to appear rebellious against King Saul, but also because he was an obnoxious person who was behaving according to his churlish nature.

1. What did David and his men request from Nabal (vv. 4-9)?
2. How did Nabal characterize David (v. 10)?

> "I could never draw the line between meanness and dishonesty. What is mean, so far as I can see, slides by indistinguishable gradations into what is dishonest."—George MacDonald

---

C. David's Furious Reply (vv. 12-13)

**12 So David's young men turned their way, and went again, and came and told him all those sayings. 13 And David said unto his men, Gird ye on every man his sword. And they girded on every man his sword; and David also girded on his sword: and there went up after David about four hundred men; and two hundred abode by the stuff.**

When David heard of Nabal's scornful, insulting refusal, he reacted with fury. His immoderate course was to leave two hundred men with the supplies and to take four hundred men with him on a mission that, if completed, would have proved highly unwise and permanently injurious to his reputation and cause. He intended to literally wipe out the males in Nabal's household. Nabal, however wicked, was a wealthy, well-known man of Judah, David's own tribe—a tribe whose support David needed as a base during his rise to power and as the foundation for his eventual rule over Israel. This intended action by David would have soon been known throughout Judah and might well have caused him to be branded as a hothead, given to excessive violence.

---

- How did David respond to Nabal's snub?

---

D. A Servant's Intervention (vv. 14-17)

**14 But one of the young men told Abigail, Nabal's wife, saying, Behold, David sent messengers out of the wilderness to salute our master; and he railed on them. 15 But the men were very good unto us, and we were not hurt, neither missed we any thing, as long as we were conversant with them, when we were in the fields: 16 They were a wall unto us both by night and day, all the while we were with them keeping the sheep. 17 Now therefore know and consider what thou wilt do; for evil is determined against our master, and against all his household: for he is such a son of Belial, that a man cannot speak to him.**

Providentially, one of Nabal's servants told his mistress about David's request and his master's rude rejoinder. The servant also informed Abigail about the relationship he and his fellow shepherds had enjoyed with David and his men. David's followers had been good to them, had never harmed them, and had never taken anything from them. Instead, David's men had been a constant "wall" of protection for the shepherds and their flocks (v. 16). Likely, this meant preventing wild animals from snatching the sheep and keeping thieves from even approaching the shepherds, who were caring for their master's flocks at some distance from his compound.

The servant advised Abigail to consider carefully what she must do in order to prevent the retaliation determined against Nabal and his household. The servant characterized his evil master to his mistress with plainness and accuracy; to put it in contemporary parlance, he *nailed* him. Nabal, said the servant, was "such a son of Belial" (v. 17)—such a *worthless person*—that he and his fellow servants could not even address him without a vile reaction. Fortunately for the servant, Abigail, a perceptive woman who lived every day with this difficult man, knew well his character.

---

1. What did one of Nabal's servants report about David's men (vv. 14-16)?
2. How did this servant characterize Nabal (v. 17)?

> "Your reputation is what people say about you. Your character is what God and your wife know about you."—Billy Sunday

---

II. INTELLIGENT AND DISCERNING ABIGAIL (1 Sam. 25:18-35)

A. Abigail's Decision and David's Determination (vv. 18-22)

(1 Samuel 25:19-20, 22 is not included in the printed text).

**18 Then Abigail made haste, and took two hundred loaves, and two bottles of wine, and five sheep ready dressed, and five measures of parched corn, and an hundred clusters of raisins, and two hundred cakes of figs, and laid them on asses.**

**21 Now David had said, Surely in vain have I kept all that this fellow hath in the wilderness, so that nothing was missed of all that pertained unto him: and he hath requited me evil for good.**

Without consulting or contending with her hateful husband, and without any delay, Abigail prepared a generous gift for David and his men. Nabal, of course, would have forbidden this largesse had he known, so Abigail acted unilaterally. As mistress of the household, she would have enjoyed some degree of discretion in the disposition of foodstuffs, and there was such plentitude that even a large amount would not soon be missed. So the discreet but decisive Abigail assembled a generous supply sufficient to feed several hundred men, loaded it on donkeys, and prepared to take it to David's camp.

David's fury had not subsided; indeed, he still burned with anger. He had acted benevolently toward Nabal and his men, never taking anything from them and constantly protecting them from trepidations by men or beasts. Now he had been repaid with insults. He rashly invoked a divine curse upon himself, inviting God to destroy him and his men if he had not wiped out Nabal and his men by nightfall (see v. 22 NIV).

In the wrathful David, we can see a lesson for all God's faithful. We should never act suddenly in angry response to provocation. Leviticus 19:18 instructs Israel concerning vengeance, "You shall not take vengeance, nor bear any grudge against the children of your people, but you shall love your neighbor as yourself: I am the Lord" (NKJV). The God of covenant forbade the taking of vengeance. If David had persisted in this vengeful response, he would have deprived innocent wives and children of their husbands and fathers, caused harm to his own cause, and, in fact, been guilty before God. The apostle Paul reminds New Testament believers that vengeance belongs to God (Rom. 12:19-20).

---

1. Why did Abigail "make haste" (v. 18)?
2. Why didn't Abigail speak to her husband (v. 19)?
3. What was David's plan (vv. 21-22)?

> **Suzanna Wesley**
> Among the great women of church history is Suzanna Wesley, mother of nineteen children, ten of whom reached adulthood—seven daughters and three sons. Her three sons, following in their father's footsteps, all became Anglican ministers. Suzanna's Christian example and her devotion to the careful training of her children in the Christian faith were largely responsible for the direction and achievement for God of the lives of John and Charles Wesley. They modeled their highly methodical approach to Christian living after their mother's example, and their influence continues to impact the contemporary church.

---

B. Abigail's Gracious Intercession (vv. 23-31)

(1 Samuel 25:23-24, 26-29 is not included in the printed text.)

**25 Let not my lord, I pray thee, regard this man of Belial, even Nabal: for as his name is, so is he; Nabal is his name, and folly is with him: but I thine handmaid saw not the young men of my lord, whom thou didst send.**

**30 And it shall come to pass, when the Lord shall have done to my lord according to all the good that he hath spoken concerning thee, and shall have appointed thee ruler over Israel; 31 That this shall be no grief unto thee, nor offence of heart unto my lord, either that thou hast shed blood causeless, or that my lord hath avenged himself: but when the Lord shall have dealt well with my lord, then remember thine handmaid.**

As David is setting out with his four hundred men to perpetrate his act of revenge on Nabal and his male servants, Abigail approaches him with her servants bearing generous gifts on donkeys behind her (in some ways, reminiscent of Jacob's approach to Esau long before). This gracious lady falls to the ground before David in humble intercession, requesting that he allow her to speak to him (vv. 23-24). Abigail's address to David is opposite to that of her scornful husband to David's men. She acknowledges that Nabal is a scoundrel and a fool, and she points out to David that she had not seen the young men who had visited their compound.

Abigail speaks subtly as she suggests that the Lord has prevented David from vengeful shedding of blood (v. 26). She implies that the Lord himself will take care of Nabal, as He will of all who are David's enemies and who seek to harm him. Abigail speaks out of deep understanding both of the defective character of her husband and of God's covenant with Israel and His support of just causes. She offers her generous gift and asks forgiveness *for herself*—as if she had been the perpetrator of wrongdoing instead of her husband (v. 28). This is a remarkable act of voluntary identification with the wrongdoing done in her household—a stance calculated to cause David to pause and take thought before proceeding with his rash plan.

Some see Abigail as speaking prophetically as she predicts David's accession to the kingship of Israel and views him as fighting "the battles of the Lord" (v. 28). Abigail reminds David that, to this point, evil has never been found in him, a subtle inducement to calm consideration. She is well aware of King Saul's pursuit of David and employs a fascinating image when she states, "The life of my lord shall be bound in the bundle of the living with the Lord your God" (v. 29 NKJV). This image, which appears on the tombstones of many Jewish dead (*Wycliffe Bible Commentary*), refers to the reality that our living and our dying are under divine control; hence, we are not ultimately under the power of any human agent. Abigail sees David's enemies as stones to be slung out by God "as from the pocket of a sling" (v. 29 NKJV).

Abigail climaxes her appeal to David with the statement that, if he behaves honorably in the current situation, once he has come to power through God's providence, he will have no regret, guilt, or bad consequences from having behaved vengefully toward Nabal and his servants (vv. 30-31). In short, Abigail's plea to David is a masterpiece of diplomacy and psychology that reveals her own strength of character and depth of wisdom and perception.

---

1. How did Abigail approach David, and why (vv. 23-24)?
2. How did Abigail describe her husband (v. 25)?
3. What did she ask David to do (vv. 26-28)?
4. List three statements Abigail makes about David (vv. 29-31).

> "We must guard against allowing anger to drag us into sin."—Joyce Meyer

---

C. David's Change of Heart (vv. 32-35)

**[32] And David said to Abigail, Blessed be the Lord God of Israel, which sent thee this day to meet me: [33] And blessed be thy advice, and blessed be thou, which hast kept me this day from coming to shed blood, and from avenging myself with mine own hand. [34] For in very deed, as the Lord God of Israel liveth, which hath kept me back from hurting thee, except thou hadst hasted and come to meet me, surely there had not been left unto**

Nabal by the morning light any that pisseth against the wall. **³⁵ So David received of her hand that which she had brought him, and said unto her, Go up in peace to thine house; see, I have hearkened to thy voice, and have accepted thy person.**

Abigail's intercessory words had great impact on David. The soft, but firm and wise, voice of this courageous woman stilled the heart of a man capable of great extremes of emotion. It is estimated that about half of the psalms in the Old Testament were composed by this gifted man whose harp could chase away the evil spirits troubling Saul, and whose inspired words have brought hope to countless tormented souls ever since David's own time. However, David was also a man of war, physically strong and in some ways rough-hewn—able to inspire men to battle and to lead them to military victory. He was never afraid of a fight, yet unwilling to use any advantage to destroy the divinely rejected but still reigning king (Saul) who would in a moment have destroyed him—a mark of David's integrity before God.

The powerful eloquence of a perceptive woman had brought David to his senses—an unusual occurrence in an age when women were normally confined to the garden, the kitchen, and the nursery. David praised the Lord of Israel that her advice had kept him from needless violence. Part of David's response is couched in rough, masculine vocabulary, but the clear evidence is that Abigail had conquered David through reason and the persuasive power of calm, eloquently expressed truth when nothing else might have stopped him. David now accepted Abigail's pacifying gifts and assured her of his personal respect for her.

## III. NABAL'S DEMISE; ABIGAIL'S ASCENT (1 Sam. 25:36-42)

### A. Abigail's Report; Nabal's Response (vv. 36-38)

**³⁶ And Abigail came to Nabal; and, behold, he held a feast in his house, like the feast of a king; and Nabal's heart was merry within him, for he was very drunken: wherefore she told him nothing, less or more, until the morning light. ³⁷ But it came to pass in the morning, when the wine was gone out of Nabal, and his wife had told him these things, that his heart died within him, and he became as a stone. ³⁸ And it came to pass about ten days after, that the Lord smote Nabal, and he died.**

Abigail returned home to find Nabal feasting as if he were royalty. Scripture here points a diametric contrast between the struggling David, already anointed king of Israel, yet in hiding and periodically fleeing for his life, and the obnoxious Nabal, living like a king and, as it were, pretending to be a king. The man was merry of heart, but deprived of his higher faculties through the excessive drinking of wine. Abigail knew better than to attempt to address her drunken husband. It would be hard enough when he was sober. But in the morning, when Nabal had sobered up, Abigail related to him the result of his foolish behavior—the fact that only her intercession had prevented every male in the compound from being wiped out by the wrathful David.

Nabal's response was either a massive heart attack or a massive stroke—"his heart died within him" (v. 37). He likely never regained consciousness, and Scripture pointedly relates that, ten days afterward, "the Lord struck Nabal, and he died" (v. 38 NKJV). Clearly, in an appropriate climactic conclusion to Nabal's folly, the Lord pronounced judgment on him and ended his life.

---

- Describe Nabal's demise.

> "Let a man meet a bear robbed of her cubs, rather than a fool in his folly" (Prov. 17:12 NASB).

---

B. David's Offer; Abigail's Acceptance (vv. 39-42)

(1 Samuel 25:40-41 is not included in the printed text.)

**39 And when David heard that Nabal was dead, he said, Blessed be the Lord, that hath pleaded the cause of my reproach from the hand of Nabal, and hath kept his servant from evil: for the Lord hath returned the wickedness of Nabal upon his own head. And David sent and communed with Abigail, to take her to him to wife.**

**42 And Abigail hasted, and arose, and rode upon an ass, with five damsels of her's that went after her; and she went after the messengers of David, and became his wife.**

David's reaction to news of Nabal's death was recognition of God's hand in it and praise to God for preventing him from an evil response to human folly. David thought in scriptural terms—an indication that he had been well instructed in the Mosaic Law and therefore understood that God worked out His will for His covenant people at every level.

David understood the omnipresence, omniscience, and omnipotence of God and the implications of that truth for his life and the lives of those around him. God had irrevocable plans for David and for Israel, and no rebellious mortal, whether rejected king or man of folly, would prevent the achievement of the divine purpose. It was also clear to David that sin had inevitable consequences and that an almighty, just God was entirely able to deal temporally and ultimately with sin.

New Testament believers are equally under divine oversight. We fight an implacable Enemy who hates God and His eternal truth, and who marshals his powerful spiritual forces against every redeemed man, woman, and child, determined either to destroy us or to render us useless in the kingdom of God. Romans 8:28 records a truth not only intended to comfort struggling believers, but also to assure them of their important position in God's economy: "We know that all things work together for good to those who love God, to those who are the called according to His purpose" (NKJV).

There are at least five personally applicable truths in this verse: (1) our identity in God; (2) our calling by God; (3) God's purpose—larger than us, but including us; (4) God's control of everything pertaining to us; and (5) God's unremitting benevolence toward us as His children. We need not resort to human devices in an effort to achieve God's purposes, which are in His hand and under His direction. Our part in the working out of God's plan is trust, obedience, and availability.

David invited the widowed Abigail to join his growing retinue as a second wife. He had been deprived by Saul of Merab, the king's eldest daughter (1 Sam. 18:19), and he had lost Michal when Saul took her from him and gave her to another man (25:44). David had afterward married Ahinoam (v. 43), and now he took Abigail as a second wife. Deuteronomy 17:14-20 instructed Israel concerning kings God knew they would later choose to lead them. God expressly forbade plurality of marriage: "Neither shall he multiply wives for himself, lest his heart turn away" (v. 17 NKJV). David was continuing a wrongful practice begun by King Saul, and it was a choice which would lead to contention, rebellion, and heartbreak in David's household. Abigail, nonetheless, was a choice lady, wise and perceptive, one whose wisdom, if sought and followed by David, might well have kept him from the needless pain he incurred in days to come.

1. How did David explain the death of Nabal (v. 39)?
2. In her acceptance of David's proposal, how did Abigail describe herself (vv. 40-41)?

"Pride builds walls between people; humility builds bridges."—Rick Warren

## CONCLUSION

Abigail was the wife of Nabal, a man of folly who incurred the wrath of David through his scornful rejection of a reasonable request by David and his men for remuneration for generous acts of service. David's rash intention to destroy every male in Nabal's compound was fortunately prevented by the gracious intercession of the remarkably intelligent, wise, and perceptive Abigail, whose persuasive words, generous gifts, and humility brought David to his senses and changed his ill-conceived course of action. Nabal, a moral and spiritual fool in the biblical sense, perished in an act of divine judgment, while David survived to become king of Israel, and the beautiful, wise, and courageous Abigail became his wife.

## GOLDEN TEXT CHALLENGE

"SHE [ABIGAIL] WAS A WOMAN OF GOOD UNDERSTANDING, AND OF A BEAUTIFUL COUNTENANCE: BUT THE MAN [NABAL] WAS CHURLISH AND EVIL IN HIS DOINGS" (1 Sam. 25:3).

Here is a candid description of both the husband and his wife. *Nabal*, whose name means "fool," was an obdurate and stubborn individual who resented any suggestion that he ought to reciprocate David's care over his flocks. Abigail, on the other hand, was a woman of tact and understanding as well as beauty.

People are not born with these little acts of life over the years. Thoughts, actions, habits—these combine to form a character. Whether we end up like Nabal or Abigail will depend on what we continually do with our time.

**Daily Devotions:**

- M. A Rash Vow
  Judges 11:30-40
- T. The Legacy of Fools
  Proverbs 3:31-35
- W. Wicked or Wise?
  Proverbs 9:7-12
- T. Prayerful Decision
  Acts 1:15-26
- F. Foolish Wisdom
  1 Corinthians 3:18-23
- S. Live Wisely
  Ephesians 5:15–21

October 5, 2014 (Lesson 5)
# Elisha the Prophet
**1 Kings 19:19-21; 2 Kings 2:1-25; 4:38-41; 13:14-25**

> **Unit Theme:**
> Great Stories of the Bible
>
> **Central Truth:**
> God empowers us to fulfill our callings.
>
> **Focus:**
> Consider the ministry of Elisha and follow God's call.
>
> **Context:**
> Elisha ministers in Israel around 850 to 800 BC.
>
> **Golden Text:**
> "Who hath saved us, and called us with an holy calling, not according to our works, but according to his own purpose and grace, which was given us in Christ Jesus before the world began" (2 Tim. 1:9).
>
> **Study Outline:**
>   I. Elisha's Call and Anointing
>      (1 Kings 19:19-21; 2 Kings 2:1-15)
>  II. Miracles With Water and Food
>      (2 Kings 2:19-25; 4:38-41)
> III. Final Prophecy; Final Miracle
>      (2 Kings 13:14-19, 22-25, 20-21)

## INTRODUCTION

The leadership of the nation of Israel, after the period of the judges, included the roles of king, priest, prophet, and elder. The king ruled the nation—ideally, *under God*. The high priest headed institutional religion, and the other priests and the Levites assisted him—until the division of the kingdom under King Rehoboam. Then only the southern kingdom even pretended to honor the Mosaic covenant, while in the northern kingdom Jeroboam established an idolatrous system. The elders ruled in the local communities. Prophets of God acted outside established institutions, though not in contradiction to those institutions if they were operating according to stipulations of Israel's covenant with God (which never happened in the northern kingdom). The prophet occupied a unique role in Hebrew culture because, if he spoke authentically, he spoke directly at the behest of God.

The kings of Israel and Judah had a close relationship with the prophets of God, whether they wanted it or not, for God often gave specific instructions and pronounced specific judgments through His anointed prophets. When kings and priests veered away from requirements of Israel's unchanging covenant instituted by the Lord, and when the people of God turned to idolatry, usually it was a true prophet of the Lord who called them back to fidelity to covenant.

The prophet had no other office—no position of secular power like the king, no institutional role like the priest. *Nabi*, the Hebrew word translated as *prophet*, derives from the root of *call* in Hebrew. Indeed, central to the prophet's role was his *calling by the Lord*. Typically, he (or rarely she) was called out from an ordinary lifestyle to speak and act on behalf of the Lord. The prophet's authority, then, rested solely in his relationship with Yahweh and in the authentication of that relationship through fulfilled prophecy and visible miracles that caused his audience, whether king or peasant, to trust his voice, even when their inclination was to act in ways contrary to the law of God contained in the Mosaic Code.

The prophet sometimes was called a *seer* because he saw visions or apprehended a spiritual dimension of the external environment beyond the perspective of the ordinary man or woman (see 2 Kings 6:20; 2:11-12). The prophet was very often called "man of God" because he spoke and acted at the direct command of the Lord. Even an idolatrous king who hated the genuine prophet of Jehovah often would call on him in times of crisis, seeking knowledge about the potential outcome of a battle or about some aspect of his own future.

From the time of Samuel forward, there were *sons of the prophets*—schools of young prophets under the direction of a recognized prophet-leader such as Samuel, Elijah, or Elisha. There is no scriptural evidence, however, that Elisha was schooled with the "sons of the prophets." At the time of his call by Elijah, Elisha was working for his father, a prominent farmer in northern Israel. Through a directive from God to Elijah, Elisha was called to leave the plow and accompany Elijah as his attendant and apprentice, a relationship to some extent like that of one of the twelve disciples to Jesus.

## I. ELISHA'S CALL AND ANOINTING (1 Kings 19:19-21; 2 Kings 2:1-15)

Elijah the prophet, after his outstanding victory over the prophets of Baal at Mount Carmel (1 Kings 18), had fearfully fled from the fury of Queen Jezebel, traveling three hundred miles south and ending up in a cave on Mount Sinai (ch. 19). God met the discouraged prophet there and gave him a vision in which he saw a whirlwind, an earthquake, and a fire; God, however, was not in these spectacular phenomena, though He might have chosen to act so. Instead, He spoke to the prophet in a *gentle whisper* ("still small voice," v. 12), questioning why he was holed up there. God gave him precise instructions for future activity, assuring him that he was indeed not alone, but one among seven thousand in Israel who had not bowed the knee to the Baal, Canaan's false fertility god.

Elijah was instructed to anoint Hazael as king of Syria, Jehu as king of Israel, and Elisha as his own successor. In the strength of this spiritual encounter, Elijah went forth to obey God's precise instructions and to continue his ministry until God translated him to heaven. Elijah had long since learned total obedience, one important key to power with God. His emotions might fluctuate, but his will belonged to Yahweh. God's servants today must first have a spiritual encounter with God; then they must obey Him fully as they pursue the ministry to which He has called them.

## A. Called (1 Kings 19:19-21)

**¹⁹ So he departed thence, and found Elisha the son of Shaphat, who was plowing with twelve yoke of oxen before him, and he with the twelfth: and Elijah passed by him, and cast his mantle upon him. ²⁰ And he left the oxen, and ran after Elijah, and said, Let me, I pray thee, kiss my father and my mother, and then I will follow thee. And he said unto him, Go back again: for what have I done to thee? ²¹ And he returned back from him, and took a yoke of oxen, and slew them, and boiled their flesh with the instruments of the oxen, and gave unto the people, and they did eat. Then he arose, and went after Elijah, and ministered unto him.**

Elijah immediately set about completing the first task assigned him by the Lord. He went to Abel Meholah (see v. 16), where he found Elisha plowing in his father's field, supervising workers who (with him) were plowing twelve yoke of oxen. Elijah abruptly removed his mantle—his outer garment made of animal skins, or haircloth—and threw it over Elisha's shoulder. This symbolic action was properly interpreted by Elisha as a call to service under the prophet's command. Some commentators believe the prophets wore a distinct outer garment easily discerned as different from that worn by others. This mantle became a symbol of spiritual anointing.

Elisha immediately set about to prepare for his change of vocation. He asked for leave to bid his parents farewell before joining his new master. Elijah replied cryptically, "Go back again, for what have I done to you?" (v. 20 NKJV). Some think he was remonstrating with Elisha for hesitating, but perhaps he was instead saying, "Make your necessary preparations, but be well aware of the import of the action I have performed on you, and don't linger." When God issues a call, we must make due preparations . . . but not hesitate and endlessly ask questions, while God's harvest field remains unreaped (see Jesus' comparable calls to action in Luke 9:57-62).

Elisha noticeably cut his ties by taking two of the oxen used for plowing, preparing a farewell meal for his family and friends, and cooking the meat with wood from the plow. In effect, he was boldly stating that he was taking a diametric turn, no longer to engage in a secular occupation, but instead to serve the man of God as his called assistant. Elisha was teaming up with God's man, placed in northern Israel to be His spokesman to a rebellious king and people.

Elisha's answer to God's call serves as an example to the people of God today. We must be sensitive to the voice of God's Spirit and ready to take whatever steps He directs. At times, family and friends may fail to understand and/or sympathize with the spiritual priorities God has brought to the forefront of our attention through the Holy Spirit. We might indeed find it necessary to proceed with God's plans for us, despite the nay-saying of those we might have expected to give support. Complacent believers often fail to share the burden of the believer answering God's call. Nonetheless, as believers at the outset of a call to ministry, we must recognize established spiritual authority, respect it, and follow it after applying appropriate scriptural tests.

---

1. Explain Elijah's actions in verse 19.

2. How did Elisha demonstrate his commitment to follow Elijah (vv. 20-21)?

> "His voice leads us not into timid discipleship but into bold witness." —Charles Stanley

### B. Tested (2 Kings 2:1-6)

(2 Kings 2:2-6 is not included in the printed text.)

**¹ And it came to pass, when the Lord would take up Elijah into heaven by a whirlwind, that Elijah went with Elisha from Gilgal.**

Elijah had done God's bidding for a generation and was now nearing the remarkable conclusion of his long, lonely, and difficult mission. Among the sons of the prophets whom Elijah had directed and instructed, his imminent homegoing was general knowledge, communicated either directly by Elijah or from God himself. Elijah was heading for the place of his departure. Elisha had accompanied and served him for some time now. Elijah and Elisha were at Gilgal, in the hills of Ephraim slightly north of Bethel. Elijah suggested that Elisha remain at Gilgal while he went to Bethel, but Elisha insisted that he had no intention of separating himself from his master. Elijah was giving Elisha a series of tests, obviously designed to determine the extent of his dedication to God and his fitness to assume the mantle of prophetic leadership.

The sons of the prophets were men of God, but not as spiritually attuned as was Elisha. After all, they had not accompanied Elijah on every recent mission for God as had Elisha. They knew essentially what was to happen, but not exactly when, where, or how. Elisha had no patience with their probing of his mind and no intention of entering into a discussion with them regarding God's plans for his master. Indeed, knowing that his earthly relationship with Elijah was nearing its end, he likely was grieving.

Elijah's test of Elisha continued. The elder prophet urged the younger associate to remain at Bethel while he went to Jericho. But Elisha was adamant. He repeated his earlier assertion, "As the Lord lives, and as your soul lives, I will not leave you!" (v. 4 NKJV). I remember a Pentecostal saint who would testify, "My face is set like a flint." She was expressing her determination not to be deflected from her mission to serve Christ and to be ready should she die or He return. The church needs such stalwart saints in every generation. The sons of the prophets, at every stop, expressed their certainty that Elijah was to be "taken away today," and Elisha repeatedly expressed his own certainty and need for their silence.

At Jericho, Elijah asked Elisha to remain there while he went on to the Jordan. The crossing of the Jordan is an age-old symbol for death and going to meet the Lord. African-American spirituals such as "Deep River" have enshrined it in our cultural memory in America. Given the associations of Israel with the Jordan River as the point of entrance into Canaan, it was most appropriate that Elisha go with his master to this crossing of the Jordan.

- How was Elisha tested, and how did he respond?

> "The supreme test of goodness is not in the greater but in the smaller incidents of our character and practice."—F. B. Meyer

C. Empowered (vv. 7-15)

(2 Kings 2:7-12 is not included in the printed text.)
**[13] He took up also the mantle of Elijah that fell from him, and went back, and stood by the bank of Jordan; [14] And he took the mantle of Elijah that fell from him, and smote the waters, and said, Where is the Lord God of Elijah? and when he also had smitten the waters, they parted hither and thither: and Elisha went over. [15] And when the sons of the prophets which were to view at Jericho saw him, they said, The spirit of Elijah doth rest on Elisha. And they came to meet him, and bowed themselves to the ground before him.**

Elisha insisted that he would accompany Elijah across the river. In his final performance of a miracle, Elijah struck the waters of the river with his mantle, and they divided so that the two crossed over on dry ground (v. 8). Meanwhile, fifty sons of the prophets observed at a distance. Elisha had passed a crucial spiritual test by his adamant refusal to remain behind as Elijah moved from town to town. Elisha understood the spiritual import of accompanying Elijah until the end, and he perceived that he was prepared to assume the mantle of anointed leadership Elijah was to leave behind.

Now Elijah asked, "What may I do for you, before I am taken away from you?" (v. 9 NKJV). Elisha asked for a "double portion" of Elijah's spirit. He was not asking for *twice as much*, though Elisha's fourteen recorded miracles are twice as many as Elijah's seven. The younger prophet was asking for the portion of the firstborn (double that of other male heirs), which, in this case, entailed leadership over the sons of the prophets—a position as spokesman for God to the coming generation, and accompanying miraculous power. Elijah could not himself grant that request, but he gave Elisha a sign that would indicate God's granting of the request—Elisha's seeing him as he was taken away.

As the two walked on and talked, "a chariot of fire appeared with horses of fire" (v. 11 NKJV), and Elijah was taken to heaven in a whirlwind. Elisha exclaimed, "My father, my father, the chariot of Israel and its horsemen!" (v. 12 NKJV). Elisha was expressing his profound respect for his master, indicating his insight into the role Elijah had performed for his generation in northern Israel, and revealing his own spiritual vision as a *seer*, a God-imparted ability to see into the spiritual realm.

Elisha now picked up Elijah's mantle which had fallen as he ascended into heaven, smote the waters of the Jordan with the mantle as he exclaimed, "Where is the Lord God of Elijah?" (v. 14), and crossed back over the Jordan on dry land. The sons of the prophets, observing at a distance, were now ready to accept Elisha's leadership as they admitted that "the spirit of Elijah rests on Elisha" (v. 15 NKJV). The *spirit*, of course, was the Spirit of God, that special anointing for God-appointed service necessary to the spokesman for God for the next generation.

1. Describe Elijah's final miracle (vv. 7-8).
2. Why did Elijah call Elisha's request "a hard thing" (vv. 9-10)?
3. Why do you suppose Elijah's exit was so elaborate (vv. 11-12)?
4. What was Elisha's first miracle, and what was its impact (vv. 13-15)?

> "The remains of great and good men, like Elijah's mantle, ought to be gathered up and preserved by their survivors; that as their works follow them in the reward of them, they may stay behind in their benefit."—Matthew Henry

---

II. MIRACLES WITH WATER AND FOOD (2 Kings 2:19-25; 4:38-41)

A. Authentication Through Healed Waters (2:19-22)

**19 And the men of the city said unto Elisha, Behold, I pray thee, the situation of this city is pleasant, as my lord seeth: but the water is naught, and the ground barren. 20 And he said, Bring me a new cruse, and put salt therein. And they brought it to him. 21 And he went forth unto the spring of the waters, and cast the salt in there, and said, Thus saith the Lord, I have healed these waters; there shall not be from thence any more death or barren land. 22 So the waters were healed unto this day, according to the saying of Elisha which he spake.**

The sons of the prophets assumed that Elijah's body had been left by the Lord somewhere in the wilderness after the prophet's separation from Elisha; so, they requested permission to search for the body, thereby showing the limitations of their spiritual perception (v. 16). Elisha knew better and advised against the search, but allowed it when they persisted. They, of course, did not find a corpse since Elijah had ascended to heaven without dying (v. 17). These sons of the prophets had settled in a pleasant location which unfortunately had bad water and barren soil. Elisha asked for a bowl containing salt and, receiving it, cast it into the water source, proclaiming that the water would no longer cause death or barren soil. God was showing the sons of the prophets that He could supply their needs miraculously through His anointed servant Elisha.

---

- Describe the healing depicted in this passage and the reason for it.

> "Miracles are always designed to authenticate the human instrument God has chosen to declare a specific revelation to those who witness the miracle."—John MacArthur

## B. Authentication Through Judgment (vv. 23-25)

**²³ And he went up from thence unto Bethel: and as he was going up by the way, there came forth little children out of the city, and mocked him, and said unto him, Go up, thou bald head; go up, thou bald head. ²⁴ And he turned back, and looked on them, and cursed them in the name of the Lord. And there came forth two she bears out of the wood, and tare forty and two children of them. ²⁵ And he went from thence to mount Carmel, and from thence he returned to Samaria.**

Leaving the sons of the prophets, Elisha walked toward Bethel. As he traveled up the road, he was met by some youths from Bethel who mocked him, saying, "Go up, you baldhead! Go up, you baldhead!" (v. 23 NKJV). These were not mere children, but, rather, *young men* who were well aware of what they were saying. Very likely, they were followers of Baal who recognized Elisha as a prophet of the Lord by his distinctive outer garment, and proceeded to show profound disrespect for the man and the God he served.

Elisha's response was severe, but not unjust; else God would not have honored it. He cursed them in the name of the Lord. Two female bears came from the woods and "mauled forty-two of the youths" (NKJV). Some find this account hard to explain and accept, but the disrespectful young men and all Israel must understand the power of the Lord God and the authority of His prophet.

---

- Why were these young people judged so harshly?

> "Punishment is justice for the unjust."—Augustine

---

## C. Authentication Through Purified Food (4:38-41)

**³⁸ And Elisha came again to Gilgal: and there was a dearth in the land; and the sons of the prophets were sitting before him: and he said unto his servant, Set on the great pot, and seethe pottage for the sons of the prophets. ³⁹ And one went out into the field to gather herbs, and found a wild vine, and gathered thereof wild gourds his lap full, and came and shred them into the pot of pottage: for they knew them not. ⁴⁰ So they poured out for the men to eat. And it came to pass, as they were eating of the pottage, that they cried out, and said, O thou man of God, there is death in the pot. And they could not eat thereof. ⁴¹ But he said, Then bring meal. And he cast it into the pot; and he said, Pour out for the people, that they may eat. And there was no harm in the pot.**

As Elisha was making his circuit of the schools of the prophets, he came to Gilgal, where there was widespread famine. The men there were hard-pressed to find adequate food for the group. When Elisha instructed his servant (likely Gehazi) to make a stew in a large pot, one of the young prophets found some wild gourds, which he added to the stew. When the men began to eat, they discovered that these wild gourds had poisoned the stew. Elisha instructed someone to bring some flour and add it to the pot, upon which the stew became entirely edible.

Elisha, during more than fifty years of prophetic ministry, performed a number of miracles—miracles of transformation, multiplication, healing, judgment, and raising of the dead. Thereby, God stamped His approval on His servant, as He had on his predecessor Elijah. Both the populace of northern Israel and the kings reigning in Samaria during the prophet's lifetime, despite their persistence in idolatrous rebellion against the Lord, knew Elisha was an anointed spokesman for God who manifested miraculous spiritual power.

During the early days of Pentecost at the beginning of the twentieth century, when persecution against ministers and laity alike was strong, God repeatedly showed Himself mighty through signs and wonders. In fact, healings and exorcisms of demons are happening today in nations where Christians are being oppressed, imprisoned, and killed.

---

1. What terrible mistake was made, and how was it remedied?
2. Describe a time God intervened for you when you made an error in judgment.

### A Pentecostal Prophet

W. J. Cothern was a rough-hewn, stalwart, humble Pentecostal prophet who had been a pioneer planter of churches and an overseer of mission states. When my dad was dying of a strangulated hernia which had been improperly diagnosed, God gave Pastor Cothern a dream vision which was tantamount to an x-ray of my dad's abdomen. On the strength of this revelation of Dad's condition, he was moved to another hospital, where life-saving surgery was performed. In fact, according to the surgeon, Dad would have died of gangrene within twenty-four hours without this divine intervention.

There were also words of knowledge often given by Pastor Cothern. On one occasion, without any known reason, I prepared an outline for a message and took it with me on Sunday morning. Brother Cothern met me at the side door of the church, saying, "Brother Sabc, the Lord told me that you have the message for today." Exposure to this kind of sensitivity to the Spirit cements one's faith in God's Word, despite the opposite pull of intellect and competing pressure to conform to modern culture.—Sabord Woods

---

III. FINAL PROPHECY; FINAL MIRACLE (2 Kings 13:14-19, 22-25, 20-21)

A. Challenge From a Dying Prophet (vv. 14-19)

(2 Kings 13:14-17 is not included in the printed text.)

¹⁸ **And he said, Take the arrows. And he took them. And he said unto the king of Israel, Smite upon the ground. And he smote thrice, and stayed. ¹⁹ And the man of God was wroth with him, and said, Thou shouldest have smitten five or six times; then hadst thou smitten Syria till thou hadst consumed it; whereas now thou shalt smite Syria but thrice.**

Elisha continued his prophetic ministry until the reign of Joash in Israel. At that time, Elisha became sick with his final illness. The king visited Elisha and wept in his grief over the coming loss to the nation. The king uttered a cryptic phrase, "O my father, my father, the chariots of Israel and their horsemen!" (v. 14 NKJV; cf. 2:12). Joash was expressing both his deep respect for the dying prophet and his recognition that Israel's victories over Syria had come through the fulfilled prophecy of the Lord's anointed servant.

Elisha gave a challenge to Joash. He instructed him to take a bow and some arrows and put his hands on the bow. Elisha placed his hands over those of the king. The king opened the east window, at the prophet's command, and shot an arrow. Elisha was giving a powerful object lesson to Joash as he called this "the arrow of the Lord's deliverance" and told the king that he must strike the Syrians at Aphek until he had destroyed them (13:17). Then he had Joash take the arrows and strike the ground with them. Joash struck three times and stopped. Elisha told him he should have struck five or six times, for then he would have struck Syria until he had totally destroyed that nation, but now would gain only three victories over Syria. Perhaps Joash's limited determination and effectiveness of leadership were symbolically indicated by his striking only three times.

---

1. What does verse 14 show about Joash's relationship with Elisha?
2. Explain Elisha's final prophecy.

> "A strong will, a settled purpose, an invincible determination, can accomplish almost anything; and in this lies the distinction between great men and little men."—Thomas Fuller

---

B. Authentication of the Prophet's Word (vv. 22-25)

(2 Kings 13:22-25 is not included in the printed text.)
After the prophet's death, Hazael, king of Syria, oppressed Israel repeatedly during Joash's reign. God, however, did not allow total destruction of northern Israel at this time because He was still honoring His covenant with the patriarchs of Israel (see v. 23). In fact, after the death of Hazael, Joash, in confirmation of Elisha's word, defeated Ben-Hadad, the new king of Syria, three times, in the process recapturing cities that had been taken by the Syrians.

C. Dead Prophet; Living Lord (vv. 20-21)

²⁰ **And Elisha died, and they buried him. And the bands of the Moabites invaded the land at the coming in of the year. ²¹ And it came to pass, as they were burying a man, that, behold, they spied a band of men; and they**

cast the man into the sepulchre of Elisha: and when the man was let down, and touched the bones of Elisha, he revived, and stood up on his feet.

Unlike his predecessor Elijah, Elisha died soon after his encounter with King Joash. Despite temperamental weaknesses, Elijah had been a strong, uncompromising spokesman for God during the reign of the heinous King Ahab, his evil Phoenician queen Jezebel, and their son Ahaziah. Elijah's successor, Elisha, was a bold, effective spokesman for God to several kings of northern Israel, including Jehoram, Jehu, Jehu's son Jehoahaz, and Jehu's grandson Joash. Elisha's word was credible to these idolatrous kings because what he prophesied came to pass without fail—the test in Deuteronomy 18:20-22 of authenticity for a prophet who spoke in the name of the Lord.

God granted a wonderful miracle in honor of the dead Elisha. As defenders of Israel fleeing from Moabite invaders quickly buried a dead soldier in the tomb of Elisha, the man immediately revived upon touching the bones of the dead prophet. There was no divine power in the bones, but there was infinite power in the God whom Elisha had served.

- Why do you suppose God performed this resurrection?

> "The Lord intends us to be powerful people—mighty in optimism and hopeful of spirit, powerful in evangelistic zeal, potent in influence, sturdy in moral fiber and purity. We can be powerhouses in prayer and preaching."—David Jeremiah

## CONCLUSION

Elisha was called by God through Elijah the Tishbite to assume his mantle of prophetic leadership for the ensuing generation in northern Israel. Elijah had been used greatly by God as spokesman to kings and as a minister to the people, but Elisha, who received the double portion of the eldest son at Elijah's death, had a ministry even more powerful than that of Elijah. He had the ear of several kings of Israel, and he performed fourteen miracles—of multiplication, transformation, purification, healing, judgment, and raising of the dead. These great men of God served as types of how God would minister through John the Baptist as well as Jesus Christ and His apostles. Our miracle-working God is still active in His church and within twenty-first-century culture today.

## GOLDEN TEXT CHALLENGE

"WHO HATH SAVED US, AND CALLED US WITH AN HOLY CALLING, NOT ACCORDING TO OUR WORKS, BUT ACCORDING TO HIS OWN PURPOSE AND GRACE, WHICH WAS GIVEN US IN CHRIST JESUS BEFORE THE WORLD BEGAN" (2 Tim. 1:9).

As encouragement to Timothy when suffering came, Paul points out two great things God has done for us. First, He has saved us. That purpose was in the divine mind before the world began and was designed entirely independent of any works of our own. This is the gospel of salvation, and we must not think it too much to suffer for what we hope to be saved by.

Second, though we were sinners, God called us to the holy calling of preaching the gospel of salvation, which will bring affliction upon us. This call came from God and claimed us wholly for God. By the appearing of Christ, the gracious purpose of the Father is made plain to us. As He said, any who have "seen Him"—discerned His tender, loving purpose in offering Himself as the sacrifice for the sin of the world—have seen the divine purpose in the heart of the Father.

**Daily Devotions:**

M. Gifted Artisans
   Exodus 36:1-4
T. Deborah the Prophetess
   Judges 4:4-10
W. Call of a Shepherd
   Amos 7:10-17
T. Sent by Jesus
   Matthew 10:1-8
F. Gifted by the Spirit
   Romans 12:3-8
S. Charged to Minister
   1 Timothy 4:11-16

October 12, 2014 (Lesson 6)
# John the Baptist

**Matthew 3:1-12; 14:1-12; Luke 1:5-80; 7:28**

**Unit Theme:**
Great Stories of the Bible

**Central Truth:**
Believers in Christ should faithfully follow God's will.

**Focus:**
Survey and follow John the Baptist's example of faithfulness to God.

**Context:**
The life of John the Baptist (about 4 BC to AD 30)

**Golden Text:**
"This is he, of whom it is written, Behold, I send my messenger before thy face, which shall prepare thy way before thee" (Luke 7:27).

**Study Outline:**
I. Incredible Beginning
   (Luke 1:5-15, 57-66, 76-80)
II. Powerful Prophetic Preaching
   (Matt. 3:1-12)
III. Martyr's Death; Faithful Legacy
   (Matt. 14:1-12; Luke 7:28)

## INTRODUCTION

John the Baptist was the last of the Old Testament prophets. He was in the tradition of the great non-writing prophets who declared the will and wisdom of God to many generations of Israelites who were perennially unfaithful to God's covenant. Among these prophets were Nathan, Ahijah, Micaiah, Elijah, and Elisha. But John was also the herald of the coming Messiah. John appeared in the first century AD in fulfillment of Old Testament prophecy. Isaiah 40:3 foretold John's crucial role as forerunner of the Messiah: "The voice of one crying in the wilderness: 'Prepare the way of the Lord; make straight in the desert a highway for our God'" (NKJV).

Malachi, the last book of the Old Testament, encouraged God's faithful people as it predicted John's preparatory role for the Messiah. The prophet recorded the following word of the Lord to former exiles in Babylon back home in Judah: "Behold, I send My messenger, and he will prepare the way before Me. And the Lord, whom you seek, will suddenly come to His temple, even the Messenger of the covenant, in whom you delight" (3:1 NKJV).

Malachi 4:5-6 foretold that Elijah the prophet would herald the coming of the day of the Lord: "Behold, I will send you Elijah the prophet before the coming of the great and dreadful day of the Lord. And he will turn the hearts of the fathers to the children, and the hearts of the children to their fathers, lest I come and strike the earth with a curse" (NKJV). The angel Gabriel, in his message to Zacharias, associated this scripture with the yet-unborn John the Baptist (Luke 1:17). Also, Jesus himself declared that John the Baptist had fulfilled prophecy foretelling Elijah's role (Matt. 17:11-12).

John was born to aging godly parents, previously unable to have a child, in direct fulfillment of a prediction by the angel Gabriel, who specified John's role and directed how he should be prepared by his parents for that role. The Old Testament contains several precedents for John's divinely enabled birth. When God had a special mission to be undertaken, He often announced it to parents previously unable to conceive and then enabled supernaturally the birth of the coming leader. Two examples are Samson and Samuel.

John was, by heredity, a priest since his father and mother were descendants of Aaron. Also, by special calling, he was a prophet who bridged the Old Testament and the New as he prepared the people of God for the coming Messiah by calling them to repentance.

## I. INCREDIBLE BEGINNING (Luke 1:5-15, 57-66, 76-80)

### A. A Righteous Couple (vv. 5-7)

(Luke 1:5-7 is not included in the printed text.)

Near the beginning of what later became known as the first century AD, a godly priest named Zacharias and his righteous wife, Elizabeth, lived near Jerusalem—possibly about twenty miles to the south in Hebron, a city among those reserved for priests and Levites when Joshua divided Canaan among the tribes. Zacharias was by heredity a priest of the division of Abijah. A thousand years earlier, King David, with the assistance of the high priests Zadok and Ahimelech, had separated the priests into twenty-four divisions. The division of Abijah was the eighth. These divisions had probably been reconstituted after the return from the Babylonian Captivity around 538 BC.

Luke asserts that Zacharias and Elizabeth were "both righteous before God" (v. 6)—not *flawless*, but *faithful* in their obedience to "the commandments and ordinances of the Lord." The word *commandments* refers to the ten great moral absolutes given by God to Moses; *ordinances* are specific regulations for worship and conduct spelled out in detail in the Mosaic Law.

Elizabeth had been unable to bear a child. In a culture in which having a son to pass the family heritage to the succeeding generation was a sign of God's blessing, the inability to bear children was a cause for great sorrow. Indeed, some acquaintances would have questioned whether some flaw in their character might have caused God to render the couple childless. Zacharias and Elizabeth, moreover, were now well past the normal age for child bearing.

---

- Characterize Zacharias and Elizabeth's relationship with God.

> "Little children are God's ongoing witness of His kingdom: a perpetual reminder of what it means to belong to the Father."—Winkie Pratney

### B. Zacharias' Priestly Duties (vv. 8-10)

(Luke 1:8-10 is not included in the printed text.)

Zacharias had been accorded the greatest honor of his life as a priest. He had been chosen to preside in the Temple at the altar of incense, which stood immediately in front of the curtain separating the Holy Place from the Holy of Holies. Only the high priest entered the Holy of Holies, and that on one occasion each year—the Day of Atonement. But the priest officiating at daily worship in the Temple would offer incense twice each day, an act that symbolized the prayers of the people of God ascending to the heavenly throne. There were numerous priests in the division of Abijah eligible to perform this office, so Zacharias had likely been chosen by lot to perform the duty on this particular day. Only the priest was inside the Temple when this worship ritual was under way. Meanwhile, the assembled worshipers prayed in the Temple courts in front of the bronze altar on which animal sacrifices were offered each day.

---

- Describe the priestly responsibility Zacharias was carrying out.

---

### C. Visitation by an Angel (vv. 11-15)

(Luke 1:11-12 is not included in the printed text.)

**¹³ But the angel said unto him, Fear not, Zacharias: for thy prayer is heard; and thy wife Elisabeth shall bear thee a son, and thou shalt call his name John. ¹⁴ And thou shalt have joy and gladness; and many shall rejoice at his birth. ¹⁵ For he shall be great in the sight of the Lord, and shall drink neither wine nor strong drink; and he shall be filled with the Holy Ghost, even from his mother's womb.**

As Zacharias performed his office at the altar of incense, an angel of the Lord appeared at the right side of the altar just outside the entrance into the Holy of Holies, where the ark of the covenant rested. A thick curtain veiled this most sacred area of the Temple from the Holy Place. The Holy Place contained the bread of the Presence (showbread), the ever-burning candelabra, and the altar of incense. When Zacharias saw the angel, he was troubled and fearful. The angel, likely far larger than life size and bearing wings, must have been a terrifying sight to Zacharias. Angels did not always appear with wings and as larger than ordinary men. At times angels appeared in human form, while at other times they had wings and appeared to have enormous stature (see Gen. 18:2; Isa. 6:2; Dan. 9:21; Rev. 10:1). Since it was evident to Zacharias that he was seeing an angel, the angel's awe-inspiring appearance must have made his identity obvious.

The angel, who later identified himself as Gabriel (Luke 1:19), immediately addressed Zacharias, conveying to him a specific message which assured him that his prayer for a child had been answered. (We learn at this point that the aging priest and his wife had, as we would expect, long prayed for a son.) Gabriel stated that Elizabeth would bear Zacharias a son who should be named *John*, meaning "God has been gracious." John would bring his parents great joy and gladness, and many would rejoice at his birth. Imagine the consternation of gossipy neighbors at signs of Elizabeth's pregnancy and the sheer joy throughout the community when the unexpected child was born!

The angel specified one requirement and several promises regarding the life and ministry of John. He would be "great in the sight of the Lord" (v. 15), experiencing not secular success but true success as measured by God alone. John was to abstain from all alcoholic beverages as evidence of being set apart to God. John would be filled with the Holy Spirit "from his mother's womb." The Holy Spirit throughout the Old Testament was given as special anointing for special purposes, but never upon a child not yet born.

The angel predicted that John would "turn many of the children of Israel to the Lord their God" (v. 16 NKJV). This prophecy was fulfilled during the ministry of John in the wilderness of Judea. John also would go before the Lord "in the spirit and power of Elijah" (v. 17 NKJV)—not reincarnation, but a similarity of anointing for powerful ministry introductory to the advent of Messiah. John would come with great anointing reminiscent of that of Elijah and with a commission to *turn* the hearts of fathers to their children. John's powerful anointing would spark genuine repentance with a far-reaching impact on family relationships. The assumption by fathers of their God-appointed role in the home, resulting from true repentance, would have a healthy spiritual and emotional effect on the subsequent development of their children. True repentance is a diametric change, an abrupt turning around so as to move in an entirely new moral and spiritual direction. John's Spirit-anointed ministry would "make ready a people prepared for the Lord" (Luke 1:17).

Zacharias questioned Gabriel, "How shall I know this? For I am an old man, and my wife is well advanced in years" (v. 18 NKJV). Apparently, despite envisioning an angel, Zacharias simply could not believe his ears. Gabriel declared that because Zacharias had not believed his words, he would be mute until the prophecy was fulfilled (v. 20). The assembled worshipers marveled that the priest remained so long in the Temple and perceived that he had seen a vision (vv. 21-22).

---

- List three promises the angel made concerning John.

> "The child must know that he is a miracle, that since the beginning of the world there hasn't been, and until the end of the world there will not be, another child like him."—Pablo Casals

---

D. Gabriel's Promise Fulfilled (vv. 57-66)

(Luke 1:57-61, 65-66 is not included in the printed text.)

**⁶² And they made signs to his father, how he would have him called. ⁶³ And he asked for a writing table, and wrote, saying, His name is John. And they marvelled all. ⁶⁴ And his mouth was opened immediately, and his tongue loosed, and he spake, and praised God.**

Elizabeth soon conceived a child in accordance with Gabriel's message. Perhaps because of embarrassment at her pregnancy when she was an aging woman, she remained in hiding for five months (v. 24). In the sixth month she was visited by her cousin Mary, pregnant with the infant Jesus. Their shared miraculous experiences would have encouraged both women—the very young and the already-aging mothers-to-be. At the expected time, Zacharias and Elizabeth's son was born to the delight of their family and friends.

On the day of the child's circumcision, when he was to be named, it was assumed that he would be called *Zacharias* after his father (v. 59). But Elizabeth insisted that he be called *John*. When those present protested that no one in Elizabeth and Zacharias' family was called John, signs were made to Zacharias (now revealed to us to be deaf as well as mute) to discover his choice of a name for his son. The priest wrote on a tablet, "His name is John" (v. 63), in accordance with Gabriel's instructions in the vision. Immediately, Zacharias' tongue was loosed and he glorified God. Those who witnessed this event spread their knowledge of it widely so that it was discussed throughout Judea (v. 65). The result was a deeply felt impression that caused people to wonder "what manner of child" John would be (v. 66).

---

1. How did Elizabeth and Zacharias break tradition, and why (vv. 59-63)?
2. With his speech restored, what were Zacharias' first words (v. 64)?
3. How did John's birth impact the community (vv. 65-66)?

> "A name is a kind of face whereby one is known."—Thomas Fuller

---

E. Zacharias' Prophecy (vv. 76-80)

**76 And thou, child, shalt be called the prophet of the Highest: for thou shalt go before the face of the Lord to prepare his ways; 77 To give knowledge of salvation unto his people by the remission of their sins, 78 Through the tender mercy of our God; whereby the dayspring from on high hath visited us, 79 To give light to them that sit in darkness and in the shadow of death, to guide our feet into the way of peace. 80 And the child grew, and waxed strong in spirit, and was in the deserts till the day of his shewing unto Israel.**

Zacharias, filled with the Holy Spirit, delivered to those assembled in his home a prophecy that predicted the imminent coming of Messiah in fulfillment of the words of prophets of the past (vv. 67-79). In his adulthood, the infant John would become a prophet of God and a herald of the Messiah, who would save His people from their sins and fulfill God's covenant with Abraham. The Messiah was envisioned by Zacharias as if already present, giving spiritual light to those in the darkness of sin and unbelief and guidance of His people into "the way of peace" (v. 79).

John grew up to become a man of God who was "strong in spirit" (v. 80)—that is, he developed strong moral character, or perhaps was strengthened by the Holy Spirit with the result of spiritual and moral maturity. Once an adult, John lived in the desert until he began his ministry. Some think he was associated with the community of Essenes at Qumran, but there is no certainty of this since that group is not even mentioned in Scripture. Moreover, John's ministry shows no evidence of influence from this community.

---

1. What did Zacharias prophesy regarding his son (vv. 76-79)?
2. Describe John's development (v. 80).

> "John the Baptist never performed any miracles. Yet, he was greater than any of the Old Testament prophets."—Leonard Ravenhill

---

## II. POWERFUL PROPHETIC PREACHING (Matt. 3:1-12)

### A. The Man and His Message (vv. 1-4)

(Matthew 3:1-2 is not included in the printed text.)

**³ For this is he that was spoken of by the prophet Esaias, saying, The voice of one crying in the wilderness, Prepare ye the way of the Lord, make his paths straight. ⁴ And the same John had his raiment of camel's hair, and a leathern girdle about his loins; and his meat was locusts and wild honey.**

Luke specifies that John began his ministry in the fifteenth year of the Roman emperor Tiberius Caesar (3:1), which would be approximately AD 26. John wore clothes typically worn by the poor, but also characteristic of prophets and particularly of Elijah (*Expositor's Bible Commentary*; see also 1 Kings 19:19; 2 Kings 2:8, 13-14). A leather belt bound together the loose folds of John's rough outer garment made of camel's hair. John's diet was also that of the very poor—locusts (large grasshoppers, roasted) and wild honey obtained directly from honeycombs, foods that would provide protein and energy.

John came "preaching" a gospel of repentance—as preparation for the imminent advent of "the kingdom of heaven" (Matt. 3:1-2). The *kingdom of heaven* is the sphere ruled by a sovereign God. Because God created human beings with free moral agency, and they (from the Garden of Eden) have made bad moral choices, political entities and institutions most often do not function according to the divine intention. However, God was about to break in on those rebellious agencies with a change in malleable human hearts that would one day result in the rule of God's Messiah, Jesus Christ. The Kingdom would begin inwardly and long exist in partial realization before a climactic change at the end of the church age brings about Christ's millennial rule on earth.

John the Baptist understood that his role was as a herald of the coming Messiah, who would establish God's kingdom (v. 3). He likely had limited understanding of the dual role of the Messiah, first appearing as the God-man before ultimately becoming ruler of a millennial kingdom. John could not have known there would be a long delay between the beginning of the Kingdom in prepared hearts and minds and the earthly kingdom ruled by Christ. But he comprehended well that the Christ was "the Lamb of God who takes away the sin of the world" (John 1:29 NKJV).

John, moreover, understood well that the kingdom of heaven must begin in prepared hearts transformed by repentance. He also knew it was his mission to proclaim fearlessly the sins of his contemporaries and lead them to a genuine transformation of heart and character that translated into changed daily living. He would thereby be paving the way for the work of the Messiah, which would immediately follow his work.

---

1. Where did John preach, and why?
2. What was his message?

---

### Sold Out to God

One great lesson we can learn from John the Baptist is his total dedication to his God-appointed task. Pentecostal believers often use the term "sold out" to characterize such consecration. One such example was M. B. Norris. While serving as pastor of a Church of God congregation in Columbus, Georgia, he organized nine churches in the area and, upon accepting a new pastoral appointment, presented the deeds to all these properties to the general officials of the denomination. Brother Norris organized the first Church of God congregation in Jesup, Georgia, in 1937 while he was also serving the Blanton Grove Church of God and, for a brief time, the Piney Grove Church of God. He also was constantly preaching revivals. This kind of dedication helped build the Church of God as well as other evangelical and Pentecostal organizations.

---

B. The Audience (vv. 5-7)

**⁵ Then went out to him Jerusalem, and all Judaea, and all the region round about Jordan. ⁶ And were baptized of him in Jordan, confessing their sins. ⁷ But when he saw many of the Pharisees and Sadducees come to his baptism, he said unto them, O generation of vipers, who hath warned you to flee from the wrath to come?**

John was preaching in the desert country descending from the Judean hills toward the Jordan River and the Dead Sea. His preaching was a phenomenon that attracted universal attention in the capital city and the entire province of Judea. Prophetic garb and fearless proclamation of truth cannot alone explain it. It was the ordained work of God in fulfillment of Old Testament Scripture as preparation for the Messiah. Only the Spirit working within the hearts of the hearers caused them to see themselves as sinners and induced them to come forward for baptism accompanied by confession of their sins. John's baptism was not convert baptism—a rite undergone by adult converts to Judaism—nor was it an example of those ritual cleansings mandated by the Mosaic Law. It was an immersion in water signifying purification of the heart and lifestyle.

John was highly suspicious when Pharisees and Sadducees came to his preaching and baptism of the repentant. These establishment groups were more than likely checking out this strange nonconformist to be sure he was not proclaiming heretical teachings. John fearlessly called them out as the hypocrites and cynics they typically were—a generation of snakes, venomous in their legalism, disregard for the poor, and cynical courting of Roman power.

---

1. How effective was John's preaching?
2. How did he address the religious leaders who came to hear him?

> "Just as the angel's announcement to Joseph declared Jesus' primary purpose to be to save His people from their sins, so the first announcement of the Kingdom (delivered by John the Baptist) is associated with repentance and confession of sin."—D. A. Carson

---

C. John's Uncompromising Stance (vv. 8-12)

(Matthew 3:12 is not included in the printed text.)

**⁸ Bring forth therefore fruits meet for repentance: ⁹ And think not to say within yourselves, We have Abraham to our father: for I say unto you, that God is able of these stones to raise up children unto Abraham. ¹⁰ And now also the axe is laid unto the root of the trees: therefore every tree which bringeth not forth good fruit is hewn down, and cast into the fire. ¹¹ I indeed baptize you with water unto repentance: but he that cometh after me is mightier than I, whose shoes I am not worthy to bear; he shall baptize you with the Holy Ghost, and with fire.**

John insisted that leaders within the religious establishment respond with the same moral and spiritual honesty that was demanded of every hearer—appropriate evidence of true repentance. Ethnic identity with Abraham, the venerated father of the race, was not sufficient. Our omnipotent God could create new inheritors of the blessings of Abraham. Moreover, the alternative to genuine repentance would eventually be judgment—an uprooting and destruction of hypocrites, claiming they were spiritual leaders when their lives showed no proof of relationship with God.

John contrasted his requirement of immersion in water (to indicate repentance) with the coming Messiah's baptism with "the Holy Ghost and with fire" (v. 11). Some see this spiritual baptism as regeneration, which certainly is a spiritual change brought about through the agency of the Spirit. As a Pentecostal, I believe John's reference is to the post-conversion baptism in the Holy Spirit. Moreover, the baptism of fire surely accompanies the descent of the

Spirit into human lives, bringing continuing purification and dynamic power. Just prior to His ascension, Jesus used the same words as John the Baptist, promising His already-regenerated assembled disciples, "John truly baptized with water, but you shall be baptized with the Holy Spirit not many days from now" (Acts 1:5 NKJV). John, then, was prophesying that already-repentant followers of Christ would receive a powerful infusion of Holy Spirit power (see v. 8).

1. What "fruits" did John demand (vv. 8, 10)?
2. Explain John's statement about Abraham (v. 9).
3. What did John declare about the coming Messiah (v. 11)?

> "A baptism of holiness, a demonstration of godly living is the crying need of our day."—Duncan Campbell

### III. MARTYR'S DEATH; FAITHFUL LEGACY (Matt. 14:1-12; Luke 7:28)

A. Herod's Assessment of Jesus (Matt. 14:1-2)

**¹ At that time Herod the tetrarch heard of the fame of Jesus. ² And said unto his servants, This is John the Baptist; he is risen from the dead; and therefore mighty works do shew forth themselves in him.**

When Herod Antipas (son of Herod the Great, and Roman tetrarch of Galilee and Perea) heard of Jesus' "miraculous powers" (v. 2 NIV), in his guilt he assumed that John the Baptist, whom he had murdered, had been reincarnated in Jesus of Nazareth and, for that reason, was performing miracles. His reaction, of course, is an evidence of Herod's ignorance and superstition, and what seems to be his obsession with the Baptist indicates a fear of divine reprisal for his infamous beheading of the prophet.

- What mistaken idea did Herod have, and why?

B. Herod's Imprisonment of John (vv. 3-5)

**³ For Herod had laid hold on John, and bound him, and put him in prison for Herodias' sake, his brother Philip's wife. ⁴ For John said unto him, It is not lawful for thee to have her. ⁵ And when he would have put him to death, he feared the multitude, because they counted him as a prophet.**

Matthew presents the sad account of John's imprisonment and death parenthetically as an event previous to Jesus' presentation of parables of the Kingdom in chapter 13. Herod's reaction to John the Baptist had been mixed. Hearing that John had denounced his marriage to the wife of his half-brother Philip, Herod had arrested and imprisoned John. But Herod apparently had afterward visited with the imprisoned prophet and dialogued with him, for Mark 6:20 states,

"Herod was afraid of John, knowing that he was a righteous and holy man, and he kept him safe. And when he heard him, he was very perplexed; but he used to enjoy listening to him" (NASB).

---

1. Why had John been imprisoned?
2. What was the common perception of John (v. 5)?

> "If we walk in righteousness He will carry us through."—A. B. Simpson

---

C. Herod's Beheading of John (vv. 6-12)

(Matthew 14:10, 12 is not included in the printed text.)
**⁶ But when Herod's birthday was kept, the daughter of Herodias danced before them, and pleased Herod. ⁷ Whereupon he promised with an oath to give her whatsoever she would ask. ⁸ And she, being before instructed of her mother, said, Give me here John Baptist's head in a charger. ⁹ And the king was sorry: nevertheless for the oath's sake, and them which sat with him at meat, he commanded it to be given her.
¹¹ And his head was brought in a charger, and given to the damsel: and she brought it to her mother.**

Herod's wife Herodias, however, continued to seethe because of John's denunciation of their marriage. On his birthday, Herod gave a great feast—with all the nobility, military officers, and important government officials of Galilee in attendance. Salome, Herodias' young daughter, performed for her uncle/stepfather a sensual dance that excited the lusts of all the males in attendance, and particularly of Herod. In his frenzied state, he promised to give to Salome anything she might ask, up to half of his kingdom.

Not knowing what to ask, the young girl asked her mother's advice. Herodias, seeing her chance to get revenge on the prophet she so hated, told her daughter to ask for the head of John the Baptist on a platter. Herod, trapped by his extravagant promise, granted the request, and soon the grisly sight of the head of John the Baptist appeared before him. John's disciples, in a final act of loyalty, obtained and entombed his body (v. 12).

---

- Why do you suppose God allowed John to be executed?

> "There is an essential difference between the decease of the godly and the death of the ungodly. Death comes to the ungodly man as a penal infliction, but to the righteous as a summons to his Father's palace. To the sinner it is an execution, to the saint an undressing from his sins and infirmities. Death to the wicked is the King of terrors. Death to the saint is the end of terrors, the commencement of glory."—Charles Spurgeon

D. Jesus' Assessment of John the Baptist (Luke 7:28)

**²⁸ For I say unto you, Among those that are born of women there is not a greater prophet than John the Baptist: but he that is least in the kingdom of God is greater than he.**

Jesus, after John had been imprisoned and had sought clarification from Him regarding His appointed role (v. 19), spoke to His disciples about John's great significance as prophet and forerunner of Messiah. Then He made the following cryptic comment: "Assuredly, I say to you, among those born of women there has not risen one greater than John the Baptist; but he who is least in the kingdom of heaven is greater than he" (Matt. 11:11 NKJV). John, who himself had said of Jesus, "He must increase, but I must decrease" (John 3:30), was a transitional figure at the end of the old covenant and the outset of the earthly ministry of Jesus Christ.

John had been used mightily by God to challenge his hearers to prepare for the advent of Messiah. But he had been removed from this world early in Christ's earthly ministry and therefore could not experience the privileges and benefits to be accorded every participant in the new covenant mediated by the crucified, resurrected, and ascended Christ (Heb. 4:14-16; 6:19-20; 9:23-28). Participants in the kingdom of God can enjoy direct access to the throne of God through our great High Priest in the heavens, know the fellowship of the redeemed by the blood of Christ, and experience opportunities for service under the banner of Christ. Nonetheless, John, along with all Old Testament saints, will enjoy millennial blessings when Christ returns to earth.

---

- Explain Jesus' statement about who is "least" and who is "greater."

---

## CONCLUSION

When we view the entire network of prophecy and fulfillment, beginning in Genesis and continuing throughout the sixty-six books of canonized Scripture, we are warranted in reaching certain bedrock conclusions. God has a plan formed in eternity past and climaxing in the birth, crucifixion, resurrection, and ascension of Jesus Christ. That plan is still in progress and is moving inevitably toward its final fulfillment at the end of the gospel age, when the previously raptured Church returns to reign with Christ a thousand years and to enjoy afterward eternal blessings in the presence of God. John the Baptist had a crucial role in God's plan, prophesied by Isaiah and Malachi, and brought to fruition through John's supernaturally enabled birth and obedient service as prophet and as forerunner of Christ.

### GOLDEN TEXT CHALLENGE

"THIS IS HE, OF WHOM IT IS WRITTEN, BEHOLD, I SEND MY MESSENGER BEFORE THY FACE, WHICH SHALL PREPARE THY WAY BEFORE THEE" (Luke 7:27).

Here, Jesus makes clear John's distinction. He is a prophet, but beyond that, he is a reformer. He is the special messenger of the Lord—a special advance man for the King. He is to work among the people, making appropriate preparations for the coming of their Sovereign to dwell for a time in their midst.

As followers of Christ in the twenty-first century, it is our responsibility to point others back to what the Messiah accomplished through His life, death, and resurrection and to testify of His ministry in our lives today.

**Daily Devotions:**
M. Preservation of the Faithful
   Psalm 31:19-24
T. Promise for the Faithful
   Psalm 111:1-8
W. Search for the Faithful
   Jeremiah 5:1-5
T. Faithful Steward
   Matthew 24:45-51
F. Faithful Lydia
   Acts 16:11-15
S. Faithful Church
   Colossians 1:1-8

October 19, 2014 (Lesson 7)
# Philip the Evangelist
### Acts 6:1-7; 8:4-40; 21:8-9

**Unit Theme:**
Great Stories of the Bible

**Central Truth:**
Proclaiming the gospel is the primary mission of the church.

**Focus:**
Study Philip's ministry and be witnesses of Christ.

**Context:**
Scenes from the ministry of Philip from AD 35 to 57

**Golden Text:**
"The people with one accord gave heed unto those things which Philip spake, hearing and seeing the miracles which he did" (Acts 8:6).

**Study Outline:**
  I. Deacon and Family Man
     (Acts 6:1-7; 21:8-9)
 II. Evangelizing Samaria
     (Acts 8:4-13)
III. Ministering to the Ethiopian
     (Acts 8:26-40)

## INTRODUCTION

Among the men selected as deacons by the Jerusalem church (Acts 6), two stand out because of their powerful spiritual anointing and total dedication—Stephen, the first martyr of the church; and Philip, like Stephen, chosen to serve among the seven in the distribution of food to discontented widows, but quickly widening his sphere of service. The apostle John, in the fourth Gospel, highlighted the service to Jesus by Philip the apostle. Philip the evangelist, doubtless so named to distinguish him readily from the apostle of the same name, was also distinctive and valuable in the service of God.

In Acts 1:4-8, Jesus gave a final message to His apostles before ascending to His Father. He first reiterated the promise of John the Baptist, who had said, "I indeed baptize you with water; but One mightier than I is coming, whose sandal strap I am not worthy to loose. He will baptize you with the Holy Spirit and fire" (Luke 3:16 NKJV). Jesus said, "John truly baptized with water; but ye shall be baptized with the Holy Ghost not many days hence" (Acts 1:5). The disciples were anticipating an immediate restoration of the political kingdom of Israel. But Jesus ended this preoccupation and redirected their focus to the planting of the kingdom of God in human hearts. He asserted, "You shall receive power when the Holy Spirit has come upon you, and you shall be witnesses to Me in Jerusalem, and in all Judea and Samaria, and to the end of the earth" (v. 8 NKJV).

The deacon Stephen became a mighty preacher of the gospel, worker of miracles, and defender of the Christian faith. Upon being falsely accused and arrested, Stephen contended for the faith against haughty Jewish religious leaders, including the high priest, and was stoned, giving a powerful final witness as he took his last breath. The young rabbi and zealot Saul, who held the garments of those stoning Stephen, led an intense wave of persecution that enveloped the church. Saul, a relentless persecutor, would eventually become Paul—the utterly committed missionary-evangelist and apostle. Meanwhile, the onslaught of opposition had an effect not anticipated by the persecutors. Instead of being silenced, zealous preachers of the faith spread across Judea and Samaria, goaded by opposition into fulfillment of Jesus' promise, prediction, and mandate in Acts 1:8.

Jesus had promised His followers an immersion in the Spirit for the specific purpose of powerful witnessing to His person and work. Now, scattered by persecution, they enthusiastically fulfilled His command. Among those who "went every where preaching the word" (8:4) was Philip the deacon, now become Philip the evangelist.

## I. DEACON AND FAMILY MAN (Acts 6:1-7; 21:8-9)

### A. Dissension in the Church (6:1)

**¹And in those days, when the number of the disciples was multiplied, there arose a murmuring of the Grecians against the Hebrews, because their widows were neglected in the daily ministration.**

On the Day of Pentecost, after the anointed preaching of Peter, three thousand people were converted and added to the 120 disciples who had been baptized in the Holy Spirit early in the morning of that same day. From Pentecost forward, people continually joined the fellowship of believers in Christ. Powerful apostolic ministry with accompanying miraculous signs resulted in numerous conversions and, as a result, several thousand believers were soon added to the Jerusalem church. Despite the fact that all of these earliest believers were Jewish in ethnicity, problems in interaction soon surfaced.

Many of the earliest Christians were Aramaic-speaking Jews who had been born and reared in Palestine. Also among them, however, were believers whose primary language was the colloquial Greek, a prominent tongue throughout the Mediterranean basin area—even more so in the first century than Latin, the language spoken by Roman government officials and military officers. By the first century AD, many Jews had become, to various degrees, assimilated into Grecian (also called Hellenic) culture—some because, after Alexander the Great had conquered so much of the known world of his age, they had migrated to Greek colonies and there absorbed the Greek language and culture. Over the generations, some of these Hellenized Jews returned to Judea, but continued to speak Greek as their primary language. Other Jews left Judea while young, but returned with a strong tinge of Greek influence in their old age. Moreover, some Jewish believers in Jesus who were born and reared in Judea had still absorbed considerable Hellenic cultural influence.

In the infant church at Jerusalem, these Jewish Christians from diverse backgrounds were attempting to worship Christ and live together in the close intimacy of people rejected by adherents of traditional Jewish religion and strongly committed to the radically different lifestyle of the church. Complicating further this diversity within the church was the communal living practiced by the earliest Christians (4:34-37).

Apparently, many destitute widows were among the constituents of the church in Jerusalem—some traditional Jews and others of Hellenic cultural background. There developed the perception, perhaps justifiable, that Aramaic-speaking widows (more traditionally Jewish) were being preferred over Greek-speaking widows in the distribution of food to the indigent. It would be easy for individuals of Aramaic Judean ethnicity to recognize more readily the needs of people very much like themselves than those of the culturally different. The resulting dispute was occupying an inordinate amount of the apostles' time and attention.

- Explain the early church's growing pains.

"God is pleased with no music below so much as with the thanksgiving songs of relieved widows and supported orphans; of rejoicing, comforted, and thankful persons."—Jeremy Taylor

B. Apostolic Leadership (vv. 2-6)

(Acts 6:2 is not included in the printed text.)

**³ Wherefore, brethren, look ye out among you seven men of honest report, full of the Holy Ghost and wisdom, whom we may appoint over this business. ⁴ But we will give ourselves continually to prayer, and to the ministry of the word. ⁵ And the saying pleased the whole multitude: and they chose Stephen, a man full of faith and of the Holy Ghost, and Philip, and Prochorus, and Nicanor, and Timon, and Parmenas, and Nicolas a proselyte of Antioch: ⁶ Whom they set before the apostles: and when they had prayed, they laid their hands on them.**

The twelve apostles knew their primary calling was spiritual leadership of the church, a calling to be pursued through much prayer and through the teaching and preaching of God's Word. Administration was not a task to be despised; rather, it was essential to the ongoing life of the church. But it must not consume the energies of men appointed by God primarily to a different area of service. The apostles, therefore, called a congregational meeting rather than attempting to solve the problem themselves. They called on the larger body of believers to select the needed assistants, or deacons, likely believing this larger group would have better knowledge of those who would be qualified to accomplish the tasks.

This particular scriptural context does not employ the word *deacon* (Greek, *diakonos*—servant, helper, minister). However, the tasks of service to which the men selected were appointed match the definition of *deacon* as the word is employed elsewhere in the New Testament (1 Tim. 3:8-13; Rom. 16:1). Also, throughout the long tradition of the Christian church, these seven men have been so called.

The apostles set three qualifications for the seven men to be chosen (Acts 6:3): (1) *good reputation* ("honest report")—so their decisions would be respected; (2) *wisdom*—careful judgment that would be apparent in a man after he had been observed for an extended time period; and (3) *Holy Spirit fullness*—true spirituality, or a life marked by the fruit and gifts of the indwelling Holy Spirit.

The assembly of believers accepted the apostles' mandate and chose seven men whom they deemed to possess the appropriate qualifications. Interestingly, all seven of these men had Greek names. They were not all necessarily immigrants from the colonies, for it was not uncommon for first-century Jews to have Greek names, but this particular selection of men must nonetheless have brought comfort to the Grecian widows. Stephen is singled out for his outstanding spiritual qualifications, but we must assume that each of the seven met the requirements of reputation, wisdom, and Holy Spirit fullness listed in verse 3.

The apostles treated the appointment of the seven deacons as a spiritual calling. They laid their hands on them and prayed over them, invoking God's blessing on them. Every task necessary to the function of God's church is ultimately a spiritual one, and each performer of these tasks needs the guidance of the Holy Spirit so that judgment is sound, attitudes are appropriate, and the required work is accomplished conscientiously and competently. Philip, the subject of our lesson, was among the exemplary men selected to be deacons.

---

1. What was "not right" (v. 2 NIV) for the apostles to do?
2. Describe those chosen to be deacons.

> "The authority by which the Christian leader leads is not power but love, not force but example, not coercion but reasoned persuasion. Leaders have power, but power is safe only in the hands of those who humble themselves to serve."—John Stott

---

C. Growth Through the Word (v. 7)

**⁷And the word of God increased; and the number of the disciples multiplied in Jerusalem greatly; and a great company of the priests were obedient to the faith.**

When problems are solved appropriately—in this case, when hindrances to unity within God's church are removed—great spiritual growth can occur. Luke employs here a phrase pregnant with meaning: "the word of God spread" (NKJV). In Acts 4:31, after Peter and John had been released from custody, the reader is told that Spirit-filled believers "spake the word of God with boldness." After the death of the persecutor Herod, we read that "the word of God grew and multiplied" (12:24 NKJV). Further, after informing the reader of miracles performed in Ephesus "by the hands of Paul" (19:11), Luke states that "the word of the Lord grew mightily and prevailed" (v. 20 NKJV).

First, we observe that the preached word, anointed by the Holy Spirit, is the agent of growth. Second, we note that the human instrument is not unduly exalted. Third, we see that persecution does not paralyze the early Christians into inactivity; instead, they are stimulated to Spirit-empowered service for God. Fourth, we can assert that the promise by Jesus, just prior to His ascension, of power to witness through the Holy Spirit was evidently being continually fulfilled.

That a large number of Jewish priests became believers in Christ testifies to the authenticity and supernatural reality of the ministry and lifestyle of apostles, deacons, evangelists, and ordinary disciples alike. For priests to give up the prerogatives and duties ingrained in them from early childhood would require a deep spiritual impact. These men relinquished much but gained immensely more.

- Describe the spiritual breakthrough that took place.

### Divinely Arranged Encounters

John Wesley went as an Anglican missionary to colonial Georgia before he was converted. There he had a series of failures before returning to England. But Moravian missionaries to the Native Americans made a deep impression on Wesley. When he returned to London, he encountered another Moravian, Peter Bohler, who also influenced him significantly. Wesley was also introduced by Moravians to Luther's commentary on Paul's epistle to the Romans. Finally, at a meeting, mainly of Moravians, on Aldersgate Street, Wesley accepted justification by faith, and his "heart was strangely warmed." This spiritual experience transformed his life and started him on his lifelong ministry across the British Isles.

We can see that God used this series of encounters with the pietistic Moravians, among other life-transforming forces, to awaken John Wesley spiritually and set him on his spiritual mission to eighteenth-century England.

### D. Philip the Evangelist and His Spirit-Led Daughters (21:8-9)

**⁸And the next day we that were of Paul's company departed, and came unto Caesarea: and we entered into the house of Philip the evangelist, which was one of the seven; and abode with him. ⁹And the same man had four daughters, virgins, which did prophesy.**

Years after the selection of the seven deacons, the apostle Paul was concluding his third missionary journey, having disembarked at Ptolemais. He and his companions—including Luke, the writer of the Book of Acts—went overland to Caesarea, a coastal city rebuilt by Herod the Great and dedicated to Caesar Augustus, which had later become the official seat of Roman governors, including Pontius Pilate. Paul's traveling party rested up for a while in Caesarea at the home of Philip the evangelist, the same fervent preacher of the gospel mentioned in Acts 6:5 and 8:4-40.

Philip had four daughters who were *prophetesses*—that is, they were used by the Holy Spirit to give utterances directly inspired by the Holy Spirit. These daughters evidently identified strongly with their deeply committed father. Their prophetic messages, as explained by Paul in 1 Corinthians 12—14, might either apply Scripture to current conditions or foretell future occurrences. That these consecrated young women were singled out as exercising this gift indicates they were so used by the Spirit frequently and were recognized by their church as holding the prophetic office. This is a direct fulfillment of Joel 2:28, quoted by the apostle Peter in Acts 2:17 as being fulfilled on the Day of Pentecost, but also directly pertinent here. Clearly, as this text indicates, the New Testament shows women in spiritual leadership roles—under proper spiritual authority, but freely exercising their spiritual gifts.

- How were Philip's four daughters like their father?

> "No doubt [women of faith in the past] were reproached for His name's sake, and accounted mad women; but they had a faith which enabled them at that time to overcome the world, and by which they climbed up to heaven."—George Whitefield

## II. EVANGELIZING SAMARIA (Acts 8:4-13)

A. Evangelism Stimulated by Persecution (vv. 4-8)

**⁴ Therefore they that were scattered abroad went every where preaching the word. ⁵ Then Philip went down to the city of Samaria, and preached Christ unto them. ⁶ And the people with one accord gave heed unto these things which Philip spake, hearing and seeing the miracles which he did. ⁷ For unclean spirits, crying with loud voice, came out of many that were possessed with them: and many taken with palsies, and that were lame, were healed. ⁸ And there was great joy in that city.**

Persecution usually results when dominant religious or political groups or authorities are challenged by fervent believers in the gospel who disturb the status quo by personal witness in public places, or organized worship with dynamic preaching and powerful results—conversions, miracles, and baptisms in the Holy Spirit with undeniable visible evidence. Such persecution also attended the beginnings of Pentecostalism early in the twentieth century, as well as long before, in and around Jerusalem soon after the Day of Pentecost in the New Testament era. Such persecution may be primarily verbal, or it may be characterized by physical abuse, legal proceedings, and even martyrdom.

When such abuse began to happen at Jerusalem, it caused that city to become a dangerous place for Christians, particularly after Saul began his relentless pursuit of followers of Jesus. As a result, they began to fan out across Judea and into Samaria, thereby directly fulfilling the words of Jesus in Acts 1:8.

Philip, likely in the capital city of the province of Samaria, fulfilled Mark 16:15-18 as he preached the gospel with signs following. Some present-day Christians would limit the performing of miracles to the twelve apostles, or to the apostolic age, asserting that they occurred only until the canon of New Testament Scripture was completed. However, miracles accompanied the preaching of New Testament believers other than apostles, as this text makes clear. And subsequent church history is replete with reports of the miraculous. Sometimes such reported miracles may have been superstitious, as in the case of some purported miracles of the Middle Ages, but often they were direct answers to prayer on behalf of human need. In the Pentecostal Movement, which began early in the twentieth century, great revivals have frequently been accompanied by divine healing resulting from "the prayer of faith" (James 5:15).

During Philip's ministry in Acts 8:7, "unclean spirits," or demons, were disturbed by challenges to their domain and shrieked loudly as they were cast out. Noticeable physical debilities such as "palsies" (tremors) and "lameness" (perhaps arthritis, broken bones not properly set, or spinal problems) were immediately healed. These physical changes were *visible* to the multitudes in attendance. Such miracles are properly called *signs* because they point to the spiritual power behind the miracle. They also often point to the inward spiritual change that God is bringing about.

---

1. How did persecution help the church?
2. What happened "with one accord" (v. 6), and what was the result (vv. 7-8)?

> "It has become a settled principle that nothing which is good and true can be destroyed by persecution, but that the effect ultimately is to establish more firmly, and to spread more widely, that which it was designed to overthrow. It has long since passed into a proverb that 'the blood of the martyrs is the seed of the church.'"—Albert Barnes

---

B. Simon the Sorcerer Professing Faith (vv. 9-13)

(Acts 8:9-11 is not included in the printed text.)

**12 But when they believed Philip preaching the things concerning the kingdom of God, and the name of Jesus Christ, they were baptized, both men and women. 13 Then Simon himself believed also: and when he was baptized, he continued with Philip, and wondered, beholding the miracles and signs which were done.**

That the miracles were authentic and served the dual purpose of relieving human suffering and pointing to Christ is evident in verse 12. Philip preached about various aspects of the sovereign rule of God on earth, inaugurated by Jesus the Messiah. His kingdom began in human hearts and will be fully realized during the millennial reign of Christ. Philip emphasized the divine authority inherent in the name of Jesus. Many trusted in Christ as Savior and Lord and were baptized in water without respect to gender.

The man known as "Simon the sorcerer," who had impressed gullible crowds through his "sorcery" (v. 9), whether by sleight of hand or actual manipulation through demonic powers, appeared to believe in Christ upon hearing Philip's preaching and was baptized (v. 13). Was he truly converted, or was he merely fascinated by the external signs of an inner spiritual reality he did not comprehend? Scripture does not specifically say.

---

1. What did people believe about Simon, and what was the result (vv. 9-11)?
2. How did Philip's preaching change the situation (vv. 12-13)?

> "The preaching of Christ is the whip that flogs the devil. The preaching of Christ is the thunderbolt, the sound of which makes all hell shake."—Charles Spurgeon

---

### III. MINISTERING TO THE ETHIOPIAN (Acts 8:26-40)

A. Divinely Ordered Encounter (vv. 26-28)

**26 And the angel of the Lord spake unto Philip, saying, Arise, and go toward the south unto the way that goeth down from Jerusalem unto Gaza, which is desert. 27 And he arose and went: and, behold, a man of Ethiopia, an eunuch of great authority under Candace queen of the Ethiopians, who had the charge of all her treasure, and had come to Jerusalem for to worship, 28 Was returning, and sitting in his chariot read Esaias the prophet.**

Philip apparently returned to Jerusalem after completing his ministry in Samaria. There he had an encounter with an angel of the Lord. The writer of the epistle to the Hebrews asks rhetorically of angels, "Are they not all ministering spirits sent forth to minister for those who will inherit salvation?" (1:14 NKJV). On this occasion the angel accosted Philip, a spiritually sensitive man ready to obey, who then ministered to an honest seeker after salvation. The angel instructed Philip to go south along an isolated stretch of road that eventually ended at Gaza, a seacoast city, expecting obedience without first understanding God's purpose.

As Philip journeyed in obedience to the angel's message, he came upon an Ethiopian royal official who served as treasurer to the powerful queen mother, whose official title was *Candace*. This distinguished man was returning home from Jerusalem, where he likely had been worshiping at the Temple as a Gentile God-fearer.

1. How did Philip respond to an angelic command?
2. Who was in the chariot, where had he been, and why?

> "The only Jesus that unbelievers ever see on this earth is the one reflected in those who already know Him. By mirroring Christ, we should be ready to turn any conversation or meeting with an unbeliever into a divine encounter."—David Jeremiah

---

B. A Sincere Inquiry (vv. 29-35)

(Acts 8:32-34 is not included in the printed text.)

**29 Then the Spirit said unto Philip, Go near, and join thyself to this chariot. 30 And Philip ran thither to him, and heard him read the prophet Esaias, and said, Understandest thou what thou readest? 31 And he said, How can I, except some man should guide me? And he desired Philip that he would come up and sit with him.**

**35 Then Philip opened his mouth, and began at the same scripture, and preached unto him Jesus.**

The Holy Spirit instructed Philip to run up to the chariot. When he reached the chariot, he overheard the Ethiopian traveler reading Isaiah 53:7-8. Philip asked the man if he understood what he was reading, whereupon the man asked in return, "How can I, unless someone guides me?" (Acts 8:31 NKJV). Then he invited Philip to join him, and the fervent evangelist was provided with a divinely arranged opening to tell the Ethiopian the good news about salvation through Jesus the Messiah. The passage being read was perfect as an entry point into a discussion of the basic truths of the gospel, since the prophet Isaiah described there the suffering Messiah who would give His life for the sins of unredeemed people.

---

1. Why did the Ethiopian answer Philip's question with a question (vv. 30-31)?
2. What did the passage being read (Isa. 53:7-8) prophesy about Jesus?
3. How did Philip help the man?

> "Only Christianity and its teachings can explain the purpose and meaning of this world—and also gives the basis for right and wrong, good and evil."—Ken Ham

---

C. The Ethiopian's Conversion and Baptism (vv. 36-38)

**36 And as they went on their way, they came unto a certain water: and the eunuch said, See, here is water; what doth hinder me to be baptized?**

**37** And Philip said, If thou believest with all thine heart, thou mayest. And he answered and said, I believe that Jesus Christ is the Son of God. **38** And he commanded the chariot to stand still: and they went down both into the water, both Philip and the eunuch; and he baptized him.

Upon hearing a full explanation of salvation by grace through faith in Christ, the Ethiopian requested water baptism. Philip ascertained that he had truly accepted Jesus Christ as the Son of God. This was not mere intellectual assent but *trust*, a leaning of the entire personality on Christ as Savior and Lord (see Acts 16:31 Amp.). Then both men left the chariot and went down into the nearby water, where Philip baptized him. We note that an inner spiritual change preceded the external symbolic act.

---

- What is the qualification for water baptism?

> "Let me address all of you, high and low, rich and poor, one with another, to accept of mercy and grace while it is offered to you. Now is the accepted time, now is the day of salvation; and will you not accept it, now it is offered unto you?"—George Whitefield

---

D. Philip's Spirit-Controlled Ministry (vv. 39-40)

**39** And when they were come up out of the water, the Spirit of the Lord caught away Philip, that the eunuch saw him no more: and he went on his way rejoicing. **40** But Philip was found at Azotus: and passing through he preached in all the cities, till he came to Caesarea.

Philip had appeared suddenly and disappeared with equal suddenness, the Lord controlling this crucial encounter from beginning to end. On four occasions in Scripture, God *translated* a human servant from one place to another—Enoch, Elijah, and Jesus to heaven; and Philip from one earthly locale to another. The ministry of Philip must have been highly important to the kingdom of God if the Holy Spirit was unwilling to allow him to trudge slowly through the desert to the beginning of his next series of appointments which stretched along the coast from Azotus to Caesarea. Meanwhile, the Ethiopian continued to experience the joy of his newfound relationship with Christ as he continued his journey through Egypt into his home country. We can speculate safely that he shared his transforming encounter with others in his homeland since an ancient Christian church still exists there today.

---

1. As the Ethiopian "went on his way," how did he act and why?
2. What did Philip keep doing?

## CONCLUSION

Philip progressed from disciple to deacon to evangelist, under Holy Spirit direction, constantly widening his sphere of influence. He preached to large crowds and witnessed to individuals. He also influenced his own daughters by his example, and they became prophetesses. This New Testament spiritual leader deserves our own study and emulation as we seek to find God's will for our lives in a culture needing desperately to witness vital Christianity.

## GOLDEN TEXT CHALLENGE

"THE PEOPLE WITH ONE ACCORD GAVE HEED UNTO THOSE THINGS WHICH PHILIP SPAKE, HEARING AND SEEING THE MIRACLES WHICH HE DID" (Acts 8:6).

The response to Philip's preaching in Samaria was extraordinary. The language here implies that great crowds of people gave their faith and consent to Philip's message and appeal.

The readiness with which his proclamation was accepted shows that in spite of radical and religious prejudice, and in spite of the adverse influence upon that community since the Lord Jesus was there (John 4:39-42), Jesus' ministry at that time was not in vain. Thus, in a sense, Philip reaped where Jesus and His disciples, and the woman of Sychar, had sown some years before.

**Daily Devotions:**

M. Tell About God's Works
   Psalm 92:1-8
T. Tell About God's Righteousness
   Psalm 94:14-19
W. Don't Quench the Fire
   Jeremiah 20:7-13
T. Jesus Testifies
   John 8:25-30
F. Peter Testifies
   Acts 10:34-44
S. Paul Testifies
   Acts 26:12-20

October 26, 2014 (Lesson 8)
# Story About Forgiveness
### Matthew 18:21-35; Luke 17:3-4

> **Unit Theme:**
> Parables of Jesus (Stories Jesus Told)
>
> **Central Truth:**
> Because God forgives us, we must forgive others.
>
> **Focus:**
> Seriously consider what Jesus said about forgiveness and have a forgiving attitude toward others.
>
> **Context:**
> Jesus teaches His disciples about forgiveness.
>
> **Golden Text:**
> "If ye forgive men their trespasses, your heavenly Father will also forgive you: but if ye forgive not men their trespasses, neither will your Father forgive your trespasses" (Matt. 6:14-15).
>
> **Study Outline:**
> I. Peter's Question About Forgiveness
>    (Luke 17:3-4; Matt. 18:21-22)
> II. Jesus Teaches Forgiveness
>    (Matt. 18:23-27)
> III. Consequences of Not Forgiving
>    (Matt. 18:28-35)

## INTRODUCTION

Today's lesson presents a story that illustrates the extent of God's forgiveness, the necessity of believers forgiving others, and the consequences of failing to forgive.

Someone has said God has a big eraser. When we consider the enormity of our transgressions, we tend to agree. But that eraser came at a great cost. To find its source, we must go to Calvary and see the Savior in His suffering as the weight of our sins presses down upon Him. Not only is there the physical agony of unthinkable torture, but there is also the emotional and mental grief of being forsaken by His Father. Hear His cry from the cross: "My God, My God, why have You forsaken Me?" (Matt. 27:46 NKJV). Out of that anguish, suffering, and death came our redemption and the forgiveness of our sins. This is the eraser, as it were, that blots out our sins and sets us on the path of righteousness.

How can we possibly fail to forgive others of the petty things they do to us, when we have been forgiven so much? The Scriptures are replete with statements that show the need to forgive others. Jesus included the call to forgive in what is called the Lord's Prayer, and followed it with an admonition: "And forgive us our debts, as we forgive our debtors. . . . For if you forgive men their trespasses, your heavenly Father will also forgive you. But if you do not forgive men their trespasses, neither will your Father forgive your trespasses" (Matt. 6:12, 14-15 NKJV).

On another occasion, Jesus said, "Whenever you stand praying, if you have anything against anyone, forgive him, that your Father in heaven may also forgive you your trespasses" (Mark 11:25 NKJV).

The apostle Paul also addressed this subject in these words: "Be kind to one another, tenderhearted, forgiving one another, even as God in Christ forgave you" (Eph. 4:32 NKJV).

## I. PETER'S QUESTION ABOUT FORGIVENESS (Luke 17:3-4; Matt. 18:21-22)

### A. The Necessity of Forgiveness (Luke 17:3-4)

**³ Take heed to yourselves: If thy brother trespass against thee, rebuke him; and if he repent, forgive him. ⁴ And if he trespass against thee seven times in a day, and seven times in a day turn again to thee, saying, I repent; thou shalt forgive him.**

Jesus issues a warning to believers not to offend others, nor to be offended by others. In the two preceding verses, He declares that dire consequences will come to those who cause offenses—especially those who offend "little ones" (those weaker or younger in the faith). If by our conduct, our words, or our attitude we cause weaker ones to stumble, we will be held accountable. The punishment for causing such an offense is so great that it would be better for us to die before we can commit such an offense.

Not only are we not to give offense, we are also not to take offense. This does not mean if someone has done us wrong, we are to do nothing. On the contrary, we are to go to the person, instead of going behind his or her back, and call to their attention the wrong they have done. Jesus said, "If a fellow believer hurts you, go and tell him—work it out between the two of you. If he listens, you've made a friend" (Matt. 18:15 TM).

If confronting an offender and forgiving them seems difficult, remember the words of Jesus in the Sermon on the Mount: "But I say unto you, Love your enemies, bless them that curse you, do good to them that hate you, and pray for them which despitefully use you, and persecute you" (5:44).

The idea of forgiving an offending believer occurs several times in Scripture (see Matt. 6:15; 18:35; Mark 11:26; Luke 6:37; Eph. 4:32). An attitude of forgiveness should be common and the daily practice of believers. We should never give place to any thought of, or desire for, revenge. There should be no limits to the forgiveness we offer to those who truly repent. This means that we lay aside all malice and allow God to be glorified through a right reaction to the situation. If there is no desire for forgiveness on the part of the offender, the matter should be left in God's hands. He is our defender and says that vengeance belongs to Him.

---

1. When should a Christian "rebuke" a fellow believer?
2. When is a Christian obligated to forgive another person?

> "Has someone wronged you recently? Resist the urge to judge that person. Instead, pray that God might use you to reach the offender."—Warren Wiersbe

## B. Peter's Question (Matt. 18:21)

**²¹ Then came Peter to him, and said, Lord, how oft shall my brother sin against me, and I forgive him? till seven times?**

In verses 15-20, Jesus discusses the procedure to take when dealing with an offending brother or sister in the church. This raises a question in Peter's mind. He wants to know how many times we are to forgive someone who hurts us. He suggests that maybe we should forgive them seven times. Peter considers this to be very generous, since the rabbis only required that those offended should forgive three times, and on the fourth offense no forgiveness was to be offered.

Let's give Peter his due. At least he understood that forgiving others is the right thing to do. Before we criticize Peter, perhaps we should ask ourselves where we stand on this question of forgiveness. Can we recall how long it has been since we forgave someone seven times for the same offense? Have we really taken Christ's teaching on forgiveness to heart?

- Why isn't "seven" enough times to forgive someone?

> "Forgive, forget. Bear with the faults of others as you would have them bear with yours. Be patient and understanding. Life is too short to be vengeful or malicious."—Phillips Brooks

## C. Forgiveness Without Limit (v. 22)

**²² Jesus saith unto him, I say not unto thee, Until seven times: but, Until seventy times seven.**

Jesus wants to impress on Peter's mind that there is no limit to the times we are to forgive a wrong against us. In Peter's thought, if someone offends him seven times in the same day for the same thing and he forgives him each time, this is quite significant. But Jesus' words must have astonished him when He told Peter that he was not only to forgive seven times but "seventy times seven." Peter was probably wondering, *How could I even keep up with forgiving that many times?* Of course, the Lord is trying to get him to understand that we are to forgive others, regardless of how many times we have been wronged. We are to never stop forgiving.

The greatest example of forgiveness is found at Calvary. Paul wrote, "But God showed his great love for us by sending Christ to die for us while we were still sinners" (Rom. 5:8 NLT). Christ did not go to the cross because we were good people who were loyal to Him. He died for us while we were His enemies and while we were still in our sins. He continues to forgive, and will for all time, those who accept His work on the cross and receive His forgiveness into their heart.

Two of Jesus' words from the cross had to do with forgiveness. The first scenario is when He speaks to the Father about those responsible for His crucifixion. Looking out at the crowd, He prays, "Father, forgive them; for they know not what they do" (Luke 23:34). The second scene occurs when the dying thief asked to be remembered. Jesus' response was immediate: "Assuredly, I say to you, today you will be with Me in Paradise" (v. 43 NKJV). While forgiveness is not mentioned in this exchange, it is obvious forgiveness took place.

## II. JESUS TEACHES FORGIVENESS (Matt. 18:23-27)

### A. The Servant's Debt (vv. 23-24)

**23 Therefore is the kingdom of heaven likened unto a certain king, which would take account of his servants. 24 And when he had begun to reckon, one was brought unto him, which owed him ten thousand talents.**

Having told Simon Peter, in effect, that there is to be no limit to the times we are to forgive those who have wronged us, Jesus now illustrates this truth. In this story, He also shows the importance of forgiving others so that we may be forgiven.

Jesus uses a parable of a king and his servants to express, in the clearest possible terms, what it means to forgive unconditionally. If Peter ever had doubts about what the Lord was teaching, all he had to do was recall this story.

The story begins with a king who has decided to settle the accounts he has with his servants—that is, to collect from them what they owe him. It was not unusual for officials who operated in the service of the king to borrow large sums of money ostensibly to operate the affairs of the area where they served. They were under the king's absolute authority and were to put the revenues from their province into the king's treasuries.

One of the servants who came before the king is represented as owing an enormous amount of money. Various commentators describe the amount in different terms. One said it was an amount that could not have been repaid in a thousand lifetimes of labor. Another said it was more than the total budget of an entire province. Still another said this man's debt was beyond commutation. One commentator attempted to calculate the amount in present-day currency, saying that the debt would come to $3,150,000,000. All of this is important when we consider what this servant did when a debtor asked forgiveness of him of a much smaller amount of money.

Since this is a parable of the Kingdom, we have a picture of a people who owe a debt that is beyond their ability to pay, and of a Sovereign who operates in grace and offers forgiveness to all who ask. Nothing we can do will be enough to pay the debt for our sins, but God has made a provision for us through Christ's death on the cross and His subsequent resurrection from the grave.

---

- If you could place a dollar figure on your sin, how high would it be?

> "When you forgive, you must cancel the debt. Do not spend your life paying and collecting debts."—Joyce Meyer

## B. The Servant's Plight (vv. 25-26)

**25 But forasmuch as he had not to pay, his lord commanded him to be sold, and his wife, and children, and all that he had, and payment to be made. 26 The servant therefore fell down, and worshipped him, saying, Lord, have patience with me, and I will pay thee all.**

The man was unable to repay the enormous debt he had accumulated. This situation left him in the unfortunate plight of having him and his family auctioned off at the slave market. In that day, this was a common way to recover some of the debt one owed. This does not mean the family would bring enough at the auction to pay off the debt, but only that whatever was paid for them would be put in the king's treasury.

This man's inability to pay the debt he owed is a picture of every individual's condition regarding sin. Nothing we can offer is sufficient to cover our sins. Only the provision God has made through the shed blood of Jesus is adequate to take away our sin and redeem our soul.

There is a second lesson here. This man's debt not only impacted his life; it touched the lives of every member of his family. The effects of sin are never singular. They are felt by all who are around us. No man ever sins in isolation. Though it may be inadvertent, others who are influenced by our lives may be affected adversely by our unrighteous deeds.

Now the day of reckoning has come. Until this point, the man seems to have given little thought to the debt he was accumulating or to how he would repay it. Now that the king has confronted him, he realizes how desperate his situation is. He throws himself at the king's feet, begs him for another chance, and promises to pay the debt in full. Obviously, this is a promise he cannot keep; the debt is too great.

How did you feel when you first realized how great the weight of your sin was? Had it ever occurred to you that your sins cost the Savior His life? How did you react when the full impact of your condition dawned on you? Did you run to the Lord and fling yourself on His mercy?

- How should we be like this servant?

> "When you've experienced grace and you feel like you've been forgiven, you're a lot more forgiving of other people. You're a lot more gracious to others."—Rick Warren

C. The Master's Compassion (v. 27)

**²⁷ Then the lord of that servant was moved with compassion, and loosed him, and forgave him the debt.**

Everything about this man's accumulation of debt was wrong. He had misused the king's investments, ignoring the fact that this money did not belong to him; he was only to be a steward of it, and with reckless abandon he accumulated a debt he could never repay. Yet, when he asked the king for more time and promised to repay the entire debt, the king was moved with compassion toward him. He asked the king for patience. The king, in mercy, issued him a pardon freeing him of his debt.

The king's heart went out to this man who was utterly undeserving of the consideration he was given. The king acted with mercy when he withheld the punishment this debtor deserved. While the king had the power to mete out punishment when it was necessary, he also had a tender heart that could be touched by a servant's plight.

What a picture of humanity's hopeless condition and God's tender mercy! We were in a state of helplessness in regard to changing our spiritual condition. We had no power or goodness that could lift us from the pit of sin and place us in good standing with God. Our best efforts in this regard were as "filthy rags" (Isa. 64:6). It was only the pure mercy and free grace of God that made it possible for us to be freed from the guilt of sin and cleansed by the precious blood of Jesus.

The forgiveness the Lord extends to us is free and complete. John Gill wrote: "When God forgives sin, He forgives all sin—original and actual, secret and open, sins of omission and commission; of heart, lip, and life; of thought, word, and deed . . . and that freely, according to His abundant mercy, and the riches of His grace; without any regard to any merits, motives, and conditions in the creature." Gill must have read Isaiah 55:1: "Ho! Everyone who thirsts, come to the waters; and you who have no money, come, buy and eat. Yes, come, buy wine and milk without money and without price" (NKJV). How beautiful that we can come to Christ without money and without price and obtain, by His grace, the priceless gift of salvation!

---

- How is God like the king in this story?

> "God pardons like a mother, who kisses the offense into everlasting forgiveness."—Henry Ward Beecher

---

III. CONSEQUENCES OF NOT FORGIVING (Matt. 18:28-35)

A. Forgiven but Unforgiving (vv. 28-30)

**²⁸ But the same servant went out, and found one of his fellowservants, which owed him an hundred pence: and he laid hands on him, and took him by the throat, saying, Pay me that thou owest. ²⁹ And his fellowservant**

fell down at his feet, and besought him, saying, Have patience with me, and I will pay thee all. ³⁰ And he would not: but went and cast him into prison, till he should pay the debt.

Still basking in the warmth of the mercy shown to him by the king, this man searched out a fellow servant who owed him a much smaller amount, and demanded payment from him. This should have been a time when the man was still rejoicing over his good fortune and his heart was tender toward others. This, however, was not the case.

Not only did the forgiven man not show any mercy to his servant, but he treated him in the cruelest manner possible. The statement that the man "took him by the throat" (v. 28) pictures a furious man almost strangling or choking another person.

His fellow servant made essentially the same plea to him that he had made to the king. He pleaded for patience and promised to pay the debt he owed. The response the man gave to his peer was the exact opposite of that shown to him by the king. Instead of extending mercy to him, he ordered him cast into prison until the debt was paid.

The sins of which we are guilty before God are too great for us to ever be able to purchase our redemption. Only by an act of mercy and grace on God's part can we find forgiveness. Despite God's immeasurable forgiveness toward us, we may find difficulty in forgiving others and sometimes carry a grudge against them. How can we hope to have the favor of God as long as we harbor this attitude in our heart?

Let us pause again to remember how great was the payment the Father made for our sin, even the giving of His Son freely and willingly when there was not one ounce of merit on our part. The sins others have committed against us might be weighty, yet they are small compared to the sin debt we owe to the Father. However, His completed forgiveness has been extended to us.

---

- When is it difficult for you to forgive another person, and why?

> "Every day God patiently bears with us, and every day we are tempted to become impatient with our friends, neighbors, and loved ones. And our faults and failures before God are so much more serious than the petty actions of others that tend to irritate us! God calls us to graciously bear with the weaknesses of others, tolerating them and forgiving them even as He has forgiven us."—Jerry Bridges

---

B. The Cost for Not Forgiving (vv. 31-34)

³¹ **So when his fellowservants saw what was done, they were very sorry, and came and told unto their lord all that was done.** ³² **Then his lord, after that he had called him, said unto him, O thou wicked servant, I forgave thee all that debt, because thou desiredst me:** ³³ **Shouldest not thou also have had compassion on thy fellowservant, even as I had pity on thee?** ³⁴ **And**

his lord was wroth, and delivered him to the tormentors, till he should pay all that was due unto him.

Other servants who saw what happened were greatly upset. They went to the king and reported to him exactly what had taken place. The king was astonished at what he heard. This man, who had been forgiven an enormous debt simply because he pleaded with the king for mercy, is now guilty of unmerciful action against the man who owed him so little. The king was baffled. He could not understand why this man had not shown mercy, even as mercy was shown to him. When the king fully realized what had happened, he was furious. He reversed his decision to show mercy and had the man arrested, thrown into prison, and tortured until he had repaid the debt he owed the king.

The lesson here is obvious. Christians are to forgive unconditionally, even as God has forgiven us in that manner. Forgiveness should condition us to forgive others. Something is drastically wrong when we who have been forgiven cannot find it in our heart to forgive others. How far this is from both the teaching and example of Jesus! What a dreadful thought that one day those who cannot forgive will stand before God with the burden of unforgiveness hanging over their head.

- What did the unforgiving servant learn about the cost of unforgiveness?

> "Many people ruin their health and their lives by taking the poison of bitterness, resentment, and unforgiveness. Matthew 18:23-35 tells us that if we do not forgive people, we get turned over to the torturers."—Joyce Meyer

### C. Forgiven and Forgiving (v. 35)

**35 So likewise shall my heavenly Father do also unto you, if ye from your hearts forgive not every one his brother their trespasses.**

Peter wanted to know how many times he should forgive someone who had wronged him. Jesus concludes this account by suggesting we are to forgive as often as the heavenly Father forgives. Not only that, the Father forgives us as many times as we sin against Him if we confess and ask His forgiveness, and repent.

Jesus indicates that an unforgiving spirit stems from an unregenerate heart. He underscored this when He said that forgiveness must come from the heart; it must be genuine. Empty words to placate someone is not forgiveness. There must be a demonstration of forgiveness that is lived out in future relationship with the individual.

Jesus is talking about a lifestyle. There are many facets of conduct that identify believers as true followers of Christ, and forgiveness is one of them. When we accept Jesus as our personal Savior, we are given a new nature. The divine nature becomes a part of our being, so the forgiveness we show stems from

God's own forgiving nature. This new nature expresses itself in what we do, including our forgiveness of others.

---

- What does it mean to forgive "from your hearts"?

### Only With God's Help

When Andrew Jackson was being interviewed for church membership, the pastor said, "General, there is one more question which I must ask you. Can you forgive all your enemies?"

Andrew Jackson was silent as he recalled his stormy life of bitter fighting. Then he responded, "My political enemies I can freely forgive, but as for those who attacked me for serving my country and those who slandered my wife—Doctor, I cannot forgive them!"

The pastor made it clear to Jackson that before he could become a member of that church and partake of the broken bread and the cup, his hatred and bitterness must be confessed and dealt with before God.

Again there was an awkward silence. Then Jackson affirmed that if God would help him, he would forgive his enemies.—George Sweeting
*Great Quotes and Illustrations*

---

## CONCLUSION

Since an unforgiving spirit stems from an unregenerate heart, we cannot claim to be children of God if we refuse to forgive others. We must relate to others in the same way the Lord has related to us. We are saved only because of the undeserved mercy of God. Therefore, we must show mercy to others whether or not they seem to deserve it.

## GOLDEN TEXT CHALLENGE

"IF YE FORGIVE MEN THEIR TRESPASSES, YOUR HEAVENLY FATHER WILL ALSO FORGIVE YOU: BUT IF YE FORGIVE NOT MEN THEIR TRESPASSES, NEITHER WILL YOUR FATHER FORGIVE YOUR TRESPASSES" (Matt. 6:14-15).

Forgiveness must somehow be interwoven into the fabric of the heart—an attitude that makes us forgiving, being reconciled to other men and women, even as we are reconciled to God. We who are forgiven must be forgiving toward others. There may be times when we are wronged so much that to have a forgiving heart seems impossible; in such times, it is a Christian discipline to intentionally begin to forgive.

Further, it is not the offense against us that creates those feelings of anger, hurt, and frustration. The Bible says, "As he thinketh in his heart, so is he" (Prov. 23:7). The feelings, then, are actually a result of what we "think in our heart," or say to yourselves, about the circumstances! We may base a theology of forgiveness on this truth. Although a deep hurt received at the end of another might come into our thoughts "seventy times seven" in a day (Matt. 18:21-35), the heart that is disciplined in God's loving, intentional forgiveness will be able to cope with remembering and still have forgiving thoughts.

Jesus cautions us in His explanation of the Lord's Prayer that we must institute a self-talk of forgiveness lest we, through an ungodly attitude, block God's forgiveness for us. It is the nature of God to love enough to be first in granting us forgiveness. As we walk with Him, let us extend to others the olive branch of peace, having a heart so bathed in God's love and so disciplined by that love that we easily forgive.

**Daily Devotions:**

M. Prayer for Forgiveness
    2 Chronicles 6:24-31
T. Blessing of God's Forgiveness
    Psalm 32:1-5
W. Greatness of God's Forgiveness
    Psalm 103:8-14
T. Jesus Forgives Sins
    Mark 2:1-12
F. Forgive One Another
    Colossians 3:12-17
S. How to Be Forgiven
    1 John 1:7 through 2:2

November 2, 2014 (Lesson 9)
# Stories About the Kingdom

Matthew 13:24-30, 36-43; 21:28-32; Mark 4:26-32; John 3:1-5

**Unit Theme:**
Parables of Jesus (Stories Jesus Told)

**Central Truth:**
Followers of Jesus Christ are citizens of God's kingdom.

**Focus:**
Highlight what Jesus said about the kingdom of God and live as citizens of the Kingdom.

**Context:**
In various settings, Jesus illustrates the kingdom of God.

**Golden Text:**
"Jesus answered and said unto him, Verily, verily, I say unto thee, Except a man be born again, he cannot see the kingdom of God" (John 3:3).

**Study Outline:**
I. Who Enters the Kingdom?
   (John 3:3, 5; Matt. 21:28-32)
II. The Kingdom Grows
   (Mark 4:26-32)
III. Christ Will Cleanse the Kingdom
   (Matt. 13:24-30, 36-43)

## INTRODUCTION

One of Jesus' favorite teaching methods was to ask questions. There are over one hundred questions asked in the four Gospels. Another method He used was to tell stories. There is the story of the prodigal son, the rich man and Lazarus, the rich young ruler, and others. A third method He employed was object lessons based on familiar items: a bird flying through the air, the lilies of the field, a city set upon a hill, and so on.

In today's lesson, Jesus uses the story of a grain of mustard seed and the growing of wheat and tares to illustrate the workings of the kingdom of God. This is both the telling of stories and the use of objects familiar to His hearers.

The life and influence of Jesus illustrates the principle of the mustard seed becoming a mighty tree. Born in an obscure village to an unknown woman, Jesus brought little attention to Himself for thirty years. The people of His day had so much on their minds: an oppressive empire, unreasonable taxation, the spiraling price of food, places to live, and clothes to wear.

When Jesus began preaching His message of repentance, love, and righteousness, it reached some but was ignored by others. Finally, He caused enough stir to prompt leaders to put a stop to His ministry. Their animosity toward Him led to His crucifixion, which they thought would bring His impact to an end and He would soon be forgotten. How wrong they were! His followers kept talking about Him even amid growing persecution. As a result, His church grew. It grew from the size of a mustard seed to a massive tree. The Roman Empire that tried to stop this movement has long since perished, but the Church lives on. As Jesus said, "I will build my church; and the gates of hell shall not prevail against it" (Matt. 16:18). He is still building His Church.

I. WHO ENTERS THE KINGDOM? (John 3:3, 5; Matt. 21:28-32)

A. The New Birth (John 3:3, 5)

(John 3:3 is not included in the printed text.)

**⁵ Jesus answered, Verily, verily, I say unto thee, Except a man be born of water and of the Spirit, he cannot enter into the kingdom of God.**

Nicodemus recognized by the deeds Jesus performed that He was from God and God was with Him. Perceiving Nicodemus' limited knowledge of the truth, Jesus told him, "Unless one is born again, he cannot see [enter or share in] the kingdom of God" (v. 3 NKJV). Jesus was saying a person must be regenerated, but Nicodemus was puzzled by this answer. He wanted to know how a grown person could reenter his mother's womb and be born again (v. 4). So Jesus repeated His statement, expressing it in different terms (v. 5).

Knowing Nicodemus was a religious man schooled in Old Testament teachings, Jesus used an expression that would take him back to one of the prophets. Through Ezekiel, God promised the people of Israel: "I will sprinkle clean water on you, and you shall be clean; I will cleanse you from all your filthiness and from all your idols. I will give you a new heart and put a new spirit within you; I will take the heart of stone out of your flesh and give you a heart of flesh. I will put My Spirit within you and cause you to walk in My statutes, and you will keep My judgments and do them. Then you shall dwell in the land that I gave to your fathers; you shall be My people, and I will be your God" (36:25-28 NKJV).

Jesus' reference to "born of water" speaks of a baptism of repentance. Through repentance, the sins of the past are forgiven. Being "born of the Spirit" enables us to walk in God's way and keep His instructions. Only being born of the Spirit will make us new creations. God's Spirit can make us what we could otherwise never be.

---

- Who cannot enter the kingdom of God, and why not?

> "Even to earnest minds the difficulty of grasping the truth at all has always proved extreme. Philosophically, one scarcely sees either the necessity or the possibility of being born again. Why a virtuous man should not simply grow better and better until in his own right he enter the kingdom of God is what thousands honestly and seriously fail to understand."—Henry Drummond

## B. The Repentant Son (Matt. 21:28-30)

**28 But what think ye? A certain man had two sons; and he came to the first, and said, Son, go work to day in my vineyard. 29 He answered and said, I will not: but afterward he repented, and went. 30 And he came to the second, and said likewise. And he answered and said, I go, sir: and went not.**

In the verses preceding this passage (vv. 23-27), Jesus had an encounter with the chief priests and elders of the people. They challenged His authority to teach and perform the wonderful works He was doing. Since His mission was not complete, He could not tell them He was the Son of God acting under the direct authority of the heavenly Father. So He answered their question with a question. He asked them by what authority John had performed his ministry of baptism. Was he acting at the behest of God or men? Any answer they gave would trip them up. If they acknowledged that John acted under orders of heaven, Jesus would ask why they did not believe him. On the other hand, the people believed John to be a prophet; if they said he was acting on human authority, the authorities would have to answer to the people. In frustration, they took the easy way out and said, "We don't know." So Jesus responded to them by telling them He would not divulge by what authority He acted.

Then Jesus told them a story about two sons. Their father gave the same instructions to both of them: they were to work in the vineyard for a day. The first son refused to go; he didn't want to dirty his hands in the vineyard. Perhaps he thought himself too good for day labor. But after he had time to think about it, he changed his mind. Whether out of a desire to please his father or out of the conviction that it was the right thing to do, he went to work in the vineyard. The second son readily agreed to go work in the vineyard. But as soon as he was out of his father's sight, he changed his mind and never went to work.

---

- Contrast the words and deeds of the two sons.

> "Conviction should actually grow throughout our Christian lives. In fact, one sign of spiritual growth is an increased awareness of our sinfulness."—Jerry Bridges

---

## C. The Way of Righteousness (vv. 31-32)

**31 Whether of them twain did the will of his father? They say unto him, The first. Jesus saith unto them, Verily I say unto you, That the publicans and the harlots go into the kingdom of God before you. 32 For John came unto you in the way of righteousness, and ye believed him not: but the publicans and the harlots believed him: and ye, when ye had seen it, repented not afterward, that ye might believe him.**

After telling the chief priests and leaders of the people the story of the two sons, Jesus asked them which of the sons did what his father asked. They correctly answered the first son, but there is nothing to indicate they understood the message Jesus was trying to convey. So Jesus explained the meaning of the story.

First, Jesus said that tax collectors and prostitutes, represented by the first son, would enter the kingdom of God before the religious leaders. Why? Because they believed the message John the Baptist preached. And what was John's message? That Jesus Christ is the Son of God, who takes away the sin of the world. They believed that message, repented, and their lives were changed. Second, the religious leaders, represented by the second son, heard the same message and refused to believe and repent, even though they saw the change the gospel had brought to the lives of those who embraced the truth.

Have you noticed that those who live an overtly sinful life are often more easily won to Christ that those who lead a religious, moral life? Both are sinners, but one recognizes their lostness while the other does not. When confronted with the need for the Savior, one acknowledges the need while the other does not.

The self-righteous religious leaders in this narrative seem to be clueless. They do not understand that, as one commentator says, "promises can never take the place of performance, and fine words are never a substitute for fine deeds. Profession and practice must meet and match." All their long, public prayers—to be seen of men—would not bring them one step closer to the kingdom of God.

Elsewhere, Jesus spoke of a Pharisee who considered himself so much better than a penitent tax collector standing nearby. The tax collector, realizing his plight, could not even lift his eyes toward heaven, but buried his face in his hands and pled for God's mercy and forgiveness. Jesus said that man went home right with God rather than the religious leader (see Luke 18:11-14).

1. What is shocking about Jesus' statement in verse 31?
2. How were the religious leaders like the second son (v. 32)?

> "If you look at God with the eye of the lawyer, the least sin makes you ineligible for mercy; but if you look at him in Christ, or with an evangelical eye, the greatest sinner may receive mercy; yes, the sense of unworthiness makes a man the more receptive."—Ralph Erskine

## II. THE KINGDOM GROWS (Mark 4:26-32)

### A. Seed Scattered (vv. 26-27)

**²⁶ And he said, So is the kingdom of God, as if a man should cast seed into the ground; ²⁷ And should sleep, and rise night and day, and the seed should spring and grow up, he knoweth not how.**

Interestingly, Mark is the only Gospel writer who records this story. These verses teach us there are some things we can do in the kingdom of God and some things we have no control over. They are to be left in the hands of God. We only bring frustration on ourselves when we try to do the things only He can do. It is our business to discover what we can do to the best of our ability and trust God for the results.

So, what can we do? We can plant the seed of the gospel in people's hearts. Even this must be done with care under the guidance of the Holy Spirit. There are times when a person's heart is more ready to receive the gospel than at other times. For example, sickness is a time when people have a sense of how weak and susceptible they are and how much they need God. Another circumstance when hearts are softened and thoughts may turn toward God is when a loved one dies. On those and other occasions, we may find an opportunity to graciously and tenderly speak to them about the love of God. So, this is what we can do: sow the seed of the gospel.

We can no more understand how grace works to bring a soul to salvation than we can understand how a seed sown can produce fruits and vegetables. Once we have communicated the Word of God, grace takes over and the result is God's doing. We cannot see what grace is doing in the inward being, but we can see the reflection of that work on the countenance of individuals as they experience new life! We cannot create, quicken, transform, regenerate, or save, but God can and does. And we marvel at this great mystery.

---

- What is the mystery of the seed?

> "Since Scripture imparts salvation, effective evangelism depends on the faithful proclamation of the Word. God will prepare the soil and bring forth the fruit. We must be faithful to plant the seed."—John MacArthur

---

B. Seed Ripening (vv. 28-29)

**[28] For the earth bringeth forth fruit of herself; first the blade, then the ear, after that the full corn in the ear. [29] But when the fruit is brought forth, immediately he putteth in the sickle, because the harvest is come.**

Once the farmer has planted seed and properly cultivated the soil, the seed germinates and the leaf bursts through the crust of the earth and grows from stage to stage. The sun, the dew, and other elements of nature—all outside human influence—combine to influence its growth. There is a steady progression from the blade to the ear to the full corn in the ear. Only when the fruit is ripe and ready does the farmer step in and harvest the crop.

We have here a picture of the work of grace in the heart. It is our responsibility to sow the seed of the Word; it is the work of grace to apply the Word and accomplish the redemption of the soul. The sown seed may not produce visible results immediately. Like the seed planted in the ground, there may be a period of time before there is any visible evidence that it will bring forth fruit. Once grace begins to work in an individual's life, the spiritual growth may be slow. The individual begins to understand and apply the Word and learn more about living in the Spirit and power of God. In the process of time, the believer learns more about what it means to rely on the Lord and to walk by faith. Nurtured by the

Word and led by the Spirit, he or she will grow strong in the Lord and eventually produce a rich and full harvest to the glory of God. At that point, the believer will understand what Paul meant when he said, "Work out your own salvation with fear and trembling; for it is God who works in you both to will and to do for His good pleasure" (Phil. 2:12-13 NKJV).

> "While we worry about how fast we grow, God is concerned about how strong we grow."—Rick Warren

### C. Seed Growing (vv. 30-32)

**30 And he said, Whereunto shall we liken the kingdom of God? or with what comparison shall we compare it? 31 It is like a grain of mustard seed, which, when it is sown in the earth, is less than all the seeds that be in the earth: 32 But when it is sown, it groweth up, and becometh greater than all herbs, and shooteth out great branches; so that the fowls of the air may lodge under the shadow of it.**

Jesus is interested in communicating His message in a way His listeners can clearly understand. So He ponders, *What is the best way to describe the kingdom of God?* He chose the method He so often used: a story. He selects an object that His hearers would be familiar with and uses that to illustrate what the kingdom of God is like.

Jesus uses a grain of mustard seed which, when planted, becomes a huge tree. These are figures every Jew would understand. To their mind, the grain of mustard seed represented the smallest possible thing, and the tree represented a great empire. The picture is that the kingdom of God had a very small beginning, but was growing into a massive movement.

When John the Baptist came preaching the kingdom of God, its numbers were very small. Jesus started out with twelve apostles. After His ascension, there were 120 followers gathered in the Upper Room. When they came out of the Upper Room filled with the Holy Spirit, thousands joined the Kingdom. From there, the Kingdom spread throughout the then-known world. Today, the kingdom of God has reached every corner of the globe. I am thankful to be a part of such a vast family of believers. Thus, the grain of mustard seed, and the tree it becomes, is an apt picture of the kingdom of God.

The growth of the kingdom of God we *have* seen is nothing compared to what we *will* see. When Christ returns and sets up His kingdom on earth, "the glory of the Lord" will cover the globe "as the waters cover the sea" (Hab. 2:14). What had been the tiniest beginning will grow greater in glory than the mightiest kingdoms of the earth. It will provide strength and protection for all those who live within its reach. What a glorious prospect!

- How is God's kingdom like a mustard seed?

---

III. CHRIST WILL CLEANSE THE KINGDOM (Matt. 13:24-30, 36-43)

A. The Parable Related (vv. 24-30)

(Matthew 13:26-29 is not included in the printed text.)

**24 Another parable put he forth unto them, saying, The kingdom of heaven is likened unto a man which sowed good seed in his field: 25 But while men slept, his enemy came and sowed tares among the wheat, and went his way.**

**30 Let both grow together until the harvest: and in the time of harvest I will say to the reapers, Gather ye together first the tares, and bind them in bundles to burn them: but gather the wheat into my barn.**

Jesus chose another story to illustrate an important point. This is the story of a farmer sowing good seed and an enemy coming along behind him and sowing seed that will produce bad results. When the crop grows, there are good plants and bad plants—wheat and tares—mingled together. Some of the man's servants want to extract the tares immediately, but the farmer objects, saying that to do so would destroy some of the wheat. The better solution is to wait until harvest time and then separate the worthless tares from the wheat. The tares could then be burned and the wheat stored in the barn.

We live in a world where good and evil coexist: sickness and health, wealth and poverty, sunny days and hurricanes, sin and righteousness, life and death. Why does God tolerate the existence of evil? Carlyle wrote: "God sits in heaven, and does nothing." The psalmist cried out, "O God, do not keep silent; be not quiet, O God, be not still. See how your enemies are astir, how your foes rear their heads. With cunning they conspire against your people; they plot against those you cherish" (83:1-3 NIV).

God has the power to do away with evil immediately, but He has a better way. Instead of pulling out the "tares" (i.e., removing the evil), He enables us to overcome it. Jesus said, "Here on earth you will have many trials and sorrows. But take heart, because I have overcome the world" (John 16:33 NLT). The apostle Paul added, "Be not overcome of evil, but overcome evil with good" (Rom. 12:21).

James S. Stewart tells of a woman who faced deep sorrow in her life. She declared, "I wish I'd never been made!" Her friend quietly replied, "My dear, you're not made yet. You're only being made—and this is the Maker's process." God has an eternity to finish making us all He intends us to be. Through faith we are made overcomers. Wait until harvest time and see what God has in store for His people.

---

- Describe various "tares" Satan uses to fight against God's kingdom.

> "My principal method for defeating error and heresy is by establishing the truth. One purposes to fill a bushel with tares; but if I can fill it first with wheat, I may defy his attempts."—John Newton

---

## B. The Parable Explained (vv. 36-40)

**³⁶ Then Jesus sent the multitude away, and went into the house: and his disciples came unto him, saying, Declare unto us the parable of the tares of the field. ³⁷ He answered and said unto them, He that soweth the good seed is the Son of man; ³⁸ The field is the world; the good seed are the children of the kingdom; but the tares are the children of the wicked one; ³⁹ The enemy that sowed them is the devil; the harvest is the end of the world; and the reapers are the angels. ⁴⁰ As therefore the tares are gathered and burned in the fire; so shall it be in the end of this world.**

After Jesus sent the multitudes away, His disciples followed Him into the house and asked Him to explain the parable of the wheat and tares. Interestingly, they did not inquire about two other parables (the mustard seed and the leaven) He had just told. Perhaps they understood their meaning without further explanation.

Jesus described for them the individuals and elements represented in this third parable. The *sower of the good seed* is Christ himself. He went about the countryside preaching the gospel and seeing sinners converted. The *field* represents the world in which the good seed is sown. The spread of the good news was not limited to the small area where Jesus ministered but, through His followers, includes the whole wide world. The *good seed* are the children of the Kingdom, who have tasted of the grace of God and become heirs of His glory and joint heirs with Jesus Christ.

The *tares* are the children of the devil who prove their identity by their principles and practices. The *enemy* (sower of the bad seed) is the devil himself. He is the enemy of Christ, the enemy of the Church, and the enemy of humanity. His mission is to destroy peace and comfort and to doom as many souls as he possibly can. The *harvest* represents the end of the world—the final judgment when the righteous will enter into eternal joy, and the wicked go into everlasting punishment. The *reapers* (end-time agents) will be the angels. They will be the executors of God's wrath on the wicked. Hypocrites, false prophets, and unbelievers will be cast into everlasting fire prepared for the devil and his angels.

---

1. What is the source of the "good seed," and what is that seed (vv. 37-38)?
2. When will God's harvest occur (vv. 39-40)?

> "And when God comes to reckon with his workmen, the plowman and the sower shall have his penny, as well as the harvest-man and the reaper."—William Gurnall

**Crippled but Not Useless**

Norman Vincent Peale once told of a man who often came to his church in a wheelchair. He had been in that chair since he was seventeen, when he was crippled by rheumatic fever. Sitting in his chair, he said to himself ceaselessly: *Useless, useless, useless.* Then, one day, he said to himself: *I am not useless.* He picked up the Bible and began to read. Finally, he was saying to himself: *So what, if I have no leg power, no arm or hand power. I have a sound mind. There is nothing crippled in my mind.*

He decided he could make greeting cards. With his gnarled and crippled hands, it took him a week to make the first card. And he suffered indescribable pain. But he sold the card at a profit. Today, he has a company making these cards by the thousands.

Clearly, a tiny mustard seed can become a massive tree.—*In God We Trust*

---

C. The Parable Applied (vv. 41-43)

**⁴¹ The Son of man shall send forth his angels, and they shall gather out of his kingdom all things that offend, and them which do iniquity; ⁴² And shall cast them into a furnace of fire: there shall be wailing and gnashing of teeth. ⁴³ Then shall the righteous shine forth as the sun in the kingdom of their Father. Who hath ears to hear, let him hear.**

A day of reckoning is coming. Christ will call on the angels to carry out His mission of separating the wheat from the tares. Anyone who has been an instrument of Satan to hinder the children of God from being fruitful will be separated out and dealt with. Those who have been motivated by wicked principles and evil practices will be gathered up and forever separated from the saints. Whether their deeds of iniquity have been done secretly or openly, they will be held accountable and judged accordingly.

The word *separate* is used several times in the preceding paragraph because being separated from God and all that is good is a major part of the torment the wicked will face. They will be ultimately cast into hell, where there will be "wailing and gnashing of teeth" (vv. 42, 50). This will be a place of mental torture, inexpressible pain, and utter despair.

What a different picture we have for the future of the righteous! The saints will find themselves in a glorious state too wonderful for words to express. Jesus' description of that future state is reminiscent of the words of Daniel: "Those who are wise will shine like the brightness of the heavens, and those who lead many to righteousness, like the stars for ever and ever" (12:3 NIV). Wrapped in the robes of Christ's righteousness, God's people shall move from glory to glory in the Father's kingdom.

---

1. Explain the phrase "those who practice lawlessness" (v. 41 NKJV).

2. What role will the angels play in this harvest?
3. Who will "shine forth as the sun" (v. 43)?

## CONCLUSION

Every individual is faced with a choice that leads to a certain destiny. The lines are clearly drawn. Those who choose Christ as Savior and Lord are following a path that leads to unspeakable joy, resplendent glory, and life everlasting. Those who reject Him face a future marked by eternal torture, eternal separation, and eternal damnation. Where do you stand?

## GOLDEN TEXT CHALLENGE

"JESUS ANSWERED AND SAID UNTO HIM, VERILY, VERILY, I SAY UNTO THEE, EXCEPT A MAN BE BORN AGAIN, HE CANNOT SEE THE KINGDOM OF GOD" (John 3:3).

The concept of being "born again" almost always strikes those who are not accustomed to it as an unusual figure of speech. Nicodemus was among this number. He stumbled over the striking word-picture that the term "born again" conjured up, and he remarked about the apparent idiocy of the whole concept.

There are many modern-day Nicodemuses. If the gospel were comprised of a series of lofty philosophical statements, they would perhaps be challenged to find out more about it. But Jesus spoke of entering the Kingdom in simple, if rather mind-boggling, figures of speech. "Become like a little child," He said, "and God will become a Father to you. Be born again as an entirely new person, and the old man that you have been will slip away."

The new birth is a total change by virtue of a new beginning, and that is what the gospel is all about.

**Daily Devotions:**

M. The Kingdom Is the Lord's
   1 Chronicles 29:10-13
T. Christ's Kingdom Foretold
   Isaiah 9:2-7
W. The Indestructible Kingdom
   Daniel 2:36-45
T. Christ's Unending Kingdom
   Luke 1:26-33
F. Future of the Kingdom
   1 Corinthians 15:20-28
S. Receiving the Kingdom
   Hebrews 12:22-29

November 9, 2014 (Lesson 10)
# Stories About Prayer
**Luke 11:5-13; 18:1-14**

**Unit Theme:**
Parables of Jesus (Stories Jesus Told)

**Central Truth:**
Prayer is foundational to every aspect of Christian living.

**Focus:**
Examine and practice principles Jesus taught for effective prayer.

**Context:**
Jesus uses stories to teach truths about prayer.

**Golden Text:**
"If we ask any thing according to his will, he heareth us: and if we know that he hear us, whatsoever we ask, we know that we have the petitions that we desired of him" (1 John 5:14-15).

**Study Outline:**
  I. Believe Prayer Is Effective
     (Luke 11:5-13)
 II. Persevere in Prayer
     (Luke 18:1-8)
III. Pray With the Right Attitude
     (Luke 18:9-14)

## INTRODUCTION

Prayer involves talking to God: praising Him, petitioning Him, honoring Him; but it also includes listening to Him. We expect that when we pray, God will answer. How He will answer, we may not know; but that He will answer, we can be certain. The answer may not be the one we are looking for, or it may be delayed in coming, but it will come. It may be "yes," or "no," or "later," or "I have something better for you," but we will hear from God.

In Psalm 5:3, David said, "In the morning I will direct [my prayer] to You, and I will look up" (NKJV). The *New English Translation* reads: "In the morning I will present my case to you and then wait expectantly for an answer." We can conclude that David began each morning with prayer. The time of day when we pray is not as important as our consistency in doing so. Notice that David said he directed his prayers to the Lord. He did not pray randomly; he had a clear objective in mind when he prayed. After he prayed, he looked up expectantly, waiting for an answer.

How many times have we been guilty of praying and never thinking about it again? That is just going through the motion and not really expecting an answer.

What a difference it makes if, after we pray, we look up day after day—waiting, expecting—until the answer comes.

Jesus is not mocking us when He said in Matthew 7:7-8: "Keep on asking, and you will receive what you ask for. Keep on seeking, and you will find. Keep on knocking, and the door will be opened to you. For everyone who asks, receives. Everyone who seeks, finds. And to everyone who knocks, the door will be opened" (NLT). The Lord is willing to hear and answer us when we pray. In fact, we have tapped into one of God's greatest delights when we pray. R. C. Trench wrote, "Prayer is not overcoming God's reluctance; prayer is laying hold of God's highest willingness."

## I. BELIEVE PRAYER IS EFFECTIVE (Luke 11:5-13)

### A. A Friend's Persistence (vv. 5-8)

**⁵ And he said unto them, Which of you shall have a friend, and shall go unto him at midnight, and say unto him, Friend, lend me three loaves; ⁶ For a friend of mine in his journey is come to me, and I have nothing to set before him? ⁷ And he from within shall answer and say, Trouble me not: the door is now shut, and my children are with me in bed; I cannot rise and give thee. ⁸ I say unto you, Though he will not rise and give him, because he is his friend, yet because of his importunity he will rise and give him as many as he needeth.**

Jesus opens this story with a question: What would you do if a friend came to you with a request at the most unreasonable time and under the most unreasonable circumstances? He presents this story to teach us there is no unreasonable time with God for hearing and answering prayer. For this reason, we are encouraged not only to pray, but to continue in prayer until an answer comes. The apostle Paul gave the same advice to the Colossians: "Continue earnestly in prayer, being vigilant in it with thanksgiving" (4:2 NKJV). Also, to the Ephesians, Paul calls for Spirit-guided prayer and perseverance in praying for believers: "Pray in the Spirit at all times and on every occasion. Stay alert and be persistent in your prayers for all believers everywhere" (Eph. 6:18 NLT).

Now to the story. The man in this story had a guest come to his house at the midnight hour. As was customary, he wanted to feed his guest, but there was no food in the house. Since it was midnight and the shops were closed, the man decided to go to his friend's house and borrow some bread. When he knocked on the door and called out to his friend for help, he got an unexpected answer. His friend called back to tell him the lights were out, the kids were in bed, and he could not rise and give him what he asked for. Think of what the friend was facing: he might wake up the kids, and it could be that he had problems getting them to sleep; there were no light switches, so he had to find and light a lamp. It was just too much trouble. But his neighbor would not give up. Finally, the man arose to help his neighbor, not because of their friendship but because of the man's persistence.

Persistence in prayer pays off. Jesus admonished His disciples, "Behold, I send the Promise of My Father upon you; but tarry in the city of Jerusalem until you are endued with power from on high" (Luke 24:49 NKJV). Regarding his "thorn in the flesh," Paul said, "Three different times I begged the Lord to take it away. Each time he said, 'My grace is all you need. My power works best in weakness'" (2 Cor. 12:8-9 NLT). Look at how Jesus prayed in Gethsemane: "And being in agony, He prayed more earnestly. Then His sweat became like great drops of blood falling down to the ground" (Luke 22:44 NKJV).

---

- What finally motivated the neighbor to respond?

> "It is not enough to begin to pray, nor to pray aright; nor is it enough to continue for a time to pray; but we must pray patiently, believing, continue in prayer until we obtain an answer."—George Mueller

---

B. A Believer's Persistence (vv. 9-10)

**⁹ And I say unto you, Ask, and it shall be given you; seek, and ye shall find; knock, and it shall be opened unto you. ¹⁰ For every one that asketh receiveth; and he that seeketh findeth; and to him that knocketh it shall be opened.**

When Jesus encourages believers to keep on asking, seeking, and knocking in prayer, He is not suggesting that God is like the neighbor who was slow to respond to the request of his friend. He wants us to understand the secret to power in prayer is persistence. Church members used to encourage fellow believers to "pray through." This meant praying until there was an inner assurance that our prayer had been heard and the answer was on the way. "Praying through" sometimes required lengthy periods of prayer. At other times, "praying through" meant praying until the answer we were looking for gave way to God's answer.

The tense of the words used in these verses indicates it is those who keep asking, keep seeking, and keep knocking who have their prayers answered. An all-wise God responds to our prayers in the manner that is best for us. Sometimes He answers immediately in the affirmative; at other times, He answers in the negative. His answer is "No" when we ask for the wrong motives and selfish reasons. He also answers "No" when He has something better for us. When the mother of Zebedee's sons asked Jesus to show favoritism to them when He came into His kingdom, Jesus responded, "You don't know what you are asking" (Matt. 20:22 NIV). We are guilty of praying in the same manner sometimes and then we wonder why our prayers get a negative response.

Occasionally, God tells us to wait as an answer to our prayer. Jacob is a good example. He came to God asking for His favor and promising God something in return. Later, as he wrestled with an angel, Jacob changed his petition from wanting God to give him something to wanting God. That night, Jacob was given the greatest possible blessing. In his plea, the angel said to Jacob, "Let Me go, for the day breaks." But Jacob said, "I will not let You go unless You bless me!" (Gen. 32:26 NKJV). The blessing that came from his waiting was this: "So Jacob called the name of the place Peniel: 'For I have seen God face to face, and my life is preserved'" (v. 30 NKJV).

- Why does prayer sometimes require "seeking" and "knocking"?

> "The goal of prayer is the ear of God, a goal that can only be reached by patient and continued and continuous waiting upon Him, pouring out our heart to Him and permitting Him to speak to us. Only by so doing can we expect to know Him, and as we come to know Him better, we shall spend more time in His presence and find that presence a constant and ever-increasing delight."—E. M. Bounds

### C. A Believer's Greatest Gift (vv. 11-13)

**11 If a son shall ask bread of any of you that is a father, will he give him a stone? or if he ask a fish, will he for a fish give him a serpent? 12 Or if he shall ask an egg, will he offer him a scorpion? 13 If ye then, being evil, know how to give good gifts unto your children: how much more shall your heavenly Father give the Holy Spirit to them that ask him?**

Jesus uses the relationship between a father and his son to illustrate the relationship between the heavenly Father and His children. It is natural for a son when he is hungry to ask food of his father. If a son asked bread of his father and he gave him a stone instead, the father's heart would be harder than the stone. If a son asked fish of his father and he gave him a poisonous snake, we would consider him a monster. The same thing would be true if a son asked for an egg and his father gave him a venomous scorpion.

Now comes the contrast. If an earthly father, marred with sins and shortcomings, gives his son the things necessary to life and sustenance, and denies him anything that would injure him, how much more will the perfect heavenly Father give His children what they need when they call on Him? Surely, every believer knows that when he or she comes to this loving Father with a genuine need, their prayers will be heard and answered. To believe otherwise would be to see God as less compassionate and less caring than an earthly father.

Not only do we have a picture of a heavenly Father who will gladly meet our every need, He is also shown as willingly giving to us the most important and indispensable gift possible—the Holy Spirit. The Spirit comes to indwell us, walk along beside us, and direct our steps. He will lead us into all truth. He is our ever-present Comforter who aids us when we pray. He enables us to offer prayers that the Father will honor and answer. James wrote, "Every good gift and every perfect gift is from above, and comes down from the Father of lights, with whom there is no variation or shadow of turning" (1:17 NKJV). But no other gift can compare with the gift of the Holy Spirit.

1. How is God different than a heartless father (vv. 11-12)?
2. What gift does God long to give (v. 13)?

> "Prayer means rushing to the Father as His child. It means asking and receiving, loving and thanking Him."—Basilea Schlink

## II. PERSEVERE IN PRAYER (Luke 18:1-8)

### A. Introduction (vv. 1-2)

**¹ And he spake a parable unto them to this end, that men ought always to pray, and not to faint; ² Saying, There was in a city a judge, which feared not God, neither regarded man.**

Luke 18 is rich with stories that illustrate gospel truths. It includes stories of the unjust judge and the persistent widow, the Pharisee and the publican, the rich young ruler, and the healing of the blind man. It also addresses Jesus' care for little children, the promise of rewards for those who put Christ first in their life, and foretells the death and resurrection of Jesus.

Jesus taught that believers ought to pray "always"—meaning we are not necessarily to be always on our knees, but rather that we should maintain a spirit of prayer at all times. We should always be ready to pray if the moment calls for it, and there should be no place where prayer is off limits. Our morning prayer and our evening prayer ought to be linked together by the prayers we offer throughout the day. In a symbolic way, our prayer life ought to resemble the morning and evening sacrifices referred to in Exodus 29:42 as a continual burnt offering.

The second principle the Lord teaches us in this story is that in prayer we are never to lose heart and we are never to give up. When we consider to whom we are praying, the infinite resources He has to meet our every need, and the promise of His Word that He will do exactly that, we should be faithfully persistent in prayer. The fact that a prayer is not answered as quickly as we had hoped, or in the exact manner we had expected, is no reason to grow faint or weary so as to quit praying. We can rest assured that, in His time, God will respond to our prayers according to our best interest.

---

- Describe a time you "fainted" for lack of prayer.

> "Oh, how strenuous is life! I know a little of it. Men 'ought always to pray, and not to faint.' How fierce the battle! I know something of the conflict, but I ought not to faint, because I can pray."—G. Campbell Morgan

---

### B. The Widow (vv. 3-5)

**³ And there was a widow in that city; and she came unto him, saying, Avenge me of mine adversary. ⁴ And he would not for a while: but afterward he said within himself, Though I fear not God, nor regard man; ⁵ Yet because this widow troubleth me, I will avenge her, lest by her continual coming she weary me.**

This woman comes to the judge asking for justice in a case in which she feels she has been defrauded. The judge is under divine mandate to deal fairly with her, to be certain that her rights are upheld, and to give careful attention to her situation. Among other requirements the Lord placed upon judges was to "learn to do good; seek justice, rebuke the oppressor; defend the fatherless, [and] plead for the widow" (Isa. 1:17 NKJV). Through Jeremiah, the Lord gave these instructions: "Execute judgment and righteousness. . . . Do no wrong and do no violence to the stranger, the fatherless, or the widow" (22:3 NKJV).

This judge, however, has no regard for God or His Word. It doesn't matter to him what God thinks about what he is doing, and he cares even less what people think. So the pleading of this woman did not even register with him at first. But this was no ordinary woman who came to him. She was determined to see justice done and to see that he was the one to carry it out. Because of her continual pleading and repealed requests, he finally confesses something like this: "This woman is driving me crazy with her badgering. If I don't see that justice is done, she is going to wear me out." Although he would not act justly out of fear of God or respect for man, he granted her petition because of her persistence.

Whatever else this passage teaches, its spiritual application is to show the importance and force of prayer. When prayer is engaged in with a view to persisting until an answer comes, it gets results. James wrote, "The effective, fervent prayer of a righteous man avails much. Elijah was a man with a nature like ours, and he prayed earnestly that it would not rain; and it did not rain on the land for three years and six months. And he prayed again, and the heaven gave rain, and the earth produced its fruit" (5:16-18 NKJV).

- How should we be like the widow?

> "Intensity is a law of prayer. God is found by those who seek Him with all their heart. Wrestling prayer prevails. The fervent effectual prayer of the righteous is of great force."—Samuel Chadwick

C. Divine Justice (vv. 6-8)

**⁶ And the Lord said, Hear what the unjust judge saith. ⁷ And shall not God avenge his own elect, which cry day and night unto him, though he bear long with them? ⁸ I tell you that he will avenge them speedily. Nevertheless when the Son of man cometh, shall he find faith on the earth?**

Jesus calls upon us to consider this situation. Here is a corrupt judge who responded to the persistent pleadings of a poor widow for whom he had the lowest regard. How much more can we expect from a good and merciful God who loved us so much that He gave His only begotten Son to save us? If we diligently seek Him, He will hear and answer prayer. The writer of Hebrews said, "But without faith it is impossible to please Him, for he who comes to God must believe that He is, and that He is a rewarder of those who diligently seek Him" (11:6 NKJV).

Having given assurance that God will provide justice for those who cry out to Him, the Lord asks a pertinent question: "When the Son of Man comes, will He find [persistence in] faith?" (Luke 18:8 Amp.). Peter states that many scoffers will say, "Where is the promise of His coming? For since the fathers fell asleep, all things continue as they were from the beginning of creation" (2 Peter 3:4 NKJV). Peter responds to their skepticism by reminding them, "The Lord is not slack concerning His promise, as some count slackness, but is longsuffering toward us, not willing that any should perish but that all should come to repentance" (v. 9 NKJV).

The important question for each of us is, Will He find us faithful at His coming? Does our heart beat for the hour of His appearing?

---

1. Answer the question about God's justice (v. 7).
2. "When the Son of Man returns, how many will he find on the earth who have faith?" (v. 8 NLT)?

> "Many are called, few are chosen, but fewer still are faithful. These are the overcomers spoken of ten times in the Book of Revelation."—Zac Poonen

---

## III. PRAY WITH THE RIGHT ATTITUDE (Luke 18:9-14)

A. The Self-Righteous (vv. 9-10)

**⁹ And he spake this parable unto certain which trusted in themselves that they were righteous, and despised others: ¹⁰ Two men went up into the temple to pray; the one a Pharisee, and the other a publican.**

Jesus speaks to a group of people who trusted in their works to produce the righteousness that made them acceptable in the sight of God. Their trust was not in God or in Christ, but in their own ability to live out the requirements of the Law. This self-righteous attitude led them to believe they were holier than other people. Those who are trusting Christ for their righteousness see themselves as sinners in need of a Savior—as spiritually bankrupt in need of a Redeemer. They see nothing within themselves that makes them worthy of acceptance before God. So, in humility, they come to Christ seeking forgiveness and praying to be made worthy by His grace to become a follower of His. What a contrast!

Another undesirable characteristic of the self-righteous is that they look down their nose at everybody else. They don't want those who are not in their group around them. The Bible uses such words as *scorn* and *despise* to describe their true feelings about others. They consider others as unworthy to be compared with themselves and that God would be wasting His time to be concerned about them.

Those who are truly righteous do not share this viewpoint. They see all people as eternity-bound and in need of a Savior. While they may not love the deeds of unbelievers, they love all people and want to lead lives that will encourage the lost to seek the Savior. Nothing pleases them more than to have others join them on the journey to a better world.

The two characters in this story are a Pharisee and a "publican," or tax collector. The Pharisee was outwardly clean but unaware of his need to be changed inwardly. He depended on his own righteousness. On the other hand, the publican knew he was a sinner.

---

1. Why did Jesus tell this parable?

2. Why did the two men go to the Temple?

> "Human legalism leads to human self-righteousness. Human self-righteousness denies the need for the saving, enabling grace of Christ."—Paul David Tripp

---

### B. The Pharisee (vv. 11-12)

**11 The Pharisee stood and prayed thus with himself, God, I thank thee, that I am not as other men are, extortioners, unjust, adulterers, or even as this publican. 12 I fast twice in the week, I give tithes of all that I possess.**

It is interesting that the Pharisee stands alone as he prayed. He probably feels he would be contaminated if he mingled with the other worshipers. He reflects the attitude expressed by the people referred to in Isaiah 65:5: "Who say, 'Keep to yourself, do not come near me, for I am holier than you!'" (NKJV).

Although he stands alone, he speaks loud enough so the worshipers in the Temple could hear his boastful words. This Pharisee is the personification of pride. He expresses words of praise, but not unto God; rather, it is praise of himself. He alleges he is "not like other men" (Luke 18:11 NKJV), meaning he is not a sinner like everybody else. He spells out his opinion of others by labeling them as robbers, crooks, and adulterers. He adds that he is certainly not like this tax collector praying nearby.

Having spoken in the most negative terms of others, showing his utter contempt for them, the Pharisee now turns to the commendable qualities he sees in himself. In his mind, he excels in holiness above all others, boasting how he does more than the Law requires of him in fasting, and bragging about the extent of his tithing. However, neither of these should be done in an ostentatious manner. Of giving and fasting, Jesus said, "Don't do your good deeds publicly, to be admired by others, for you will lose the reward from your Father in heaven. . . . And when you fast, don't make it obvious, as the hypocrites do, for they try to look miserable and disheveled so people will admire them for their fasting. I tell you the truth, that is the only reward they will ever get" (Matt. 6:1, 16 NLT).

---

1. How did the Pharisee compare himself with the tax collector?
2. Why is it unwise to compare oneself with others?

> "Many have passed the rocks of gross sins—who have suffered shipwreck upon the sands of self-righteousness."—William Secker

---

### C. The Publican (vv. 13-14)

**13 And the publican, standing afar off, would not lift up so much as his eyes unto heaven, but smote upon his breast, saying, God be merciful to me a sinner. 14 I tell you, this man went down to his house justified rather**

than the other: **for every one that exalteth himself shall be abased; and he that humbleth himself shall be exalted.**

The Pharisee stood apart from the other worshipers because he thought himself too good to associate with them; the publican stood afar off from others because he felt unworthy to be in their company. Further, the publican turned his face toward the ground, not feeling worthy to look up as he called upon the Lord. He beat his chest in anguish as he called out for mercy. His whole demeanor expressed a public acknowledgment of his great transgressions for all within view of him to see. Unlike the Pharisee, the publican confessed no good traits but openly acknowledged he was a sinner in need of God's mercy. He saw himself as such a grievous sinner that his only hope was in a gracious Savior.

This publican, who readily acknowledged that he was a sinner and who felt unworthy of divine favor in any way, was accounted righteous in the eyes of God and was forgiven of all his sins. He went home "justified" by God, while the Pharisee who had such a high opinion of himself left without being changed. Jesus then explained that a humble attitude is well pleasing and acceptable to God, while pride and arrogance are abhorred. On another occasion, Jesus said, "Those who exalt themselves will be humbled, and those who humble themselves will be exalted" (Matt. 23:12 NLT). The Virgin Mary saw this principle at work in God's dealings with humanity. She said of God, "His mighty arm has done tremendous things! He has scattered the proud and haughty ones. He has brought down princes from their thrones and exalted the humble" (Luke 1:51-52 NLT).

---

1. How did the tax collector see himself (v. 13)? Was this accurate?
2. What does it mean to be "justified," and how does it happen (v. 14)?

> Prayer is the soul's sincere desire,
> Uttered or unexpressed;
> The motion of a hidden fire
> That trembles in the breast.
>
> Prayer is the burden of a sigh,
> The falling of a tear;
> The upward glance of an eye
> When none but God is near.
>
> Prayer is the simplest form of speech
> That infant lips can try;
> Prayer the sublimest strains that reach
> The majesty on high.
> —James Montgomery

---

### CONCLUSION

The stories in this lesson teach how to live and how not to live; how to pray and how not to pray. In prayer, as in life, we are to render praise to God and not to ourselves. We are to walk humbly and not with pride and arrogance. We are to live and pray in a God-centered manner, which will result in a God-blessed life.

## GOLDEN TEXT CHALLENGE

"IF WE ASK ANY THING ACCORDING TO HIS WILL, HE HEARETH US: AND IF WE KNOW THAT HE HEAR US, WHATSOEVER WE ASK, WE KNOW THAT WE HAVE THE PETITIONS THAT WE DESIRED OF HIM" (1 John 5:14-15).

The apostle John here affirms his confidence in God in the strongest terms. "We have," not merely a belief in a remote God, but "confidence," absolute trust, unshaken assurance in a God who is ever near at hand. Such confidence, says John, inspires a sense of boldness (2:28), an attitude of intimacy with God—toward Him, face to face. One who is thus positioned and privileged may "ask" for himself.

"According to his will," is the qualifying condition to answered prayer, even in the case of Jesus our Savior (Luke 22:42). God "heareth us" even when His answers take the form of denials. Our asking must always be subject to God's good and perfect will.

We know that God hears our prayers; and even as we ask, we know that we have, anticipatively, the answers to our petitions. Such is the utter confidence that we may claim now—gifts that are yet to be bestowed in the future. In effect, we have the answer already, as in Mark 11:24, and the assured answer is equal, so far as faith is concerned, to the gift itself!

**Daily Devotions:**
M. Example of Prevailing Prayer
   Genesis 32:24-30
T. Praying for God's Help
   Nehemiah 4:1-9
W. Prayer of Confession
   Daniel 9:3-6, 17-19
T. The Spirit Intercedes for Us
   Romans 8:24-28
F. Pray Always, With All Prayer
   Ephesians 6:14-20
S. Effective Prayer
   James 5:13-18

November 16, 2014 (Lesson 11)
# Stories About Stewardship
**Luke 12:16-21; 16:1-13**

**Unit Theme:**
Parables of Jesus (Stories Jesus Told)

**Central Truth:**
We ought to use responsibly all that God has given us.

**Focus:**
Assess our stewardship responsibilities to God and be faithful to Him.

**Context:**
Jesus presents divine perspectives on handling what God has entrusted to us.

**Golden Text:**
"It is required in stewards, that a man be found faithful" (1 Cor. 4:2).

**Study Outline:**
I. Be Rich Toward God
   (Luke 12:16-21)
II. Wisely Prepare for Eternity
   (Luke 16:1-9)
III. Be a Faithful Steward
   (Luke 16:10-13)

## INTRODUCTION

The business of a steward is to manage the affairs of one over him or her. For believers, it means properly handling what God has entrusted to us—God requires stewards to be found faithful. Today's lesson presents two men who were called on to account for their stewardship. The lesson begs the question of how we would fare if we were called into account for the way we are living.

Suppose we were called into account for the stewardship of our time. How much of our time do we spend wastefully? How much do we spend in bringing glory to God and honoring His name? Do we ever pause to consider that we will give an account for what we do with the time God has given us on this earth? For every moment since we began to understand right from wrong, we will have to give an account to God.

What if we were called into account for the stewardship of the abilities God has given us? Have we made any effort to develop our natural abilities so we can better serve Him? Have we perverted those abilities by using them only for personal gain and in selfish interests? Or, can we confidently say we are using our God-given abilities in a way that will bring glory to Him, make holiness attractive to those who observe us, and make the truth appealing to those around us?

There are many other areas of our life for which we may be called on to give an account for the way we have managed them. For example, have we been good stewards of our influence? Have we lived in such a sinful way before others that we have lost any influence for good and God that we might have otherwise had? What about our finances? Have we been guilty of robbing God by not paying our tithe and/or not giving offerings as were the people addressed in Malachi 3:8?

The Bible says, "It is appointed unto men once to die, but after this the judgment" (Heb. 9:27). Whether one stands before the judgment seat of Christ or the Great White Throne Judgment, all will give an account of their service as stewards. Sinners will utterly fail that accounting, and believers will either be rewarded or lose their rewards.

## I. BE RICH TOWARD GOD (Luke 12:16-21)

### A. A Very Rich Man (vv. 16-17)

**¹⁶ And he spake a parable unto them, saying, The ground of a certain rich man brought forth plentifully: ¹⁷ And he thought within himself, saying, What shall I do, because I have no room where to bestow my fruits?**

This is a story about a farmer. Making a living by farming goes all the way back to the Garden of Eden. Can you think of a profession more important to the survival of man? Why, the planet would face starvation if all the farmers let their land lay fallow for just one year!

This man was a successful farmer—his land produced fine crops. His fortune seems to have been built on diligent labor and honest endeavor. His crops were so abundant that he no longer had a place to store the produce.

One danger in being successful is forgetting that God owns all things and that He is the source of all blessings. The psalmist said, "The earth is the Lord's, and the fulness thereof; the world, and they that dwell therein" (24:1). The Lord God declared, "Every beast of the forest is mine, and the cattle upon a thousand hills" (50:10). David captured this truth so beautifully in his prayer to the Lord before the assembly of all the people: "All that is in heaven and in earth is Yours; Yours is the kingdom, O Lord, and You are exalted as head over all. Both riches and honor come from You, and You reign over all. In Your hand is power and might; in Your hand it is to make great and to give strength to all" (1 Chron. 29:11-12 NKJV).

Clearly, God doesn't need to be helped, supported, or subsidized. He made and owns all things. This is God's world. Everything in it belongs to Him. Understanding everything belongs to God leads to a life of peace and joy. It involves letting Christ control and direct us in all things. He becomes the center of our lives. It means using our possessions, our time, talents, influence, and property for His glory.

---

- Restate the rich man's question in contemporary terms.

> "The person who thinks the money he makes is meant mainly to increase his comforts on earth is a fool, Jesus says. Wise people know

that all their money belongs to God and should be used to show that God, and not money, is their treasure, their comfort, their joy, and their security."—John Piper

---

B. A Selfish Attitude (vv. 18-19)

**[18] And he said, This will I do: I will pull down my barns, and build greater; and there will I bestow all my fruits and my goods. [19] And I will say to my soul, Soul, thou hast much goods laid up for many years; take thine ease, eat, drink, and be merry.**

Seeing that his crops have produced more product than he can store, the farmer decides to build bigger barns to take care of all his crops and goods. Is not this logical? Is not this something anyone facing this situation would commonly do? He then concludes that he has accumulated enough to retire on. Is this not what most live to do? We spend a lifetime putting back an amount that will enable us to retire at a certain age.

Notice how self-centered the farmer is. He is trusting in his abundance for his future security and, in doing so, has forgotten God. He talks about "my fruits," "my goods," "my barns," even "my soul." He vainly believed that what he had accumulated was enough to keep him secure for the days and years ahead. He could foresee no calamity that would take away what he had provided for himself. He feels he has enough now to relax and enjoy the years ahead without fear of anything going wrong. He forgot two things: (1) Only the care and providence of God can secure our future; and (2) "life is not defined by what you have, even when you have a lot" (Luke 12:15 TM).

J. B. Phillips tells a parable about some little field mice who settled in a field of corn. Everything they needed was there. One day the farmer who owned the field came to reap his harvest. This turn of events meant tragedy for the mice. What seemed so smug and secure suddenly came crashing down around them. It never occurred to them that the field did not belong to them.

Likewise, we must not be guilty of the attitude of the farmer in the story Jesus tells. This is God's world, and everything in it belongs to Him. What we trust of our own making can be gone overnight; what we trust to God will last for an eternity.

---

- Describe the rich man's plan for the future.

### Mine or God's?

A little boy was given two quarters—one for Sunday school and another for himself. As he was running down the street, he dropped one of them and watched it roll into the sewer. "Well," he muttered, "there goes God's quarter." But the truth is, all the quarters are God's.

---

C. A Flawed Perspective (vv. 20-21)

**[20] But God said unto him, Thou fool, this night thy soul shall be required**

of thee: then whose shall those things be, which thou hast provided? **²¹ So is he that layeth up treasure for himself, and is not rich toward God.**

God has startling news for this farmer: he is going to die that night. He then confronts the man with the question, "Who will get all you have worked for?" The farmer would no longer have any control over it. Most likely, his relatives would be left to squabble over it.

Jesus then gives the application of the story. The farmer's fate is the same for all who trust in their personal treasure for security. On the other hand, to be in a rich relationship with God means placing our confidence and trust in Him. Only as we walk in His favor do we find hope and stability. When a man has deposited his treasure in the hands of God, he knows it will continue to bear results in another and better world. Elsewhere Jesus admonished, "Do not lay up for yourselves treasures on earth, where moth and rust destroy and where thieves break in and steal; but lay up for yourselves treasures in heaven, where neither moth nor rust destroys and where thieves do not break in and steal. For where your treasure is, there your heart will be also" (Matt. 6:19-21 NKJV).

This story should remind us of our accountability to God. David prayed, "Everything we have has come from you, and we give you only what you first gave us! We are here for only a moment, visitors and strangers in the land as our ancestors were before us. Our days on earth are like a passing shadow, gone so soon without a trace" (1 Chron. 29:14-15 NLT). The apostle Paul wrote, "So then every one of us shall give account of himself to God" (Rom. 14:12).

Daniel Webster, secretary of state under President Fillmore, attended a dinner gathering at the Hotel Astor in New York City. One man approached him and asked, "Mr. Webster, what is the most important thought that you ever had?" Webster answered, "The most serious thought that has ever occupied my mind was that of my individual responsibility to God."

Where do you stand on this: Do you try to avoid your responsibility to God, or do you readily acknowledge that you are accountable to Him?

---

1. Answer the question in verse 20.
2. What does it mean to be "rich toward God," and how does this happen (v. 21)?

---

"If rich people only knew when they died—how their relations would scramble for their money, the worms for their bodies, and the devils for their souls—they would not be so anxious to save money!"—William Tiptaft

---

II. WISELY PREPARE FOR ETERNITY (Luke 16:1-9)

A. A Dishonest Manager (vv. 1-2)

**¹ And he said also unto his disciples, There was a certain rich man, which had a steward; and the same was accused unto him that he had**

wasted his goods. ² And he called him, and said unto him, How is it that I hear this of thee? give an account of thy stewardship; for thou mayest be no longer steward.

Jesus now tells the story of a rich man who had a manager over his affairs who proved to be dishonest. He forgot that the money belonged to his master and not to himself.

Truit Gannon, pastor of a church in Georgia, tells of an incident in his boyhood. A man named Hugh, who worked for his father, owned a beautiful Harley Davidson motorcycle. Truit says it was his greatest thrill as a teenager to ride that motorcycle. One day he asked, "Hugh, can I ride your motorcycle again today?" Hugh's words have stuck with him ever since: "You can ride it anytime you want to, anywhere you want to, and as often as you want to. Just remember to ride it like it was mine and not yours." Reflecting on that statement, Gannon says, "God has given us full and free use of this world. All He asks is that we use it like it was His and not ours. That's stewardship."

We are daily confronted with the question, "Do I live for God or for myself?" The man in our story forgot he was working for someone else and not for himself. If we are not careful, we can adopt the same attitude in relation to God. Frank Sinatra sang, "I did it my way." Unfortunately, that could be the theme song of many people's lives. But our way often leads to difficulty and heartbreak, as the man in this story is soon to find out. On the other hand, God's way leads to life, peace, and joy. There is true contentment in doing God's will and fulfilling His purpose for our lives.

The steward in this story was trusted by the master to handle his goods in a way that was to the advantage of the master. Word came to the master that his manager had been embezzling his goods. So the master called him to account. He asked for a complete report of his activities and an audit of his books. He then informed him that he was fired.

---

- What accusation was brought against a manager?

---

> "A steward manages assets for the owner's benefit. The steward carries no sense of entitlement to the assets he manages. It's his job to find out what the owner wants done with his assets, then carry out his will."—Randy Alcorn

---

B. A Shrewd Rascal (vv. 3-7)

³ Then the steward said within himself, What shall I do? for my lord taketh away from me the stewardship: I cannot dig; to beg I am ashamed. ⁴ I am resolved what to do, that, when I am put out of the stewardship, they may receive me into their houses. ⁵ So he called every one of his lord's debtors unto him, and said unto the first, How much owest thou unto my lord? ⁶ And he said, An hundred measures of oil. And he said unto him, Take thy bill, and sit down quickly, and write fifty. ⁷ Then said he to another,

And how much owest thou? And he said, An hundred measures of wheat. And he said unto him, Take thy bill, and write fourscore.

Having been caught cheating and consequently dismissed from his job, the unjust steward ponders his situation. He concludes that he cannot "dig"—he was not strong enough to be a farmer. He had spent years in delicate and luxurious living and was not accustomed to manual labor. Also, he had too much pride to beg, although his pride didn't bother him when it came to cheating.

So the man devised a clever plan to ingratiate himself to those who owed his master money or goods. He offered to arrange for them to pay back only a percentage of what they owed. Their notes were altered to show them owing only this smaller amount. The amount he saved them was substantial and put them under lasting obligation to him. He did this so when he needed a place to live, they would invite him into their homes. Having been cast out of one setting, he resolved to position himself to be received in another.

We are not told how the manager planned to justify his actions to his master. Was he simply squandering the master's money? Was he illegally reducing debt? Was he subtracting interest that had accrued on the debt in violation of biblical teaching? Was he sacrificing his own commission for long-term gain? Jesus did not condone what this man was doing. It is clear the manager's plan was to have friends indebted to him when he needed them.

This man's plan may have provided a temporary fix for him when he was banished from his master's employment, but it was a flawed plan; it did not take into account the eternal consequences of his action. He might outsmart his master, but he still had to answer to *the* Master. More important than earthly provisions is eternal habitation. On another occasion, Jesus asked the all-important question, "What shall it profit a man, if he shall gain the whole world, and lose his own soul? Or what shall a man give in exchange for his soul?" (Mark 8:36-37).

1. How did the manager describe his dilemma (v. 3)?
2. What did he resolve to do (v. 4)?
3. How did the manager win the favor of his boss' customers (vv. 5-7)?

C. A Crafty Steward (vv. 8-9)

**⁸ And the lord commended the unjust steward, because he had done wisely: for the children of this world are in their generation wiser than the children of light. ⁹ And I say unto you, Make to yourselves friends of the mammon of unrighteousness; that, when ye fail, they may receive you into everlasting habitations.**

How did the master of the estate react when he heard of the clever maneuvering of his manager? While not condoning his action, he showed grudging admiration for what the manager had done. What is commended here is the steward looking after himself by making friends who would later help him—not the method he used to accomplish this.

Through this story, Jesus wishes to teach that those who live with a view to eternity should be as prudent in their activities as are those who live only for this world. We are to live out the principles of the gospel in such fashion that sinners will see Christ in us and desire to know Him. We are also charged to "do good . . . especially to those who are of the household of faith" (Gal. 6:10 NKJV).

This story teaches us that the best use we can make of the financial gains God has blessed us with is to use those means to take the message of salvation to sinners. If we use our abilities and spend our money bringing sinners to Christ, we will have the gratitude of the heavenly host who rejoices every time a sinner is converted. When we enter heaven, we will rejoice that we invested our money in things of eternal value.

Sometimes we do not realize how much good we can do and how far-reaching our efforts can be even when we pay our tithe. Thomas Lane Butts said: "One of the miracles of the organized church is that you can be busy at your daily tasks at home and at the same time be preaching the gospel in Africa, feeding the hungry in Haiti, or helping the homeless in India. You can win some victory for humanity, wherever you are, by your tithe."

---

1. What does Jesus say about shrewdness (v. 8)?
2. Explain Jesus' statement in verse 9.

---

> "A dreadful thing is the love of money! It disables both eyes and ears, and makes men worse to deal with than a wild beast, allowing a man to consider neither conscience nor friendship nor fellowship nor salvation."—John Chrysostom

---

### III. BE A FAITHFUL STEWARD (Luke 16:10-13)

A. The Reward of Faithfulness (v. 10)

**10 He that is faithful in that which is least is faithful also in much: and he that is unjust in the least is unjust also in much.**

The principle Jesus puts forth here is simple: If you can be trusted to handle small things, you have proven yourself capable of handling much greater things. If you are honest in dealing with natural, temporal matters, you will be honest in spiritual matters. With little or with much, what God wants from us is faithfulness.

One of the clearest ways to show our faithfulness is in how we handle money. Charles Spurgeon said, "Much of the unhappiness and discontent in the lives of many Christian people is their basic dishonesty when it comes to their honoring God with their substance." Our substance is money, but much more. Giving is only part of stewardship, and the tithe is only a part of giving. There are also other areas of our life in which we need to be faithful stewards.

As faithful stewards, we will seek to use our time wisely. We will ask God to teach us to number our days so that our minutes, hours, and days count for Him (see Pss. 39:4-5; 90:12). We will also use our body wisely and care for it. Immoralities and habits that degrade the body will be refused and disdained. The apostle Paul wrote: "I beseech you therefore, brethren, by the mercies of God, that you present your bodies a living sacrifice, holy, acceptable to God, which is your reasonable service" (Rom. 12:1 NKJV).

As faithful stewards, we will use our spiritual gifts for God's glory and in the service of humanity. Further, we will share the gospel by word of mouth and by the life we lead. Our lifestyle will say to others, "Jesus Christ is the most important priority in my life, and I want you to know Him and love Him as I do."

---

- Explain this principle.

> "Since my money is God's money, every spending decision I make is a spiritual decision."—John Hagee

---

B. The True Riches (vv. 11-12)

**¹¹ If therefore ye have not been faithful in the unrighteous mammon, who will commit to your trust the true riches? ¹² And if ye have not been faithful in that which is another man's, who shall give you that which is your own?**

Jesus asks a rather startling question: If you cannot be trusted in handling worldly wealth, how can you be trusted with the riches of the heavenly kingdom? Further, Jesus asked, If you cannot be trusted with another person's money, who will trust you with your own?

The steward in Christ's parable was in possession of his master's money, but possession does not mean ownership. This is true in relation to the kingdom of God. The Lord retains title to everything in His world, but He allows us to possess some portion of it. How we use those possessions will impact our future. Consider the money God has enabled us to accrue. Some people think tithing is just some method the church created to raise money. Nothing could be further from the truth. Tithing is God's plan for financing the work of His kingdom. When we tithe, we have a sense of being in partnership with God; He has promised to reward our faithfulness. In this way, tithing impacts our future.

It is important that we remember who we are. We are only stewards of what God has given us and, no matter how much we accumulate or how high we climb in this world, we and all that we have belong to Him. We would do well to heed the advice of Roland Hayes' mother. Roland was invited to sing before the king in Buckingham Palace. His parents had been slaves, and he was born in a tiny cabin in Georgia. After a music teacher heard him sing, doors began to open for him. Among the amazing opportunities that came his way was to perform at Buckingham Palace. He sent his mother a cablegram telling her about it. She cabled back to him a message of just four words: "Remember who you are."

That was a message for Roland Hayes, but it is also a message for us. No matter how much of this world's goods we acquire, let us remember that we were made of the dust of the earth and we will return to dust. Only what our soul possesses will live forever. We are stewards.

---

- What do possessions reveal about us?

> "Most people fail to realize that money is both a test and trust from God."—Rick Warren

## C. The Two Masters (v. 13)

**¹³ No servant can serve two masters: for either he will hate the one, and love the other; or else he will hold to the one, and despise the other. Ye cannot serve God and mammon.**

We cannot serve God and pursue the ways of the world at the same time. The apostle John addressed this issue by admonishing, "Do not love the world or the things in the world. If anyone loves the world, the love of the Father is not in him. For all that is in the world—the lust of the flesh, the lust of the eyes, and the pride of life—is not of the Father but is of the world. And the world is passing away, and the lust of it; but he who does the will of God abides forever" (1 John 2:15-17 NKJV).

So, we have a choice to make: Will the Lord be our God, or will money be our god? Will we serve God, or will we serve the world? To serve God is to have a view toward eternity; to serve the world is to embrace the temporary and fleeting. Can we say with Joshua, "As for me and my house, we will serve the Lord" (Josh. 24:15 NKJV)?

Life is made up of choices. Wherever you are in your life, the choices you have made have brought you to this place. Your life choices reveal what is important to you and what direction you are going to follow.

In Death Valley, California, there is a place known as Dante's View. From there, you can look down into the lowest spot in the United States—a depression in the earth two hundred feet below sea level called Black Water. From the same location, you can also look up to the highest peak in California, Mount Whitney, rising to a height of 14,494 feet. From Dante's View, travelers must decide which direction they will take: to the lowest spot in the United States, or to one of the highest.

In life, there is no middle ground when it comes to the most important choice we can make. Will we take the high road and follow Jesus, or will we take the low road and embrace the world and its ways?

- What will happen to a person who tries to serve both God and money?

> "If a person gets his attitude toward money straight, it will help straighten out almost every other area in his life."—Billy Graham

## CONCLUSION

The manager in today's lesson made some poor choices. He thought he could defraud his master and get by with it. Even his efforts to befriend those indebted to his master provided a temporary fix. Are the decisions you are making tailored to this world only? Or are you looking at the big picture and deciding for eternity? When God breathed life into man, he became a living soul. In the decisions you make, don't forget your soul.

## GOLDEN TEXT CHALLENGE

"IT IS REQUIRED IN STEWARDS, THAT A MAN BE FOUND FAITHFUL" (1 Cor. 4:2).

*Newsweek* ran an article titled "Letters in the Sand," a compilation of letters written by military personnel to family and friends in the States during the Gulf War.

One was written by Marine Corporal Preston Coffer. He told a friend, "We are talking about Marines, not the Boy Scouts. We all joined the service knowing full well what might be expected of us." He signed off with the Marine motto, *Semper Fi*—Latin for "always faithful."

As soldiers in God's service (or stewards in His household), He demands our faithfulness.

**Daily Devotions:**

M. Jacob's Stewardship
   Genesis 31:36-42
T. Joseph's Stewardship
   Genesis 39:1-6
W. Moses' Stewardship
   Deuteronomy 34:7-12
T. Faithfulness Rewarded
   Matthew 25:14-23
F. Faithfulness Acknowledged
   Philippians 2:19-30
S. Faithfulness Encouraged
   Hebrews 10:19-25

November 23, 2014 (Lesson 12)
# Stories About Finding the Lost
### Luke 15:1-24

**Unit Theme:**
Parables of Jesus (Stories Jesus Told)

**Central Truth:**
Christ seeks and saves the lost.

**Focus:**
Give thanks for Christ's love for the lost and endeavor to bring the unsaved to Him.

**Context:**
Jesus Christ explains salvation through three parables.

**Golden Text:**
"I [Jesus] say unto you, there is joy in the presence of the angels of God over one sinner that repenteth" (Luke 15:10).

**Study Outline:**
I. Finding a Lost Sheep
   (Luke 15:1-7)
II. Finding a Lost Coin
   (Luke 15:8-10)
III. Finding a Lost Son
   (Luke 15:11-24)

## INTRODUCTION

In Israel, the people known as "publicans and sinners" were despised by some and, at the least, ostracized from a certain level of society. The religious leaders, particularly the Pharisees and scribes, had nothing to do with them. Further, these leaders were not interested in bringing them into their religious circles.

Jesus, on the other hand, took a completely different point of view. He made it His business to reach out to them, to show them the way to salvation, and to help them find abundant life. Because they sensed His genuine love and care for them, they came out to hear Him on many occasions. The religious leaders took note of this and criticized Jesus severely. They should have been happy that someone was burdened for the lost souls in Israel and was seeking to lead them out of darkness into the light of life.

So, Jesus tells three stories that demonstrate the scribes and Pharisees are wrong in criticizing Him and that they, in fact, should be doing what He was doing. At the least, they should be rejoicing that lost ones were being saved.

These three stories show us a picture of the love of God manifested in Christ. The greatest possible expression of the love and grace of God is seen in the redemptive work of Christ on the cross. There He shed His precious blood so that every lost soul could find salvation. What He did on Calvary shows us that every individual is of infinite value to the Lord. Because of His redemptive work, the door that leads to heaven is open to everyone who chooses to enter.

The story of the Prodigal Son especially teaches us that Christ forgets our past, gives us direction and purpose for the future, and lets us know He will always be there for us. We can claim as our own the beautiful song, "What a Friend We Have in Jesus."

Notice that individuals are at the center of each of these stories. Someone said, "Winning people one at a time is the best way of winning the world, in time." The stories tell of one sheep, one coin, and one son.

## I. FINDING A LOST SHEEP (Luke 15:1-7)

### A. Registering a Complaint (vv. 1-2)

**¹ Then drew near unto him all the publicans and sinners for to hear him. ² And the Pharisees and scribes murmured, saying, This man receiveth sinners, and eateth with them.**

Among those who came to hear Jesus on this occasion were a large number of tax collectors and sinners. The Master received them courteously, and sometimes even went to their homes to visit and dine. Undoubtedly, He saw these visits as opportunities to share the truth with those who needed it the most.

These people who might be termed "outcast" came to hear what Jesus had to say. They were not there just to swell the numbers of those who came out; they listened to His message. This explains why the Scriptures tell us "tax collectors and harlots enter the kingdom of God before [the self-righteous]" (Matt. 21:31 NKJV). They came to Christ thirsting for His salvation, and He gave them "living water" (John 4:10).

The outcasts were not the only ones present that day. Scribes (interpreters of the Law) and Pharisees (rigid observers of their decrees and interpretations) were there. They were not there to hear what Jesus had to say as much as to criticize and complain. They were displeased that Jesus would associate with individuals they considered of low degree. In their thinking, this kind of behavior was beneath the dignity of a prophet. So, Jesus tells the three stories in this lesson to demonstrate that every sinner ought to be sought after. Of all people, the religious leaders should put forth the greatest possible effort to rescue those who are in the grip of sin.

Jesus described His mission in these words: "The Son of man is come to seek and to save that which was lost" (Luke 19:10). Everything He did, including His death on the cross, was designed to fulfill that purpose. Even Daniel, in the Old Testament, realized the wisdom of that purpose when he wrote, "They that be wise shall shine as the brightness of the firmament; and they that turn many to righteousness as the stars for ever and ever" (12:3).

---

1. What caused the religious leaders to grumble and complain?
2. Do we ever voice similar complaints? If so, why?

"The church is not a select circle of the immaculate, but a home where the outcast may come in. It is not a palace with gate attendants and challenging sentinels along the entrance-ways holding off at arm's length the stranger, but rather a hospital where the brokenhearted may be healed, and where all the weary and troubled may find rest and take counsel together."—James H. Aughey

---

B. Searching for a Sheep (vv. 3-6)

**³ And he spake this parable unto them, saying, ⁴ What man of you, having an hundred sheep, if he lose one of them, doth not leave the ninety and nine in the wilderness, and go after that which is lost, until he find it? ⁵ And when he hath found it, he layeth it on his shoulders, rejoicing. ⁶ And when he cometh home, he calleth together his friends and neighbours, saying unto them, Rejoice with me; for I have found my sheep which was lost.**

In this story of the lost sheep, there are ninety-nine sheep safely in the fold and one who has strayed away. We are not told how the sheep came to be lost. One possible scenario has the sheep eating grass and enjoying it so much that he forgets about the shepherd. When he finally looks around, the shepherd is not there. Since the shepherd leads the sheep and is not there to guide him, the sheep does not know which way to turn. As soon as the shepherd realizes the sheep is missing, he leaves the ninety-nine who are safely in the fold, and cannot rest until he finds the lost one. As soon as he finds the sheep, the shepherd tenderly and joyfully hoists the sheep on his shoulders and carries him home. He tells his friends and neighbors he has found the lost sheep that they might rejoice with him.

What a powerful example this story gives the church! We must not be content only to enjoy the company of those who are of like precious faith and are safe within the walls of the church. There are lost souls in our communities who would choose to follow Christ if believers would take the time and effort to witness to them of His great love. The Lord has specifically commanded His followers to go find others. He said, "Go out into the highways and hedges, and compel them to come in, that my house may be filled" (Luke 14:23).

Another thought this story conveys is the importance of one soul. In a day when there is so much talk about megachurches, we must not forget that souls enter the kingdom of God one at a time. Do not consider it a small matter when you lead one soul to Christ. Your fellow believers will rejoice with you as will the inhabitants of heaven.

---

- How did it feel when you were a "lost sheep"? How did the Good Shepherd find you?

"The ravages of sin are not pleasant—but they are what Jesus came to forgive and heal. 'The Son of Man came to seek and to save what was lost' (Luke 19:10 NIV). Yet Christians often hesitate to reach out to those who are different. They want God to clean the fish before they catch them."—Jim Cymbala

---

### C. Rejoicing in Heaven (v. 7)

**7 I say unto you, that likewise joy shall be in heaven over one sinner that repenteth, more than over ninety and nine just persons, which need no repentance.**

In the application of this story, Jesus gives us a glimpse into heaven, or at least what happens in heaven when a sinner repents on earth. We are not talking about someone who has gained a head knowledge of the way of salvation, but someone who has experienced a complete change in heart and life. The moment that occurs, heaven bursts into rejoicing. Apparently God, who knows what is in the heart of all people and knows when a heart is changed, reveals to the angels when a conversion has taken place, and they join Him in unspeakable joy.

What a picture we have of God in this story! He is as pleased when a sinner repents as a shepherd is when a sheep that has wandered away is found and brought back to the fold. He is a God who never gives up on people, no matter how grievous their sin or how far they have strayed from Him. Isaiah recorded, "As the bridegroom rejoices over the bride, so shall your God rejoice over you" (62:5 NKJV). The heart of God experiences the joy of joys when a sinner turns from his or her ways and comes home to Him.

In other religions, there is no hint of grace that seeks out the lost to save them from their sins. But in Christ, God seeks to save all people for time and eternity. The value God puts on a soul is evident from the price He was willing to pay for its salvation. That price was the precious blood of Christ. Every time a soul receives salvation, it is another triumph for His work on the cross, and all heaven rejoices with Him in that victory.

---

- How valuable is a single human being to God?

"I think, beloved, it will not be hard for you to learn. The angels of heaven rejoice over sinners that repent: saints of God, will not you and I do the same? I do not think the church rejoices enough."—Charles Spurgeon

---

## II. FINDING A LOST COIN (Luke 15:8-10)

### A. Losing One Coin (v. 8)

**8 Either what woman having ten pieces of silver, if she lose one piece, doth not light a candle, and sweep the house, and seek diligently till she find it?**

This is the story of a woman who was in possession of ten silver coins and lost one of them. That may not sound like much, but the coin she lost was equal to one day's wages. Considering she was probably not a person of means, it is more likely that she lived as it were "from paycheck to paycheck"—just one step away from poverty and hunger.

William Barclay suggests a second possibility: The coin she lost could have been part of a headdress made of ten silver coins linked together by a silver chain. This headdress was the mark of a married woman. It would have been almost the equivalent of a wedding ring. If that should be the case, she would search for it as if she had lost her marriage ring.

Barclay goes on to explain that finding a lost coin in a Palestinian peasant's house would require a diligent search. The houses were very dark; the floor was beaten earth covered with dried reeds and rushes. About the only hope the woman had was that she might see the coin glint or hear it tinkle as it moved.

It was not the coin's fault that it was lost—it was lost because the woman either carelessly or accidentally dropped it. We are lost because of Adam's fall, resulting in all humanity being born with a sin nature. However, when we are mature enough to understand we are sinners in need of a Savior, we become responsible for the sins in our life and have need to turn to Christ. Another matter to consider is that although the coin was lost, it was still in the house. Not every lost person is out in the world somewhere; some are in the church. Confession does not always mean possession. Perhaps some in the church are lost and don't even realize it. Jesus speaks of those who call Him "Lord" and boast of mighty works for Him, to whom He will say, "I never knew you" (see Matt. 7:22-23).

---

- How can the church "seek diligently" to reach lost people?

> "Our god is the thing, or person, which we think most precious, for whom we would make the greatest sacrifice, and who moves our heart with the warmest love. He is the person or thing that if lost would leave us desolate."—Alan Redpath

---

B. Finding One Coin (v. 9)

**9 And when she hath found it, she calleth her friends and her neighbours together, saying, Rejoice with me; for I have found the piece which I had lost.**

Jesus points out how diligently this woman went about her search for the lost coin. The longer it was on the floor, the more dirt and dust would cover it and the harder it would be to find. This points out the importance of diligently seeking the salvation of the lost around us. The longer they continue in sin and the stronger its hold on them becomes, the more difficult it will be to win them to Christ.

The woman lights the brightest lamp in the house, finds her broom, and sweeps the floor, carefully searching for the coin. Finally, as the dirt and dust is removed, she sees the coin lying on the floor. Can you image her joy as she reaches down to pick up this precious possession of hers?

This scene reminds us of how God shines the light of His Word into our heart that we may no longer walk in darkness. Paul wrote, "God, who said, 'Let there be light in the darkness,' has made this light shine in our hearts so we could know the glory of God that is seen in the face of Jesus Christ. We now have this light shining in our hearts" (2 Cor. 4:6-7 NLT). Throughout the Christian experience, the Word continues to chase the darkness from before us and shine upon our path. The psalmist said, "Your word is a lamp to guide my feet and a light for my path" (119:105 NLT).

Can you imagine the joy that fills this woman's heart when she finds the lost coin? Her distress turns into rejoicing! Immediately, she calls her friends and neighbors together and tells them it is time to celebrate because she has found the lost coin. What a picture of how we should react when a sinner comes to God and is converted. Think of the mother who has prayed for years that her child would find Christ, or the husband who has prayed for his unsaved wife. When such a prayer is answered, crying turns to laughter and joy overwhelms the soul.

- Why should helping reach a lost person for Christ be our greatest joy?

> "It is the consciousness of the threefold joy of the Lord: His joy in ransoming us, His joy in dwelling with us as our Savior and power for fruit-bearing, and His joy in possessing us, as His Bride and His delight; it is the consciousness of this joy which is our real strength. Our joy in Him may be a fluctuating thing: His joy in us knows no change."—Hudson Taylor

### C. Reacting in Heaven (v. 10)

**10 Likewise, I say unto you, there is joy in the presence of the angels of God over one sinner that repenteth.**

Dr. Lyman Beecher was once asked, "What do you count the greatest thing a human being can do?" He replied, "The greatest thing a human being can do is to bring another human being to Jesus Christ as Savior."

The apostle Paul found his greatest joy in those he had led to Christ. He wrote to the Philippians, "Therefore, my dear brothers and sisters, stay true to the Lord. I love you and long to see you, dear friends, for you are my joy and the crown I receive for my work" (4:1 NLT). Winning souls to Christ and helping them succeed in the Christian life was the crowning experience of Paul's life.

Every preacher who has preached a sermon that touched a life for God . . . every believer who has witnessed to another about the grace of God . . . every saint who has lived Christ before others in a way that made them say, "I want to know this Christ too," knows exactly how Paul felt.

This joy that believers feel on earth extends to heaven, for there is joy in the presence of the angels every time a sinner repents. It is as though the Lord calls the whole celestial family together and says, "Rejoice with Me, for another lost soul has been found!" When we think of what has happened, no wonder there is such joy! Another soul has been rescued from the devil and his angels; another subject has been added to the kingdom of God; and another heir has been born into the family of God. I believe the Father, the Son, and the Holy Spirit take the lead in this moment of great jubilation.

## III. FINDING A LOST SON (Luke 15:11-24)

### A. Claiming an Inheritance (vv. 11-13)

**11 And he said, A certain man had two sons: 12 And the younger of them said to his father, Father, give me the portion of goods that falleth to me. And he divided unto them his living. 13 And not many days after the younger son gathered all together, and took his journey into a far country, and there wasted his substance with riotous living.**

The story of the prodigal son shows forth the beauty of the grace of God, who is willing to receive and treat with kindness the most grievous sinner who repents and turns to Him. There are other pictures here as well. For example, there is the portrait of a son who has all the comforts of home and the provisions of a loving father, much like Adam and Eve had in the Garden of Eden, but who forfeits these blessings (as they did) to go his own way. He decides, "It is my life and I will live it the way I please, and nobody can dictate to me." Then we see how miserable a person can be when he lives in rebellion and goes to great excess in undisciplined living, wasting everything on a wild lifestyle.

The story begins when this son comes to his father and requests his share of the estate immediately. He does not want to wait until his father dies. He must have thought he could take his portion of the estate, make his own way in the world, and live a better life than his father could offer. He wanted his freedom; he no longer wanted to be under his father's control. It is interesting that the father did not deny that the boy had the right to claim his inheritance, and neither did he try to keep the boy at home. People leave God for the same reason this son left home: they do not feel they need Him . . . they can make it on their own.

---

- What motivated the youngest son to ask for his inheritance, and what was the result?

> "We can create as magnificent an environment as we like, but unless we change the heart, it's all a waste of time."—John Hagee

---

### B. Losing an Inheritance (vv. 14-19)

**14 And when he had spent all, there arose a mighty famine in that land; and he began to be in want. 15 And he went and joined himself to a citizen of that country; and he sent him into his fields to feed swine. 16 And he would fain have filled his belly with the husks that the swine did eat: and no man gave unto him. 17 And when he came to himself, he said, How many hired**

servants of my father's have bread enough and to spare, and I perish with hunger! ¹⁸ I will arise and go to my father, and will say unto him, Father, I have sinned against heaven, and before thee, ¹⁹ And am no more worthy to be called thy son: make me as one of thy hired servants.

    The Prodigal Son gives us a picture of what sin does to a man. It strips him of all that is good and valuable, leaving him miserable and wrecked. He finds himself in a "far country"; spiritually speaking, it is a place where there is a famine of the Word. The unregenerate have no interest in the Word, but instead live on the bread of deceit. They labor for that which brings no satisfaction. Isaiah 55:1-2 describes the remedy: "Ho! Everyone who thirsts, come to the waters; and you who have no money, come, buy and eat. Yes, come, buy wine and milk without money and without price. Why do you spend money for what is not bread, and your wages for what does not satisfy? Listen carefully to Me, and eat what is good, and let your soul delight itself in abundance" (NKJV).

    When the Prodigal Son lost his money, he also lost his friends. Abandoned by those who had helped him come to ruin, he seeks employment from a pig farmer and is sent into the field to slop the pigs. He is so hungry that even the pods he was feeding the pigs looked good to him. All the zest was gone from his life, and he hated the job he had been given to do—a job that would have been especially repugnant to Jews (see Deut. 14:8). But, in one sense, it was a blessing to him because it forced him to take a look at himself and see just how far he had fallen.

    Under these dire circumstances, the young man realizes that even the servants in his father's house were far better off than he was. In a contrite spirit, he decides to return to his father with the confession that he had sinned against God and against his earthly father. He didn't make excuses for himself, or blame somebody else, or make light of what he had done. The Prodigal acknowledges that he had forfeited every right to be called his father's son, and so he would ask just to be made a hired servant.

---

1. How did the young man stay alive in a terrible famine (vv. 14-16)?
2. Why did the son want to become a servant (vv. 17-18)?
3. How had his attitude changed (v. 19)?

> "You will not be in heaven two seconds before you cry out, Why did I place so much importance on things that were so temporary? What was I thinking? Why did I waste so much time, energy, and concern on what wasn't going to last?"—Rick Warren

---

C. Returning Home (vv. 20-24)

    ²⁰ And he arose, and came to his father. But when he was yet a great way off, his father saw him, and had compassion, and ran, and fell on his neck, and kissed him. ²¹ And the son said unto him, Father, I have sinned against heaven, and in thy sight, and am no more worthy to be called thy son. ²² But the father said to his servants, Bring forth the best robe, and

put it on him; and put a ring on his hand, and shoes on his feet: ²³ And bring hither the fatted calf, and kill it; and let us eat, and be merry: ²⁴ For this my son was dead, and is alive again; he was lost, and is found. And they began to be merry.

The Prodigal Son has now made his decision to leave the far country and return to his father's house. As he heads toward home, can you imagine what is on his mind? He is probably feeling shame for the way he has lived. He may even have doubts about how his father will receive him. But, whatever he is thinking, his need to get out of the mess he is in drives him homeward.

How does the father react when he sees his son coming a great distance away? Does he hold him in contempt, go inside the house, slam the door, and refuse to let him enter? Does he set the boy down and lecture him, humiliate him, and put him on probation? No. Even at a great distance, though he is wearing ragged clothes and is emaciated, his father recognizes this is his son coming, and he is moved with compassion and love. The son may have been walking slowly, wondering what would happen when he got home; but the father runs to him, throws his arms around him, embraces him, and kisses him. This kiss is a sign of affection and reconciliation. If the son wondered if his father would forgive him and receive him, this should have erased all of his doubts.

Here is the point of the story. Who could blame a father for forgiving a son who came to him in such humility? Not even a Pharisee could fault him for that. Surely, they could see it was right for Jesus to treat the lost with tenderness and joyfully receive those who turn to God for salvation.

Upon the son's confession of sin and expressing his unworthiness to be called a son, the father responds by calling for the best robe to be put on the son. This was a garment the servants never wore, and it signaled to the son that he had no intention of treating him like a servant. The father orders a ring for his son's finger and shoes for his feet. The ring signified membership in the family. Slaves went barefoot, but this was his son, so he must have shoes. To show his heartfelt joy, the father orders the preparing of the best calf for a time of feasting. He wants all to know that his son is alive again. To come back to God means to begin living again!

---

1. Describe the father's love of his wayward son (v. 20).
2. Describe the son's repentance (v. 21).
3. How does the heavenly Father "clothe" and "feed" repentant sinners (vv. 22-23)?
4. How does verse 24 describe the status of all Christians?

## The Wicked Doctor

A certain doctor had the reputation of being the most wicked man in the most wicked town in England. He was dying and knew he had but a short time to live. Someone sent for a minister who came and led the doctor to Christ. Some of the people who knew the doctor were indignant. They couldn't understand why the doctor should escape the punishment he deserved. One of them asked, "Do you think that a deathbed conversion atones for a whole life of sin?" Another replied, "No, but Calvary does." The father in the story of the lost son gives us a picture of Calvary love.

## CONCLUSION

When sinners come to God in brokenness of heart and genuine contrition for their sins, they are received with open arms. When they place their faith in Christ, His grace becomes their portion and they are welcomed into the kingdom of God. When that happens, all heaven explodes with rejoicing.

## GOLDEN TEXT CHALLENGE

"I [JESUS] SAY UNTO YOU, THERE IS JOY IN THE PRESENCE OF THE ANGELS OF GOD OVER ONE SINNER THAT REPENTETH" (Luke 15:10).

In all of the three parables of grace in Luke 15, there is an emphasis on *joy*: (1) the joy of the shepherd and his friends and neighbors when, after long seeking, he brought his lost sheep back; (2) the joy of the woman with her friends and neighbors when, after diligent searching with lamp and broom, she found her precious coin; (3) the joy of the father and his household when, possibly after years of agonized waiting, praying, and yearning, the Prodigal Son came home.

In all three parables, the earthly joy with which all of Christ's hearers could identify was a mirror in which was reflected the greater joy which is experienced in heaven "over one sinner that repenteth."

Thus, Christ gives us a glimpse into heaven, both now and on the day of resurrection. We witness the rejoicing of God himself and of His angelic hosts as they gaze upon the multitude of lost souls found and redeemed and restored. The Lord said to Job, "[Where were you] when the morning stars sang together, and all the sons of God [the angelic beings] shouted for joy?" (38:7). So, it was when God laid the foundations of the earth (v. 4).

Jesus, however, paints a picture of the angelic choirs shouting with even greater joy as they behold the wondrous products of redeeming grace. Jesus himself (the Good Shepherd) will share that joy, for "he shall see of the travail of his soul, and shall be satisfied" (Isa. 53:11). He was strengthened in His earthly life and ministry during the years of searching and suffering and dying for the lost, by "the joy that was set before him" (Heb. 12:2), the hope of rescued sheep, found coins, and reconciled prodigals.

Paul cherished the same blessed hope. He said to the Thessalonian Christians, "For what is our hope, or joy, or crown of rejoicing? Are not even ye in the presence of our Lord Jesus Christ at his coming?" (1 Thess. 2:19).

Shall not all who seek with determination and sacrifice for lost sheep, and search diligently with the lamp of the Word and the broom of the Spirit for lost human coins stamped with the image of God, enjoy celebrations in the eternal presence of God? Shall not all who pray and mourn and wait with hearts of love for lost prodigals, have their part in those joyful celebrations as well?

**Daily Devotions:**

M. Jesus, the Messiah-Savior
Isaiah 53:1-12
T. Salvation of the Gentiles
Isaiah 60:1-5
W. God's Mercy to Sinners
Jonah 3:1-10
T. Jesus, the Good Shepherd
John 10:10-18
F. All Saved by Grace
Acts 15:1-11
S. Seeking the Salvation of Sinners
1 Corinthians 9:16-22

November 30, 2014 (Lesson 13)
# Stories About Responding to Christ
Matthew 20:1-16; Luke 14:15-24

**Unit Theme:**
Parables of Jesus (Stories Jesus Told)

**Central Truth:**
Responding to Christ with faith and obedience brings salvation.

**Focus:**
Acknowledge the call of Christ and respond with obedience to Him.

**Context:**
Jesus illustrates God's call to serve in His kingdom.

**Golden Text:**
"Behold, I [Jesus] stand at the door, and knock: If any man hear my voice, and open the door, I will come in to him, and will sup with him, and he with me" (Rev. 3:20).

**Study Outline:**
I. Responding Early and Late
   (Matt. 20:1-7)
II. All Who Respond Are Rewarded
   (Matt. 20:8-16)
III. Ignoring Christ's Call Is Inexcusable
   (Luke 14:15-24)

## INTRODUCTION

Matthew 20 is an action-packed chapter. It begins with the story of the owner of a vineyard going out to find laborers. It continues with Jesus speaking of His death and resurrection. In the meantime, He replies to the mother of Zebedee's children concerning their place in the future kingdom. That response causes a stir among the rest of the disciples, which Jesus has to deal with. This chapter also tells the inspiring story of two blind men who received their sight.

To some extent, the vineyard story comes as an answer to a question Peter asked in chapter 19: "We've given up everything to follow you. What will we get [out of it]?" (v. 27 NLT). Jesus assured him of the place of the disciples in His current and future kingdom, saying, "Everyone who has given up houses or brothers or sisters or father or mother or children or property, for my sake, will receive a hundred times as much in return and will inherit eternal life" (v. 29 NLT). Jesus' followers would gain authority, friendship, and eternal life. These are incredible dividends for those who invest their lives in the Lord's service.

We have before us a story that addresses service and rewards. Those who entered the vineyard had an opportunity to render service to the landowner, and they were all paid according to their faithfulness to the task. Reading this story, we are challenged to ask what opportunities we have had to serve the Lord, and what we have done with them.

Billy Graham has preached the gospel in person to millions of people. It appears he was faithful to fulfill that mission and he will, no doubt, be rewarded accordingly. On the other hand, think about the wife who is abandoned by her husband and left to provide for their children. She lives a godly life before them, works two jobs to take care of them, and sees that they have an opportunity in life. We never hear of her; nobody ever reports her deeds. But, in the eyes of the Lord, great is her reward.

I. RESPONDING EARLY AND LATE (Matt. 20:1-7)

A. Early Laborers (vv. 1-2)

¹ **For the kingdom of heaven is like unto a man that is an householder, which went out early in the morning to hire labourers into his vineyard.**
² **And when he had agreed with the labourers for a penny a day, he sent them into his vineyard.**

The story begins with the landowner, the head of family affairs, getting out of bed at daybreak, to find laborers to cultivate his vineyard. The salary offered to the laborers was a "penny," a Roman coin equal to a Greek *drachma*, or about fourteen cents in American money. This was then the usual pay for a day's labor. While this sounds cheap, it must be remembered that what a person could buy with this salary was about as much as can be bought with a day's wages now.

A large portion of Judea was planted in grapevines. The land was favorable to the cultivation of grapes. The vineyard is often used in Scripture to represent the people of Israel and/or the Church. Isaiah spoke of what God expected of Israel and in what ways He was disappointed: "The vineyard of God-of-the-Angel-Armies is the country of Israel. All the men and women of Judah are the garden he was so proud of. He looked for a crop of justice and saw them murdering each other. He looked for a harvest of righteousness and heard only the moans of victims" (5:7 TM). Jeremiah also spoke of how the Lord was disappointed at the failure of the rulers to properly care for His vineyard: "Many rulers have destroyed My vineyard, they have trodden My portion underfoot; they have made My pleasant portion a desolate wilderness" (12:10 NKJV).

Notice that the master of the household called the laborers to come into his vineyard and work. They did not enter the vineyard until they were called by the master. Likewise, the disciples of Christ are called by the Master to enter the kingdom of God and to labor in His service. Jesus said, "You did not choose Me, but I chose you and appointed you that you should go and bear fruit, and that your fruit should remain" (John 15:16 NKJV).

---

- Describe some of the work that takes place in the kingdom of heaven.

"Jesus organized the church, which is His vineyard. He commands all to go into the vineyard and work. All who are united to Christ by faith, and are thus members of His mystical body, should be members of His visible church."—James H. Aughey

## B. Other Laborers (vv. 3-5)

**3 And he went out about the third hour, and saw others standing idle in the marketplace, 4 And said unto them; Go ye also into the vineyard, and whatsoever is right I will give you. And they went their way. 5 Again he went out about the sixth and ninth hour, and did likewise.**

The landowner went out at 6:00 in the morning (called by the Romans and Jews the "first hour") to find workers for his vineyard. Throughout the day, he continued to look for workers: at 9:00 a.m., the "third hour"; noon, the "sixth"; and 3:00 p.m., the "ninth." At the first hour, he told the workers how much he would pay them; however, thereafter he only told them that he would pay a fair wage at the end of the day.

Throughout the day, the landowner returned to the marketplace in search of workers. The individuals were not just standing around; they were there because they wanted to work. They would have already been working, but they lacked opportunity. They are to be commended for their persistence. When hired, they did their best for the rest of the day.

The opportunity you are looking for may not have come yet, but don't give up. When it comes, it will be worth the wait. When you render your best service for the Master, the reward will be great.

The Bible says much about the rewards that await believers who are faithful to the Lord. It speaks about both forfeiting and sustaining rewards. Paul wrote, "Each one's work will become clear; for the Day will declare it, because it will be revealed by fire; and the fire will test each one's work, of what sort it is. If anyone's work which he has built on it endures, he will receive a reward. If anyone's work is burned, he will suffer loss; but he himself will be saved, yet so as through fire" (1 Cor. 3:13-15 NKJV).

The Scriptures list several rewards (called crowns) that are available to believers. They include the "crown of life" for faithfulness (James 1:12), the "crown of glory" for the faithful pastor (1 Peter 5:4), the "crown of righteousness" for those who love Christ's appearing (2 Tim. 4:7-8), the "incorruptible crown" for self-mastery (1 Cor. 9:25-27), and the "crown of life" for those who die a martyr's death (Rev. 2:10).

---

- Why are so many Christians "standing idle" instead of actively serving God?

---

"If God only used perfect people, nothing would get done. God will use anybody if you're available."—Rick Warren

---

## C. Later Laborers (vv. 6-7)

**6 And about the eleventh hour he went out, and found others standing idle, and saith unto them, Why stand ye here all the day idle? 7 They say unto him, Because no man hath hired us. He saith unto them, Go ye also into the vineyard; and whatsoever is right, that shall ye receive.**

The landowner comes to workers who had still not found work at 5:00 o'clock in the afternoon. There was only one hour left before the end of the Jewish day. They had waited eleven hours before being hired.

Sometimes individuals have to wait until later in life to accomplish their mission, or they may even have to give up their dream and pursue another course in life. Suppose two people have decided to spend their life in full-time ministry. One of them does whatever is necessary to qualify to fulfill this dream and enters into a flourishing work for the Kingdom. The other individual has a family member who becomes very ill and is dependent on this man or woman to provide the necessary care. The service this person renders does not claim attention or praise the way the first one experiences. Yet, are not both worthy of divine recognition?

Those who are forced to take what is perceived to be a lesser role in life must resist the temptation to become bitter and resentful. It can be harder and take more faith and courage to fulfill a role outside of the limelight than it is to have a high-profile role that garners a lot of attention.

On a football field, quarterbacks, running backs, and receivers are given loud applause for their exploits. But the most difficult position to play is sitting on the bench. This position gets no attention. All this player can do is wait and hope to get a chance to play.

You might feel like the football player on the bench, or the laborers who were not called until the eleventh hour, but rest assured that God has not forgotten you. Do the best you can where you are, and leave the reward for your service up to the Master.

---

"If the Lord Jehovah makes us wait, let us do so with our whole hearts; for blessed are all they that wait for Him. He is worth waiting for. The waiting itself is beneficial to us: it tries faith, exercises patience, trains submission, and endears the blessing when it comes. The Lord's people have always been a waiting people."—Charles Spurgeon

---

II. ALL WHO RESPOND ARE REWARDED (Matt. 20:8-16)

A. Payday for the Laborers (vv. 8-11)

**⁸ So when even was come, the lord of the vineyard saith unto his steward, Call the labourers, and give them their hire, beginning from the last unto the first. ⁹ And when they came that were hired about the eleventh hour, they received every man a penny. ¹⁰ But when the first came, they supposed that they should have received more; and they likewise received every man a penny. ¹¹ And when they had received it, they murmured against the goodman of the house.**

At the close of the day, the landowner tells his foreman to pay the workers. His instructions are to begin with those who were hired last. The foreman pays those hired at the eleventh hour with a day's wages. When those who were hired at the first hour come before the foreman, they are paid the same. They strongly object, thinking they should be paid more.

Bear in mind that the landowner paid the workers who started at the first hour exactly what they had agreed to work for. They voiced no objection to this salary when it was offered. Had they been paid first and gone home, probably nothing more would have come of it. However, since the eleventh-hour workers were paid first and everyone knew how much they received, the first-hour workers grumbled and said it was not fair. Although the way the landowner paid the other workers may have seemed unfair, he honored the contract he had with the first-hour workers.

Having done what he said he would do for the first-hour workers, the landowner was free to pay the other workers whatever he chose. That his payment to them was generous is a right the vineyard owner had. After all, it was his vineyard.

---

1. What caused some of the workers to grumble?
2. What causes some Christians today to complain about others' service to God?

> "God dispenses gifts, not wages. None of us gets paid according to merit, for none of us comes close to satisfying God's requirements for a perfect life. If paid on the basis of fairness, we would all end up in hell. . . . In the bottom line realm of ungrace, some workers deserve more than others; in the realm of grace, the word *deserve* does not even apply."—Philip Yancey

---

### B. Explanation From the Landowner (vv. 12-15)

**12 Saying, These last have wrought but one hour, and thou hast made them equal unto us, which have borne the burden and heat of the day. 13 But he answered one of them, and said, Friend, I do thee no wrong: didst not thou agree with me for a penny? 14 Take that thine is, and go thy way: I will give unto this last, even as unto thee. 15 Is it not lawful for me to do what I will with mine own? Is thine eye evil, because I am good?**

Those who worked all day complained that the landowner had paid the others who worked a shorter amount of time the same wages as they received. They felt they had an exclusive right to this salary. A similar attitude emerged among the Jewish Christians when Peter took the gospel to the Gentiles. The Jews seemed to think they had a monopoly on the truth. But Peter declared that when the Gentiles responded to the truth, God "made no distinction between us and them, purifying their hearts by faith" (Acts 15:9 NKJV). Eternal life is available to both the Jew and the Gentile through the shed blood of Jesus Christ, and there is plenty room in heaven for all.

The landowner responded to these first-hour workers by reminding them he had done for them exactly what he had promised; therefore, they had no cause to complain. He then told them to take their money and go home and not to cause him any more trouble. He reminded them that there was no law against doing what he pleased with his money. He then chided them for being jealous because he was doing something good for the others.

The landowner was sovereign over what he owned. Likewise, God is the undisputed Master of the universe. He originated, created, and controls this world. It is in His power to do good for all those who trust and obey Him. James said, "Every good gift and every perfect gift is from above, and comes down from the Father of lights, with whom there is no variation or shadow of turning" (1:17 NKJV).

The spirit of jealousy that surfaced among the first-hour workers can sometimes be seen in the church. Some people think because they have been members of a local church for a long time, they should be able to dictate its policies. They are resentful when newcomers arrive and begin to take an active part in the operation of the church. Seniority can be a good thing when exercised in the right spirit, but it does not automatically deserve respect and honor. That has to be earned.

---

1. What does God "have the right to do" (v. 15 NIV)?
2. When does God's generosity have a negative impact on some people?

> "When you take care of your job, God will take care of the paycheck."—Woodrow Kroll

---

C. A Lesson for the Laborers (v. 16)

**16 So the last shall be first, and the first last: for many be called, but few chosen.**

This phrase referred to how the Romans went about recruiting their armies—something Jesus' hearers readily understood. No greater honor could come to an individual than to be chosen to serve in the Roman army. Our little boys are sometimes heard to say they want to be firemen or policemen when they grow up, but every Roman boy wanted to be chosen to serve in the army. Young people did not volunteer to serve; rather, they were chosen. When there was a vacancy, several boys would be called to take an examination, but only one of them might be chosen. Those who were not chosen might come another time and try again.

In this story, some were not chosen for the vineyard until the eleventh hour, but at the end of the day their reward was as great as the others. In Kingdom work, those who are faithful to the end will hear the Master say, "Well done, good and faithful servant; you were faithful over a few things, I will make you ruler over many things. Enter into the joy of your lord" (Matt. 25:21 NKJV).

Jesus does not say *all* who are first will be last, or *all* who are last will be first. Some who are first will still be first, and some who are last will still be last. It is all in the spirit of the service we render. It behooves us to trust and serve the

Lord for the sheer joy of doing so, and not in the hope of receiving a reward. Those who work only with an eye for receiving earthly recognition will find that to be all they will receive. They will go to the back of the line in the Kingdom. It is somewhat ironic that those who are only concerned with receiving a reward lose it, and those who are not seeking a reward find it.

- When and where will "the last . . . be first"?

> **All of Me**
> When asked the secret of his success in the Salvation Army, General William Booth said: "I will tell you the secret. God has had all there was of me. There have been men with greater brains than I, men with greater opportunities. But I made up my mind God should have all of William Booth there was."

## III. IGNORING CHRIST'S CALL IS INEXCUSABLE (Luke 14:15-24)

A. Refusing the Invitation (vv. 15-20)

**15 And when one of them that sat at meat with him heard these things, he said unto him, Blessed is he that shall eat bread in the kingdom of God. 16 Then said he unto him, A certain man made a great supper, and bade many: 17 And sent his servant at supper time to say to them that were bidden, Come; for all things are now ready. 18 And they all with one consent began to make excuse. The first said unto him, I have bought a piece of ground, and I must needs go and see it: I pray thee have me excused. 19 And another said, I have bought five yoke of oxen, and I go to prove them: I pray thee have me excused. 20 And another said, I have married a wife, and therefore I cannot come.**

Jesus had been invited into the house of one of the rulers of the Pharisees for a meal, perhaps even a feast. During the course of the evening, the Lord set forth some principles that should govern such an occasion (vv. 7-14). In response to what Jesus said, one of the guests said, in effect, "What a blessing it is to eat dinner in the kingdom of God" (v. 15). Apparently, this guest grasped the meaning and the beauty of the principles He had spoken, and responded with this expression.

Jesus replied to the man by telling a story. He says a man prepares a great supper, invites many people to attend, sends his servant out to tell those who had been invited that the supper is ready, and encourages them to come and eat. Their reaction to this news is surprising. They all begin to make excuses as to why they could not attend.

One of them had bought some land and needed to inspect it. Can you imagine buying land unforeseen and waiting until dark to go and check it out? Another person had bought some oxen and wanted to try them out. Can you imagine buying some animals and waiting until night to see if they can do the job? The third one had married a wife and needed to get home to her. This is probably the most trifling excuse of all because he probably could have brought his wife with him to the supper.

The door of entry into the kingdom of God is open and free. Christ made the provision of entrance at Calvary. If individuals do not enter, it is because of their own refusal and whatever excuse they may bring. They have put other things between themselves and God. If only they would come to know Him, and understand Him, they would embrace Him with their whole heart.

---

1. Who is "blessed" (v. 15)?
2. Describe the foolishness of each excuse (vv. 18-19).
3. Name some foolish excuses people make today for not following Christ.

> "When a person refuses to come to Christ, it is never just because of lack of evidence or because of intellectual difficulties: at root, he refuses to come because he willingly ignores and rejects the drawing of God's Spirit on his heart."—William Lane Craig

---

B. Extending the Invitation to Others (vv. 21-22)

**21 So that servant came, and shewed his lord these things. Then the master of the house being angry said to his servant, Go out quickly into the streets and lanes of the city, and bring in hither the poor, and the maimed, and the halt, and the blind. 22 And the servant said, Lord, it is done as thou hast commanded, and yet there is room.**

The servant returns to the master of the house and reports that those who were invited had spurned his invitation, refusing to come to the feast. The master is furious. He orders his servant to go out and invite people living in the streets and alleys to the supper. He commissioned him to go to the poor, the crippled, the blind, and the lame with the supper invitation. These people who had it hard in life understood what it was like to do without. So, when an opportunity is presented to enjoy warm fellowship and delicious food, they gladly come. The servant reports he had followed the master's orders and that this group had accepted his invitation. But, even with their coming, there was still room at the banquet table for others.

The reason for having a supper is to satisfy hunger. Apparently, the first group invited were not hungry. So the master reaches out to others who are hungry and they come. People not only hunger for food; they also hunger for love, shelter, and security. More important is for the soul to hunger and thirst for God. David wrote, "As the deer longs for streams of water, so I long for you, O God. I thirst for God, the living God" (Ps. 42:1-2 NLT).

Those who turn a deaf ear to the voice of God need to know that, at some point, they will no longer hear His call. But as long as the heart is hungry, the soul can find hope and help in God. Once the soul has been enriched by the marvelous grace of God, it would rather give up anything than to lose a seat at the Lord's table.

---

1. Why was it important for the servant to "go out quickly," and where was he sent (v. 21)?
2. What should motivate us to reach the poor and the needy for Christ?

> "The kingdom of God is for the spiritually sick who want to be healed, the spiritually corrupt who want to be cleansed, the spiritually poor who want to be rich, the spiritually hungry who want to be fed, the spiritually dead who want to be made alive. It is for ungodly outcasts who long to become God's own beloved children."—John MacArthur

---

C. Going to the Highways and Hedges (vv. 23-24)

**23 And the lord said unto the servant, Go out into the highways and hedges, and compel them to come in, that my house may be filled. 24 For I say unto you, That none of those men which were bidden shall taste of my supper.**

Since enough people had not been found in the city to fill the banquet table, the master orders his servant to go to "the roads and country lanes" (v. 23 NIV) and compel those living there to come. These were people of the lowest class who were steeped in poverty. His servant is to persuade them to come and sit at the master's table by addressing any objections they might have and urging them to accept the invitation. They might complain that they are too poor or do not have the proper attire to sit at the master's table, but the servant is to overcome these concerns.

The master was in earnest about getting those who were invited to the banquet he had prepared. Likewise, God is earnest about reaching the lost, presenting the gospel to them, and one day seeing them sit down at the Marriage Supper of the Lamb.

There is one group who will be absent from that glorious gathering: those who were first invited but refused to come. Individuals who do not want God or feel a need for Him will have no part in the future of the kingdom of God—not because God does not want them, but because they refuse Him. Christ has opened the door of heaven to all who will receive Him. The banquet table is spread, and believers can walk right in.

Can you imagine the joy around the supper table that night in the master's house when people of all walks of life gathered together to enjoy the feast that had been prepared? Imagine what heaven will be like when people from every tribe, language, and nation—people from all over the earth who have been purchased by the blood of Jesus—assemble around the table in that glorious realm to worship God!

---

1. Who else was invited to the supper?

2. Whom are you inviting to join God's kingdom?

> "The reward of being 'faithful over a few things' is just the same as being 'faithful over many things'; for the emphasis falls upon the same word; it is the 'faithful' who will enter 'into the joy of their Lord.'"—Charles S. Robinson

## CONCLUSION

In every generation, when the affluent and the ruling class have refused to acknowledge a need of God, the poor have been open to the gospel. Jesus listed as part of His mission to "preach the gospel to the poor" (Luke 4:18). Believers still have an obligation to share the truth with all who will listen. The two sources we have to persuade people is the Word of God and love. When the Word is presented in love, it is a powerful force for moving individuals toward God.

## GOLDEN TEXT CHALLENGE

"BEHOLD, I [JESUS] STAND AT THE DOOR, AND KNOCK: IF ANY MAN HEAR MY VOICE, AND OPEN THE DOOR, I WILL COME IN TO HIM, AND WILL SUP WITH HIM, AND HE WITH ME" (Rev. 3:20).

This touching and tender call has, for centuries, been the foundation of Christian song and sermon. The scene has Christ standing outside the door of the heart. He both knocks and speaks. What a rich display of grace!

This scene is repeated in the history of the Church. It is a present and continuous action. Today, He stands and knocks.

The words of invitation Jesus speaks apply not only to the Church, but also to the sinner. His voice has the ring of the Christ of quickening power, the Christ who knocks at the door of every sinner's heart urging him or her to be saved. While He knocks at the door of the sinner's heart, there is an ever-open door by which people may enter into eternal life. Jesus said, "I am the door: by me if any man enter in, he shall be saved" (John 10:9).

So, He continues standing and knocking at the door of the human heart. He wants to enter and to have His rightful place in the soul of humanity. He will make a feast for anyone who will receive Him.

**Daily Devotions:**

M. Choose Life and Blessing
   Deuteronomy 30:15-20
T. Danger in Rejecting Wisdom
   Proverbs 1:20-33
W. Respond to Wisdom's Call
   Proverbs 8:1-11
T. Jesus' Invitation
   Matthew 11:25-30
F. Respond to the Gospel
   Acts 2:36-41
S. Confess Faith in Christ
   Romans 10:6-13

# Introduction to Winter Quarter

"Law and Grace in the New Testament" comprises the first unit (lessons 1-2, 4-6). Scripture passages are from John's Gospel, Romans, Galatians, Ephesians, 1 Timothy, and Jude.

The expositions were written by the Reverend Dr. Thomas Doolittle (Ph.D., Southern Baptist Theological Seminary; M.A., M.Div., Church of God Theological Seminary; B.A., Lee College), who is chairperson of the Department of Christian Ministries and associate professor of Pastoral Ministry at Lee University. He served as a pastor in the Church of God for over twenty-four years, including pastorates in Georgia, Alaska, and Kentucky.

---

The Christmas lesson (3) was compiled by Lance Colkmire (B.A., M.A.), editor of the *Evangelical Commentary* and the *Church of God Evangel* for Pathway Press. He also serves the South Cleveland (TN) Church of God as missions pastor.

---

The second unit (lessons 7-12), "God's Moral Law (Genesis-Deuteronomy)," explores the sacredness of human life, the command to worship the Lord God, honoring God's name, justice, sexual purity, and treating others fairly.

The expositions were written by the Reverend Joshua F. Rice (B.A., M.A., Th.M.), who earned his Ph.D. in New Testament Studies from Lutheran School of Theology. He serves as teaching pastor of Mount Paran North Church of God in Marietta, Georgia, and is an adjunct professor at Lee University and Pentecostal Theological Seminary. Josh and his wife, Johanna, have two children.

December 7, 2014 (Lesson 1)
# Why Do We Need Grace?

John 1:14-17; Romans 5:1-2; Galatians 5:1-11; Ephesians 1:3-10; 2:4-9

**Unit Theme:**
Law and Grace in the New Testament

**Central Truth:**
God's grace makes salvation possible.

**Focus:**
Explore why God made grace available by Christ and receive God's grace by faith.

**Context:**
Various New Testament passages declaring the necessity of divine grace

**Golden Text:**
"God, who is rich in mercy, for his great love wherewith he loved us, even when we were dead in sins, hath quickened us together with Christ, (by grace ye are saved)" (Eph. 2:4-5).

**Study Outline:**
I. The Law Was Insufficient
   (Gal. 5:1-11)
II. God's Grace Is Sufficient
   (John 1:14-17; Eph. 1:3-10)
III. Grace Is Received by Faith
   (Rom. 5:1-2; Eph. 2:4-9)

## INTRODUCTION

In this lesson, we begin our study on *law* and *grace* as these terms are discussed in the New Testament. The Old Testament provides us with detailed accounts of the creation of the Law that God gave to the Israelites, which is sometimes referred to as the Mosaic Law. The creation and explanation of the Law is found in the first five books of the Bible, which are called the *Pentateuch*. The Law of the Old Testament is often viewed as legalistic and rigid, without much emphasis on grace. Grace also is found in the Old Testament and is embedded in the Law itself. As we study how these two terms are presented in the New Testament, we will begin to understand the dynamic relationship between *law* and *grace*.

In the Old Testament, the Law was emphasized and presented clearly, whereas grace was presented in a less obvious manner. Then, the opposite is true in the New Testament. Grace is a central theme in the New Testament, while the Law receives much less attention. In the New Testament, God's plan of redemption is revealed in Christ Jesus, who made God's grace available to all humanity so that we could receive redemption from sin. What the Law was unable to provide in the Old Testament became available in the New Testament: salvation by grace!

As we proceed in this lesson, we will be exploring the reason we need grace and how we receive grace through faith in Jesus Christ. We need grace because we cannot earn our salvation. We simply cannot be good enough to satisfy the requirements of the Law. Our only hope is found in God's abundant grace that was revealed through Christ. The question "Why do we need grace?" might seem simple, but the answer is profound and somewhat complex. Thankfully, the apostle Paul provides some invaluable insights, and his starting point concerns the insufficiency of the Old Testament Law for providing liberation from sin.

## I. THE LAW WAS INSUFFICIENT (Gal. 5:1-11)

### A. The Liberty of Grace (vv. 1-6)

**¹ Stand fast therefore in the liberty wherewith Christ hath made us free, and be not entangled again with the yoke of bondage. ² Behold, I Paul say unto you, that if ye be circumcised, Christ shall profit you nothing. ³ For I testify again to every man that is circumcised, that he is a debtor to do the whole law. ⁴ Christ is become of no effect unto you, whosoever of you are justified by the law; ye are fallen from grace. ⁵ For we through the Spirit wait for the hope of righteousness by faith. ⁶ For in Jesus Christ neither circumcision availeth any thing, nor uncircumcision; but faith which worketh by love.**

This passage presents both a comforting promise and a disturbing warning to believers. Paul begins this section by declaring that Christ has made or set us free by liberating us from sin's horrific bondage. However, he cautions us to "stand fast" so we can persevere in the freedom or liberty that only comes through the vicarious death of Jesus on the cross. The Greek noun for "liberty" is *eleutheria,* and the Greek verb for "made us free" is *eleutheroo*. The apostle's use of two words from the same root emphasizes the true freedom believers have in Christ, while providing a stark contrast with "the yoke of bondage" that Christ destroyed when He saved us from sin (v. 1).

Paul warns the Galatians that it is possible for them to become "entangled again" in the bondage that separates one from the liberating power of Christ. It is impossible for anyone to free himself or herself from such entanglement. The only hope is in Christ Jesus. He has the power to set us free and to keep us free from sin when we obey Him and stand firmly on His promises. The Galatians are being tempted to forsake their freedom in Christ by adopting the legalism of the Old Testament laws (vv. 2-3). Certain Jewish Christians (called *Judaizers*) are demanding that the Galatians adopt the Mosaic laws to truly be saved. If they do this, Paul argues they will be abandoning their freedom in Christ to adopt a religion based on works, which cannot save anyone (v. 4). This will render the work of Christ ineffective for their redemption if they reject His liberty to adopt a salvation contingent on personal works. They must beware, lest they fall from grace and lose their relationship with Christ.

Verses 4 and 5 reveal the basis of our salvation and the key for standing firm in our liberty. Our hope of righteousness and redemption only comes by faith in Jesus Christ, and we can endure in this faith through the work of the Holy Spirit! The Lord not only has set us free, He also sent the Holy Spirit to ensure that we can persevere faithfully until we realize the hope of His coming (John 14:1-4, 16, 26).

Whether one is circumcised does not really matter (Gal. 5:6). What does matter is "faith expressing itself through love" (NIV). This is the ultimate calling for faithful service to Christ and others. It is the fulfillment of the two greatest commandments: (1) loving God with all of our being, and (2) loving others as ourselves (Matt. 22:34-40).

---

1. What has Christ done for those who have put their trust in Him (v. 1)?
2. What are believers commanded to do (v. 1)?
3. Explain the error Paul warned the Galatians not to make (vv. 2-4).
4. What is available "through the Spirit," and how (v. 5)?
5. What is "the only thing that counts" (v. 6 NIV), and why?

> "Christian liberty then does not teach that there are things in the world in which you are free to indulge yourself. It does not suggest that you may do anything you wish with God's creation. But it teaches that there are things which you are free to enjoy and use as you serve the Lord."—Walter J. Chantry

---

B. The Offense of the Cross (vv. 7-11)

**⁷ Ye did run well; who did hinder you that ye should not obey the truth? ⁸ This persuasion cometh not of him that calleth you. ⁹ A little leaven leaveneth the whole lump. ¹⁰ I have confidence in you through the Lord, that ye will be none otherwise minded: but he that troubleth you shall bear his judgment, whosoever he be. ¹¹ And I, brethren, if I yet preach circumcision, why do I yet suffer persecution? then is the offence of the cross ceased.**

In this section we read some disturbing news. After the Galatians accepted Christ, at first they had "run well" (v. 7), which is a metaphor for the athletic tracks of the ancient Greek world. Apparently, pressure from the Judaizers had a negative impact on the Galatian believers, and they had not been faithful in following the "plain truth of the gospel, whether they know it or not" (Alan Cole, *The Epistle of Paul to the Galatians*). They had neglected their calling from God (v. 8) due to the "leaven," or heretical doctrine of the false teachers (v. 9). God does not take such behavior and teachings lightly, and a warning concerning judgment is declared (v. 10). Some of the Judaizers had even accused Paul of teaching the need for circumcision to be saved. But Paul refutes this adamantly by pointing out the persecutions he received from preaching salvation only through faith in the grace of the Lord Jesus, which he calls "the offence of the cross" (v. 11).

Even today, secular people are often offended at the thought that Jesus' death on the cross is humanity's only hope for redemption. Fortunately for the Galatians, Paul's words indicate he had hope that they would respond to his letter and change so they could "stand fast" once again in the liberating grace of God (v. 1).

1. How had some Galatians gotten off course (vv. 7-8)?
2. Explain the meaning of verse 9.
3. Describe the warning in verse 10.

> "All God's plans have the mark of the cross on them, and all His plans have death to self in them. . . . But men's plans ignore the offence of the cross or despise it. Men's plans have no profound, stern or self-immolating denial in them. Their gain is of the world."—E. M. Bounds

---

## II. GOD'S GRACE IS SUFFICIENT (John 1:14-17; Eph. 1:3-10)

### A. Grace for Grace (John 1:14-17)

**14 And the Word was made flesh, and dwelt among us, (and we beheld his glory, the glory as of the only begotten of the Father,) full of grace and truth. 15 John bare witness of him, and cried, saying, This was he of whom I spake, He that cometh after me is preferred before me: for he was before me. 16 And of his fulness have all we received, and grace for grace. 17 For the law was given by Moses, but grace and truth came by Jesus Christ.**

John 1:14 is one of the most significant verses in Scripture regarding the incarnation of Jesus Christ. In this statement, the apostle John confesses that the Word, Jesus, left His rightful place in heaven as God's only Son to take upon Himself flesh to become fully human. We often refer to Jesus as the God-man, meaning that Jesus was fully human and fully God. This is the marvelous mystery of the Incarnation! God the Son became a human and graced the world with His physical presence so He could redeem humanity.

John declares that he and the other disciples were privileged to see the glory of Christ that belongs to the "only begotten" Son of God. Jesus, being filled with "grace and truth," redeemed the world through His grace (John 1:17; 3:16) and liberated all who believed with His truth (8:32). In verse 15 of our text, John the Baptist proclaims that Jesus is the eternal Son of God who has always been, which reflects the beginning of John's Gospel (1:1-4).

The phrase "grace for grace" (v. 16) is an interesting usage of words that emphasizes the inexhaustible nature of Christ's redeeming grace. Thus, "fresh grace replaces grace received, and will do so perpetually," always providing the grace we need every day and in every situation (George R. Beasley-Murray, *Word Biblical Commentary: John*). One commentator described the profound implications of John's phrase with these words:

> God's grace to His people is continuous and is never exhausted. Grace knows no interruption and no limit. In contrast to the Law, it stresses the dynamic character of the Christian life. . . . *Grace* means an ever-deepening experience of the presence and the blessing of God (Leon Morris, *The Gospel According to John*).

---

1. Describe the "glory" of Jesus Christ (v. 14).

2. What does Christ provide for His followers (v. 16)?
3. How does verse 17 contrast Moses with Jesus?

> "Believing the right things about Jesus isn't enough. You're not adopted as God's child until you confess and turn away from your wrongdoing and receive the freely offered gift of forgiveness and eternal life that Jesus purchased with his death on the cross. Until you do that, you'll always be on the outside looking in."—Lee Strobel

B. The Grace of Adoption (Eph. 1:3-6)

**³ Blessed be the God and Father of our Lord Jesus Christ, who hath blessed us with all spiritual blessings in heavenly places in Christ: ⁴ According as he hath chosen us in him before the foundation of the world, that we should be holy and without blame before him in love: ⁵ Having predestinated us unto the adoption of children by Jesus Christ to himself, according to the good pleasure of his will, ⁶ To the praise of the glory of his grace, wherein he hath made us accepted in the beloved.**

This passage begins with a threefold blessing of praise that Paul extends in worship to God and declares to the church at Ephesus: (1) God is to be "blessed" through our praise and worship; (2) believers are abundantly "blessed" that God has extended grace and blessings to His people through Christ; and (3) the "blessings" Christ bestows on us extend beyond the physical world into the "spiritual" and "heavenly" realm. All three words come from the same root word in Greek, and the verb form, *eulogeo*, means to "celebrate with praises" in addressing God, or to "invoke blessings upon a person" (W. E. Vine). In this sense, "spiritual" does not refer to "otherworldly" gifts, but relates to "all that God's Spirit brings to life." Likewise, "heavenly places," or "heavenlies," is more concerned with our present enjoyment of our life in Christ and implies a spirituality that extends beyond the physical world: God's reality (Klyne Snodgrass, *The NIV Application Commentary: Ephesians*).

In Christ, we already enjoy the spiritual blessings of God that come through Christ Jesus. The kingdom of God is already in existence, and we are partakers of all He promised. Even now, we are sitting with Jesus in the "heavenly realms" (2:6 NIV)!

Even before the world was created, God chose us to be His holy and blameless people (1:4). The message God told Jeremiah applies to believers today: "Before I formed you in the womb I knew you, before you were born I set you apart; I appointed you as a prophet to the nations" (Jer. 1:5 NIV).

In verse 5 of our text, Paul states we are "predestined" (NKJV) for adoption as children of God through the saving work of Jesus Christ. Here, *predestined* does not mean our fate was determined without any will on our part. Instead, we are predestined based on our choice to accept Christ as our Savior. In other words, all who accept Jesus as Lord and Savior have a common predestination: adoption into the family of God. Based on our faith in Christ, we fully become heirs of Christ and receive complete acceptance as members of His family (v. 6).

1. Name some "spiritual blessings" (v. 3) you have received.
2. When did God choose us, and for what purpose (vv. 4-6)?

---

**Secure in Our Adoption**

A few years ago, my wife and I adopted Bethany—a five-year-old who needed a new home. This was a major decision for us, since our other two daughters were grown and married. We were enjoying the freedom that comes with an empty nest. Then, we adopted Bethany and our nest drastically changed.

We have worked aggressively to teach Bethany that she is as much our daughter as our two natural daughters, and she will always be our daughter. This has been a difficult concept for her to grasp, since she has not been in stable situations previously. It is extremely difficult for a small child to grasp the full implications of adoption. Bethany can recite what we tell her *adoption* means and even explain it to some degree, but her understanding is limited. She will need to grow and mature to feel secure as our daughter.

We, as Christians, sometimes struggle to grasp fully the significance of our adoption into God's family. However, God is still welcoming us home into His loving arms of grace and mercy, waiting for us to fully realize what we have received in Christ. Knowing we are His children should overwhelm us with praise and love for our God and Savior! This is the peace Christ promised us (John 14:27).—Thomas Doolittle

---

C. The Grace of Redemption (vv. 7-10)

**⁷ In whom we have redemption through his blood, the forgiveness of sins, according to the riches of his grace; ⁸ Wherein he hath abounded toward us in all wisdom and prudence; ⁹ Having made known unto us the mystery of his will, according to his good pleasure which he hath purposed in himself: ¹⁰ That in the dispensation of the fulness of times he might gather together in one all things in Christ, both which are in heaven, and which are on earth; even in him.**

Our adoption has been purchased through the redemptive death of Christ on the cross, whereby God forgave our sins through the abundant "riches of his grace" (v. 7). There is no greater gift than the forgiveness of sins, for this cleanses us from all past transgressions and ushers us into the glorious liberty of God's saving grace. In the Old Testament, Israel had an elaborate sacrificial system for killing animals so they could be forgiven of their sins and restored to fellowship with God. The shedding of blood was necessary for the forgiveness of sins (Heb. 9:22); however, the animal sacrifices could not effectively remedy the problem of sin (10:4). The Israelites had to repeat these sacrifices due to their inadequacy, but they also pointed toward the coming Messiah who would offer Himself as the final sacrifice for sin (Isa. 53; Heb. 9:12).

Through God's "wisdom and understanding" (Eph. 1:8 NIV), Jesus became the ultimate sacrifice for the sins of the world when He lay down His life for all humanity on the cross of Calvary (Heb. 9:23-28). This "mystery" of God's plan has been revealed to us and demonstrated as God's "good pleasure" (Eph. 1:9). We should exuberantly rejoice that our spiritual adoption brings great pleasure to God! The good news gets even better: "When the times will have reached their fulfillment" (v. 10 NIV), God will gather all of His family together in Christ and we will live and rejoice in His presence forever!

1. Describe "the riches of [Christ's] grace" (vv. 7-8).
2. What divine mystery has been revealed to us (vv. 9-10)?

"We are adopted into God's family through the resurrection of Christ from the dead in which He paid all our obligations to sin, the law, and the devil, in whose family we once lived. Our old status lies in His tomb. A new status is ours through His resurrection."—Sinclair B. Ferguson

## III. GRACE IS RECEIVED BY FAITH (Rom. 5:1-2; Eph. 2:4-9)

A. Faith Provides Access to Grace (Rom. 5:1-2)

**¹Therefore being justified by faith, we have peace with God through our Lord Jesus Christ: ²By whom also we have access by faith into this grace wherein we stand, and rejoice in hope of the glory of God.**

When we receive the grace of God through faith, God declares that we are then "justified." *Justification* refers to a judicial pronouncement of "legal and formal acquittal from guilt by God as judge, the pronouncement of the sinner as righteous, who believes on the Lord Jesus Christ" (W. E. Vine). An old saying was coined years ago to describe what *justification* means: "Just as if I'd never sinned." As Christians, we should be greatly comforted and filled with peace by knowing God has completely forgiven us of our sins (see 1 John 1:9; Ps. 103:11-12).

Through faith in Christ, we also have access to His grace that enables us to stand faithfully (Rom. 5:2), which echoes Paul's words in Galatians 5:1. Throughout his epistles, Paul emphasizes the concept of grace in relation to our salvation and Christian life. As French Arrington notes, Paul's focus "on grace is an indication to us that the 'amazing grace' of which we often sing actually defines our existence as the people of God" (*The Greatest Letter Ever Written: A Study of the Book of Romans*).

The term *access* (Greek, *prosagoge*) had two basic usages. It was used for introducing someone to a person of royal lineage, which could refer to Jesus providing access to God's throne for all believers (Heb. 4:16). Also, *prosagoge* has been used to describe access to a harbor. This type of access could emphasize the safety that a harbor provided for storm-weary sailors in ancient coastal areas (Arrington). We too have safety in Christ Jesus, no matter what storms of this life may come our way. He calms the storms and says "Peace, be still!" (Mark 4:39).

1. When does someone receive "peace with God," and how (v. 1)?
2. Why should Christians be joyful (v. 2)?

> "Paul's claim [was] that the message he preached was the authentic gospel of Christ. It is this: two things on which Paul preeminently insisted—that salvation was provided by God's grace and that faith was the means by which men appropriated it."—F. F. Bruce

---

### B. Grace Provides Mercy for Salvation (Eph. 2:4-9)

**⁴ But God, who is rich in mercy, for his great love wherewith he loved us, ⁵ Even when we were dead in sins, hath quickened us together with Christ, (by grace ye are saved;) ⁶ And hath raised us up together, and made us sit together in heavenly places in Christ Jesus: ⁷ That in the ages to come he might shew the exceeding riches of his grace in his kindness toward us through Christ Jesus. ⁸ For by grace are ye saved through faith; and that not of yourselves: it is the gift of God: ⁹ Not of works, lest any man should boast.**

Paul begins this passage by describing the rich mercy of God that was revealed in His amazing love for us. Our hope for redemption stems from His "great love" that reached out to us even when we were "dead in sins" (vv. 4-5). We were powerless to save ourselves and deserved the wrath of God (vv. 1-3), but God intervened in Christ Jesus! He "quickened" (v. 5), or "raised us up" together (v. 6). Once again, "heavenly places" indicates the spiritual nature of our salvation that we actually enjoy today as we serve and worship our Lord. "In the ages to come" establishes the everlasting aspects of our redemption that will culminate in the return of Christ and our physical resurrection to be with Him forever. God's "kindness" (goodness) will usher us into His eternal kingdom (v. 7)!

Paul reemphasizes that our salvation is dependent on the grace of God that we receive through faith in Christ (v. 8). We have no basis for boasting, since we did nothing to earn our redemption (v. 9). The salvation we enjoy is entirely a gift from God! This is our great reason to rejoice and celebrate! Now that we are free, let's be sure to stand firmly in this glorious liberty God gives us through Jesus Christ.

---

1. Describe the "riches" of God (vv. 4-7).
2. Why shouldn't we boast about our "works" (vv. 8-9)?

> "God's mercy is so great that you may sooner drain the sea of its water, or deprive the sun of its light, or make space too narrow, than diminish the great mercy of God."—Charles Spurgeon

### CONCLUSION

We need grace for salvation, grace for help in troubling times, and grace to live faithfully for Christ. We cannot earn grace, and we certainly do not deserve it. This is what makes grace so amazing! It is the free gift of God through Christ Jesus, His only begotten Son. Through grace, we have received God's forgiveness of sin through faith in Christ. We have been adopted into God's family, and we are heirs of His promises. Where would we be without grace? We would be lost and dead in sin. Where are we with grace? We are standing firmly on His Word, trusting Him for salvation, and waiting for Christ's return! Rejoice in His grace and enjoy your salvation. The One who saved you will be faithful and keep you if you will stand on His promises.

## GOLDEN TEXT CHALLENGE

"GOD, WHO IS RICH IN MERCY, FOR HIS GREAT LOVE WHEREWITH HE LOVED US, EVEN WHEN WE WERE DEAD IN SINS, HATH QUICKENED US TOGETHER WITH CHRIST, (BY GRACE YE ARE SAVED)" (Eph. 2:4-5).

Because of sin, we were spiritually destitute. Yet God—who is rich in mercy—looked on us with love.

Because of sin, we were "dead." Yet God—who is the source of all life—sent His Son to make us alive.

God's gifts of mercy and life flow from His grace.

**Daily Devotions:**

M. Cursed Because of Disobedience
   Deuteronomy 27:15-26
T. Blessing of Forgiveness
   Psalm 85:1-9
W. Praise the Compassionate God
   Psalm 103:1-7
T. Saved by Grace
   Acts 15:6-11
F. Gospel of Grace
   Galatians 1:3-10
S. Grow in Grace
   2 Peter 3:14-18

December 14, 2014 (Lesson 2)
# Saved by Grace

Romans 3:19-31; 7:7-11; 8:1-4; Galatians 2:20-21; 1 Timothy 1:12-16

**Unit Theme:**
Law and Grace in the New Testament

**Central Truth:**
Through faith in Jesus Christ, we are saved by God's grace.

**Focus:**
Contrast the results of law and grace, and accept life—spiritual and eternal—by grace.

**Context:**
Studies on saving grace from three Pauline epistles

**Golden Text:**
"This is a faithful saying, and worthy of all acceptation, that Christ Jesus came into the world to save sinners; of whom I am chief" (1 Tim. 1:15).

**Study Outline:**
I. The Law Exposed Sin
 (Rom. 3:19-20; 7:7-11)
II. Grace Provides Justification
 (Rom. 3:21-31)
III. Grace Produces Life
 (Rom. 8:1-4; Gal. 2:20-21; 1 Tim. 1:12-16)

## INTRODUCTION

This week we are studying one of the most exciting themes in Scripture: "salvation through grace." The lesson title encapsulates several profound concepts of the gospel. The word *saved* indicates that at one time we were in a hopelessly lost condition, but someone intervened and we were saved. The word *grace* lets us know we were saved by an unmerited action that we did not deserve or earn. This phrase has become a simple statement that summarizes the marvelous mercies God extends to all believers through His Son, Jesus Christ.

"Saved by grace" is the theme of the redeemed people of God! Jesus saved us when we could not save ourselves. This is the story we have heard time and time again, but it is still fresh. Our hymnals are filled with songs that declare this wonderful truth. We love to sing about God's "Amazing Grace," because only one thing could wash our sin away: "Nothing but the Blood" of Jesus!

These songs ring true because they identify with our experience. People who have not been saved may not be able to understand our witness of salvation by the grace of God. Skeptics, atheists, and liberals may not even think we need saving. However, those of us who have been saved know beyond any doubt that we are saved by the glorious riches of God's grace in Jesus Christ. We love to sing songs about salvation because they remind us of the transformation God has produced in our lives. As we study about our salvation this week, we should praise God for His gift of grace and think of how we can share the gospel with others. To understand fully our need for salvation, we must first understand the role of the Law in God's salvation plan.

## I. THE LAW EXPOSED SIN (Rom. 3:19-20; 7:7-11)

### A. The Law Revealed Sin (3:19-20)

**[19] Now we know that what things soever the law saith, it saith to them who are under the law: that every mouth may be stopped, and all the world may become guilty before God. [20] Therefore by the deeds of the law there shall no flesh be justified in his sight: for by the law is the knowledge of sin.**

The apostle Paul begins this section by relating the impact the Law of the Old Testament had on the world. The Law revealed sin. God gave the Law to His people so they would know what righteousness was and how they must live if they were going to please Him. More importantly, the Law exposed our inability to completely fulfill the requirements of the Law. Everyone was "guilty before God" (v. 19). No one was good enough to keep all of the Law. As Martin Luther noted, Paul's claim includes all people, even "the best and most excellent men most of all" (*The Bondage of the Will*). Thus, we all came under the condemnation of the Law and were deserving of judgment.

Verse 20 declares no person could be justified before God by obeying the Law. Our "deeds" betrayed our inability to keep the demands of righteousness, so we failed in attaining personal righteousness through our actions and behaviors. However, the Law provided an invaluable service to us. Through it, we gained "the knowledge of sin." This means the Law was our teacher; it taught us that we were lost and in need of God's grace. In Galatians 3:24, Paul calls the law a "schoolmaster," or a type of tutor. If we had not learned about sin, we would not have turned to God for deliverance from our sinfulness.

---

- What did the Old Testament Law accomplish?

> "The Law tells me how crooked I am. Grace comes along and straightens me out."—D. L. Moody

---

### B. The Law Could Not Bring Life (7:7-11)

**[7] What shall we say then? Is the law sin? God forbid. Nay, I had not known sin, but by the law: for I had not known lust, except the law had said, Thou shalt not covet. [8] But sin, taking occasion by the commandment, wrought in me all manner of concupiscence. For without the law sin was dead. [9] For I was alive without the law once: but when the commandment came, sin revived, and I died. [10] And the commandment, which was**

ordained to life, I found to be unto death. ¹¹ For sin, taking occasion by the commandment, deceived me, and by it slew me.

Paul begins this section by asking a provocative rhetorical question: "Is the law sin?" The question has an obvious answer: "Of course not!" The words "God forbid" (v. 7) provide an authoritative rebuke of any such notion. Then, Paul provides some clarifying statements to reinforce his contention that the Law was the means by which we became aware of our own sin. For example, the command that prohibits coveting created the awareness that lust is sinful. In verse 8, the apostle contends that sin produced much "concupiscence," or sinful desires, that the law exposed. Indeed, without the Law, Paul said "sin was dead," indicating that we would not be aware of sin except for the commands of God.

In verse 9, Paul compares his life before salvation to his life after redemption. He is describing the self-deception characterizing those who are not born again. However, when God's truth shines on their lives, their sinfulness is exposed, revealing they are spiritually dead.

Even though God's commandment was designed to give life to those who obey it, it brings death (separation from God for eternity), because no one could fulfill all its demands (v. 10). Paul then laments that the deceitfulness of sinful desires led him away from God into the consequences that disobedience brings: spiritual death (v. 11). Paul's words also reflect the original sin of Adam and Eve in the Garden of Eden. God only gave one law or restriction to the first couple He created, forbidding them to eat of the Tree of Knowledge of Good and Evil. Through their transgression, sin entered into their lives, bringing with it the condemnation of death (Gen. 3).

---

1. How do we know it is sinful to covet (v. 7)? In what sense is coveting the essence of sin?
2. Explain this statement: "Without the law sin was dead" (v. 8).
3. What "deceived" Paul, and how (v. 11)?

> "Lust, in one form or another, is the common sin that plagues all of mankind."—George Sweeting

---

## II. GRACE PROVIDES JUSTIFICATION (Rom. 3:21-31)

### A. Justification by Grace (vv. 21-26)

²¹ **But now the righteousness of God without the law is manifested, being witnessed by the law and the prophets; ²² Even the righteousness of God which is by faith of Jesus Christ unto all and upon all them that believe: for there is no difference: ²³ For all have sinned, and come short of the glory of God; ²⁴ Being justified freely by his grace through the redemption that is in Christ Jesus: ²⁵ Whom God hath set forth to be a propitiation through faith in his blood, to declare his righteousness for the remission of sins that are past, through the forbearance of God; ²⁶ To declare, I say,**

**at this time his righteousness: that he might be just, and the justifier of him which believeth in Jesus.**

Even though the Law exposed sin and pronounced judgment for disobedience, the Old Testament provides ample witness to the "righteousness of God" that was made available to His people (v. 21). God's righteousness was prophesied by the prophets and other writers of the Old Testament in such passages as Isaiah 53; Psalms 2:7; 45:6-7; 118:22-26; Genesis 3:15; 49:10. This righteousness only comes through faith in Jesus Christ. It is available to all people through His vicarious death on the cross, but it is received only by those who "believe" in Jesus Christ. In the Greek, *believe* connotes the idea of trust and faith and indicates that one must truly trust Jesus completely for salvation (Rom. 3:22). It is an abandonment of all attempts to save oneself and a declaration that our salvation is a work of His grace, because all people are under the curse of sin and "come short" of God's glory (v. 23).

The expression "come short" emphatically declares we have no glory that can compare to God's glory. In every aspect, we fall short qualitatively and quantitatively. This language emphasizes Paul's contention that, without Christ, all people are without any hope of salvation or justification. Our only hope resides in the One who embodies the glory of God (John 1:14) and who gave Himself as a ransom for our sin (Mark 10:45). This would be reason for despair if the apostle's words ended here. However, Paul quickly progresses to the good news.

The next three verses of our text proclaim the wonderful news of the gospel. We have been "justified freely"! The word *freely*, so closely connected with *grace*, should remove any doubt as to the reason for our justification as sinners. Jesus Christ died for our sins and justified us before God, redeeming us from the horrific consequences of sin (v. 24). Jesus' vicarious death was the *propitiation* (appeasement) that resulted in the *remission* (forgiveness) of our sin when we accepted Christ as Lord and Savior (v. 25). Then, Paul declares Jesus is *just*, meaning He is righteous and has no sin. Jesus does not need for anyone to justify Him, because He is just by nature, which qualifies Him to justify those who believe in Him (v. 26).

---

1. What is available "unto all," and how (vv. 21-22)?
2. What does it mean to "fall short of the glory of God" (v. 23 NKJV)?
3. How does God treat the repentant person (v. 24)?
4. Explain the term "forbearance of God" (v. 25), and why we should be thankful for it.
5. How is God both "just" and "justifier" (v. 26)?

---

> "To be *justified* means more than to be declared 'not guilty.' It actually means to be declared righteous before God. It means God has imputed or charged the guilt of our sin to His Son, Jesus Christ, and has imputed or credited Christ's righteousness to us."—Jerry Bridges

---

B. Justification Through Faith (vv. 27-31)

(Romans 3:28-30 is not included in the printed text.)
**²⁷Where is boasting then? It is excluded. By what law? of works? Nay: but by the law of faith.**
**³¹ Do we then make void the law through faith? God forbid: yea, we establish the law.**

Our justification is not based on the Law, which would require us to fully obey all aspects of the Law. If we could perfectly obey all of God's commands, we would have grounds for boasting due to our self-merit. However, our justification comes through "the law of faith," which is based on the grace of Jesus Christ and removes all grounds for boasting or pride (v. 27). This justification by faith is not dependent on any works we can do (v. 28). Also, it is available to both Jews and Gentiles, to the circumcised and uncircumcised (vv. 29-30). According to Paul, this does not invalidate the Old Testament law, but demonstrates the need for it in revealing the need and means of salvation (v. 31).

1. Why do Christians have no reason to boast (vv. 27-28)?
2. How are Jews and Gentiles alike (vv. 29-30)?
3. Answer the question in verse 31: "If we emphasize faith, does this mean that we can forget about the law?" (NLT).

"When a person becomes a Christian and has authentic faith, he has a real mystical union with Christ, so that Christ really comes to indwell the believer. When we exercise faith in Jesus Christ, His righteousness is counted towards us and we are justified."—R. C. Sproul

III. GRACE PRODUCES LIFE (Rom. 8:1-4; Gal. 2:20-21; 1 Tim. 1:12-16)

A. The Spirit of Grace (Rom. 8:1-4)

**¹ There is therefore now no condemnation to them which are in Christ Jesus, who walk not after the flesh, but after the Spirit. ² For the law of the Spirit of life in Christ Jesus hath made me free from the law of sin and death. ³ For what the law could not do, in that it was weak through the flesh, God sending his own Son in the likeness of sinful flesh, and for sin, condemned sin in the flesh: ⁴ That the righteousness of the law might be fulfilled in us, who walk not after the flesh, but after the Spirit.**

In Romans 8, we discover the marvelous declaration that we who are saved are free from condemnation! We have liberty in Christ through our justification by faith. Verse 1 inserts a qualifying phrase that clarifies who is being described: "who walk not after the flesh, but after the Spirit." At first glance, we may wonder if we really walk after the Spirit since we all have struggles and temptations. However, those who walk after the Spirit will not be immune from struggles and trial. The Spirit leads us as we respond positively to His guidance. When we make a mistake or fail, the Spirit corrects us and calls us to follow Christ. This correction and calling is evidence we are walking after the "Spirit of life" who set us free from the power of sin and death through Christ Jesus (v. 2). As French Arrington observes:

> Christians are free because God sees them in Christ. The power of the law to condemn them has been decisively broken. Sin has been dealt with at Calvary, and through the indwelling presence of the Holy Spirit, the Christian can live victoriously (*The Greatest Letter Ever Written: A Study of the Book of Romans*).

The Law was unable to set us free from sin because the flesh is weak. Through the Incarnation, God sent His Son, Jesus, in "the likeness of sinful flesh" to condemn sin and free us from its power (v. 3). Jesus appeared in the "likeness" of sinful flesh, but not the fallen state of the flesh, for He was "without sin" (Heb. 4:15). Through Jesus, the righteousness requirements of the Law are fulfilled through the work of the Holy Spirit in us (Rom. 8:4).

When the Holy Spirit lives in us, we will no longer be controlled by the flesh or sin. We will be led by the Spirit to follow Christ and to serve Him fully, free from condemnation. The Holy Spirit is the Spirit of grace because He brings God's grace into our life and keeps us on the path of righteousness when we follow Him.

---

1. What does it mean to "walk . . . after the Spirit" (v. 1)?
2. How does being "free from the law of sin and death" (v. 2) affect daily living?
3. What did Jesus Christ do "in the flesh" (v. 3), and why (v. 4)?

---

> "Within each of us exists the image of God, however disfigured and corrupted by sin it may presently be. God is able to recover this image through grace as we are conformed to Christ."—Alister McGrath

---

B. The Life of Grace (Gal. 2:20-21)

**[20] I am crucified with Christ: nevertheless I live; yet not I, but Christ liveth in me: and the life which I now live in the flesh I live by the faith of the Son of God, who loved me, and gave himself for me. [21] I do not frustrate the grace of God: for if righteousness come by the law, then Christ is dead in vain.**

In this passage, Paul describes some aspects of our life of grace in Christ Jesus, beginning with a startling declaration: "I am crucified with Christ" (v. 20). Paul is asserting that his flesh and will have died to Christ. He has taken up the cross as Jesus instructed His followers to do (Matt. 10:38). This may sound like a sacrifice, but Paul does not see it that way. He readily adds that he is more alive than ever because Jesus lives in him. Even though he is still in the physical body, he lives by the faith of Christ, who is "the Son of God." Paul then personalizes the gospel with the assertion that Jesus "loved me, and gave himself for me" (Gal. 2:20). We, too, should realize the gospel is for "me." We must first experience Christ for ourselves. Then, we will want to share Christ with others.

The message of justification by faith in Christ has an evangelistic application that should not be neglected. Since salvation is for all people, the implication is that all people are lost without Christ. If we do not accept this biblical truth, can we effectively reach others with the gospel? Scot McKnight contends that if we are going to evangelize the world with the message of "justification by faith through Christ," then, along with the apostle Paul, we must acknowledge the lost condition of all people:

> We need to be willing with Paul, to see all people as sinners. Ours is a conscientious and sensitive world. Consequently, we are afraid to let the world know that there is sin and that all people are sinners. Thus, the sweet work of Christ that forgives, reconciles, justifies, and redeems can have no impact because we refuse to take the first step: admit that we are all sinners (*Galatians: The NIV Application Commentary*).

This realization of the personal applications of Christ's sacrifice compels Paul to trust Jesus for salvation and to not "frustrate," or render ineffective, God's grace by trying to merit salvation through obedience to the Law. If it had been possible to gain righteousness through good works, then Jesus' death was totally unnecessary (v. 21). However, Jesus did not die in vain, because the only way we could be saved was for Him to die in our place. He gave Himself for us.

---

1. What does it mean to be "crucified with Christ," and why is it necessary?
2. How do some religions try to "nullify the grace of God" (v. 21 NASB)?

> "Between here and heaven, every minute that the Christian lives will be a minute of grace."—Charles Spurgeon

---

C. The Ministry of Grace (1 Tim. 1:12-16)

**¹² And I thank Christ Jesus our Lord, who hath enabled me, for that he counted me faithful, putting me into the ministry; ¹³ Who was before a blasphemer, and a persecutor, and injurious: but I obtained mercy, because I did it ignorantly in unbelief. ¹⁴ And the grace of our Lord was exceeding abundant with faith and love which is in Christ Jesus. ¹⁵ This is a faithful saying, and worthy of all acceptation, that Christ Jesus came into the world to save sinners; of whom I am chief. ¹⁶ Howbeit for this cause I obtained mercy, that in me first Jesus Christ might shew forth all longsuffering, for a pattern to them which should hereafter believe on him to life everlasting.**

In verse 12, Paul is rejoicing that God considered him faithful and placed him in the ministry so he can share the message of God's grace with others. This is especially noteworthy because of the sinfulness of Paul's life before Christ. He describes himself as blaspheming God, persecuting Christians, and deliberately inflicting injury on God's people (v. 13). Nevertheless, Paul received mercy from God! If God could transform Paul and call him into the ministry, we should never think God cannot use us to reach others. Through His grace, God will provide an abundance of "faith and love" so we can minister to others (v. 14).

In verse 15, Paul relates that he considers himself to be the "chief," or greatest, of all sinners. This may seem to be an unmerited claim, but Paul is expressing his unworthiness to receive God's grace and call to ministry. This should be everyone's attitude. We can rejoice in our salvation while recognizing we were not worthy of God's goodness. This is the beauty of God's grace.

In verse 16, Paul testifies that he received God's longsuffering and mercy so his life could be a "pattern" (Greek, *hypotypōsis*) for others. *Hypotypōsis* could be translated as "example" or "model," and emphasizes that one is expected to embrace and copy the pattern that has been placed before him or her (Joseph Henry Thayer, *Thayer Greek-English Lexicon of the New Testament*). Today we are still studying the "pattern" of God's grace in the life of Paul so we might learn from him and live as patterns for others.

Praise the Lord for all of the great people of faith who have inspired and encouraged us to live faithfully for Christ. We, too, must become patterns for the generations who are coming after us. This is the way we pass on the faith and continue the building of Christ's church. We all should ask ourselves, What pattern are we providing for others to follow?

---

1. Why did Paul become a minister of the gospel (v. 12)?
2. List three words Paul used to describe himself before meeting Christ (v. 13), and then list three traits of Christ which transformed Paul (v. 14).
3. How was Paul a "pattern," or "example" (NASB), for others (v. 16)?

### A Pattern to Follow

When I first accepted Christ as my Savior, I looked to my pastor for guidance and direction. Although I did not realize it, I was seeking a pattern to follow so I could develop as a believer. I was fortunate to have pastors who were faithful to God and could guide me on my Christian journey.

Even now, over forty years since I received Jesus, I still pay attention to the patterns that my first pastors provided for me as a young believer. I admire their consistency as Christians and their commitment to faithful ministry. May we all seek to be a "faithful pattern" to those who are watching. —Thomas Doolittle

---

### CONCLUSION

Sometimes we may feel we are the "chief" sinner of all, just as Paul did. This should lead us to greater celebration for the abundance of mercy and grace we have received as followers of Christ. No longer are we condemned. Now, we are justified and free from all condemnation. The Holy Spirit resides in us and guides us into all truth! Praise the Lord for God's grace!

Now that we have received grace, let us become a "pattern" by which others can see Christ and desire to follow Him. Our world is filled with pain, war, evil, and despair. However, we have a message of hope that can bring peace and joy into the lives of those who do not know Jesus. We are saved by grace, and we have a responsibility to share this grace with those who do not know Christ. After this life on earth, we will enjoy everlasting life with all of God's people, including those we helped lead to Christ.

## GOLDEN TEXT CHALLENGE

"THIS IS A FAITHFUL SAYING, AND WORTHY OF ALL ACCEPTATION, THAT CHRIST JESUS CAME INTO THE WORLD TO SAVE SINNERS; OF WHOM I AM CHIEF" (1 Tim. 1:15).

Here the apostle quotes some unknown early Christian saying, probably from a hymn or written treatise commonly known among the Christians: "Christ Jesus came into the world to save sinners." In order to emphasize his acceptance of this truth, Paul calls it "a faithful saying" and adds that it is "worthy of all acceptation." These words of Paul are very much like the words of Christ himself, who first declared "the Son of man is come to seek and to save that which was lost" (Luke 19:10), and "I came not to call the righteous, but sinners to repentance" (Mark 2:17).

Paul adds his own testimony to his assurance that Jesus came to earth to save sinners, by declaring himself to be the chief of sinners. He never hesitated to acknowledge the magnitude of his former sinful nature and to declare himself to be an example of God's grace. The fact that Jesus would save him was proof that His grace is sufficient for all.

## Daily Devotions:

M. No One Is Good
   Psalm 14:1-7
T. Prayer of Confession
   Psalm 51:1-12
W. Promise of Everlasting Life
   Daniel 12:1-3
T. Justified by Faith in Christ
   Galatians 2:14-21
F. Purpose of the Law
   Galatians 3:19-24
S. Heirs of Eternal Life
   Titus 3:3-7

December 21, 2014 (Lesson 3)
# The Savior Is Born (Christmas)
Luke 2:1-40

**Unit Theme:**
The Birth of Jesus

**Central Truth:**
Jesus was born to be the Savior of the world.

**Focus:**
Examine the events surrounding Christ's birth and accept Him as Savior.

**Context:**
Bethlehem in 4 BC. It seems strange to say Christ was born four years "Before Christ," but this is due to a four-year error in our calendar.

**Golden Text:**
"For unto you is born this day in the city of David a Saviour, which is Christ the Lord" (Luke 2:11).

**Study Outline:**
  I. Humble Birth
     (Luke 2:1-7)
 II. Angelic Announcement
     (Luke 2:8-20)
III. Seeing God's Salvation
     (Luke 2:21-38)

## INTRODUCTION

The second chapter of Luke presents a picture of Romans and angels and shepherds and parents and a baby—not just any baby, but the infant Jesus. What do we learn from these individuals concerning the coming of Christ?

*The Romans.* From the Romans we see the government of that ancient world continued to make its demands even when the birth of Christ was imminent. The ruling authorities were only concerned with the functioning of government; it had not been revealed to them that the birth of the Messiah was imminent. And even if Caesar himself had been aware of the impending birth of a Savior in one small part of his empire, it is doubtful he would have blinked. Similarly today, we should not expect secular government to pay much attention to Jesus Christ or His claims. It is up to the Church to lift up Jesus Christ as Lord.

*The Angels.* The message of eternal hope was delivered by the angels in the announcement that Jesus had been born. Their supernatural appearance and communication with the shepherds reminds us God does whatever it takes to get His message to humanity. He primarily speaks through His written Word and His Spirit, but God also speaks through people, circumstances, miracles, angels, and many other means.

*The Shepherds.* The perfect response to the Gospel message was evidenced by the shepherds, who believed the angels' amazing message, went to see the evidence for themselves, and then spread the good news to others. This is the same pattern God wants His children to follow today: believe His message, draw close to Jesus, and take the good news to other people.

*The Parents.* Mary and Joseph provided the tender and special care that any infant should receive and which this infant especially deserved. They set the example which every parent and everyone else who deals with holy things should follow.

*The Baby.* Unlike the image depicted in some paintings, there was no halo encircling the head of the baby Jesus. There was nothing extraordinary about His appearance, and His resting place was the humblest of beds—a feeding trough. Yet angels led shepherds to Him, and they went away "praising God for all the things that they had heard and seen" (Luke 2:20). Today God is still revealing Himself in the mundane aspects of life, and it take spiritual ears to hear His voice and learn His lessons.

I. HUMBLE BIRTH (Luke 2:1-7)

A. The Decree (vv. 1-3)

**¹ And it came to pass in those days, that there went out a decree from Caesar Augustus that all the world should be taxed. ² (And this taxing was first made when Cyrenius was governor of Syria.) ³ And all went to be taxed, every one into his own city.**

Censuses were carried out in the Roman world for two reasons: to assess taxes and to discover who was eligible for military service. Since the Jews were exempt from military service, a census conducted in Palestine would be for taxation purposes.

Discoveries have been made which provide definite information about the censuses. The information has come from actual census documents written on papyrus and discovered in the dustheaps of Egyptian towns and villages and in the sands of the desert. It is almost certain that what happened in Egypt happened in Syria, too, and Judea was part of the province of Syria.

At one time, critics questioned the thought of every person going to his own city to be enrolled, but now people possess documents proving that this is what happened. We have here another instance of additional knowledge confirming the accuracy of the New Testament record.

Christianity is sometimes accused of being behind the times and the Bible of being irrelevant. The facts are that the Bible and Christianity are very much up-to-date and speak to the burning issues of the day. Instead of disproving the message of Scripture, modern discoveries confirm what the Word says. This should be a source of special encouragement to the believer. The truths we have known all along are now attested by sources outside Christendom.

---

1. How could one man tax "all the world" (v. 1)?
2. What was the response to Caesar's decree (v. 3)?

> "Christmas began in the heart of God. It is complete only when it reaches the heart of man."—*The Encyclopedia of Religious Quotations*

## B. The Journey (vv. 4-5)

**⁴ And Joseph also went up from Galilee, out of the city of Nazareth, into Judaea, unto the city of David, which is called Bethlehem; (because he was of the house and lineage of David:) ⁵ To be taxed with Mary his espoused wife, being great with child.**

Actors on the stage of the world don't always know how to evaluate their role. Caesar Augustus, the first Roman emperor, issues a decree; it is obeyed and he is in control. Joseph and Mary, peasants from Nazareth, answer his decree and make their way to Bethlehem. How insignificant they seem amid the many who are returning to their hometown. Yet this woman, marching under the orders of Caesar, is carrying in her womb the Son of God. This man traveling by her side is protecting her.

The significance of the actors in this drama changes when we read the words of the prophet Micah: "But thou, Bethlehem Ephratah, though thou be little among the thousands of Judah, yet out of thee shall he come forth unto me that is to be ruler in Israel; whose goings forth have been from of old, from everlasting. Therefore will he give them up, until the time that she which travaileth hath brought forth: then the remnant of his brethren shall return unto the children of Israel. And he shall stand and feed in the strength of the Lord, in the majesty of the name of the Lord his God; and they shall abide: for now shall he be great unto the ends of the earth" (5:2-4).

No longer is the big man in the city on seven hills, Caesar Augustus, the main character in this drama. Joseph and Mary become the most significant personalities on the stage. Caesar is only an instrument that God is using to prepare the way for the fulfillment of prophecy. Things are not always as they appear to be.

**espoused** (v. 5)—"betrothed" (RSV) or "engaged" (NASB)

- What does verse 4 reveal about Joseph?

> "He [Joseph] was a 'just' (Matt. 1:19) and yet merciful and tenderly considerate man."—*Fausset's Bible Dictionary*

## C. The Birth (vv. 6-7)

**⁶ And so it was, that, while they were there, the days were accomplished that she should be delivered. ⁷And she brought forth her firstborn son, and wrapped him in swaddling clothes, and laid him in a manger; because there was no room for them in the inn.**

Prior to this time, Mary had been living at the wrong address for the birth of the

Christ child. Caesar's decree had changed all of that. She arrived in Bethlehem in the nick of time. Soon upon her arrival, the time of her delivery came.

Jesus was born in a stable. It is probable that the stable was built out of a cave. Travelers were put up in such places, that is, in the open areas, while the back parts were used for animals. When the child was born, Mary wrapped Him in swaddling clothes, which consisted of a square of cloth with a long bandage-like strip coming diagonally off from one corner. The infant was first wrapped in the square of cloth and then the long strip was wound around Him. Jesus was then laid in a manger—a place where animals feed.

The reason Jesus was born in a stable was because there was no room in the inn when Joseph and Mary arrived in Bethlehem. In Mary's condition the journey was a very slow one. By the time they arrived, the rooms in the inn were already occupied. This experience anticipated the reception He would receive from people. John recorded, "He came unto his own, and his own received him not" (1:11). Then he added: "But as many as received him, to them gave he power to become the sons of God, even to them that believe on his name" (v. 12).

- Describe the birth of Jesus.

"The best Christmas gift was wrapped in a manger."—*Marquee Messages*

II. ANGELIC ANNOUNCEMENT (Luke 2:8-20)

A. The Shepherds (vv. 8-9)

**⁸ And there were in the same country shepherds abiding in the field, keeping watch over their flock by night. ⁹ And, lo, the angel of the Lord came upon them, and the glory of the Lord shone round about them: and they were sore afraid.**

Now enter the shepherds into this drama. They were tending their flocks. Most biblical scholars agree these were probably Temple shepherds, watching flocks intended for sacrifice.

The announcement of the birth of Jesus came at night as shepherds discharged their duty. This shows us God's regard for people of every station in life. The message did not come to Caesar's palace, nor to the Temple, but to lowly shepherds. When at a later time Jesus described His mission, He declared: "The Spirit of the Lord is upon me, because he hath anointed me to preach the gospel to the poor; he hath sent me to heal the brokenhearted, to preach deliverance to the captives, and recovering of sight to the blind, to set at liberty them that are bruised, to preach the acceptable year of the Lord" (Luke 4:18-19).

As the shepherds were busy at their task, an angel of the Lord appeared to them, and the glory of the Lord shone around them. The immediate reaction of the shepherds was one of fear; they were terrified.

1. Describe the scene in verse 8.

2. How did the scene change (v. 9)?

_____

B. The Angel (vv. 10-12)
**¹⁰ And the angel said unto them, Fear not: for, behold, I bring you good tidings of great joy, which shall be to all people. ¹¹ For unto you is born this day in the city of David a Saviour, which is Christ the Lord. ¹² And this shall be a sign unto you; Ye shall find the babe wrapped in swaddling clothes, lying in a manger.**

The angel's first act was to still the fear that was in the heart of the shepherds. The angel said, "Do not be afraid." The shepherds mistakenly feared that hurt would come to them from the one who had come to help. How often do we make that same mistake? How often do we misinterpret God's hand in our lives? We must learn "that all things work together for good to them that love God, to them who are the called according to his purpose" (Rom. 8:28).

The message of the angel was good news for all people of all time. It was the joyful news that the Savior had been born. That Savior is Christ the Lord, the Messiah. He would confront all the sin of the world with regal authority, based on redeeming power. Of Him, the angel told Joseph, "And she [Mary] shall bring forth a son, and thou shalt call his name Jesus: for he shall save his people from their sins" (Matt. 1:21). Christ has confronted all the chaos of the world as the Messiah and has established the true kingdom of God. He is Lord and as such confronts all eternity and all ages, and does so triumphantly.

The angel announced to the shepherds that the Baby could be found "wrapped in cloths and lying in a manger" (Luke 2:12 NIV).

_____

1. What was for "all people" (v. 10)?
2. Why is the phrase "unto you" significant (vv. 11-12)?

> "The angel's message was that God had come, redemption was possible, the Lord had visited His people with salvation." —Billy Graham

_____

C. The Heavenly Host (vv. 13-14)
**¹³ And suddenly there was with the angel a multitude of the heavenly host praising God, and saying, ¹⁴ Glory to God in the highest, and on earth peace, good will toward men.**

The terrified shepherds hardly had time to respond before the angel was joined by a great company of the heavenly host, praising God and shouting praise unto Him. What a picture! All heaven breaking forth, sweeping down, and hovering over Bethlehem's plains to declare the meaning of the coming of the Child.

The anthem is twofold. It speaks of heaven and earth. It exalts God who is above. The expression is a descriptive word for heaven, the dwelling place of God: "Glory to God in the highest." The message it bears for earth is one of peace—not just any kind of peace, but the peace which God alone can give. His peace comes only to people in whom He is well pleased, those on whom His favor rests.

Peace comes through Jesus Christ. It will come to the earth when people are like Him. That is the way to peace, and there is no other way. Negotiations, disarmament, peace treaties, and the like will never produce lasting peace. We applaud the efforts of world leaders in their quest for peace, but we put our hope for ultimate and complete peace in the Prince of Peace—Jesus Christ.

---

1. How does the scene change in verse 13?
2. What is the message for earth's inhabitants (v. 14)?

> "The better acquainted you become with God, the lesser tensions you feel and the more peace you possess."—Charles Allen

---

D. The Response (vv. 15-20)

**15 And it came to pass, as the angels were gone away from them into heaven, the shepherds said one to another, Let us now go even unto Bethlehem, and see this thing which is come to pass, which the Lord hath made known unto us. 16 And they came with haste, and found Mary, and Joseph, and the babe lying in a manger. 17 And when they had seen it, they made known abroad the saying which was told them concerning this child. 18 And all they that heard it wondered at those things which were told them by the shepherds. 19 But Mary kept all these things, and pondered them in her heart. 20 And the shepherds returned, glorifying and praising God for all the things that they had heard and seen, as it was told unto them.**

The message to the shepherds was that God in Christ had begun His earthly sojourn. The Babe they would find in the manger is the Son of God. So, as soon as the angels had departed, the shepherds said, "Let's go to Bethlehem, and see for ourselves what the Lord has told us" (see v. 15).

The shepherds hurried off to Bethlehem, and when they had seen Jesus they spread the word concerning Him. What was their message? "Unto you is born this day . . . a Savior." Joseph Parker wrote: "The world did not want an adviser. The world had advised itself almost into hell. The world did not ask for a speculator. Everything that man could do had been done, and men sat in the darkness of their own wisdom. The world did not want a reformer, a man who could change his outward and transient relations, an engineer that would continually devote this time (for appropriate remuneration) to the readjustment of the wheels and the pulleys and the various mechanical forces of society. The world wanted a Savior."

It is not surprising that all who heard what the shepherds said to them were amazed. The story they conveyed was good news of the highest order. We can easily understand that Mary treasured in her heart and pondered over the heavenly messages. And what is more natural than that the shepherds would return to their tasks with gratitude and praise? In their memories, their lingered a song that expresses still the hope of all humanity.

---

1. What did the shepherds find (v. 16), and how did they respond (v. 17)?
2. How did people respond to the shepherds' message (v. 18)?
3. Describe Mary's reaction to "all these things" (v. 19).

> "Christ was born in the first century, yet He belongs to all centuries. He was born a Jew, yet He belongs to all races. He was born in Bethlehem, yet He belongs to all countries."—George W. Truett

---

## III. SEEING GOD'S SALVATION (Luke 2:21-38)

### A. Fulfillment of the Law (vv. 21-24)

(Luke 2:23-24 is not included in the printed text.)

**21 And when eight days were accomplished for the circumcising of the child, his name was called JESUS, which was so named of the angel before he was conceived in the womb. 22 And when the days of her purification according to the law of Moses were accomplished, they brought him to Jerusalem, to present him to the Lord.**

When Jesus was eight days old, He was circumcised according to Jewish law and given the name Jesus (v. 21). The Hebrew form of *Jesus* was *Joshua*, meaning "savior." This name was given to Jesus by the angel Gabriel even before He was conceived (Matt. 1:21; Luke 1:31).

The period of purification for the mother of a newborn child was forty days. At the expiration of this forty-day period, Mary and Joseph took Jesus to Jerusalem for dedication in the Temple. There He would be "called holy [set apart] to the Lord" (2:23; see also Ex. 13:2, 12).

A lamb was the usual sacrifice as a burnt offering. Persons too poor to offer a lamb were allowed to bring two turtledoves, or two pigeons, which cost considerably less than a lamb (Lev. 12:8). The fact that Joseph and Mary offered doves or pigeons instead of a lamb indicates the degree of their poverty. Joseph was a carpenter, not a prosperous merchant or landowner. For God's purposes, Jesus began His earthly life in the most ordinary and humble station of life.

---

1. When was it determined that Mary would name the child "Jesus" (v. 21)?
2. Why was Jesus taken to Jerusalem (vv. 22-23)?

---

### B. Simeon's Words About Jesus (vv. 25-32)

**25 And, behold, there was a man in Jerusalem, whose name was Simeon; and the same man was just and devout, waiting for the consolation of**

Israel: and the Holy Ghost was upon him. ²⁶ And it was revealed unto him by the Holy Ghost, that he should not see death, before he had seen the Lord's Christ. ²⁷ And he came by the Spirit into the temple: and when the parents brought in the child Jesus, to do for him after the custom of the law, ²⁸ Then took he him up in his arms, and blessed God, and said, ²⁹ Lord, now lettest thou thy servant depart in peace, according to thy word: ³⁰ For mine eyes have seen thy salvation, ³¹ Which thou hast prepared before the face of all people; ³² A light to lighten the Gentiles, and the glory of thy people Israel.

Few people in the Temple would likely have paid any attention to the infant in Mary's arms. The fact that His parents had given the offering of the poor would have made Him even less noticed by either the people or religious leaders. One who did notice Him, however, was Simeon, a man of deep devotion, who lived in anticipation of the Messiah. This is the meaning of "waiting for the consolation of Israel" (v. 25). The fact that "the Holy Ghost was upon him" means he frequently prophesied and spoke by revelation of the Spirit.

It had been revealed to this devout man that he would not see death until he had seen the Messiah. Although the Scripture does not indicate Simeon's age, it has been believed from earliest time he was a very old man.

Just as Simeon came into the Temple by the Holy Spirit, so he recognized Jesus by the same Spirit. He took the infant in his arms and blessed the Lord with a beautiful hymn of praise. His words "Now lettest thou thy servant depart in peace" (v. 29) meant he could now conclude his life without regret or sense of incompleteness. His life had been perfectly fulfilled, and Simeon yielded his place to the infant in his arms. Simeon was like a guard whose responsibility was to hold the fort in faith and prayer until the Deliverer arrived; he then could end his vigil and retire in peace.

Simeon recognized in Jesus the salvation that was to come to all people. The Jews had long awaited their Messiah, who would be their salvation and their glory. They expected Him to be strictly a Jewish redeemer and ruler, taking vengeance on all except themselves. Simeon's prophecy was far more inclusive and showed deep spiritual insight. This was the greatest lesson the Jews had to learn: the messianic salvation could not be held to themselves alone. There had now come together a light that would lighten the world.

---

1. What does verse 25 reveal about Simeon?
2. What had been "revealed unto him" (v. 26)?
3. Explain Simeon's statement, "My eyes have seen your salvation" (v. 30 NIV).
4. How is Jesus described in verse 32?

"I am persuaded that all of our problems are conceived and born in the sinful belief that something or someone other than Jesus Christ can quench the thirst of our souls."—C. Samuel Storms

## C. Simeon's Words to Mary (vv. 33-35)

**33 And Joseph and his mother marvelled at those things which were spoken of him. 34 And Simeon blessed them, and said unto Mary his mother, Behold, this child is set for the fall and rising again of many in Israel; and for a sign which shall be spoken against; 35 (Yea, a sword shall pierce through thy own soul also,) that the thoughts of many hearts may be revealed.**

Joseph and Mary's amazement (v. 33) was twofold. First, they marveled that a devout stranger such as Simeon should recognize the divine nature of their Son. Then, they marveled at such deep insight into the things He was destined to do.

In verse 34 Simeon blessed both Joseph and Mary, and then emphasized to Mary that her child was the great hope of Israel. What the Jewish people had awaited for more than three centuries, she had brought into the world Yet, His ministry would bring division to the nation. Those who would reject Him would fall, and those who would accept Him would rise to great glory. This child was a sign to Israel, a clear evidence of God's visitation to humanity.

Simeon further revealed that the child would be cruelly treated, and that the sword of His suffering would pierce into Mary's heart as well (v. 35). This is a prediction of the sacrifice of Christ's life for the salvation of all people. Simeon foretold the sorrow that would come to Mary when she saw the suffering of her child (see John 19:25-27).

---

1. How would Jesus cause "the falling and rising of many" (v. 34 NIV)?
2. What is the "sword" of verse 35?

---

## D. Anna's Praise (vv. 36-38)

**36 And there was one Anna, a prophetess, the daughter of Phanuel, of the tribe of Aser: she was of a great age, and had lived with an husband seven years from her virginity; 37 And she was a widow of about fourscore and four years, which departed not from the temple, but served God with fastings and prayers night and day. 38 And she coming in that instant gave thanks likewise unto the Lord, and spake of him to all them that looked for redemption in Jerusalem.**

There was a woman in the Temple who, like Simeon, was endowed with the spirit of prophecy. Anna had been a woman of importance; the mention of her father's name indicates he had been a man of some renown. She was an extraordinary woman about eighty-four years of age who no longer left the Temple. She very likely lived in a small chamber of the Temple. The kingdom of God has been advanced greatly by saintly women who make precious their declining years with fasting and prayers. Such women have always been choice handmaidens of the Lord.

Like Simeon, Anna spoke praise to the Lord for the dawning of the day of redemption. It is not likely that she saw the extent of this redemption, but she clearly saw the beginning of the messianic age. She recognized in Jesus the redemption for which Israel had been waiting.

1. Who was Anna (vv. 36-37)?
2. What did Anna declare (v. 38)?

> "Jesus was God and man in one person, that God and man might be happy together again."—George Whitefield

## CONCLUSION

There was a European monarch who worried his court by often disappearing and walking incognito among his people. When he was asked not to do so for security's sake, he answered, "I cannot rule my people unless I know how they live." It is the great thought of the Christian faith that we have a God who knows the life we live because He too lived it and claimed no special advantage over common people.

## GOLDEN TEXT CHALLENGE

"FOR UNTO YOU IS BORN THIS DAY IN THE CITY OF DAVID A SAVIOUR, WHICH IS CHRIST THE LORD" (Luke 2:11).

A baby was born in Bethlehem many years ago. His parents were poor, and He had no unusual advantages. He raised no army, He conquered no kingdoms, He owned no real estate, and He had no bank account. Neither did He write books or paint pictures or compose music. He was mocked by the great and died a criminal's death. Yet this Man has revolutionized the civilized world.

Multitudes have lived and died triumphantly by the power of their faith in Him and obedience to the doctrines He inculcated, and He has more followers in the world today than ever before. His maxims are acknowledged, even by those who reject His authority, to be the noblest and purest that ever have been uttered, and no man has ever been able to pick a flaw with His character. What will you do with Jesus who is called the Christ?—Phillips Brooks

**Daily Devotions:**
M. God's Anointed Son
   Psalm 2:1-12
T. Sure Prophecy
   Isaiah 9:2-7
W. Source of Our Peace
   Isaiah 53:1-5
T. Virgin Birth
   Matthew 1:18-25
F. Cause for Rejoicing
   Matthew 2:1-11
S. Miraculous Conception Foretold
   Luke 1:26-35

December 28, 2014 (Lesson 4)
# Grace Demands Righteous Living
**Romans 5:12 through 6:4**

**Unit Theme:**
Law and Grace in the New Testament

**Central Truth:**
God's grace demands and enables righteous living.

**Focus:**
Reflect on the sanctifying effect of God's grace and live righteously in Christ.

**Context:**
In AD 58, the apostle Paul writes from Corinth to the church in Rome.

**Golden Text:**
"We are buried with him by baptism into death: that like as Christ was raised up from the dead by the glory of the Father, even so we also should walk in newness of life" (Rom. 6:4).

**Study Outline:**
I. Abundant Grace Through Christ
   (Rom. 5:12-17)
II. Grace Reigns Through Christ's Righteousness
   (Rom. 5:18-21)
III. Walk in Newness of Life
   (Rom. 6:1-4)

## INTRODUCTION

We have been studying grace and emphasizing the work of God through Christ in purchasing our salvation. We will now turn our attention to our responsibility after we are born again. As we proceed in our study, we must remember we are saved only by grace. We cannot do anything to augment God's grace in Christ Jesus. However, once we are saved, we cannot relax and assume we have no further responsibility. To do so would be to disregard God's instruction for us to pursue a righteous lifestyle in Christ. When we receive God's grace, we also accept the demands that grace places on us for righteous living.

When my oldest daughter turned sixteen, we handed her a set of keys to our family car. We did this because we loved her and she was our child. She did not *earn* the keys to the car; we just *gave* them to her. It was an act of grace. However, with the gift of our keys came great responsibility. If she wanted to keep the keys to the car, she had to follow our family guidelines, which she did. In a similar manner, God expects us to follow His guidelines after we receive His gift of grace.

Prior to salvation, we could not fulfill the Law and merit salvation. We accepted Jesus as our Savior and committed our life to Him. Now, the Holy Spirit is working in our lives and we have power to live righteously, which we did not have before salvation. We do not seek righteousness to be saved; we seek righteousness because we *are* saved!

Righteous living involves relationships, emotions, behaviors, attitudes, spiritual disciplines, and service. When we are saved, Jesus comes into our hearts and brings His righteousness into our lives. A righteous lifestyle is the overflow of Christ's righteousness that lives within our heart. As we pursue Christ, His love and light radiates out through our actions and thoughts so others see Christ in us. The more we love Jesus, the more we want to live like Him and to love like Him. Ultimately, righteous living is the fulfillment of loving God with all our heart, all our soul, and all our mind; and loving our neighbor as ourself (Matt. 22:37-40). Jesus declared that these are the two great commandments.

## I. ABUNDANT GRACE THROUGH CHRIST (Rom. 5:12-17)

### A. The Reign of Death (vv. 12-14)

**[12] Wherefore, as by one man sin entered into the world, and death by sin; and so death passed upon all men, for that all have sinned: [13] For until the law sin was in the world: but sin is not imputed when there is no law. [14] Nevertheless death reigned from Adam to Moses, even over them that had not sinned after the similitude of Adam's transgression, who is the figure of him that was to come.**

To comprehend the abundant grace we have through Christ, we must first consider the reign of death that dominated the world prior to the birth of Jesus. After Adam and Eve were created, they enjoyed the beautiful Garden of Eden and intimate fellowship with God. God intended for them to live forever, but they sinned and disobeyed the one command God gave them. Through their transgression, sin entered into the world and they were excluded from the Garden (Gen. 3:1-24). The most dreadful consequence of their sin was the curse of death that was "passed upon all" people (Rom. 5:12). Because all people have sinned, all will die.

French Arrington describes the universal guilt of sin due to Adam's transgression as "corporate solidarity." All humanity exists in unity with Adam through his sin and disobedience to God's commands (Gen. 3; Rom. 5:12-21; 1 Cor. 15:22, 45). The entire human race has experienced the condemnation of Adam's failure, because Adam's act was a corporate action of all humanity (*The Greatest Letter Ever Written*).

Through the commands God gave in the Old Testament, sin was exposed and people were held accountable for their transgressions (Rom. 5:13). Thus, sin was being "imputed" to all people. The Greek word for *impute* is *ellogao*, which means "to charge to one's account" and indicates the guilt all people bear regarding sin (W. E. Vine).

Verse 14 describes the grip sin had over all people from Adam until Moses. All people sinned and all were under its curse as "death reigned" over the generations. The Old Testament is filled with stories that reflect the reign of death that covered the world. Then, during Moses' time, God gave Israel the Law which brought hope. Tragically, Israel's history illustrates the inability of people to fulfill the requirements of God's commands.

1. How could Adam's sin be considered the greatest disaster in human history?
2. What changed with Moses' coming?
3. How was Adam "a type of Him who was to come" (v. 14 NKJV)?

> "Augustine teaches us that there is in each man a serpent, an Eve, and an Adam. Our senses and natural propensities are the *serpent*; the excitable desire is the *Eve*; and reason is the *Adam*. Our nature tempts us perpetually; criminal desire is often excited; but sin is not completed till reason consents."—Blaise Pascal

B. The Abundance of Grace (vv. 15-17)

**¹⁵ But not as the offence, so also is the free gift. For if through the offence of one many be dead, much more the grace of God, and the gift by grace, which is by one man, Jesus Christ, hath abounded unto many. ¹⁶ And not as it was by one that sinned, so is the gift: for the judgment was by one to condemnation, but the free gift is of many offences unto justification. ¹⁷ For if by one man's offence death reigned by one; much more they which receive abundance of grace and of the gift of righteousness shall reign in life by one, Jesus Christ.**

Praise the Lord for good news! The pervasive nature of death required drastic intervention for its reign to be demolished. Just as sin came into the world through one person, Adam, the grace of God came through one person also, Jesus Christ (v. 15). The "gift by grace" overcame the reign of death and was made available to the whole world through Jesus.

Verse 16 compares the judgment that came through sin with the "justification" that is the "free gift" of God. Sin brought condemnation and separation from God. Likewise, God's grace delivered us from condemnation through justification. Though our offenses were many, God's free gift of salvation set us free from sin's condemnation!

As Isaiah proclaimed, "Come now, and let us reason together, saith the Lord: though your sins be as scarlet, they shall be as white as snow; though they be red like crimson, they shall be as wool" (1:18). God's wonderful grace covers a multitude of transgressions. His grace can transform the greatest sinner into a beautiful testimony of the redemptive power of Christ. The psalmist described our forgiveness as being so complete that it is as though our sins have been completely forgotten by God: "As far as the east is from the west, so far hath he removed our transgressions from us" (103:12). Once we are saved, God no longer holds us accountable for our past sins. His forgiveness is complete and everlasting. Jesus came to earth so we could have abundant living that begins when we believe in Christ and receive His gift of grace.

The apostle Paul, in Romans 5, is establishing the veracity of Jesus' dying for our sins. If sin could enter the world through one person, salvation could also, and did in Christ. The redeemed of God have received "abundance of grace" and "the gift of righteousness" (v. 17). Grace is given in abundance to overcome the reign of death that came through Adam's transgression. This abundance of grace is more than sufficient to provide the remedy for all of the offenses that came though sin. God not only gifted us with grace, He also provided us with righteousness that will allow us to "reign in life." We reign because we belong to Christ, and we share in His reign in this life and the life to come. Only Jesus could provide such ultimate redemption.

---

1. In verse 15, what is the "free gift," and what is the "offence"?
2. How does the gift counteract the offence (vv. 16-17)?

> "We must not limit the mighty grace of God."—D. L. Moody

---

## II. GRACE REIGNS THROUGH CHRIST'S RIGHTEOUSNESS (Rom. 5:18-21)

### A. The Means of Grace (vv. 18-19)

**18 Therefore as by the offence of one judgment came upon all men to condemnation; even so by the righteousness of one the free gift came upon all men unto justification of life. 19 For as by one man's disobedience many were made sinners, so by the obedience of one shall many be made righteous.**

Verse 18 reemphasizes that judgment came upon all people through the offense of Adam and Eve. If they had not sinned, judgment would not have been declared and sin would not have been imputed to humanity. Nevertheless, they did sin and all people came under condemnation for sin. The Greek word for *condemnation* indicates that a harsh legal pronouncement has been given to the one receiving judgment. This is the reason God sent His only begotten Son into the world: so all could be set free from sin. Only Jesus Christ could provide freedom from sin, because He was and still is truly righteous. Only through Christ's righteousness could we receive the "free gift" that provides justification for eternal life (v. 18). This gift is available to anyone who accepts Christ as Lord and Savior.

Note the poignant contrast between those who are under condemnation and those who are liberated from sin. As French Arrington notes, "People who love darkness rather than light come under God's holy displeasure or judgment. For those who are in Christ there remains no holy displeasure or divine judgment. For them Christ has borne God's holy displeasure toward their sins" (*The Greatest Letter Ever Written*).

Then, Paul reminds the readers that the disobedience of Adam ushered sin into the human race, and all people became sinners. If one man's disobedience could have such a devastating effect on humanity, then one man's obedience could rectify the situation (v. 19). Jesus Christ was the only person who could do this. In 1 Corinthians 15:22, Paul stated, "For as in Adam all die, even so in

Christ shall all be made alive." Later, in verses 45-47, Jesus is called "the last Adam," indicating He alone could undo the condemnation that sin brought upon all people.

1. Name two ways "all men" are alike (v. 18).
2. Describe the fresh start available to every human being (v. 19).

> "Perhaps the most wonderful thing of all is this: God lifts us not only from what we are by nature to what Adam was in the Garden of Eden, but to what Adam was to become in the presence of God, and would have been had he persevered in obedience. The gospel does not make us like Adam in his innocence—it makes us like Christ, in all the perfection of His reflection of God."—Sinclair B. Ferguson

B. The Reign of Grace (vv. 20-21)

**20 Moreover the law entered, that the offence might abound. But where sin abounded, grace did much more abound: 21 That as sin hath reigned unto death, even so might grace reign through righteousness unto eternal life by Jesus Christ our Lord.**

Through Adam, sin entered the human race and brought judgment on everyone. Then, the law of God was introduced to point the way to righteousness and to reveal sin. However, the Law also exposed sin and clearly pronounced the offenses people were committing. Through the Law, people became conscious of their sins and the displeasure of God because of sin. As people increased in number, so did their sinful disobediences. Indeed, the apostle states that "sin abounded" due to the sinful nature of the people (v. 20).

One would think the abundance of sin would result in another global judgment from God, similar to the Flood during Noah's time. Instead, God in His infinite wisdom and mercy responded with an unexpected act: He gave His only Son so the world could be saved (John 3:16). Though "sin abounded, grace did much more abound" (Rom. 5:20). The Greek word for the first "abound" is *pleonazō*, which means "to increase or to become greater in quantity" (Joseph Henry Thayer, *A Greek-English Lexicon of the New Testament*). The second "abound," which is a translation of the Greek word *hyperperisseuō*, describes abundance beyond measure (Thayer). Obviously, God's provision of grace through Jesus Christ is abundantly available for all who come to Him in faith.

In verse 21, the effects of sin brought death into the world. God warned Adam and Eve that they would die if they ate of the Tree of Knowledge of Good and Evil (Gen. 2:17). Rejecting God's instructions, they plunged headlong into disobedience that would ultimately lead to their deaths and to many painful experiences in their family (chs. 3-4). Through their transgression, death reigned from their day until Jesus (1 Cor. 15:22). Through Jesus' vicarious death on the cross and His triumphant resurrection, grace became available to the world. Christ triumphed over death, ending its reign and establishing the promise of the resurrection that has become the hope of all followers of Christ (vv. 54-58). We now live under the "reign of grace," which came through the free gift of salvation in Christ. This reign is characterized by the righteousness of God's only Son, and leads to "eternal life" for all who accept Him as their Lord and Savior. Through God's grace, we are called to live righteous lives that reflect our commitment to Jesus Christ and His reign in our lives.

1. What did the Law accomplish?
2. Why is abundant grace necessary?

"Christ's death to sin and His satisfaction of God's justice opened the way for the reign of grace in our lives."—Jerry Bridges

## III. WALK IN NEWNESS OF LIFE (Rom. 6:1-4)

### A. A New Baptism (vv. 1-3)

¹ **What shall we say then? Shall we continue in sin, that grace may abound?** ² **God forbid. How shall we that are dead to sin, live any longer therein?** ³ **Know ye not, that so many of us as were baptized into Jesus Christ were baptized into his death?**

This passage begins with a series of rhetorical questions that have obvious answers. The questions are designed to lead the readers to the proper conclusions. Paul is concerned that some people may misinterpret his teachings and think we should continue in sin so God's grace may abound even more (v. 1).

In verse 2, Paul vehemently renounces this idea by declaring "God forbid." The apostle is repulsed by the idea that the followers of Christ should continue in sin. He is even more repulsed by the idea that Christians should sin so that God's grace can be more abundant. This is contrary to the redemptive life that believers enjoy in Christ. To be alive in Christ is to be "dead to sin." It is inconceivable to live habitually in sin after salvation, because salvation involves dying to sin and coming alive in Christ.

Then, Paul invokes the imagery of baptism to clarify his message. Water baptism represents a spiritual experience by which the believer shares a "faith-union" with Christ in His death, resurrection, and exaltation. Baptism into Christ "seals the believer's exodus, his deliverance from the bondage of sin" (F. F. Bruce, *The Epistle of Paul to the Romans*). The believer's baptism into Jesus Christ and His death results in resurrection from sin and spiritual empowerment to live for Christ.

This freedom from sin liberates us from the inability to live righteously. Through God's grace, we are ushered into Kingdom living that starkly contrasts with worldly philosophies. Paul declared, "For the kingdom of God is not meat and drink; but righteousness, and peace, and joy in the Holy Ghost" (14:17). Our new life in Christ enables us to live in accordance with Kingdom principles!

1. In these verses, what does "God forbid"?

2. What is the Christian's relationship with sin?

> "Come and see the victories of the cross. Christ's wounds are thy healings, His agonies thy repose, His conflicts thy conquests, His groans thy songs, His pains thine ease, His shame thy glory, His death thy life, His sufferings thy salvation."—Matthew Henry

### B. A New Life (v. 4)

**⁴ Therefore we are buried with him by baptism into death: that like as Christ was raised up from the dead by the glory of the Father, even so we also should walk in newness of life.**

Historically, Jesus died and was buried. Our participation in His death and burial occurs through faith. As Christ sacrificed Himself, we are to sacrifice ourselves, including our sinful desires and motives. In Romans 12:1-2, it is described as becoming a "living sacrifice" to God that reflects a rejection of this present sinful world and transformation that only comes through faith in Christ:

> I beseech you therefore, brethren, by the mercies of God, that you present your bodies a living sacrifice, holy, acceptable to God, which is your reasonable service. And do not be conformed to this world, but be transformed by the renewing of your mind, that you may prove what is that good and acceptable and perfect will of God (NKJV).

Jesus was raised from the dead by the "glory of the Father" (6:4), which represents the Father as "active agent in Christ's resurrection" (John Murray, *The Epistle of Romans*). The "glory of the Father" is a unique phrase that Paul used to describe "the glory through which Christ was raised. . . . The glory of God is the majesty of God, the sum of His perfections" that was manifested in Jesus' resurrection (Murray).

Since Christ was raised to life through the glorious power of God the Father, our lifestyle should reflect the resurrected life that has been given to us. We should "walk in newness of life." The word *walk* refers to the manner in which we conduct our lives. *Newness* indicates believers are to live in a consistent, Christlike manner that contrasts with our former life before Christ (Vine).

Walking in a Christlike manner is a recurring theme found in most of Paul's epistles. The following passage from Colossians 1 encapsulates Paul's claim that Christians should maintain a lifestyle that reflects the character of Christ and is "worthy of the Lord":

> For this reason we also, since the day we heard it, do not cease to pray for you, and to ask that you may be filled with the knowledge of His will in all wisdom and spiritual understanding; that you may walk worthy of the Lord, fully pleasing Him, being fruitful in every good work and increasing in the knowledge of God; strengthened with all might, according to His glorious power, for all patience and longsuffering with joy (vv. 9-11 NKJV).

"Walk" (v. 10; Rom. 6:4) is a figurative expression to signify the entire range of the activities in which one may engage throughout life. This concept is further employed by Paul in several other passages (Rom. 8:1, 4; 13:13; 1 Cor. 7:17;

2 Cor. 4:2; Gal. 2:14; 5:16, 25; 6:16; Eph. 2:10; 4:1, 17; 5:8, 15; Phil. 3:16-18; Col. 2:6; 3:7; 4:5; 1 Thess. 4:1, 12; 2 Thess. 3:6). Obviously, Paul expects that the believer's walk, or manner of conduct, will reflect the transformation that occurs at salvation.

We need grace for salvation, and we need grace so we can walk in the new life we received through Jesus. Our life has become new because Jesus redeemed us from sin and regenerated us through the power of the Holy Spirit. We now can live holy and righteous lives because Jesus lives within us. As Paul declared in Galatians 2:20, "I am crucified with Christ: nevertheless I live; yet not I, but Christ liveth in me: and the life which I now live in the flesh I live by the faith of the Son of God, who loved me, and gave himself for me."

---

1. What does water baptism illustrate?
2. Describe the "newness of life" Christ gives.

---

### Costly Grace

When I was a young minister, I asked one of my mentors how we should understand the relationship between grace and good works in the Christian life. He said, "We are saved by grace. We can do nothing to save ourselves, but Jesus paid the full price for our pardon from sin. However, once you receive grace, then it costs you everything you have!" Those words have guided me throughout my Christian life. I am saved by grace, and now I belong to God. I must strive to live a righteous life because I have received His grace.—Thomas Doolittle

---

## CONCLUSION

Too often we emphasize that we are saved by grace and then we neglect, or even forget, our responsibility to live righteously after we are saved. Our salvation is dependent solely on the grace of the Lord Jesus Christ, and we can do nothing to earn it. Paul declared we are saved by grace through faith and not by any works we can do; it is the gift of God (Eph. 2:8-9). However, once we are saved, good works should follow. In verse 10, Paul went on to say: "For we are his workmanship, created in Christ Jesus unto good works, which God hath before ordained that we should walk in them."

Prior to salvation, we could not live righteously. Now that we have received Christ, we can follow Him faithfully and live righteously through His grace and power. Praise the Lord for saving us and enabling us to live righteously in Christ Jesus!

### GOLDEN TEXT CHALLENGE

"WE ARE BURIED WITH HIM BY BAPTISM INTO DEATH: THAT LIKE AS CHRIST WAS RAISED UP FROM THE DEAD BY THE GLORY OF THE FATHER, EVEN SO WE ALSO SHOULD WALK IN NEWNESS OF LIFE" (Rom. 6:4).

*Therefore*, as a consequence of this death, which Paul assumes as a settled fact, *burial* follows. The figure of *baptism* points back to Christ's death and burial, and our identification with Him in both; it points forward to His resurrection and our participation in His resurrection life.

As our Lord's resurrection revealed God's mighty power and His excellent glory, so the rebirth of a soul—involving death to sin, burial, and resurrection, dramatically symbolized and portrayed in the rite of baptism—is a work of divine power designed to glorify God.

**Daily Devotions:**

M. A Righteous Lifestyle
   Psalm 15:1-5
T. A God-Pleasing Lifestyle
   Psalm 19:7-14
W. Righteous and Wicked Lifestyles Contrasted
   Psalm 37:5-17
T. New Life in Christ
   Ephesians 4:17-24
F. Live as God's Children
   1 John 3:1-10
S. Encouragement to Live Righteously
   Jude 17-25

January 4, 2015 (Lesson 5)
# Dead, Yielded, and Free

**Romans 6:5-23; 12:1-2; Jude 3-4**

**Unit Theme:**
Law and Grace in the New Testament

**Central Truth:**
Christians are set free from sin's dominion so they can live righteously.

**Focus:**
Describe and practice the freedom from sin that God's grace makes possible.

**Context:**
Spirit-inspired insights from Paul and Jude concerning righteous living

**Golden Text:**
"Reckon ye also yourselves to be dead indeed unto sin, but alive unto God through Jesus Christ our Lord" (Rom. 6:11).

**Study Outline:**
  I. Dead to Sin
     (Rom. 6:5-11)
 II. Yielded to God
     (Rom. 6:12-14; 12:1-2)
III. Set Free by Grace
     (Jude 3-4; Rom. 6:15-23)

## INTRODUCTION

Today we will focus on three key words that relate to our salvation and Christian walk: *dead*, *yielded*, and *free*. Each word pertains to our journey of faith that began when Christ first came into our lives while we were dead in our former sinful life. As Paul stated in Ephesians 2:1, "And you hath he quickened, who were dead in trespasses and sins." Here is a paradox for us to contemplate: Prior to salvation, we were dead. Then, when we were saved, we died again! Although this may seem confusing, as we proceed in our study the meaning of these two statements will become much clearer.

At the heart of this lesson is the concept of Christian liberty and what that means for us as believers. Too often, Christian liberty has been interpreted to mean that Christians continue sinning even after salvation. We all know that Christians can still sin after they are saved. However, this should not be taken lightly. As disciples of Jesus, we are instructed not to sin. Thankfully, Christians who succumb to temptation can be forgiven of their sins. However, we should not become comfortable with sin, nor should we assume we all will sin frequently. On different occasions when Jesus pronounced someone forgiven of their sins, He instructed them to "sin no more" (John 5:14; 8:11). The apostle John wrote: "My dear children, I write this to you so that you will not sin. But if anybody does sin, we have an advocate with the Father—Jesus Christ, the Righteous One" (1 John 2:1 NIV).

We must never allow the assurance of God's forgiveness to make us comfortable with sin in our lives. On the contrary, the goodness of God should motivate us to avoid sin and, if we do sin, to quickly repent and realign ourselves to pursue righteous living in Christ. This does not mean we will not be tempted after we are saved or that we will not have any struggles. However, it does mean we must actively pursue a righteous lifestyle that is in alignment with the teachings of God's Word. We can live righteously because, through God's grace, we are dead to sin and alive in Christ Jesus.

I. DEAD TO SIN (Rom. 6:5-11)

A. Crucified With Christ (vv. 5-7)

**⁵ For if we have been planted together in the likeness of his death, we shall be also in the likeness of his resurrection: ⁶ Knowing this, that our old man is crucified with him, that the body of sin might be destroyed, that henceforth we should not serve sin. ⁷ For he that is dead is freed from sin.**

In our last lesson, we ended by studying the "Walk in the Newness of Life" that is described in Romans 6:1-4. This week we begin by continuing to examine chapter 6 as we explore our new life in Christ. The apostle Paul begins this passage by describing how we are "planted together in the likeness of his death" (v. 5), which can be translated as "united with him in a death like his" (NIV). We are united with Christ through His death in a spiritual sense, through "baptism," which refers to our acceptance of Jesus as Lord and Savior (vv. 3-4). Our "death" is like Jesus' death, because we surrendered our will to the will of the Father as Jesus prayed in the Garden of Gethsemane (Matt. 26:36-39). Our life is no longer our own, since we now live for God through faith in His Son, Jesus (Gal. 2:20).

Our death also is distinctly different from Jesus' death because we did not physically die with Him, and our death was not a vicarious act. However, we do participate spiritually in His death, which allows us to "be united with him in a resurrection like his" (Rom. 6:5 NIV). Four distinct characteristics of our resurrection demonstrate how it will be like Christ's:

1. *It will be physical.* Jesus' resurrection was not just a spiritual one. The Lord physically was raised from the dead in such a manner that even His most skeptical disciples were persuaded that He was alive (John 20:24-29; Acts 1:3). We too will be resurrected physically and receive a new body (1 Cor. 15:51-55).

2. *It will be permanent.* Jesus rose from the dead and triumphed over death forever (Matt. 28:18-20; Rev. 1:18). Our resurrection will be permanent also, and we will never die after we are raptured or resurrected (1 Thess. 4:14-17).

3. *It will be glorious.* Jesus' resurrection was glorious as He openly triumphed forever over Satan, death, and darkness (Col. 2:15). Our resurrection will be glorious because we participate in His triumph as His redeemed people (2 Cor. 2:14).

4. *It will be everlasting.* Through His resurrection, Jesus is alive forever and will reign forever and ever throughout all eternity (Luke 1:33; Rev. 11:15). We will

enjoy everlasting life that began at salvation and will be fully realized at our resurrection. We will forever be united with Jesus and all of His saints (Rev. 7:9-17).

In Romans 6:6, Paul describes our former nature as the "old man" that was crucified with Christ. When we accepted Jesus as our Savior, our sinful nature was "crucified" with Him and could no longer control us. Prior to salvation, we were helpless to live righteously and please God. Our old nature held us in its grip of death. At salvation, Jesus broke the hold of our sinful nature and delivered us from sin and death. The dominating sinful nature died with Jesus on the cross, and we received new life in Christ! Jesus redeemed us so that our bodies that were "ruled by sin might be done away with" (NIV). Even though we still are tempted and sometimes struggle, sin no longer controls us. We are free to follow Christ and to serve Him wholeheartedly. We could not do this before we were saved, but now we are free to live as children of God (8:14).

As born-again believers, we no longer "serve sin" (6:6). Instead, we have died to sin and our selfishness. Nevertheless, we are more alive than ever! How is this possible? It is a marvelous paradox. The only way we could be free was to die! We died to sin through faith in Jesus Christ. Through this death, our old nature, the flesh, was crucified with Jesus. Through this process, we were set free from sin and introduced to true liberty that is only available in Christ (v. 7). As Jesus declared, "If the Son therefore shall make you free, ye shall be free indeed" (John 8:36).

---

1. Explain the union mentioned in verse 5.
2. How do "our old man," "the body of sin," and slavery to sin all reflect the same idea (vv. 6-7)?

> "The presence of the flesh is not, however, an excuse for walking in it."—C. I. Scofield

---

B. Alive Unto God (vv. 8-11)

**⁸ Now if we be dead with Christ, we believe that we shall also live with him: ⁹ Knowing that Christ being raised from the dead dieth no more; death hath no more dominion over him. ¹⁰ For in that he died, he died unto sin once: but in that he liveth, he liveth unto God. ¹¹ Likewise reckon ye also yourselves to be dead indeed unto sin, but alive unto God through Jesus Christ our Lord.**

Our death "with Christ" is the foundation to believing that we also will "live with him" (v. 8). This may seem logical to us as contemporary believers, but this would have been a difficult concept for the Christians at Rome to comprehend. They lived in the shadow of the Roman emperor, who controlled most of the known world. The idea that a king would invite his followers to live with him forever contradicted everything they had understood about life. Generally, Christians were poor people who often were oppressed and persecuted. The rulers may have let them live, but they did not invite them into personal relationships or allow them into close proximity. However, Jesus is the King who has a different set of rules. He invites His followers to live with Him and to be in His presence forever! The realization of this truth must have brought abundant joy to the believers at Rome.

Since Jesus was raised from the dead, death does not have any "dominion," or power, over Him (v. 9). Acting under the authority of Rome, Pilate had Jesus crucified at the wishes of the corrupt Jewish religious leaders in Jerusalem. They exercised their "dominion" over Jesus and unlawfully executed Him. Now, Paul proclaims, death no longer has dominion over Christ. The resurrection of Jesus revealed the limitation of earthly powers and unveiled the unlimited power of God. The dominion of Roman government relates to the physical realm, but God's reign extends to all realms—earthly and heavenly. Thus, the Christians at Rome did not need to be fearful of the empire's dominion, for they served the Lord who triumphed over all creation through His resurrection.

Jesus "died to sin once for all" (v. 10 NIV), and He will never die again. Now, He is alive, and "he liveth unto God," indicating that Jesus has risen to His rightful place as God's only Son who is exalted above all. Eventually, all people and all creation will acknowledge the lordship of Jesus Christ (Phil. 2:9-11).

Paul expected the knowledge of Jesus' triumph to encourage and strengthen the Roman believers, because they shared in His victory. In the same manner, the believers can consider themselves dead to sin and alive to God through Jesus Christ (Rom. 6:11). We do not have to wait until our death or until the resurrection to enjoy our life in God. Right now, in this present life, the children of God enjoy the wonderful life in Christ that begins at salvation.

---

1. How have living Christians already "died with Christ" (v. 8 NKJV)?
2. How did Jesus gain dominion over death (vv. 9-10)?
3. How must Christians view themselves (v. 11)?

> "Only as we accept our responsibility and appropriate God's provisions will we make any progress in our pursuit of holiness."—Jerry Bridges

---

II. YIELDED TO GOD (Rom. 6:12-14; 12:1-2)

A. Yielded for Righteousness (6:12-14)

**¹² Let not sin therefore reign in your mortal body, that ye should obey it in the lusts thereof. ¹³ Neither yield ye your members as instruments of unrighteousness unto sin: but yield yourselves unto God, as those that are alive from the dead, and your members as instruments of righteousness unto God. ¹⁴ For sin shall not have dominion over you: for ye are not under the law, but under grace.**

As Christians, we must not allow sin to reclaim its dominion over our lives. At salvation, we were set free from sin. However, sin will return if we do not strive to live for Christ. Sin always seeks to find fertile ground. We must be careful to cultivate a fruit-filled life in the Spirit so sin cannot invade our life again.

Verse 12 indicates we will still be tempted, but we can overcome if we do not allow sin to "reign" in our bodies by succumbing to the lusts we may encounter. After salvation, our "mortal body" is still susceptible to lusts, or "evil desires" (NIV). If unchecked, those enticements will lead to sin (see James 1:14-15).

In verse 13 of the text, Paul expands his warning by cautioning that yielding any part of ourselves for sinful activities can lead to disaster. The Greek word for *yield* means "to put at the service of" (*Vincent's New Testament Word Studies*). We must not think that a little sinful behavior is acceptable. If we think we can control sin, we are deceiving ourselves. Sin always seeks to extend its influence in an effort to totally dominate a person. Instead, we must yield or give ourselves over to God so we can become "instruments of righteousness." Our manner of behavior must reflect our new life in Christ. We are "alive from the dead," and sin should never characterize our lifestyle. Instead, our lives should be characterized by the life of Christ that comes through the power of the Holy Spirit.

Verse 14 declares "sin shall no longer be your master" (NIV). Sinful living is not an option for the children of God. We are no longer "under the law," but we are "under grace." Being under grace frees us to live righteously as believers in Christ and as citizens of the kingdom of God. This is true freedom! We are free to yield ourselves to God so we can live a life pleasing to Him that is characterized by righteous living. We cannot do this through our own abilities or self-righteousness, but only through the transformative work of God in Christ.

---

1. Even if you are a Christian, what will sin try to do (v. 12)?
2. What does God want us to offer Him, and why (v. 13)?
3. How can we overcome sin (v. 14)?

> "Lord, I am no longer my own, but Yours. Put me to what You will, rank me with whom You will. Let me be employed by You or laid aside for You, exalted for You or brought low by You. Let me have all things, let me have nothing, I freely and heartily yield all things to Your pleasure and disposal."—John Wesley

---

B. Yielded for Transformation (12:1-2)

**¹ I beseech you therefore, brethren, by the mercies of God, that ye present your bodies a living sacrifice, holy, acceptable unto God, which is your reasonable service. ² And be not conformed to this world: but be ye transformed by the renewing of your mind, that ye may prove what is that good, and acceptable, and perfect, will of God.**

This passage provides the manner by which believers are dramatically transformed to become the instruments of righteousness described above. This passage is an urgent plea from Paul to the believers at Rome and applies to all Christians in all times. He affirms that his instructions can only be fulfilled through the grace of God and His "mercies." The initial focus is on our "bodies," which are the "temple of God" (see 1 Cor. 6:19-20). The body includes our whole being and is emphasized to preclude any misconceptions that one can be righteous in a spiritual sense while living a sinful lifestyle in the body. As believers, we are to give our bodies as "living sacrifices"—a poignant phrase capturing the freedom of grace that allows us to live "holy" in Christ. Such righteous living is "acceptable" (NIV, "pleasing") to God and is our "reasonable service," which can be translated as "spiritual act of worship" (NIV).

Paul warns the church not to be "conformed" to this world. If they do, they will hinder the powerful transformation God designed for His born-again people. The focus of the transformative work of God is in our "minds" through the "renewing" work of the Holy Spirit. This is the will of God for all His people. Here we have a threefold description of the will of God that He has ordained for Christ's followers: (1) *good*, because its origin is God; (2) *acceptable*, because it is pleasing to God; and (3) *perfect*, because all God does is perfect and cannot be improved.

---

1. Describe the "sacrifice" God calls us to make (v. 1).
2. What is genuine "spiritual worship" (v. 1 RSV)?
3. Why is it so easy to be "conformed to this world" (v. 2)?
4. How can we have a renewed mind, and why do we need it?

> "This is the glory and miracle of grace, that God, through the Holy Spirit, is able to transform a stubborn, rebellious, and unbelieving will into a passionate, obedient, believing will without violating the integrity of the individual or diminishing the voluntary nature of one's decision to trust Christ for salvation."—Sam Storms

---

III. SET FREE BY GRACE (Jude 3-4; Rom. 6:15-23)

A. Free to Contend for the Faith (Jude 3-4)

(Jude 3-4 is not included in the printed text.)

We have been set free by grace, which gives us the freedom and ability to live a righteous life before God. Today, as during the times of the apostles, we face many challenges in fulfilling God's call to live righteously. Before considering verse 3, we will focus on the issues Jude addresses in the next verse. He warned that ungodly people would seek to deceive God's children by "turning the grace of our God into lasciviousness" (v. 4), which refers to unrestrained, lustful behavior. It connotes the idea of loose morals and unrestrained sensuality. According to Jude, when believers depart from the true faith and regress into libertinism, they are denying the Lord Jesus Christ.

To prevent this deterioration in the church, Jude calls for Christians to "earnestly contend for the faith" that was proclaimed by the apostles and embraced by the churches of the Lord Jesus Christ (v. 3). The deception facing the church was so devious that only heartfelt contention would suffice for preserving the faithful. However, through deliberate efforts at preserving the true faith, the church could maintain the teaching of Christ and pass the faith on to future generations. Our own conversion and commitment to Christ are evidence that Jude's words had their desired effect. Now it is up to us to pass on the faith to the generations of believers who will follow us.

---

1. Explain the term "common salvation" (v. 3).
2. What is the "faith" we must fight for, and how can we do it?
3. In Jude's day, how was sound doctrine being undermined (v. 4)?
4. Today, what attacks against the faith are taking place within the church?

> "Press forward. Do not stop, do not linger in your journey, but strive for the mark set before you."—George Whitefield

---

B. Free to Obey God (Rom. 6:15-20)

**15 What then? shall we sin, because we are not under the law, but under grace? God forbid. 16 Know ye not, that to whom ye yield yourselves servants to obey, his servants ye are to whom ye obey; whether of sin unto death, or of obedience unto righteousness? 17 But God be thanked, that ye were the servants of sin, but ye have obeyed from the heart that form of doctrine which was delivered you. 18 Being then made free from sin, ye became the servants of righteousness. 19 I speak after the manner of men because of the infirmity of your flesh: for as ye have yielded your members servants to uncleanness and to iniquity unto iniquity; even so now yield your members servants to righteousness unto holiness. 20 For when ye were the servants of sin, ye were free from righteousness.**

Our freedom as Christians must not lead to sin. The phrase "God forbid" (v. 15) reveals the danger inherit in returning to sin and demonstrates God's displeasure with backsliding. If believers fall back into sin, they are in danger because sin leads to separation from God, as it did for Adam and Eve in the Garden of Eden (Gen. 3).

In Romans 6:16, Paul echoes the position he established in verse 13, but here he includes the concept of servanthood. Those who continue in sin are actually servants of sin. However, those who are God's servants will be servants of "obedience unto righteousness," and their service flows from the freedom of grace.

In verse 17, Paul gives thanks because the believers at Rome had obeyed God from their "heart," indicating there were many faithful believers in the church. Next, the apostle validates the importance of being faithful to the doctrine that was "delivered" to the church. The Christ-followers at Rome were obedient to God because Jesus set them free from sin (v. 18). Since salvation, their obedience made them servants of righteousness that leads to "holiness" (v. 19), which comes through the sanctifying work of God by the Holy Spirit (15:16).

Prior to their salvation and deliverance from sin, Christians were servants of sin and were "free from righteousness" (v. 20). This phrase does not indicate they had an enjoyable freedom prior to salvation. Instead, this phrase presents a tragic description of the believers' prior state when they were enslaved to sin and were not concerned about righteousness. Thankfully, their status dramatically changed at salvation.

---

1. What decision does every individual have to make (v. 16)?
2. Contrast slavery to sin with slavery to righteousness (vv. 17-20).

> "The call of God to salvation requires separation from sin. This separation begins with justification (new birth) and continues in sanctification throughout the life of the believer."—French L. Arrington

---

C. Free to Bear Fruit (vv. 21-23)

**21 What fruit had ye then in those things whereof ye are now ashamed? for the end of those things is death. 22 But now being made free from sin, and become servants to God, ye have your fruit unto holiness, and the end everlasting life. 23 For the wages of sin is death; but the gift of God is eternal life through Jesus Christ our Lord.**

Verse 21 presents a vivid reminder of the Roman believers' past lifestyle. Paul reminds them that they were unrighteous and are now "ashamed" of their sinful past, which would have led to death had they not received Christ. Many of us can identify with this statement, due to the sins of our past. However, we can rejoice that Christ set us free, and we are now God's servants (v. 22)! As John Murray notes, "Bondservice to God . . . must exemplify itself in obedience to the concrete and practical demands of righteousness" (*The Epistle of Romans*).

Since salvation, we can bear the good fruit that reflects "holiness" (v. 22). This fruit will result in "everlasting life," starkly contrasting with the fruit of verse 21, which leads to death. This is the good fruit that comes from righteous living through faith in Christ. Perhaps the best brief description of such fruit is found in Galatians 5:22-23: "The fruit of the Spirit is love, joy, peace, longsuffering, gentleness, goodness, faith, meekness, temperance: against such there is no law."

Our study concludes with a well-known verse that compares the final outcome of a life of sin with the wonderful blessing that awaits all God's faithful people (Rom. 6:23). *Wages* comes from the Greek word *opsōnion*, which was used in ancient time to describe a soldier's pay. This imagery indicates sin is a hard master that provides a harsh final payday: *death*. This death ultimately results in eternal separation from God and enduring torment.

In contrast, the final status of the servants of God is declared to be a "gift" from God: "eternal life through Jesus Christ our Lord." We cannot earn this gift, nor do we merit this marvelous blessing. The gift is "eternal" and will never end nor diminish throughout future eons. Christians will live forever in the presence of the gift's source: the Lord Jesus Christ.

The use of the inclusive *our* ("Christ our Lord") leaves us with two revealing thoughts. First, our faith is not some abstract religion in which God is far removed from His people. We have a personal relationship with God through faith in Jesus Christ. Our Lord promised to always be with us until He returns for His people (Matt. 18:20; 28:20). Second, we belong to a vast host that includes all those who have believed in God throughout history! One day we will join with them to enjoy eternal life forever (Heb. 12:1-2; Rev. 21:1-7)!

---

1. Answer the question in verse 21.
2. Describe the "fruit" of serving God (v. 22).
3. What is earned by our actions, and what cannot be earned (v. 23)?

> "God dispenses gifts, not wages. None of us gets paid according to merit, for none of us comes close to satisfying God's requirements for a perfect life. If paid on the basis of fairness, we would all end up in hell."—Philip Yancey

---

## CONCLUSION

"*Dead, Yielded,* and *Free*" describe the process by which God liberated us from sin and enabled us to live righteously before Him. We are *dead* because we died to sin when we accepted Jesus as our Lord and Savior. We are *yielded* when we submit ourselves to God as servants of righteousness in obedience to Christ. We are *free* through the grace of God and faith in Christ so we can bear the good fruit of righteousness that leads to everlasting life. All of these blessings are the wonderful gift of God through His Son, Jesus.

## GOLDEN TEXT CHALLENGE

"RECKON YE ALSO YOURSELVES TO BE DEAD INDEED UNTO SIN, BUT ALIVE UNTO GOD THROUGH JESUS CHRIST OUR LORD" (Rom. 6:11).

*Sin* contains three letters:
- *S* stands for *serpent*, who brought sin into the world.
- *I* is for my sinful human nature. *I* am my own worst enemy.
- *N* stands for *nothing*, for sin is emptiness.

The only safe thing to do with this heart-center of sin in my life, the *I*, is to put it to death; let it be crucified with Christ, so that it is no longer "I" that lives, but Christ lives in me (Gal. 2:20). Not until that miracle is wrought—the death of self—am I safe from sin.

**Daily Devotions:**
- M. Follow Paths of Righteousness
   Psalm 23:1-6
- T. Repent and Live
   Ezekiel 18:24-32
- W. Spirit-Empowered Living
   Ezekiel 36:22-27
- T. The Son Sets Free
   John 8:31-36
- F. Stand Fast in Freedom
   Galatians 5:1-6, 13
- S. Live as Servants of God
   1 Peter 2:11-17

January 11, 2015 (Lesson 6)
# What Does God's Grace Promise?

**Romans 4:13-25; Galatians 3:10 through 4:7**

**Unit Theme:**
Law and Grace in the New Testament

**Central Truth:**
Followers of Christ share in His inheritance.

**Focus:**
Affirm that grace makes us God's heirs and receive our inheritance by faith.

**Context:**
The Holy Spirit inspires the apostle Paul with deep insights on God's grace.

**Golden Text:**
"Wherefore thou art no more a servant, but a son; and if a son, then an heir of God through Christ" (Gal. 4:7).

**Study Outline:**
I. The Law and the Promise
   (Gal. 3:10-25)
II. Heirs of God Through Christ
   (Gal. 3:26—4:7)
III. The Promise Is Received by Faith
   (Rom. 4:13-25)

## INTRODUCTION

Recent studies by the Barna group and other researchers indicate that the forces of secularism, postmodernism, and pluralism are contributing to a continuing decline in church membership and attendance. Some people think the church is no longer relevant or necessary. Over 70 percent of the Millennial Generation—those born between 1980 and 1990—think American churches are irrelevant, and 65 percent of this group rarely or never attends church (Rainer and Rainer). One way the church can relate to this younger generation is to make sure the message of grace is communicated to them. The grace of the Lord Jesus Christ is always relevant!

The term *grace* refers to those gifts and blessings God gives to us. We could never earn grace, and we certainly do not merit any blessings from God. *Grace* is an umbrella term under which we can place all God gives us through His Son. The greatest promise of grace is salvation through faith in the Lord Jesus Christ. Through God's grace, we can enjoy the peace of God, fellowship with Christ, and the joy of the Holy Spirit.

God has given us many promises throughout the Bible. Every promise is given to us through His grace. Every time we quote a scripture with promise or we praise God for answering prayers, we are giving witness to the Lord's abundant grace. As John Newton stated in "Amazing Grace":

> Through many dangers, toils and snares,
> I have already come;
> 'Tis grace that brought me safe thus far,
> And grace will lead me home.

As believers in Christ, we have received the promise of God's grace that will lead us through this life into the everlasting presence of the Lord. We are not under the curse of the Law, because we enjoy the promise of grace!

## I. THE LAW AND THE PROMISE (Gal. 3:10-25)

### A. The Curse of the Law (vv. 10-14)

(Galatians 3:10-12 is not included in the printed text.)

**¹³ Christ hath redeemed us from the curse of the law, being made a curse for us: for it is written, Cursed is every one that hangeth on a tree: ¹⁴ That the blessing of Abraham might come on the Gentiles through Jesus Christ; that we might receive the promise of the Spirit through faith.**

Think about how grace has affected your life. Do you remember how your life was before you accepted Jesus as Savior? Do you remember the transformation that occurred when Christ came into your life? During your Christian journey, have there been times when you were especially aware of God's grace for you or your family? As you reflect on how grace has permeated your life, you may want to consider sharing with others a personal story or testimony of God's grace. Now, let us consider Paul's letter to the church at Galatia to gain more insights into the relationship between the Law and the promise of God's grace.

In Galatians 3:10-18, the apostle Paul expounds on the curse that came through the Law. The Law provided a complex set of requirements for living righteously. The *curse* refers to the requirement that if one lived by the Law, then he or she also must obey every part of the Law. If one failed to fulfill any aspect of the Law, then that person was "under the curse" (v. 10). This means no one has ever been "justified by the law in the sight of God" (v. 11).

In the eyes of other people, a person may appear justified through the Law. Jesus often confronted the Pharisees with their self-righteousness and inconsistencies in obeying the Law. The Pharisees sought to be justified through their obedience of the Law. Thus, their commitment to the Law placed them under its curse because they could not fulfill its every requirement.

Justification only comes by grace through faith in Christ. As Paul contends, "The just shall live by faith" (v. 11). This cannot be accomplished through the Law, which is "not of faith" (v. 12). If one seeks justification through the Law, that person will live under its curse rather than in grace. Jesus Christ redeemed us from the Law's curse by providing grace through His vicarious death on the cross (v. 13). This gracious act of Jesus liberates us from the need to fulfill the requirements of the Law, because we are saved by grace when we accept Jesus as Savior.

Through grace, all of Christ's followers have received the same blessing Abraham received: "the promise of the Spirit through faith" (v. 14). In verse 13, the curse of the Law is revealed in Christ's crucifixion. In verse 14, the blessing of grace is revealed through Christ Jesus' atoning work on the cross. The Cross is the transformational event when the curse of the Law was eradicated by the blessing of God's grace through His Son's sacrifice for the world and the giving of His redeeming promise (John 3:16). The content of God's promise is "nothing less than the gift of the Spirit, the distinguishing mark of the child of God" (Alan Cole, *The Epistle of Paul to the Galatians*).

---

1. Who is living under a curse (v. 10)?
2. How is a person justified in the sight of God (v. 11)?
3. What has Christ "become . . . for us," and why (v. 13 NKJV)?

> "Behold, what manner of love is this, that Christ should be arraigned and we adorned, that the curse should be laid on His head and the crown set on ours."—Thomas Watson

---

B. The Blessing of Abraham (vv. 15-18)

(Galatians 3:15, 17-18 is not included in the printed text.)

**¹⁶ Now to Abraham and his seed were the promises made. He saith not, And to seeds, as of many; but as of one, And to thy seed, which is Christ.**

To strengthen his argument, Paul draws from "the manner of men," which can be translated as taking "an example from everyday life" (v. 15 NIV). The example here is the binding nature of human covenants or contracts. A legally established covenant cannot be altered through any means, including rejection of the terms or by altering the contents. Verse 16 asserts this is exactly the case concerning God's covenant with His people. God established His covenant with Abraham and his "seed." The promise was to only one "seed," who is Christ. Paul drives home his point by declaring that God's promise to Abraham was given 430 years prior to the introduction of the Law (v. 17). Thus, the Law could not "disannul," or negate, the previous covenant of promise God established with Abraham.

Verse 18 refers to the *inheritance* that came through God's promise to Abraham. This "promised possession" not only included the land promised to Abraham, but especially extended to "the expression of God's favor and blessing" (Ernest De Witt Burton, *A Critical and Exegetical Commentary on the Epistle to the Galatians*). This inheritance is the promise of God passed on to all of God's people through Jesus Christ. This covenant can never be violated or annulled, and the promise cannot be attained by adhering to the Law. It is only available by God's grace through faith in Christ.

---

1. What is Christ called in verse 16, and why?
2. How did the giving of the Law affect God's promise to Abraham (vv. 17-18)?

> "There is no more blessed way of living, than the life of faith based upon a covenant-keeping God—to know that we have no care, for He cares for us; that we need have no fear, except to fear Him; that we need have no troubles, because we have cast our burdens upon the Lord, and are conscious that He will sustain us."—Charles Spurgeon

---

C. The Promise of Faith (vv. 19-25)

**19 Wherefore then serveth the law? It was added because of transgressions, till the seed should come to whom the promise was made; and it was ordained by angels in the hand of a mediator. 20 Now a mediator is not a mediator of one, but God is one. 21 Is the law then against the promises of God? God forbid: for if there had been a law given which could have given life, verily righteousness should have been by the law. 22 But the scripture hath concluded all under sin, that the promise by faith of Jesus Christ might be given to them that believe. 23 But before faith came, we were kept under the law, shut up unto the faith which should afterwards be revealed. 24 Wherefore the law was our schoolmaster to bring us unto Christ, that we might be justified by faith. 25 But after that faith is come, we are no longer under a schoolmaster.**

If we can only receive the promise through faith in Christ, then what purpose does the Law serve? The Law was given because of "transgressions," or the sinfulness, of people (v. 19). The Law acted to restrain sin and reveal its consequences. The Law served a necessary purpose until the "seed," or Jesus, came into the world. Paul's reference to angels indicates they were involved in transmitting the content of the Law (see Acts 7:53; Heb. 2:2).

Verses 19 and 20 of the text recognize that Moses was the mediator for the Law, which indicates the Law was inferior to the promise. However, God gave the promise directly to Abraham without the assistance of a mediator, establishing His promise forever.

To clarify the relationship between the Law and the promise, Paul asserts there is not a conflict between the two. Instead, the Law simply could not provide "life" or "righteousness" (v. 21). Both the Law and the promise are equally from God and should be valued while recognizing the limitations of the Law. However, the promise of God is not limited in providing abundant life and righteousness (John 10:10; Rom. 3:22). According to God's Word, "the whole world is a prisoner of sin" (Gal. 3:22 NIV). However, those who believe in Jesus Christ through faith have received the promise of grace and are no longer under the condemnation of sin (Rom. 6:23).

Prior to salvation, we were all enslaved to sin and under its curse until the faith that comes through Christ should be revealed (Gal. 3:23). The Law served as our "schoolmaster" to teach us we were in need of Christ for justification through faith (v. 24). Since we have faith in Christ, we are no longer under the "supervision of the law" (v. 25 NIV). Now we are under grace and recipients of God's promise!

1. What was the purpose of the Law (v. 19)?
2. How were we imprisoned, and how can we be freed (vv. 22-23)?
3. What is called our "tutor," and why (vv. 24-25 NKJV)?

> "God gave the Law originally as a railroad track to guide Israel's obedience. The engine that was supposed to pull a person along the track was God's grace, the power of the Spirit. And the coupling between our car and the engine was faith, so that in the Old Testament, like the New Testament, salvation was by grace, through faith, along the track of obedience (or sanctification)."—John Piper

---

II. HEIRS OF GOD THROUGH CHRIST (Gal. 3:26—4:7)

A. Heirs by Baptism (3:26-29)

(Galatians 3:27-28 is not included in the printed text.)

**²⁶ For ye are all the children of God by faith in Christ Jesus.**

**²⁹ And if ye be Christ's, then are ye Abraham's seed, and heirs according to the promise.**

As recipients of the promise of God, we have become God's children by believing in Jesus (v. 26). We have been "baptized into Christ," which refers to our acceptance of Christ through faith as Lord and Savior, and we "have put on," or "been clothed," with Christ (v. 27). This twofold emphasis on spiritual baptism and being clothed indicates the security and sufficiency of Christ for our justification.

All believers are "clothed" equally in Christ and there are no distinctions spiritually in our status before the Lord. The promise of God removes all religious, social, and gender barriers so that all are equal in Christ: "There is neither Jew nor Greek, slave nor free, male nor female, for you are all one in Christ Jesus" (v. 28 NIV). Verse 29 then declares if we belong to Christ, we are also Abraham's "seed" and share in the inheritance of God's promise through Abraham. The promise made to Abraham is our promise!

---

1. What does it mean to "put on Christ" (v. 27)?
2. Describe the equality shown in verses 28 and 29.

> "My worth is what I am worth to God; and that is a marvelous great deal, for Christ died for me. Thus, incidentally, what gives to each of us His highest worth gives the same worth to everyone; in all that matters most are we equal."—William Temple

---

B. Heirs Through Adoption (4:1-7)

(Galatians 4:1-3 is not included in the printed text.)

**⁴But when the fulness of the time was come, God sent forth his Son, made of a woman, made under the law, ⁵To redeem them that were under the law, that we might receive the adoption of sons. ⁶And because ye are sons, God hath sent forth the Spirit of his Son into your hearts, crying, Abba, Father. ⁷Wherefore thou art no more a servant, but a son; and if a son, then an heir of God through Christ.**

The apostle Paul compares an heir with a servant by observing that as long as the heir is a child, he or she is not really free, but is dependent on others for their care and instruction (vv. 1-2). This dependency continues until the parent determines the child is ready to assume the role of an heir. In similar fashion, when we were "children," or were not yet believers, we were enslaved to "the basic principles of the world," which were contrary to the promise (v. 3 NIV). However, in God's appointed time, He sent His Son Jesus into the world to redeem us from the curse of the Law (v. 4), so through faith in Him we could have the "full rights" (NIV) as God's adopted children (v. 5).

Upon our adoption into the family of God, He poured forth His Spirit into our hearts. The indwelling Spirit "calls out, 'Abba, Father'" (v. 6 NIV). This declaration by the Holy Spirit announces we are no longer servants, but we are now fully heirs of God through the work of Christ (v. 7). God has adopted us into His family, and we now enjoy the promise fully as His children and heirs. As Romans 8:15 declares, "For you did not receive a spirit that makes you a slave again to fear, but you received the Spirit of sonship. And by him we cry, 'Abba, Father'" (NIV).

---

1. When does a child become an heir (vv. 1-3)?
2. How is Jesus Christ described in verse 4?
3. What did Christ accomplish for us (v. 5)?
4. How do you know you have transitioned from slave to son (vv. 6-7)?

> "A man adopts one for his son and heir that does not at all resemble him; but whosoever God adopts for His child is like Him; he not only bears his heavenly Father's name, but His image (Col. 3:10)."
> —Thomas Watson

---

## III. THE PROMISE IS RECEIVED BY FAITH (Rom. 4:13-25)

### A. Promise Given Through Grace (vv. 13-16)

**¹³For the promise, that he should be the heir of the world, was not to Abraham, or to his seed, through the law, but through the righteousness of faith. ¹⁴For if they which are of the law be heirs, faith is made void, and the promise made of none effect: ¹⁵Because the law worketh wrath: for where no law is, there is no transgression. ¹⁶Therefore it is of faith, that it might be by grace; to the end the promise might be sure to all the seed; not to that only which is of the law, but to that also which is of the faith of Abraham; who is the father of us all.**

In Romans 4 we find a wonderful discussion regarding the faith of Abraham in relation to the salvation of all believers. The promise Abraham received did not come through the Law or through righteousness that could be attained by keeping the Law. Instead, the promise delivered to Abraham as God's heir came through "the righteousness of faith" (v. 13). It is impossible to become heirs of God's promise through the Law. If this were possible, then our "faith has no value and the promise is worthless" (v. 14 NIV). However, we know our faith is invaluable: "to those who through the righteousness of our God and Savior Jesus Christ have received a faith as precious as ours" (2 Peter 1:1 NIV).

Trusting in the Law and our own righteousness leads to the "wrath" of God, because it is a rejection of His promise in Christ Jesus. By trusting in God's grace through faith in Christ, we escape from "wrath," because God forgives our transgressions (Rom. 4:15). Verse 16 declares the promise of God came through faith, so it is by grace alone. The reason is so the promise "may be guaranteed to all Abraham's offspring" (NIV), which includes all who "are of the faith of Abraham." Paul clearly is including Gentile believers in the offspring of Abraham. Abraham is first a *father of faith*, and all who have faith as Abraham's are his heirs. Abraham's relationship with God was not based on his status, connections, or position; it was based on his trust in God. We should remember that "between the time of Abraham and Christ, God has not changed His way of saving" people and bringing them "into a right relationship with Himself" (French L. Arrington, *The Greatest Letter Ever Written*).

---

1. Explain the term "the righteousness of faith" (v. 13).
2. What does the Law produce, and why (vv. 14-15)?
3. Describe the Christian's relationship with Abraham (v. 16).

---

"True faith rests upon the character of God and asks no further proof than the moral perfections of the One who cannot lie. It is enough that God has said it."—A. W. Tozer

---

B. Promise Received by Faith (vv. 17-25)

(Romans 4:17-22 is not included in the printed text.)

**23 Now it was not written for his sake alone, that it was imputed to him; 24 But for us also, to whom it shall be imputed, if we believe on him that raised up Jesus our Lord from the dead; 25 Who was delivered for our offences, and was raised again for our justification.**

Abraham had great faith in God, who "gives life to the dead and calls things that are not as though they were" (v. 17 NIV). Here God is described as "both the Creator and Life-Giver," because He created life in the beginning, and at the end of the age He will bestow everlasting life on all who trust in Christ (French Arrington). In the following verses, Paul provides a detailed description of Abraham's faith regarding God's promise. We should all seek to follow Abraham's example and have faith that is filled with hope (v. 18), does not weaken over time (v. 19), refuses to "waver" (v. 20 NIV), and is "fully persuaded" that God can and will fulfill His promise (v. 21). Due to Abraham's unwavering faith, it was "imputed" to him as righteousness (v. 22). The Greek word for *imputed* means "to credit to one's account" (*Vine's Expository Dictionary of Old and New Testament Words*).

For Abraham and all believers, righteousness only comes by faith through the grace of the Lord Jesus Christ. Verse 24 leaves no doubt as to who has been credited with righteousness: those "who believe in him who raised Jesus our Lord from the dead" (NIV). The promise of grace must be received by heartfelt faith in the Lord Jesus. No other religion or god can provide salvation. As Acts 4:12 states, "Salvation is found in no one else, for there is no other name under heaven given to mankind by which we must be saved" (NIV).

Paul concludes this passage in Romans 4 by reminding the readers that Jesus died because of our "offences"—our sins or transgressions—and He was resurrected for our justification (v. 25). This verse probably was part of a doctrinal confession of the early church that they recited to declare this crucial belief. This confessional declaration "unites the death and the resurrection of our Lord and sees the two events, though separated by two days, as an inseparable action of God in providing salvation for us" (Arrington). We needed justification due to our "offences," and the Lord's resurrection provided the foundation for our justification and salvation (John Murray, *The Epistle of Romans*). Salvation through faith in the Lord Jesus Christ is the ultimate promise of grace! What better promise could we possibly receive?

---

1. How does verse 17 describe God's power?
2. What did Abraham's faith in God accomplish (vv. 18-22)?
3. Who receives the righteousness of God (vv. 23-24)?
4. How does verse 25 summarize the ministry of Jesus?

---

### The Tune of Grace

Grace comes free of charge to people who do not deserve it, and I am one of those people. I think back to who I was—resentful, wound tight with anger, a single hardened link in a long chain of ungrace learned from family and church. Now I am trying in my own small way to pipe the tune of grace. I do so because I know, more surely than I know anything, that any pang of healing or forgiveness or goodness I have ever felt comes solely from the grace of God. I yearn for the church to become a nourishing culture of that grace.—Philip Yancey, *What's So Amazing About Grace?*

---

### CONCLUSION

We began today's lesson with a question: What does God's grace promise? To explore the answer to this question, we focused on the faith of Abraham and God's promise to him. Thankfully, everyone who is born again through faith in Christ is an heir to the promise God gave to Abraham. We have inherited the promise of everlasting faith that belongs to all of God's children throughout the ages. We should testify of our salvation to those who do not know Christ, and pass on the gospel of grace to the next generation, so we can all share in the joys of the promise of God forever!

## GOLDEN TEXT CHALLENGE

"WHEREFORE THOU ART NO MORE A SERVANT, BUT A SON; AND IF A SON, THEN AN HEIR OF GOD THROUGH CHRIST" (Gal. 4:7).

The gospel brings sonship; law inflicts bondage. The sonship of the new order involves liberty and heirship. Consider some of the privileges this implied.

The slave is ordered to do this or that without his master condescending to tell him the reason for his mandates. He is bound to a blind, implicit obedience. Nothing is done to develop his understanding and to help him to decide on his own judgment. But the son is admitted to his father's counsels, and educated so as to reason for himself and to act on the dictates of his own conscience.

The slave may hate his master and only obey in fear of the lash. The true son is above this abject, servile obedience. He has learned to love his father and, from love, to seek to anticipate his father's wishes and willingly endeavor to please him. The law commands, threatens, drives, compels. The gospel persuades and attracts. The Christian obeys God because he or she first loves God. The secret is that law cannot change our hearts, while the gospel does create a new heart within us, so that we no longer need the restraints of law, but earnestly desire to please God.

The slave is kept at a distance from his master, holds an inferior position, and is excluded from fellowship. The son lives at home in the presence of his father and enjoys close companionship with him. Law keeps us at a distance from God. Christians are brought near through Christ and belong to the family of God.

The slave can own nothing. All he earns and his very person are the property of his master. Sons are heirs. Law allows us to gain nothing—it is a hard master; but the gospel offers the richest gifts. Christians, being God's sons, become fellow heirs with Christ.—**W. F. Adeney**

## Daily Devotions:

- M. God's Promise Believed
  Genesis 15:1-6
- T. Promised Child the Heir
  Genesis 21:3-12
- W. God Delights in Mercy
  Micah 7:18-20
- T. Children of Promise
  Galatians 4:21-31
- F. Faith and Patience Rewarded
  Hebrews 6:10-20
- S. Results of Faith
  Hebrews 11:8-12

January 18, 2015 (Lesson 7)
# Hold Human Life Sacred

Genesis 9:5-6; Exodus 20:13; Leviticus 19:16; 20:1-3, 9-10, 22-24, 26; Numbers 35:29-34; Deuteronomy 19:1-13; 21:1-9

**Unit Theme:**
God's Moral Law (Genesis-Deuteronomy)

**Central Truth:**
Christians' words and actions should affirm the sacredness of human life.

**Focus:**
Affirm and respect the sacredness of human life.

**Context:**
Scripture passages from the Pentateuch show God has also deeply valued human life.

**Golden Text:**
"Whoso sheddeth man's blood, by man shall his blood be shed: for in the image of God made he man" (Gen. 9:6).

**Study Outline:**
I. Do Not Murder
   (Gen. 9:5-6; Ex. 20:13; Lev. 19:16)
II. Protect the Innocent
   (Deut. 19:1-10; 21:1-9)
III. Promote Righteousness
   (Lev. 20:1-3, 9-10, 22-24, 26; Num. 35:29-34; Deut. 19:11-13)

## INTRODUCTION

It is difficult to translate a sense of the sacredness of the Torah from the ancient Jewish community into our modern world today. *Torah* is a Hebrew word representing what is often referred to as the Pentateuch, the first five books of the Old Testament. Our English Bibles translate the Hebrew word *Torah* as *Law*. Even this poses problems; for when we think of "law," we often imagine cold legalism and needless rules. For the ancient Jews, however, the Torah represented the definitive revelation of God at that moment in time. For them, Torah was eternally relevant. In ancient sources such as the Bavli, which preserve the sayings of the rabbis, we find rabbinic teachings such as these:
- "Torah study is superior to the saving of life."
- "Torah study is superior to building the Temple."
- "Torah study is superior to the honor of father and mother."

How can we make sense of such an elevation of the Torah? In some places, the rabbis even speak of the Torah using erotic language, as if the Torah is their first love, even their spouse. One ancient Jewish sermon quotes God as saying, "Would that they would forsake Me, but obey My Torah."

Ancient Jews so cherished the Torah because it was a document detailing the profound liberation of God. The Torah was not given as the means of liberation, but as the way of life for a liberated people. By this we mean that God did not give the Jewish people the Torah in Egypt as if to say, "Follow these laws and you will find liberation." God first redeemed His people from Egypt, and then gave them the Torah to keep them living liberated lives. Torah was meant to be an explosively life-giving reality from the start.

This is why the Torah places such a high value on all human life. Its context is liberating a people thought to be worthless slaves by the reigning Egyptian empire. God's moral law springs from this context of oppression and seeks to create a people who will embody His life and value system.

I. DO NOT MURDER (Gen. 9:5-6; Ex. 20:13; Lev. 19:16)

One of the most widely recognized commandments in all the Bible is this: "Do not murder." Many people, however, do not recognize the depth of this prohibition. It was not only planted in the Ten Commandments, but exists at key turning points of the Torah. It is to these turning points that we now give our attention.

A. The Noahic Covenant (Gen. 9:5-6)

**⁵ And surely your blood of your lives will I require; at the hand of every beast will I require it, and at the hand of man; at the hand of every man's brother will I require the life of man. ⁶ Whoso sheddeth man's blood, by man shall his blood be shed: for in the image of God made he man.**

Of all the covenants in the Bible, the one commonly called the "Noahic covenant" remains the least known. We know of the covenant of Abraham in Genesis 12; the Mosaic covenant, which describes the Torah as a whole; the Davidic covenant, which God declares in 2 Samuel 7; and finally the new covenant, which Jesus introduces at the Last Supper. But before these stood God's covenant with Noah.

The Noahic covenant is unique in the Scriptures because it marks the beginning of a literally new humanity. It begins with a blessing over Noah's family and the promise that they will repopulate the earth and will rule over it for the provision of food. Nonetheless, there are limits to man's rule.

God has decided He will no longer stand for unnecessary violence in His created order. This prohibition even extends to the animal world. Why such strong language? Because the fallout from Adam and Eve's sin had been extreme violence. Cain ruthlessly killed his brother, Abel (Gen. 4), leading to a world that was "corrupt in God's sight and was full of violence" (6:11 NIV). God's only hope of a new world is to stop such violence before it could break out again.

The most horrific form of violence in God's sight is murder. Here, the text inserts a poetic verse, probably very ancient: "Whoever sheds man's blood, by man his blood shall be shed, for in the image of God He made man" (9:6 NASB).

The covenant with Noah and his bloodline stretches back to the Creation story, seeking to reestablish a world in which people understand one another as created in God's own image (1:27).

- Why is murder so offensive to God?

> "When you murder a human, you attack God, who makes every human in His image."—John Piper

---

B. The Mosaic Covenant (Ex. 20:13)
**¹³ Thou shalt not kill.**

The centerpiece of the Mosaic covenant is the Ten Commandments. This covenant commonly bears Moses' name because it was he who ascended Mount Sinai to receive the legislation of this covenant directly from God. Although the laws of God are explained more fully throughout the covenant, they revolve around the sacred Ten Commandments.

It is important to remember the historical context of the Ten Commandments. They are not ethics or philosophy disconnected from the real situation that gave them birth. Instead, they are rooted in Israel's experience of oppression in Egypt. This is the power of the commandments to observe the Sabbath, to refuse idolatrous images, to refuse to steal. This is exactly the opposite of the way life had worked for dozens of generations of Jews in Egypt!

Violence begets violence. The Jews had endured centuries of brutal violence at the hands of the Egyptians. God fears that when they are given their own nation-status, they will replicate the violence they have seen. So He lays down a hard-and-fast rule: "Thou shalt not kill" (v. 13). So simple, so stark, leaving no room for questioning. The people of Israel are to fulfill the covenant of Noah, avoiding murder at all costs. Martin Luther King Jr., a champion of this ethic of nonviolence, extended it, as Jesus did, even to enemies: "For through violence you may murder a murderer, but you can't murder *murder*. Through violence you may murder a liar, but you can't establish truth. Through violence you may murder a hater, but you can't murder hate through violence. Darkness cannot put out darkness; only light can do that."

Of course, Dr. King received this line of thinking from Jesus, who perfectly fulfilled this spirit of this great commandment by taking it further: "But I tell you: Love your enemies and pray for those who persecute you" (Matt. 5:44 NIV).

---

> "Nothing good ever comes of violence."—Martin Luther

---

C. The Priestly Covenant (Lev. 19:16)
**¹⁶ Thou shalt not go up and down as a talebearer among thy people: neither shalt thou stand against the blood of thy neighbour; I am the Lord.**

The Book of Leviticus represents a priestly covenant between God and the people of Israel. The most popular viewpoint on the authorship of the Torah is that four communities of Jews shared its origins. One of these communities was the priestly class, who produced Leviticus. Many of these priestly laws take the Ten Commandments and expand on them. In Leviticus 19, this priestly source recasts the Ten Commandments from a priestly viewpoint.

The Ten Commandments here are given in a different order and often expanded upon. For example, the command to honor one's father and mother appears first (v. 3), while the command to honor the Sabbath is placed toward the back of the list (v. 30). There are commandments suited to the world of the priests, such as the proper method of animal sacrifice (vv. 5-8). These commandments are brought together, however, by their rootedness in the character of God as "holy" (v. 2). This is the soil from which all of these commandments flow. The commandment against murder, in this list (v. 16), is heightened from its appearance in the Noahic and Mosaic covenants.

The commandment here is not simply to refuse to murder, but to refuse to endanger the life of the neighbor in any way. We see, then, in the covenants in the Old Testament, a remarkable value of the sacredness of human life.

---

- Describe two actions we must guard against.

### Not a Trivial Matter

In his book *From the Maccabees to the Mishnah*, Shaye Cohen tells the story of Caesar Augustus' smart policies toward the Jews during the days surrounding the birth of Jesus. Seeking to gain their favor, he decreed that any Roman who improperly touched a Torah scroll would be penalized. A Roman soldier subsequently desecrated a scroll, and in order to calm the disorder, Augustus had him beheaded. To the ancient Jews, the Torah was nothing to be played with.

---

## II. PROTECT THE INNOCENT (Deut. 19:1-10; 21:1-9)

"Am I my brother's keeper?" Cain asked God in reference to his brother, Abel, in Genesis 4:9. It is a profound question when it is taken from its murderous context. To what degree do I bear responsibility for my neighbor? Is obedience to the commandment not to murder worth anything apart from its opposite—the lifestyle of loving one's neighbor? The Book of Deuteronomy answers these questions.

### A. Cities of Refuge (19:1-10)

(Deuteronomy 19:4-9 is not included in the printed text.)

**1 When the Lord thy God hath cut off the nations, whose land the Lord thy God giveth thee, and thou succeedest them, and dwellest in their cities, and in their houses; 2 Thou shalt separate three cities for thee in the midst of thy land, which the Lord thy God giveth thee to possess it. 3 Thou shalt prepare thee a way, and divide the coasts of thy land, which the Lord thy God giveth thee to inherit, into three parts, that every slayer may flee thither.**

**10 That innocent blood be not shed in thy land, which the Lord thy God giveth thee for an inheritance, and so blood be upon thee.**

Deuteronomy is a single, final speech of Moses that he delivers to the children of Israel before his death. The nation is on the verge of taking the Promised

Land. It will not be long before they are a genuine nation. Much of Deuteronomy is concerned with the details of what that nation will look like. Moses has limited time to deliver this speech. And, in a non-literary society, only very important things get written down. It is fascinating, therefore, that Moses takes considerable time to set up institutions and laws that will protect the innocent.

One of these institutions is the "cities of refuge." They were original creations from the mind of God. Nothing else like them exists in all of ancient history. In Numbers 35:6, the Lord told Moses to set aside six cities as places "to which a person who has killed someone may flee" (NIV). In Deuteronomy 19:2, Moses commands the designation of three such places—apparently referring to the three to be established west of the Jordan River (see Josh. 20:7). The other three were set up east of the Jordan (v. 8). All were to be easy to reach.

In verses 4-7 of our lesson text, we discover that the cities of refuge were meant to protect those who had accidentally killed a fellow Israelite. We can imagine this was not terribly uncommon in ancient agrarian societies, where hard manual labor with heavy tools was necessary for every facet of life. Moses gives an example in verse 5—an ax head that flies off the handle and strikes a bystander. In order for such an accidental murder to be forgiven, cities of refuge were constructed.

What is God's overall purpose in demanding cities of refuge? "So innocent blood will not be shed . . . and bloodguiltiness be on you" (v. 10 NASB).

God's desire that the value of life be preserved among His people is so strong that He demands places of refuge in a start-up nation. Interestingly, there were no prisons constructed in the Promised Land. The money we use to build prisons, they could use for the cities of refuge.

---

1. Explain the roadwork God ordered (vv. 2-3).
2. Who were the cities of refuge designed to protect (vv. 4-6)?
3. What was God's underlying concern in establishing these cities (v. 10)?

---

"Where does your security lie? Is God your refuge, your hiding place, your stronghold, your shepherd, your counselor, your friend, your redeemer, your savior, your guide? If He is, you don't need to search any further for security."—Elisabeth Elliot

---

B. Unsolved Murders (21:1-9)

(Deuteronomy 21:1-4 is not included in the printed text.)
**⁵ And the priests the sons of Levi shall come near; for them the Lord thy God hath chosen to minister unto him, and to bless in the name of the Lord; and by their word shall every controversy and every stroke be tried: ⁶ And all the elders of that city, that are next unto the slain man, shall wash their hands over the heifer that is beheaded in the valley: ⁷ And they shall answer and say, Our hands have not shed this blood, neither have our**

eyes seen it. ⁸ Be merciful, O Lord, unto thy people Israel, whom thou hast redeemed, and lay not innocent blood unto thy people of Israel's charge. And the blood shall be forgiven them. ⁹ So shalt thou put away the guilt of innocent blood from among you, when thou shalt do that which is right in the sight of the Lord.

Every society has its forgotten members. To be forgotten places a person at the bottom of the social ladder. These are precisely the sorts of people for whom God has special concern: "He defends the cause of the fatherless and the widow, and loves the alien, giving him food and clothing" (10:18 NIV). This mighty compassion of God extends to the victim whose name may not be remembered by the community.

Chapter 21 begins by setting up a curious case. In the early days of Israel's settlement, there would be few urban centers. The people would spread out in the land, with plenty of farming soil to go around. As a result of the widespread population, secret murders of peasants could occur. These are no less significant to God than violence among the known and powerful. For this reason, He prescribed that careful rituals be performed by the elders, judges, and priests of Israel to communicate the gravity of the shedding of innocent blood:

- Determine which city is nearest the site of the killing (v. 2).
- That city's elders will select and kill an unworked heifer (vv. 3-4).
- The priests shall come near (v. 5).
- The city's elders will wash their hands over the slain man and declare their ignorance and innocence concerning his death (v. 6).

On first glance, this pomp and circumstance seems unnecessary. Apparently, the scenario describes the uncertain death of a solitary individual. No family or friends are mentioned. He is completely alone. Nonetheless, God requires the entire town to gather in order to proclaim the significance of his life.

All of this ceremony was so that the Jews would understand the seriousness of shed human blood (vv. 7-9)! While other ancient nations are sacrificing humans, even children, to appease the neighboring Canaanite gods, the God of Israel is demonstrably pro-life, guaranteeing the value of even the forgotten peasants.

---

1. How did God order elders, priests, and judges to work together (vv. 1-8)?
2. What did God promise in verse 9?

---

> "I can do no other than be reverent before everything that is called life. I can do no other than to have compassion for all that is called life. That is the beginning and the foundation of all ethics."—Albert Schweitzer

---

III. PROMOTE RIGHTEOUSNESS (Lev.20:1-3, 9-10, 22-24, 26; Num. 35:29-34; Deut.19:11-13)

In the Torah, punitive measures are taken to ensure that human life is protected. God is in the business of ordering a new society, and functional societies always require penalties for the most heinous crimes. In studying these penalties, we discover values that matter most to God. Foremost among these is a respect for the sacredness of human life.

A. Worship of Molech Condemned (Lev. 20:1-3)

(Leviticus 20:1-2 is not included in the printed text.)

**³ And I will set my face against that man, and will cut him off from among his people; because he hath given of his seed unto Molech, to defile my sanctuary, and to profane my holy name.**

It is remarkable, in its ancient context, that the Old Testament unilaterally prohibits the sacrifice of children to gods. With a singular biblical voice, this is declared an abomination. While this seems abhorrent to modern ears, child sacrifice was commonly practiced in the ancient Near East. In fact, in 1971, an archaeologist discovered a stone tower dating to around 500 BC, with a drawing of the ancient practice of child sacrifice. In the inscription, a banquet of a child is set before a two-headed monster. In the great city of Carthage, archaeologists have uncovered what they call the "Carthaginian Tophet"—a massive burial ground in which they estimate 20,000 child corpses were deposited, the victims of child sacrifice.

God would not allow such practices among His people. In fact, one of the biggest ancient take-aways from the story of Abraham and Isaac is that it marks a definitive moment when God would not receive child sacrifice, thus setting Himself apart from all other gods (see Gen. 22:9-14). In Leviticus 20, we see this prohibition in the laws of the Torah.

Interestingly, not much is known about the ancient pagan deity called Molech. In many cases, the term is used for a type of offering or sacrifice. In Leviticus 20, however, we meet the god Molech. The name bears a great resemblance to the Hebrew Malek, meaning "king." The Old Testament is, in fact, one of our best sources for understanding this mysterious god and how he was worshiped. In many places, the people of Israel are denounced for allowing their children to "pass through the fire" in worship to Molech, suggesting that children were sacrificed by immolation (2 Chron. 33:6; Jer. 32:35; Ezek. 16:21). Yahweh will not tolerate this.

In Leviticus 20:3, we see God takes the worship of Molech personally. God gives three reasons for the seriousness of this criminal act: the killing of children, the loss of the sacredness of the sanctuary, and the loss of the holiness of God's name.

- Why does God prescribe the death penalty in this situation?

> "Legalized abortion is a national holocaust . . . a stench in the nostrils of Almighty God."—Chuck Baldwin

B. Righteous Living Commanded (Lev. 20:9-10, 22-24, 26)

(Leviticus 20:23-24 is not included in the printed text.)

⁹ For every one that curseth his father or his mother shall be surely put to death: he hath cursed his father or his mother; his blood shall be upon him. ¹⁰ And the man that committeth adultery with another man's wife, even he that committeth adultery with his neighbour's wife, the adulterer and the adulteress shall surely be put to death.

²² Ye shall therefore keep all my statutes, and all my judgments, and do them: that the land, whither I bring you to dwell therein, spue you not out.

²⁶ And ye shall be holy unto me: for I the Lord am holy, and have severed you from other people, that ye should be mine.

In the remainder of the chapter, the Torah lists heinous crimes, most of which are capital offenses. They often reach back to the Ten Commandments, and show us how the ancient Israelite community implemented those commandments into their everyday lives.

Interestingly, Jesus deals specifically with the teachings in verses 9 and 10 in two vastly different situations of His ministry. First, at the beginning of Mark 7, Jesus has become embroiled in a controversy with the Pharisees and teachers of the Torah over the ceremonial washing of hands. Indignant, Jesus declares to them, "You have let go of the commands of God and are holding on to the traditions of men" (Mark 7:8 NIV). In His scathing denunciation of these religious leaders (vv. 9-12), Jesus actually quotes from Leviticus 20, and then says, "You nullify the word of God by your tradition that you have handed down. And you do many things like that" (Mark 7:13 NIV).

Second, in John 8, a woman caught in the act of adultery is brought before Jesus. For Jews schooled in the law of Leviticus 20, the problem before Jesus is clear. Verse 10 of the text requires that both parties caught in adultery are equally guilty. But where is the man? As a result of this breach in the Torah, Jesus declares, "If any one of you is without sin, let him be the first to throw a stone at her" (John 8:7 NIV). None of them is without sin, for in that very instance they were clearly breaking the Torah of Leviticus 20.

A key foundation of the Torah is that obedience is required to dwell successfully in the land that God will give to Israel (v. 22). Another key foundation, articulated in verses 23 and 24, is that the Israelites are to be "separated," or "set apart," from other nations. They are to live differently. This difference is rooted in the holiness of God. In verse 26, God's language is violent. He has "severed," or "cut off," the nation of Israel from all other peoples, in order to make them His shining light in the world.

---

1. To God, how important are parent/child and husband/wife relationships (vv. 9-10)?
2. What did God warn His people against, and what would happen if they disobeyed (vv. 22-24)?
3. What is God's will for His children (v. 26)?

> "The Holy Spirit cannot conquer the world with unbelief, nor can He save the world with a worldly church. He calls for a crusade, a campaign, and adventure of saving passion. For this enterprise He wants a separated, sanctified, and sacrificial people."—Samuel Chadwick

C. Make Righteous Judgments (Num. 35:29-34; Deut. 19:11-13)

(Numbers 35:29-30, 34 is not included in the printed text.)

**Numbers 35:31 Moreover ye shall take no satisfaction for the life of a murderer, which is guilty of death: but he shall be surely put to death. ³² And ye shall take no satisfaction for him that is fled to the city of his refuge, that he should come again to dwell in the land, until the death of the priest. ³³ So ye shall not pollute the land wherein ye are: for blood it defileth the land: and the land cannot be cleansed of the blood that is shed therein, but by the blood of him that shed it.**

**Deuteronomy 19:11 But if any man hate his neighbour, and lie in wait for him, and rise up against him, and smite him mortally that he die, and fleeth into one of these cities: ¹² Then the elders of his city shall send and fetch him thence, and deliver him into the hand of the avenger of blood, that he may die. ¹³ Thine eye shall not pity him, but thou shalt put away the guilt of innocent blood from Israel, that it may go well with thee.**

Although the Torah metes out stiff penalties for murder, there is still an appropriate process to be followed. This is a time before our modern judicial system, but pains were still taken to ensure that criminals were treated properly. We see this first in Numbers 35:30, where multiple witnesses are required to punish a murderer. In addition, the murderer cannot be saved by bribery under any circumstances (v. 31).

The penalty for breaking such just laws will be the pollution of the land itself (v. 33). This agrarian society, so dependent on the fertility of the land for their survival, was reminded of the interconnectedness of the land and their behavior. These laws were necessary for a fruitful life. The Lord declared, "You shall not defile the land in which you live, in the midst of which I dwell" (v. 34 NASB).

In the same way that these laws are generally applied in Numbers 35, in Deuteronomy 19:11-13, Moses turns his attention to problems that might arise in the improper use of the cities of refuge. "The cities of refuge were not to be as safe for criminals who were deserving of death nor to afford protection to those who had slain a neighbor out of hatred. If such murderer should flee to the free city, the elders of his own town were to fetch him out, and deliver him up to the avenger of blood, that he might die" (*Keil and Delitzsch Commentary*).

"That it may go well with thee" (v. 13) is God's heart for His people, and these stiff laws were given to preserve that preferred future for them.

---

1. Describe a legal protection God put into place for the accused (Num. 35:30).
2. Based on verse 33, would you say our nation today is a polluted land? Why or why not?
3. Who was worthy of capital punishment (Num. 35:31; Deut. 19:11-13)?

> "Justice cannot be for one side alone, but must be for both."—Eleanor Roosevelt

## CONCLUSION

The sacredness of human life is one of the most prominent themes of Scripture. We see it most prominently in the ministry of Jesus, but it begins in the Bible's first pages. Through the Torah's teachings about murder, innocent blood, and justice, God's heart is revealed. He is unmistakably a God who is intensely pro-life.

## GOLDEN TEXT CHALLENGE

"WHOSO SHEDDETH MAN'S BLOOD, BY MAN SHALL HIS BLOOD BE SHED: FOR IN THE IMAGE OF GOD MADE HE MAN" (Gen. 9:6).

After the Flood, God made a covenant with Noah and his family, promising never to destroy the human race again by water. Also, as long as the earth and human history should last, there would be regular seasons, day and night, planting time and harvest time (Gen. 8:22). This in itself shows God's concern for man's well-being. Despite man's sinful condition, there would be constants he could depend on for making life easier.

God then commanded that human life be held sacred. Even the animals would be, to a certain extent, responsible if they killed a human (see Ex. 21:28-29). God explained that murder is wrong. Killing another person destroys someone else who is also made in His image. God then instituted capital punishment, a requirement of the life of the murderer for the life he had taken.

**Daily Devotions:**
- M. You Are Your Brother's Keeper
  Genesis 4:8-12
- T. Ways of the Wicked
  Psalm 10:2-11
- W. Fearfully and Wonderfully Made
  Psalm 139:13-18
- T. High Standard for Relationships
  Matthew 5:20-26
- F. Oppressors Condemned
  James 5:1-6
- S. Love One Another
  1 John 3:11-18

January 25, 2015 (Lesson 8)
# Worship Only the Lord God
**Exodus 20:2-6; Deuteronomy 4:15-40**

**Unit Theme:**
God's Moral Law (Genesis-Deuteronomy)

**Central Truth:**
Only the One True God is to be worshiped.

**Focus:**
Acknowledge and worship only the One True God.

**Context:**
Moses receives the Ten Commandments around 1440 BC, and then reviews God's demands some thirty years later.

**Golden Text:**
"Know therefore this day, and consider it in thine heart, that the Lord he is God in heaven above, and upon the earth beneath: there is none else" (Deut. 4:39).

**Study Outline:**
I. Know the Lord Is God
   (Ex. 20:2-3; Deut. 4:32-40)
II. Do Not Worship False Gods
   (Ex. 20:4; Deut. 4:15-23)
III. God Is Jealous and Merciful
   (Ex. 20:5-6; Deut. 4:24-31)

## INTRODUCTION

One of the most challenging themes of Scripture is the exclusivity that God demands. The peoples of the Old and New Testaments were steeped in idol worship. References to polytheism even appear in the Old Testament itself. In Psalm 82:1, for example, Yahweh is portrayed as presiding over the great pantheon of gods: "He gives judgment among the 'gods'" (NIV). In 1 Kings 22, the prophet Micaiah describes a vision of Yahweh giving orders to a host of gods in order to destroy Ahab. There are other references of this nature in the Old Testament, and they bring to mind the specific picture of polytheism among ancient peoples. Yet, from cover to cover, the Bible demands this radical requirement: Yahweh alone is worthy of worship.

It is easy to leap from the ancient world to the modern world. Are we any less polytheistic today? Perhaps people today do not typically adhere to the belief in a multiplicity of gods, but neither do they proclaim the truth of only one God either. The mantra of our present world is simple: "Pick what works for you." This, of course, is ludicrous. There is no more opportune time to reclaim this central commandment of Scripture: "You shall have no other gods before Me" (Ex. 20:3 NKJV).

Remarkably, the first commandment in the Old Testament is taken up by Jesus in the New Testament. He proclaims in John 14:6, "I am the way, the truth, and the life. No one comes to the Father except through Me" (NKJV). This exclusive claim became a hallmark of early Christianity. In fact, Roman critics of the movement often persecuted the Christians on the charge of "atheism," due to their refusal to participate in festivals or worship practices of local temples. We see this in the early Christian story of the martyrdom of Polycarp, where Christians are being killed in the arena at a festival honoring Caesar. "All the crowd, astonished at the noble conduct of the God-beloved and God-fearing race of Christians, cried out, 'Away with the atheists'" (Henry Bettenson, ed., *Documents of the Christian Church*). Yet, they did not back down from their exclusive allegiance to Christ, even at the cost of their lives.

## I. KNOW THE LORD IS GOD (Ex. 20:2-3; Deut. 4:32-40)

We have noted previously how important it is to recognize that the Ten Commandments are not disconnected from the real life of ancient Israel. They are not simply abstract rules to live by. To view them in such a way sucks the life from them. Instead, they come to us from an elaborate, gripping, historical narrative. They come to us from the particular story of Jewish oppression in Egypt.

### A. The Context of Egypt (Ex. 20:2-3)

**² I am the Lord thy God, which have brought thee out of the land of Egypt, out of the house of bondage. ³ Thou shalt have no other gods before me.**

The Ten Commandments are a rebuttal and a contradiction to the way of life the Jews had known for dozens of generations in Egypt.

- The commandment to abstain from idolatry was a rebuttal of Egyptian culture, which depicted their gods in all sorts of physical forms and drawings.
- The commandment to not misuse the name of God was a rebuttal of Egyptian religion, which cited the power of their gods as justification for their oppression of the Jews.
- The commandment to honor the Sabbath was a rebuttal of the Egyptian economy, which valued the Jews only as production units to increase their national prosperity.
- The commandment to honor one's father and mother was a rebuttal of Egyptian tyranny, which broke down the family unit.
- Each commandment can and should be seen against this context of imperial Egypt.

Old Testament scholar Walter Brueggemann describes this radical shift in this way: "The reality emerging out of the Exodus is not just a new religion or a new religious idea or a vision of freedom but the emergence of a new social community in history, a community that has historical body, that had to devise laws, patterns of governance and order, norms of right and wrong, and sanctions of accountability. The participants in the Exodus found themselves, undoubtedly surprising to them, involved in the intentional formation of a new social community to match the vision of God's freedom. That new reality, which is utterly discontinuous with Egypt, lasted in its alternative way for 250 years" (*The Prophetic Imagination*). This new community was principally to stand against the previous context of Egypt in the way that they worshiped God.

The worship practices of the Egyptians maintained a strong hold on the Jewish community, even though God had freed them from Egypt. This is one of the reasons an entire generation of Jews would die before their children could rightly inherit the Promised Land. Just days after their release through the Red Sea, the famous story of the golden calf put the children of Israel to shame. It is important to recognize that when the Jews demanded that the golden calf be fashioned (Ex. 32), they were not necessarily falling into the sin of worshiping another deity. They probably did not understand themselves to be exchanging the worship of Yahweh for the worship of another god. They had simply been living in Egypt for so long that they had grown accustomed to gods they could see! Images of calves and bulls were prominent in Egyptian depictions of their deities. It is these default images and understandings of God that Yahweh must break from the forefront of the Ten Commandments.

Before one word of the Ten Commandments was uttered, they were situated within the context of how the God who speaks these words can be known by His people Israel: "I am the Lord your God, who brought you out of the land of Egypt, out of the house of bondage" (20:2 NKJV). Whereas the Egyptians defined the primary characteristics of their gods around appearances and powers, the God of Israel defines Himself around His story—the story which became the Jews' story. How did they know the attributes of Yahweh? The answer is simple: because He delivered them from Egyptian bondage.

This is the meaning of the Passover festival: "When you enter the land that the Lord will give you as he promised, observe this ceremony. And when your children ask you, 'What does this ceremony mean to you?' then tell them, 'It is the Passover sacrifice to the Lord, who passed over the houses of the Israelites in Egypt and spared our homes when he struck down the Egyptians'" (12:25-27 NIV). The point of the Passover is also the first point of the Ten Commandments: God is known by way of His story of liberating the people of Israel.

That theme of liberation set the stage for the Ten Commandments. Because God had revealed Himself to the nation as the Deliverer, they could trust that these commandments would liberate them to lead productive lives. This would be completely different from the oppressed lives they had known in Egypt. Therefore, God required exclusive allegiance.

The commandment in 20:3—"You shall have no other gods before Me" (NKJV)—is not prideful or demanding; it is logical. None of the other commandments would carry any weight if the people of Israel were not committed to the God of these commandments. Most importantly, none of the other commandments would carry any weight if the Jews were not rooted in the story of Yahweh which gave to these commandments the power of liberation. God's laws were freeing only because they stemmed from a liberating God who had proven Himself in history.

---

1. How does God identify Himself (v. 2)?
2. List some "other gods" people serve today (v. 3).

*"Begin where we will, God is there first."*—A. W. Tozer

B. The Self-Revelation of God (Deut. 4:32-40)

(Deuteronomy 4:36-38 is not included in the printed text.)

**32** For ask now of the days that are past, which were before thee, since the day that God created man upon the earth, and ask from the one side of heaven unto the other, whether there hath been any such thing as this great thing is, or hath been heard like it? **33** Did ever people hear the voice of God speaking out of the midst of the fire, as thou hast heard, and live? **34** Or hath God assayed to go and take him a nation from the midst of another nation, by temptations, by signs, and by wonders, and by war, and by a mighty hand, and by a stretched out arm, and by great terrors, according to all that the Lord your God did for you in Egypt before your eyes? **35** Unto thee it was shewed, that thou mightest know that the Lord he is God; there is none else beside him.

**39** Know therefore this day, and consider it in thine heart, that the Lord he is God in heaven above, and upon the earth beneath: there is none else. **40** Thou shalt keep therefore his statutes, and his commandments, which I command thee this day, that it may go well with thee, and with thy children after thee, and that thou mayest prolong thy days upon the earth, which the Lord thy God giveth thee, for ever.

Theologians often refer to God's revelation of Himself in two categories: *general revelation* and *special revelation*. By *general revelation*, we mean the fingerprints of God that we see all around us in nature, in our capacities, and in the laws of morality. Paul the apostle describes this mode of general revelation in Romans 1:20: "For since the creation of the world God's invisible qualities—his eternal power and divine nature—have been clearly seen, being understood from what has been made, so that men are without excuse" (NIV).

However, Scripture affirms that general revelation was not enough. God had a more specific story to tell. Theologian Millard J. Erickson comments: "Why was special revelation necessary? The answer lies in the fact that the humans had lost the relationship of favor which they had with God prior to the Fall. It was necessary for them to come to know God in a fuller way if the conditions of fellowship were once again to be met. This knowledge had to go beyond the initial or general revelation that was still available, for now in addition to the natural limitation of human finiteness, there was also the moral limitation of human sinfulness. It was now insufficient simply to know of God's existence and something of what He is like" (*Christian Theology*). This *special revelation* takes an accelerated form as God shapes His fledgling people Israel, preparing them to live a new life in the Promised Land.

In Deuteronomy 4, Moses reminds the people of Israel of the goodness of God. His proclamation rings out like a grand sermon. Moses declares that from the beginning of time, what God is doing in choosing Israel is unheard of; it has never happened before! This is why they owe Yahweh exclusive allegiance (vv. 32-35).

Because this allegiance is substantiated in Israel's history with the liberating God, Yahweh, Moses can demand that they recognize the futility of other gods.

Israel must not just listen to these commands. They must "take [them] to heart" (v. 39 NIV), allowing them to be impressed upon their deepest thoughts, attitudes, and emotions. By following God's commandments, "it might be well with them and their descendants, and they might have long life in Canaan . . . for all the future" (*Keil and Delitzsch Commentary*).

1. What unique acts of God are described in verses 33 and 34?
2. Describe something you have witnessed that only God could have done.
3. How did God express love for His people (vv. 36-38)?
4. Explain God's promise in verse 40.

> "God does not reveal information by communication: He reveals Himself by communion."—Sam Storms

## II. DO NOT WORSHIP FALSE GODS (Ex. 20:4; Deut. 4:15-23)

The lure of idolatry was the norm in the ancient world. This persisted into the New Testament period. For the people of Israel to be non-idolatrous was revolutionary in their context. Yet God is unrelenting in this demand.

A. The Temptations of Canaanite Religion (Ex. 20:4)

**⁴ Thou shalt not make unto thee any graven image, or any likeness of any thing that is in heaven above, or that is in the earth beneath, or that is in the water under the earth.**

The most ancient archaeological discovery from the land of Egypt is not the pyramids or the relics of the pharaohs. Instead, a small idol of a head of cattle, dated to 3500 BC, was discovered in a grave in southern Egypt over a century ago. In that era, the gods of the ancient Near East were taking the form of cows. Neil MacGregor, the curator of the British Museum, comments:

> Along the Nile Valley, the cow, a source of blood, meat, security and energy, eventually transformed human existence and became such a central part of Egyptian life that it was widely venerated. Whether actual cow worship started as early as the time of our little model is still a matter of debate, but in later Egyptian mythology the cow takes on a prominent role in religion, as the powerful cow-goddess Bat. She is typically shown with the face of a woman and the ears and horns of a cow. And the clearest sign of just how far cattle rose in status over the centuries is that Egyptian kings were subsequently honored with the title "Bull of his Mother." The cow had come to be seen as the creator of the pharaohs (*History of the World in 100 Objects*).

In the context of this culture, the Ten Commandments set a new precedent.

The first and second commandments address two differing problems that are interrelated. The first addresses polytheism; it is not allowed. But the second addresses a manner in which the Jews might get around polytheism and still incorporate the worship practices of neighboring peoples into the worship of Yahweh. They might do this, of course, by fashioning idols that would represent Yahweh.

So the listeners would get the point fully, in verse 4 God reiterated the prohibition of the various forms that idols might take. They should not aspire toward a heavenly vision of God, or an earthly vision, or an ocean vision. The gods of Egypt were depicted in such ways. The God of Israel, however, would faithfully guard His invisible image.

---

- What does God prohibit, and why?

> "The essence of idolatry is the entertainment of thoughts about God that are unworthy of Him."—A. W. Tozer

---

B. The Remembrance of Egypt (Deut. 4:15-23)

(Deuteronomy 4:17-18, 21-22 is not included in the printed text.)

**15 Take ye therefore good heed unto yourselves; for ye saw no manner of similitude on the day that the Lord spake unto you in Horeb out of the midst of the fire: 16 Lest ye corrupt yourselves, and make you a graven image, the similitude of any figure, the likeness of male or female.**

**19 And lest thou lift up thine eyes unto heaven, and when thou seest the sun, and the moon, and the stars, even all the host of heaven, shouldest be driven to worship them, and serve them, which the Lord thy God hath divided unto all nations under the whole heaven. 20 But the Lord hath taken you, and brought you forth out of the iron furnace, even out of Egypt, to be unto him a people of inheritance, as ye are this day.**

**23 Take heed unto yourselves, lest ye forget the covenant of the Lord your God, which he made with you, and make you a graven image, or the likeness of any thing, which the Lord thy God hath forbidden thee.**

Once again, when Moses stood to address the people in Deuteronomy 4, his teachings on abstaining from idol worship were rooted in the history between God and Israel. Moses reminded them of the giving of the Ten Commandments at Mount Horeb, where God spoke invisibly from a fire (v. 15). This invisibility was necessary to Torah theology. Should the children of Israel break this creed of divine invisibility, they would begin to ascribe false attributes to Yahweh (v. 16).

What Moses seemed to be guarding against here is what scholars call religious *syncretism*. This term refers to what happens when elements of differing faiths become mixed. Moses feared the worship of Yahweh might become watered down, powerless. Therefore, he went into great detail (v. 19).

Worshiping the heavenly bodies was common among the peoples of the ancient Near East. In fact, the Egyptian sun god, Ra, was paramount in the Egyptian religion which the Jews had witnessed for so many centuries. But God would allow no syncretism, for He revealed Himself definitively to His people (v. 20).

The imagery Moses uses in verse 23 is graphic. He challenges the children of Israel to never forget the harsh life of Egypt, which was sanctioned by Egypt's gods. They serve a different God who will not be revealed in graven images.

1. What reminder does God give (v. 15), and why (vv. 16-18)?
2. What might God's people feel "driven" to do (v. 19), and what should encourage them to resist (v. 20)?
3. Explain Moses' status (vv. 21-22).
4. What must God's people remember (v. 23)?

> "How quickly we forget God's great deliverances in our lives. How easily we take for granted the miracles He performed in our past."—David Wilkerson

### III. GOD IS JEALOUS AND MERCIFUL (Ex. 20:5-6; Deut. 4:24-31)

The commandments of God are not disconnected from the character of God. In fact, each reveals the other. It is not surprising, then, to see God describing His own character traits in the middle of the delivery of key commandments. It is to these character traits of jealousy, mercy, and covenant love that we now turn.

A. The Jealousy of God (Ex. 20:5-6)

**⁵ Thou shalt not bow down thyself to them, nor serve them: for I the Lord thy God am a jealous God, visiting the iniquity of the fathers upon the children unto the third and fourth generation of them that hate me; ⁶ And shewing mercy unto thousands of them that love me, and keep my commandments.**

What do we mean by the "jealousy of God"? After all, we typically view *jealousy* as a negative character trait. We see in Romans 13:13 and 1 Corinthians 3:3 the commands against jealousy in these early churches. However, we also see Paul claiming that he is "jealous" for the Corinthians "with godly jealousy" (2 Cor. 11:2). This "godly jealousy" is most famously represented in God's commentary on the second commandment.

The jealousy of God in the Old Testament is related to the commitment that God has made to His people, Israel. This is no elastic commitment. God has delivered them from Egypt and shepherded them toward liberation. Therefore, He expects allegiance. The emotions of God are caught up in this passion.

God does not make a general pronouncement in Exodus 20:5-6, but one targeted toward the people God has specifically delivered. His benefits reach a thousand generations. Should the children of Israel resent God's jealousy, they will see ramifications for several generations. So we see God's jealousy is merciful. The scales are not balanced. His mercy prevails!

In the New Testament, we see the jealousy of God in the weeping of Jesus. In Matthew 23:37 and Luke 13:34, Jesus laments the fate of Jerusalem, which will be destroyed by the Romans in just a few decades' time: "O Jerusalem,

Jerusalem, you who kill the prophets and stone those sent to you, how often I have longed to gather your children together, as a hen gathers her chicks under her wings, but you were not willing" (NIV). This lament is part and parcel of the character of a jealous God who longs for the hearts of His people.

---

1. How does God describe Himself in verse 5, and why?
2. What is the consequence of hating God, and the benefit of loving Him?

> "When properly understood, [God's] jealousy isn't inconsistent with His love and holiness; it's required by it."—Dan Vander Lugt

---

B. Long-Term Commitment (Deut. 4:24-31)

(Deuteronomy 4:25-28 is not included in the printed text.)

**24 For the Lord thy God is a consuming fire, even a jealous God.**
**29 But if from thence thou shalt seek the Lord thy God, thou shalt find him, if thou seek him with all thy heart and with all thy soul. 30 When thou art in tribulation, and all these things are come upon thee, even in the latter days, if thou turn to the Lord thy God, and shalt be obedient unto his voice; 31(For the Lord thy God is a merciful God;) he will not forsake thee, neither destroy thee, nor forget the covenant of thy fathers which he sware unto them.**

The Book of Deuteronomy is forward-looking. As Moses reaches the end of his journey with the people of Israel, his mind turns toward their future. He realizes that soon he will no longer have day-to-day administration over their problems and successes. The Torah and its commandments will take his place.

Moses wants to impress upon the people that the commandments of the Torah are always immediate and relevant. There will not come a day when compromise is acceptable. This is especially significant when it comes to the possibility of idolatry in the Jewish community.

In verse 24, Moses calls God "a consuming fire." Why is this significant? There are at least three reasons: (1) Fire cannot be constructed in idolatrous form. Ancient peoples constructed idols in a variety of animal and human likenesses (often combinations of both), but one cannot sculpt fire out of stone. God cannot be likened with wood or stone. (2) Fire is untamable. Moses reminds the people that they cannot "manage" God. They will do well to heed His word. (3) Fire is life-giving. When early man began experimenting with fire, great leaps were made in human civilization. In the same way, God seeks to give them life.

Moses also warns the people of what will happen if they ignore the jealousy of God. As he contemplates the future, he fears that the centrality of God and His Word in the life of the nation will "leak" over time. This priority must be adequately passed down from generation to generation. Mincing no words, Moses declares an oath formula—"I call heaven and earth to witness against you" (v. 26)—so the nation may never forget the gravity of his challenge. If they seek to worship idols, God will hand them over to their own devices . . . but in a foreign land. However, there is a promise beginning in verse 29: "If from there you seek the Lord your God . . ." (NIV). Scripture always carries a divine "if." There is always a turning point that will decide the future. That turning point is a moment of decision. Even in exile, in a foreign land, God promises that He can always be sought . . . and found. Even in distress, there is the possibility of return.

We can imagine how significant these words were to the Jewish people during the period of the Exile, when they were forcibly removed from their land by the Babylonian Empire in 587 BC. They depended on this text as they turned back to God who, once again, gave to them their land.

---

1. How would God prove to be "a consuming fire" (vv. 24-28)?
2. Who finds God (v. 29)?
3. How would God prove Himself to be "merciful" (vv. 30-31)?

### Protest of Beauty

In the days of the Bosnian conflict, cellist Vedran Smailovic was devastated to lose twenty-one friends in a single bomb crater when his city, Sarajevo, was under siege. In response, he played his cello for twenty-one straight days in the carnage of the bomb crater, even at threats to his life. Some have called his act a "protest of beauty."

When we worship God exclusively, we engage in such protest. We protest the brokenness of this world when we worship, knowing that God is a healing, liberating God.

---

### CONCLUSION

The commandment of the exclusive worship of God is coupled with the revelation of God's attributes of jealousy, passion, and mercy. God is not an emotionless force, but a loving Father, longing to cherish, protect, and prosper His children. In Exodus 20 and Deuteronomy 4, we find that idolatry threatens this intimate relationship with God. Still today, these commandments are piercing, relevant, and applicable.

### GOLDEN TEXT CHALLENGE

"KNOW THEREFORE THIS DAY, AND CONSIDER IT IN THINE HEART, THAT THE LORD HE IS GOD IN HEAVEN ABOVE, AND UPON THE EARTH BENEATH: THERE IS NONE ELSE" (Deut. 4:39).

Since God is "in heaven above and on the earth beneath" (NKJV)—that is, in all creation—no other god could possibly exist. For He is everywhere present and fills all things. There is no room for another, because He is uncircumscribed. The true God exists outside creation, for nothing can contain Him; rather, He contains all things in Himself, and is present everywhere (*Orthodox Study Bible*).

**Daily Devotions:**
M. Commit to Worship Only God
   Joshua 24:14-24
T. Follow God
   1 Kings 18:20-24, 36-39
W. Acknowledge the True God
   2 Kings 5:9-19
T. The Unknown God Made Known
   Acts 17:22-31
F. Idols Are Nothing
   1 Corinthians 8:1-6
S. Whose Friend Are You?
   James 4:1-10

February 1, 2015 (Lesson 9)
# Honor God's Name

Exodus 20:7; 22:28; Leviticus 19:12; 24:10-16; Numbers 15:30-31; 2 Samuel 12:14; Proverbs 14:31; Matthew 5:33-37; Romans 2:17-24; 2 Corinthians 9:12-13

**Unit Theme:**
God's Moral Law (Genesis-Deuteronomy)

**Central Truth:**
God's name is to be honored by our speech and actions.

**Focus:**
Consider what it means to honor God's name and revere His name by how we live.

**Context:**
Variety of Scripture passages lifting up the greatness of God's name

**Golden Text:**
"Thou shalt not take the name of the Lord thy God in vain; for the Lord will not hold him guiltless that taketh his name in vain" (Ex. 20:7).

**Study Outline:**
I. Do Not Misuse God's Name
   (Ex. 20:7; 22:28; Lev. 19:12; 24:10-16)
II. Sin Dishonors God
   (Num. 15:30-31; 2 Sam. 12:14; Prov. 14:31)
III. Integrity Honors God
   (Matt. 5:33-37; Rom. 2:17-24; 2 Cor. 9:12-13)

## INTRODUCTION

Perhaps you have come across a Jewish individual who refers to God in a peculiar way: *hashem*. We have often heard God referred to according to His traditional Jewish names—*Yahweh* and *Jehovah*—but these names are not used in modern Jewish communities today. In fact, when these names are encountered in modern synagogue readings, the rabbis will not pronounce them, but will substitute a different name for God, such as *Adonai*. When speaking about God in conversation, however, *hashem* is preferred. This term, in Hebrew, literally means "he name." God's name has historically been so revered by the Jews that they refuse to say it, speaking of it reverently in the third person: *hashem*.

Why such reverent emphasis on the name of God? The ancient Jews always understood that God's law was inseparable from God's personhood. This is something largely lost on the modern world. We live in a world of ideas. A good idea, we often figure, is good for most anyone, anytime, anyplace. We mix and match all sorts of ideas to achieve the lives we want to possess. The Bible leads us away from this trap.

One of the most important stories in the Old Testament, the troubling story of Abraham's near sacrifice of Isaac, has the powerful meaning that God is the only source of ethics. There is no ethic that exists outside God. God sets the standard, and even if that standard were to include child sacrifice, nothing could be done about it. All goodness comes from God. Therefore, child sacrifice is inappropriate because God has made His will on the matter so clear in the gripping account of Abraham. The name (or identity) of God, therefore, is the soil from which all teachings of the Bible grow.

This reality also applies directly to Jesus, who claimed to be the truth (John 14:6). The great theologian Paul Tillich comments: "Jesus is not the truth because His teachings are true. But His teachings are true because they express the truth which He Himself is" (*The New Being*).

The Bible's reverence for the name of God points to God's self as the very rule for living.

## I. DO NOT MISUSE GOD'S NAME (Ex. 20:7; 22:28; Lev. 19:12; 24:10-16)

The misuse of God's name can be connected to some of the greatest evils in human civilization. The Roman Empire proclaimed its bloody triumphs to be the result of the state gods that sanctioned and delivered their conquests. Adolf Hitler and his court theologians developed elaborate theories for justifying the Nazi ideology in the name of a Jew-hating "God." Totalitarian regimes in our day justify the power of the state by denying the name of God altogether. Even political parties in modern democracies fight over the name of God, each wanting to be identified as the Christian voice. In the Torah, however, God will not allow such name-dropping. His name is to be reverenced, not leveraged for human purposes.

### A. Taking God's Name in Vain (Ex. 20:7)

**⁷ Thou shalt not take the name of the Lord thy God in vain; for the Lord will not hold him guiltless that taketh his name in vain.**

The third commandment is the most stripped-down commandment among the first six. Commandments 7-9 are terse, because they outline behavior that can be avoided in simple terms. Not only the brevity, but also the placement of the third commandment is important. It is the third in a list of three prohibitive commandments before God gives the active commandments of honoring the Sabbath and honoring parents. Additionally, the fact that this commandment comes on the heels of the prohibition against idolatry gives us a key to its meaning. There is more here than first meets the eye.

This commandment probably has nothing to do with profanity. It has been interpreted this way in much of the church today, but this is not likely the third commandment's target. The context of Egypt is paramount. In the words of Old Testament professor Walter Brueggemann, this commandment is a statement that God is "the holy one who will have no competitor or be made 'useful'" (*Mandate to Difference: An Invitation to the Contemporary Church*). This commandment addresses the leveraging of God as a means to an end.

Idols, addressed in the preceding commandment, were used as means to all sorts of ends in the ancient world. They were used in the courts of kings and rulers to communicate divine sanction and authority. They were hauled to battlegrounds to communicate the protection of a nation's gods over its armies. Idols were even themselves a business, enriching the skilled artisans who built them. Since the use of idols was not allowed for the people of Israel via the second commandment, there might have been the temptation to attempt a different form of leveraging the power of God—through using His name in idolatrous ways. What is an idolatrous use of God's name? Whenever His name is used for purposes that are not completely His, the sacred name is disrespected.

- List ways a person could violate this command.

> "When are Christian folks going to remember that every time you call yourself a Christian, you invoke the name of God, and that if you then walk a walk that does not reflect the presence of Christ in your life, cast a vote that does not reflect the presence of Christ in your life, then you are taking the name of the Lord your God in vain?"—Alan Keyes

B. Blaspheming the Name of God (Ex. 22:28; Lev. 19:12; 24:10-16)

(Leviticus 24:10-14 is not included in the printed text.)

**Exodus 22:28 Thou shalt not revile the gods, nor curse the ruler of thy people.**

**Leviticus 19:12 And ye shall not swear by my name falsely, neither shalt thou profane the name of thy God: I am the Lord.**

**24:15 And thou shalt speak unto the children of Israel, saying, Whosoever curseth his God shall bear his sin. [16] And he that blasphemeth the name of the Lord, he shall surely be put to death, and all the congregation shall certainly stone him: as well the stranger, as he that is born in the land, when he blasphemeth the name of the Lord, shall be put to death.**

There is a specific form of misusing the name of God that is especially out of bounds in Scripture. This form is called *blasphemy*. The sin of blasphemy comes to us from a context in which words matter. For the ancient Hebrews, words themselves created realities. The Hebrew term *dabar* meant both "word and deed." Words wielded power and accomplished things in Hebrew thought. Therefore, blasphemy represented a terrible sin. To misuse words when speaking of the Holy One was harmful to the human soul and to the entire society.

We begin our study of the dangers of blasphemy with a difficult verse. Exodus 22:28 has been translated in different ways, depending on how one reads the manuscript traditions. Consider two options for properly interpreting this verse: (1) It may be a verse about blaspheming God, which would make it similar to other verses in the Old Testament. Many newer translations take this path. (2) The Hebrew phrase for "the gods" may be rendered in terms of "judges," which would make the verse about human rulers. In fact, terms for human rulers and for God are often interchangeable. Whichever interpretation is chosen, the emphasis of the verse remains firm. Words about God and rulers should be carefully guarded. This is a common injunction in Scripture.

In Leviticus 19, a much different form of blasphemy is highlighted. Oath formulas were common during this period of history. We often read in the Old Testament of someone "swearing an oath" (i.e., Gen. 26:31; Josh. 2:17; Judg. 21:1). Oath-making was closely tied to the concept of covenant in the ancient world, and various covenants might be struck between individuals, families, tribes, and even nations. The names of gods were commonly used in such oaths.

Interestingly, in Leviticus 19:12, God seems to allow for the use of His name in oaths, as long as the vow is taken with utter seriousness. The problem here is not in the swearing, but in the falsity of the swearing. God reminds the Israelites of His name in the second part of this commandment: "I am the Lord." The term *Lord* in the Old Testament is not a general term. It is the specific name of God. Typically represented in capital letters in English Bibles, this is the four-letter Hebrew name for God known as the *tetragrammaton*. It literally spells YHWH, with no vowels, rendering it unpronounceable. God reminds the Israelites of the solemnity of His name. They should think twice before they speak it in an oath.

---

1. What is prohibited in Exodus 22:28, and why?
2. What does it mean to "swear . . . falsely" by God's name (Lev. 19:12)?

> "God's name is qualified by the adjective *holy* in the Old Testament more often than all other qualities or attributes combined."—Sam Storms

---

C. Dealing With a Blasphemer (Lev. 24:10-16)

(Leviticus 24:10-16 is not included in the printed text.)

In this passage, we find a graphic portrayal of the gravity of how the name of God should be treated. A half-Jew finds himself in a fight with a full Jew. Apparently more influenced by the culture of his Egyptian father rather than his Jewish mother, this young man curses the name of the God of Israel. This would have been an ultimate form of shaming the belief system, the culture, and the ethnic identity of his Jewish rival. In verse 12, we find one of the few instances in the Torah of an early form of incarceration (prisons were not invented yet). The people of the community are so perplexed as to what to do that they put the perpetrator "in ward," or "in custody" (NKJV), and bring the situation to the attention of Moses.

The Lord tells Moses, "Let all who heard him lay their hands on his head, and let all the congregation stone him" (v. 14 NKJV). The name of God is to be protected at all costs. Punishment for this crime does not discriminate between Jews and immigrants (vv. 15-16). It is significant that Jews are treated no differently than aliens in this regard. The people of God are called to ultimately reverence His name.

Jesus reminds us of this truth in Mark 3:28-29 when He is questioned about the motives of His healing ministry: "I tell you the truth, all the sins and blasphemies of men will be forgiven them. But whoever blasphemes against the Holy Spirit will never be forgiven; he is guilty of an eternal sin" (NIV). As a Torah-keeping rabbi, Jesus knows the dangers of blaspheming God's name. To blaspheme God's name is to blaspheme His character. It is mistaking the holy for the evil, and seeking to skew these categories. When the holiness of the name of God is lost, all is lost.

1. Why was a man brought into custody (vv. 10-12)?
2. What did "all that heard him" do, and why (v. 14)?
3. Why was the penalty for blasphemy so harsh (v. 16)?

> "By laying their hands upon the head of the blasphemer, the hearers or witnesses were to throw off from themselves the blasphemy which they had heard, and return it upon the head of the blasphemer, for him to expiate."—*Keil & Delitzsch Commentary on the Old Testament*

II. SIN DISHONORS GOD (Num. 15:30-31; 2 Sam. 12:14; Prov. 14:31)

One of the most significant and misunderstood themes in Scripture is *sin*. This is because in modern thought, *sin* is often associated with rule-breaking, as opposed to an act that is contrary to the heart of God. Because of this, the language of *sin* in modern societies has been exchanged for the language of sickness and disorders. Barbara Brown Taylor writes:

> There are words in the Christian language that have no equivalent in the other languages we speak, such as the languages of business, law, or psychology. When we lose the religious words, we lose the hold they have on the realities they represent. *Sin* does not translate simply as rule-breaking. . . . It is a bigger word than that, with deeper roots, and if we drop it from our vocabulary then our language, not to mention our experience, will be diminished (*Speaking of Sin: The Lost Language of Salvation*).

The Old Testament introduces us to a world of thought in which the ultimate "thumbing the nose" at the commands of God is labeled as *sin*, and it is deadly.

A. The Penalty for Sin (Num. 15:30-31; 2 Sam. 12:14)

**Numbers 15:30 But the soul that doeth ought presumptuously, whether he be born in the land, or a stranger, the same reproacheth the Lord; and that soul shall be cut off from among his people. <sup>31</sup> Because he hath despised the word of the Lord, and hath broken his commandment, that soul shall utterly be cut off; his iniquity shall be upon him.**

**2 Samuel 12:14 Howbeit, because by this deed thou hast given great occasion to the enemies of the Lord to blaspheme, the child also that is born unto thee shall surely die.**

In the early nation of Israel, when national unity was critical, sins were seen to threaten the stability of the entire community. So we see, for example, the "sin in the camp" of Achan in Joshua 7. The most grievous sins were punished in dramatic ways in order to protect the community. We see these penalties in action in Numbers 15:30-31 and 2 Samuel 12:14.

In Numbers 15, the Torah addresses various issues concerning sacrificial offerings. The practice of sacrifice in the ancient Jewish community was typically an act of reunification. In verses 22-29, Moses gives attention to unintentional sins, which might take hundreds of forms. These should be addressed through a sacrifice offered by the "whole community" (v. 24 NIV) so the effects of the sin did not threaten society.

In verses 30-31, a different penalty is stated for the one who sins intentionally. Again, privileged Jews are given no priority when it comes to honoring the commands of God. The picture here is not one of complacency, but of pride—a person who breaks God's commands as if nothing is on the line. This is the ultimate danger to the community, which is why such an individual must be "cut off." His guilt cannot be taken away by sacrifice, for he has sought to live apart from God.

In 2 Samuel 12:14-15, we catch a glimpse of the gravity of sin in the imperial court of David. This is a real-world example of God's lack of favoritism. In the account, David has reached the peak of his success, and so sins "presumptuously" against Bathsheba, even ordering the death of her husband. Incredibly, he brushes the situation away and goes on like nothing ever happened.

Confronted by the court prophet, Nathan, King David is finally stricken with guilt. Nonetheless, Nathan declares the judgment of God over the king's sin—his son-to-be-born child will die. In verse 14, Nathan identifies David's sin as blasphemy (in accordance with Num. 15:30). David's sin was intentional and methodical. It would be met, therefore, with a stiff penalty.

1. Describe the sober equality shown here (Num. 15:30-31).
2. Why wouldn't David and Bathsheba's first son survive (2 Sam. 12:14)?

"God does not exalt His mercy at the expense of His justice."—Jerry Bridges

B. The Promise of Repentance (Prov. 14:31)

**³¹ He that oppresseth the poor reproacheth his Maker: but he that honoureth him hath mercy on the poor.**

The Book of Proverbs esteems the good neighbor:

The neighborly qualities which Proverbs urges on the reader add up to nothing less than *love*, though the word itself is not prominent. He is to be notably a man of peace: not only reluctant to start strife (3:29) or to spread it (25:8-9), but disarmingly kind (see the rising sequence in 24:17, 19; 25:21-22), and generous in his judgments (Derek Kidner, *The Proverbs: An Introduction and Commentary*).

Neighborliness was considered to be at the heart of a fruitful and happy society, and so we see these points of emphasis throughout Solomon's writings. In 14:31, we find a particular instance of neighborliness that is said to honor God—being gracious to the needy.

Contrarily, this proverb warns, "He who oppresses the poor taunts his Maker" (NASB). God is not only concerned with individual sins of blasphemy, but with social sins that God also interprets as blasphemy/reproach. The truth of this scripture is graphically depicted in Job 31:16-23, in which Job declared:

If I have denied the desires of the poor or let the eyes of the widow grow weary, if I have kept my bread to myself, not sharing it with the fatherless—but from my youth I reared him as would a father, and from my birth I guided the widow—if I have seen anyone perishing for lack of clothing, or a needy man without a garment, and his heart did not bless me for warming him with the fleece from my sheep, if I have raised my hand against the fatherless, knowing that I had influence in court, then let my arm fall from the shoulder, let it be broken off at the joint. For I dreaded destruction from God, and for fear of his splendor I could not do such things (NIV).

The good news here is that repentance is possible. By showing mercy toward the poor, reproach toward God is immediately transformed into worship.

- How does God identify with the needy?

> "He alone loves the Creator perfectly who manifests a pure love for his neighbor."—Venerable Bede

III. INTEGRITY HONORS GOD (Matt. 5:33-37; Rom. 2:17-24; 2 Cor. 9:12-13)

The theme of *sin* is equally important to the New Testament as it is to the Old. The difference, however, is that the New Testament proclaims the beginning of the ultimate demise of sin. Christ has become a new temple, a perfect sacrifice, and has sent the Holy Spirit to sanctify the believer. Because of this, a profound focus on personal and communal integrity becomes the norm in the early Christian message. It is to this message we now turn.

A. New Testament Prohibitions (Matt. 5:33-37; Rom. 2:17-24)

(Matthew 5:35-36 and Romans 2:17-22 are not included in the printed text.)
**Matthew 5:33 Again, ye have heard that it hath been said by them of old time, Thou shalt not forswear thyself, but shalt perform unto the Lord thine oaths: [34] But I say unto you, Swear not at all; neither by heaven; for it is God's throne.**

**[37] But let your communication be, Yea, yea; Nay, nay: for whatsoever is more than these cometh of evil.**

**Romans 2:23 Thou that makest thy boast of the law, through breaking the law dishonourest thou God? [24] For the name of God is blasphemed among the Gentiles through you, as it is written.**

Jesus is a Torah-studying, Torah-teaching, Torah-observant Jewish rabbi. We should not be surprised to witness His passion for the name of God. In His day, the misuse of God's name had grown all too common. As a result, Jesus prohibited all oaths in His movement (Matt. 5:33-36). He preserves the emphasis on the holiness of the name of God by canceling the practice of oaths altogether, adding, "But let your statement be, 'Yes, yes' or 'No, no'; anything beyond these is of evil" (v. 37 NASB). For Jesus, the reverence of the name of God took precedence over this cultural practice.

The specificity of Jesus in the New Testament often gives way to the general focus of Paul. In the Book of Romans, Paul writes to a church that he has never visited before. In this letter, he introduces both himself and his gospel. In the first chapter, Paul begins with the problem of sin, showing its results in the predicament of humanity. In chapter 2, Paul castigates the Jewish community for assuming all too often that they existed above this problem. He insists that the problem of sin has infected even God's chosen people. French Arrington summarized (vv. 17-24):

> Some Jews of Paul's day failed to practice what they professed. They were proud of possessing the law, but habitually broke it and caused others (the Gentiles) to doubt and dishonor God. While offering to guide others toward the light, the hypocrites among the Jews turned them away from God. They heartily approved the truths of the Old Testament, but did not consistently live by them (*The Greatest Letter Ever Written*).

This is truly a shocking conclusion! Paul indicts the Jewish community for the sin of blasphemy, since their elevation of the Torah has been at the expense of actually living the Torah.

---

1. Why is it unnecessary and unwise to make an oath (Matt. 5:33-36)?
2. How does verse 37 describe a person of integrity?
3. How did some Jews view themselves (Rom. 2:17-20)?
4. What was the problem with these Jewish teachers (vv. 21-23)?
5. How did these people hinder non-Jews (v. 24)?

> "No oath is necessary for the truthful person. Their word is so reliable that nothing more than a statement is needed from them."
> —D. A. Carson

---

B. New Testament Promises (2 Cor. 9:12-13)

**¹² For the administration of this service not only supplieth the want of the saints, but is abundant also by many thanksgivings unto God; ¹³ Whiles by the experiment of this ministration they glorify God for your professed subjection unto the gospel of Christ, and for your liberal distribution unto them, and unto all men.**

Paul's conclusion in the opening chapters of Romans is that "all have sinned and fall short of the glory of God" (3:23 NIV). The counterpart to this verse, though, is full of life: "and are justified freely by his grace through the redemption that came by Christ Jesus" (v. 24 NIV). Yes, the Bible dramatically condemns sin, even requiring the death of God's own Son to pay its penalty. But there is a counterpart to the story of sin in the New Testament: God has made a way for humanity to be free from sin and so to experience life with God.

In 2 Corinthians 8 and 9, Paul encourages generosity among the members of the Corinthian church. Specifically, he is raising financial support for a great offering for the church in Jerusalem. In Paul's mind, this would be an amazing expression of how God has repaired the breach between Jews and Gentiles. In 1 Corinthians 16:1-3, we find that the church at Corinth had been participating in this great offering. Here, Paul calls for further participation. Just as in Proverbs 14:31, participation in blessing the poor comes with a promise—"many thanksgivings unto God" and "glorify[ing] God" (2 Cor. 9:12-13).

Perhaps the Corinthians could not see past the offering to the theology of the offering. They understood themselves to be aiding the mother church of Jerusalem, but Paul sees much more happening. Their integrity as generous givers is honoring and worshipful to God. This honor will result in the praise of God from more people, as the early church expands its vibrant ministry.

---

1. What brought "many thanksgivings unto God" (v. 12)?
2. How does your giving "glorify God" (v. 13)?

> **The Human Condition**
> In William Shakespeare's famous play *Julius Caesar*, Cassius colludes with another Roman nobleman to assassinate the emperor. The climax of their conversation reads, "The fault, dear Brutus, is not in our stars, but in ourselves." The Bible names this fault in the human condition as *sin*, so that God might win the victory over it in Christ.

---

## CONCLUSION

Reverence for the name of God is a key requirement in the Old and New Testaments. This command calls for the recognition of the dangers and destructive powers of sin, as well as the grand promises of God that are offered for those who repent. *Penalty* and *promise* are two sides of the same coin in Christian theology. Christ took upon Himself the penalty of sin so we might inherit the promise of God's good news.

## GOLDEN TEXT CHALLENGE

"THOU SHALT NOT TAKE THE NAME OF THE LORD THY GOD IN VAIN; FOR THE LORD WILL NOT HOLD HIM GUILTLESS THAT TAKETH HIS NAME IN VAIN" (Ex. 20:7).

More is meant in this commandment than meets the eye. Not only is the name of God not to be used in angry and hateful oaths and cursing, but it is not to be used lightly or carelessly either. We ought to call His name reverently and deliberately, and we should not use His name so frequently that it becomes ordinary and meaningless.

Another way God's name is profaned is when people make vows or promises in His name and then don't keep them. God remembers these matters and "will not hold [them] guiltless."

Individuals also profane the name of the Lord when they profess to be Christians and then do not live holy and godly lives. When the name is taken in vain (uselessly, without cause), it is robbery of respect due to God.

**Daily Devotions:**

M. God's Covenant Name
   Exodus 3:13-17
T. Actions Can Profane God's Name
   Leviticus 20:1-7
W. Do Not Despise God's Name
   Malachi 1:6-14
T. Power in Jesus' Name
   Mark 16:14-20
F. May God's Name Be Glorified
   2 Thessalonians 1:3-12
S. Bring Honor to God
   1 Tim. 6:12-16

February 8, 2015 (Lesson 10)

# Justice for All

**Exodus 18:13-26; 20:16; 21:22-25; 22:21; 23:6-9; Leviticus 19:15; Deuteronomy 16:18-20; 17:8-13; 19:15-21; 25:1-3**

**Unit Theme:**
God's Moral Law (Genesis-Deuteronomy)

**Central Truth:**
God commands nations and individuals to be just.

**Focus:**
Conclude that God commands us to be just and practice social justice.

**Context:**
Old Testament perspectives on social justice

**Golden Text:**
"He hath shewed thee, O man, what is good; and what doth the Lord require of thee, but to do justly, and to love mercy, and to walk humbly with thy God?" (Mic. 6:8).

**Study Outline:**
I. A Biblical Legal System
   (Ex. 18:13-26; Deut. 16:18-20; 17:8-13)
II. Justice Requires Truthfulness
   (Ex. 20:16; Deut. 19:15-21)
III. Justice Must Be Evenhanded
   (Ex. 21:22-25; 22:21; 23:6-9; Lev. 19:15; Deut. 25:1-3)

## INTRODUCTION

Contemporary thinking on the biblical theme of *justice* is often shaped exclusively by Martin Luther and the Protestant Reformation in sixteenth-century Europe. For Martin Luther, justice was an individual problem between man and God that was solved by the blood of Christ. This was a groundbreaking realization in Christendom, but biblical justice is broader than atonement alone. New Testament scholar N. T. Wright calls this "God's project of justice within a world of injustice." He further says:

> This project is a matter of setting the existing creation to rights rather than scrapping it and doing something else instead. God decides, for that reason, to work through human beings as they are—even though their hearts think only of evil—and through Israel, even though from Abraham onward they make as many mistakes as they do acts of obedience. Both in the grand narrative itself, and in many smaller moments within it, we observe a pattern of divine action, to judge and punish evil and to set bounds to it without destroying the responsibility and agency of human beings themselves; and also both to promise and to bring about new moments of grace, events which constitute new creation (*Evil and the Justice of God*).

In the Torah, the first five sacred books of the Old Testament, the "new creation" is the new nation of Israel itself. There, we find God's passion for a justly ordered society.

What are the differences between our modern concept of justice and the biblical theme of justice? There are three differences at the forefront of this discussion: (1) *Our modern concept of justice is impersonal, whereas biblical justice is personal.* We imagine justice to look like an impersonal judge making a decision based on an abstract law, with little regard for the person being judged. Biblical justice, on the other hand, is about God's love for the person being judged. (2) *Our modern concept of justice is retributive, whereas biblical justice is restorative.* God is not simply focused on punishing, but restoring to health. (3) *Our modern concept of justice is individual, whereas biblical justice is communal.* God's justice restores not just individuals, but whole communities to live His purposes.

I. A BIBLICAL LEGAL SYSTEM (Ex. 18:13-26; Deut. 16:18-20; 17:8-13)

When studying the Torah, it is important to remember that these documents functioned not just as documents of faith, but also charters of government. In them, God was setting up a theocracy with no king, so they operated something like a cross between the Bible and a national constitution. Because of this, the Torah takes pains to rightly order a just society. This includes a massive number of laws to ensure that justice prevailed. Sometimes these laws can seem tedious to us, but the Torah leaves no stone uncovered when it comes to rooting out the possible causes of injustice that would dilute God's dream for the nation of Israel.

A. The Need for a Justice System (Ex. 18:13-26)

(Exodus 18:15-24 is not included in the printed text.)

**$^{13}$ And it came to pass on the morrow, that Moses sat to judge the people: and the people stood by Moses from the morning unto the evening. $^{14}$ And when Moses' father in law saw all that he did to the people, he said, What is this thing that thou doest to the people? why sittest thou thyself alone, and all the people stand by thee from morning unto even?**

**$^{25}$ And Moses chose able men out of all Israel, and made them heads over the people, rulers of thousands, rulers of hundreds, rulers of fifties, and rulers of tens. $^{26}$ And they judged the people at all seasons: the hard causes they brought unto Moses, but every small matter they judged themselves.**

In the Book of Exodus, the nation of Israel might be referred to as a grand experiment. It is difficult for us to imagine the degree to which they were learning to be a nation along the journey. Remember, no one had any recollection of what it was like to live in a functional society. They had been the victims of state-sponsored, institutional slavery for four centuries. That was their only point of reference. Because of this complete lack of the tools necessary to build a healthy society, features of culture that we take for granted virtually happened upon the children of Israel. Nowhere is this better depicted than in the sudden need for a justice system.

In Exodus 18, we find a fascinating depiction of the relationship between Moses and Jethro, his father-in-law. Jethro had taken Moses into the Midianite community back in chapter 2. However, we learn little about him in the opening scenes of Exodus. He obviously had a loving relationship with Moses, as he gave him his daughter Zipporah in marriage (2:21). This officially brought Moses into Jethro's family. Moses worked directly for Jethro, tending his flock (3:1). And Jethro allowed Moses to return to Egypt to check on his people (4:18). Beyond all this, however, we read nothing more about Jethro until chapter 18.

It had been some time since Moses had seen his family, and it was a humble and joyous reunion, with Moses bowing down to the ground in respect to his father-in-law (see vv. 1-7). What an example of Numbers 12:3, which tells us Moses was "more humble than anyone else on the face of the earth" (NIV)! The leader of a nation of hundreds of thousands humbly bowed before the shepherd from Midian. Although Jethro was called "priest of Midian" (Ex. 18:1), he came to believe in Yahweh only when Moses shared the deeds of Yahweh's deliverance of the children of Israel (see vv. 9-12).

The heart of Exodus 18 opens up the day after Jethro's arrival, when he begins to observe Moses' daily routine (v. 13). Moses understood being a judge as one of his primary roles as leader of the nation. Unfortunately, judging various disputes was dominating his time. After all, these people had only known the harshness of Egyptian oppression. Such an environment created factions, infighting, and strife. Jethro could hardly believe his eyes.

It is striking that Moses was surprised by Jethro's question, "Why do you alone sit as judge?" (v. 14 NASB). He explains to his father-in-law that he followed this routine because the people kept coming to him. Moses was simply reacting to the needs of the people, but Jethro had a plan to help him become a proactive leader.

Jethro's plan was simple. He probably learned it by dividing up his many flocks among his employee shepherds. One person cannot do all the work, whether tending flocks or judging a nation. Therefore, Jethro encouraged Moses to find capable men that he could train in the Torah so they might serve as judges, according to their ability, over groups of thousands, hundreds, fifties, and tens (v. 21). God used Jethro to enlighten Moses' mind. Suddenly, Moses is only faced with the infrequent "hard case," and he is freed to lead the nation more efficiently (vv. 25-26).

---

1. How did Moses describe his role as judge (vv. 13-16)?
2. What was Jethro's concern (vv. 17-18)?
3. Describe Jethro's plan (vv. 19-23).
4. How did Israel's judicial system change (vv. 24-26)?

> "It is theoretically and practically impossible to build any community apart from love and justice. If only one of these two is focused upon, an inevitable extremism and perversion follow."—Ravi Zacharias

---

B. The Justice System Develops (Deut. 16:18-20)

**¹⁸ Judges and officers shalt thou make thee in all thy gates, which the Lord thy God giveth thee, throughout thy tribes: and they shall judge the people with just judgment. ¹⁹ Thou shalt not wrest judgment; thou shalt**

not respect persons, neither take a gift: for a gift doth blind the eyes of the wise, and pervert the words of the righteous. **20** That which is altogether just shalt thou follow, that thou mayest live, and inherit the land which the Lord thy God giveth thee.

In the Book of Deuteronomy, Moses prepares the nation of Israel not just to take the Promised Land, but to do so without him. Moses is preparing them for his death. This preparation is painstaking, involving many details. One of the most important facets of Jewish culture Moses wants to strengthen is their legal system. Since he will no longer be serving as "chief justice," he must devise new methods and develop new leaders for legal disputes to be mediated.

In Exodus 18, Moses was free to select the judges of thousands, hundreds, fifties, and tens. Now he must pass off the important task of selecting adequate judges. Moses frames the role around the command for fairness/justice, because he knows that a society left to its own devices will stray from this rule (Deut. 16:18). Because the role of judge is so powerful—holding the fate of individuals, communities, and societal morality in the balance—Moses wants to particularly safeguard against the possibility of bribery (v. 19). The King James Version translates the term for *bribe* as "gift," showing how it might be justified in the eyes of the receiver. Moses knows that such "gifts" can be blinding. They skew the evidence in the mind of the judge, and this is not in accordance with the administration of justice.

Finally, Moses caps off the command to reject gifts/bribes, with the ultimate rule for the Jewish justice system: "Follow justice and justice alone" (v. 20 NIV). The point of "justice" in this verse is emphatic. Every piece of the legal system should be built on the foundation of this singular principle of justice. The children of Israel will ignore this command at their own peril.

---

1. List three things Israel's judges were not to do (v. 19).
2. What did God promise (v. 20)?

> "Human progress is neither automatic nor inevitable. Every step toward the goal of justice requires sacrifice, suffering, and struggle; the tireless exertions and passionate concern of dedicated individuals."—Martin Luther King Jr.

---

C. Deciding Difficult Cases (17:8-13)

(Deuteronomy 17:10-11 is not included in the printed text.)

**8 If there arise a matter too hard for thee in judgment, between blood and blood, between plea and plea, and between stroke and stroke, being matters of controversy within thy gates: then shalt thou arise, and get thee up into the place which the Lord thy God shall choose; 9 And thou shalt come unto the priests the Levites, and unto the judge that shall be in those days, and enquire; and they shall shew thee the sentence of judgment.**

**12 And the man that will do presumptuously, and will not hearken unto the priest that standeth to minister there before the Lord thy God,**

or unto the judge, even that man shall die: and thou shalt put away the evil from Israel. <sup>13</sup> And all the people shall hear, and fear, and do no more presumptuously.

As Jethro had set up the legal system, Moses alone was the arbiter of the most difficult legal cases. With Moses' imminent death, a new system was needed. In this passage, Moses introduced such a system.

Moses pointed out three types of cases that often proved exceedingly difficult (v. 8). In agrarian societies, murders could often be hidden. Assaults could be committed with no witnesses. And lawsuits, as today, could take a variety of complex forms. Interestingly, Moses did not create a new band of judges for such disputes, but assigned these duties to the priests (v. 9). Difficult decisions would be left to them, since they were the primary interpreters of the Torah. Their verdicts would be final, and there would be no court of appeals.

The danger was that the people not accord to the priests the respect they had placed in Moses. Cries of foul play or incompetence were to be expected. Moses cut these possibilities off at the root, declaring that showing contempt for the judge would warrant a death penalty (v. 12). For society to function justly, respect for the judges of the Torah mattered more than anything.

---

1. How were the more difficult cases to be handled (vv. 8-9)?
2. How must people respond to the verdict (vv. 10-11)?
3. What was worthy of death, and why (vv. 12-13)?

> "The moral law of God is the only law of individuals and of nations, and nothing can be rightful government but such as is established and administered with a view to its support."—Charles Finney

---

II. JUSTICE REQUIRES TRUTHFULNESS (Ex. 20:16; Deut. 19:15-21)

The commandments of the Torah, which we sometimes read as individualistic, are consistently related to the health of the nation at large. Healthy individuals create healthy societies, and unhealthy individuals create unhealthy societies. This is why any society built on the foundation of justice will encourage a profound emphasis on telling the truth. We see this first and foremost in the Torah.

A. The Commandment Against False Testimony (Ex. 20:16)

**<sup>16</sup> Thou shalt not bear false witness against thy neighbour.**

In the Old Testament, there were no photographs, fingerprints, or forensic evidence. *The only evidence for determining crimes was the verbal testimony of individuals!* For this reason, the Bible safeguards the sacredness of testimony as the truth on which an effective justice system operates.

We see this safeguarding of testimony in the Ten Commandments. It is commonly assumed that one of the Ten Commandments in Exodus 20 is "Thou shalt not lie." In reality, this is a caricature of the actual commandment, which is not so general. It refers to the specifics of the justice system.

This law is sandwiched between commandments that foster the formation of healthy relationships within society. In the same way that the Israelites must avoid murder, adultery, stealing, and coveting, they must also speak the truth in court if they are to live productively in the land God is giving them.

- What does it mean to "bear false witness"?

> "The effects of slander are always long-lived. Once lies about you have been circulated, it is extremely difficult to clear your name. It's a lot like trying to recover dandelion seeds after they have been thrown to the wind."—John MacArthur

B. The Need for Witnesses (Deut. 19:15-21)

**15** One witness shall not rise up against a man for any iniquity, or for any sin, in any sin that he sinneth: at the mouth of two witnesses, or at the mouth of three witnesses, shall the matter be established. **16** If a false witness rise up against any man to testify against him that which is wrong; **17** Then both the men, between whom the controversy is, shall stand before the Lord, before the priests and the judges, which shall be in those days; **18** And the judges shall make diligent inquisition: and, behold, if the witness be a false witness, and hath testified falsely against his brother; **19** Then shall ye do unto him, as he had thought to have done unto his brother: so shalt thou put the evil away from among you. **20** And those which remain shall hear, and fear, and shall henceforth commit no more any such evil among you. **21** And thine eye shall not pity; but life shall go for life, eye for eye, tooth for tooth, hand for hand, foot for foot.

The Torah does not demand truth with no regard for the problems of the human condition. Knowing that dishonesty is always possible, further safeguards are given to ensure that those accused of committing crimes are treated with fairness. The need for multiple witnesses was created to achieve this.

It is a common commandment in the legal codes of the Torah that one witness is not sufficient grounds to convict a person. In the case of a single witness, the verdict is simple: case closed. At least two witnesses are required to convict (v. 15).

Yet, not even this demand for multiple witnesses solves every problem the courts might face. What about a witness with a clear hatred for the defendant? In verse 16, the term for "false" can also mean "malicious." Whatever the motive, the witness can be identified as potentially twisting his testimony in order to swing the case. In such an event, additional judges and priests should be brought in for further examination (v. 17). If he is guilty of perjury, the consequence should be stiff—"do to him as he intended to do to his brother" (v. 19 NIV).

Without such a dire penalty, justice might never take its course. The entire system rested on truthful testimony. False testimony could not be tolerated.

1. Describe protections implemented for the accused (vv. 15-18).
2. How was a lying witness to be handled (vv. 19-21)?

> "Responsibility is measured, not by the amount of injury resulting from wrong action, but by the distinctness with which conscience has the opportunity of distinguishing between the right and the wrong."—Frederick W. Robertson

---

### III. JUSTICE MUST BE EVENHANDED (Ex. 21:22-25; 22:21; 23:6-9; Lev. 19:15; Deut. 25:1-3)

For justice to be truly just, it must be the same for all people. Yet, Moses lived and wrote in the ancient world where it was assumed that people were not equal. Some were born to lead lives of privilege, often above the law, while most were born peasants. The beauty of the Torah is that it would not allow favoritism between classes of people on any grounds.

#### A. Ultimate Fairness (Ex. 21:22-25)

(Exodus 21:22-24 is not included in the printed text.)

**25 Burning for burning, wound for wound, stripe for stripe.**

In Exodus 21:22-25, we find a disturbing scenario. Before the days of modern medicine, pregnancies were constantly touch and go. In this hypothetical scene, a pregnant woman is accidentally struck so that she prematurely gives birth. This leads to one of two scenarios. If the baby is fine, the woman's husband, in conjunction with the local court, will levy a fine against the man who caused the premature birth. However, if there is serious injury to the woman or to the fetus, or, worse, if the fetus is stillborn, the offender is to be punished. Here we find one of the most staggering pronouncements of ultimate fairness in the Bible: "Eye for eye, tooth for tooth" (v. 24).

How do we make sense of this penal code? As Christians, the matter is complicated by Matthew 5:38-42, where Jesus appears to overturn this commandment. When interpreting this, we must keep in mind the vastly different contexts of Moses and Jesus. Moses is setting up a just society from scratch. There can be no compromises in the fairness of the legal system. By the time of Jesus, however, the people of Israel have lost the justice system to the Romans. This is why Pontius Pilate must be involved in sentencing Jesus. Jesus' teaching in Matthew 5 concerns how His followers are to live in an occupied territory, where "eye for eye" and "tooth for tooth" is no longer plausible.

---

1. If a woman gave birth prematurely (but safely) due to an altercation, what was the proper verdict (v. 22)?
2. If injury resulted from the altercation, what was the proper verdict (vv. 23-25)?

> "In our addresses therefore unto God, let us so look upon Him as a just God, as well as a merciful; and not either despair of or presume upon His mercy."—Abraham Wright

B. Mercy in the Legal Code (Deut. 25:1-3)
**¹ If there be a controversy between men, and they come unto judgment, that the judges may judge them; then they shall justify the righteous, and condemn the wicked. ² And it shall be, if the wicked man be worthy to be beaten, that the judge shall cause him to lie down, and to be beaten before his face, according to his fault, by a certain number. ³ Forty stripes he may give him, and not exceed: lest, if he should exceed, and beat him above these with many stripes, then thy brother should seem vile unto thee.**

Even in the Torah we find mercy in the legal code. A prime example is in the case of beatings in this passage. There are no prisons mentioned in the Torah and so no prison sentences. Instead, there were instances in which beatings might serve as the proper punishment (vv. 1-3).

Even in the midst of a penalty that might strike us as barbaric, there is a concern for the perpetrator. The criminal is not to be degraded before the eyes of the court or the witnesses. Once the beating has been completed, he is to be restored to his community.

- Explain the limit imposed on beating as a form of punishment.

### Your Own Calcutta
Mother Teresa was one of the greatest emissaries of justice for the poor in the twentieth century. Because of her fame and dogged commitment to the poor of Calcutta, India, foreign dignitaries and devout church leaders often visited her. One visitor asked her, "How can I be like you?" Her response was simple: "Find your own Calcutta."

C. Justice for the Disadvantaged (Ex. 22:21; 23:6-9; Lev. 19:15)
(Exodus 22:21; 23:6-9; Leviticus 19:15 are not included in the printed text.)
One of the most enduring characteristics of the Torah is its concern for the foreign-born. This concern stems from the fact that the Jewish people remembered what it was to be foreigners in the distant land of Egypt. Because of this, God expected them to treat aliens with respect. We see this especially in the justice system.

Often in the Torah, the command to remember the foreign-born is peppered between seemingly unrelated laws. This command is essentially a touchstone that God trains the children of Israel to turn to again and again. In Exodus 22:21, this commandment is found between rules about sexuality, pagan worship, and lending money.

The sin of racism is as old as time, and the Jews were liable to this sin. There might be many ways to mistreat or oppress a Gentile living in Israel. In the same way God would not allow the oppression of the widow or orphan, one was not to be improperly treated on the basis of race.

Exodus 22:21 was not written with specific reference to the courts. In 23:6-9, however, the courts come into a view again. Once again, we face a problem that we tend to see as modern, but in fact it is as old as humanity itself. "Do not deny justice to your poor people" (v. 6 NIV) forms one of the foundational elements of modern justice systems in the Western world. In the United States, for example, legal representation is provided by the state for those who cannot afford it. Yet, even in this system there is always the possibility of "buying justice." Imagine such difficulties in the ancient world! Then, as now, poor people were involved in lawsuits. Then, as now, their voices might be squelched in a variety of ways. Therefore, God forbids bribes, false charges, and incorrect sentences (vv. 7-8). He holds His people accountable for doing justice (v. 9).

In the priestly document of Leviticus, we find a similar refrain. Once again, the commandment of justice pops up constantly in the Torah text. Leviticus 19:15 includes all the necessary safeguards for justice to be rightly administered. There should be no assumptions of guilt or innocent toward any party on the basis of their social status. The poor should not be seen in a better light because they are poor, nor the mighty because they are mighty. Instead, people should be considered neighbors, and therefore judged fairly.

---

1. What were the Israelites to remember (Ex. 22:21)?
2. According to 23:6 and 9, who must be protected?
3. Why is bribery so terrible (v. 8)?

> "The great can protect themselves, but the poor and humble require the arm and shield of the law."—Andrew Jackson

---

## CONCLUSION

Amos 5:24 says, "Let justice roll on like a river" (NIV). This is the cry of the Torah. In Exodus, Leviticus, and Deuteronomy, we see the blueprint for a well-ordered society. This blueprint includes a widespread legal system that is based on accurate testimony and fair, evenhanded sentencing. In this way, the Bible laid the foundations for just judicial systems in our time.

### GOLDEN TEXT CHALLENGE

"HE HATH SHEWED THEE, O MAN, WHAT IS GOOD; AND WHAT DOTH THE LORD REQUIRE OF THEE, BUT TO DO JUSTLY, AND TO LOVE MERCY, AND TO WALK HUMBLY WITH THY GOD?" (Mic. 6:8).

God had delivered His people, Israel, from Egyptian bondage, but they had failed to respond to His mighty saving acts. They had turned aside from God and had trusted in external forms of worship to no avail. The popular view was that

God demanded an unceasing supply of offerings to atone for sins. So people asked the prophet Micah, "Will the Lord be pleased with thousands of rams, or with ten thousands of rivers of oil?" (6:7).

As always, God did not want more and more offerings, but heartfelt devotion to Him. Our response to the living God is to be grounded in His great mercy.

What God has done prompts us to live the life of faith. That requires us to do justly, to love mercy (or kindness), and to walk humbly with God. "To do justly" requires righteous living. The Scripture teaches us to "trust in the Lord, and do good" (Ps. 37:3). Genuine concern and love for others are to spring from personal faith in God. "To love mercy" requires a right heart. Only the person with a pure and sanctified heart abides with God (15:1-2). Regardless of how noble our deeds may be, without pure motives we cannot please God. "To walk humbly" requires the forsaking of pride and self-will and developing a wholehearted devotion to walk carefully with God.

Faith without works is dead. Good deeds are important, but basic is the devotion of the heart to God. Our hearts should be set on fire with love in response to God's grace and mercy in Christ. The fruit of this is the doing of justice, the pursuit of kindness, and the exercise of a humble walk with the Lord.

## Daily Devotions:

M. Just Judge
   Genesis 18:22-33
T. Injustice Rebuked
   Psalm 82:1-8
W. Do Justly
   Micah 6:6-16
T. Don't Seek Revenge
   Matthew 5:38-48
F. Government to Promote Just Society
   Romans 13:1-7
S. The Righteous Judge
   Revelation 19:11-16

February 15, 2015 (Lesson 11)
# Be Sexually Pure

Genesis 2:18-25; Exodus 20:14; Leviticus 18:1-30;
Deuteronomy 24:5; Proverbs 5:1-23

**Unit Theme:**
God's Moral Law (Genesis-Deuteronomy)

**Central Truth:**
God created us as sexual beings and commands us to be sexually pure.

**Focus:**
Acknowledge and obey God's commands for sexual purity.

**Context:**
God's creation of man and woman, God's laws, and Solomon's teaching lift up sexual purity.

**Golden Text:**
"Nevertheless, to avoid fornication, let every man have his own wife, and let every woman have her own husband" (1 Cor. 7:2).

**Study Outline:**
I. Sexual Immorality Defiles
   (Lev. 18:1-5, 17-18, 20, 22, 24-30)
II. Dangers of Sexual Immorality
   (Prov. 5:1-14, 20-23)
III. God's Plan for Sexuality
   (Gen. 2:18-25; Ex. 20:14; Deut. 24:5; Prov. 5:15-19)

## INTRODUCTION

In the first century BC, a famous Roman politician and orator named Cicero wrote about his culture's current sexual practices. In fact, he mocked anyone who would champion a commitment to abstinence outside of marriage:

> If anyone thinks that youth should be forbidden affairs even with courtesans [prostitutes], he is extremely severe. That view is contrary not only to the license of this age, but also to the custom and concessions of our ancestors (*Pro Caelio*).

Yet, in the middle of the pagan Roman Empire, early Christianity emerged and expanded. Ironically, one of the classic Christian virtues is *chastity*. From the early days of the Christian movement, it was understood that Christians have something to say about human sexuality. We see teachings on human sexuality throughout the New Testament, from Jesus to His apostles. But such teaching did not begin with Jesus and His early followers. Instead, we see a commitment to sexual purity within the pages of the Old Testament.

Why would a focus on human sexuality be such a prime subject in the religious documents of early Judaism? We can pick out three primary reasons: (1) *The Bible's teachings on human sexuality preserve the fruitfulness of humanity.* The Torah, for example, is written to a primitive agrarian economy. Households are able to function and prosper based on the number of children, especially sons, which they are able to produce. Sexuality within the confines of marriage serves this end. (2) *The Bible's teachings on human sexuality preserve the bonds of family.* This not only includes marital bonds, but also healthy bonds between parents and children. When these bonds break down, society suffers. (3) *The Bible's teachings on human sexuality preserve the health of the human soul.* God knows that sexuality is a matter of the heart, and should be handled with sacred care. We see this sacred care proclaimed in Paul's first letter to the Thessalonian church: "It is God's will that you should be sanctified: that you should avoid sexual immorality; that each of you should learn to control his own body in a way that is holy and honorable, not in passionate lust like the heathen, who do not know God" (4:3-5 NIV). As we study the teachings of Scripture on human sexuality, we discern the will of God for our lives.

I. SEXUAL IMMORALITY DEFILES (Lev. 18:1-5, 17-18, 20, 22, 24-30)

Leviticus reflects the perspective and concerns of the priestly class of Israel. At the beginning of the nation's history, God raised up Aaron to serve alongside Moses as the first high priest of Israel. This divine choice meant the political power of the nation would always exist alongside the priestly power of the nation. Priests, then, serve vital functions in ruling over Israel. They are the moralists, the educators, and the spiritual teachers of the nation. The priestly teaching on human sexuality creates important boundaries that will lead the Jewish people in the will of God.

A. A People Set Apart (vv. 1-5)

(Leviticus 18:1-2 is not included in the printed text.)

**³ After the doings of the land of Egypt, wherein ye dwelt, shall ye not do: and after the doings of the land of Canaan, whither I bring you, shall ye not do: neither shall ye walk in their ordinances. ⁴ Ye shall do my judgments, and keep mine ordinances, to walk therein: I am the Lord your God. ⁵ Ye shall therefore keep my statutes, and my judgments: which if a man do, he shall live in them: I am the Lord.**

The ethical teachings of the Bible are always related to the sort of people that God has called into being. That is, God is not laying out a set of moral laws so much as He is calling forth a people to embody His character. There is a tremendous difference between these two approaches. If we treat the commands of Scripture as moral truth alone, we will miss their goal and will give into lifeless legalism. We will see the Scripture as a list of rules to be followed. However, if we seek to *embody* these commandments as the natural extension of our lives as God's people, the result will be "life . . . more abundantly" (John 10:10). Their point is to bring us into vital relationship with God.

This abundant life, of course, is lived in the body, so the Scripture focuses heavily on what we do with our bodies. Christian author Dallas Willard comments:

> If salvation is to affect our lives, it can only do so by affecting our bodies. If we are to participate in the reign of God, it can only be by our actions. And our actions are physical—we live only in the processes of our bodies. *To withhold our bodies from religion is to exclude religion from our lives.* Our life is a bodily life, even

though that life is one that can be fulfilled solely in union with God (*The Spirit of the Disciplines: Understanding How God Changes Lives*).

In Leviticus 18, the Lord gave to Moses an extended teaching on human sexuality. In the Torah, the children of Israel were constantly reminded of their past. This occurred for two reasons. First, the remembrance of Egypt framed the life-giving relationship God established with His people. God was not giving them strict commands out of legalism, but out of love. Second, the remembrance of Egypt taught the Israelites what *not* to do. God recontrasts His word with the way society functioned in Egypt. This is also the rule when it comes to the Torah's teachings on human sexuality.

Not only did God ask His people to look backward to Egypt, but He asked that they look to the future as well. In the same way that Egypt was not their reference point for how to live, neither would Canaan be (v. 3). They could not simply replace a moral dependence on Egypt with a moral dependence on any Canaanite system of thinking or living. God knew this would be the most difficult challenge for the new nation: to look to God alone, rather than their neighbors, for a model. God's injunction here is total: neither the Egyptian nor the Canaanite lifestyle held any promise for the new nation of Israel. To hammer this point, God twice repeated the focus on His decrees and laws, followed by the double-proclamation of His identity (vv. 4-5). He is Yahweh, the God whom they knew and who had delivered them. They must look to Him alone as their pathway to life.

---

1. What did the Lord God prohibit (v. 3)?
2. How did God want His commands to affect His people (vv. 4-5)?

---

"Premarital sex defrauds the future marriage partner of the person with whom you are involved. You are robbing that person of the virginity and single-minded intimacy that ought to be brought into a marriage. Thus, sexual impurity is as much a social injustice against others as it is a personal sin against God."—Sam Storms

---

B. Various Sexual Boundaries (vv. 17-18, 20, 22, 24-30)

(Leviticus 18:17-18, 20, 22, 26-29 is not included in the printed text.)

**²⁴ Defile not ye yourselves in any of these things: for in all these the nations are defiled which I cast out before you: ²⁵ And the land is defiled: therefore I do visit the iniquity thereof upon it, and the land itself vomiteth out her inhabitants.**

**³⁰ Therefore shall ye keep mine ordinance, that ye commit not any one of these abominable customs, which were committed before you, and that ye defile not yourselves therein: I am the Lord your God.**

After the strong introduction in which God claims a special relationship and the primary role as father over the nation of Israel, the Torah launches into a lengthy list of sexual prohibitions that form boundaries around the sexual behavior of the nation. Eighteen offenses are listed, and many seem grotesque to us in the modern world. However, they are found in Leviticus because they existed in the culture of the day. Many of these sexual practices were connected to various forms of cult worship, and God wanted to root them all out.

Interestingly, almost all of the prohibitions against sexuality involve some form of incest. Verse 6 lays this out explicitly, and verses 7-18 detail the various arrangements that ancient incest might take. Keep in mind that this was a time in which polygamy was the norm. Also, marriage was not solely for the purposes of love and childbearing, but also for peacemaking. Marriage brought various clans together. The combination of polygamy with marriage as a community bond could certainly lead to the scenarios that Leviticus prohibits. The Scriptures are clear: such practices are out of bounds in the community of God.

After the lengthy prohibitions against incest, the Scriptures do not leave out adultery. Verse 20 reminds the Jews that adultery is as serious as incest. Additionally, sacrificing children to the god Molech (v. 21) is found in this list of sexual sins. We do not know much from history about this practice, but the placement of this verse suggests there may have been sexual rites connected with the worship of Molech. Likewise, homosexuality (v. 22) and beastiality (v. 23) are strictly condemned as "detestable" and "a perversion" (NIV).

Verses 24 and 25 connect these prohibitions to the defilement of the land itself. This is a strange comparison to modern minds, but in a primitive agrarian economy the livelihood of all the people depended on the fertility of the land. Human sexuality is, of course, all about fertility. Many of the practices that Leviticus prohibits were engaged in by neighboring peoples in the hopes of producing a greater degree of fertility, thus more children. Ironically, God declared that, in their rush toward greater fertility, the land lost its fertility and expelled them. This leads to a foundational truth in the Torah: "the fertility of the Promised Land is found not in religious ritual, but in God himself." These teachings on human sexuality will test that truth in the hearts of the Israelites. They must exercise the faith to follow all of God's decrees in order that God might bless their fertile land.

Just as Leviticus 18 began with the commandment to be set apart, it ends with the same (v. 30). Scripture often duplicates those points that God wants to be the strongest. Here we find the duplication of God's personal standard as the only template for the Israelites to follow. This is followed by the re-proclamation of His divine name. He alone is Yahweh, the nation's only God.

---

1. Why do you suppose these specific sexual sins are listed (vv. 17-18, 20)?
2. What is called "detestable" (v. 22 NIV)?
3. Which "nations" were an example for Israel, and how (vv. 24-28)?
4. What could violators of God's law expect (v. 29)?

> "We should embrace biblical language regarding sexuality. Terms like *fornication* and *adultery* should not be sugarcoated, but instead be used to demonstrate God's condemnation of sex outside of marriage."—Lance Colkmire

## II. DANGERS OF SEXUAL IMMORALITY (Prov. 5:1-14, 20-23)

The Book of Proverbs might be considered an educational curriculum in the life of Solomonic Israel. Solomon ruled during a time when the nation was flourishing economically, culturally, and religiously. This resulted in a class of educators, or what Old Testament scholar Walter Brueggemann called "intelligentsia":

> There arose in this model of the people of God an intelligentsia that was in part civic bureaucracy and in part the lobby of higher education . . . the sages of the Book of Proverbs who permeate and pervade the literature of the Old Testament, likely were influential in establishment thought in this period. This intellectual opinion accepted the formal presuppositions of temple religion; that is, the rule of Yahweh and the moral coherence of the world were assumptions of this community of reflection (*Cadences of Home: Preaching Among Exiles*).

This focus on education is preserved in the Book of Proverbs. Here we find important teachings on human sexuality that were passed down to the young men and women of Solomon's Israel.

### A. The Allure of Adultery (vv. 1-14)

(Proverbs 5:1-2, 6-7, 12-14 is not included in the printed text.)

**³ For the lips of a strange woman drop as an honeycomb, and her mouth is smoother than oil: ⁴ But her end is bitter as wormwood, sharp as a two-edged sword. ⁵ Her feet go down to death; her steps take hold on hell.**

**⁸ Remove thy way far from her, and come not nigh the door of her house: ⁹ Lest thou give thine honour unto others, and thy years unto the cruel: ¹⁰ Lest strangers be filled with thy wealth; and thy labours be in the house of a stranger; ¹¹ And thou mourn at the last, when thy flesh and thy body are consumed.**

The Book of Proverbs is initially laid out as Solomon's instructions to his son. This reflects a time period in which education was considered the domain of the family and the household. Fathers were expected to faithfully pass on the teaching of the Torah to their sons. In this environment, the most potent educational curriculum was also the most vivid. To this end, Solomon painted a vivid picture of the dangers of adultery.

Adultery served many functions in the ancient world. Often sexual liaisons were methods of gaining political power. Solomon knew this might be the case with his son, so he painted a horrifying picture of adultery (vv. 3-5). The power of this text is in the poetry. Rather than simply reciting the well-known Ten Commandments, which include the prohibition of adultery, Solomon wanted his son to think about the character of the adulteress. On the outside, she is enticing and alluring, like honey and oil, but following her path leads to bitterness, pain, and death.

Solomon's hope is to elicit an internal response from his children—"Do not turn aside from what I say" (v. 7 NIV). This terrifying picture goes on through verse 14. The way of adultery leads to a mountain of regret through the wasting of one's vigor, possessions, and health. The future image of the end of such a life is enough to bring a young student to tears. The way of the adulteress leads to momentary pleasure, but a lifetime of ruin and shame in front of the entire community.

1. What did Solomon wish for his son (vv. 1-2)?
2. Describe the deceitfulness of an adulterous woman (vv. 3-6).
3. List three losses an adulterer might experience (vv. 9-11)?
4. How do verses 12 and 13 characterize the sexually immoral person?

> **Not Right Now**
> In one of the great literary works of the Western world that survives from the fourth century AD, Saint Augustine describes his moral failures before he turned to Christ. He writes that he often prayed as a teenager, "Make me chaste, make me continent, but not right now" (Confessions, 8.7). In the same way, our culture tempts us to spurn the freedom that God is offering us in the Bible's teaching on sexuality.

---

B. The Awareness of God (vv. 20-23)

**20 And why wilt thou, my son, be ravished with a strange woman, and embrace the bosom of a stranger? 21 For the ways of man are before the eyes of the Lord, and he pondereth all his goings. 22 His own iniquities shall take the wicked himself, and he shall be holden with the cords of his sins. 23 He shall die without instruction; and in the greatness of his folly he shall go astray.**

Given the beauty of marriage and the horrible consequences of adultery, why would anyone choose the latter path? "Why be captivated . . . by an immoral woman?" (v. 20 NLT).

Up to this point, the whole of Proverbs 5 focuses on humanity, but verses 21-23 focus on God. Solomon reminds his son that God is watching, and God is just. He has set forth moral laws that include definite consequences. Man is not alone, which is both a great hope and a great warning. The final picture is tragic—the son who dies for simple lack of discipline. Matthew Henry observed: "Though secret sins may escape the eyes of our fellow creatures, yet a man's ways are before the eyes of the Lord, who not only sees, but ponders all his goings. Those who are so foolish as to choose the way of sin, are justly left of God to themselves, to go on in the way to destruction."

---

1. Why is the question in verse 20 relevant today?
2. How is God depicted in verse 21?
3. How might an artist draw the picture in verses 22 and 23?

> "The man who receives 'with meekness the engrafted word' (James 1:21) discerns the source of temptation that comes his way. He understands that, behind the beautiful illusion of pleasure, there is a snake—coiled and ready to strike."—Steve Gallagher

III. GOD'S PLAN FOR SEXUALITY (Gen. 2:18-25; Ex. 20:14; Deut. 24:5; Prov. 5:15-19)

God has planned fruitful human living down to the minutest detail. A traditional wedding ceremony calls Jesus Christ "the Master of the art of living." This divine plan for human life includes God's plan for human sexuality. We find this plan unfolding throughout Scripture, from its appearance in the first pages of Genesis.

A. The First Marriage (Gen. 2:18-25)

(Genesis 2:19-22, 25 is not included in the printed text.)

**¹⁸ And the Lord God said, It is not good that the man should be alone; I will make him an help meet for him.**

**²³ And Adam said, This is now bone of my bones, and flesh of my flesh: she shall be called Woman, because she was taken out of Man. ²⁴ Therefore shall a man leave his father and his mother, and shall cleave unto his wife: and they shall be one flesh.**

It is a powerful truth that Genesis 2 comes before Genesis 3. Genesis 3, of course, is when creation goes haywire due to the fall of Adam and Eve. What often goes unnoticed, however, is that God finds an imperfection in creation before the introduction of sin. That imperfection is the solitude of man (2:18).

In contrast to God's proclamation over the close of natural creation "that it was good" (1:25), there is something less than good after man is set forth to steward the creation (2:15). God has given him great responsibility that requires a helper. Thus, the story of man and woman is born.

In verses 19-20, the text expounds on the need Adam has for a helper, based on the scope of the work God has given him. Sometimes religious artwork gives us the impression that the Garden of Eden was a perpetual vacation for Adam. In fact, God kept Adam busy cataloguing the creation and discovering its wonders. Finally, God takes action, putting Adam to sleep and taking a rib (vv. 21-22). The point of this act is to forge a close identity between man and woman, which is summarized in the poem of verse 23: "This is now bone of my bones, and flesh of my flesh."

Genesis then does something rare—offering a verse of commentary that translates *the meaning* of this text for all future audiences. "Therefore" (v. 24) is sometimes translated "for this reason." This text provides God's original reason for marriage. Woman was literally made from man, and therefore, they were made for each other. They were "both naked," and this was no reason to be ashamed (v. 25). The uniqueness of the marital relationship stems from its unique authorship. The bond between parent and child can only be trumped by the bond between husband and wife.

---

1. What was "not good" (v. 18), and how did God change matters (vv. 21-22)?
2. Name two commonalities of every beast and bird (v. 19).
3. What is God's plan for husband and wife (v. 24)?
4. Why weren't Adam and Eve ashamed of their nakedness (v. 25)?

"Marriage itself is consummated with the literal bodily union of husband and wife. From that point on, the husband should regard the wife as his own flesh. If she hurts, he ought to feel the pain. If she has needs, he should embrace those needs as his own. He should seek to feel what she feels, desire what she desires, and in effect, give her the same care and consideration he gives his own body."—John MacArthur

B. The Preservation of Marriage (Ex. 20:14; Deut. 24:5)

**Exodus 20:14 Thou shalt not commit adultery.**

**Deuteronomy 24:5 When a man hath taken a new wife, he shall not go out to war, neither shall he be charged with any business: but he shall be free at home one year, and shall cheer up his wife which he hath taken.**

Because marriage was created and ordained by God in Genesis 2, the remainder of Scripture takes pains to preserve its sanctity and its fruitfulness. The Scriptures sometimes even speak of God's relationship to His people Israel using marital language. In Isaiah 54:5, for example, the prophet declares to Israel that "your Maker is your husband" (NKJV). The New Testament takes over this language, with the Church as the bride of Christ. In this section, we see the care that is taken in the Torah to preserve this God-given relationship of marriage.

Many of the teachings of the Old and New Testament lead right back to the Ten Commandments. It is remarkable how these simple statements serve as the moral touchstone of the whole of Scripture. In fact, much of the Torah is essentially further commentary on these Commandments. The ordination of marriage in Genesis 2:24 is dealt with by two of the Ten Commandments—the fifth commandment, preserving the relationship between children and parents; and the seventh, preserving the marriage relationship.

There are some truths that require no elaboration, so that their punch might be felt. "Thou shalt not commit adultery" (Ex. 20:14) is brief and direct. Adultery must not be justified, explained, or tolerated.

However, Scripture never leaves the complexities of morality at "thou shalt not." More is needed to preserve marriage than the prohibition of adultery alone. In Deuteronomy 24:5, we find one of many commandments meant to preserve the happiness of a marriage so it remains unthreatened by the sin of adultery. The marriage relationship is so valued by God that it should be valued by the nation of Israel even at the expense of military force. If they must go to battle without vital soldiers, so be it. In this instance, God is more interested in the happiness of the soldier's marriage than the strength of the soldier's battalion. What a portrayal of the character of God!

1. Why is Exodus 20:14 broken so frequently?
2. Why is Deuteronomy 24:5 good advice?

"Sex is more than pleasure; it is a covenant—a covenant between a man, a woman, and God."—DeWayne Moree

C. The Beauty of Marriage (Prov. 5:15-19)

**¹⁵ Drink waters out of thine own cistern, and running waters out of thine own well. ¹⁶ Let thy fountains be dispersed abroad, and rivers of waters in the streets. ¹⁷ Let them be only thine own, and not strangers' with thee. ¹⁸ Let thy fountain be blessed: and rejoice with the wife of thy youth. ¹⁹ Let her be as the loving hind and pleasant roe; let her breasts satisfy thee at all times; and be thou ravished always with her love.**

Solomon instructs his son with this powerful truth: the antidote to adultery is a fruitful marriage. He speaks of a happy marriage as a gift from God. The wife that God has given to a husband should not be exchanged for the adulteress.

The depiction of water arouses the son's interest. No prosperous ruler would spill the natural resource of water out into the streets. This is the point of harnessing that water in a well. In the same way, sexual instincts are to be harnessed, and wives are to be cherished. This statement of the beauty of marriage is among the most majestic in the Bible.

---

1. Explain the meaning of verses 15 and 16.
2. What is to be "yours alone" (v. 17 NIV)?
3. What should bring joy (vv. 18-19)?

> "Husbands and wives, recognize that in marriage you have become one flesh. If you live for your private pleasure at the expense of your spouse, you are living against yourself and destroying your joy."—John Piper

---

## CONCLUSION

Hebrews 13:4 commands that "the marriage bed [be] kept pure" (NIV). This is a consistent focus of Scripture. God lays out healthy sexuality within the confines of marriage from the start of the Creation story. Even before the fall of man, God sees the need to perfect the human experiment by creating the institution of marriage. When the commands and prohibitions that God sets out for our human sexuality are heeded, the result is fruitfulness, happiness, and contentment.

## GOLDEN TEXT CHALLENGE

"NEVERTHELESS, TO AVOID FORNICATION, LET EVERY MAN HAVE HIS OWN WIFE, AND LET EVERY WOMAN HAVE HER OWN HUSBAND" (1 Cor. 7:2).

By the direct creative act of God, both "male and female" compose the race (Gen. 1:27). The Lord could have continued to create people by direct action as in the case of Adam, but instead He gave the power of procreation to the race. The entire teaching in the Bible is one man for one woman, and one woman for one man. This is conjugal love, and the Scriptures teach that any sexual involvement outside of the lawful marriage contract is sin.

The writer of Proverbs stated, "Whoso findeth a wife findeth a good thing, and obtaineth favour of the Lord" (18:22). The apostle Paul, in that spiritually fragrant portion on husbands and wives in Ephesians 5, said, "So ought men to love their wives as their own bodies. He that loveth his wife loveth himself. . . . Nevertheless let every one of you in particular so love his wife even as himself; and the wife see that she reverence her husband" (vv. 28, 33).—**Paul Van Gorder, *The Church Stands Corrected***

**Daily Devotions:**
- M. Adulterous King Judged
  2 Samuel 12:7-14
- T. Avoid Immorality
  Proverbs 6:23-32
- W. Marital Intimacy
  Song of Solomon 4:9-16
- T. Impure Fantasies Condemned
  Matthew 5:27-30
- F. Gift of Sexuality
  1 Corinthians 7:1-7
- S. Purity Commanded
  Ephesians 5:3-12

February 22, 2015 (Lesson 12)

# How Should We Treat Others?

Exodus 20:15; 22:1-27; Leviticus 6:1-7; 25:14-17; Deuteronomy 15:7-11; 24:10-15, 19-22; 25:13-16

**Unit Theme:**
God's Moral Law (Genesis-Deuteronomy)

**Central Truth:**
God commands us to treat others with respect and fairness.

**Focus:**
Review and observe God's laws about how to treat others fairly.

**Context:**
Old Testament passages regarding property rights, fair transactions, and generosity

**Golden Text:**
"As ye would that men should do to you, do ye also to them likewise" (Luke 6:31).

**Study Outline:**
I. Respect Property Rights
   (Ex. 20:15; 22:1-15; Lev. 6:1-7)
II. Engage in Fair Transactions
   (Ex. 22:25-27; Lev. 25:14-17; Deut. 24:10-15; 25:13-16)
III. Give Generously to the Poor
   (Deut. 24:19-22; 15:7-11)

## INTRODUCTION

There is a famous criticism of living "too heavenly-minded to be any earthly good." In the Bible, there is hardly a line of separation between the two orientations. Instead, to be oriented toward the things of God is also to be oriented toward the good of this world. Jesus drew this connection most famously in His teaching on the two greatest commandments:

> "Love the Lord your God with all your heart and with all your soul and with all your mind." This is the first and greatest commandment. And the second is like it: "Love your neighbor as yourself." All the Law and the Prophets hang on these two commandments (Matt. 22:37-40).

Jesus, of course, was not asked about the two greatest commandments, but in His theology, you cannot talk about love for God without likewise talking about love for neighbor. As He said, the whole of Scripture hangs on this vital link.

There are two fundamental questions that make up theology: (1) "What is God like?" and (2) "What difference does this make?" The biblical answer to those questions is "God is love" (1 John 4:8), and therefore calls us to live a life of love toward Him and toward the object of His love—all people. If we do not believe God is love, there is no reason to treat others in any particular way. If we do not believe God exists at all, there is no reason for anything. Dietrich Bonhoeffer said, "Without Christ we should not know God. . . . But without Christ we also would not know our brother, nor could we come to him. The way is blocked by our own ego" (*Life Together: The Classic Exploration of Faith in Community*).

The commandment to love one's neighbor was not original to Jesus. We will see in this study that He pulled it directly from the Torah. In the Bible's opening books, we are given a clear picture as to how we should treat others . . . as God treats us.

I. RESPECT PROPERTY RIGHTS (Ex. 20:15; 22:1-15; Lev. 6:1-7)

The right to personal property is one of the revolutionary components of the Torah. The children of Israel had been delivered from slavery in Egypt, where they themselves were considered the property of the Egyptian state. Since God freed them from being the possessions of the Egyptians, they must forge a new relationship toward possessions. We will see that this relationship strikes a balance between the right to own personal property (individual betterment) and the good of the community (social justice). This balance also includes a strong attentiveness to the poor. Taken as a whole, the Torah paints the picture of a just and equitable society.

A. Stealing Forbidden (Ex. 20:15)

**15 Thou shalt not steal.**

As we have seen often in our study of God's moral law in the Torah, the Ten Commandments set out general principles that are elaborated on in other biblical passages. The principle never changes, but sometimes the methods for employing the principle in the life of the nation of Israel develop and progress. The Israelites have been living at the very bottom of a slave economy for over four centuries. They have cultivated an attitude of sheer survival. The need to survive led to all sorts of immoral behavior, including stealing. As God prepares them to live as a new nation in a new land, however, there will be no need for stealing. God will provide everything they need. The commandment "Thou shalt not steal" is among the most simple in the Bible.

The motive to steal comes from a worldview of scarcity which says, "There are not enough resources in the world to go around . . . to meet the needs of everyone. Therefore, I have to take what I need any way I can get it." God challenges this worldview in the Ten Commandments. If stealing is forbidden, then God is promising that He will supply the needs of His people, so they will not need to take from others. This was revolutionary!

Historians tell us the ancient world was driven by a "limited goods" mentality. That is, unlike many societies now, in which there is the perception that money is limitless and anyone might strike it rich, people in the ancient world thought oppositely.

> By "Image of Limited Good" I mean that broad areas of peasant behavior are patterned in such fashion as to suggest that peasants view their social, economic, and natural universes—their total environment—as one in which all of the desired things in life such as land, wealth, health; friendship and love; manliness and honor; respect and status; power and influence; security and safety, exist in finite

quantity and are always in short supply, as far as the peasant is concerned. Not only do these and all other "good things" exist in finite and limited quantities, but in addition there is no way directly within peasant power to increase the available quantities. It is as if the obvious fact of land shortage in a densely populated area applied to all other desired things: not enough to go around (George Foster, "Peasant Society and the Image of Limited Good," *American Anthropologist 67*).

It is to a formerly enslaved people who embody this mentality that God imparts a new worldview. In this worldview, there are enough material resources for everyone, because God is enough for everyone.

---

- List various reasons people break this command.

> "Money exerts a certain control over us because it seems to hold out so much (false) promise of happiness. It whispers with great force, 'Think and act so as to get into a position to enjoy my benefits.' This may include stealing, borrowing, or working. Money promises happiness, and we serve it by believing the promise and walking by that faith."—John Piper

---

B. Restitution for Stealing (Ex. 22:1-15; Lev. 6:1-7)

(Exodus 22:2-15; Leviticus 6:6-7 are not included in the printed text.)

**Exodus 22:1** If a man shall steal an ox, or a sheep, and kill it, or sell it; he shall restore five oxen for an ox, and four sheep for a sheep.

**Leviticus 6:1** And the Lord spake unto Moses, saying, ² If a soul sin, and commit a trespass against the Lord, and lie unto his neighbour in that which was delivered him to keep, or in fellowship, or in a thing taken away by violence, or hath deceived his neighbour; ³ Or have found that which was lost, and lieth concerning it, and sweareth falsely; in any of all these that a man doeth, sinning therein: ⁴ Then it shall be, because he hath sinned, and is guilty, that he shall restore that which he took violently away, or the thing which he hath deceitfully gotten, or that which was delivered him to keep, or the lost thing which he found, ⁵ Or all that about which he hath sworn falsely; he shall even restore it in the principal, and shall add the fifth part more thereto, and give it unto him to whom it appertaineth, in the day of his trespass offering.

The Bible deals with life as it is, not just life as it should be. Although the prohibition against stealing is simple, strong, and straightforward, God knows the human heart is sinful. This commandment will not always be kept. As a result, the Torah stipulates how restitution should be made when the sin of stealing is committed.

The most common form of stealing treated in the Torah is the robbery of livestock. It is easy to imagine why this form of stealing was addressed so often. As livestock grazed across the land of Israel, herds and flocks often intermingled. Fences and barriers were not always put up to delineate where one farmer's land began and another farmer's land ended. As a result, there were opportune moments for an unethical shepherd to steal an animal undetected. The Torah metes out stiff penalties for such behavior, such as quadrupling or quintupling a stolen animal's value if it was slaughtered (Ex. 22:1).

Cases would go before the local judge for a decision, as we see in verses 7-9. Such a sentence would detract would-be thieves. In fact, verse 3 demands that a poor thief be himself sold into slavery if he cannot make restitution for the robbery. However, if the animal is found in his possession unharmed, he must only pay back double (v. 4). We see in the specificities of these sentences a pronounced focus on making a just judgment, so the punishment properly meets the crime. There are even differing sentences concerning self-defense in verse 2.

What about in cases that are impossible to judge accurately? Such a case is laid out in verses 10-13. Here we find a potential scene in which an animal dies or is injured or stolen while being safeguarded by a neighbor. If the owner of the animal believes the neighbor has done wrong, the defendant may swear an oath before Yahweh that he did the animal no harm. This will settle the matter. If the defendant is unwilling to do this, he must make restitution. The name of God was so revered in ancient Jewish society that this litmus test was a reliable means of getting to the truth of the matter.

In Leviticus 6:1-7, we find a more general rule for dealing with stolen property. For personal property disputes that are mediated by the priests, a single penalty is laid down for stolen goods of all types. In this scenario, the penalty of one-fifth is sufficient to remunerate the damage from the theft. In addition, a guilt offering of considerable value must be presented as a sacrifice.

---

1. List situations where people were required to "pay double" (Ex. 22:4, 7, 9 NKJV).
2. When were people required to "make restitution" (vv. 3, 5, 6, 10-14)?
3. When would someone be "sold for his theft" (v. 3)?
4. What steps would a thief have to take to make things right with God (Lev. 6:4-7)?

> "Law, without force, is impotent."—Blaise Pascal

---

## II. ENGAGE IN FAIR TRANSACTIONS (Ex. 22:25-27; Lev. 25:14-17; Deut. 24:10-15; 25:13-16)

Property theft is not the only form of stealing. The Torah takes pains to disallow all forms of stealing, to cut it off at the root, and to enforce penalties when those laws are broken. In the following passages, taken from Exodus, Leviticus, and Deuteronomy, we find the Bible's emphasis on fairness in one's professional and personal transactions.

A. The Prohibition of Interest (Ex. 22:25-27)

**²⁵ If thou lend money to any of my people that is poor by thee, thou shalt not be to him as an usurer, neither shalt thou lay upon him usury. ²⁶ If thou at all take thy neighbour's raiment to pledge, thou shalt deliver it unto him by that the sun goeth down: ²⁷ For that is his covering only, it is his raiment for his skin: wherein shall he sleep? and it shall come to pass, when he crieth unto me, that I will hear; for I am gracious.**

One distinctive of the Jewish community is the practice of refusing to charge interest to one another. Throughout history, the Jewish people have been able to so quickly prosper around the world because of this commitment. Access to capital is key to the success of a people. If everyone has access, the playing field of business and life is leveled, allowing more people to participate and prosper. This is why the prohibition of interest is so strong in Exodus 22. Verse 25 is focused on the poor, but Deuteronomy 23:20 expands this command to include the entire Jewish community: "You may charge a foreigner interest, but not a brother Israelite, so that the Lord your God may bless you in everything you put your hand to in the land you are entering to possess" (NIV).

The leveling of interest was not only tied to monetary loans. In the ancient world, money was not the only type of financial exchange. Property was valuable in its own right. Therefore, all sorts of collateral might be used, including one's own clothing (Ex. 22:26). Interest and collateral are serious business to the heart of God. To this day they are used to take advantage of the poor and weak, but God will have none of this among the people of Israel. His compassion causes Him to hear those who are mistreated—He will not remain on the sidelines when injustices are perpetrated (v. 27).

---

1. If money was loaned, what did God require (v. 25)?
2. If a person's garment was taken in pledge, what did God require (vv. 26-27)?
3. What might God say today to companies that charge exorbitant interest?

> "Interest works night and day, in fair weather and in foul. It gnaws at a man's substance with invisible teeth."—Henry Ward Beecher

---

B. The Problem of Jubilee (Lev. 25:14-17)

**¹⁴ And if thou sell ought unto thy neighbour, or buyest ought of thy neighbour's hand, ye shall not oppress one another: ¹⁵ According to the number of years after the jubile thou shalt buy of thy neighbour, and according unto the number of years of the fruits he shall sell unto thee: ¹⁶ According to the multitude of years thou shalt increase the price thereof, and according to the fewness of years thou shalt diminish the price of it: for according to the number of the years of the fruits doth he sell unto thee.**

**¹⁷ Ye shall not therefore oppress one another; but thou shalt fear thy God: for I am the Lord your God.**

In Leviticus 25, we find what was the most utterly leveling event in the nation of Israel. Although free to amass personal property and wealth, the Year of Jubilee was instituted to prevent monopolies of God's land. The central proclamation of the Year of Jubilee is verse 23: "the land is mine." To this agrarian society, land equaled wealth, prosperity, and the future. God would not give up His ownership of the land. Therefore, since He is a gracious God, every fifty years the land was redistributed to the original layout of the Promised Land. No families were left out of this redistribution.

Putting this redistribution on a timetable introduced an obvious problem. The Jews were not stupid, but shrewd. Jewish businessmen with any financial savvy would be careful to time their transactions so as not to incur losses from the Year of Jubilee. God strictly warned against this kind of cold calculation (v. 14).

How might such oppression take place? Verses 15 and 16 explain such a scenario, in which financial numbers are insured against the Year of Jubilee. God calls this practice exactly what it is: *oppression*.

The reverence which the people of Israel were called to show toward the Lord would be evidenced in their refusal to oppress one another (v. 17). Even when vast amounts of land were at stake, God's Word was to take precedence over building wealth.

---

1. Why was "Jubilee" an appropriate name for this particular year (vv. 14-15)?
2. What does God warn against (vv. 16-17)?

> "Since my money is God's money, every spending decision I make is a spiritual decision."—John Hagee

---

C. Do Not Oppress or Extort (Deut. 24:10-15; 25:13-16)

(Deuteronomy 24:11-13; 25:13-14 are not included in the printed text.)

**24:10 When thou dost lend thy brother any thing, thou shalt not go into his house to fetch his pledge.**

**¹⁴ Thou shalt not oppress an hired servant that is poor and needy, whether he be of thy brethren, or of thy strangers that are in thy land within thy gates: ¹⁵ At his day thou shalt give him his hire, neither shall the sun go down upon it; for he is poor, and setteth his heart upon it: lest he cry against thee unto the Lord, and it be sin unto thee.**

**25:15 But thou shalt have a perfect and just weight, a perfect and just measure shalt thou have: that thy days may be lengthened in the land which the Lord thy God giveth thee. ¹⁶ For all that do such things, and all that do unrighteously, are an abomination unto the Lord thy God.**

In Deuteronomy 24:10-13, we find a situation similar to, but broader, than we saw in Exodus 22. There, the scenario involves a cloak that has been taken as collateral for some kind of loan. Here, the collateral might be anything in the borrower's house. The Torah shows great respect for the borrower, forbidding the lender from entering his house. The lender is to assume the risk for the loan based on the character of the borrower. If the borrower provides his cloak for collateral, the righteous lender should return it by nightfall so the man is not left without his cloak to sleep in (Deut. 24:12-13).

In the same way that the Jews were not to oppress one another in matters of lending, they were also to pay fair wages to hired laborers (vv. 14-15). God is interested in fair labor practices, including the speedy disbursement of daily salaries. At this time, hired hands were typically day laborers, dependent on the wage at the end of the day for their survival. If a Jewish landholder oppressed such a laborer, God would get involved.

A common form of ancient oppression was the manipulation of weights and measures (25:13-14). Various metals, foods, and other goods would be weighed so their value could be assessed. An unscrupulous dealer could tweak the scales in order to cheat the buyer. God strictly forbade this, lumping financial misdealing into the same category as sexual immorality and idolatrous worship—they were all abominations before God (v. 16). However, using "accurate and honest weights and measures" would be rewarded with long life (v. 15 NIV).

---

1. What protection was provided to the borrower (24:10-11)?
2. What is called a "righteous act" (vv. 12-13 NIV)?
3. Name ways the principles in 25:13-15 are violated today.
4. How does God view dishonesty (v. 16)?

> "He who allows oppression shares the crime."—Desiderius Erasmus

---

### III. GIVE GENEROUSLY TO THE POOR (Deut. 24:19-22; 15:7-11)

God's Word pays special attention to people who are oppressed. We see this attention highlighted in the Book of Deuteronomy.

#### A. The Tradition of Gleaning (24:19-22)

(Deuteronomy 24:20-22 is not included in the printed text.)

**[19] When thou cuttest down thine harvest in thy field, and hast forgot a sheaf in the field, thou shalt not go again to fetch it: it shall be for the stranger, for the fatherless, and for the widow: that the Lord thy God may bless thee in all the work of thine hands.**

The tradition of gleaning in the fields is well known in the Bible because of the Book of Ruth, where Boaz is recognized as a righteous man because he allowed Ruth to glean the leftover harvests from his fields. In Deuteronomy 24:19, we find the origination of that tradition as it relates to care for the poor.

The three categories referenced are at the bottom of the social ladder: (1) The *stranger* (alien or migrant) has no Jewish inheritance, no Jewish land, no Jewish family. (2) The *fatherless* has been deprived of the family's primary breadwinner. (3) The *widow* has been left alone. These voices are important to God, so He repeats the same commandment with regard to olive trees (v. 20) and grape vineyards (v. 21). He justifies these commandments with the call to remember the days of slavery (v. 22). As God rescued the children of Israel from Egyptian slavery, the Israelites were to protect the poor from oppression.

---

1. Whom were landowners to help, and how (vv. 19-21)?
2. What were God's people to "remember," and why (v. 22)?

> "Watch lest prosperity destroy generosity."—Henry Ward Beecher

---

B. Unmistakable Conviction (15:7-11)

**7 If there be among you a poor man of one of thy brethren within any of thy gates in thy land which the Lord thy God giveth thee, thou shalt not harden thine heart, nor shut thine hand from thy poor brother: 8 But thou shalt open thine hand wide unto him, and shalt surely lend him sufficient for his need, in that which he wanteth. 9 Beware that there be not a thought in thy wicked heart, saying, The seventh year, the year of release, is at hand; and thine eye be evil against thy poor brother, and thou givest him nought; and he cry unto the Lord against thee, and it be sin unto thee. 10 Thou shalt surely give him, and thine heart shall not be grieved when thou givest unto him: because that for this thing the Lord thy God shall bless thee in all thy works, and in all that thou puttest thine hand unto. 11 For the poor shall never cease out of the land: therefore I command thee, saying, Thou shalt open thine hand wide unto thy brother, to thy poor, and to thy needy, in thy land.**

The call to remember the poor is sounded over and over again in the Torah. As in Leviticus 25, where it addresses potential scenarios of oppression in the Year of Jubilee, so we see the same dynamic occurring in Deuteronomy 15. Here, Moses is instituting a different festival—the year of canceling debts. The Year of Jubilee was to take place every fifty years; the year of canceling debts, every seven. This was a purely financial jubilee, in which all debts were canceled. The same hazard of calculating lending practices based on this year was likely.

Verse 7 specifies the man in question to be a fellow Jew, so there is great urgency about his proper treatment. Stinginess was not an option, but notice the passage is not about almsgiving, but lending. The poor man is being given capital, the chance to begin his life again (v. 8). The greatest obstacle to this could be the very thing meant to create the poor man's freedom—the year of canceling debts (v. 9). So, God warned the Jews to beware of the greed that might crop up in their heart. It was sinful to withhold a loan to a brother in need.

In all of these transactions, we are assured God was watching the heart. While man might be calculating based on numbers, property values, and the calendar, God was paying attention to one's internal disposition (v. 10). If the Lord saw a heart of pure generosity, He would bless the giver all the more.

Why was this issue so important? Because the problem of poverty would always persist, the people of God must always give (v. 11). God called the people to address the problem with open hearts and open hands.

---

1. Describe the godly person's "heart" and "hand" (vv. 7-8).

2. Whom did God promise to bless (vv. 9-10)?

> "Too often we think of being tempted as being enticed to do big things like stealing, murdering, or committing adultery. But most often we're tempted to be impatient, stingy, jealous, greedy, or any number of other things that we consider lesser sins."—Joyce Meyer

## CONCLUSION

God has given us a world full of resources that He means to be used for human betterment. Unfortunately, power-grabbing and greed can quickly sap these resources. As a result, God lays out commandments in Scripture to order society in a just and equitable way. Through respecting property rights, engaging in fair transactions, and remaining open-handed toward the poor, we fulfill God's will for treating other people with love.

## GOLDEN TEXT CHALLENGE

"AS YE WOULD THAT MEN SHOULD DO TO YOU, DO YE ALSO TO THEM LIKEWISE" (Luke 6:31).

Christian love demands sacrificial action that far surpasses the world's standard of love. It means giving to others with no demands or expectation that they will return the favor.

How do we want others to treat us? Then treat them the same way we want to be treated, regardless of how they may respond. Do the good to them that we desire they do to us.

We who reflect the love of God to the world are promised, "Your reward will be great, and you will be sons of the Most High" (Luke 6:35 NKJV). God will reward our love, and we will show ourselves to be His children. The Most High delights toward us who yield to the Holy Spirit and have generous hearts like our heavenly Father. Our likeness to Him will reveal that we are His children.—**French Arrington**

**Daily Devotions:**
M. Do Not Steal
   Leviticus 19:11-13
T. The Righteous Are Generous
   Psalm 37:21-26
W. Treat Others With Love
   Luke 6:27-36
T. Generosity Exemplified
   Acts 4:32-37
F. Generosity Brings God Praise
   2 Corinthians 9:6-15
S. Have a Good Work Ethic
   1 Thessalonians 4:9-12

# Introduction to Spring Quarter

"Life of Samuel" (lessons 1-5, 7) moves from the calling of young Samuel to David's anointing as king (1 Samuel 1—16).

The lessons were written by Dr. Lee Roy Martin (D.Th., University of South Africa; M.Div., Pentecostal Theological Seminary), professor of Hebrew and Old Testament at the Pentecostal Theological Seminary in Cleveland, Tennessee. He has pastored for eighteen years, and has written books on Jonah and the Book of Judges.

---

The Easter lesson (6) and the Pentecost lesson (13) were compiled by Lance Colkmire (see biographical information on page 156).

---

The second unit, "The Early Church (Acts, Part 1)" covers events from the first twelve chapters of Acts (lessons 8-12, 14).

This unit was written by French L. Arrington, Ph.D. He taught and mentored ministerial students for decades at the Pentecostal Theological Seminary and Lee University. Dr. Arrington is the author of *Encountering the Holy Spirit*; the three-volume *Christian Doctrine: A Pentecostal Perspective*; *Unconditional Eternal Security: Myth or Truth?*; and commentaries on Luke, Acts, Romans, 1 and 2 Corinthians, and 1 Timothy.

March 1, 2015 (Lesson 1)
# God Calls Young Samuel
**1 Samuel 1:8-28; 3:1-21**

**Theme:**
Life of Samuel

**Central Truth:**
God hears the prayers of His children and directs their lives.

**Focus:**
Consider God's providence for Samuel's call and trust God to direct our lives.

**Context:**
About 1080 to 1070 BC in Ramah and Shiloh

**Golden Text:**
"The Lord came, and stood, and called as at other times, Samuel, Samuel. Then Samuel answered, Speak; for thy servant heareth" (1 Sam. 3:10).

**Study Outline:**
  I. Hannah's Prayer Answered
      (1 Sam. 1:10-20)
 II. Samuel Dedicated to the Lord
      (1 Sam. 1:21-28)
III. Called to Be a Prophet
      (1 Sam. 3:1-21)

## INTRODUCTION

It has been said that the Bible is a roadmap for the Christian, but that is not the best description of the Bible because a roadmap is too impersonal. The Bible is the story of God and His people—people and their daily lives, as God seeks to mold and shape them. Yes, the Bible is "a lamp unto [our] feet and a light unto [our] path" (Ps. 119:105); and yes, the Bible contains doctrine, teachings, and instruction. However, most of the Bible's teaching is done in the form of stories—stories of success and failure, victory and defeat, struggle and attainment, love and hate, conflict and reconciliation.

The Book of 1 Samuel tells the story of three major characters and their walk with God: Samuel, Saul, and David. In the next few weeks, we will get to know these characters. We will listen with Samuel for the voice of God, and we will reply with him, "Speak, for Your servant hears" (3:10 NKJV). We will grieve over Saul, the first king of Israel, whose reign rapidly vanishes from his hands. We will feel the flow of anointing oil as it is poured on David's head, as we hear God say, "Man looks at the outward appearance, but the Lord looks at the heart" (16:7 NKJV).

The Book of 1 Samuel follows the books of Joshua, Judges, and Ruth. The Book of Joshua recounts Israel's great victories over Jericho and the other cities of Canaan. Throughout this book, the people of Israel were obedient and faithful, and God rewarded their faithfulness with His blessings. The Book of Judges narrates Israel's downward spiral from victory to defeat, from unity to fragmentation, and from faithfulness to idolatry. Judges concludes on a tragic note: "In those days there was no king in Israel; everyone did what was right in his own eyes" (21:25 NASB). The Book of Ruth takes place during the days of the judges, and it tells a story that eventually leads to King David.

First Samuel picks up the story of Judges in midstream (both Eli and Samuel functioned as judges), and we learn in the opening chapters that a deep darkness had fallen on the land. "The word of the Lord was rare in those days—there was no revelation breaking forth" (see 3:1). Furthermore, even the priests did not know the Lord. They were "scoundrels" who "treated the Lord's offerings with contempt" (2:12, 17 NLT), and who used their office to procure sexual favors (v. 22).

However, in the midst of the darkness, a flicker of light began to shine. The prayer of Hannah was the spark that lit the fires of revival which would sweep over the land through the ministry of her son, the prophet Samuel.

## I. HANNAH'S PRAYER ANSWERED (1 Sam. 1:10-20)

The days of the judges were distressing times, but it is during those times of moral and spiritual darkness that God's people stand out as beacons of light. Elkanah, a righteous man, would take his family each year to the town of Shiloh, where the tabernacle of the Lord was located, and there he would offer sacrifices to the Lord (1 Sam. 1:3). Elkanah married a woman named Hannah, but she was unable to have children (v. 2). Apparently, because of Hannah's barrenness, Elkanah pursued the custom of marrying a second wife, Peninnah, who was able to have children. In the biblical world, children were highly valued, and it was considered a disgrace for a woman to be barren. Hannah's condition, therefore, caused her great pain. In addition to her own feelings of inferiority, she was also humiliated by Peninnah, who would mock Hannah and torment her (v. 6).

When Elkanah went to the Tabernacle, he sacrificed a *peace offering* (see Lev. 7:11-36). Unlike the *whole burnt offering*, in which the entire animal is consumed on the altar, the *peace offering* consists only of the blood and the parts of the animal that were not normally eaten by humans. The flesh of the animal would be cooked, and the family would eat it as an act of celebration and thanksgiving. A portion would be given to the priest who had officiated at the sacrifice (v. 32). Elkanah gave a portion of the sacrificial animal to each member of the family, but he gave a double portion to Hannah because he loved her and wanted her to feel special, even though she was unable to bear children (1 Sam. 1:4-5).

Hannah's pain finally got the best of her, and she wept and refused to eat. Her husband tried to comfort her, but she was beyond comfort (vv. 7-8).

A. Hannah's Prayer (vv. 10-16)

(1 Samuel 1:12-14 is not included in the printed text.)

**¹⁰ And she was in bitterness of soul, and prayed unto the Lord, and wept sore. ¹¹ And she vowed a vow, and said, O Lord of hosts, if thou wilt indeed look on the affliction of thine handmaid, and remember me, and not forget thine handmaid, but wilt give unto thine handmaid a man child,**

then I will give him unto the Lord all the days of his life, and there shall no razor come upon his head.

¹⁵ And Hannah answered and said, No, my lord, I am a woman of a sorrowful spirit: I have drunk neither wine nor strong drink, but have poured out my soul before the Lord. ¹⁶ Count not thine handmaid for a daughter of Belial: for out of the abundance of my complaint and grief have I spoken hitherto.

The emotional pain of Hannah's condition moved her to action. In her desperation she went to the Tabernacle to present her case before God in prayer (vv. 10-11). Even though Hannah's inability to have children was caused by the Lord himself (vv. 5-6), she did not accept her situation as final. She was desperate for divine help. She poured out her soul to God in "fervent prayer," as we also are encouraged to do (James 5:16). She wept until she could weep no more. Like David, she "cried [unto God] with [her] whole heart" (Ps. 119:145).

In addition to her passionate prayer, Hannah made a vow to the Lord. She promised that if the Lord would give her a son, she would give him back to the Lord as a Nazirite, consecrated unto God. The promise that no razor would come upon his head is a part of the Nazirite vows found in Numbers 6:1-8. Normally, this vow was only for a short, specified period of time; but Hannah promised to give her son as a Nazirite for his entire life.

Eli was the high priest at that time, and he was stationed at the entrance to the Tabernacle. As he watched Hannah praying, he saw her mouth moving but did not hear her speaking, because she was praying silently. Assuming that she was drunk, he rebuked her (1 Sam. 1:12-14). She protested, however, insisting that she was not filled with wine or strong drink; rather, she was filled with sorrow, and she had "poured out [her] soul before the Lord" (v. 15). She pleaded with Eli that he would not consider her to be a "daughter of Belial" (v. 16), which means a worthless, degenerate woman. She explained to Eli that her prayers were not worthless or degenerate, for they had emerged from thoughtful contemplation on her situation and from the provocation of Peninnah, who had grieved her deeply.

---

1. Describe Hannah's emotional state (v. 10).
2. Describe Hannah's vow (v. 11).
3. What was Eli's wrong idea, and how did Hannah change his mind (vv. 12-16)?

### Influential Prayers

The preaching of John Wesley sparked a worldwide revival in the eighteenth century, and the impact of that revival endures today, most specifically in the Pentecostal Movement. Wesley attributed his success in ministry to the powerful influence of his praying mother, Suzanna. God's providence and calling in the lives of people like Wesley (and Samuel) often emerges out of the prayers and consecrated lives of their parents and grandparents. Like Suzanna Wesley, we must live in such a way that our children will be greater servants of the Lord than we have been.

B. Hannah's Peace (vv. 17-20)

**¹⁷ Then Eli answered and said, Go in peace: and the God of Israel grant thee thy petition that thou hast asked of him. ¹⁸ And she said, Let thine handmaid find grace in thy sight. So the woman went her way, and did eat, and her countenance was no more sad. ¹⁹ And they rose up in the morning early, and worshipped before the Lord, and returned, and came to their house to Ramah: and Elkanah knew Hannah his wife; and the Lord remembered her. ²⁰ Wherefore it came to pass, when the time was come about after Hannah had conceived, that she bare a son, and called his name Samuel, saying, Because I have asked him of the Lord.**

Hannah apparently made an impression on Eli, and he realized he had misjudged her motives. Therefore, he spoke a word of assurance to her; he told her to "go in peace." He also affirmed that the God of Israel would grant the petition she had asked of Him. Hannah received Eli's assurance as a word from the Lord, and she returned to her family with confidence that God had heard her prayer. She ceased her fasting, and she was no longer sad.

The next day, Hannah, Elkanah, and all the family departed from Shiloh and returned to their home in Ramah. The Lord "remembered her" (v. 19), which means He took notice of her prayers, and soon she conceived and gave birth to a son.

Hannah called her son "Samuel, saying, Because I have asked him of the Lord" (v. 20). The Hebrew name *Samuel* does not exactly match any Hebrew phrase, but it comes closest to meaning "heard of the Lord." Hannah asked and the Lord heard. From his birth until the end of his life, prayer would be an important part of Samuel's life. Just as the Lord heard Hannah's prayer, He would also hear the prayers of Samuel.

---

1. Describe Hannah's change (vv. 17-18).
2. Explain the naming of Samuel (vv. 19-20).

> "O God, make us desperate, and grant us faith and boldness to approach Your throne and make our petitions known, knowing that in doing we link arms with Omnipotence and become instruments of Your eternal purposes being fulfilled on this earth."—Nancy Leigh DeMoss

---

II. SAMUEL DEDICATED TO THE LORD (1 Sam. 1:21-28)

A. Samuel With His Mother (vv. 21-23)

(1 Samuel 1:21-23 is not included in the printed text.)

After Samuel was born, his father, Elkanah, continued to make his annual pilgrimage with his family to Shiloh, where he would offer sacrifices to the Lord. However, Hannah kept Samuel at home. She wanted to make every minute count while she had her son with her. She intended to remain at home with Samuel until he was weaned. Then she would take him to the Tabernacle, where she would fulfill her vow and Samuel would enter the service of the Lord.

---

- Explain Elkanah's statement, "Only may the Lord confirm His word" (v. 23 NASB).

---

### B. Samuel Brought to the Temple (vv. 24-25)

**24 And when she had weaned him, she took him up with her, with three bullocks, and one ephah of flour, and a bottle of wine, and brought him unto the house of the Lord in Shiloh: and the child was young. 25 And they slew a bullock, and brought the child to Eli.**

The *weaning* that is spoken of here was most likely a figure of speech that refers to the completion of childhood at the age of twelve. A child was normally weaned from his mother's milk at the age of two or three. At the age of seven, he was weaned from children's food; and at the age of twelve, he was weaned from his mother's care and placed into the apprenticeship of his father or a male relative. In Samuel's case, he may have entered into the service at the Tabernacle when he was as young as three or as old as twelve.

Hannah brought Samuel to the Tabernacle along with three bullocks. One was for a whole burnt offering as a sign of Samuel's consecration. The second was for a sin offering, and the third was for a peace offering. She also brought flour and wine, which were offered along with the animals (see Lev. 23:13).

After they had offered up the first bull as a burnt offering, Hannah presented Samuel to Eli the high priest, who would instruct and train Samuel in the service of the Tabernacle.

---

- List everything Hannah took to the Tabernacle, and why.

> "He that chooses God, devotes himself to God as the vessels of the sanctuary were consecrated and set apart from common to holy uses, so he that has chosen God to be his God, has dedicated himself to God, and will no more be devoted to profane uses."—Thomas Watson

---

### C. Samuel Given to the Lord (vv. 26-28)

**26 And she said, Oh my lord, as thy soul liveth, my lord, I am the woman that stood by thee here, praying unto the Lord. 27 For this child I prayed; and the Lord hath given me my petition which I asked of him: 28 Therefore also I have lent him to the Lord; as long as he liveth he shall be lent to the Lord. And he worshipped the Lord there.**

Several years had passed since Eli had observed Hannah's prayer in the Tabernacle. Therefore, she takes care to remind him of her identity and to testify of God's answer to her prayer. In her recounting of the story, she states that she had "stood" praying. The Hebrew word for *stood* (*natsav*) is not the normal word for a standing posture, which would be *amad*. The Hebrew term used here signifies more than posture; it is often used in military contexts with the meaning "to place oneself, to be positioned, to take a stand." Hannah is saying she engaged in spiritual warfare and her prayer was one of urgency and commitment. She took a stand in prayer just as Paul encourages us to do: "Put on the whole armour of God, that ye may be able to stand against the wiles of the devil. . . . Wherefore take unto you the whole armour of God, that ye may be able to withstand in the evil day, and having done all, to stand. Stand therefore . . ." (Eph. 6:11-14).

Hannah testifies that she had prayed for a son, and God had answered. Therefore, just as God had been faithful to her, she would be faithful to Him and would fulfill her vow by giving Samuel back to God. All the days of his life, Samuel would belong to God. How many times have we made promises to God that we failed to keep? God is faithful, and we must be faithful to Him as well.

After Hannah had presented Samuel to Eli at the Tabernacle, Samuel bowed down before the Lord as a sign of his submission and his commitment.

The birth of a child is reason for celebration within any culture, but it was especially so in ancient Israel. Children were considered to be a great blessing. The psalmist wrote, "Children are a heritage from the Lord, the fruit of the womb is a reward" (Ps. 127:3 NKJV). In response to God's gift of a son, Hannah praises God with a song (1 Sam. 2:1-10). Our prayers should be accompanied by thanksgiving (Phil. 4:6), and every answer should be celebrated with fervent praise (Ps. 103:1-4). Like Miriam, Deborah, Elizabeth, and the Virgin Mary, Hannah's song was prophetic, inspired by the Holy Spirit.

---

1. What was Hannah's testimony to Eli (v. 27)?
2. Describe an answered prayer to which you can testify.
3. In verse 28, what did Hannah do? What did Samuel do?

---

> "Consecration is only possible when we give up our will about everything."—F. B. Meyer

---

## III. CALLED TO BE A PROPHET (1 Sam. 3:1-21)

After Samuel enters the service of the Tabernacle, he undergoes a period of training and preparation (1 Sam. 2:11-36). The story emphasizes the contrast between Samuel and the sons of Eli (Hophni and Phinehas). Three times we read that Samuel "ministered" to the Lord (2:11, 18; 3:1), but the sons of Eli were "sons of Belial" (which means "worthless"), and they "knew not the Lord" (2:12). They would take by force parts of the sacrifices that were not theirs (vv. 13-17);

they would seduce the women who served at the door of the Tabernacle (v. 22); and they would not submit to correction (v. 25).

The contrast between Samuel and Eli's sons is suggested further by a play on words, using the term *great* (Hebrew *gadol*). While the sin of Hophni and Phinehas was "great" (v. 17), Samuel "grew before the Lord" (v. 21). Inasmuch as the word translated "grew" can also mean "was great," the contrast is between the greatness of Samuel in the presence of God and the greatness of Hophni and Phinehas in sin.

A. The Prophetic Word Was Rare (vv. 1-9)

(1 Samuel 3:2-6 is not included in the printed text.)

**¹ And the child Samuel ministered unto the Lord before Eli. And the word of the Lord was precious in those days; there was no open vision.**

**⁷ Now Samuel did not yet know the Lord, neither was the word of the Lord yet revealed unto him. ⁸ And the Lord called Samuel again the third time. And he arose and went to Eli, and said, Here am I; for thou didst call me. And Eli perceived that the Lord had called the child. ⁹ Therefore Eli said unto Samuel, Go, lie down: and it shall be, if he call thee, that thou shalt say, Speak, Lord; for thy servant heareth. So Samuel went and lay down in his place.**

Not only was the priesthood corrupt, but the prophetic word of God was not reaching the people of God. The "word of the Lord" (v. 1) refers to the word that was delivered by the prophets, and in those days the word of the Lord was *precious*, which means "rare." The word *vision* signifies prophecy in its widest sense, a revelation of God's will to His people (see Isa. 1:1; Obad. 1:1; Nah. 1:1; Jer. 14:14; 23:16). The Israelites had the written Law of Moses, but it was not "open." Instead, it was a closed book that lacked the unction of the Holy Spirit. The Bible is not sufficient without the Holy Spirit to breathe life into the Word: "The letter kills, but the Spirit gives life" (2 Cor. 3:6 NKJV). As a symbol of Israel's lack of spiritual vision, we read twice that Eli the high priest "could not see" (1 Sam. 3:2; 4:15). Both the people and their leaders lacked vision, and "where there is no vision, the people perish" (Prov. 29:18).

After Samuel had served for some years in the Tabernacle, and he had grown into a young man of God, the Lord spoke to him. Both Samuel and Eli had lain down for the night when the Lord called to Samuel (3:4); but Samuel thought it was Eli who was calling to him. Eli denied calling out to Samuel, so Samuel went back to his bed. The Lord called again, "Samuel," and Samuel went to Eli once more.

Samuel had never received a revelation, and he had never heard God speak to him; therefore, he did not know how to recognize the voice of the Lord. However, after God called to Samuel the third time, Eli discerned that it must be the Lord who was calling Samuel. Eli instructed Samuel to lie down, and if God called him again, to respond with the words, "Speak, Lord; for thy servant heareth" (v. 9).

---

1. What was "rare in those days" (v. 1 NASB), and why?
2. What was Eli slow to perceive?

> "A spiritual leader will first and foremost, have a calling from God. His work will not be his profession, but his calling."—Zac Poonen

## B. Samuel Receives the Prophetic Word (vv. 10-18)

(1 Samuel 3:11-18 is not included in the printed text.)

**10 And the Lord came, and stood, and called as at other times, Samuel, Samuel. Then Samuel answered, Speak; for thy servant heareth.**

Samuel obeyed Eli's instructions, and when the Lord called to him, he responded. Then the Lord gave Samuel a prophetic word of judgment against the household of Eli (vv. 11-14)—a word that confirmed the previous judgment that had been delivered sometime earlier by an anonymous prophet (2:27-36). Because Eli had not restrained his sons in their evil, God would destroy the line of Eli, and others would take on the priestly role in his place.

Samuel was afraid and he did not immediately tell Eli about the word of judgment. He stayed in his bed until the morning, when he arose and opened the doors to the house of God. Eli, however, asked Samuel about the Lord's word, and Samuel revealed everything. Knowing that the will of God is for the best, Eli accepted the Lord's verdict (vv. 15-18).

1. How did Samuel answer the Lord (v. 10)?
2. What did the Lord reveal to Samuel (vv. 11-14)?
3. How did Eli reply to the word from God (vv. 17-18)?

> "Sound doctrine and holy living are the marks of true prophets."—J. C. Ryle

## C. Destined to Be a Prophet (vv. 19-21)

**19 And Samuel grew, and the Lord was with him, and did let none of his words fall to the ground. 20 And all Israel from Dan even to Beersheba knew that Samuel was established to be a prophet of the Lord. 21 And the Lord appeared again in Shiloh: for the Lord revealed himself to Samuel in Shiloh by the word of the Lord.**

As the story of Samuel's birth and calling comes to a close, we are given five statements about Samuel that prepare us for his subsequent ministry as a prophet: (1) Once again, we are told "Samuel grew." (2) We are assured "the Lord was with him." (3) None of Samuel's words fell "to the ground," meaning that every word Samuel spoke was received by the people. (4) Everyone knew Samuel was confirmed to be a prophet. (5) The Lord continued to speak to Samuel, which was evidence of the Lord's abiding presence at the Tabernacle in Shiloh.

## CONCLUSION

In the story of Samuel's birth, consider the central role of the Lord. In the first scene, we learn it was the Lord who had closed Hannah's womb" (1:5-6). In the second scene, we hear the high priest Eli promise Hannah, "May the God of Israel grant your petition" (v. 17 NASB). In the third scene, we are told "the Lord remembered her" (v. 19). And in the fourth scene, Hannah testifies, "The Lord has granted me my petition" (v. 27 NKJV). At every stage of the story, the Lord stands at the center of the action, teaching us that through all of our problems and our challenges, it is the faithfulness and power of God that brings life, hope, and a future.

Samuel's birth came as an answer to prayer, and his life and ministry were directed by the Lord. Out of her pain, Hannah pleaded with God for a son, but God is able to do "exceeding abundantly above all that we ask or think" (Eph. 3:20). Therefore, God gave Hannah more than a son—He gave her a prophet who would bring revival to Israel. Like Hannah, we must turn our pain into prayer, and trust God to transform our situation and create new possibilities for the future.

## GOLDEN TEXT CHALLENGE

"THE LORD CAME, AND STOOD, AND CALLED AS AT OTHER TIMES, SAMUEL, SAMUEL. THEN SAMUEL ANSWERED, SPEAK; FOR THY SERVANT HEARETH" (1 Sam. 3:10).

With anticipation in his young mind, Samuel lay down again in his place. But this time there is something more than a mysterious voice that arrests his attention. In some mysterious way, "the Lord came, and stood" in the presence of Samuel, so that he must have recognized a kind of divine manifestation.

The call came in the same way as on the three previous occasions, only that Samuel's name is called twice here. With Eli's instructions fresh in mind, and with both eye and ear aware of the Lord's call, Samuel responds: "Speak; for thy servant heareth." This response probably meant more than the child knew. It indicated a willingness to hear and to heed any message the Lord might give, whatever the cost; it was a full surrender to God. It was to be the beginning of a prophet's career at a tender age.

It should be the same with us today, because surrender to God is the secret of peace and usefulness, and nothing else is valid and eternal. "The world passeth away, and the lust thereof: but he that doeth the will of God abideth for ever" (1 John 2:17).

**Daily Devotions:**
M. Noah Finds Grace
   Genesis 6:8-13; 7:1
T. God's Promise; Abraham's Faith
   Genesis 15:1-6
W. Gideon Recruited by God
   Judges 6:11-16
T. Jeremiah Called to Prophesy
   Jeremiah 1:4-10
F. Jesus Calls Philip and Nathanael
   John 1:43-50
S. Matthias Chosen
   Acts 1:15-17, 21-26

March 8, 2015 (Lesson 2)
# Samuel's Ministry Established
### 1 Samuel 6:1 through 7:17

**Theme:**
Life of Samuel

**Central Truth:**
God desires to minister through us for His glory.

**Focus:**
Observe that God established Samuel's ministry and allow God to minister through us.

**Context:**
About 1050 to 69 1030 BC in the towns of Mizpeh, Bethcar, and Ramah

**Golden Text:**
"All Israel from Dan even to Beersheba knew that Samuel was established to be a prophet of the Lord" (1 Sam. 3:20).

**Study Outline:**
I. Samuel Calls Israel to Repentance
   (1 Sam. 7:1-6)
II. Samuel's Intercession; God's Intervention
    (1 Sam. 7:7-13)
III. Restoration and Peace
     (1 Sam. 7:14-17)

## INTRODUCTION

Jesus promised He would build His church and "the gates of hell" would not "prevail against it" (Matt. 16:18). The Church has never been defeated; however, it has suffered serious setbacks. Those setbacks are possible because the Church is made up of people, and people are subject to weakness, mistakes, and failure. Looking back, we can see how our mistakes have caused some of the contemporary problems in the Church. Nevertheless, we cannot undo the past—once mistakes are made, we are doomed to suffer the consequences until God restores His power and presence to the Church.

In 1 Samuel 4, Israel suffered a terrible setback. They made the mistake of trusting in their own strength, disobeying God, and bowing to idols. Their failure to fully trust and obey God resulted in their defeat at the hands of the Philistines, who captured the ark of the covenant (vv. 10-11). Israel's loss of the ark meant that the glory of God had been taken from their midst, a fact that was symbolized by the name *Ichabod,* which was given to Eli's newborn grandson (v. 21).

Israel's loss of the ark to the Philistines stands in the background of today's lesson. Until now, the story of Samuel has illuminated Israel's internal spiritual problems, but it has not revealed the presence of external threats. In chapter 4 the focus changes, with the emphasis falling on the invading Philistines, who had oppressed Israel from the time of Samson. The Philistines apparently entered the west coast of Palestine from the sea at about the same time the Israelites entered the eastern hill country from the desert. As the Philistines grew stronger, they became Israel's primary enemy during the time of Samson, Eli, Samuel, Saul, and David. They were subdued under the reigns of David and Solomon and were required to pay tribute money to Israel.

When the Philistines captured the ark of the covenant, it was clear that Israel's defeat in battle was linked to her backslidden spiritual condition. Therefore, before Samuel can lead Israel in a plan to defeat the Philistines, he must first lead them to spiritual renewal. In this lesson, we learn that Samuel's approach includes prayer and repentance as key elements in revival.

I. SAMUEL CALLS ISRAEL TO REPENTANCE (1 Sam. 7:1-6)

When the Philistines captured the ark of the covenant, they took it to the Philistine city of Ashdod and placed it on prominent display in the temple of their god Dagon (ch. 5). They were proud of their new trophy, but the thrill of victory was quickly displaced by the agony of God's judgment. Although the Lord had allowed the Philistines to capture the ark, He would not allow them to keep it. They set the ark beside the statue of the god Dagon and left it there overnight. The next morning, they found the statue of Dagon fallen on its face to the ground before the ark of God, with his head and his hands severed from his body. Next, God caused tumors to break out on all the Philistine men in Ashdod, and this was repeated in Gath when the ark was taken there, and again in Ekron when the ark was moved there.

In chapter 6, the Philistines hitched two milk cows to an ox cart and sent the ark of the covenant back to Israel. Along with the ark, they included a guilt offering in the hopes God would heal them. The cows took the ark to the Israelite town of Bethshemesh, and the Levites took the ark and placed it on a large stone, and they offered sacrifices. But, because some of the men of Bethshemesh looked into the ark, God struck them down. They feared to keep the ark there, so they sent it to the nearby town of Kirjathjearim.

A. The Ark Remains With Abinadab (vv. 1-2)

**¹ And the men of Kirjathjearim came, and fetched up the ark of the Lord, and brought it into the house of Abinadab in the hill, and sanctified Eleazar his son to keep the ark of the Lord. ² And it came to pass, while the ark abode in Kirjathjearim, that the time was long; for it was twenty years: and all the house of Israel lamented after the Lord.**

For some unknown reason, the Israelites did not return the ark to the Tabernacle in Shiloh. Perhaps it was because Shiloh was close to Philistine territory, and they were afraid the Philistines would return to Shiloh and capture the ark again. Kirjathjearim was the nearest town to Bethshemesh, and Abinadab's house stood on a hill. Therefore, it was a strong place where the ark would be the safest, and also it was visible from some distance, which was important to the people as they would turn toward the ark when they prayed.

Abinadab must have been a man of faith. Apparently he was unafraid to have the ark on his property, even though its presence had caused so much destruction at other locations. Abinadab may have realized the presence of God can bring judgment when God is disobeyed and disrespected, but it can bring blessing when God is honored and worshiped. Eleazar, the son of Abinadab, was consecrated as keeper of the ark. Kirjathjearim was not a Levitical city, so Eleazar was probably not a Levite; nevertheless, he was set apart to attend to the ark.

The ark remained with Abinadab for twenty years, a very long time for it to be absent from the Tabernacle (v. 2). King David would later retrieve the ark, bring it into Jerusalem, and restore it to its proper place in the Tabernacle (2 Sam. 6).

When all the Israelites became aware that the ark had been returned and was resting at Abinadab's house, they began to lament and mourn after the Lord as an expression of their grief and deep sorrow. It was the beginnings of repentance. The near loss of the ark awakened them to the fragility of their relationship with the Lord. They also realized they must turn back to God if they were to be safe from the threat of the Philistines and other invaders.

---

1. Describe Eleazar's role (v. 1).
2. Describe Israel's lament (v. 2).

> "The coming of God's reign either demands repentance or brings judgment."—D. A. Carson

---

B. Israel Forsakes Their Idols (vv. 3-4)

**³ And Samuel spake unto all the house of Israel, saying, If ye do return unto the Lord with all your hearts, then put away the strange gods and Ashtaroth from among you, and prepare your hearts unto the Lord, and serve him only: and he will deliver you out of the hand of the Philistines. ⁴ Then the children of Israel did put away Baalim and Ashtaroth, and served the Lord only.**

As the Israelites begin to grieve and repent over their backsliding, Samuel reenters the scene. With prophetic authority, Samuel instructs the people how to repent genuinely. If they want to return to the Lord with all their hearts, actions must accompany their words. They must put aside the "strange gods and Ashtaroth." *Strange gods* refers to any of the gods of the Canaanites, Egyptians, or other peoples nearby. *Ashtaroth* (also known as *Astarte* or *Ishtar*) was a female god who was worshiped by many Mesopotamian peoples. True repentance includes a turning away from all that is evil.

Not only must the Israelites forsake the worship of foreign gods, they must also "direct [their] hearts to the Lord and serve Him alone" (v. 3 NASB). The Hebrew word translated *direct* (or "prepare") means "to be intent on, be firmly resolved." True repentance includes the setting of the heart firmly on God so it cannot be drawn away to other things. Moses advised us how to seek after God. He said, "You will find Him if you seek Him with all your heart and with all your soul" (Deut. 4:29 NKJV). Furthermore, God demands that we serve only Him. One of the Ten Commandments states, "You shall have no other gods before Me" (Ex. 20:3 NKJV). It is not enough that we include God in our lives for a few minutes each day and for an hour on Sundays. God wants all of our time and all of our heart.

If the Israelites would obey Samuel's directive, the Lord would deliver them from the power of the Philistines. It is implied, therefore, that if they did not turn to the Lord with all their hearts, He would not deliver them. The lesson is clear: our devotion to the Lord affects our ability to engage in effective spiritual warfare.

The Israelites received Samuel's message and acted upon it immediately. They put aside their "Baalim and Ashtaroth, and served the Lord only" (1 Sam. 7:4). *Baalim* is another term that refers to the various gods of the ancient Near East. Literally meaning "lords," these local gods were thought to control various natural phenomena such as rain, wind, and the sun. Israel was tempted to serve the gods of their neighbors. Similarly, we are tempted to worship the gods of this world—"the lust of the flesh, and the lust of the eyes, and the pride of life" (1 John 2:16).

- What did Samuel demand, and how did the people respond?

> "There is nothing so abominable in the eyes of God and of men as idolatry, whereby men render to the creature that honor which is due only to the Creator."—Blaise Pascal

C. Samuel Gathers Israel for Prayer (vv. 5-6)

**⁵ And Samuel said, Gather all Israel to Mizpeh, and I will pray for you unto the Lord. ⁶ And they gathered together to Mizpeh, and drew water, and poured it out before the Lord, and fasted on that day, and said there, We have sinned against the Lord. And Samuel judged the children of Israel in Mizpeh.**

In a move reminiscent of the intercession of Moses (Num. 11:2; 21:7), Samuel calls the people together to pray for them. He knew the Philistines would attack soon, and he wanted the Israelites to be spiritually prepared for battle.

He called the people together at the town of Mizpeh, a place where they had met in times past (see Judg. 20:1). *Mizpeh*, which means "watchtower," was located on the western boundary of the mountains. Therefore, it was a fitting geographical location for entering into battle with the Philistines.

They drew water, but instead of drinking the water, they poured it out to the Lord. They also fasted, and together these two acts served as a sign of their self-denial and willingness to give everything to the Lord in repentance. In the Bible, fasting is often associated with confession and repentance (see Judg. 20:26; 2 Sam. 12; 1 Kings 21:27; Dan. 9:3). The Day of Atonement was Israel's annual occasion of national repentance, and on that day they fasted for twenty-four hours (Lev. 16). Thus, they confessed their sins to the Lord.

Until now, Samuel had been known as a prophet, but on this day, he expanded his leadership role beyond that of prophet to the position of judge. As both prophet and judge, he was a powerful spiritual leader.

1. What did Samuel do for Israel (v. 5)?
2. What was the significance of the pouring out of water (v. 6)?

> "Repentance is the tear in the eye of faith."—D. L. Moody

---

## II. SAMUEL'S INTERCESSION; GOD'S INTERVENTION (1 Sam. 7:7-13)

### A. Samuel Cries Out to God (vv. 7-9)

**7 And when the Philistines heard that the children of Israel were gathered together to Mizpeh, the lords of the Philistines went up against Israel. And when the children of Israel heard it, they were afraid of the Philistines. 8 And the children of Israel said to Samuel, Cease not to cry unto the Lord our God for us, that he will save us out of the hand of the Philistines. 9 And Samuel took a sucking lamb, and offered it for a burnt offering wholly unto the Lord: and Samuel cried unto the Lord for Israel; and the Lord heard him.**

The Philistine leaders gathered their armies for battle against Israel, and the Israelites were afraid—they had every reason to be. Even though Samson had killed many Philistines with his own hands, the Israelite army had never defeated the Philistines in battle. They knew they must have the Lord's help if they were to win. Therefore, they begged Samuel to continue praying for victory. Their plea to Samuel reminds us of Paul's admonition, "Pray without ceasing" (1 Thess. 5:17). Paul himself practiced unceasing prayers for those under his spiritual care (Rom. 1:9; 1 Thess. 1:2-3; 2 Tim. 1:3).

In a sign of faith and dedication, Samuel offered up a whole burnt offering to the Lord. As the smoke of the offering ascended to heaven, so did the prayers of Samuel. In the New Testament we read, "The smoke of the incense, with the prayers of the saints, ascended before God" (Rev. 8:4 NKJV). Like Moses before him, Samuel became known for his ability to move God in prayer (see Ps. 99:6; Jer. 15:1). Later in his life, he would say to the Israelites, "God forbid that I should sin against the Lord in ceasing to pray for you" (1 Sam. 12:23). Samuel's life of prayer may be one reason he is included among the greatest men and women of faith (Heb. 11:32).

---

1. Explain the Philistines' plot (v. 7).
2. How did Israel, and then Samuel, respond to the crisis (vv. 8-9)?

### Courage in Crisis

While camping in Wyoming, the Kelly family saw a bear approaching their campsite. Immediately, eleven-year-old Baden began screaming to distract the bear while the family rushed into a cabin. He grabbed his little sister, who stood frozen, and ran with her, but the bear was closing in fast. Suddenly, Baden's brother Logan darted out of the cabin shouting and running straight toward the bear. The startled bear turned away and everyone was saved. During a crisis, God uses people who have the courage to act on behalf of others. Just as Samuel arose during a crisis, so also we must stand up for God today.

### B. The Lord Delivers Israel (vv. 10-11)

**¹⁰ And as Samuel was offering up the burnt offering, the Philistines drew near to battle against Israel: but the Lord thundered with a great thunder on that day upon the Philistines, and discomfited them; and they were smitten before Israel. ¹¹ And the men of Israel went out of Mizpeh, and pursued the Philistines, and smote them, until they came under Bethcar.**

The Lord heard Samuel's prayer with no time to spare. While the offering was still on the fire and prayers were still being prayed, the Philistines attacked. The Lord intervened with a miraculous noise of thunder that was so loud the Philistines became confused. In the midst of their confusion, the Israelites attacked and struck them down. The Philistines fled for their lives, and the Israelites pursued them and continued to destroy their army until they reached Bethcar—a city that was apparently near Philistine territory.

- How did the Lord intervene?

### C. Samuel Erects a Memorial (vv. 12-13)

**¹² Then Samuel took a stone, and set it between Mizpeh and Shen, and called the name of it Ebenezer, saying, Hitherto hath the Lord helped us. ¹³ So the Philistines were subdued, and they came no more into the coast of Israel: and the hand of the Lord was against the Philistines all the days of Samuel.**

Samuel realized the power of remembrance; therefore, he set up a memorial stone and called it *Ebenezer*, which is translated literally "the stone of help." The stone monument would continually remind Israel that the Lord had helped them to defeat the Philistines on that day. Furthermore, if the Lord could give them victory on that day, He could give them victory on every other occasion when enemies attacked.

It is important for us to remember the Lord does not change (Mal. 3:6) and that just as He helped us in the past, He can help us today. Whenever we face tests and trials, we must remind ourselves that the Lord answers prayer. We must remember His past acts of salvation, healing, and deliverance. The psalmist tells us, "Forget not all His benefits: who forgives all your iniquities, who heals all your diseases, who redeems your life from destruction, who crowns you with lovingkindness and tender mercies" (103:2-4 NKJV).

Although the Philistines continued to live in what is today the Gaza Strip, and they continued to attack Israel, they never again subdued and ruled over Israel as they had done in the past. Any time they came against Israel, "the hand of the Lord was against" them so they were driven back to their own land (1 Sam. 7:13).

1. Explain the purpose of the stone.
2. How did God bless Samuel's leadership?

> "To me, it has been a source of great comfort and strength in the day of battle, just to remember that the secret of steadfastness, and indeed, of victory, is the recognition that 'the Lord is at hand.'"—Duncan Campbell

---

## III. RESTORATION AND PEACE (1 Sam. 7:14-17)

### A. Israel Is Restored (v. 14)

**14 And the cities which the Philistines had taken from Israel were restored to Israel, from Ekron even unto Gath; and the coasts thereof did Israel deliver out of the hands of the Philistines. And there was peace between Israel and the Amorites.**

This shows the power and success of Samuel's leadership. Not only did Israel win the battle described here, they went on to attack the Philistines and take from them the cities which properly belonged to Israel. The term *Amorites* is a general designation that refers to various people who inhabited Canaan before the Israelites arrived. Many of them remained in the land during the time of Samuel. These Amorites chose to align themselves with Israel rather than with the Philistines, and assisted the Israelites in their battles against the Philistines.

God is able to restore everything the Enemy has stolen from us (Joel 2:25). He can restore our joy (Ps. 51:12), our comfort (Isa. 57:18), our homes (Jer. 27:22), and our health (30:17).

---

- Describe a divine restoration you have witnessed.

> "When by the malice of enemies God's people are brought to greatest straits, there is deliverance near to be sent from God unto them."—David Dickson

---

### B. Samuel Judges Israel (vv. 15-16)

**15 And Samuel judged Israel all the days of his life. 16 And he went from year to year in circuit to Bethel, and Gilgal, and Mizpeh, and judged Israel in all those places.**

Samuel's ministry as judge was confirmed by the victory over the Philistines that had been obtained through his prayers. He continued in that role for the rest of his life. Even after Saul became king, Samuel exercised leadership and authority, as evidenced by his removal of Saul and his anointing of David as king in Saul's place.

Samuel's style of leadership kept him close to the people. Rather than setting up a headquarters and requiring the people to come to him, Samuel would go to where the people lived. He would make yearly rounds of the towns in the central region of the country.

- Describe Samuel's ministry.

### C. Samuel Builds an Altar (v. 17)

**¹⁷ And his return was to Ramah; for there was his house; and there he judged Israel; and there he built an altar unto the Lord.**

After completing his annual circuit, Samuel would return to his home in Ramah. There he would continue to judge Israel, and he built an altar to facilitate his guidance of the religious affairs of the nation. From his home in Ramah, Samuel would minister as a prophet, bringing the word of the Lord to the people. He also served as a judge, much like a governor, guiding them on a daily basis. Finally, as a descendant of the Levites, he was authorized to offer up sacrifices to the Lord on the altar he had built.

- What did Samuel build in Ramah, and why?

### CONCLUSION

God used Samuel to bring revival and restoration to broken and backslidden Israel. Samuel stands in sharp contrast to the judges who served immediately before him. Jephthah, Samson, and Eli certainly deserve commendation for some areas of their lives, but they were often driven by their own desires, fears, and weaknesses. The success of Samuel can be attributed to four important elements.

1. *The influence of a godly family.* His father was a faithful man who went every year to the Tabernacle to offer sacrifices. His mother was devoted to the Lord and to her family.

2. *The power of prayer.* Samuel was born in answer to prayer, and throughout his ministry he prayed with faith. Samuel was recognized as a man of effective prayer.

3. *The call of God.* Samuel was gifted both as a prophet and as a judge. Because of the manner in which God appeared to him, Samuel never doubted that he was called of God. As Christians, we are told to make our calling and election sure (2 Peter 1:10). That is, we must be certain that we have surrendered to God's will for our lives and that we are following the path He has set before us.

4. *Obedience.* Nowhere do we read that Samuel ever resisted God's will or disobeyed God's directions. Samuel was faithful and obedient to God at all times. The influence of a godly family, the power of prayer, and the calling of

God are not sufficient to produce an effective ministry (whether clergy or laity). We must be faithful and obedient. As we will hear Samuel say later, "Behold, to obey is better than sacrifice" (1 Sam. 15:22).

## GOLDEN TEXT CHALLENGE

"ALL ISRAEL FROM DAN EVEN TO BEERSHEBA KNEW THAT SAMUEL WAS ESTABLISHED TO BE A PROPHET OF THE LORD" (1 Sam. 3:20).

Beersheba represented the far south, while Dan was in the far north. Thus, all the tribes of Israel, from north to south, knew that a new spiritual leader was arising in their midst. It signaled a dimension of God's representation that had been lacking for many years.

Samuel was a Levite by tribal lineage. But his ministry task was not limited to that provided by his bloodline. God selected him to fulfill the office of a prophet. The prophet's task included both predicting future events and forthtelling the words of God that had already been spoken. Prophets provided a constant emphasizing of what God had said in the past and expected His people to follow in the present and the future.

Samuel's establishment as a prophet began the rise of a line of prophets. He established the school of the prophets and became the spiritual ancestor of prophets whose ministry would span the centuries of Israel's existence.

**Daily Devotions:**

- M. Chosen to Preserve
  Genesis 45:1-7
- T. Called to Deliver
  Exodus 3:1-10
- W. Burdened to Rebuild
  Nehemiah 2:11-18
- T. Anointed to Prepare the Way
  Matthew 3:1-6
- F. Commended for Service
  Romans 16:1-7
- S. Encouraged to Restore
  Philemon 10-17

March 15, 2015 (Lesson 3)
# Israel Demands a King
### 1 Samuel 8:1 through 10:27

**Theme:**
Life of Samuel

**Central Truth:**
God remains faithful even when we fail Him.

**Focus:**
Perceive how Israel rebelled against God and submit to God's will.

**Context:**
Around 1030 BC in Ramah, Beersheba, Mizpeh, and Gibeah

**Golden Text:**
"The Lord said unto Samuel, Hearken unto the voice of the people in all that they say unto thee: for they have not rejected thee, but they have rejected me, that I should reign over them" (1 Sam. 8:7).

**Study Outline:**
I. Israel's Rebellious Demand
   (1 Sam. 8:1-22)
II. God's Providence Demonstrated
   (1 Sam. 9:15-24)
III. Saul Anointed and Proclaimed King
   (1 Sam. 9:25—10:27)

## INTRODUCTION

God's way is the best way, but when we face difficulties, we are tempted to question His way, to take shortcuts, or to invent what we think is a better way. Sometimes our dissatisfaction with God's way comes as a result of envying the prosperity of unbelievers. We want what they have: money, possessions, status, power, pleasure. Christ taught us, however, that we must not be influenced and shaped by the forces of the world around us; rather, we must be an influence for good. That is, we are in the world, but we are "not of the world" (John 17:16).

God's way is the best way, and to stray from His way is to bring trouble upon ourselves. Therefore, whenever we are tempted to choose our way instead of God's way, we should recall the wise words of Solomon, who said, "Trust in the Lord with all thine heart; and lean not unto thine own understanding. In all thy ways acknowledge him, and he shall direct thy paths. Be not wise in thine own eyes: fear the Lord, and depart from evil" (Prov. 3:5-7). We should remind ourselves that the "way of a fool is right in his own eyes" (12:15).

We are encouraged to be "steadfast" in our walk with God (1 Cor. 15:58), but still we fall short at times. However, even when we are unfaithful, God remains faithful (2 Tim. 2:13). Even in our disobedience, God continues to work in our lives to bring us back into conformity to His will. Although every act of disobedience carries serious consequences, we can be restored, and that one act of disobedience does not necessarily prevent us from fulfilling God's plan for our lives.

In this week's lesson, we will learn that Israel strayed from God's perfect will. God had established the nation under the leadership of twelve tribes who were ruled by elders and judges like Samuel. However, Israel grew dissatisfied with God's plan of government. They saw that other nations were ruled by kings; therefore, they wanted a king like those other nations. Even though their desire for a king was an act of rebellion against the will of God, God was gracious to grant their desire and to continue His guidance and care of His rebellious people.

## I. ISRAEL'S REBELLIOUS DEMAND (1 Sam. 8:1-22)

Samuel lived in a transitional period in Israel's history. He was the last of the judges, and he was instrumental in instituting the monarchy as the new form of leadership in Israel. When God brought Israel out of Egypt, He established a government for His people that was very different from the governments of the surrounding nations. Nations in the ancient Near East were ruled by kings, who exercised supreme authority and who built their own kingdoms and amassed their own wealth. In the process of establishing their authority, these kings were known for their tyranny and for their oppression of the weak and the poor.

The Pharaoh of Egypt was the greatest example of the oppressive power of the kings of that age. When God delivered Israel from Egypt, He also delivered them from the brutality of the Egyptian form of government. When the Lord made a covenant with Israel at Mount Sinai in the wilderness, He proclaimed a new form of government in which God himself served as Israel's king. The twelve tribes of Israel would come together under the common bond of worship at the Tabernacle and under the common leadership of the priests, the prophets, the elders, and the judges. This new form of government would prevent any concentration of power in the hands of a few people and would thus ensure freedom from oppression.

### A. The Wickedness of Samuel's Sons (vv. 1-3)

**¹ And it came to pass, when Samuel was old, that he made his sons judges over Israel. ² Now the name of his firstborn was Joel; and the name of his second, Abiah: they were judges in Beersheba. ³ And his sons walked not in his ways, but turned aside after lucre, and took bribes, and perverted judgment.**

Samuel arose during a dark time in Israel and served the nation well for many years. His positive spiritual influence brought about a revival in the land and freedom from the power of the Philistines. As with all leaders, however, Samuel grew old and the time came for him to introduce new leaders who would replace him. Samuel served as a judge, and the office of judge was not hereditary. The appointment of judges was usually based on their divine calling or on their reputation for leadership potential. However, rather than waiting on God's choice and rather than searching among Israel's elders, Samuel made his sons judges over Israel.

At first, his sons served in a limited capacity, only "in Beersheba." That is, they did not travel across the land ministering to the entire nation as Samuel had done. The Israelites soon learned that Samuel's sons did not have the integrity and the depth of character found in Samuel. Samuel had left a good example for his sons to follow, but they instead "turned aside after lucre," which means they attempted to acquire dishonest gain, perhaps even using violence to obtain money. More specifically, they went against the basic requirements of their office by taking bribes and perverting justice. The office of the judge was instituted to ensure that everyone in society received fair and equal treatment in regard to the Law. But Samuel's sons violated their obligation for fairness and equality by receiving bribes and giving preferential treatment to individuals who would pay for the judgment to go in their favor.

---

- Compare Samuel's sons (vv. 1-3) with Eli's sons (2:12, 17).

> "He that boasts of being one of God's elect, while he is willfully and habitually living in sin, is only deceiving himself, and talking wicked blasphemy."—J. C. Ryle

---

### B. Israel Demands a King (vv. 4-6)

**4 Then all the elders of Israel gathered themselves together, and came to Samuel unto Ramah, 5 And said unto him, Behold, thou art old, and thy sons walk not in thy ways: now make us a king to judge us like all the nations. 6 But the thing displeased Samuel, when they said, Give us a king to judge us. And Samuel prayed unto the Lord.**

The elders of Israel were unhappy with the performance of Samuel's sons, and we might expect that they would demand that Samuel search for better candidates to replace him. However, the elders went beyond the demand for new judges; they demanded a change in the entire leadership structure. The failure in leadership of Samuel's sons caused the people to seek an alternative form of government. Apparently, the elders believed their form of government was not adequate for the times in which they lived. They felt it was time to reorganize along the lines of the other nations around them. Therefore, they asked Samuel to appoint a king over them.

As we might expect, their request for a king was displeasing to Samuel. God had created the nation of Israel to be a different kind of people. Other nations were ruled by human monarchs and human laws, but Israel was ruled by God himself according to His divine laws. For four hundred years, Israel had suffered at the hands of the Egyptian king; but God had delivered Israel from that bondage and oppression. Now, however, Israel was asking to be brought under the same kind of government that was known to oppress and abuse the citizenry.

Demonstrating his great spiritual depth, Samuel's response to their request was to pray to the Lord. Even though Samuel had made the mistake of appointing his own sons as judges, he knew at this point that he needed the strength and guidance of the Lord. Whenever faced with opposition or criticism, prayer is always in order. A spiritual leader will always rely on God.

- Was the Israelites' demand justifiable? Why or why not?

> "The authority by which the Christian leader leads is not power but love, not force but example, not coercion but reasoned persuasion. Leaders have power, but power is safe only in the hands of those who humble themselves to serve."—John Stott

---

## C. The Lord Heeds Their Request (vv. 7-9)

**7 And the Lord said unto Samuel, Hearken unto the voice of the people in all that they say unto thee: for they have not rejected thee, but they have rejected me, that I should not reign over them. 8 According to all the works which they have done since the day that I brought them up out of Egypt even unto this day, wherewith they have forsaken me, and served other gods, so do they also unto thee. 9 Now therefore hearken unto their voice: howbeit yet protest solemnly unto them, and shew them the manner of the king that shall reign over them.**

The Lord's answer to Samuel is a bit surprising. First, the Lord agrees to the people's request for a king. He tells Samuel to listen to the voice of the people; that is, he should give the people what they want.

Second, He addresses Samuel's anxiety by explaining that the people have not rejected Samuel; they have rejected the Lord. Their rejection of God's preferred form of government was a rejection of God's authority and leadership.

Third, the Lord reminds Samuel that Israel had been a rebellious people from their beginning. Ever since the Lord brought Israel out of Egypt and to that very day, Israel had forsaken the Lord repeatedly and served other gods. The charge of ongoing idolatry is verified by looking back at the Book of Judges, which recounts numerous times in which the Israelites abandoned the Lord and worshiped the gods of the Canaanites. Therefore, the Lord is telling Samuel that Israel's misbehavior is nothing new. Forsaking God had become a pattern.

Fourth, the Lord again instructs Samuel to give the people what they wanted; however, before surrendering to their will, Samuel should solemnly warn the people. He should inform them of the many dangers in having a king.

---

1. How did God characterize the Israelites (vv. 7-8)?
2. What did God instruct Samuel to do (v. 9)?

### Living Illustration

The life of the prophet Hosea was a living illustration of God's faithfulness. Hosea's wife was unfaithful to him on repeated occasions, but Hosea always rescued her and restored her as his wife. In the same way, Israel rebelled against God time and time again, but despite their unfaithfulness, God continued to be faithful to His people. The New

Testament puts it this way: "If we are faithless, He remains faithful, for He cannot deny Himself" (2 Tim. 2:13 NASB).

---

D. The Dangers of Kingship (vv. 10-18)

(1 Samuel 8:12-18 is not included in the printed text.)

**10 And Samuel told all the words of the Lord unto the people that asked of him a king. 11 And he said, This will be the manner of the king that shall reign over you: He will take your sons, and appoint them for himself, for his chariots, and to be his horsemen; and some shall run before his chariots.**

Samuel explained that God would give the Israelites what they wanted, even though it was not His will. The change from tribal leadership to a centralized monarchy meant that the new king would demand very much from the people, and he would enrich himself at the people's expense. He would draft their children into military and domestic service. He would even appropriate their land, property, and animals for his own use. He would inflict heavy taxes upon them, and they would be oppressed. Samuel warned them further, "Then you will cry out in that day because of your king whom you have chosen for yourselves, but the Lord will not answer you in that day" (v. 18 NASB).

---

1. List the warnings Samuel gave about being ruled by a king (vv. 11-17).

2. In verse 18, what did Samuel predict?

---

E. Israel's Refusal to Listen to Samuel (vv. 19-22)

(1 Samuel 8:21-22 is not included in the printed text.)

**19 Nevertheless the people refused to obey the voice of Samuel; and they said, Nay; but we will have a king over us; 20 That we also may be like all the nations; and that our king may judge us, and go out before us, and fight our battles.**

All of Samuel's warnings fell on deaf ears; the people had already made up their minds, and they would not listen to reason. They were intent on forsaking God's will. They insisted, "Give us a king; we want to be like all the nations. We want a standing army and a king ready to lead us in battle." Apparently, the Israelites had become afraid of the Philistines and believed their security rested in the establishment of a strong military. However, even a quick survey of Israel's history demonstrates the Lord had always given them the victory over their enemies as long as they remained faithful to Him. It was not a strong military that would give them security, but the presence of the Lord. Thus, their demand for a king demonstrates their lack of faith in the Lord's ability to protect them from their enemies.

Samuel went back to the Lord in prayer and shared with Him all that the people said. Once again, the Lord told Samuel to give them a king, and Samuel asked everyone to return to their homes until the new king was chosen.

1. Why did the Israelites want a king?
2. Why do you suppose God granted their request?

## II. GOD'S PROVIDENCE DEMONSTRATED (1 Sam. 9:15-24)

At the beginning of chapter 9, we are introduced to Saul, the young man who will become king. Saul is described as a "choice young man" from the tribe of Benjamin (vv. 1-2). He was strikingly handsome, and he was a head taller than any other person in Israel.

Saul enters the story as he and his servant are sent on a mission to find the lost donkeys of Saul's father (vv. 3-14). They search for some time but are unable to locate the donkeys. As a last resort, they decide to consult with the prophet Samuel and ask for his advice on finding the donkeys.

### A. The Lord Chooses Saul as Leader (vv. 15-16)

**15 Now the Lord had told Samuel in his ear a day before Saul came, saying, 16 To morrow about this time I will send thee a man out of the land of Benjamin, and thou shalt anoint him to be captain over my people Israel, that he may save my people out of the hand of the Philistines: for I have looked upon my people, because their cry is come unto me.**

Saul and his servant enter the city to inquire of Samuel, and Samuel is expecting them. The Lord had told Samuel that He would send a man from the tribe of Benjamin, whom Samuel should anoint to be "captain" over the Israelites.

It is significant that the Lord does not describe Saul as king; rather, He calls him *captain*, which means "leader." Although the Lord agrees to give the people a king, God is not willing to relinquish His role as the ultimate King of Israel. Therefore, when God speaks of Saul, He calls him "leader" instead of "king."

It is also significant that God's decision is based on Israel's urgent request. The Lord says, "Their cry is come unto me." God's way is always the best way, but sometimes God allows us to have our own way, even though He knows it is hazardous.

- What did the Lord promise Samuel?

> "A spiritual leader will first, and foremost, have a calling from God. His work will not be his profession, but his calling."—Zac Poonen

### B. Saul Is Introduced to Samuel (vv. 17-24)

(1 Samuel 9:18-24 is not included in the printed text.)
**17 And when Samuel saw Saul, the Lord said unto him, Behold the man whom I spake to thee of! this same shall reign over my people.**

As soon as Samuel saw Saul, the Lord said to the prophet, "This is the man who will govern My people." We are not told why the Lord chose Saul as the new leader; we can only speculate about the reasons behind the Lord's decision.

Saul came seeking advice on finding his lost donkeys, but Samuel had more important news for him. Samuel informed Saul that all of Israel's hopes were focused on him, but Saul deferred, reminding Samuel that Saul's family was small and insignificant (vv. 20-21). Saul did not understand why Samuel was speaking to him in such a way.

Samuel insisted that Saul and his servant join him in a feast at the high place—a place of worship. Therefore, Samuel made worship a part of his first meeting with Saul. Samuel gave Saul the best seat at dinner and gave him a choice piece of meat (vv. 22-24). After dinner, they went down to Samuel's house, and they continued their conversation on the housetop. All the houses in the ancient Near East had flat roofs, and people would walk, talk, and sleep there to enjoy the fresh, cool air.

---

1. What role did lost donkeys play in this account (vv. 18-20)?
2. How did Saul describe himself (v. 21)?
3. Describe Samuel's special treatment of Saul (vv. 22-24).

---

"According to Scripture, virtually everything that truly qualifies a person for leadership is directly related to character. It's not about style, status, personal charisma, clout, or worldly measurements of success. Integrity is the main issue that makes the difference between a good leader and a bad one."—John MacArthur

---

III. SAUL ANOINTED AND PROCLAIMED KING (1 Sam. 9:25—10:27)

A. Samuel Prepares to Anoint Saul (9:25-27)

(1 Samuel 9:25-27 is not included in the printed text.)
They arose early the next morning, and Samuel called for Saul to send him on his way. It was customary that as a visitor departed, the host would walk for some distance along with the visitor, and they would say their goodbyes. As they reached the edge of the city, Samuel asked the servant to go on ahead so Samuel could speak privately to Saul and give him a message from God.

---

- Why did Samuel send Saul's servant ahead of them?

---

B. Samuel Anoints Saul as Leader (10:1-8)

(1 Samuel 10:2-8 is not included in the printed text.)
**¹ Then Samuel took a vial of oil, and poured it upon his head, and kissed him, and said, Is it not because the Lord hath anointed thee to be captain over his inheritance?**

As soon as they were alone, Samuel anointed Saul with oil, kissed him, and proclaimed him to be the "captain" over God's people. The private anointing service was to be only the first sign of Saul's new authority. Later in the day, Saul would meet a group of young prophets who would be singing and worshiping the Lord (v. 5). The Spirit of the Lord would come upon Saul, he would prophesy with them, and he would be "turned into another man" (v. 6). After the Holy Spirit had come upon Saul, he would be led by the Spirit to begin his time of leadership over Israel.

- Describe what Samuel did, and why.

C. God's Spirit Comes Upon Saul (vv. 9-16)

(1 Samuel 10:11-16 is not included in the printed text.)

**9 And it was so, that when he had turned his back to go from Samuel, God gave him another heart: and all those signs came to pass that day. 10 And when they came thither to the hill, behold, a company of prophets met him; and the Spirit of God came upon him, and he prophesied among them.**

Everything happened just as Samuel had promised. As Saul turned to leave Samuel, "God gave him another heart," which means Saul accepted the call of God upon his life. Soon, Saul met the group of prophets who were worshiping and prophesying, and he began to prophesy with them. All of the people saw what was happening to Saul, and they recognized the Holy Spirit was upon him.

When Saul finished prophesying, his uncle saw him and asked where he had been. "'We were looking for the donkeys,' Saul replied, 'but we couldn't find them. So we went to [the prophet] Samuel to ask him where they were.' . . . But Saul didn't tell his uncle [that Samuel had anointed him to be king]" (vv. 14, 16 NLT).

1. How did God transform Saul (v. 9)?
2. How did God's Spirit act through Saul (v. 10)?
3. What did Saul tell his uncle, and what information did he withhold (v. 16)? Why?

> "A leader must have a servant's heart. And if he has a servant's heart, he will act like a servant and react like a servant when he is treated like a servant."—Wayne Mack

D. Samuel Presents Saul to the People (vv. 17-27)

(1 Samuel 10:17-19, 25-27 is not included in the printed text.)

²⁰ And when Samuel had caused all the tribes of Israel to come near, the tribe of Benjamin was taken. ²¹ When he had caused the tribe of Benjamin to come near by their families, the family of Matri was taken, and Saul the son of Kish was taken: and when they sought him, he could not be found. ²² Therefore they enquired of the Lord further, if the man should yet come thither. And the Lord answered, Behold, he hath hid himself among the stuff. ²³ And they ran and fetched him thence: and when he stood among the people, he was higher than any of the people from his shoulders and upward. ²⁴ And Samuel said to all the people, See ye him whom the Lord hath chosen, that there is none like him among all the people? And all the people shouted, and said, God save the king.

Samuel called the people together at Mizpeh in order to present Saul to them as their new leader (v. 17). Before presenting Saul, however, Samuel first rebuked the people for rejecting God's plan and for demanding a king (vv. 18-19).

Samuel went through a process of selecting Saul by first calling the tribe of Benjamin to step forward. He then narrowed his choice to the family of Matri. Finally, Samuel singled out Saul as the Lord's chosen leader, but Saul was nowhere to be found. For some reason, Saul had hidden himself among the "stuff" (v. 22), which can refer to equipment, baggage, or supplies. Apparently, Saul believed he should not present himself openly, lest he be accused of arrogance.

Samuel then declared to all the people how the kingdom of Israel should operate, and he wrote everything in a book (v. 25). After the ceremony was finished, everyone went home. God touched the hearts of several men, who went along with Saul to aid him in leading the people (v. 26). "But some troublemakers said, 'How can this fellow save us?'" (v. 27 NIV).

---

1. How had the Lord helped Israel in the past, and why did He bring that to the people's attention (vv. 18-19)?
2. What do Saul's actions say about his attitude (vv. 21-22)?
3. Describe the mixed reactions to Saul's appointment (vv. 26-27).

> "Nobody is fit to be a leader unless he would rather be a follower instead of a leader."—Jack Hyles

---

## CONCLUSION

Israel found an excuse to stray from God's perfect will. Like Israel, we can always excuse our disobedience. One famous TV comedian would say, "The devil made me do it." Whatever reasons may present themselves, they are never sufficient to justify our departure from God's will. Disobedience will always lead to suffering and regret.

However, if we have turned away from full obedience, God is ready to hear our cries of repentance. If we will humble ourselves before God, He will restore us to His presence and set us again upon His path of life.

## GOLDEN TEXT CHALLENGE

"THE LORD SAID UNTO SAMUEL, HEARKEN UNTO THE VOICE OF THE PEOPLE IN ALL THAT THEY SAY UNTO THEE: FOR THEY HAVE NOT REJECTED THEE, BUT THEY HAVE REJECTED ME, THAT I SHOULD REIGN OVER THEM" (1 Sam. 8:7).

Samuel had not long to wait for the Lord's answer to his prayer. Just how the Lord spoke to Samuel is not made clear, but that Samuel recognized the divine message is certain. God answers sincere prayer in His own way and time. And if our hearts are attuned to His voice, we will hear Him. His answer may not be according to our notion. It may even be disappointing at the first.

It is very likely here that Samuel was perplexed and perhaps disappointed at the Lord's response. Instead of rigid rebuke for the people, there is concession. Doing as they wish, Samuel must step down from his office as judge and let them have their king. They must learn, too, from experience what it is really like to have a king. So it often is with people who persist in their demands without seeking divine counsel.

## Daily Devotions:

M. Israel's Rebellion
   Numbers 14:1-6
T. Consequences of Rebellion
   Numbers 14:26-35
W. Israel Forsakes God
   Judges 2:10-15
T. Jesus Rejected by His Own
   John 1:6-13
F. Spiritual Blindness
   John 9:39-41
S. God Is a Reconciler
   2 Corinthians 5:17-21

March 22, 2015 (Lesson 4)
# Samuel, Example of Integrity
### 1 Samuel 11:1 through 12:25

**Theme:**
Life of Samuel

**Central Truth:**
Christians are called to lead lives of integrity.

**Focus:**
Examine and be influenced by the integrity of Samuel in order to glorify God by our living.

**Context:**
About 1025 BC in Gilgal

**Golden Text:**
"Moreover as for me [Samuel], God forbid that I should sin against the Lord in ceasing to pray for you: but I will teach you the good and the right way" (1 Sam. 12:23).

**Study Outline:**
I. Samuel's Testimony of Integrity
   (1 Sam. 11:12—12:5)
II. Samuel Calls Israel to Faithfulness
   (1 Sam. 12:6-15)
III. God's Faithfulness Affirmed
   (1 Sam. 12:16-25)

## INTRODUCTION

In recent years, the Church has faced an integrity crisis as one prominent Christian leader after another has fallen into immorality. For some, the besetting sin was greed; for others, it was sex. Whatever the particular sin, some Christian leaders have lost their integrity, and now their witness and their ministry is in question. Furthermore, because Christian leaders represent the body of Christ, whenever a leader falls, the integrity of the entire Church is called into question. Leaders should be an example "in word, in conduct, in love, in spirit, in faith, in purity" (1 Tim. 4:12 NKJV).

However, integrity is a necessity not only for leaders, but also for every believer. Each of us is called to be a witness, and to share with others what the Lord has done for us. Therefore, our lives are constantly being watched; we face intense scrutiny by the world. We must maintain our integrity in order for our witness to be effective. We must both "talk the talk" and "walk the walk."

Furthermore, our integrity is something we must maintain until the end of our days. The prophet Ezekiel warns us if a person lives a righteous life, but then falls away into a life of sin, "none of the righteous things that person has done will be remembered" (18:24 NIV).

In this week's lesson, we learn that the integrity of Samuel continued into his old age. He maintained his witness in both word and deed until the end of his life. Samuel knew he did not have very long to live, and he gathered the people together to bring them into unity of heart under the leadership of Saul, who had recently been appointed as king over Israel. Samuel used the occasion to testify and to invite open examination of his life. Samuel defended his own integrity and asked the people to follow his example in serving the Lord. The quality of Samuel's spiritual leadership is an example to us all.

I. SAMUEL'S TESTIMONY OF INTEGRITY (1 Sam. 11:12—12:5)

Soon after Saul was anointed as the new leader of Israel, his leadership was tested. The Ammonites besieged the town of Jabesh Gilead, and the town surrendered and offered to be subject to the Ammonites. The Ammonites, however, wanted more than surrender from the men of Jabesh; they wanted to humiliate them and "bring reproach on all Israel" (11:2 NKJV). They demanded that the men of Jabesh have their right eyes gouged out.

Saul heard of this threat to Jabesh Gilead, and he was very angry. The Spirit of God came upon him and he sent word throughout Israel that he was raising an army to fight the Ammonites. "The fear of the Lord fell on the people" (v. 7), and 330,000 men came out to fight with Saul and Samuel. The next day, Saul attacked and defeated the Ammonites; and, in the process, delivered the town of Jabesh Gilead.

A. Samuel Confirms Saul's Leadership (11:12-15)

**12 And the people said unto Samuel, Who is he that said, Shall Saul reign over us? bring the men, that we may put them to death. 13 And Saul said, There shall not a man be put to death this day: for to day the Lord hath wrought salvation in Israel. 14 Then said Samuel to the people, Come, and let us go to Gilgal, and renew the kingdom there. 15 And all the people went to Gilgal; and there they made Saul king before the Lord in Gilgal; and there they sacrificed sacrifices of peace offerings before the Lord; and there Saul and all the men of Israel rejoiced greatly.**

Saul's great victory confirmed his anointing as leader of Israel. After the battle, some of the people wanted to call out everyone who had opposed Saul and have them put to death. It was quite normal in those days for a king to execute all of his opposition as soon as he had the power to do so.

Saul, however, showed great restraint and wisdom by refusing to harm those who had resisted his leadership. He announced that he would put no one to death because it was a day of great rejoicing. It was a day in which the Lord brought salvation to Israel.

The attack of the Ammonites was Saul's first test of leadership, and he had proven himself worthy of his new office. Therefore, Samuel decided the Israelites should gather together and reaffirm Saul as the nation's leader and commander.

With Samuel leading the ceremony, the Israelites assembled in Gilgal and unanimously installed Saul as king over Israel. Two statements in verse 15 suggest that Samuel wanted the ceremony to center on the Lord rather than on Saul alone. First, it is said that Saul was enthroned "before the Lord," that is, in the presence of the Lord. Saul's inauguration was a religious ceremony recognizing that ultimate authority rested in God.

Second, the people "sacrificed sacrifices of peace offerings before the Lord." The peace offerings would have been offered on a newly built altar and would have served at least three purposes: (1) The offerings were in thanksgiving for the victory over the Ammonites. (2) The offerings were in commemoration of the renewal of the kingdom under the leadership of Saul. (3) The offerings signified Israel's dependence on God for future blessings, peace, and prosperity.

---

- Describe the positive beginning to Saul's leadership of Israel.

> "True leadership is tested and proved in crises. The real leader is the one who can handle the stress."—John MacArthur

---

## B. Samuel Affirms Himself as an Example (12:1-5)

**¹ And Samuel said unto all Israel, Behold, I have hearkened unto your voice in all that ye said unto me, and have made a king over you. ² And now, behold, the king walketh before you: and I am old and grayheaded; and, behold, my sons are with you: and I have walked before you from my childhood unto this day. ³ Behold, here I am: witness against me before the Lord, and before his anointed: whose ox have I taken? or whose ass have I taken? or whom have I defrauded? whom have I oppressed? or of whose hand have I received any bribe to blind mine eyes therewith? and I will restore it you. ⁴ And they said, Thou hast not defrauded us, nor oppressed us, neither hast thou taken ought of any man's hand. ⁵ And he said unto them, The Lord is witness against you, and his anointed is witness this day, that ye have not found ought in my hand. And they answered, He is witness.**

Now that Saul has demonstrated his ability to lead the Israelites, and he has been reaffirmed in his position as leader, and the nation has celebrated together in unity, Samuel takes the opportunity to remind the Israelites of their role in the leadership transition. Samuel declares he has done as the people wanted—he has given them a king who now walks before them.

Furthermore, as outgoing leader, Samuel affirms his lifelong integrity as prophet and judge. He states that he has served the people (and the Lord) from his childhood until now, when he is old, gray-headed, and with adult children. In all of the years he served Israel, Samuel never took anyone's property, was never dishonest, never accepted a bribe, and never oppressed anyone. In other words, he served faithfully and established justice. The people agree with everything Samuel says—he has served with integrity.

There is a ring of finality to Samuel's words. He insists on repeating the word *witness*. He asks the people to give "witness" before the Lord. He adds that "the

Lord is witness" to his life of integrity (v. 5). The people testify in agreement, "Yes, He is a witness."

- Describe Samuel's life of integrity.

> "Few things are more infectious than a godly lifestyle. The people you rub shoulders with every day need that kind of challenge. Not prudish. Not preachy. Just crackerjack-clean living. Just honest-to-goodness, bone-deep, non-hypocritical integrity."—Chuck Swindoll

## II. SAMUEL CALLS ISRAEL TO FAITHFULNESS (1 Sam. 12:6-15)

A. God's Faithfulness (vv. 6-11)

(1 Samuel 12:8-11 is not included in the printed text.)

**6 And Samuel said unto the people, It is the Lord that advanced Moses and Aaron, and that brought your fathers up out of the land of Egypt. 7 Now therefore stand still, that I may reason with you before the Lord of all the righteous acts of the Lord, which he did to you and to your fathers.**

After confirming his own integrity, Samuel now reminds the Israelites of the Lord's integrity. It is not enough that the people accept Saul as their new leader and affirm Samuel's integrity as their old leader. Samuel knows the people must also acknowledge God's ultimate authority, which stands behind all of His chosen leaders. Samuel served faithfully, but it is God who called and empowered Samuel. Saul has proven his fitness as the new leader, but it is God who anointed Saul for his leadership role.

In order to compel the Israelites to recognize the Lord's position as ultimate king over Israel, Samuel narrates the history of Israel and highlights the central role of the Lord's integrity and faithfulness in that history. Beginning with the Lord's deliverance of Israel from Egyptian bondage, when the Lord raised up Moses and Aaron, Samuel describes how the Lord saved Israel over and over again. His description matches that of the Book of Judges, which depicts how Israel rebelled repeatedly against the Lord, but when they cried out for help, the Lord was faithful to save them from their enemies.

1. What did Samuel emphasize about Moses' and Aaron's leadership, and why (vv. 6-8)?
2. Contrast the faithfulness of Israel with God's faithfulness (vv. 9-11).

> "The more you praise God, the more you become God-conscious and absorbed in His greatness, wisdom, faithfulness, and love. Praise reminds you of all that God is able to do and of great things He has already done."—Wesley L. Duewel

### B. Samuel Speaks of Israel's Demand (vv. 12-13)

**¹² And when ye saw that Nahash the king of the children of Ammon came against you, ye said unto me, Nay; but a king shall reign over us: when the Lord your God was your king. ¹³ Now therefore behold the king whom ye have chosen, and whom ye have desired! and, behold, the Lord hath set a king over you.**

Even though the Lord had saved the Israelites from all their past enemies, the recent attack by Nahash, the Ammonite king, had caused them to doubt God's plan of government. They acted out of fear, again demanding that Samuel set up a king to rule over Israel. God was their King, but they wanted a human king instead—someone visible to them.

In response to their request, Samuel had anointed Saul as their leader and they had accepted him. Samuel now says to the people, "Here is the king you have chosen; the Lord has given you what you wanted."

The purpose of Samuel's statement is to draw attention to the continued faithfulness of the Lord. Time and time again, Israel had rebelled and served other gods; yet when they cried out for help, the Lord came to their rescue. They cried out and begged for a king, and the Lord gave them a king. He has never failed them nor forsaken them. He has always been faithful in His covenant relationship with Israel.

---

- Who was responsible for Saul becoming king?

---

> "God is faithful even when His children are not."—Max Lucado

---

### C. Call to Serve the Lord (vv. 14-15)

**¹⁴ If ye will fear the Lord, and serve him, and obey his voice, and not rebel against the commandment of the Lord, then shall both ye and also the king that reigneth over you continue following the Lord your God: ¹⁵ But if ye will not obey the voice of the Lord, but rebel against the commandment of the Lord, then shall the hand of the Lord be against you, as it was against your fathers.**

Samuel pleads with the Israelites to be faithful to God just as God has been faithful to them. This call to faithfulness is expressed in several ways. First, Israel must "fear the Lord" (v. 14), rather than fearing their enemies and the gods of the Canaanites. Jesus later commanded, "Do not fear those who kill the body but cannot kill the soul. But rather fear Him who is able to destroy both soul and body in hell" (Matt. 10:28 NKJV). To *fear* the Lord is to respect, revere, honor, and worship Him as God while excluding all others.

Second, Israel must "serve" the Lord (1 Sam. 12:14). To serve God is to devote our time, talents, and energy to doing God's will. It is to love God with all our heart, all our soul, and all our strength (Matt. 22:37). To serve the Lord is to be a good steward of our resources, abilities, and time. To serve the Lord is to deny ourselves, take up our cross, and follow Him (16:24).

Third, Israel must "obey his voice" (1 Sam. 12:14). When the Lord speaks, Israel must listen and obey. To obey the voice of God is to follow His Word in every respect, at all times, and in every situation. True obedience means we obey Him in both the large things and the small things. It means obeying Him in the areas of our lives where it is easy, as well as in the areas where it is difficult. True obedience means we walk in the Spirit and allow Him to guide us continually (Gal. 5:16; Rom. 8:14).

Fourth, Israel must not "rebel against the commandment of the Lord" (1 Sam. 12:15). To not rebel against God's commandment is another way of saying they should be obedient, faithful, and loyal. *Rebellion* signifies an intentional disobedience. It is not a sin of weakness or a sin of ignorance, but a willful and intentional disregard for the commands of God.

Samuel assures the Israelites that if they will be faithful to the Lord, they will find themselves in a position to "continue following the Lord" (v. 14). As obedient sheep follow the shepherd, so obedient Israel will follow the Lord. As loving children follow their parents, so faithful Israel will follow the Lord. By fearing the Lord, hearing His voice, and serving Him, Israel will be able to stay close to God and walk where He leads. As the writer of Hebrews put it, we must run the race with patience, "looking unto Jesus the author and finisher of our faith" (12:2).

Finally, Samuel warns Israel that if they choose to disobey God, they will find themselves in deep trouble: "the hand of the Lord" will be against them as it was against their ancestors (1 Sam. 12:14). Samuel is referring to the times in the past when Israel disobeyed God, and God turned them over to their enemies (e.g., Judg. 2:14). The Israelites were hoping that a king would be able to keep them safe from their enemies, but Samuel sounds a word of caution. It is the Lord, not the king, who ensures Israel's safety; and if Israel chooses to disobey the Lord, then they will lose His protection. In fact, their disobedience would cause the hand of God to turn against them and cause them to be defeated.

---

1. What promise does Samuel make to Israel?
2. What warning does Samuel give Israel?

### Hitler's Hypocrisy

A certain political leader made frequent use of Christian vocabulary. He talked about the blessing of the Almighty and the Christian beliefs which would become the pillars of the new government. He spoke of his spirituality to the press, especially to the church papers. He displayed his tattered Bible and declared that he drew the strength for his great work from it as many Christians welcomed him as a man sent from God. Who was this leader? It was Adolf Hitler, a master of religious hypocrisy! (*Today in the Word*, June 3, 1989).

## III. GOD'S FAITHFULNESS AFFIRMED (1 Sam. 12:16-25)

### A. God Proves His Faithfulness (vv. 16-18)

**16 Now therefore stand and see this great thing, which the Lord will do before your eyes. 17 Is it not wheat harvest to day? I will call unto the Lord, and he shall send thunder and rain; that ye may perceive and see that your wickedness is great, which ye have done in the sight of the Lord, in asking you a king. 18 So Samuel called unto the Lord; and the Lord sent thunder and rain that day: and all the people greatly feared the Lord and Samuel.**

In order to emphasize his message and ensure its lasting effect on the people, Samuel called for a sign from the Lord. He tells the people to "stand and see" (v. 16), which means they should give Him their complete attention. The sign consists in the Lord's sending "thunder and rain" (v. 17), which would be very unusual during the time of wheat harvest. The wheat harvest occurs in Palestine between the middle of May and the middle of June, and during this time it almost never rains. Therefore, when God sent thunder and rain on that day in answer to Samuel's prayer, everyone knew it was a miracle of divine omnipotence. The sign was intended to show to the people their sin by demanding a king and that God was calling them to obedience.

The Lord sent the thunder and rain as Samuel had prayed for, and the people were astonished. Therefore, they "greatly feared the Lord and Samuel" (v. 18).

- Why did God send a supernatural sign?

> "Our need is not to prove God's faithfulness but to demonstrate our own, by trusting Him both to determine and to supply our needs according to His will."—John MacArthur

### B. The Israelites Repent (v. 19)

**19 And all the people said unto Samuel, Pray for thy servants unto the Lord thy God, that we die not: for we have added unto all our sins this evil, to ask us a king.**

Samuel's preaching in conjunction with the miraculous sign of the thunderstorm brought the Israelites to their knees in repentance. Their response was to ask Samuel to pray that God would not strike them down. In addition to their general disobedience and sin, they also admitted their rebellion in asking for a king. The miraculous storm convinced the people that God might judge them at any time, and they asked Samuel to intervene for them in prayer.

Samuel was known as a man of prayer, and the people trusted in his relationship with God. Apparently, they did not have confidence that God would hear their own prayers. They did not even refer to God as "our God," but rather they called Him "your God" (NKJV), that is, Samuel's God.

- What did the people acknowledge?

> "It is not the objective proof of God's existence that we want but the experience of God's presence. That is the miracle we are really after, and that is also, I think, the miracle that we really get."—Frederick Buechner

### C. Samuel Declares God's Love for Israel (vv. 20-25)

**20 And Samuel said unto the people, Fear not: ye have done all this wickedness: yet turn not aside from following the Lord, but serve the Lord with all your heart; 21 And turn ye not aside: for then should ye go after vain things, which cannot profit nor deliver; for they are vain. 22 For the Lord will not forsake his people for his great name's sake: because it hath pleased the Lord to make you his people. 23 Moreover as for me, God forbid that I should sin against the Lord in ceasing to pray for you: but I will teach you the good and the right way: 24 Only fear the Lord, and serve him in truth with all your heart: for consider how great things he hath done for you. 25 But if ye shall still do wickedly, ye shall be consumed, both ye and your king.**

In response to the panic of the people, Samuel declares the Lord's love for His people. First, he reiterates what the people must do. He advises them that they should not be afraid because, even though they have "done all this wickedness" (v. 20), God still cares for them as His people. It is important that they do not move away from God out of fear; rather, they should move closer to God and serve Him with all their heart. "Vain things" (v. 21, meaning "idols") cannot help Israel in any way. They "cannot profit nor deliver," for gods are empty and powerless.

Second, Samuel declares what the Lord will do: He will remain faithful to His people (v. 22). The Lord chose Israel as His people, and He will not forsake them. To abandon His people would be to desecrate His own name. God did not choose Israel to now forsake them.

Third, Samuel declares what he himself will do: he will never stop praying for his fellow Israelites (v. 23). To cease praying for them would be a sin. Samuel was born in answer to prayer, and his ministry was marked by prayer. Now, near the end of his days, he will not cease his ministry of intercession. Samuel's dedication and determination to pray for his people is proof of his deep spiritual life. Samuel is a model and a pattern for Christian leaders, and he resembles closely the ministry of the apostle Paul, who often spoke of his prayers for believers. Paul wrote to the Roman church, "For God is my witness, whom I serve with my spirit in the gospel of his Son, that without ceasing I make mention of you always in my prayers" (Rom. 1:9; see also 10:1; 2 Cor. 13:7-9; Eph. 1:15-16; Phil. 1:4-9; Col. 1:3; 1 Thess. 1:2).

Finally, Samuel challenges Israel once again to be faithful. In light of all God has done for them, they should serve the Lord "in truth" with all their hearts (2 Sam. 12:24). To serve the Lord "in truth" means they must not make a pretense of their devotion. God knows their hearts, and He is not pleased with hypocritical worship. If they do not serve the Lord truly, they will suffer the consequences of God's judgment (v. 25).

1. List some "futile things" (v. 21 NASB) people seek after today. What does this accomplish?
2. What had God chosen to do, and why (v. 22)?
3. List two promises made by Samuel (v. 23).

"God's not forsaking us is the work He does in us to keep us from forsaking Him."—John Piper

## CONCLUSION

David prayed, "Search me, O God, and know my heart: try me, and know my thoughts: and see if there be any wicked way in me" (Ps. 139:23-24). David knew how easy it is to lose our integrity. First, *we must worship God with integrity*. Our relationship with God must be genuine—our love for Him must be real. Second, *we must serve God with integrity*. Our works of service should not bring glory to ourselves but should give glory to God (1 Cor. 10:31). Third, *we must reach out to others with integrity*. Our witness, our prayers, and our ministry must flow out of our love for our neighbor. Paul warns that we may preach, prophesy, give, and sacrifice; but if we do it without love, it is of no profit (13:1-3).

Samuel was a model of integrity. His life is an example to us all.

## GOLDEN TEXT CHALLENGE

"MOREOVER AS FOR ME [SAMUEL], GOD FORBID THAT I SHOULD SIN AGAINST THE LORD IN CEASING TO PRAY FOR YOU: BUT I WILL TEACH YOU THE GOOD AND THE RIGHT WAY" (1 Sam. 12:23).

The prophet Samuel was known for his prayers of intercession. The psalmist lists him with Moses and Aaron, as "Samuel among them that call upon his name; they called upon the Lord, and he answered them" (Ps. 99:6). The prophet Jeremiah alludes to the wonderful power which Samuel exercised in intercession, when he pleaded for his people (Jer. 15:1).

This aspect of Samuel's ministry reminds us of Moses (Num. 11:2; 21:7); Daniel (Dan. 9:3-19); Elijah (1 Kings 17:17-24); and Paul, who interceded daily for the churches (Rom. 1:9; Eph. 1:16). Most of all, we are reminded of our heavenly High Priest, Jesus Christ, who "ever liveth to make intercession" for us (Heb. 7:25).

In our Golden Text, Samuel pledged his continued intercession as his sacred duty, plus his continued instruction in the good and the right way.

**Daily Devotions:**
- M. A Good Name
  Ruth 2:8-12
- T. A Great Testimony
  2 Kings 23:21-25
- W. A Reputation of Integrity
  Daniel 6:1-4
- T. A Great Faith
  Matthew 8:5-13
- F. A Faithful Church
  Philippians 1:3-7
- S. A Faithful Mother
  2 John 1:1-6

March 29, 2015 (Lesson 5)
# Disobedience to God Brings Judgment
### 1 Samuel 13:1-23; 15:1-35

**Theme:**
Life of Samuel

**Central Truth:**
We must serve God on His terms.

**Focus:**
Highlight the consequences of Saul's moral failure and avoid the sins he committed.

**Context:**
About 1020 to 1010 BC

**Golden Text:**
"Samuel said, Hath the Lord as great delight in burnt offerings and sacrifices, as in obeying the voice of the Lord? Behold, to obey is better than sacrifice, and to hearken than the fat of rams" (1 Sam. 15:22).

**Study Outline:**
I. God Rejects Saul as King
 (1 Sam. 13:1-14)
II. Saul's Grievous Disobedience
 (1 Sam. 15:1-11)
III. Obedience Is Better Than Sacrifice
 (1 Sam. 15:12-29)

## INTRODUCTION

Obedience to God is a basic and essential characteristic of the Christian faith. Although salvation comes by "grace through faith" and not by our works of righteousness (Eph. 2:8-9), even our repentance and response to the gospel can be called the "obedience of faith" (Rom. 16:26). Our salvation can be compared to God's deliverance of Israel from Egyptian bondage and His subsequent covenant with Israel. The Ten Commandments begin with the words, "I am the Lord your God, who brought you out of the land of Egypt, out of the house of bondage. You shall have no other gods before Me" (Ex. 20:2-3 NKJV). Salvation came first, but salvation is followed immediately with a call for unqualified obedience and faithfulness.

*Obedience* is a defining element of our identity and our mission as God's people. The apostle Paul often spoke of himself as a "servant" of the Lord Jesus Christ (Rom. 1:1), and Christians are called "servants" of God (6:22). The sole duty of a servant is to obey the commands of the master; therefore, we no longer serve sin, nor do we serve our own carnal desires. Instead, we serve the Lord Jesus Christ (Col. 3:24). A disobedient servant cannot be trusted.

The necessity of obedience extends to the individual believer, to church leaders, and to the Church as a whole. Therefore, it is vital that we examine our own lives, pray for our leaders, and take responsibility for our role in the local church.

This week's lesson draws special attention to obedience in the life of an individual leader—King Saul. The previous chapters of 1 Samuel have shown us Saul was qualified to be Israel's leader and he was chosen by God. He was installed and approved by the people, and he was divinely anointed by the Holy Spirit. His initial efforts at leading Israel proved successful as he raised an army and soundly defeated the enemy.

Last week's lesson, however, ended on an ominous note, in which the people, along with Saul, were warned that they must fear the Lord and serve Him with all their heart. If they disobeyed God, they would be swept away (1 Sam. 12:24-25). Unfortunately, we learn this week that Saul had a rebellious heart, and he did not fully obey the Lord.

I. GOD REJECTS SAUL AS KING (1 Sam. 13:1-14)

A. Saul Faced With Difficulty (vv. 1-7)

(1 Samuel 13:1-5 is not included in the printed text.)

**[6] When the men of Israel saw that they were in a strait, (for the people were distressed,) then the people did hide themselves in caves, and in thickets, and in rocks, and in high places, and in pits. [7] And some of the Hebrews went over Jordan to the land of Gad and Gilead. As for Saul, he was yet in Gilgal, and all the people followed him trembling.**

Saul began his reign with a great victory over the enemy, and Israel followed him enthusiastically. After two years, Saul decided to attack the Philistines in hopes that he might rid Israel of their most dreaded enemy. He chose an elite group of three thousand fighting men and attacked the Philistines on two flanks. Saul led one attack in Michmash, and his son Jonathan led a second attack in Gibeah. Jonathan's troops defeated a garrison of the Philistines, and Saul blew the trumpet to call Israel together for full battle. He wanted to take advantage of Jonathan's victory and press the attack against the Philistines.

Unfortunately, the Philistines also gathered all of their army together and came against Saul and his forces at Michmash. Saul and his men realized they were badly outnumbered and they panicked and fled to hiding places in the rocks, caves, thickets, and so on (v. 6). Saul's army was not experienced and not well-disciplined. When they saw the size of the Philistine army, they ran in every direction. In addition to those who hid themselves, others sought refuge by crossing the Jordan River and escaping into the land of Gad and Gilead.

A certain number of Saul's army remained with him in Gilgal. Although they were faithful to stay with him, they "followed him trembling" (v. 7), that is, they were fearful. Saul and his army must have been quite surprised when they were unable to defeat the Philistines. This setback was surely a great challenge to the faith of Saul and to his position as leader.

---

1. What caused Israel to "become a stench to the Philistines" (v. 4 NIV)?
2. How did Saul's soldiers respond to the Philistine threat (vv. 6-7)?

"Be assured that, if God waits longer than you could wish, it is only to make the blessing doubly precious! . . . Our times are in His hands."—Andrew Murray

---

B. Saul Disobeys Samuel's Instructions (vv. 8-12)

⁸And he tarried seven days, according to the set time that Samuel had appointed: but Samuel came not to Gilgal; and the people were scattered from him. ⁹ And Saul said, Bring hither a burnt offering to me, and peace offerings. And he offered the burnt offering. ¹⁰ And it came to pass, that as soon as he had made an end of offering the burnt offering, behold, Samuel came; and Saul went out to meet him, that he might salute him. ¹¹And Samuel said, What hast thou done? And Saul said, Because I saw that the people were scattered from me, and that thou camest not within the days appointed, and that the Philistines gathered themselves together at Michmash; ¹² Therefore said I, The Philistines will come down now upon me to Gilgal, and I have not made supplication unto the Lord: I forced myself therefore, and offered a burnt offering.

Samuel had made arrangements to come to Gilgal and offer a sacrifice to gain the Lord's favor in the battle, but he did not arrive at the time that had been agreed upon. As Saul and his men waited for Samuel to come, the men began to get restless and many of them "scattered" (v. 8). Saul realized that if he did not act soon, he would have no army left. Therefore, instead of waiting any longer for Samuel, Saul brought forth the animals for the burnt offering and peace offerings, and made the sacrifices himself.

Just as soon as Saul had completed the burnt offering, Samuel arrived at Gilgal; and when Saul saw Samuel in the distance, he went out to meet him. Samuel probably saw the smoke rising from the altar and realized immediately that Saul had already presented the burnt offering to the Lord. Therefore, he asked Saul, "What have you done?" (v. 11 NIV).

Saul replied that because of the urgency of the situation, he had indeed offered the sacrifice. Saul believed he had been justified in disobeying Samuel's instructions. The people were scattering, Samuel had not arrived on time, and the Philistines were gathering for battle. He was afraid the Philistines might attack before he and his men had "made supplication unto the Lord" (v. 12). Therefore, as leader, Saul believed he should take action, even if his action was in violation of Samuel's commands. When Saul said, "I forced myself . . ." (v. 12), he meant that he had acted with great reluctance; but apparently, he had not been reluctant enough to prevent himself from disobeying God's will.

---

1. Describe the crisis Saul faced (vv. 8, 11).
2. How did Saul explain his actions to Samuel (v. 12)?

"Do not let the loud utterances of your own wills anticipate, nor drown, the still, small voice in which God speaks. Bridle impatience until He does. If you cannot hear His whisper, wait until you do."—Alexander MacLaren

---

## C. Saul Rejected by God (vv. 13-14)

**¹³ And Samuel said to Saul, Thou hast done foolishly: thou hast not kept the commandment of the Lord thy God, which he commanded thee: for now would the Lord have established thy kingdom upon Israel for ever. ¹⁴ But now thy kingdom shall not continue: the Lord hath sought him a man after his own heart, and the Lord hath commanded him to be captain over his people, because thou hast not kept that which the Lord commanded thee.**

Saul thought he had acted wisely under the circumstances, but Samuel declared otherwise. Saul's actions were foolish; and they revealed his impatience, his disregard for Samuel, and his distrust of God. He should have waited patiently until Samuel arrived. Some commentators have suggested Saul's sin was that he intruded into the office of the priest, but Saul is never charged with that sin. Instead, Saul's sin is about not keeping the commandment of the Lord.

Samuel not only declared Saul's transgression, he also pronounced Saul's punishment. The Lord had intended to establish Saul's kingdom for all time, but because of Saul's disobedience, his kingdom would not continue.

Saul's independent spirit and disobedient heart made him unqualified to serve as the Lord's chosen "captain over his people." Saul met many of the qualifications for leader of Israel, but he did not meet the most important qualification—"the Lord has sought for Himself a man after His own heart" (v. 14 NKJV). Rather than pursuing the heart and will of God, Saul pursued his own will and heart.

Saul offered no response to Samuel's message, and Samuel departed for Gibeah, while Saul and Jonathan remained to fight the Philistines. Although He had rejected Saul from being king, the Lord brought victory to Israel in their battle against the Philistines. However, the victory was accomplished primarily through the faith of Jonathan, who declared, "Nothing can hinder the Lord from saving, whether by many or by few" (14:6 NIV).

---

- What did Samuel discover about Saul, and what were the consequences?

### Listen and Live

Cindy was a beautiful three-year-old child, but she often ignored her parents' instructions. One day the front gate was inadvertently left open, and Cindy ran out of the yard and headed toward the street. The parents screamed at her to stop and turn back. She paused for a second, looked back at her parents, then gleefully laughed as she turned and ran directly into the path of an oncoming car. The parents rushed their little girl to the hospital, but she died from her injuries.

> We must not only be able to recognize God's voice, but we also must immediately obey His voice when we hear it. It is life (adapted from Henry Blackaby, *Hearing God's Voice*).

## II. SAUL'S GRIEVOUS DISOBEDIENCE (1 Sam. 15:1-11)

A. Commanded to Destroy the Amalekites (vv. 1-6)

(1 Samuel 15:1, 4-6 is not included in the printed text.)
**² Thus saith the Lord of hosts, I remember that which Amalek did to Israel, how he laid wait for him in the way, when he came up from Egypt. ³ Now go and smite Amalek, and utterly destroy all that they have, and spare them not; but slay both man and woman, infant and suckling, ox and sheep, camel and ass.**

Although Saul's kingdom would not continue forever, he continued to serve as Israel's leader for several years. Samuel came to Saul and reminded him he had been anointed as king over the Lord's people, and he informed Saul the Lord had a mission for him to accomplish. That mission was to destroy the Amalekites.

The Lord had not forgotten how the Amalekites had attacked Israel as they journeyed from Egypt to the Promised Land. Israel had requested permission to pass through the land of Amalek, but the Amalekites would not allow them to pass through (Ex. 17). The Lord had given Israel a great victory over the Amalekites at that time, but they had continued as enemies of Israel and had attacked Israel on other occasions (Judg. 3:13; 6:3; 10:12).

The Lord commanded Saul to gather his army and attack Amalek. All of the Amalekites and all of their animals were to be destroyed. Saul was to execute God's judgment on this evil people, just as God himself had brought judgment against the entire world in Noah's day, and just as God had executed judgment against Sodom and Gomorrah by raining down fire and brimstone upon the evil cities. Sin must be punished. All of God's judgments in the present world are symbolic forewarnings of the Final Judgment (Rev. 20:11-15).

1. How had the Amalekites abused the Israelites (v. 2; also see Deut. 25:17-18)?
2. Describe the judgment against Amalek (1 Sam. 15:3).
3. How were the Kenites treated, and why (v. 6)?

> "God is not obligated to save anybody, to make any special act of grace, to draw anyone to Himself. He could leave the whole world to perish, and such would be a righteous judgment."—R. C. Sproul

B. Disregarding God's Command (vv. 7-9)

**⁷ And Saul smote the Amalekites from Havilah until thou comest to Shur, that is over against Egypt. ⁸ And he took Agag the king of the Amalekites**

alive, and utterly destroyed all the people with the edge of the sword. ⁹ But Saul and the people spared Agag, and the best of the sheep, and of the oxen, and of the fatlings, and the lambs, and all that was good, and would not utterly destroy them: but every thing that was vile and refuse, that they destroyed utterly.

In response to the word of the Lord, Saul gathered his army and attacked the Amalekites. The Lord gave Israel a great victory, and they destroyed the Amalekites. It appeared that Saul had obeyed the Lord's command, but upon closer inspection, we learn Saul's obedience was incomplete.

The Lord had ordered Saul to destroy the Amalekites completely, along with all of their livestock; but Saul and his people spared Agag, king of the Amalekites. They also spared the best of the livestock, especially the sheep and oxen, which were sacrificial animals.

Saul had not learned from his earlier mistake when he had disobeyed Samuel's instructions. Again Saul disregarded God's clear command and chose to pursue his own way instead of God's way. Saul decided he would destroy the animals that were "despised and worthless" (v. 9 NKJV), but he would not destroy the good animals. After all, why should all of those good animals go to waste? Saul demonstrated once again that he was not a man after God's heart.

- How did Saul disobey the Lord?

C. Samuel Notified of Saul's Sin (vv. 10-11)

¹⁰ Then came the word of the Lord unto Samuel, saying, ¹¹ It repenteth me that I have set up Saul to be king: for he is turned back from following me, and hath not performed my commandments. And it grieved Samuel; and he cried unto the Lord all night.

When the Lord saw what Saul had done, He revealed Saul's disobedience to Samuel. The Lord told Samuel He was sorry for appointing Saul as king over Israel. The Hebrew word translated *repenteth* signifies "to regret" or "to be sorry." It is the same word used in Genesis 6:6: "The Lord was sorry that He had made man on the earth" (NKJV). The sin of the early human race made the Lord regret that He had ever created humanity. Similarly, Saul's disobedience made the Lord regret that He had ever made Saul king.

Saul had been anointed as Israel's leader and had been given one basic commandment—to follow the Lord with all his heart. However, Saul's actions demonstrate that he had "turned back" from following the Lord. Saul's heart was not right with God.

Saul's disobedience and the Lord's judgment upon him caused Samuel much grief and pain. Samuel was known throughout his ministry as a man of prayer, and in the time of trouble, his habit was to take everything to the Lord in prayer. In this case, Samuel prayed to the Lord all night long. Apparently, Samuel hoped his intercession might change God's mind and bring about forgiveness and restoration for Saul. However, Saul had passed the point of no return; he would not change, and God would not change His mind about His punishment of Saul.

How did Samuel's feelings mirror the Lord's?

"The most tremendous judgment of God in this world is the hardening of the hearts of men."—John Owen

---

## III. OBEDIENCE IS BETTER THAN SACRIFICE (1 Sam. 15:12-29)

### A. Samuel Confronts Saul (vv. 12-16)

(1 Samuel 15:12-16 is not included in the printed text.)

The Lord sent Samuel to deliver His message of judgment to Saul. Meanwhile, Saul "set up a monument for himself" (v. 12 NKJV) following his defeat of the Amalekites. When Samuel found Saul, Saul greeted him cheerfully and declared confidently, "I have performed the commandment of the Lord" (v. 13). Samuel, however, knew better; and he responded, "If you have obeyed the Lord, then why do I hear the sounds of sheep and oxen?" (see v. 14). Saul then admitted he had saved the "best of the sheep and of the oxen, to sacrifice unto the Lord" (v. 15). However, Saul was not willing to take the blame. He told Samuel it was "the people" who had spared the animals.

---

- How did Saul try to justify his disobedience?

---

### B. Saul Refuses to Repent (vv. 17-23)

(1 Samuel 15:23 is not included in the printed text.)

**17 And Samuel said, When thou wast little in thine own sight, wast thou not made the head of the tribes of Israel, and the Lord anointed thee king over Israel? 18 And the Lord sent thee on a journey, and said, Go and utterly destroy the sinners the Amalekites, and fight against them until they be consumed. 19 Wherefore then didst thou not obey the voice of the Lord, but didst fly upon the spoil, and didst evil in the sight of the Lord? 20 And Saul said unto Samuel, Yea, I have obeyed the voice of the Lord, and have gone the way which the Lord sent me, and have brought Agag the king of Amalek, and have utterly destroyed the Amalekites. 21 But the people took of the spoil, sheep and oxen, the chief of the things which should have been utterly destroyed, to sacrifice unto the Lord thy God in Gilgal. 22 And Samuel said, Hath the Lord as great delight in burnt offerings and sacrifices, as in obeying the voice of the Lord? Behold, to obey is better than sacrifice, and to hearken than the fat of rams.**

In light of Saul's disobedience, Samuel brought a message from the Lord. He began by reminding Saul of the Lord's blessings upon his life. Saul had been an unknown farmer, with no particular prospects for the future; but God had taken him and made him "head of the tribes of Israel" (v. 17). The Lord had lifted up Saul and promoted him to the highest position in the land. The Lord had anointed Saul with the Holy Spirit and made him king. Saul was expected to obey the Lord's assignments, taking God's commandment seriously.

The assignment regarding the Amalekites was simple and straightforward. Saul was commanded to "utterly destroy" (v. 18) them because of their sin. Saul, however, had other ideas. Instead of destroying the livestock of the Amalekites, Saul had spared the best of the sheep and oxen. Saul's decision was judged as "evil" (v. 19) in the Lord's sight.

It is not surprising that Saul refused to acknowledge his sin. He believed that partial obedience equaled obedience. He insisted, "Yea, I have obeyed the voice of the Lord" (v. 20). Saul did not consider his saving of Agag and the animals as disobedience. He had come to the conclusion that he should take the best animals and offer them as sacrifices to the Lord. He probably planned a big party in which he would celebrate his victory and sacrifice the sheep and oxen.

Samuel explained that Saul was flawed in his understanding of how to please God. Although God's plan for worship included times and places for burnt offerings and other sacrifices, those outward rituals were not as important as the inward qualities of the heart. Whenever God commanded sacrifices to be made, then He was pleased with sacrifices; but whenever God commanded some other kind of action, He was not pleased with sacrifices. God asks for obedience above all else.

To rebel against God's clear command is just as heinous as the sin of witchcraft, and "stubbornness is as iniquity and idolatry" (v. 23). Even though he may have had good intentions, Saul had rebelled against God's command. His refusal to see things from God's perspective shows Saul was stubborn in his heart. Samuel declares that because Saul had "rejected the word of the Lord, [God] also has rejected" Saul from being king (v. 23 NKJV).

---

1. What was Saul like when God first chose him (v. 17)?
2. What brings God delight, and what does He despise (vv. 22-23)?

---

"If He has said 'Do this,' let me do it, not because I dread Him, but because I love Him. And if He forbids me to do anything, let me avoid it."—Charles Spurgeon

---

C. Samuel Pronounces Judgment on Saul (vv. 24-29)

(1 Samuel 15:24-29 is not included in the printed text.)

Finally, Saul confessed his wrongdoing. He admitted he had "transgressed the commandment of the Lord" because he "feared the people" (v. 24). Saul was more concerned with what people thought of him than what the Lord thought of him.

Saul asked Samuel for forgiveness, and he invited Samuel to return with him to the altar that they might worship the Lord together. Samuel, however, would no longer give his support to Saul, and he turned to leave. As Samuel turned, Saul grabbed his robe and tore it; whereupon Samuel said, "The Lord has torn the kingdom of Israel from you today" (v. 28 NIV). Samuel concluded his rebuke of Saul by insisting that Saul's repentance was too late. God would not change His mind on this matter. Saul was finished.

1. What does Saul continue to do in verse 24?
2. Describe the impromptu object lesson and its meaning (vv. 27-28).
3. How does Samuel contrast God with man (v. 29)?

## CONCLUSION

God is love, and His grace is sufficient to cover all of our sins. However, if we intentionally disobey God again and again, we can reach the point where our hearts are rebellious and stubborn. At that point, our relationship with the Lord is in jeopardy. The apostle Paul declared, "Where sin abounded, grace abounded much more" (Rom. 5:20 NKJV), but does that mean we can continue to sin without penalty? Paul answered, "Certainly not! How shall we who died to sin live any longer in it?" (6:2 NKJV).

Disobedience is dangerous, and Saul discovered disobedience will be punished. We should examine our hearts and confess any areas in which we are not living in complete obedience to the Lord. Are we worshiping according to God's Word? Are we doing to others as we would have them do to us? Are we loving our neighbor as ourselves? Are we walking in the Spirit? Are we sharing the good news of Christ? No matter how creative or exciting our ideas are, if they are not in conformity to God's commands, then our ideas must be abandoned. Let us surrender our lives and our hearts to God's will.

## GOLDEN TEXT CHALLENGE

"SAMUEL SAID, HATH THE LORD AS GREAT DELIGHT IN BURNT OFFERINGS AND SACRIFICES, AS IN OBEYING THE VOICE OF THE LORD? BEHOLD, TO OBEY IS BETTER THAN SACRIFICE, AND TO HEARKEN THAN THE FAT OF RAMS" (1 Sam. 15:22).

Our true desires and motives can be hidden under the cloak of religious zeal and claims of gratitude to God. Saul proved this to be the condition of his own heart. He was sent to destroy Amalek, but he rendered only partial obedience to the command of the Lord, sparing King Agag and the best of the spoils. Under the pretext that he had reserved the animals for a thanksgiving offering to God, he sought to conceal his pride, disobedience, and rebellion against the commands of God.

Sacrifice without full obedience to God and His word is of no value. Throughout the Bible, obedience to the Lord is of supreme importance. The saving work of Jesus Christ was characterized by unreserved obedience. When He defined His purpose for coming, the Lord said, "I came down from heaven, not to do mine own will, but the will of him that sent me" (John 6:38).

Christ's supreme act of obedience is the means by which our sins are forgiven. By faith, we participate in the saving benefits of His perfect obedience. Our humble participation in the Lord's obedience calls us to a life of obedience—a life free of pride, pretext, and deception, but devoted to holiness and the truth of the gospel.

**Daily Devotions:**

M. Confronted by One's Sin
   Genesis 38:24-26
T. Disobedience Leads to Death
   Joshua 7:19-26
W. Obedient to God's Call
   Amos 7:10-17
T. Adam's Disobedience; Jesus' Obedience
   Romans 5:12-21
F. Children of Disobedience
   Ephesians 5:1-7
S. Children of Light
   Ephesians 5:8-14

April 5, 2015 (Lesson 6)
# Empty Tomb; Living Savior
### John 20:1-31

**Theme:**
Easter

**Central Truth:**
Christ's resurrection is the foundation of Christian faith and practice.

**Focus:**
Review the events of Christ's resurrection and worship and serve Him as our risen Lord.

**Context:**
In AD 30, Jesus Christ rises from the dead and commissions His disciples.

**Golden Text:**
"Ye seek Jesus of Nazareth, which was crucified: he is risen; he is not here: behold the place where they laid him" (Mark 16:6).

**Study Outline:**
I. An Empty Tomb
   (John 20:1-9)
II. The Risen Lord
   (John 20:10-16)
III. The Great Commission
   (John 20:17-23)

## INTRODUCTION

The hallmark of the Christian faith is the resurrection of Jesus Christ. Take it away and Christianity falls apart. As Paul wrote in 1 Corinthians 15:14, "And if Christ has not been raised, our preaching is useless and so is your faith" (NIV).

In recent years, theological fads have arisen to contort the bodily resurrection of Jesus. Papers, books, and even television programs have attested to a "spiritual interpretation" of the Resurrection, arguing that the Resurrection narratives in the Gospels need not be taken literally. This viewpoint believes that the disciples interpreted their ongoing commitment to Jesus' teachings as Jesus' continued presence. They then invented the Resurrection story to communicate this. Not only is such a position logically ludicrous, in that people will not die for something they know is a lie, it is also not new.

In the second century, a Roman named Celcus wrote vehemently against the faith of the Christians. He especially mocked the Resurrection story:

> While he was alive he did not help himself, but after death he rose again and showed the marks of his punishment and how his hands had been pierced. But who says this? A hysterical female and perhaps some other one of those who were deluded by the same sorcery, who either dreamt in a certain state of mind

and through wishful thinking had a hallucination due to some mistaken notion . . . or, which is more likely, wanted to impress others by telling this fantastic tale.

Those who contest the evidence behind Jesus' resurrection are completely unoriginal. From the day He went missing from the tomb, lies began to spread about His resurrection being nothing more than a farce.

Not only is the evidence for Jesus' resurrection compelling, it is also brilliantly interwoven into the whole of Christian theology. While reading through the rest of the New Testament, it becomes clear that Jesus' resurrection is not an isolated event. Although it certainly vindicates Him as God's Son, the Resurrection is larger than that. Specifically, Jesus' resurrection is a prelude to the general resurrection of believers. Because Jesus rose from the grave, we also will rise. Such truth inspires worship in the hearts of all true believers.

I. AN EMPTY TOMB (John 20:1-9)

One of the most compelling pieces of evidence for the literal bodily resurrection of Jesus Christ is the undisputed nature of the empty tomb. This piece of evidence withstood the test of the "wrong-tomb theory" of the early twentieth century, which postulated that the women, suffering from grief and looking for the tomb in the darkness of early morning, simply found the wrong tomb and assessed that Jesus had risen from the dead. The Romans, and at least some Jewish religious leaders, such as Nicodemus, knew exactly where Jesus was buried. If the disciples had found the wrong tomb, the enemies of Jesus needed only to produce the corpse and carry it through the streets of Jerusalem to put Christianity to death once and for all. The fact that this never happened is clear evidence that Jesus' tomb was indeed empty. The Resurrection story shows that even the disciples initially mistook the reason for its emptiness.

A. The Missing Body (vv. 1-2)

**[1] The first day of the week cometh Mary Magdalene early, when it was yet dark, unto the sepulchre, and seeth the stone taken away from the sepulchre. [2] Then she runneth, and cometh to Simon Peter, and to the other disciple, whom Jesus loved, and saith unto them, They have taken away the Lord out of the sepulchre, and we know not where they have laid him.**

The story of the Resurrection does not begin with great faith, but great confusion. Indeed, if the story were a forgery it would certainly be a very poor one. In a forgery, faith would overcome all traces of confusion. However, in the Resurrection accounts of the Gospels, virtually everyone has to be convinced of Jesus' resurrection by clear and incontrovertible evidence. Although Jesus had spoken of His resurrection, the Gospels are clear that none of His followers understood what He was talking about. In fact, it is quite late in the Resurrection narratives that they recall those teachings. Even faced with an empty tomb, they do not expect that He has risen. They clearly expect to complete the requisite days of Jewish mourning around His tomb, and then to return to their former ways of life. Thankfully, that is not allowed to happen.

In the first century, women were considered second-class citizens across all cultures. They were often without what we would now call basic human rights, and their testimony was invalid in any Roman or Jewish court. It is scandalous that a woman who could not stand as a witness in a court of law is nevertheless the first witness to Jesus' empty tomb. This is clear evidence for the historicity of the Resurrection. If John was inventing the story, he would never have Mary Magdalene as the empty tomb's first witness. She is known as "Magdalene" probably because she was from a notorious town in Galilee called Magdala or Migdol. A *Magdalene* was another word for a woman who let her hair down in public, which was the primary way a prostitute identified herself for sale, and Magdala was full of such women. However, this does not necessarily mean Mary was such a woman. Whatever her background, she was now a Christ-follower and the first witness of the empty tomb.

It was alarming that the stone was rolled away from the tomb, but there is more at stake than just a missing body. We know that the Roman seal had been placed on the stone in front of Jesus' tomb. The penalty for disturbing a Roman seal was crucifixion upside down—the harshest torture that the Romans ever invented. By even being near the scene of a disturbed Roman seal, Mary Magdalene is placing herself at great risk. But seeing the stone rolled away, she jumps to an immediate conclusion. In fact, the text does not say that she ever even entered or looked into the tomb.

Mary figures that "they" (v. 2)—either the Romans or the Jewish religious leaders—had taken Jesus' body. She has no idea of Jesus' whereabouts. The theory of resurrection never dawns on her. Initially, she believes the body has been stolen.

---

1. Why do you suppose Mary Magdalene came to the tomb so early?
2. What was her response to the empty tomb?

> "You are not asked to trust in a dead Jesus, but in One who, though He died for our sins, has risen again for our justification."—Charles Spurgeon

---

B. No Evidence of Grave Robbery (vv. 3-9)

**³ Peter therefore went forth, and that other disciple, and came to the sepulchre. ⁴ So they ran both together: and the other disciple did outrun Peter, and came first to the sepulchre. ⁵ And he stooping down, and looking in, saw the linen clothes lying; yet went he not in. ⁶ Then cometh Simon Peter following him, and went into the sepulchre, and seeth the linen clothes lie, ⁷ And the napkin, that was about his head, not lying with the linen clothes, but wrapped together in a place by itself. ⁸ Then went in also that other disciple, which came first to the sepulchre, and he saw, and believed. ⁹ For as yet they knew not the scripture, that he must rise again from the dead.**

Mary Magdalene's observation of the scene at the tomb was the most believable option. Jesus was a hotly contested prophet that the Romans and the Jewish religious leaders wanted to get rid of once and for all. Stealing the body would accomplish this and would also be a final act of dishonor toward Jesus, given that this culture took the rites of burial so seriously. In fact, it was rare for crucifixion victims to be allowed a burial. As Peter and another disciple hear Mary's news and race toward the tomb, there is no evidence that they think anything different has happened . . . until they look closer at the items in the tomb.

The "other disciple" (v. 4) in John's Gospel is most likely John himself. He consistently refers to himself in the third person throughout the Gospel. Although he starts out by running alongside Peter, John soon outruns him and reaches the tomb first. For some reason, though, John does not enter the tomb. Impetuous Peter is the first to rush in.

The reader has been set up for a scene of chaos and destruction. Grave robbers would have entered the tomb quickly, grabbed the body messily, and hurried away. But that is not at all the scene that Simon Peter encounters. Instead, the linen sheets which were wrapped around Jesus' body and the burial cloth which had been placed around His face are neatly separated into piles. This is not the work of someone who was making haste to steal anything. We do not know how this strikes the heart of Peter. It is John who begins to hold out hope in something great.

The order in verses 8 and 9 is noticeably strange. If John has no clue that the Scriptures contain prophecies about Jesus' resurrection, what exactly does he believe in when he sees the burial cloths neatly folded? We cannot know. Perhaps he instantly remembers Jesus' words about His resurrection. Perhaps a visceral hope inspired by the Holy Spirit wells up in him. Wherever this hope has come from, John suddenly has the sense that Jesus' story was not over.

---

**napkin** (v. 7)—"face-cloth" (NASB)

1. How did Peter respond to Mary Magdalene's message (vv. 3-4)?
2. Describe the items Peter saw in the tomb (vv. 6-7).
3. What do Peter and John not understand (v. 9)?

> "It was inevitable that Jesus Christ should be crucified; it was also inevitable that He should rise again."—H. R. L. Sheppard

---

## II. THE RISEN LORD (John 20:10-16)

Each of the four Gospels tells the story of Jesus' resurrection very deliberately. Although they do not provide all the detail that we want to know, the writers take their time in such a way that builds anticipation and tells us all that we need to know. In each account, great confusion is followed by the unmistakeable appearance of Jesus. In fact, at the end of Mark's Gospel, the appearance of Jesus is foretold, but not actually narrated. Note that Jesus does not immediately appear onto the scene of His resurrection. Instead, He allows His disciples and the women to doubt, testing their faith. He does not rush onto the scene with the evidence of the scars on His hands and feet, nor does He thunder the news about His resurrection from the heavens. Jesus realizes that great faith is often born from great confusion, even great doubt.

## A. Uncontrollable Mourning (vv. 10-13)

**¹⁰ Then the disciples went away again unto their own home. ¹¹ But Mary stood without at the sepulchre weeping: and as she wept, she stooped down, and looked into the sepulchre, ¹² And seeth two angels in white sitting, the one at the head, and the other at the feet, where the body of Jesus had lain. ¹³ And they say unto her, Woman, why weepest thou? She saith unto them, Because they have taken away my Lord, and I know not where they have laid him.**

Incredibly, the disciples are struck with fear at the discovery of the empty tomb. Only John has shown evidence of believing that something more than a terrible grave robbery may have happened. Upon the discovery of the empty tomb, however, the disciples flee to their homes. This is already a dangerous time for them, and they probably fear being implicated in the robbery. After all, they would be the prime suspects. Perhaps they have been framed! They are the ones with an interest in continuing Jesus' ministry. Within this situation of terror, only Mary Magdalene has the courage to continue at the tomb. It may be that she is too overwhelmed with grief to return home.

Mary Magdalene has already mistaken the emptiness of the tomb for a scene of grave robbery. She now mistakes the presence of holy angels for mundane groundskeepers. Groundskeepers would certainly not be dressed in gleaming white, nor would they be tending to the inside of tombs. Apparently, Mary is weeping so hysterically that she is unable to process what is going on in front of her. Her sense of logic is being overwhelmed by her sense of grief. Why would two men suddenly be sitting where Jesus' body had been laid? Yet the angels are incredulous at her weeping, as if they are the confused ones.

The angels' question, "Why are you crying?" belies the triumph of the day that they have come to announce. It is certainly not a day for weeping! Poor Mary, however, cannot presently understand this. She reiterates to the angels the same words she had cried out to Peter and John in verse 2. It is all that she can say—the body has been stolen, and she does not know where it can be.

---

1. Contrast Peter and John's actions with Mary Magdalene's actions (vv. 10-11).
2. What did Mary witness (v. 12)?
3. How did she explain her tears (v. 13)?

> "It wasn't a tomb at all—it was a room for a transient. Jesus just stopped there a night or two on His way back to glory."—Herbert Smith

---

## B. A Miraculous Reunion (vv. 14-16)

Throughout the post-resurrection Gospel narratives, Jesus appears in unexpected ways. He suddenly shows up in locked rooms, to cook breakfast on the beach, or to reveal His physical body to a doubter. The Gospels take pains to establish that the same body that was crucified is the same body that was resurrected, even though this resurrected body is newly constituted in some way that is probably impossible to understand. When Jesus finally meets Mary Magdalene face-to-face, we do not know for sure if His resurrected body gives Him an appearance that is not immediately recognizable, or if Mary is too overcome with grief and hysteria to recognize Him. The evidence points to this second explanation. At the mention of her name, she is convinced that Jesus has risen.

**¹⁴ And when she had thus said, she turned herself back, and saw Jesus standing, and knew not that it was Jesus. ¹⁵ Jesus saith unto her, Woman, why weepest thou? whom seekest thou? She, supposing him to be the gardener, saith unto him, Sir, if thou have borne him hence, tell me where thou hast laid him, and I will take him away.¹⁶ Jesus saith unto her, Mary. She turned herself, and saith unto him, Rabboni; which is to say, Master.**

The story of Mary Magdalene's miraculous reunion with Jesus begins with the two of them standing in the same vicinity, yet she remains clueless as to what is actually going on. In fact, she does not even recognize Him (v. 14). The resurrected Son of God is standing in front of her, yet she does not have the vision to see Him. This is itself evidence for Jesus' bodily resurrection. In false apocryphal versions of the Resurrection, which were popular in the Gnostic heresy of the second century AD, Jesus' appearance at the empty tomb is the scene of a cosmic spectacle. We know from this account in John, however, that His resurrection appearance was as humble as His ministry had been. His character has not changed.

Jesus does not force Himself upon Mary in her broken state. Instead, He echoes the exact question of the angels (v. 15). Mary remains fixated on the corpse. She wants only to fulfill the proper Jewish burial customs by caring for the body. That is precisely why she arrived at the tomb early in the morning. She initially has no idea that the corpse she is seeking is living and breathing before her very eyes.

It is at the mention of her name that she realizes it is Jesus (v. 16). What a humble and touching beginning to this Easter drama! Easter doesn't begin with a proclamation of Christian doctrine or with a pumped-up Jesus busting out of the tomb like a superhero. Easter begins when Jesus walks into the life of mourning Mary, a woman from Magdala, and calls her name. Her Aramaic response, "Rabboni," is appropriate. He is her rabbi, and she addresses Him as such. But there is even more in this response. Leon Morris notes:

> In the older Jewish literature [Rabboni] appears to be used, but seldom with reference to men, and as a mode of address it is mostly used of addressing God in prayer. John may want us to understand Mary's reaction to the presence of the risen Lord as similar to that of Thomas who said, "My Lord and my God" (*The Gospel According to John*).

Mary's recognition of Jesus' divine nature will carry into the responses of each of the disciples as they are faced with the resurrection of their Lord.

---

1. In verse 14, what did Mary Magdalene fail to perceive?
2. What did Mary tell the "gardener" she was willing to do (v. 15)?

3. Describe the significance of the one word Jesus spoke to Mary and her one-word response in verse 16.

> "Remember that the living God is everything. Not success, not victory—but God. Not winning, not losing—but God."—A. W. Tozer

## III. THE GREAT COMMISSION (John 20:17-23)

It can reasonably be said that Jesus' resurrection is a prelude to His Great Commission. This is not to downplay the massive impact of His resurrection, of course, but simply to emphasize that the Resurrection is not the end of the story. It is the close of the story of Jesus' life on earth which the disciples are then to take and incorporate into the existing stories of every culture, every people group, in every time period. We know this because of the forceful commission which the resurrected Jesus gives to His disciples. He has not returned to them simply to continue their ministry together as it was before. He has returned to empower them to transform the world.

### A. Mary Magdalene's Testimony (vv. 17-18)

**¹⁷ Jesus saith unto her, Touch me not; for I am not yet ascended to my Father: but go to my brethren, and say unto them, I ascend unto my Father, and your Father; and to my God, and your God. ¹⁸ Mary Magdalene came and told the disciples that she had seen the Lord, and that he had spoken these things unto her.**

The Great Commission that Jesus will give to His entire band of disciples is foreshadowed in the instructions He gives to Mary. Upon their reunion, Jesus does not explain to her the mysteries of His resurrection. He tells her in simple terms that she must tell the Eleven that Jesus will be returning to the Father, as He had told them before His trial. It is as if Jesus wants to prevent any of them from imagining that life can ever be normal again. His resurrection has changed everything, and Mary Magdalene becomes the first herald of this earth-shattering news. As Paul Tillich wrote, "A new state of things has appeared, it still appears; it is hidden and visible, it is there and it is here. Accept it, enter into it, let it grasp you" (*The New Being*). This is the message that Mary announces to the cowering disciples after she meets Jesus. Against all odds, Jesus has risen from the dead to change their lives yet again!

1. What message did Jesus charge Mary Magdalene to take to His disciples (v. 17)?
2. What was her testimony to the disciples (v. 18)?

### B. Reunion With the Resurrected Jesus (vv. 19-23)

**¹⁹ Then the same day at evening, being the first day of the week, when the doors were shut where the disciples were assembled for fear of the Jews, came Jesus and stood in the midst, and saith unto them, Peace be**

unto you. [20] And when he had so said, he shewed unto them his hands and his side. Then were the disciples glad, when they saw the Lord. [21] Then said Jesus to them again, Peace be unto you: as my Father hath sent me, even so send I you. [22] And when he had said this, he breathed on them, and saith unto them, Receive ye the Holy Ghost: [23] Whose soever sins ye remit, they are remitted unto them; and whose soever sins ye retain, they are retained.

The entire day passes in silence since the discovery of the empty tomb. The only happening has been Mary Magdalene's triumphant announcement, but many of the disciples certainly thought this was little more than the ramblings of someone insane with grief. It is not until that night, with the disciples cowering in fear behind locked doors, that Jesus makes His appearance to the Eleven.

We can only speculate as to the physical nature of Jesus' appearance. We only know that all at once, they see Him. This is no illusion. Everyone sees Him. What is more, He arrives with words of greeting and blessing. He has risen to bring them His peace. They can stop fearing for their lives.

In verse 20, John once again focuses on the bodily nature of Jesus' resurrection as Jesus shows them that it is really Him. He is no phantom or ghost. He is not just a spiritual being. He inhabits the same body they had come to know—the body that had been crucified. John's terse statement about their joy seems at first glance rather trite, but how else could their joy be described? Truly, it must have been a joy that is impossible for any writer to put into adequate words.

The joyful reunion between Jesus and His disciples soon becomes serious. Once again, Jesus has marching orders for the Eleven, but these will be somewhat different than the ones they received before His death. He officially passes on the mantle of His ministry to them. Jesus declares, "As the Father has sent me, I am sending you" (v. 21 NIV).

For three years, they had been aware that Jesus was carrying out a solemn mission from God. Now a new phase of that mission is passed on to them. This is why Jesus immediately commands them to receive the Holy Spirit (v. 22). They will need the Spirit's power to accomplish such a mission, which will focus on the forgiveness of sins (v. 23).

Regarding verse 23, Adam Clarke wrote, "The apostles received from the Lord the doctrine of reconciliation, and the doctrine of condemnation. They who believed on the Son of God, in consequence of their preaching, had their sins remitted; and they who would not believe were declared to lie under condemnation."

What a huge responsibility Christ places on those who teach and preach the gospel! The Lord indwells His ministers with His Spirit and puts His Word in their mouth so they can declare His message of forgiveness to those who repent and judgment on those who refuse Christ's forgiveness. Of course, the God-called messenger's heart is always that those who hear the gospel will receive it.

---

1. What were the disciples doing when the resurrected Jesus first appeared to them (v. 19)?
2. What did Jesus show the disciples, and why (v. 20)?

3. What did Jesus command the disciples to do (v. 21), and how would they do this (v. 22)?

> "The risen Christ lingered on earth long enough fully to satisfy His adherents of the truth of His resurrection."—James Stalker

## CONCLUSION

The resurrection of Jesus Christ is the hinge upon which human history turns. The writers of the New Testament understand that something changed about the fundamental nature of human living and possibility when Jesus triumphed over the Cross by walking out of the tomb. This possibility has been realized each day since the Resurrection as Christians have walked in the power of the Holy Spirit. Easter empowerment is meant to help every disciple, across every culture and background, to fulfill the mission of Jesus.

## GOLDEN TEXT CHALLENGE

"YE SEEK JESUS OF NAZARETH, WHICH WAS CRUCIFIED: HE IS RISEN; HE IS NOT HERE: BEHOLD THE PLACE WHERE THEY LAID HIM" (Mark 16:6).

The resurrection of Christ was not witnessed by any human being. Neither was the risen Lord himself the first to communicate the news. It was announced by the angel who had rolled the stone away.

There are two features of this announcement: (1) "He is risen," and (2) "He is not here: behold the place where they laid him." These aspects are integrally linked. "He is risen" was proven by the empty tomb—the body of Jesus was gone. And the fact that the tomb was empty is explained by the fact that Jesus was risen.

Liberal thinkers endeavor to explain away the empty tomb and the missing body, claiming these matters do not prove the truth of the Resurrection. However, the Roman and Jewish authorities would have left no stone unturned to trace the body and find the explanation of the empty tomb. The stone was rolled away and Christ's body was not found because He had indeed risen.

**Daily Devotions:**

M. Living Redeemer
   Job 19:23-27
T. Resurrection Hope
   Psalm 16:1-11
W. Jesus Christ Lives
   Luke 24:36-48
T. Promise of Resurrection
   John 5:19-29
F. Resurrection Body
   1 Corinthians 15:49-58
S. Newness of Life
   Colossians 3:1-10

April 12, 2015 (Lesson 7)
# Samuel Anoints David King
**I Samuel 15:34 through 16:23**

**Theme:**
Life of Samuel

**Central Truth:**
God directs people's lives through His wisdom.

**Focus:**
Consider the selection and anointing of David and value God's wisdom.

**Context:**
About 1010 to 1000 BC in Ramah and Bethlehem

**Golden Text:**
"Samuel took the horn of oil, and anointed him in the midst of his brethren: and the Spirit of the Lord came upon David from that day forward" (1 Sam. 16:13).

**Study Outline:**
  I. God Directs Samuel
     (1 Sam. 15:34—16:5)
 II. God Chooses David
     (1 Sam. 16:6-13)
III. God Positions David
     (1 Sam. 16:14-23)

## INTRODUCTION

Although the events of life may seem to occur at random, without purpose or pattern, the Bible affirms that God directs the lives of His people. The psalmist declares, "The steps of a good man are ordered by the Lord" (37:23). The apostle Paul agrees, stating that the children of God are "led by the Spirit of God" (Rom. 8:14). Sometimes God's hand of direction is obvious, while at other times His influence is more subtle and hidden from view. God can guide His children through dreams, visions, revelations, His "still small voice" (1 Kings 19:12), and His written Word (the Bible). On a daily basis, however, most of God's guidance is behind the scenes, as God works to shape the circumstances and events of life so His plan might be accomplished.

The purposes of God are particularly relevant when it comes to the choice of spiritual leaders. Most of the Bible's great leaders did not possess obvious qualities of leadership at the time of their initial appointment. In fact, many of them appeared to be poor candidates for any position of leadership. Moses suffered from a speech impediment, but God called him to speak the Word of God. David was just a shepherd, yet the Lord made him king of Israel. Peter was an uneducated fisherman, but God made him an apostle of the early church.

We do not always know why God calls a certain person to be a pastor, while He guides another believer to be a nurse or a mail carrier. However, we trust that God's wisdom enables Him to place each of His children exactly where they need to be in the body of Christ (1 Cor. 12:12-31). We must trust that God knows what He is doing as He administers His gifts and callings in the church (see also Eph. 4:11-13).

Whenever we are allowed to participate in the process of choosing leaders (either through elections or appointments), we usually focus our attention on the outward, visible qualities of the candidates: their previous experience, gifts, abilities, education, expertise, physical condition, age, health, and so forth. In this week's lesson, however, we see that God does not judge on the basis of outward appearance. God is looking for candidates with inner, spiritual qualifications. Saul had all of the outward qualifications, but he did not meet God's high spiritual standard; therefore, he was rejected. God will now place His anointing on a new king to replace Saul—David, the son of Jesse.

## I. GOD DIRECTS SAMUEL (1 Sam. 15:34—16:5)

### A. Sadness Over Saul's Failure (15:34-35)

**³⁴ Then Samuel went to Ramah; and Saul went up to his house to Gibeah of Saul. ³⁵ And Samuel came no more to see Saul until the day of his death: nevertheless Samuel mourned for Saul: and the Lord repented that he had made Saul king over Israel.**

In our previous lesson, we studied Saul's greatest act of disobedience. The Lord had commanded Saul to destroy the Amalekites and all of their livestock. Saul, however, only obeyed God partially. He killed all of the Amalekites except for their king, Agag; and he destroyed some of the animals, but he saved the best sheep and cattle. Because of his disregard for the Lord's commands, Saul was rejected as king. The Lord would find a new king to replace Saul.

Before leaving Saul's presence, Samuel executed Agag, the king of the Amalekites (vv. 32-33). He then departed to his home in Ramah, and Saul went to his house in Gibeah. Sadly, Samuel had no more contact with Saul until the day of Samuel's death. Saul had been rejected by the Lord, and there was no longer any reason for Samuel to speak to Saul. However, Samuel continued to mourn for Saul, even as the Lord himself regretted making Saul king. Samuel's mourning for Saul is a sign of his love for others. Even though Saul had essentially replaced Samuel as the leader of Israel, Samuel did not hold any ill will against him. Samuel did not rejoice in Saul's misfortune and failure. The kingdom of God should not be a competitive environment in which ministers compete against each other and take pleasure in each other's failings.

---

- Explain Samuel's sorrow.

---

### B. God's Plan for a New King (16:1-3)

**¹ And the Lord said unto Samuel, How long wilt thou mourn for Saul, seeing I have rejected him from reigning over Israel? fill thine horn with oil, and go, I will send thee to Jesse the Bethlehemite: for I have provided me a king among his sons. ² And Samuel said, How can I go? if Saul hear**

it, he will kill me. And the Lord said, Take an heifer with thee, and say, I am come to sacrifice to the Lord. ³ And call Jesse to the sacrifice, and I will shew thee what thou shalt do: and thou shalt anoint unto me him whom I name unto thee.

We do not know how long Samuel mourned for Saul, but eventually the Lord instructed Samuel it was time to move on. The Lord had rejected Saul, and everyone must begin to look to the future and to the appointment of Saul's replacement. The Lord had found a new king for Israel. This new leader was one of the sons of Jesse, from Bethlehem. Samuel was to go to Jesse's house and anoint one of his sons to be the new king.

The Lord's instructions troubled Samuel because, even though Saul had been rejected by God, he continued on the throne, and in the eyes of the people he was still king. Saul retained his authority for the time being, and if he were to hear of Samuel's actions in anointing a new king, Saul would have him executed as a traitor.

Samuel's fear of Saul was well-founded; therefore, the Lord gave Samuel a strategy that would allow him to accomplish God's will while not draw attention to Samuel's activities. Samuel should take a heifer with him to Bethlehem, and say he had come to offer a sacrifice to the Lord. Then he should invite Jesse to the sacrifice. At that time, the Lord would give further directions to Samuel.

- How did God shake Samuel out of his grief?

"Nothing, however small, however strange, occurs without [God's] ordering, or without its particular fitness for its place in the working out of His purpose; and the end of all shall be the manifestation of His glory, and the accumulation of His praise."—B. B. Warfield

C. Samuel at Jesse's House (vv. 4-5)

⁴ **And Samuel did that which the Lord spake, and came to Bethlehem. And the elders of the town trembled at his coming, and said, Comest thou peaceably?** ⁵ **And he said, Peaceably: I am come to sacrifice unto the Lord: sanctify yourselves, and come with me to the sacrifice. And he sanctified Jesse and his sons, and called them to the sacrifice.**

Samuel did as the Lord had commanded him. When he arrived in Bethlehem, the city elders came trembling to greet him, and asked Samuel if he had come in peace. Several factors may have caused the elders to be afraid. First, in light of Samuel's recent pronouncements against King Saul, they may have wondered if more political intrigue was at hand. Second, Samuel was a prophet of the Lord, and they may have been afraid he was bringing some word of judgment against a member of their community. Third, Samuel was well-advanced in age, and he no longer traveled around the country as he had done when he was younger. Therefore, his mission must be of great importance to undertake a journey to Bethlehem.

Samuel allayed their fears and promised he had come in peace. He told them he had come to offer a sacrifice to the Lord, and he invited them to the sacrifice. He also sent word to Jesse and his sons that they too should come to the sacrifice.

It was customary for a peace offering that only the blood, entrails, and fat were burned on the altar. The flesh of the animal was cooked and eaten in celebration of God's blessings. Samuel, as the person offering the sacrifice, could invite whomever he pleased to participate in the sacrificial meal.

---

- Why were the elders of Bethlehem worried, and how did Samuel assure them?

> "This is a sane, wholesome, practical, working faith: That it is a man's business to do the will of God; second, that God himself takes on the care of that man; and third, that therefore that man ought never to be afraid of anything."—George MacDonald

---

II. GOD CHOOSES DAVID (1 Sam. 16:6-13)

A. The Lord Looks on the Heart (vv. 6-10)

(1 Samuel 16:8-9 is not included in the printed text.)

**⁶ And it came to pass, when they were come, that he looked on Eliab, and said, Surely the Lord's anointed is before him. ⁷ But the Lord said unto Samuel, Look not on his countenance, or on the height of his stature; because I have refused him: for the Lord seeth not as man seeth; for man looketh on the outward appearance, but the Lord looketh on the heart.**

**¹⁰ Again, Jesse made seven of his sons to pass before Samuel. And Samuel said unto Jesse, The Lord hath not chosen these.**

When Jesse and his sons arrived, they presented themselves before Samuel. Samuel was greatly impressed with Jesse's eldest son, Eliab, and said, "Surely this is the Lord's anointed!" (v. 6 NLT). We are not told how much information Samuel revealed to Jesse, but when Samuel made reference to "the Lord's anointed," Jesse would have known Samuel was speaking of some kind of ministry or office in service to the Lord.

Samuel's assessment of Eliab, however, was not accurate. Apparently, Samuel was considering Eliab's outward qualifications only. The Lord warned Samuel not to be swayed by Eliab's appearance or height, because the Lord had not chosen this one. In fact, the Lord explained He "does not see as man sees"; God "looks at the heart," the inner person, where qualities of character are found (v. 7 NKJV).

Earlier, the Lord had told Samuel He was looking for a new king who would be "a man after [God's] own heart" (13:14). A man after God's heart would not see leadership as a means to self-promotion or a pathway to wealth and personal gain. Instead, he would see leadership as a means to accomplish God's will on behalf of the people of God. A man after God's heart would put the needs of the people ahead of his own needs. He would act in ways that produced safety and prosperity for the community. Obedience to God's commandments would be his highest priority. A man after God's own heart would admit his own shortcomings and seek God's help and direction.

Samuel knew one of Jesse's sons was destined to be the new king. So he examined Jesse's second son, Abinadab, and then the third son, Shammah, but neither was the chosen one. Samuel continued looking at Jesse's sons until he had seen seven. However, the Lord had not chosen any of them.

---

- How did Samuel know whom not to anoint?

> "God often takes a course for accomplishing His purposes directly contrary to what our narrow views would prescribe."—John Newton

---

### B. The Lord Chooses David (vv. 11-12)

**11 And Samuel said unto Jesse, Are here all thy children? And he said, There remaineth yet the youngest, and, behold, he keepeth the sheep. And Samuel said unto Jesse, Send and fetch him: for we will not sit down till he come hither. 12 And he sent, and brought him in. Now he was ruddy, and withal of a beautiful countenance, and goodly to look to. And the Lord said, Arise, anoint him: for this is he.**

Samuel must have been a bit confused by the situation. He had been told to anoint one of Jesse's sons, but none of the seven had been chosen by the Lord. Therefore, Samuel asked Jesse, "Are these all of your boys?" Jesse said he had one other son, who was his youngest, but he was busy keeping the sheep. Samuel instructed Jesse to call his eighth son to the sacrifice. They would not sit down and eat until the youngest arrived.

Jesse's youngest son is described as "ruddy," meaning either he had red hair or he was somewhat red-faced. The Hebrew words translated "beautiful countenance" mean more literally "beautiful eyes." And he was handsome.

As soon as the boy (David) arrived, the Lord spoke to Samuel, "Arise, anoint him: for this is he." The Lord revealed no reason for his choice of David as king. Normally, the highest honor would fall on the eldest in the family, but God does not follow human methods and traditions. We can only assume the Lord had searched the heart of every young man in Israel, and David had proven to be a faithful and godly young man.

---

- Why do you suppose the youngest son had not been invited to the sacrifice?

### C. Samuel Anoints David (v. 13)

**13 Then Samuel took the horn of oil, and anointed him in the midst of his brethren: and the Spirit of the Lord came upon David from that day forward. So Samuel rose up, and went to Ramah.**

Samuel obeyed immediately. Placing David in the midst of his brothers, Samuel poured the oil on David's head. The horns of animals represented power, therefore the pouring out of the anointing oil from a horn represented the giving of power to the recipient. On this occasion, the anointing ceremony was much more than a ritual; for when Samuel poured the oil on David, the Lord poured His Spirit upon David at the same time. The Hebrew text describes the coming of the Holy Spirit in powerful terms. That is why some translations read that the Spirit of the Lord came "mightily" (NASB, RSV) or "powerfully" (NIV, NLT) upon David.

Furthermore, there were times in the Old Testament when the Holy Spirit was apparently given to leaders only temporarily, but with David we are told the Spirit of the Lord was on him "from that day forward." The Holy Spirit was a permanent endowment upon David's life and ministry.

Samuel returned to Ramah when the sacrificial meal was over, and we have no record of any instructions Samuel may have given to David or Jesse. It is likely that Samuel said nothing at the time, since he had good reason for keeping the matter secret from Saul, both for his own sake and David's. Jesse, David, and his brothers may have assumed Samuel merely intended to consecrate David as a student of the prophets. It is difficult to imagine, however, that Samuel left David in uncertainty as to the reason for the anointing he had performed. Samuel may have communicated the purpose to David and Jesse, without letting the other sons know. David remained with his father and kept the sheep as before; therefore, if David was aware of his future, he left the further development of his calling to the Lord, assured that He would prepare and show him the way to the throne in His own good time.

- Whom does God anoint today? Why? How?

> "If God called us to a task, He will then qualify us for the job."—Jack Hyles

### III. GOD POSITIONS DAVID (1 Sam. 16:14-23)

A. An Evil Spirit Torments Saul (vv. 14-17)

**14 But the Spirit of the Lord departed from Saul, and an evil spirit from the Lord troubled him. 15 And Saul's servants said unto him, Behold now, an evil spirit from God troubleth thee. 16 Let our lord now command thy servants, which are before thee, to seek out a man, who is a cunning player on an harp: and it shall come to pass, when the evil spirit from God is upon thee, that he shall play with his hand, and thou shalt be well. 17 And Saul said unto his servants, Provide me now a man that can play well, and bring him to me.**

Now that David had been anointed as the king who would replace Saul, Saul remained on the throne, ruling as king in the eyes of the people, but God's favor and anointing had left him.

For some reason, the Lord did not think it was sufficient just to remove His Spirit from Saul; He sent an evil spirit to torment him. There is no reason for us to be troubled by the statement that the Lord sent an evil spirit. It was important in Old Testament times that the people understood the sovereignty of God. That is, the Old Testament correctly teaches that even the evil spirits are subject to the sovereignty of God. Even Satan himself can do nothing without God's permission (see Job 1). This evil spirit took possession of Saul; it not only deprived him of his peace of mind, but stirred up the feelings, ideas, imagination, and thoughts of his soul to such an extent that at times it drove him even into madness.

Saul's servants saw the change in their master, and wishing to be of help, they came up with a plan to alleviate his suffering. They proposed to find a man who was gifted on the harp and bring this man into the king's court. Whenever Saul's mind would be troubled, the music of the harp would produce comfort and peace. Saul approved of the idea, and encouraged his servants to find such a man and bring him into the palace.

- Describe Saul's spiritual condition.

> "The wicked is a very coward, and is afraid of everything: of God, because He is his enemy; of Satan, because he is his tormentor; of God's creatures, because they, joining with their Maker, fight against him; of himself, because he bears about with him his own accuser and executioner."—Joseph Hall

B. David Enters Saul's Court (vv. 18-21)

(1 Samuel 16:19-20 is not included in the printed text.)

**18 Then answered one of the servants, and said, Behold, I have seen a son of Jesse the Bethlehemite, that is cunning in playing, and a mighty valiant man, and a man of war, and prudent in matters, and a comely person, and the Lord is with him.**

**21 And David came to Saul, and stood before him: and he loved him greatly; and he became his armourbearer.**

One of Saul's servants knew David was skilled at playing the harp and that he was a brave warrior who had proven himself in battle. He also was "prudent in matters" (v. 18), meaning he was wise in speech—he knew when to speak and when to be silent. He knew how to be tactful and diplomatic. Finally, he was handsome in appearance. Therefore, he would be presentable in appearance and demeanor, a fitting addition to the king's court.

Saul accepted his servant's suggestion, and he sent for David, who was keeping the sheep. Jesse sent David to serve Saul, but he did not send him empty-handed. As an introductory gift to King Saul, David brought a donkey loaded with bread and wine, and a kid goat (v. 20).

David made an immediate impression on Saul, who came to love David very much. David advanced quickly from court musician to armor-bearer, a position of great honor.

1. List four traits of David (v. 18).
2. What did Jesse send with David, and why (vv. 19-20)?
3. How did Saul receive David (v. 21)?

> "*Wise* speaks not of one who merely knows some fact, but of one who is skilled in the art of godly living. He submits to Scripture and knows how to apply it to his circumstances."—John MacArthur

C. David Ministers to Saul (vv. 22-23)

**²² And Saul sent to Jesse, saying, Let David, I pray thee, stand before me; for he hath found favour in my sight. ²³ And it came to pass, when the evil spirit from God was upon Saul, that David took an harp, and played with his hand: so Saul was refreshed, and was well, and the evil spirit departed from him.**

Saul sent word to Jesse that David had been accepted into the king's court. There David would play the harp for Saul whenever the evil spirit would torment him. David's music would bring relief to Saul and the evil spirit would leave him. This story illustrates the great power of anointed music.

- How did David minister to the king?

> "Next to theology I give to music the highest place and honor. And we see how David and all the saints have wrought their godly thoughts into verse, rhyme, and song."—Martin Luther

## CONCLUSION

The young man David kept himself busy, watching his father's sheep and learning to play the harp. Little did he know his life was about to take a radical turn. Other great leaders in the Bible and throughout history have testified to similar experiences. God is looking for men and women who are willing to serve in whatever capacity that presents itself. Whatever our hands find to do, let us do it for the Lord; and the Lord will promote us to a position of greater responsibility in His time.

While it is important that we develop our gifts, abilities, talents, and skills, it is even more important that we develop spiritually. God is searching for people whose hearts are attuned to the things of God—men and women after God's own heart. Let us trust God's wisdom to place us exactly where we need to be in the body of Christ.

## GOLDEN TEXT CHALLENGE

"SAMUEL TOOK THE HORN OF OIL, AND ANOINTED HIM IN THE MIDST OF HIS BRETHREN: AND THE SPIRIT OF THE LORD CAME UPON DAVID FROM THAT DAY FORWARD" (1 Sam. 16:13).

God may wait until He finds the person with the right potentialities for His work. He may point him or her out clearly, marking them for His service. But whatever an individual's character or talent, God must still fit him or her for His task.

Just as Saul before him, David received both a formal anointing and an actual anointing with God's Spirit. Note that the Spirit came upon David "from that day forward." This had not been said of Saul. David's dedication was a continuous, lifelong matter. Mistakes were made, even sin was yielded to at times, but David's subjection of self to the will of God always brought him safely back.

**Daily Devotions:**

M. Godly Wisdom
   Genesis 41:33-41
T. Divine Knowledge and Skill
   Exodus 31:1-6
W. Source of True Wisdom
   Job 28:20-28
T. Jesus Grows in Wisdom
   Luke 2:43-52
F. God's Unsearchable Wisdom
   Romans 11:33-36
S. Earthly Wisdom; Heavenly Wisdom
   James 3:13-18

April 19, 2015 (Lesson 8)
# Life in the Early Church
### Acts 2:42-47; 4:23-37; 5:12-16

**Theme:**
The Early Church (Acts, Part 1)

**Central Truth:**
Churches should be filled with the Spirit's presence and vitality.

**Focus:**
Study and experience the dynamics of early church life.

**Context:**
Events beginning after Pentecost, AD 30, in Jerusalem

**Golden Text:**
"They continued stedfastly in the apostles' doctrine and fellowship, and in breaking of bread, and in prayers" (Acts 2:42).

**Study Outline:**
 I. Dynamics of a Healthy Church
   (Acts 2:42-47; 4:32-37)
 II. Prayerful and Spirit-Filled Community
   (Acts 4:23-31)
 III. Power Demonstrated Through the Apostles
   (Acts 5:12-16)

## INTRODUCTION

The background for this lesson is the outpouring of the Holy Spirit on the Day of Pentecost, when 120 believers "were all filled with the Holy Ghost, and began to speak with other tongues, as the Spirit gave them utterance" (Acts 2:4).

According to our Western understanding, something full cannot be filled more, but from the standpoint of the Bible, a Spirit-filled believer can receive additional fillings with the Spirit. We will see this happen in today's study. These new fillings give the disciples extraordinary spiritual power to face the threats of the religious authorities. With boldness and great power, they continue to speak the word of God and to bear witness about the resurrection of Jesus (4:33).

Jesus promised that the heavenly Father will fill His children who ask Him for the Spirit (Luke 11:13). Therefore, God does not fail to answer the prayer of believers in Acts 4, when they ask for a fresh infilling. This prayer is a model for Luke's readers and for us. God's answer to their prayer underscores the importance of the Church faithfully proclaiming the message of salvation through the power of the Holy Spirit.

I. DYNAMICS OF A HEALTHY CHURCH (Acts 2:42-47; 4:32-37)
A. Steadfast and United (2:42)

**42 And they continued stedfastly in the apostles' doctrine and fellowship, and in breaking of bread, and in prayers.**

In addition to growth in numbers, the immediate and direct results of the outpouring of the Holy Spirit brings about other changes in the early church. There begins to emerge among the believers what may be described as a "Pentecostal lifestyle." Luke pictures the life of this community in four ways.

1. *The new converts are committed believers who devote themselves steadfastly to everything taught by the apostles.* The apostles have been eyewitnesses to the ministry of Jesus, and their teachings provide the foundation for the Church. Jesus had commanded the apostles to teach those who became disciples (Matt. 28:19-20). So they execute their commission to teach, and these new believers give themselves to the essential truths vital to a strong faith and abide by the apostles' teaching. Solid doctrine provides a sound basis for Christian living. "If you hold to my teaching," Christ said, "you are really my disciples" (John 8:31 NIV). This is precisely what believers do. Knowing and trusting Jesus does not become abstract for them. They continue daily in the apostles' teaching.

2. *The believers devote themselves to "the fellowship."* The word *fellowship* (*koinonia*) expresses the unity of the early church. No single English word fully translates its meaning, but the basic idea is fellowship. *Fellowship* involves more than a communal spirit they share with one another. It is a joint participation at the deepest level in the spiritual fellowship that is "in Christ." On the human side, believers share with one another, but the quality of their fellowship is determined by their union and fellowship with Christ. They have been called into fellowship with Him and jointly participate in His saving work. Their mutual participation in Him is effected by the Holy Spirit (2 Cor. 13:14), and "so it becomes a fellowship of the Holy Ghost." And where the Son and Spirit are, there is the Father; so it is a fellowship with the Father (R. B. Rackham, *Acts of the Apostles*). These first disciples are one by faith in Jesus Christ in their fellowship with one another. They express their love and harmony. They are united in mind and heart.

3. *The new believers continue in the "breaking of bread"—a phrase used only by Luke.* Does it refer to ordinary fellowship meals or to the Lord's Supper? An ancient custom in Palestine was the breaking of a loaf of bread with the hands rather than cutting it with a knife, but the breaking of bread is an essential feature of the celebration of the Lord's Supper. Obviously, there is more involved here than having meals together. Such a meaning would be out of place with weighty matters such as "teaching," "fellowship," and "prayer" (cf. Acts 20:11). Luke relates only significant actions of the three thousand believers, so, most likely, the "breaking of bread" refers to the observance of the Lord's Supper.

Christ himself broke bread and commanded His disciples to do likewise. After giving thanks, Jesus broke the bread and said, "This is my body, which is broken for you" (1 Cor. 11:24). These words provide the basis for calling the Supper "the breaking of bread." The breaking of the loaf represents Christ's giving Himself to suffering and death. As the bread and fruit of the vine are received, believers see them as signs that the spotless Lamb of God has been slain. The observance of the Supper points to Christ's death, but it also reminds us that Christ's blessings are constantly appropriated, that His strength is the source of our strength. The Holy Supper also calls us to look forward to Christ's return to earth. It anticipates the blessings and joy of all who participate in the Marriage Supper of the Lamb (Rev. 19:9).

4. *The daily devotions of these new believers include prayer.* In addition to special times of prayer and praise together, their devotions include prayers at the Temple (Acts 3:1). After Jesus ascends into heaven, the disciples return to Jerusalem and make the Temple a place of worship (Luke 24:51-53). They observe the Jewish hours of prayer, and before Pentecost, they are united together in prayer for baptism in the Spirit (Acts 1:14). After the outpouring of the Spirit, they continue steadfastly in prayer. Thus, prayer and praise mark the life of the church, in addition to constant devotion to the apostles' teaching, to the fellowship, and to the breaking of bread. All four elements confirm the power and the presence of the Spirit in the Church.

---

1. List four characteristics of the early church.
2. Which of these four traits is most lacking in the contemporary church, and how should we address that weakness?

> "The root of all steadfastness is in consecration to God."—Alexander MacLaren

---

B. Generous and Worshipful (2:43-47; 4:32-37)

(Acts 4:32-35 is not included in the printed text.)

**2:43 And fear came upon every soul: and many wonders and signs were done by the apostles. ⁴⁴ And all that believed were together, and had all things common; ⁴⁵ And sold their possessions and goods, and parted them to all men, as every man had need. ⁴⁶ And they, continuing daily with one accord in the temple, and breaking bread from house to house, did eat their meat with gladness and singleness of heart, ⁴⁷ Praising God, and having favour with all the people. And the Lord added to the church daily such as should be saved.**

**4:36 And Joses, who by the apostles was surnamed Barnabas, (which is, being interpreted, The son of consolation,) a Levite, and of the country of Cyprus. ³⁷ Having land, sold it, and brought the money, and laid it at the apostles' feet.**

The single-hearted devotion of these Spirit-filled disciples does not go without notice. All the people have a high regard for them. The miracles performed by God through the apostles and the dedication of the disciples to holy living inspire a profound reverence among the Jewish people (2:43). These believers manifest a remarkable fellowship. Out of spontaneous love for God and their fellows, they share their possessions in common. Rather than neglecting the poor, they voluntarily sell their "possessions and goods" to relieve the distress of those in need. There is no suggestion that they give up everything they own, but they do give goods to a common storehouse in order to meet specific needs in the Christian community.

The fact that Barnabas is singled out for selling a piece of property (4:36-37) indicates the practice of selling land is not something all the believers are doing. The new believers are willing to share their possessions when needs arise

(2:45). The term *communism* does not describe this practice. Rather, they are expressing spontaneous love that is completely voluntary.

These humble believers meet daily in the Temple. Their single-hearted devotion brings them to the "house of God," a sacred place. Likely, the Temple is more than a meeting place for them. Their presence implies that they participate in the daily worship there. Their fellowship with one another is strong because they meet in different homes for meals.

The Greek verbs in 2:43-47 have the force of repeated or continuous action. That is, all the people keep on being filled with awe, the disciples keep on selling their goods as individual needs arise and keep on sharing all things in common, and God keeps on adding to their fellowship those who are being saved. Completely dedicated to Christ, they continue to praise God and worship Him in the Temple. They have experienced the blessings of the last days: the joy, liberty, and power of the Holy Spirit, and a profound sense of being the people of God.

The influence and respect in which these Spirit-anointed disciples are held give them opportunity for witness. Their evangelistic efforts continue daily, and there are daily additions to the church. Only the forgiveness of sins entitles people to church membership. Their fellowship continues to grow, too. Day after day, God continues to add those who become believers to the Christian fellowship.

---

1. Describe the church's influence on the people of Jerusalem (vv. 43, 47).
2. Describe the unity of the church (vv. 44-46).

> "True worship and devotion will make our lives fragrant and will perfume the environment around us. Our homes, our churches, even our places of work will bear the sweet scent of our devotion."—Nancy Leigh DeMoss

---

II. PRAYERFUL AND SPIRIT-FILLED COMMUNITY (Acts 4:23-31)

A. Praying for Spiritual Boldness (vv. 23-30)

(Acts 4:25-28 is not included in the printed text.)

**23 And being let go, they went to their own company, and reported all that the chief priests and elders had said unto them. 24 And when they heard that, they lifted up their voice to God with one accord, and said, Lord, thou art God, which hast made heaven, and earth, and the sea, and all that in them is.**

**29 And now, Lord, behold their threatenings: and grant unto thy servants, that with all boldness they may speak thy word, 30 By stretching forth thine hand to heal; and that signs and wonders may be done by the name of thy holy child Jesus.**

After Peter and John were arrested, imprisoned, and then threatened for healing and preaching in Jesus' name (vv. 1-22), they were set free. After their release, the focus falls on prayer and the answer to the prayers by the believers to be refilled with the Spirit. Peter and John go to a large group of fellow

Christians (probably at the Temple), and inform them about the threats of the Jewish authorities. The immediate reaction is to join *together* in prayer (v. 24). These Christians are united in the Spirit as they worship God (cf. 1:14; 2:44). Their minds and hearts are one as they pray to the Creator. They move as one body, in unity in Christ.

Of all the prayers recorded in Luke-Acts, this prayer is the longest. It reminds us of such Old Testament prayers as 2 Kings 19:15-19 and Isaiah 37:15-20. The prayer is worthy of study and imitation.

1. *These believers begin by recognizing God as "Sovereign Lord" (Acts 4:24 NIV).* They recall His mighty power in Creation and have confidence that He has control of everything in earth and heaven.

2. *They refer to a prophecy the Sovereign Lord had given through David by the inspiration of the Holy Spirit (Ps. 2:1-2), and they apply it to the suffering of Jesus (cf. Acts 13:33; Heb. 1:5; 5:5).* Inspired by the Holy Spirit, long ago David had predicted the persecution of Christ by His enemies. Jesus did suffer at the hands of "the nations" (Romans), the people of Israel, and the rulers (who included Herod and Pilate). The Jews plotted against God's Anointed One. Even though Pilate found Him innocent three times (Luke 23:4, 14, 22), he still turned Him over to be crucified. Like David, Jesus is described as God's "servant" (Acts 4:27 NIV), but the description of Him as "holy servant" emphasizes His innocent suffering as the Suffering Servant of Isaiah 53 (cf. Acts 3:14).

At His baptism, Jesus was anointed by the Spirit as the Messiah (Luke 3:22; cf. 4:1). The plotting of His adversaries against the Spirit-anointed Savior was under God's sovereignty (Acts 4:28). What the authorities did to Jesus was in full accordance with God's purpose. The sovereign Lord remained in control and used the free, but evil, deeds of men to accomplish His plan of salvation. His ruling hand should reassure His people in the face of persecution. Like Jesus, they can expect to be vindicated by their Lord.

3. *The believers call attention to their circumstances (vv. 29-30).* They are not in danger of losing political power or privileges, but something far more precious—their freedom, even their lives. Rather than pray for deliverance from danger, they ask for boldness to preach the "word." God's Word is the message of Jesus Christ and God's saving work in Him. The word *boldness* (*parrhesia*) refers to courage and freedom of speech that results from being empowered by the Spirit (cf. Luke 21:15). The believers want to be inspired by the Holy Spirit so they will have the courage to boldly present the message of salvation without any regard for the threats of their enemies. At the same time, the believers are aware that signs and wonders aid the preached word. So they also ask that God act directly and, by His own hand, heal the sick and perform miracles by the power of Jesus. It becomes clear why the Sanhedrin's orders against mighty deeds are ineffective. They are trying to stop God's own work. The disciples' witness to the gospel cannot be suppressed, nor can the signs and wonders that attest divine approval of their ministry.

---

1. How did the Christians begin their prayer for help (v. 24)? What can we learn from this?

2. What is pointless (v. 25)?
3. Who determined the fate of Jesus Christ, and when (vv. 26-28)?
4. What did the believers request (vv. 29-30)?

> "What the disciples wanted was not numbers but an essential quality that would keep them being the church God intended. Boldness can only be imparted by the Holy Spirit."—Jim Cymbala

---

B. Receiving a Powerful Answer (v. 31)

**31 And when they had prayed, the place was shaken where they were assembled together; and they were all filled with the Holy Ghost, and they spake the word of God with boldness.**

God answers their prayer (v. 31). He gives them a visible sign of His presence: the place where they are meeting is shaken. Luke does not identify the place where they gathered, but the evidence points to the Temple mount, which would have accommodated a gathering of thousands. This external manifestation of God's power reassures the believers that the Sovereign Lord is still with them. God has heard them pray for the boldness needed to bear witness to the gospel, as well as their prayer for signs and wonders.

The believers also experience an internal filling with the Spirit. These believers, including Peter and John, had already received their initial filling with the Spirit at Pentecost (2:4). Scripture teaches that to be filled with the Spirit is not a once-for-all experience. A person already filled with the Spirit may receive a fresh filling (cf. 13:52; Eph. 5:18), especially when particular needs and challenges arise. The repetitive character of the experience is demonstrated by the fresh filling of Peter, John, and other Christians as they pray.

---

- How did God answer the church's prayer?

> "The kingdom of God is not going to be advanced by our churches becoming filled with men, but by men in our churches becoming filled with God."—Duncan Campbell

---

III. POWER DEMONSTRATED THROUGH THE APOSTLES (Acts 5:12-16)

**12 And by the hands of the apostles were many signs and wonders wrought among the people; (and they were all with one accord in Solomon's porch. 13 And of the rest durst no man join himself to them: but the people magnified them. 14 And believers were the more added to the Lord, multitudes both of men and women.) 15 Insomuch that they brought forth the sick into the streets, and laid them on beds and couches, that at the least the shadow of Peter passing by might overshadow some of them. 16 There came also a multitude out of the cities round about unto Jerusalem,**

bringing sick folks, and them which were vexed with unclean spirits: and they were healed every one.

This summary of the church's situation is similar to 2:43-47, where Luke emphasizes the apostles' magnificent ministry of signs and wonders, the awesome respect of the people for God's presence, and the harmony and unity of the Christians. In chapter 5 he covers more fully the effects of the exposure and punishment of Ananias and Sapphira, who lost their lives for trying to deceive the church (vv. 1-11). The effects are (1) a great number of signs and wonders, (2) a greater reverence felt by the people, and (3) conversion of more people.

God continues to answer the prayer of 4:29-30 for power to preach the gospel with boldness and for the preached word to be accompanied by signs and wonders. The apostles continue their powerful ministry in Solomon's Colonnade, a large portico of the Temple (cf. 3:11), and make a deep impression on the people.

Nevertheless, a paradoxical situation develops: "No one else dared join them, even though they were highly regarded by the people" (5:13 NIV). Apparently, unbelievers keep themselves at a distance from the Christians because of fears resulting from the deaths of Ananias and Sapphira. They may have been frightened by the possibility that halfhearted commitment could also lead to their judgment. At the same time, these people have high respect for the Christians, knowing that the conduct of Ananias and Sapphira has not been tolerated by the church. They can only praise them for their commitment to holy living.

In spite of the deep respect and fear that keep unbelievers at a safe distance, those men and women who earnestly desire salvation are saved and become members of the church (v. 14). News of what is happening spreads throughout Jerusalem and even to surrounding towns (v. 16). As a result, the reputation of the Christians grows, and more people bring the sick and those troubled by demons for deliverance. They place the sick in the streets, believing that healing power works through the apostles.

Again, the focus is on the apostles' leader, Peter, whose "shadow" serves as the medium of healing power (v. 15). Placing the sick so that the shadow of Peter can fall on them must not be passed off as popular superstition, especially in light of the fact that "all of them were healed" (v. 16 NIV). In Luke 1:35 and 9:34, *overshadow* refers to God's presence and power. The healings through Peter's shadow are similar to the healing power of Jesus' clothing (Mark 6:56) and cloths touched by Paul (Acts 19:12). Again, God's power saves those who believe the gospel, heals the sick, and sets free those with demons.

---

1. Describe how the church grew (vv. 12-14).
2. Describe the miracles that took place (vv. 15-16).

> "Do you ever wonder what it would be like to visit a New Testament church service? I imagine it would be a far cry from our stately sanctuaries with their crystal chandeliers and misty-mauve carpets."—John Hagee

## CONCLUSION

The practices of the early church should be at work in local churches today—fervent prayer, deep fellowship, generous giving, sincere worship, effective evangelism, and ongoing discipleship.

## GOLDEN TEXT CHALLENGE

"THEY CONTINUED STEDFASTLY IN THE APOSTLES' DOCTRINE AND FELLOWSHIP, AND IN BREAKING OF BREAD, AND IN PRAYERS" (Acts 2:42).

Genuine biblical fellowship is much more than a church social. As John put it, "That which we have seen and heard declare we unto you, that ye also may have fellowship with us: and truly our fellowship is with the Father, and with his Son Jesus Christ" (1 John 1:3). Fellowship is rooted in the idea of mutual participation, sharing in common. For the Christian, the basis of this mutual participation is Jesus Christ.

Through the new birth, Christians are joined to Jesus Christ. Because they are joined to Christ, through Him they are joined to one another; so when one member suffers, all suffer, and when one member is honored, all rejoice.

Christians build up one another as they study God's Word together, eat the Lord's Supper together, and pray corporately.

**Daily Devotions:**

- M. God Identifies His People
  Exodus 19:1-7
- T. Blessing of Unity
  Psalm 133:1-3
- W. Comfort of Fellowship
  Ecclesiastes 4:9-12
- T. Instructions for Communion
  1 Corinthians 11:23-28
- F. Pray for All People
  1 Timothy 2:1-8
- S. Basis of Our Fellowship
  1 John 1:1-10

April 26, 2015 (Lesson 9)
# Preaching, Power, and Perseverance
### Acts 3:1-26; 5:1-11, 17-42

**Theme:**
The Early Church (Acts, Part 1)

**Central Truth:**
God empowers Christians to proclaim His message without fear.

**Focus:**
Investigate how God preserved and empowered the early church and depend on Him to do the same for the church today.

**Context:**
Events in Jerusalem soon after Pentecost, AD 30

**Golden Text:**
"We are his [Jesus'] witnesses of these things; and so is also the Holy Ghost, whom God hath given to them that obey him" (Acts 5:32).

**Study Outline:**
I. Lame Man Healed; Christ Preached
   (Acts 3:1-21)
II. Power of God Exhibited
   (Acts 5:1-11)
III. Persecuted but Persevering Church
   (Acts 5:17-42)

## INTRODUCTION

Nobody in their right mind enjoys being the object of hatred and malicious opposition. The natural human desire is to seek the approval of others and live peaceably with them. Persecution, therefore, runs counter to human nature and is something to be avoided if possible.

This is as true for the Christian as it is for anyone else. The apostle Paul said, "If it be possible, as much as lieth in you, live peaceably with all men" (Rom. 12:18). Yet, the Bible tells us, particularly from the lips of the Lord Jesus Christ, that the Christian is to expect persecution (John 15:18) and that the experience should be considered a blessing (Matt. 5:11-12). Peter goes so far as to exhort us to rejoice when we are persecuted for our faith in Christ (1 Peter 4:12-16).

Persecution that is leveled against us because of our identification with Jesus Christ is actually directly against Him through us. Through the indwelling presence of the Holy Spirit, we can endure persecution and rejoice while suffering for our Savior. The apostles leftt us such an example: "They departed from the presence of the council, rejoicing that they were counted worthy to suffer shame for his name" (Acts 5:41).

I. LAME MAN HEALED; CHRIST PREACHED (Acts 3:1-21)

A. Lame Man Healed (vv. 1-10)

(Acts 3:1-5, 9-10 is not included in the printed text.)

**⁶ Then Peter said, Silver and gold have I none; but such as I have give I thee: In the name of Jesus Christ of Nazareth rise up and walk. ⁷ And he took him by the right hand, and lifted him up: and immediately his feet and ancle bones received strength. ⁸ And he leaping up stood, and walked, and entered with them into the temple, walking, and leaping, and praising God.**

At three o'clock in the afternoon—one of the regular times for prayer—Peter and John go to the Temple. The Temple had a number of gates, but the gate called Beautiful apparently was a favorite passageway into the Temple court. This man was placed here daily, where he begged from people on their way to worship.

Being a crippled man, he was not allowed to enter the Temple precincts beyond the court of the Gentiles. As Peter and John are about to enter the Temple for prayer, they encounter the man, who makes a strong appeal for money.

Looking intensely at the beggar, Peter says, "Look at us!" (v. 4 NIV). His words encourage the beggar, who feels confident these two men will give him a monetary gift. However, Peter offers him something much better—commanding him to walk "in the name of Jesus Christ." The word *name* signifies the authority and power of Jesus exercised by His followers to heal the sick and lame (3:16; 4:10). As Peter speaks, he takes the beggar's right hand and raises him to his feet. Immediately, his legs are miraculously healed.

As the man walks and leaps his way into the Temple with Peter and John, it is twice said that he is "praising God" (3:8-9). The onlookers—realizing his identity—react with "wonder and amazement" (v. 10 NIV).

1. Describe the crippled man's daily routine (v. 2).
2. How were the man's expectations exceeded (vv. 4-8)?
3. How did the onlookers respond (vv. 9-10)?

> "People pay attention when they see that God actually changes persons and sets them free. When someone is healed or released from a life-controlling bondage, everyone takes notice."—Jim Cymbala

B. Christ Preached (vv. 11-21)

(Acts 3:11, 14-18, 21 is not included in the printed text.)

**¹² And when Peter saw it, he answered unto the people, Ye men of Israel, why marvel ye at this? or why look ye so earnestly on us, as though by our own power or holiness we had made this man to walk? ¹³ The God of Abraham, and of Isaac, and of Jacob, the God of our fathers, hath glorified his Son Jesus; whom ye delivered up, and denied him in the presence of Pilate, when he was determined to let him go.**

**¹⁹ Repent ye therefore, and be converted, that your sins may be blotted out, when the times of refreshing shall come from the presence of the**

Lord; [20] And he shall send Jesus Christ, which before was preached unto you.

The healed man clings to Peter and John. His behavior attracts a crowd of people, who gather at Solomon's Colonnade—probably a porch that ran along the east side of the Temple.

The admiration of the people is directed toward the two apostles as though their own power has healed the man. Peter, instead, points the people to the true source of the extraordinary healing—the God of the patriarchs Abraham, Isaac, and Jacob (v. 13). The God of their ancestors has performed the miracle through "His Servant Jesus" (NKJV).

Peter then goes on to describe the enormity of the crime committed against Jesus in three ways:

1. The people handed Him over to Pilate to be killed (v. 13). The governor desired to let Him go, but the people and their leaders refused to release Him.

2. The people demanded that Barabbas, a murderer, be released rather than "the Holy One and the Just" (v. 14; Luke 23:18ff.).

3. Their demands caused the Romans to crucify "the author of life" (Acts 3:15 NIV). However, the climax of their evil is not what they expected—"God . . . raised [Him] from the dead." The triumph of Jesus over death was an action of God, and Peter declares he and John witnessed this undeniable reality. Peter emphasizes that by the power of the risen Jesus, the crippled man was healed (v. 16). The proclamation of Jesus' name should make it desirous for people to believe.

At this point, Peter addresses the people as "brethren," not in the Christian sense, but as fellow countrymen and as a change of tone. He recognizes the people and their leaders had acted out of ignorance (v. 17). He points out, however, that their failure to perceive the significance of their crime does not make them innocent. Their mistreatment of Jesus fulfills what God had foretold through His prophets about the suffering and death of Christ—the Crucifixion was no accident (v. 18). But neither their ignorance nor God's eternal will frees them of guilt for crucifying Jesus.

Yet, it is not too late for them to repent and make things right with God. Peter declares those who repent and had their sins blotted out will receive relief from divine displeasure and receive spiritual renewal and power—"times of refreshing" (v. 19)—through the Holy Spirit. Yet, the fullness of this renewal will not take place until the return of Christ, when everything will be restored (vv. 20-21).

---

1. How did the healed man respond to Peter and John, and why (v. 11)?
2. What did Peter make perfectly clear (v. 12)?
3. What did Peter accuse the people of doing (vv. 13-17)?
4. What offer did Peter make (vv. 19-20)?

> "Christ is the Good Physician. There is no disease He cannot heal; no sin He cannot remove; no trouble He cannot help."—James H. Aughey

## II. POWER OF GOD EXHIBITED (Acts 5:1-11)

### A. Deadly Decision (vv. 1-10)

(Acts 5:6-10 is not included in the printed next.)

**¹ But a certain man named Ananias, with Sapphira his wife, sold a possession, ² And kept back part of the price, his wife also being privy to it, and brought a certain part, and laid it at the apostles' feet. ³ But Peter said, Ananias, why hath Satan filled thine heart to lie to the Holy Ghost, and to keep back part of the price of the land? ⁴ Whiles it remained, was it not thine own? and after it was sold, was it not in thine own power? why hast thou conceived this thing in thine heart? thou hast not lied unto men, but unto God. ⁵ And Ananias hearing these words fell down, and gave up the ghost: and great fear came on all them that heard these things.**

Ananias and his wife, Sapphira, feel confident they can deceive the apostles and the whole church. They have the freedom to do whatever they want with the money from the sale of some land; but claiming to give all the proceeds, Ananias keeps "back part of the money for himself" (v. 2 NIV). His deception is detected at once. Under the prophetic inspiration of the Spirit, Peter exposes his falsehood. Ananias is not only lying to the church and its leaders, but he is also lying to the Holy Spirit.

In contrast to Jesus and His disciples who are full of the Spirit (Luke 4:1; Acts 2:4), Ananias is filled with Satan (5:3). Yielding to Satan, he lies to the Holy Spirit. The Holy Spirit has brought the Church into existence by His life-giving power, and He exercises constant oversight over the community of believers. By the authority of the Spirit, Peter rebukes Ananias: "What made you think of doing such a thing?" (v. 4 NIV).

Peter's recognition of the hypocrisy of Ananias is an example of "the word of knowledge" (1 Cor. 12:8). He is able to unmask Ananias as a liar. In questioning him, Peter does not expect answers; his questions are really declarative statements. As soon as Peter stops speaking, the heinous sin of Ananias becomes apparent. By divine power, he is struck with instant death (Acts 5:5). The sins of dishonesty and hypocrisy are always serious. It is no small matter to sin against the Holy Spirit.

Three hours after the sudden death of her husband and his burial, Sapphira arrives. The fate of her husband has not reached her ears. She has collaborated with Ananias and acts out the part agreed on between them (v. 2). Peter begins with an imperative question: "Tell me, is this the price you and Ananias got for the land?" (v. 8 NIV). Her answer reflects her agreement with Ananias, confirming that she, too, is a liar.

In his second question, Peter asks Sapphira, "How could you agree to test the Spirit of the Lord?" (v. 9 NIV). By their mutual agreement, Ananias and Sapphira have not only shared totally in the decision, but also in the guilt of their sin.

When Sapphira affirmed her husband's lie, Peter knew what was about to take place. Immediately, he issued a solemn prophetic proclamation: "Look! The feet of the men who buried your husband are at the door, and they will carry you out also" (v. 9 NIV). At once, she collapsed in death.

---

1. How was Satan involved in this event (vv. 1-3)?

2. Why was this couple's sin so serious (vv. 4, 9)?

> "Whatever is only almost true is quite false, and among the most dangerous of errors, because being so near truth, it is the more likely to lead astray."—Henry Ward Beecher

---

### B. Great Fear (v. 11)

**11 And great fear came upon all the church, and upon as many as heard these things.**

What prompted Ananias and Sapphira to fall into the deceitful use of possessions? At least two unholy desires seem to have motivated their hypocrisy—the love of money and the love of praise.

As a result of God's punishment of the couple, "great fear" comes on the whole church and everyone who hears about the event (vv. 5, 11). These two deaths warn against the love of money and unholy desires for recognition. Even unbelievers who hear about the incident tremble at the thought of the removal of the two impostors from the church.

The primary interest for Luke is not to strike fear in the hearts of people, but to teach that the Holy Spirit is active in the church. The Holy Spirit protects the church's integrity and guards it against such divisive sin as that of Ananias and Sapphira.

---

> "God's wrath arises from His intense, settled hatred of all sin and is the tangible expression of His inflexible determination to punish it."—Jerry Bridges

---

## III. PERSECUTED BUT PERSEVERING CHURCH (Acts 5:17-42)

### A. Angelic Deliverance (vv. 17-24)

(Acts 5:17, 24 is not included in the printed text.)

**18 And laid their hands on the apostles, and put them in the common prison. 19 But the angel of the Lord by night opened the prison doors, and brought them forth, and said, 20 Go, stand and speak in the temple to the people all the words of this life. 21 And when they heard that, they entered into the temple early in the morning, and taught. But the high priest came, and they that were with him, and called the council together, and all the senate of the children of Israel, and sent to the prison to have them brought. 22 But when the officers came, and found them not in the prison, they returned, and told, 23 Saying, The prison truly found we shut with all safety, and the keepers standing without before the doors: but when we had opened, we found no man within.**

Earlier, religious authorities commanded Peter and John to stop proclaiming the good news about Jesus (4:18). But Peter and John and the other apostles never stop preaching and healing the sick in the name of the Savior. Once again, their many successes arouse the hostility of the religious leaders.

Their arrest and imprisonment come as no surprise to the apostles. They know the Sanhedrin is controlled by men who are likely to carry out their threats. What happens during the night, however, must come as a great surprise to the apostles and to all Jerusalem. Before daybreak, the angel of the Lord delivers them from prison.

The angel instructs the apostles to return to the Temple and to teach "the full message of this new life" (5:20 NIV). The phrase "this new life" refers to the life initiated by the death and resurrection of Jesus. The apostles obey the angel's command and begin to preach the message of salvation that leads to the Christian life. Ironically, the Sadducees do not even believe in angels (23:8)!

Early the next morning, Caiaphas and his associates call a full meeting of the Sanhedrin. The Temple guards are sent to get the prisoners, but they find the prison empty (5:22). When the authorities hear of the disappearance of the apostles, they are distressed and feel helpless, not knowing "whereunto this would grow" (v. 24); they do not know what to do or what to say. This miracle of deliverance demonstrates that the gospel cannot be stopped by bonds or prisons (cf. 12:6-11; 16:26ff.).

---

1. Why were the religious leaders "filled with jealousy" (v. 17 NASB)?
2. Where did the apostles go upon their release, and why (vv. 18-21)?

> "The angel fetched Peter out of prison, but it was prayer that fetched the angel."—Thomas Watson

---

B. Unflinching Determination (vv. 25-32)

(Acts 5:25-28, 30-32 is not included in the printed text.)
**²⁹ Then Peter and the other apostles answered and said, We ought to obey God rather than men.**

When news comes that the apostles are in the Temple, the Temple guards arrest them (vv. 25-26). Their rearrest is peaceful, indicating the authorities recognize that the apostles are popular, and the use of force may result in a violent reaction from the people. The apostles are brought before the Sanhedrin. Caiaphas repeats the earlier injunction "not [to] teach in this name" (v. 28; cf. 4:18), but he also introduces a new theme: the apostles' attempt to make the council "guilty of this man's blood" (5:28 NIV).

The high priest avoids mentioning the name of Jesus. The Jewish leaders are aware that they are accused directly of murdering the Messiah (2:23; 3:14-15). This charge is a sensitive point. The Jewish leaders find themselves branded as murderers, and the Christians are, in effect, publicly calling for God to judge them for their crime.

The disciples have prayed for Spirit-inspired boldness to speak the Word (4:29), and God continues to answer their prayer. As the spokesman for the apostles, Peter speaks boldly, "We must obey God rather than men!" (5:29 NIV). This moral obligation assumes the divine command of the angel who set them free, as well as the commission of Christ to preach the gospel to the ends of the earth. Peter concedes that the apostles are guilty of disobeying the Sanhedrin. But God's authority is above that of human beings. With great candor, Peter stresses also that the Jewish leaders are personally responsible for the death of Jesus—they have shed innocent blood.

In his speech, Peter uses three of the major elements normally emphasized in early Christian preaching (known as the *kerygma*): Christ's death, resurrection, and ascension. As the crucified, risen Lord, Jesus Christ is the Author of salvation, offering eternal life to all sinners who repent of their sins (vv. 30-31).

---

1. Describe two concerns of the religious leaders (vv. 24-26).
2. What were the apostles accused of doing (vv. 27-28)?
3. How did Peter defend the apostles' actions (v. 29)?
4. Summarize Peter's testimony (vv. 30-32).

> "I am prepared to go anywhere, provided it be forward. I determined never to stop until I had come to the end and achieved my purpose."—David Livingstone

---

C. Reason to Rejoice (vv. 33-42)

(Acts 5:33-40 is not included in the printed text.)
**⁴¹ And they departed from the presence of the council, rejoicing that they were counted worthy to suffer shame for his name. ⁴² And daily in the temple, and in every house, they ceased not to teach and preach Jesus Christ.**

As the spokesman for the apostles, Peter provokes the anger of the Sanhedrin. "They were furious" (v. 33 NKJV) translates a Greek word that literally means "sawn asunder" or "cut to the quick." The *New English Bible* renders it, "This touched them on the raw."

At least Gamaliel, a member on the Sanhedrin, dares to offer wise counsel to this elite group to which he belongs. His argument runs like this: "If this movement (as it is thought by the Sanhedrin) is not blessed of God, it will come to nothing. On the other hand, should it prove, as the Christians believe, to be the work of God, nothing would succeed in stopping it" (see vv. 38-39). Any such efforts to end it would be futile. Still worse, the Sanhedrin would not only be opposing human beings, but also God and His judgment.

Gamaliel cites two examples of messianic movements without the blessing of God, which therefore proved unsuccessful (vv. 36-37). He insists that the Christian movement will come to the same end, as did these men's movements, if it is not inspired by God.

The advice of Gamaliel does not restrain the Sanhedrin from flogging the apostles (v. 40). This punishment is more severe than the earlier imprisonment and threats they had received. Again, the Sanhedrin forbids them from preaching about Jesus.

The beating conforms to what Jesus had told them to expect (Luke 21:12), but the Sanhedrin does not succeed in discouraging them. They go away, "rejoicing because they had been counted worthy of suffering disgrace for the Name" (Acts 5:41 NIV). In the midst of persecution, the apostles are full of joy because they consider it a great honor to suffer for the sake of Jesus Christ. They are glad for the opportunity to show that Christ's confidence in them is not misplaced. Refusing to heed the threat of the Sanhedrin, they continue to teach and preach daily that Jesus is the true Messiah. As before, they preach publicly in the Temple, but now they also teach in private homes (v. 42). Persecution does not diminish the witness of these Spirit-anointed disciples.

1. How did Peter's message affect the religious leaders (v. 33)?
2. Summarize Gamaliel's advice (vv. 38-39).
3. Explain the apostles' actions to the council's actions (vv. 40-42).

"We can catch the Spirit of Christ and zealously and enthusiastically go out each day determined to serve God and be what we ought to be! Stay on the firing line!"—Shelton Smith

## CONCLUSION

Pakistan, Turkey, and North Korea are three of many nations where Christians know what it means to experience persecution for preaching the gospel in power. We should (1) pray for persecuted peoples and (2) be prepared for opposition we will face for standing for Christ.

## GOLDEN TEXT CHALLENGE

"WE ARE HIS [JESUS'] WITNESSES OF THESE THINGS; AND SO IS ALSO THE HOLY GHOST, WHOM GOD HATH GIVEN TO THEM THAT OBEY HIM" (Acts 5:32).

The apostles were not speaking through hearsay; they were witnesses of the very things they had to say. God had verified His truth to them by the Holy Spirit.

The emphasis here was that the apostles were not speaking as mere individuals, but as men empowered by the Spirit to speak the message of Jesus. Their message was therefore not human but divine, not temporal but eternal, not earthly but heavenly.

**Daily Devotions:**
M. God Sustains His People
   Deuteronomy 8:1-10
T. God Preserves His People
   Esther 9:20-28
W. God's Goodness to His People
   Psalm 107:1-9
T. God's Provision for His People
   Luke 12:22-31
F. God's Power in the Church
   Ephesians 1:15-23
S. Jesus' Words to a Persecuted Church
   Revelation 2:8-11

May 3, 2015 (Lesson 10)
# Living and Dying for Christ

**Acts 6:1 through 7:60**

**Theme:**
The Early Church (Acts, Part 1)

**Central Truth:**
No matter the cost, Christians must declare the gospel.

**Focus:**
Describe the courageous faith of Stephen and emulate his example of steadfast faith in Christ.

**Context:**
Probably AD 34, Jerusalem and vicinity

**Golden Text:**
"Stephen, full of faith and power did great wonders and miracles among the people" (Acts 6:8).

**Study Outline:**
I. Empowered to Serve
   (Acts 6:1-18)
II. Falsely Accused
   (Acts 6:9-15)
III. First Christian Martyr
   (Acts 7:51-60)

## INTRODUCTION

The Christians in Jerusalem devoted themselves to forming a community of fellowship (Acts 2:42), which finds expression in the sharing of possessions with the needy. As a positive example of fellowship, Luke calls attention to Barnabas (4:36-37); in contrast, Ananias and his wife, Sapphira, are negative examples (5:1-11). In chapter 6, Luke reports a breakdown in fellowship because of the community's neglect of a particular group of widows. In the midst of tremendous progress of the church, this problem places the unity of the church in serious jeopardy.

Seven Spirit-empowered men are appointed to deal with this crisis. Among them are Stephen and Philip (the only two whom Luke describes in any detail). Philip emerges as a charismatic preacher (8:4-8, 26-40; 21:8). He is the first to plant a church among the Samaritans. Stephen is described as "a man full of faith" (6:5), no doubt meaning miracle-working faith. He does "great wonders and miraculous signs" (v. 8 NIV), and his opponents are unable to cope with his preaching (v. 10). Because of Stephen's powerful witness, this courageous man of God becomes the first Christian martyr.

I. EMPOWERED TO SERVE (Acts 6:1-8)

A. Chosen to Serve (vv. 1-6)

¹ And in those days, when the number of the disciples was multiplied, there arose a murmuring of the Grecians against the Hebrews, because their widows were neglected in the daily ministration. ² Then the twelve called the multitude of the disciples unto them, and said, It is not reason that we should leave the word of God, and serve tables. ³ Wherefore, brethren, look ye out among you seven men of honest report, full of the Holy Ghost and wisdom, whom we may appoint over this business. ⁴ But we will give ourselves continually to prayer, and to the ministry of the word. ⁵ And the saying pleased the whole multitude: and they chose Stephen, a man full of faith and of the Holy Ghost, and Philip, and Prochorus, and Nicanor, and Timon, and Parmenas, and Nicolas a proselyte of Antioch: ⁶ Whom they set before the apostles: and when they had prayed, they laid their hands on them.

At this time, the Christian community consists of two groups: the Grecian Jews (Greek-speaking believers) and the Hebraic Jews (Aramaic-speaking believers). The Grecian Jews of Acts 6 are believers who have been strongly influenced by Greek culture, probably while living outside of Palestine. The Hebraic Jews are Christians who have lived in their native land of Palestine.

Many devout Jews who lived outside of Palestine most of their lives moved to Jerusalem in their old age to be buried near this city. When the men died, few of the widows were capable of supporting themselves. They depended on the benevolence of religious groups for survival. Because these widows were not well known, it was easy for the leaders of the community to overlook them. The widows of the Aramaic-speaking Christians were more likely to have been better known, thus less likely to be overlooked in daily distribution of assistance.

However, something more than a different language between the two groups seems to be involved here. Social circumstances and theological differences could have played a part in the friction between the two groups.

The Christians had set aside funds for the needy (2:45; 4:34-35, 37; 5:1ff.), but they were not adequately instructed on how to care for the widows of the Greek-speaking believers. The immediate response of the apostles seems to indicate that the neglect of these widows is not intentional discrimination. Their responsibility to preach the gospel, to devote themselves to prayer, and to govern the church make it impractical for them to administer relief to the poor. It is not that the caring for widows is "beneath" them, nor do they consider it to be a lower level of ministry. Rather, their primary burden is to preach God's Word and to administer the affairs of the church.

As Spirit-led leaders, the apostles call a general meeting of "all the disciples" (6:2 NIV) and propose a solution to the problem—that the church select seven men and give them the responsibility to care for the widows. Their function will be to "serve tables." Luke does not use the word *deacon* (*diakonos*) to describe the seven men. The terms for *serve* and *deacon* come from the same Greek root. Deacons are mentioned in Philippians 1:1 and 1 Timothy 3:8-13. Thus, it seems appropriate to use the title *deacon* for the seven, especially in light of the work performed by deacons in later times (which included the handling of finances, caring for the needy, and other practical matters of ministry).

If this plan is followed, the apostles will then be able to devote themselves to prayer, preaching, and teaching (see Acts 6:4). The congregation as a whole sees the wisdom of the apostles' proposal (v. 5) and participates in the selection of these deacons. The basic qualification is *spirituality*, but they are to be distinguished in two ways: (1) They are to be "full of the Holy Spirit" (v. 3 NKJV). Rather than being merely good administrators or managers of funds, this qualification requires them to be Spirit-anointed with the power of a miracle-working faith. (2) They are also to be "full of . . . wisdom." Complementary to the acts of power is Spirit-inspired speech. The deacons are, therefore, to be powerful in works and in word.

The seven men who are chosen have Greek names, but this fails to prove they are native Greeks. At this time, many Jews have Greek names. Undoubtedly, these men speak Greek and are equipped spiritually and linguistically to deal with the problem to which they have been assigned. Stephen's name appears first in the list, followed by the words "a man full of faith and of the Holy Spirit" (v. 5 NIV). These words are not repeated after the other names, but they are understood to describe all seven deacons.

The new deacons are presented by the entire congregation to the apostles. The laying-on of hands ratifies the community's choice and signifies the giving of responsibility and the imparting of strength and blessings for the task.

---

1. Explain the "murmuring" that took place (v. 1).
2. What "pleased the whole group" (v. 5 NIV), and why (vv. 2-4)?

---

### Ministry Model
As in the early church, we should be concerned about how minorities—the poor, widows, orphans, and people of different racial origins—are treated. Such people are often powerless, and their needs can be overlooked. Each congregation should have a proper plan to minister to disadvantaged and minorities and commit this ministry to those who are spiritually gifted and committed to caring for the needs of others.

---

B. Ministry Multiplied (vv. 7-8)

**⁷And the word of God increased; and the number of the disciples multiplied in Jerusalem greatly; and a great company of the priests were obedient to the faith. ⁸And Stephen, full of faith and power, did great wonders and miracles among the people.**

Upon the resolution of a potentially dangerous rift, the Spirit-anointed church again enjoys a spirit of unity and rapid growth. An impressive number of new converts join the church, including for the first time "a large number of priests" (v. 7 NIV). Luke underscores the striking effect of the gospel on these priests. They become "obedient to the faith," indicating that faith in Jesus Christ demands a course of life in accordance with what we believe. To follow this course is to obey the faith (cf. Rom. 1:5).

In Acts 6:8 (NIV), we see the coupling of *grace* (*charis*) and *power* (*dunamis*) in Stephen's life, indicating that divine grace confers on him spiritual gifts to perform miracles. Works empowered by the Spirit are typical of Stephen's ministry. He does not perform one or two miracles, but many.

1. Describe the revival that occurred (v. 7).
2. Describe Stephen's ministry (v. 8).

> "The ministry of 'watch care' is necessary for the preservation and upbuilding of that which belongs to Christ."—Charles W. Conn

## II. FALSELY ACCUSED (Acts 6:9-15)

### A. Lying Witnesses (vv. 9-14)

⁹ **Then there arose certain of the synagogue, which is called the synagogue of the Libertines, and Cyrenians, and Alexandrians, and of them of Cilicia and of Asia, disputing with Stephen.** ¹⁰ **And they were not able to resist the wisdom and the spirit by which he spake.** ¹¹ **Then they suborned men, which said, We have heard him speak blasphemous words against Moses, and against God.** ¹² **And they stirred up the people, and the elders, and the scribes, and came upon him, and caught him, and brought him to the council,** ¹³ **And set up false witnesses, which said, This man ceaseth not to speak blasphemous words against this holy place, and the law.** ¹⁴ **For we have heard him say, that this Jesus of Nazareth shall destroy this place, and shall change the customs which Moses delivered us.**

Marvelous manifestations of the Spirit, along with Stephen's preaching, stir up opposition (vv. 8-9). The Greek-speaking Jews of the Synagogue of the Freedmen, who were probably prisoners of war set free by the Romans, argue with Stephen. None of Stephen's adversaries could "stand up against his wisdom or the Spirit by whom he spoke" (v. 10 NIV). As he speaks, Stephen is empowered by the Holy Spirit, and his message manifests the spiritual gift of wisdom. It is theologically informed, and his opponents cannot answer his arguments or repudiate his logic (cf. Ex. 4:14-16; Luke 21:15).

Stephen's adversaries charge him with blasphemy. Being more interested in vindicating themselves than in the truth, they resort to obtaining false testimony from witnesses. The authorities have so far been restrained in their actions against the disciples because of their fear of the people. But the false witnesses poison the minds of the people against the disciples, distorting certain utterances of Stephen.

The dispute between Stephen and the Greek-speaking Jews focuses on the Law and the Temple. Stephen's accusers claim that he has spoken "blasphemous words against Moses, and against God" (Acts 6:11).

First, as the bearer of the Law, Moses represents God's revelation given to the Jews at Mount Sinai. To deny Moses is to assault the divine authority and validity of the worship and practices of the Jews. Thus, Stephen is accused of changing the customs handed down by Moses (v. 14).

Second, Temple worship prescribes the divine order of worship for the people of Israel. To question Temple order is seen as a violation of God's power and majesty. A similar charge had been made against Jesus. He had predicted the destruction of the Temple. The fourth Gospel records the prophecy and its significance: "Destroy this temple, and I will raise it again in three days"; but, as John explained, "the temple he had spoken of was his body" (2:19, 21 NIV; cf. Matt. 26:61; Mark 14:58). It is quite possible that during his debate in the synagogue, Stephen cited this prophecy. Twisting Stephen's words as blasphemous, his enemies charge him with teaching that Jesus will destroy the Temple and abolish its services (Acts 6:14).

What Stephen actually teaches is in accordance with the Old Testament prophecy that God does not dwell in temples made by hands (7:48-49). Stephen sees that the saving work of Christ brings to an end the Temple order with its ceremonial and sacrificial worship. A new dimension of fellowship with God has been introduced through Jesus. Such fellowship with God far exceeds the Temple and its worship.

In other words, the old Temple is being replaced by a new temple, the Christian church (cf. 15:16-18). This transition makes clear that the last days have dawned. Through the power of the Spirit, Stephen proclaims the universal scope of salvation. But the Greek-speaking Jews, zealous defenders of tradition, see his prophetic preaching as a threat to sacrificial worship and the ceremonial law.

1. Why did the religious leaders resort to lying, and what were their lies (vv. 9-11)?
2. How was opposition built against Stephen (vv. 12-14)?

> "Freedom lies in being bold."—Robert Frost

B. Stephen's Countenance (v. 15)

**¹⁵ And all that sat in the council, looking stedfastly on him, saw his face as it had been the face of an angel.**

As charges are made against Stephen, his face appears to the court like "the face of an angel." That is, his countenance is aglow with God's glory like that of Moses (Ex. 34:29-30) and like that of Jesus (Luke 9:29). The glorious radiance of Stephen's face indicates that just as Jesus had promised His disciples (12:11-12; 21:14-15), the Holy Spirit continues to inspire him to proclaim the gospel.

III. FIRST CHRISTIAN MARTYR (Acts 7:51-60)

A. Dynamic Testimony (vv. 51-54)
   (Acts 7:52-53 is not included in the printed text.)

**⁵¹ Ye stiffnecked and uncircumcised in heart and ears, ye do always resist the Holy Ghost: as your fathers did, so do ye.**

**⁵⁴ When they heard these things, they were cut to the heart, and they gnashed on him with their teeth.**

After the high priest's question, "Are these charges true?" (7:1 NIV), a silence falls on the Sanhedrin until Stephen completes his defense (vv. 2-53). His speech has six major divisions, concentrating mainly on the history of God's people as found in the first five books of the Old Testament.

Stephen concludes his speech with scorching words directed at his accusers and the members of the Sanhedrin (vv. 51-53). Deeply stirred by his convictions and inspired of the Holy Spirit, Stephen uses vivid language to denounce them for their hardness of heart. They are "stiffnecked" (Ex. 33:3, 5) and have "uncircumcised" hearts and ears (see Lev. 26:41; Deut. 10:16). Among the Jews, the word *uncircumcised* was used as a term of reproach and contempt. David denounced Goliath as "this uncircumcised Philistine" (1 Sam. 17:26), and Ezekiel called Elam "uncircumcised" (Ezek. 32:24) and the Israelites "uncircumcised in heart" (44:7, 9).

Moses and the prophets had hurled these same two expressions—*stiffnecked* and *uncircumcised*—at pagan nations and apostate Israel. No words could be more accurate for Stephen's opponents, who are following in the steps of their fathers by closing their minds to the message of God and resisting the Holy Spirit (Isa. 63:10), under whose inspiration Stephen speaks.

There is nothing new about the Jewish leaders' rejection of Spirit-inspired leaders. Their predecessors had persecuted the prophets and killed those who prophesied of Christ's first coming (Acts 7:52). But now the leaders of Israel are guilty of having betrayed and murdered "the Just One," the Messiah himself. A definite pattern of disobedience runs throughout Israel's history. Israel has been blessed, receiving the Law through the hands of angels, but they have transgressed the Law (v. 53). Thus, Stephen is justified in applying the words of Moses to the people before him. Because the leaders oppose the Holy Spirit, they deny their spiritual heritage.

In the climax of his speech, Stephen touches on a tender spot. As a result, his prophetic words provoke the Sanhedrin to greater anger. They have been portrayed as belonging to a nation of idolaters and as being guilty of crucifying Christ. The charges against them have been sustained by a number of scriptures. There is an outburst of rage against Stephen, and they grit their teeth at him. He has presented a great defense; but even though the Sanhedrin convicts him, they are unable to withstand the wisdom and the Spirit in which Stephen speaks.

---

1. How were the religious leaders like their ancestors (vv. 51-53)?
2. How did Stephen's enemies respond to his message (v. 54)?

> "I know of nothing which I would choose to have as the subject of my ambition for life than to be kept faithful to my God till death, still to be a soul-winner, still to be a true herald of the cross, and testify the name of Jesus to the last hour."—Charles Spurgeon

## B. Heavenly Vision (vv. 55-57)

**55 But he, being full of the Holy Ghost, looked up stedfastly into heaven, and saw the glory of God, and Jesus standing on the right hand of God, 56 And said, Behold, I see the heavens opened, and the Son of man standing on the right hand of God. 57 Then they cried out with a loud voice, and stopped their ears, and ran upon him with one accord.**

Stephen has an inspired vision. Full of the Holy Spirit, Stephen looks up into heaven and sees the Lord Jesus standing at the right hand of God the Father. Stephen's vision leaves no doubt about Jesus' place in the Godhead.

Only here in the New Testament is Jesus portrayed as standing, rather than sitting, at the right hand of God. The most satisfying explanation of Jesus' standing is that He is acting in the role of intercessor, advocate, and witness. He is confessing Stephen before the heavenly Father, even as He had promised: "Whoever acknowledges me before men, I will also acknowledge him before my Father in heaven" (Matt. 10:32 NIV).

Stephen confesses the risen Lord before the Sanhedrin, declaring that he sees Jesus Christ sharing in God's glory as the exalted Son of Man. These words are "blasphemous" to the religious leaders. They cover their ears, indicating they will not listen to the "blasphemer" any longer. Their refusal to hear reflects a much deeper problem: fighting against their ears' being opened by the Holy Spirit (Acts 7:51). They drown out Stephen's voice by "yelling at the top of their voices" (v. 57 NIV) and rushing to grab him.

---

1. Describe Stephen's vision (vv. 55-56).
2. When is unity a negative thing (v. 57)?

> "The vision of the Divine Presence ever takes the form which our circumstances most require."—Alexander MacLaren

---

## C. Glorious Death (vv. 58-60)

**58 And cast him out of the city, and stoned him: and the witnesses laid down their clothes at a young man's feet, whose name was Saul. 59 And they stoned Stephen, calling upon God, and saying, Lord Jesus, receive my spirit. 60 And he kneeled down, and cried with a loud voice, Lord, lay not this sin to their charge. And when he had said this, he fell asleep.**

These violent reactions suggest a lynching, rather than an official act. The Sanhedrin has no right to impose the death penalty without the consent of the Roman governor. The reference to "witnesses" (v. 58), who are expected to cast the first stones at the condemned person (Deut. 17:7), may suggest a trial procedure; but the outburst of rage indicates that Stephen has fallen victim to a fanatical mob. They rush him outside the city and proceed to stone him, the punishment prescribed for a blasphemer (Lev. 24:14-16; Num. 15:32-36).

Among the witnesses to Stephen's death is a young man named Saul (Acts 7:58). When those who hurled the stones removed their outer garments to give them more freedom to throw the stones, they placed their garments at Saul's feet. Saul is among Stephen's opponents, and Stephen's address may have prompted him to take part in his murder. The death of Stephen makes a deep and lasting impression on young Saul/Paul (22:20), who becomes a friend of Christians when he is miraculously transformed by God's grace (9:17, 20).

The account of Stephen's death reminds us of the passion of his Lord. Like Jesus, he is rejected by his own people. As he dies, Stephen's prayer has a striking resemblance to Jesus' prayer when He faced His own death: "Lord Jesus, receive my spirit" (7:59). There is a difference, however. Jesus committed His spirit into the hands of the Father (Luke 23:46), but Stephen looks to the Lord Jesus and commits his spirit to the greatest vindicator of God's people.

Next, Stephen kneels in prayer and echoes still another utterance of Jesus on the cross: "Lord, do not hold this sin against them" (Acts 7:60 NIV; cf. Luke 23:34). With the calm confidence of a prophet, he follows the example of Jesus and remains faithful to His teaching: "Pray for those who mistreat you" (Luke 6:28 NIV). Before Stephen dies, all those present hear this inspired witness offer a prayer of forgiveness for his executioners. Only the power of the Holy Spirit can enable Stephen to pray as he does. Like Jesus, he is rejected by his own people—a rejected prophet.

Describing what is characteristic of a believer's death, Luke simply says, "He fell asleep" (Acts 7:60). The death of this Spirit-anointed deacon stands in contrast to the fanatical frenzy of the mob. His death becomes a major transition. Now the persecution of the church widens, and it is scattered throughout Judea and Samaria.

1. Why was Stephen thrown out of the city (v. 58)?
2. Contrast Stephen's actions with his enemies' actions (vv. 59-60).

"Everyone recognizes that Stephen was Spirit-filled when he was performing wonders. Yet, he was just as Spirit-filled when he was being stoned to death."—Leonard Ravenhill

## CONCLUSION

"As odd as it may sound, pastors and believers in the persecuted church have a great deal of compassion for those of us in the West. They often pray that all of our wealth and all of our distractions won't draw us away from our faith, from our first love of Jesus, or from the mission God has entrusted us with. . . . Satan never tests the Western church and the persecuted church using the same form of temptation, but the function of those individual temptations is always the same: to separate and disempower us."—Carl Moeller and David Hegg (*The Privilege of Persecution*)

### GOLDEN TEXT CHALLENGE
"STEPHEN, FULL OF FAITH AND POWER, DID GREAT WONDERS AND MIRACLES AMONG THE PEOPLE" (Acts 6:8).

Although the apostles delegated relief work to others so they might devote themselves continually to prayer and the preaching of God's Word, it is wrong to suppose that deacons needed only mediocre spiritual qualifications. In the early church and now, people involved in practical, hands-on ministries need to be "full of faith and power" to serve effectively.

**Daily Devotions:**
M. God Honors Courageous Faith
   Judges 7:15-23
T. God Empowers Those He Chooses
   1 Samuel 16:10-13
W. Remaining Faithful When Threatened
   Daniel 3:16-25
T. The Spirit Will Help
   Luke 12:11-12
F. Focus on the Eternal
   2 Corinthians 4:7-18
S. Faith Tested
   1 Peter 1:3-9

May 10, 2015 (Lesson 11)
# From Persecutor to Preacher
### Acts 9:1-31

**Theme:**
The Early Church (Acts, Part 1)

**Central Truth:**
Christ's power transformed Saul the persecutor into Paul the missionary.

**Focus:**
Discuss Paul's conversion and praise God for the transforming power of Christ.

**Context:**
Events beginning about AD 35 in Damascus and Jerusalem

**Golden Text:**
"The Lord said unto him [Ananias], Go thy way: for he [Paul] is a chosen vessel unto me, to bear my name before the Gentiles, and kings, and the children of Israel" (Acts 9:15).

**Study Outline:**
I. Life-Transforming Encounter With Christ
   (Acts 9:1-9)
II. Commissioned by Christ
   (Acts 9:10-19)
III. Preaching and Persecuted for Christ
   (Acts 9:20-31)

## INTRODUCTION

The Bible first introduces Saul as a young man who received the outer garments of those who stoned Stephen (Acts 7:58). Their clothing lay at his feet as Stephen died. Soon after the death of Stephen, Saul attempted vehemently to destroy the church. He threw both men and women in jail (8:3) and went from synagogue to synagogue in Jerusalem trying to make the Christians blaspheme the name of Jesus (26:11).

As Peter did earlier, however, Saul (Paul) becomes a Spirit-anointed, charismatic apostle. Whereas Peter is the central figure in the first twelve chapters of Acts, Paul is the dominant person in chapters 13-28. His conversion marks a major turning point in the narrative of Acts and is one of the most remarkable events in the history of the Church.

Chapter 9 is the first of three accounts of Paul's conversion in Acts (see 22:3-16; 26:9-18). More verses in Acts are devoted to this event than to any other subject, leaving no doubt about the importance of his conversion. The appearance of Christ to Paul involves both his conversion and his call to be the apostle to the Gentiles. Though these are interlocking realities, the emphasis in Acts falls more on his calling than on his conversion (9:6; 22:10; 26:16-18).

## I. LIFE-TRANSFORMING ENCOUNTER WITH CHRIST (Acts 9:1-9)

### A. A Mission of Hate (vv. 1-3)

**¹ And Saul, yet breathing out threatenings and slaughter against the disciples of the Lord, went unto the high priest, ² And desired of him letters to Damascus to the synagogues, that if he found any of this way, whether they were men or women, he might bring them bound unto Jerusalem. ³ And as he journeyed, he came near Damascus: and suddenly there shined round about him a light from heaven.**

Like a raging bull, Saul breathes out violent threats of murder against Christ's followers, but he is not satisfied to limit his persecution of them to Jerusalem. Because many Christians have fled the city, he is determined to pursue them and bring them back to Jerusalem as prisoners. Saul goes to the high priest (Caiaphas) and secures letters authorizing him to arrest and extradite the followers of "the Way" who have fled Jerusalem after the death of Stephen (9:2; 22:4; 26:11).

Only in Acts is the phrase "the Way" used as a designation for Christians (19:9, 23; 24:14). Perhaps this term stemmed from such Old Testament expressions as "the way of God" or "the way of righteousness," or it may come from Jesus' calling Himself "the Way" (John 14:6). When Paul later confesses that he persecuted "this Way" (22:4), he means the Christian community and its message of the death and resurrection of Jesus.

Having obtained letters apparently from the Sanhedrin, Saul goes to Damascus, a city about 140 miles north of Jerusalem and the home of a large Jewish community. He knows that many of the Christians can be found worshiping in the Jewish synagogues. The implication here is that the Sanhedrin had power over the members of the synagogues outside of Palestine, but scholars have disputed whether the high priest had the authority to intervene into the affairs of those synagogues. Luke does not tell us, but perhaps Saul's traveling companions are officers of the Sanhedrin.

---

1. Considering Saul's state of mind, what do you imagine he said to the high priest (vv. 1-2)?
2. When and how has God ever stopped you in your tracks, as He did Saul?

> "The suffering of sickness and the suffering of persecution have this in common: they are both intended by Satan for the destruction of our faith, and governed by God for the purifying of our faith."— John Piper

---

### B. A Blinding Light (vv. 4-9)

**⁴ And he fell to the earth, and heard a voice saying unto him, Saul, Saul, why persecutest thou me? ⁵ And he said, Who art thou, Lord? And the Lord said, I am Jesus whom thou persecutest: it is hard for thee to kick against the pricks. ⁶ And he trembling and astonished said, Lord, what wilt thou have me to do? And the Lord said unto him, Arise, and go into the city, and**

it shall be told thee what thou must do. ⁷ And the men which journeyed with him stood speechless, hearing a voice, but seeing no man. ⁸ And Saul arose from the earth; and when his eyes were opened, he saw no man: but they led him by the hand, and brought him into Damascus. ⁹ And he was three days without sight, and neither did eat nor drink.

As Saul and his companions draw near Damascus, a blinding light out of heaven suddenly surrounds him, and he hears a voice speaking to him in Aramaic (26:14 NIV). The light shows forth the glory of the exalted Lord. It is not surprising that the light blinds Saul, since no man is able to physically look at God. The voice is also characteristic of revelation (see Luke 3:22; 9:35).

The risen Jesus appears to Saul (cf. 1 Cor. 9:1; 15:8) and speaks to him: "Saul, Saul, why are you persecuting Me?" (Acts 9:4 NKJV). Attacking Jesus' disciples is not, as Saul thinks, merely a persecution of people worshiping in a heretical manner. To persecute the Christians is to persecute Christ (Luke 10:16), who was rejected but now is risen and continues to be active in history.

At first, Jesus does not identify Himself. Thus, the persecutor asks, "Who are You, Lord?" (Acts 9:5 NKJV). Saul acknowledges the One who is speaking as *Lord*, recognizing that he is speaking to a heavenly person.

The exalted Lord identifies Himself as Jesus, the One whom Saul is persecuting. There on the road to Damascus, the Crucified One, who was revealed to Saul in His divine glory, transforms him. The archenemy of the church dies spiritually to his former life and is made a new man (cf. Gal. 2:20). At the time of his miraculous change, he receives a prophetic call with a task to perform: He must get up and go into Damascus, where he will be given instructions about his future ministry. Saul offers no resistance.

Saul's companions stand speechless; they hear the sound of the Lord's voice, evidently without understanding what He says, but they do not see Him. They are puzzled. The risen Lord appeared only to Saul and gave him a command. Obeying it, he arises to go into Damascus but discovers that he is unable to see. As a result, he has to be led into the city by his companions. There he fasts for three days. Luke does not tell us why, but his abstinence from food and drink may have been due to his state of shock or his waiting to be told what to do. This zealous opponent of the church has been rendered helpless by the Lord.

---

1. How was Saul "kick[ing] against the goads" (v. 5 NKJV)?
2. How was Saul impacted, and how did he address Jesus (v. 6)? What does this indicate?
3. For three days, what did Paul refuse to do, and why (v. 9)?

"The flesh must be broken. The Lord can use us then."—G. V. Wigram

## II. COMMISSIONED BY CHRIST (Acts 9:10-19)

### A. Two Divine Visions (vv. 10-16)
(Acts 9:12-14 is not included in the printed text.)

**10** And there was a certain disciple at Damascus, named Ananias; and to him said the Lord in a vision, Ananias. And he said, Behold, I am here, Lord. **11** And the Lord said unto him, Arise, and go into the street which is called Straight, and enquire in the house of Judas for one called Saul, of Tarsus: for, behold, he prayeth.

**15** But the Lord said unto him, Go thy way: for he is a chosen vessel unto me, to bear my name before the Gentiles, and kings, and the children of Israel: **16** For I will shew him how great things he must suffer for my name's sake.

The Lord speaks to a Jewish Christian in Damascus named Ananias, who is "a devout observer of the law and highly respected by all the Jews living there" (22:12 NIV). Nothing more is known about him, but he might have been among those who fled Jerusalem after the death of Stephen. In a vision, the Lord directs Ananias to a house on Straight Street in Damascus. There he will find Saul of Tarsus earnestly praying. Saul is expecting the visit because he has been granted a vision of a man called Ananias laying "his hands on him to restore his sight" (9:12 NIV).

God has prepared Ananias to minister to Saul, but at first he is reluctant because he has heard about Saul's persecution of God's people. According to reports, Saul was throwing believers into jail in Jerusalem; now he had letters authorizing him to arrest and to extradite Christians in Damascus (vv. 13-14). Ananias speaks of the believers in two significant expressions: as "saints" and as "all who call on your name" (NIV). *Saints* is a term used frequently in the New Testament for Christians; it describes them as being consecrated to live holy in the service of the Lord. "All who call on your name" means they are people who pray and worship in the name of Jesus Christ (cf. 2:21; 22:16).

In light of the terrible suffering Saul has caused the Christians, Ananias' initial response is entirely natural. His response here serves to introduce a further statement from the Lord about His calling of Saul: "This man is my chosen instrument" (9:15 NIV; cf. Gal. 1:15f.), a statement that emphasizes the divine initiative in calling him. Despite what he has done in the past, God has future plans for Saul. His task is to proclaim the name of Jesus to Gentiles, to their kings, and to the people of Israel.

The fulfillment of Saul's mission will involve suffering for the sake of Jesus (Acts 9:16). The list of his sufferings in 2 Corinthians 11:23ff. gives us a good commentary on this facet of Jesus' message. His conversion and call bring about a radical change in Saul's life: the persecutor becomes the persecuted.

---

1. What did Ananias know about Saul (vv. 13-14)?

2. What did the Lord reveal about Saul (vv. 15-16)?

3. What is ironic about the street name (v. 11)?

> "The conversion of a soul is the miracle of a moment, but the manufacture of a saint is the task of a lifetime."—Alan Redpath

### B. Divine Impartation (vv. 17-19)

**17 And Ananias went his way, and entered into the house; and putting his hands on him said, Brother Saul, the Lord, even Jesus, that appeared unto thee in the way as thou camest, hath sent me, that thou mightest receive thy sight, and be filled with the Holy Ghost. 18 And immediately there fell from his eyes as it had been scales: and he received sight forthwith, and arose, and was baptized. 19 And when he had received meat, he was strengthened. Then was Saul certain days with the disciples which were at Damascus.**

The word Ananias receives from the Lord removes his fear of the former persecutor. Therefore, he goes to where Saul is staying. When he comes into his presence, he addresses Saul as "Brother"—not because he is a fellow Israelite, but because he is a fellow believer. The Lord sends Ananias so that Saul's sight may be restored and so that he may be filled with the Spirit. As Ananias prays for him, a flaky substance falls from his eyes, and his sight is recovered. Saul has been motivated by zeal to persecute the believers, but now he needs more than zeal to fulfill his prophetic task of preaching the gospel to the Gentiles. He must be "filled with the Spirit" as the disciples were on the Day of Pentecost.

After his healing, he is baptized by Ananias. He then ends his fast, but he does not leave Damascus. By healing Saul of his blindness, the Lord gives him a powerful sign of his calling. Through baptism in the Spirit, He empowers him to proclaim the gospel to all people (v. 15). The experience of Saul demonstrates that God gives the fullness of the Spirit to those who obey Him (5:32) and to those who earnestly pray for it. Note how after his encounter with the Lord on the road, Saul obeyed the heavenly voice by going into Damascus, where he spent three days in intense prayer and fasting.

1. What did Ananias call Saul, and why?
2. Explain the three uses of the word *receive(d)* in these verses.

> "His Spirit resides within to encourage, energize, and enable [us]. The Spirit isn't just here, He's inside."—Sam Storms

## III. PREACHING AND PERSECUTED FOR CHRIST (Acts 9:20-31)

### A. Confounding Transformation (vv. 20-22)

**20 And straightway he preached Christ in the synagogues, that he is the Son of God. 21 But all that heard him were amazed, and said; Is not this he that destroyed them which called on this name in Jerusalem, and came hither for that intent, that he might bring them bound unto the chief**

priests? ²² **But Saul increased the more in strength, and confounded the Jews which dwelt at Damascus, proving that this is very Christ.**

Saul stays several days with the Damascus Christians, who apparently receive him at once into their fellowship. Soon after his baptism in the Spirit and in water, he begins to fulfill his mission by preaching that Jesus is the Son of God. Like Peter at Pentecost, Saul is empowered by the Spirit to proclaim to unbelieving Jews that Jesus is the Initiator of salvation and that His death is the only means of reconciling people to God (cf. Rom. 5:10; Gal. 2:20; Col. 1:13-14). Evidently, on this occasion Saul has only a short ministry in the city.

Saul's preaching has a strong effect on his hearers. Now in the synagogues in Damascus, he bears witness to the same faith he has tried to destroy earlier. Saul has seen the risen Christ in His glory, and thus preaches as an eyewitness.

The Jews in Damascus are baffled by his proof "that Jesus is the Christ" (v. 22 NIV), promised by the Old Testament prophets. Inspired by the Holy Spirit, Saul becomes more and more powerful in his preaching; his opponents are thrown into confusion, unable to refute his arguments that the crucified Jesus is the Messiah. This increase in power speaks of the dynamic work of the Spirit. Such spiritual power is fundamental to the Pentecostal experience, which is basic to Paul's entire ministry, beginning in Damascus and continuing for twenty-five years or more. Paul probably spent much of the three years around Damascus, preaching in various cities and villages.

---

1. What did Saul do "immediately" (v. 20 NASB)?
2. What question was everyone asking (v. 21)?
3. Explain the phrase "Saul kept increasing in strength" (v. 22 NASB).

---

"*Repentance* is not a merely intellectual change of mind or mere grief, still less doing penance, but a radical transformation of the entire person, a fundamental turnaround involving mind and action and including overtones of grief, which result in 'fruit in keeping with repentance.'"—D. A. Carson

---

B. Narrow Escape (vv. 23-25)

(Acts 9:23-25 is not included in the printed text.)

"After many days had gone by," the Jews plan secretly to assassinate Saul (v. 23 NIV). These "many days" comprise the three years mentioned in Galatians 1:18 as lapsing before Saul goes to Jerusalem. Their plot may have been the consequence of his missionary activity in Arabia (v. 17). (At that time, the area designated as Arabia applied to the whole territory of modern Arabia, Sinai, and the inland up to Damascus.)

Luke does not tell us how Saul learns about the plot against his life. According to 2 Corinthians 11:32, the governor of Damascus under Aretas, the king of Arabia, cooperates with an attempt to arrest the apostle. His would-be assassins keep constant watch of the city gates, waiting for him to leave Damascus.

This activity becomes known to Saul's Christian friends, and they enable him to escape the clutches of his enemies by letting him down in a basket outside the city wall.

Already Saul has begun to suffer for the name of his Savior (cf. Acts 9:16). His prophetic proclamation of Jesus as the Son of God met strong resistance, but God's deliverance of him from Damascus suggests that this Spirit-anointed apostle is destined to preach the gospel to the ends of the earth. None of the efforts to obstruct his path will succeed; finally, because of God's grace and power, this "chosen instrument" (v. 15 NIV) will emerge as one through whom God's purpose is fulfilled (28:31).

---

"Like Paul, those in the persecuted church absolutely believe that the power that raised Jesus from the dead is the greatest power."—Carl A. Moeller

---

C. Return to Jerusalem (vv. 26-30)

(Acts 9:26-30 is not included in the printed text.)

Compelled to flee from the scene of his first labors in the gospel, Saul returns to Jerusalem. The twelve apostles had remained in the Holy City when Saul set out on his murderous mission. They and other disciples had not forgotten his persecution of them. When he arrives, he encounters doubt and suspicion. The believers have heard about his conversion (Gal. 1:23); but knowing his history, they are fearful of him and doubt that he is a genuine disciple. They do not rule out the possibility of a deceitful plot to take advantage of them. It seems incredible to them that such a violent persecutor had become a Christian. Thus, the Christians reject him when he attempts to join them.

Barnabas seems to be the first to have been convinced of Saul's sincerity. He introduces him to two of the apostles, Peter and James (see Gal. 1:18-24). This "son of encouragement" (see Acts 4:36) seems to have been familiar with the details of Saul's conversion and his evangelistic work in Damascus. He apparently convinces the Christian community not only of this Pharisee's conversion, but also of the Lord's calling and equipping him for ministry. Because of Barnabas' commendation, Saul is accepted as a genuine disciple and a preacher of the gospel.

Now having a close association with the apostles and the power of his ministry recognized by them, Saul preaches with the same boldness as he had in Damascus (9:28). Following in the footsteps of Stephen, he preaches to the Greek-speaking Jews and debates with them. They find their new opponent just as invincible as Stephen had been. Since they cannot repudiate Saul's reasoning from the Scriptures, they resolve that his fate will be the same as Stephen's. When the Christians learn that Saul's life is in peril, they send him to Caesarea (v. 30). He makes a short voyage north on the Mediterranean into the region of Tarsus, the place of his birth (21:39; 22:3).

Saul disappears at this point from Luke's account and reappears about ten years later (11:25-30). This is known as a "silent period," but obviously it is silent only to us. According to his own account, he goes into the regions of Syria and Cilicia, preaching the faith he once tried to destroy (Gal. 1:21-24).

1. How did Barnabas ("son of encouragement") live up to his name (vv. 26-27)?
2. What became a pattern in Paul's ministry (vv. 28-30; see vv. 22-25)?

> "To be a Christian means to forgive the inexcusable, because God has forgiven the inexcusable in you."—C. S. Lewis

## CONCLUSION

In Acts 9:31, Luke sums up the state of the Christian movement: "Then had the churches rest throughout all Judaea and Galilee and Samaria, and were edified; and walking in the fear of the Lord, and in the comfort of the Holy Ghost, were multiplied."

The church enjoys peace, since persecution has ceased. Freedom from sufferings allows the believers, through the help of the Spirit, to build up the church spiritually and numerically. Their faith is strengthened, and their way of life is determined by their reverential fear of the Lord. They are aided by the encouragement of the Holy Spirit. That is, the Spirit's work inspires anointed preaching and teaching so that the church is enriched and its number grows. As the Spirit empowers the believers, they are encouraged to push into new fields with the gospel.

## GOLDEN TEXT CHALLENGE

"THE LORD SAID UNTO HIM [ANANIAS], GO THY WAY: FOR HE [PAUL] IS A CHOSEN VESSEL UNTO ME, TO BEAR MY NAME BEFORE THE GENTILES, AND KINGS, AND THE CHILDREN OF ISRAEL" (Acts 9:15).

"As it was with Paul, so with all men—God has a mission for all to perform; and at the very heart of that mission is to bear Christ's name to those among whom He is not known or ignored" (Wilbur G. Williams).

God does not look at what a person is, but at what He can make out of him or her. The disobedient sinner is merely the raw material out of which the Lord will make one of His jewels; "For it is God which worketh in you both to will and to do of his good pleasure" (Phil. 2:13).

**Daily Devotions:**

M. Changed by God
   Genesis 32:24-32
T. Prayer for Transformation
   Psalm 119:1-10
W. Promise of Transformation
   Ezekiel 36:24-29
T. Example of Transformation
   Luke 8:26-35
F. New Creation
   2 Corinthians 5:14-17
S. Salvation Assured
   2 Peter 1:3-11

May 17, 2015 (Lesson 12)

# Including the Excluded

**Acts 10:1-48**

**Theme:**
The Early Church (Acts, Part 1)

**Central Truth:**
The message of Jesus Christ is for the whole world.

**Focus:**
Review how salvation came to the Gentiles and reach out to all with the gospel.

**Context:**
AD 41 or 42 in Jerusalem

**Golden Text:**
"Peter opened his mouth, and said, Of a truth I perceive that God is no respecter of persons: But in every nation he that feareth him, and worketh righteousness, is accepted with him" (Acts 10:34-35).

**Study Outline:**
I. Seeing and Following God's Plan
   (Acts 10:1-23)
II. Good News for All People
    (Acts 10:34-43)
III. Gentiles Receive the Holy Spirit
     (Acts 10:44-48)

## INTRODUCTION

The importance of the story of Cornelius' meeting with Simon Peter and the ensuing events is evidenced by the space Luke gives it (Acts 10:1—11:18). Luke emphasizes three main truths in this account:

1. *God approves of the early church's ever-widening evangelistic outreach, including outreach to the Gentiles.* This outreach ministry includes prayers, visions, angels, conversions, and ministry of the Spirit—all of which are the direct result of divine guidance and empowerment.

2. *Emphasis on God's initiative in ministry does not deny personal decisions or make Peter and Cornelius robots.* As occurs throughout the Book of Acts, the divine initiative calls for human response. It is a matter of divine direction and human obedience, as Peter's response to the words of the Holy Spirit illustrates in 10:19-20.

3. *When Peter reports what happened while he was praying in Joppa and later at the home of Cornelius, Luke reports that the believers at Jerusalem approve the receiving of the Gentiles in the church (11:18).* This approval is significant for extending the mission to the Gentiles, but it fails to settle the issue

of receiving uncircumcised Gentiles into the church. (This issue is settled later, as recorded in 15:1-29.)

## I. SEEING AND FOLLOWING GOD'S PLAN (Acts 10:1-23)

### A. God Speaks to Cornelius (vv. 1-8)

(Acts 10:6-8 is not included in the printed text.)

**¹ There was a certain man in Caesarea called Cornelius, a centurion of the band called the Italian band, ² A devout man, and one that feared God with all his house, which gave much alms to the people, and prayed to God alway. ³ He saw in a vision evidently about the ninth hour of the day an angel of God coming in to him, and saying unto him, Cornelius. ⁴ And when he looked on him, he was afraid, and said, What is it, Lord? And he said unto him, Thy prayers and thine alms are come up for a memorial before God. ⁵ And now send men to Joppa, and call for one Simon, whose surname is Peter.**

As a Roman centurion, Cornelius is in charge of a hundred soldiers, about one-sixth of a regiment. He lives in Caesarea—an important seaport city which served as the Roman capital for Judea and Syria.

Cornelius' regiment is designated "the Italian," which was probably a special body of Roman troops. He is a prayerful man, and though a Gentile, he observes the traditional Jewish hour of prayer (v. 3). His prayers do not fall on deaf ears, for one afternoon while he is praying, an angel of God appears to him in a vision.

The presence of the angel frightens Cornelius, a natural reaction to being confronted by the supernatural. He addresses the heavenly visitor as "Lord" and inquires what he wants. The angel calls Cornelius by name and assures him that his prayers have been heard and God has taken note of his deeds of kindness to the poor. God has accepted Cornelius' prayers and gifts to the poor as fitting sacrifices. They are like burnt offerings, and they ascend like incense (see Lev. 2:9-16). Remembering his petitions, God is about to answer Cornelius' prayers.

The angel calls upon him to act out his faith through obedience. He must send for a man in Joppa named Simon Peter. At this time, Simon Peter is staying at the home of a tanner, also named Simon. The Jews regarded the job of a tanner, which involves preserving pigs' hides, as a despised and unclean occupation (see Num. 19:11-13; Deut. 14:8). Promptly, Cornelius obeys the word of the angel and sends two household servants and a devout soldier to Joppa.

---

1. List four facts about Cornelius (vv. 1-2).
2. What encouraging message did an angel bring to Cornelius (v. 4)?
3. How did Cornelius respond to the angelic vision (vv. 5-8)?

---

"You cannot obey God without your obedience spilling out in a blessing to all those around you."—Adrian Rogers

B. God Speaks to Peter (vv. 9-16)

(Acts 10:9-10, 15-16 is not included in the printed text.)

**¹¹ And saw heaven opened, and a certain vessel descending unto him, as it had been a great sheet knit at the four corners, and let down to the earth: ¹² Wherein were all manner of fourfooted beasts of the earth, and wild beasts, and creeping things, and fowls of the air. ¹³ And there came a voice to him, Rise, Peter; kill, and eat. ¹⁴ But Peter said, Not so, Lord; for I have never eaten anything that is common or unclean.**

As the messengers from Cornelius approach Joppa, Peter goes up on the flat roof of the house to pray. It is noon and Peter becomes hungry, which prepares him for the vision. While the meal is being prepared, he prays, falls into a trance, and has a vision (v. 10). In the vision, heaven opens and Peter sees a great sheet being gradually lowered from the sky by four ropes. The sheet contains all kinds of unclean animals, reptiles, and birds (v. 12; 11:6), and he hears a heavenly voice urging him to kill the unclean animals and prepare a meal (10:13). Consistent with the importance of this event, the sheet appears to Peter three times.

Though Peter is in a trance, he is completely in touch with his thoughts and feelings. Eating meat considered unclean is strongly objectionable to him. He recoils at the thought of violating the food laws (Lev. 11; Deut. 14:1-21) and protests the command from heaven (Acts 10:14). Never in his life has he eaten anything unclean, and by abstaining, he is obeying the laws given to his ancestors. Peter fails to consider that God is now abolishing such laws.

Three times he is rebuked by the words, "Do not call anything impure that God has made clean" (v. 15 NIV). This divine corrective emphasizes the cleansing power of God's saving grace. The vision, therefore, involves more than setting aside food laws and attitudes toward ritual purity. It show that Gentiles, cleansed by the renewing grace of God, are to be included in the fellowship of God's people.

---

1. While in a trance, what did Peter see and hear, and how did he answer (vv. 11-14)? Why?
2. How did the divine voice reply (v. 15)?
3. What happened three times, and why (v. 16)?

---

> "The kingdom of God is for the spiritually sick who want to be healed, the spiritually corrupt who want to be cleansed, the spiritually poor who want to be rich, the spiritually hungry who want to be fed, the spiritually dead who want to be made alive."—John MacArthur

---

C. Peter Greets a Gentile Delegation (vv. 17-23)

(Acts 10:17-18, 21-23 is not included in the printed text.)

¹⁹ **While Peter thought on the vision, the Spirit said unto him, Behold, three men seek thee.** ²⁰ **Arise therefore, and get thee down, and go with them, doubting nothing: for I have sent them.**

Peter understands that the vision challenges his traditional beliefs about the distinction between clean and unclean animals. He is "greatly perplexed" about the possibility of a secondary meaning of the vision (v. 17 NASB), but he is unable to come to any conclusion. While he is contemplating the meaning, the delegation from Cornelius arrives. The Holy Spirit reveals to Peter that he has three visitors and bids him to go with them.

Convinced of the Spirit's direction, the apostle goes downstairs to meet the guests. The messengers make themselves known and tell Peter of their mission. To make a favorable impression on the apostle, they describe their master as "a righteous and God-fearing man, who is respected by all the Jewish people" (v. 22 NIV). They have come because a holy angel instructed Cornelius to invite Peter to preach in Caesarea. Peter goes with them.

1. What did God reveal to Peter (vv. 17-20)?
2. How did Cornelius' group explain their coming, and how did Peter respond (vv. 22-23)?

II. GOOD NEWS FOR ALL PEOPLE (Acts 10:34-43)

Upon his arrival in Caesarea, Peter immediately begins his Spirit-anointed sermon. His message has three major parts: (1) the current situation, (2) the personal career of Jesus, and (3) Christ's mandate to the apostles to preach.
A. The Specific Situation (vv. 34-35)
³⁴ **Then Peter opened his mouth, and said, Of a truth I perceive that God is no respecter of persons:** ³⁵ **But in every nation he that feareth him, and worketh righteousness, is accepted with him.**

The apostle declares that God treats all people the same. God does not judge a person on such factors as nationality or race, but on character—He "accepts men from every nation who fear him and do what is right" (v. 35 NIV). Peter goes on to teach that salvation is only possible through faith in the gospel of the death and the resurrection of Christ. Following moral rules fails to make a person acceptable to God. This gospel is offered to all without restriction, provided they are willing to repent of their sins and trust Jesus for forgiveness. In God's sight, those who fear Him and do what is right are those who are marked by faith in the Savior.

- What did people discover about the Lord?

B. The Personal Career of Jesus (vv. 36-43)
   (Acts 10:36-38 is not included in the printed text.)

⁣³⁹ **And we are witnesses of all things which he did both in the land of the Jews, and in Jerusalem; whom they slew and hanged on a tree: ⁴⁰ Him God raised up the third day, and shewed him openly. ⁴¹ Not to all the people, but unto witnesses chosen before of God, even to us, who did eat and drink with him after he rose from the dead. ⁴² And he commanded us to preach unto the people, and to testify that it is he which was ordained of God to be the Judge of quick and dead. ⁴³ To him give all the prophets witness, that through his name whosoever believeth in him shall receive remission of sins.**

God does not discriminate, for He has sent the gospel through Jesus Christ, who is the Lord of all people. The content of God's message is the "good news of peace" (v. 36 NIV), which Jesus preached to the people of Israel. Although Jesus first preached the good news to the Jews, the message was not intended for Israel alone. *Peace* refers to reconciliation with God made possible through the atoning death of Jesus Christ.

Devout people like Cornelius and his friends have known about the ministry of Jesus that began in Galilee after John the Baptist preached his baptism and that the good news of peace filled the land of Judea (v. 37). In light of the narrative of Acts, we could assume that these people heard their first Christian sermon not from Peter, but Philip, an evangelist living in Caesarea (8:40; 21:8); or some other believer could have actually introduced them to the gospel earlier. At the conclusion of Peter's sermon, he simply declares that everyone who believes in Christ receives forgiveness of sins (10:43).

The reference in 11:18 that God "granted even the Gentiles repentance unto life" (NIV) fails to indicate whether this happened before or after Peter arrived. Cornelius is reported in verse 14 to have been told to send for Peter in order that he and his people may be "saved." Yet nothing is mentioned here explicitly concerning repentance and conversion of Cornelius and his friends. Peter's preaching may have only confirmed their faith in Jesus, but Luke does not state explicitly anything to this effect. Rather, he simply describes Cornelius in Jewish terms as "God-fearing" and as a follower of the Jewish practice of almsgiving and prayer (10:2).

Another possible interpretation is that as Peter preaches to the people of Cornelius, they believe the gospel and are subsequently baptized in the Spirit. This interpretation, like the previous one, maintains a distinction between the indwelling of the Holy Spirit and the baptism in the Spirit.

Continuing the second part of his sermon, Peter gives a brief outline of what happened to Jesus:

1. "God anointed Jesus of Nazareth with the Holy Ghost and with power" (v. 38). After His baptism in the Jordan, the Holy Spirit immediately anointed Him for His ministry (Luke 3:21-22; 4:1, 14-21). By His miracles, He demonstrated God's rule over the devil and the forces of evil. The apostles had been with Jesus from the very beginning of His ministry (Acts 1:21-22), so they were eyewitnesses of what He did in the city of Jerusalem and the rest of the country of the Jews (Luke 4:31-44).

2. Jesus was put to death by the Jews, who "hanged [Him] on a tree" (Acts 10:39). But God brought Him back to life on the third day and allowed a select group of witnesses to see Him alive on earth for a period of forty days (Luke

24:13-53; Acts 1:3-11). These witnesses were chosen by God beforehand. Jesus, therefore, did not appear to all the Jewish people, but only to those who had been prepared to be witnesses through their long and intimate association with the Savior. Their testimony rested especially on the fact that they had meals with Christ after His resurrection (10:41; cf. Luke 24:13-43). Now Peter bears witness to these Gentiles about the central truth of the gospel—the resurrection of Christ.

3. Jesus ordained to the apostles to preach the gospel. As part of their message, they are to declare that God has appointed Jesus "as judge of the living and the dead" (Acts 10:42 NIV; 2 Tim. 4:1; 1 Peter 4:5). He is destined to be the judge of all people—past and present. At the end of the world, some will still be alive on the earth. They, as well as the dead, will face Christ as their ultimate judge (John 5:21-22). To this One, the Old Testament prophets testify and their witness agrees with the apostolic preaching "that everyone who believes in him receives forgiveness of sins through his name" (Acts 10:43 NIV).

---

1. Who is Jesus Christ, and what is His message (v. 36)?
2. What did Jesus do, and how (v. 38)?
3. What did Peter witness (vv. 39-41)?
4. What did Peter and the prophets declare about Jesus (vv. 42-43)?

> "To *evangelize* is to spread the good news that Jesus Christ died for our sins and was raised from the dead according to the Scriptures, and that as the reigning Lord He now offers the forgiveness of sins and the liberating gift of the Spirit to all who repent and believe."—John Stott

---

## III. GENTILES RECEIVE THE HOLY SPIRIT (Acts 10:44-48)

(Acts 10:46-48 is not included in the printed text.)

**44 While Peter yet spake these words, the Holy Ghost fell on all them which heard the word. 45 And they of the circumcision which believed were astonished, as many as came with Peter, because that on the Gentiles also was poured out the gift of the Holy Ghost.**

Peter's sermon is suddenly interrupted by the Gentile believers' receiving the baptism in the Holy Spirit. These Gentile believers receive the same gift that Jewish believers did in the Upper Room at Pentecost (Acts 2:1-4). This outpouring on Gentiles amazes the six Jewish believers who have accompanied Peter to Caesarea (10:45). As the audible, visible, initial evidence of being filled with the Spirit, Cornelius and his friends speak in tongues (v. 46)—a manifestation that later causes church leaders to glorify God and acknowledge that "God has granted even the Gentiles repentance unto life" (11:18 NIV).

The baptism in the Spirit indicates that these Gentiles are as acceptable to God as are Jewish believers. God takes the initiative in bestowing the Pentecostal gift of the Spirit, but the verb *received* (10:47) indicates the necessity of human response to the divine initiative.

On the basis of their Spirit baptism, Peter challenges anyone not to deny the Gentile believers' water baptism—the ordinance that serves as an outward sign of conversion and cleansing from sin. Since no one raises an objection, Peter commands the Gentiles to be "baptized in the name of the Lord" (v. 48).

God makes no difference between Gentile and Jewish believers. Without becoming converts to Judaism, Cornelius and his family enter the church on equal standing with the Jewish Christians, and they receive the same prophetic gift of the Spirit bestowed on the believers at Pentecost, on the Samaritans (8:14-17), and on the apostle Paul (9:17). The outpouring of the Spirit on the Gentile household of Cornelius becomes a decisive turning point in the mission of the church. The Christian church now begins to reach out to Gentiles as well as Jews.

At the end of Peter's meeting with Cornelius, rather than leaving immediately, Peter stays with the Gentile believers "for a few days" (10:48 NIV). His brief stay shows the full membership of Gentiles in the Christian community. The gospel makes it possible for people of different backgrounds and racial origins to have fellowship with one another.

---

1. Who was "astonished," and why (vv. 44-46)?
2. How was Peter's question (v. 47) answered (v. 48)?

> "Wherever God can get a people that will come together in one accord and one mind in the Word of God, the baptism of the Holy Ghost will fall upon them, like as at Cornelius' house."—William J. Seymour

---

## CONCLUSION

The vision at Joppa convinces Peter that God shows no favoritism (Acts 10:34)— even people like Cornelius are accepted by God. But the Gentiles' receiving the Spirit baptism teaches Peter a second lesson: God's impartiality applies not only to salvation; it applies to all of His gifts (Roger Stronstad, *The Charismatic Theology of Saint Luke*).

## GOLDEN TEXT CHALLENGE

"PETER OPENED HIS MOUTH, AND SAID, OF A TRUTH I PERCEIVE THAT GOD IS NO RESPECTER OF PERSONS: BUT IN EVERY NATION HE THAT FEARETH HIM, AND WORKETH RIGHTEOUSNESS, IS ACCEPTED WITH HIM" (Acts 10:34-35).

The dictionary defines *prejudice* as "judgment or opinion before the facts are known." Human prejudice seems to germinate and grow with little or no effort.

We are able to determine in this passage that Christian as well as non-Christian minds are targets for prejudice. Simon Peter seemed plagued with this problem. It was only after God gave him a vision that he was able to conquer prejudice. Until this experience, he was content to evangelize in the proximity of

Jerusalem. Following this experience, he was found in many areas speaking to both Jews and non-Jews.

Three courses of action are necessary for the Christian to destroy this dangerous malady: (1) Realize that the Bible condemns prejudice. (2) Like Peter, rise to a "housetop" experience in prayer. "The effectual fervent prayer of a righteous man availeth much" (James 5:16). (3) Like Peter, begin immediately to put into practice this newly acquired attitude.

**Daily Devotions:**

M. Plan to Bless All Nations
   Genesis 12:1-3
T. Joy for All Nations
   Psalm 67:1-7
W. The King for All Nations
   Isaiah 11:1-10
T. Gentiles Seek Jesus
   John 12:20-23
F. Gentiles Become God's People
   Romans 15:7-13
S. All Nations Around God's Throne
   Revelation 7:9-17

May 24, 2015 (Lesson 13)
# Baptism in the Holy Spirit (Pentecost)
### Acts 1:1-8; 2:1-39

**Theme:**
Pentecost

**Central Truth:**
God gave the Holy Spirit so every believer in Christ may be filled with the Spirit.

**Focus:**
Understand that the fulfillment of God's promise to give the Holy Spirit in abundance began on the Day of Pentecost, and be filled with the Spirit.

**Context:**
First days after the resurrection of Christ, AD 30, in Jerusalem

**Golden Text:**
"The promise is unto you, and to your children, and to all that are afar off, even as many as the Lord our God shall call" (Acts 2:39).

**Study Outline:**
I. Baptism in the Spirit Foretold
   (Acts 1:4-8)
II. Baptism in the Spirit Received
   (Acts 2:1-13)
III. Spirit Baptism for All Believers
   (Acts 2:14-18, 37-39)

## INTRODUCTION

*What is baptism in the Spirit?* The verb *baptize* literally means "to dip" or "to immerse." It is an intense spiritual experience through which the lives of believers are immersed into the Spirit of God. Like a garment that has been dipped into water, they find themselves surrounded, covered, and filled with the power and presence of the Spirit.

Spirit baptism is not the same as the new life that accompanies repentance and faith. We are born again by the Spirit and indwelt by the Spirit from the time of conversion. *Spirit baptism*, on the other hand, is a supernatural, charismatic empowerment that equips the Church to fulfill its mission in the world.

I. BAPTISM IN THE SPIRIT FORETOLD (Acts 1:4-8)

A. A Spiritual Baptism (vv. 4-5)

⁴**And, being assembled together with them, commanded them that they should not depart from Jerusalem, but wait for the promise of the Father, which, saith he, ye have heard of me. ⁵For John truly baptized with water; but ye shall be baptized with the Holy Ghost not many days hence.**

One of the "convincing proofs" of Jesus' being alive after His crucifixion was His presence at a meal with His disciples (v. 4). The word translated as "being assembled together" literally means "to eat salt with," probably referring to Christ's eating with the disciples in Luke 24:42-43. On that occasion, He urged them to remain in Jerusalem until they received the promised Holy Spirit (v. 49).

The *fullness of the Spirit* is called "the promise of the Father" (Acts 1:4). Many promises are given in the Bible, but "the promise of the Father" has to do directly with the outpouring of the Spirit. Ezekiel spoke of God's future outpouring of the Spirit on the house of Israel (39:29). Joel promised the outpouring would be on all people (2:28). So God, through the prophets, including John the Baptist, promised the outpouring of the Spirit.

John the Baptist had administered baptism in the waters of Jordan as an outward sign of God's cleansing power from sin to those who repented. During his ministry, John spoke of a baptism that would be administered by Christ through which believers would be empowered by the Spirit (Matt. 3:11; Mark 1:8; Luke 3:16; John 1:33). Later, Jesus promised the disciples they would be baptized with the Spirit in just a short time (Acts 1:5).

When John the Baptist baptized, he was the agent, the waters of the Jordan were the element, and the candidates were those who repented and desired baptism. In baptism with the Spirit, Christ is the agent, the Spirit is the element, and the candidate is the Christian. Most modern translations retain the phrase "with the Holy Spirit," but the preposition *with* (*en*) may be rendered *in*. "Baptized *in* the Spirit" identifies clearly the Holy Spirit as the element of this baptism, whereas "baptism *with* the Spirit" may suggest being in the company of the Holy Spirit.

---

1. Why do you suppose Christ wanted the disciples to "wait for the promise" (v. 4)?
2. When would the promise be fulfilled (v. 5)?

> "The Holy Spirit cultivates a passion to know Christ so insatiable that prayer, fasting, obedience, and the yearning to become a disciple are the overriding facts of character."—Toby Morgan

---

B. Witnesses for the Kingdom (vv. 6-8)

(Acts 1:6-7 is not included in the printed text.)

**⁸ But ye shall receive power, after that the Holy Ghost is come upon you: and ye shall be witnesses unto me both in Jerusalem, and in all Judaea, and in Samaria, and unto the uttermost part of the earth.**

During the forty days between His resurrection and ascension, Jesus spoke to the disciples concerning the Kingdom (v. 3). The disciples mistakenly think that in the Kingdom, Israel is destined for world dominion. They anticipate the fulfillment of Jesus' promise that they themselves will exercise authority over the tribes of Israel (Luke 22:30). At a fellowship meal, the disciples ask Jesus if He is going to restore the kingdom to Israel at this time (Acts 1:6). They hope for an earthly order in which Israel rules over other nations as in the period of David and Solomon. Also, according to ends-time expectation, they see the outpouring of the Spirit as a sign of the new world order.

The disciples failed to understand the nature of the Kingdom. God's rule had already been initiated through the ministry, death, and resurrection of Jesus, but they are right about one thing: a strong link exists between the Holy Spirit and the kingdom of God. The rule of God is initiated and exercised by the Holy Spirit in the last days through the ministry of Christ. Jesus does not deny the restoration of the Kingdom to Israel, but He rejects their efforts to determine the time it will occur (v. 7).

The time of the consummation of the Kingdom lies with the Father: "No one knows about that day or hour, not even the angels in heaven, nor the Son, but only the Father" (Matt. 24:36 NIV). God has reserved the dates of the outworking of His plan. It is not important for His people to know exactly when Christ will return, but it is important that they receive the power of the Holy Spirit so they may bear witness to Christ's death and resurrection until He does return (Acts 1:8).

Rather than changing the subject when the disciples ask about the Kingdom, Jesus gives them an answer: the gospel must be preached to all nations before the true blessedness for Israel and the whole world will come (cf. Matt. 24:14). They are promised power—not political power, but power for service. The word for *power* (*dunamis*) comes from a verb that means "to be able" or "to have strength."

Jesus assures the disciples that they will receive power when the Holy Spirit comes on them. The phrase "you will be my witnesses" (Acts 1:8 NIV) is not so much a command as a promise. They are the people of God, and the power of the Spirit will transform them into witnesses. Bearing witness to Jesus, therefore, identifies them as the people of God.

Their witness is to begin in the same city in which Jesus was condemned, and it is to reach "to the ends of the earth" (NIV). This phrase refers to distant lands in Acts 13:47 (quoting Isa. 49:6). Though this phrase may mean "Rome" to Jesus' disciples, it is prophetic of the spread of the gospel in the last days. So the commission embraces all humankind in every age and place, and calls attention to the task of the Church in the last days until Jesus returns.

---

1. What were the disciples anticipating (v. 6)?
2. How does Christ explain the purpose of the baptism in the Spirit (v. 8)?

> "See the Gospel Church secure,/And founded on a Rock!/All her promises are sure;/Her bulwarks who can shock?/Count her every precious shrine;/Tell, to after-ages tell,/Fortified by power divine,/The Church can never fail."—Charles Wesley

## II. BAPTISM IN THE SPIRIT RECEIVED (Acts 2:1-13)

### A. Wind, Fire, and Tongues (vv. 1-4)

**¹ And when the day of Pentecost was fully come, they were all with one accord in one place. ² And suddenly there came a sound from heaven as of a rushing mighty wind, and it filled all the house where they were sitting. ³ And there appeared unto them cloven tongues like as of fire, and it sat upon each of them. ⁴ And they were all filled with the Holy Ghost, and began to speak with other tongues, as the Spirit gave them utterance.**

On the Day of Pentecost, the disciples are praying and waiting, ready to be baptized in the Spirit. A striking characteristic of these disciples is their unity. Luke has already described them as being united in prayer, suggesting that they have one mind and purpose (1:14). The Day of Pentecost begins with them "all together in one place" (2:1 NIV)—most likely in the Temple, where they gathered daily (Luke 24:53; Acts 2:46; 5:42; cf. 6:13-14).

When the Day of Pentecost dawns, the time of praying and waiting is over for about 120 disciples. At first, there is a supernatural sound from heaven as of a violent wind. As the sound fills the house (Temple) where they are sitting, tongues like fire rest on those present. The wind and fire emphasize the greatness of the occasion and serve as an audible, visible evidence of the presence of the Spirit. The sound of the mighty wind signifies the Holy Spirit is with the disciples; the tongue-like flames of fire that rest on each of them are a manifestation of God's glory, adding splendor to the occasion.

The later accounts in Acts of filling with the Spirit give no hint that the sound of wind and the fiery tongues occur again. These signs are introductory and for one particular occasion. The constant and recurring sign of the Spirit's fullness is speaking in other tongues (10:46; 19:6). At Pentecost, Peter declares that Christ has poured out what the people see and hear (2:33). Speaking in tongues—an outward visible, audible sign—marks the disciples' enduement with supernatural power, that is, their being filled with the Spirit.

The verb for "filled" (*pimplemi*) used in 2:4 is closely linked with the Spirit (Luke 1:41, 67; Acts 4:8, 31; 9:17; 13:9). This verb is used by Luke to indicate the process of anointing with power for divine service. In Acts, being *filled with the Spirit* means the same as "baptism in the Spirit" or "the gift of the Spirit" (cf. 1:5; 2:4, 38).

The Holy Spirit enables the disciples to speak in other tongues. In full submission to the Spirit ("as the Spirit gave them utterance," v. 4), they speak and act as the Spirit leads them. Such utterances are not ecstatic speech nor mere gibberish; but, as the term *to speak with* suggests, they are mighty and authoritative (cf. v. 14; 26:25).

While believers are the mouthpieces of the Holy Spirit, they remain in full control of their faculties. The Spirit respects their freedom and seeks their cooperation. The Spirit speaks through them, but they are actively speaking in tongues and are able to stop at will. Peter, for example, speaks in tongues, but stops when he begins to address the Pentecost multitude. So, the manifestation of tongues can be understood as an active response and obedience to the Holy Spirit.

1. Why is it important for believers to come together "with one accord in one place" (v. 1)?
2. Describe the two uses of the word *filled* (vv. 2, 4).

> "The Christian religion is hopeless without the Holy Ghost."—Samuel Chadwick

---

B. Confounded Crowd (vv. 5-13)

(Acts 2:5, 9-11 is not included in the printed text.)

**⁶ Now when this was noised abroad, the multitude came together, and were confounded, because that every man heard them speak in his own language. ⁷ And they were all amazed and marvelled, saying one to another, Behold, are not all these which speak Galilaeans? ⁸ And how hear we every man in our own tongue, wherein we were born?**

**¹² And they were all amazed, and were in doubt, saying one to another, What meaneth this? ¹³ Others mocking said, These men are full of new wine.**

At Pentecost, the disciples have an international audience, because devout Jews from Jerusalem and outside of Palestine have gathered for this Jewish festival. Many hear the disciples speaking about the wonderful works of God in a variety of languages. By this time, the disciples must have left the Temple and gone into the streets. The God-fearing Jews behold the work of the Spirit and hear the Galilean disciples speaking in languages of the national groups present—a great miracle indeed! Knowing the disciples had not learned these languages, they have no reasonable explanation for the phenomenon. Luke describes their response as bewilderment, amazement, and perplexity (vv. 6, 12) to the miracle of praising God in foreign languages.

In no other place does the New Testament describe *glossolalia* as speaking in foreign languages (see Acts 10:46; 19:6; 1 Cor. 14:14). Paul emphasizes that the gift of interpretation must accompany tongues for the local church to be edified (1 Cor. 12:7-10; 14:1ff.). According to Paul, tongues is a language, but without the companion gift of interpretation, a message in tongues remains unintelligible to both the speaker and the hearer. Therefore, the gift of tongues must be interpreted in the local church.

The Pentecost crowd recognizes the miraculous nature of the manifestation. Some are seized with amazement and are troubled by what the Spirit's manifestation means. They have no idea of what purpose the miracle serves. Others are shocked by what has happened and accuse the disciples of being drunk. Not recognizing some of the particular languages in which the disciples speak, they mistake them for nonsense.

What some claim is the result of drunkenness is actually a manifestation of the outpouring of the Holy Spirit. The disciples have had a profound spiritual experience, and with joy and vigor they express their thanksgiving and praise to God for His mighty saving work in Christ and for their Spirit baptism. The same Spirit who guided the patriarchs and empowered the prophets has come to guide and empower the Church to carry the gospel to all nations.

1. Who had come to Jerusalem to observe Pentecost (vv. 5, 8-11)?
2. List the various terms used to describe the crowd's reaction (vv. 6-7, 12-13).

> "The average man is not going to be impressed by our publicity, our posters, or our programs, but let there be a demonstration of the supernatural in the realm of religion, and at once man is arrested."—Duncan Campbell

---

### III. SPIRIT BAPTISM FOR ALL BELIEVERS (Acts 2:14-18, 37-39)

The apostle Peter is now filled with the Spirit and "addresses" the crowd in a Spirit-inspired utterance. Having heard what those mocking the disciples have said, he responds to the question "What does this mean?" (v. 12 NIV) with great prophetic authority. He first denies that the disciples are drunk: "It's only nine in the morning!" (v. 15 NIV). Men may be intoxicated at any hour, but the early hour makes it highly improbable. Nine o'clock is the hour of prayer, and Jews normally do not have breakfast until ten o'clock. Instead, these disciples have been filled with the Spirit.

To disclaim the charge of drunkenness and explain the meaning of the Spirit's manifestation, Peter links the events of Pentecost with Joel 2:28-32. The multitudes have seen the prophecy of Joel fulfilled before their eyes. What has been expected "in the last days" has come to pass: the outpouring of God's Spirit. Speaking in tongues is an eschatological speech—speech that indicates the last days have dawned.

In the Old Testament, the expression "last days" refers to the coming of the Messiah (Isa. 2:2; Mic. 4:1). In the New Testament, the "last days" are initiated by the coming of Christ and the events at Pentecost. The mighty outpouring of the Spirit signals that the last days (the messianic era) are here. The last days encompass the period between the first and the second coming of Christ. The age of fulfillment has begun, though the final consummation still lies in the future. The hearers at Pentecost are living in these last days. The use of the plural in the "last days" indicates the outpouring of the Spirit encompasses more than just one day.

#### A. Prophecy Fulfilled (vv. 14-18)

**14 But Peter, standing up with the eleven, lifted up his voice, and said unto them, Ye men of Judaea, and all ye that dwell at Jerusalem, be this known unto you, and hearken to my words: 15 For these are not drunken, as ye suppose, seeing it is but the third hour of the day. 16 But this is that which was spoken by the prophet Joel; 17 And it shall come to pass in the last days, saith God, I will pour out of my Spirit upon all flesh: and your sons and your daughters shall prophesy, and your young men shall see visions, and your old men shall dream dreams: 18 And on my servants and on my handmaidens I will pour out in those days of my Spirit; and they shall prophesy.**

Basing his message on Joel's prophecy, Peter proclaims the outpouring of the Spirit is for "all people" (v. 17 NIV). It is universal in scope—on young men as well as old, on daughters as well as sons, even on those of low estate, both men and women. Instead of just kings, priests, and prophets, the Spirit is to be poured out on believers of every race, nationality, and gender—all kinds of people.

Upon receiving the baptism in the Spirit, they are to "prophesy" (v. 17). Tongues that accompany the experience of immersion in the Spirit have the character of prophetic speech, and Peter links the power of the Spirit with the universal outburst of prophecy. The same connection is made between the charismatic power of the Spirit and prophecy in Numbers 11:24-29, where the elders prophesy after the Spirit has been transferred from Moses to them. Moses then expresses the desire that all God's people might prophesy. Joel 2 promises the fulfillment of Moses' desire, and the events at Pentecost potentially fulfill that desire.

This anointing of the Spirit for prophecy is not confined to the believers at Pentecost. The words of Peter, "Your sons and your daughters shall prophesy" (Acts 2:17) point to the continuing prophetic activity of the Church. Further evidence of the works of the Spirit will be seen in "dreams" and "visions." These kinds of experiences were ways of receiving prophetic revelation (Num. 11:29). The Holy Spirit sometimes reveals divine truth to God's people through dreams and visions (Luke 1:22; 9:28-36; Acts 7:55-56; 8:29; 9:10ff.; 10:10ff.; 11:5ff., 28; 16:9; 22:17-18; 27:23-24).

---

- List characteristics of the "last days" outpouring of God's Spirit (vv. 17-18).

---

"You will do more in one year if you are really filled with the Holy Ghost than you could do in fifty years apart from Him."—Smith Wigglesworth

---

B. Promise Offered (vv. 2:37-39)

**37 Now when they heard this, they were pricked in their heart, and said unto Peter and to the rest of the apostles, Men and brethren, what shall we do? 38 Then Peter said unto them, Repent, and be baptized every one of you in the name of Jesus Christ for the remission of sins, and ye shall receive the gift of the Holy Ghost. 39 For the promise is unto you, and to your children, and to all that are afar off, even as many as the Lord our God shall call.**

Peter's inspired message reaches the hearts of the people. They understand that his words apply to them personally, for many of them have agreed with the actions of their leaders against Jesus. As they listen to Peter, they are "cut to the heart" (v. 37 NIV). Being deeply troubled, and convicted of their sins—namely, that they have killed their Messiah—they inquire, "Brothers, what shall we do?"

Peter tells them to repent and be baptized in the name of Jesus Christ. The basic meaning of *repentance* here is a change of mind and remorse for errors and sins. Repentance demands the forsaking of the old life of sin and living a life of obedience to God.

Individuals who repent should also be baptized in water. *Faith* is the means by which God grants forgiveness. The New Testament does not teach that a physical act, such as baptism, produces a spiritual change. John the Baptist refused to baptize people until they showed they were repentant (Matt. 3:7-8; Luke 3:8). Jesus taught that repentance precedes forgiveness of sins (Luke 24:47). In the Great Commission, we are told to make disciples of people before baptizing them (Matt. 28:18-20). And in his sermon, Peter puts repentance before baptism (Acts 2:38 NKJV). Water baptism must be preceded by repentance and faith.

Peter goes on to promise "the gift of the Holy Spirit" to those who repent and are baptized (v. 38 NKJV). This promise must be understood in the context of the outpouring of the Spirit at Pentecost, which Peter and his colleagues have just experienced. The initial work of the Spirit follows repentance and issues in a new life in Christ. Peter's promise here refers to a subsequent free gift of the Spirit, fulfilling Joel's promise of charismatic, Pentecostal power. Such power equips believers to be witnesses for Christ and empowers them to perform miracles (cf. v. 43). This baptism is a clothing with power—a gift that Jesus encourages His disciples to pray for (Luke 11:13).

God desires that all His people have the same momentous experience the disciples received at Pentecost. It remains a present, universal blessing: "for all whom the Lord our God will call," including "all who are far off" (v. 39 NIV).

---

1. When and how has God "pricked [your] heart" (v. 37)?
2. Who can receive the promise of the Spirit, and how (vv. 38-39)?

> "Don't let obstacles along the road to eternity shake your confidence in God's promise. The Holy Spirit is God's seal that you will arrive."—David Jeremiah

---

## CONCLUSION

At Pentecost, the disciples become members of a charismatic community, heirs to the earlier Spirit-anointed ministry of Jesus. As they miraculously speak in various languages, the believers glorify God for the great things He has done and thereby witness to the astonished crowd.

When we are baptized in the Spirit, we likewise are made heirs to the Spirit-anointed ministry of Jesus and witnesses to our world.

## GOLDEN TEXT CHALLENGE

"THE PROMISE IS UNTO YOU, AND TO YOUR CHILDREN, AND TO ALL THAT ARE AFAR OFF, EVEN AS MANY AS THE LORD OUR GOD SHALL CALL" (Acts 2:39).

It is unlikely that Peter had a full conception of how far the scope of his statement would extend. He may have visualized "all that are afar off" as the area of the Middle East or even of the then-known world. He could not have fully grasped the vast sweep of the promise of this scripture.

Many times we are too small in our thinking when it comes to the promises of God. Even while we are thinking of the infinite possibilities of what God can accomplish, we are probably underestimating Him.

An old saying states, "What the human mind can conceive, it can achieve." But God can achieve those things the human mind can never conceive or comprehend. It is impossible to cast the promises of God in such cosmic terms that they fully explore the range of His power.

**Devotions:**

M. Spirit-Filled Elders
   Numbers 11:24-29
T. Anointed by the Spirit
   Isaiah 61:1-11
W. The Holy Spirit Promised
   Joel 2:28-32
T. John Prepared the Way
   Matthew 3:1-9
F. Baptism in the Holy Ghost
   John 1:29-34
S. Baptism Into Christ
   1 Corinthians 12:12-18

May 31, 2015 (Lesson 14)
# The Church Prevails
### Acts 12:1-24

**Theme:**
The Early Church (Acts, Part 1)

**Central Truth:**
Evil cannot overcome God's plan and power.

**Focus:**
Observe how the church's influence grew in spite of persecution and testify of God's power.

**Context:**
About AD 44 in Jerusalem

**Golden Text:**
"The word of God grew and multiplied" (Acts 12:24).

**Study Outline:**
I. Delivered by Unified Prayer
   (Acts 12:1-12)
II. Surprised by Answered Prayer
   (Acts 12:13-18)
III. Arrogance Judged; the Church Expands
   (Acts 12:19-24)

## INTRODUCTION

Acts 12 depicts the last great conflict between the church at Jerusalem and her enemies. The Jerusalem church had declined because many believers had to flee for their lives during the earlier persecutions. The Jewish people who had stiffened their necks and hardened their hearts became even harder in their opposition to the remaining Christians. To make matters worse, Herod Agrippa, the Roman puppet who ruled in Jerusalem and claimed to be an Israelite, had joined the opposition. The numerically weakened church could rely on no one but God, and this they did.

## I. DELIVERED BY UNIFIED PRAYER (Acts 12:1-12)

A. Herod Agrippa Persecutes the Church (vv. 1-3)

**¹ Now about that time Herod the king stretched forth his hands to vex certain of the church. ² And he killed James the brother of John with the sword. ³ And because he saw it pleased the Jews, he proceeded further to take Peter also. (Then were the days of unleavened bread.)**

Luke introduces a new story. He does not indicate the precise time, but he suggests it "was about this time," apparently referring to Paul and Barnabas' visit to Jerusalem. The events recorded here occur in Jerusalem. Prior persecution and opposition to the gospel came from the Jewish religious authorities (4:1-6;

5:17-18, 21-28; 6:12-15; 7:54—8:3; 9:1-2). Until now, the religious leaders—especially the Sadducees—have persecuted the believers without the assistance of the civil authorities. Persecution intensifies, and now the ruler of Palestine, Herod Agrippa I, is the leader.

Herod Agrippa was the grandson of Herod the Great, who ruled Galilee at the time of Jesus' birth (Matt. 2:1). Like a number of the members of Herod's family, Agrippa served as a puppet ruler over the Jews under the Roman occupation of Palestine. He grew up in Rome, where he lived in extravagance and wasted what he had inherited. In AD 41, the emperor Claudius made him king of all the territory ruled by Herod the Great, though his reign lasted for only three years. When he returned to Palestine, he became very popular and lived in luxury. Constantly he sought the favor of the Jews and presented himself as a devotee of their religion, though the Herod family were non-Jews from Idumea. Aware that Jewish opinion was against the church, Agrippa took steps to persecute the believers to enhance his popularity.

Agrippa begins to *persecute* ("to hurt, to mistreat") "some who belonged to the church" (Acts 12:1 NIV). Those who carry out his orders persecute the believers so intensely that they suffer more than they did earlier at the hands of the Sanhedrin. Agrippa's main target seems to have been the leaders of the church. He strikes at Jesus' inner circle of disciples by having the apostle James, a son of Zebedee, executed. No reason is given for selecting James, the first apostle to suffer martyrdom. He dies by the sword (his head being placed on a block and cut off by an executioner).

The Jews as a whole take pleasure in Agrippa's persecution of the apostles. The situation in Judea has certainly changed from the earlier days when persecution involved only the Jewish leaders. Hostility toward the gospel spread. The support Agrippa receives from the people encourages him to press forward in his actions against the other apostles. So he has Peter arrested, clearly intending to do to him what he has done to James. Evidently, Agrippa is seeking to destroy the Jerusalem church by beheading its leaders.

- Why did Herod arrest Simon Peter?

"Though persecuting malice raged, yet the Gospel shone with resplendent brightness; and, firm as an impregnable rock, withstood the attacks of its boisterous enemies with success."—John Foxe

B. The Church Prays for Peter (vv. 4-6)

(Acts 12:4 is not included in the printed text.)

**5 Peter therefore was kept in prison: but prayer was made without ceasing of the church unto God for him. 6 And when Herod would have brought him forth, the same night Peter was sleeping between two soldiers, bound with two chains: and the keepers before the door kept the prison.**

Peter is seized during the Festival of Unleavened Bread, a seven-day feast after the eating of the Passover (Ex. 12:14-20). By New Testament times, these festivals had become one celebration, so that the two terms "Passover" and "Feast of Unleavened Bread" were synonyms (Luke 22:1). During this time, Jerusalem was made up of Jews who were enthusiastic for the Law. To avoid creating a disturbance or alienating the Jews, Agrippa has Peter placed in prison until after the Passover week. Should he have had a public trial or an execution during the festive week, the Jews would have felt that the feast was desecrated.

Determined that the prisoners will not escape, Agrippa places a guard of sixteen soldiers on duty. He must have heard about the previous imprisonment of the apostles and their escape from prison in the night without the knowledge of the guards (Acts 5:17-23). Divided into four squads, each squad of guards is on duty for three hours, so there is a watch around-the-clock. At all times, two of these guards are chained to Peter while the other two stand on duty at the entrance.

While Peter is in prison, the church prays on his behalf (12:5). The intensity of their prayers is indicated in two ways: (1) The verb *was praying* (NIV) reflects their persistence in prayer; they keep on praying, knowing that human impossibilities are possible with God. (2) *Without ceasing* ("earnestly," NIV) signifies they recognized the urgency of the situation; they pray with words they feel intently in their hearts. We do not know whether this prayer of the church is for Peter's deliverance or for his faith not to fail him. They may remember that earlier he had faltered in the face of danger (Luke 22:54-62). Furthermore, they may not have expected Peter to be delivered, since both Stephen and James had become martyrs. Their petitions may have taken more than one direction, including prayer for Peter's deliverance and prayer that his faith would be strong should he face the executioner's block. In any case, God's mighty act of delivering Peter takes place in the context of prayer.

---

1. Why were such extreme security measures used?
2. How did the Christians reach out to Peter?

> "Against the persecution of a tyrant the godly have no remedy but prayer."—John Calvin

---

C. An Angel Rescues Peter (vv. 7-12)

(Acts 12:10, 12 is not included in the printed text.)

**7 And, behold, the angel of the Lord came upon him, and a light shined in the prison: and he smote Peter on the side, and raised him up, saying, Arise up quickly. And his chains fell off from his hands. 8 And the angel said unto him, Gird thyself, and bind on thy sandals. And so he did. And he saith unto him, Cast thy garment about thee, and follow me. 9 And he went out, and followed him; and wist not that it was true which was done by the angel; but thought he saw a vision.**

**11 And when Peter was come to himself, he said, Now I know of a surety, that the Lord hath sent his angel, and hath delivered me out of the hand of Herod, and from all the expectation of the people of the Jews.**

The detailed description of deliverance emphasizes it was wholly a miracle. On the last night of Passover week, Peter must have been expecting to die the next morning. He lies sleeping between two guards, chained to both of them. There are also guards at the doors of the prison. God suddenly intervenes by sending an angel, who fills the prison cell with the light of divine glory. The very thing Herod wants to prevent is about to occur. The angel wakes Peter by slapping him on the side, and the chains fall off. He obeys the angel by fastening his belt and slipping on his sandals, and then he follows the heavenly visitor.

While he is being delivered, Peter thinks he is dreaming and does not realize he is actually leaving the prison. Peter and the angel pass the two guards stationed at the cell door, evidently without these men recognizing Peter. As they come to the heavy iron gate, it miraculously opens without any visible cause. The angel accompanies Peter down a street until he is beyond the pursuit of the guards. The angel then disappears.

King Agrippa has taken great precautions to prevent Peter's escape. Those efforts to restrain God's Spirit-anointed messenger only make the miracle more dramatic. When Peter realizes what has happened, his own words—"Now I know of a surety . . ." (v. 11)—interpret the significance of his deliverance. What he has seen was no vision. God has sent an angel and miraculously rescued him from the hand of Agrippa (cf. Dan. 3:19-27). Divine intervention has frustrated opponents of the church.

1. What did Peter wrongly think, and why (v. 9)?
2. When did Peter realize the truth, and what did he then do (vv. 11-12)?

"When by the malice of enemies God's people are brought to greatest straits, there is deliverance near to be sent from God unto them."—David Dickson

II. SURPRISED BY ANSWERED PRAYER (Acts 12:13-18)

A. Unexpected Knock (vv. 13-16)

(Acts 12:13 is not included in the printed text.)
**[14] And when she knew Peter's voice, she opened not the gate for gladness, but ran in, and told how Peter stood before the gate. [15] And they said unto her, Thou art mad. But she constantly affirmed that it was even so. Then said they, It is his angel. [16] But Peter continued knocking: and when they had opened the door, and saw him, they were astonished.**

After his release, Peter immediately decides to inform his Christian friends of what has happened. Thus, he goes to the house of Mary, the mother of John Mark, where many of the believers have gathered to pray on what appears to be the last night of Peter's life (v. 12). Peter enters the gateway that leads from the street to the courtyard and knocks on the outside door, interrupting the prayer of those on the inside.

A servant girl by the name of Rhoda answers the door (v. 13). She is excited when she recognizes Peter's voice. Forgetting to unlock the door, she rushes inside in amazement to tell the others. The Christians in Mary's house do not believe Rhoda's report that Peter is at the door. They insist that Rhoda is crazy, but she confidently maintains that Peter is there. The Christians then suggest that she has seen an appearance of Peter's angel, who has assumed his voice and appearance. But they are wrong; when the Christians finally open the door, they are shocked.

---

- Why didn't Rhoda open the door, and how did the other believers respond to her news (vv. 13-16)?

> "Four things let us ever keep in mind: God hears prayer, God heeds prayer, God answers prayer, and God delivers by prayer."—E. M. Bounds

---

B. Amazing Testimony (vv. 17-18)

(Acts 12:18 is not included in the printed text.)

**17 But he, beckoning unto them with the hand to hold their peace, declared unto them how the Lord had brought him out of the prison. And he said, Go shew these things unto James, and to the brethren. And he departed, and went into another place.**

After Peter finally gains entrance, with a motion of his hand, the people become quiet. He satisfies their curiosity by explaining that God has set him free. Since the other leaders of the church are not present, Peter requests that "James and the brothers" be told about the miracle (17 NIV). The James mentioned here is the brother of Jesus (Mark 6:3). The manner in which he is mentioned indicates his prominence in the church. Both Luke and Paul indicate that James has served as the head of the Jerusalem church (Acts 15:13; 21:18; Gal. 1:19; 2:9, 12).

After Peter has asked the believers to pass on the news to other church leaders, for safety reasons he leaves in the night to go to "another place" (Acts 12:17), which could have been another house in Jerusalem or, most likely, another town outside the city. He must have expected a vigorous effort to rearrest him, making it difficult for him to hide safely in Jerusalem. After a few years, Peter appears again in Jerusalem (15:4, 7), though he may have returned sooner than that, since Agrippa lived only a short time after Peter's departure (12:20-23).

The next morning, Peter's escape becomes known publicly (v. 18). By then he is safe in a secret hiding place. By daylight, when the two guards to whom Peter has been chained are awakened, they see that their prisoner has escaped. There is great confusion among the guards, not knowing what has happened to Peter. They have no idea of how he got loose from his chains and how the guards standing watch did not see anyone pass them. All they know is Peter is gone.

- How did Peter's testimony spread?

> "If you take care of yourself and walk with integrity, you may be confident that God will deal with those who sin against you. Above all, don't give birth to sin yourself; rather, pray for those who persecute you. God will one day turn your persecution into praise."—Warren Wiersbe

---

## III. ARROGANCE JUDGED; THE CHURCH EXPANDS (Acts 12:19-24)

### A. Arrogance Judged (vv. 19-23)

(Acts 12:19-20 is not included in the printed text.)

**21 And upon a set day Herod, arrayed in royal apparel, sat upon his throne, and made an oration unto them. 22 And the people gave a shout, saying, It is the voice of a god, and not of a man. 23 And immediately the angel of the Lord smote him, because he gave not God the glory: and he was eaten of worms, and gave up the ghost.**

When Agrippa hears about Peter's escape, he has his officers make a thorough search, but they fail to find a trace of the prisoner. Their inability to find Peter confirms that a stupendous miracle has occurred, but Agrippa refuses to acknowledge it. He interrogates the four guards who were on duty at the time of Peter's escape. The king then charges the guards with negligence and has them, as the text literally reads, "to be led off"—probably not to prison, but to execution (v. 19). When Roman soldiers allowed a prisoner to escape, customarily they received the same punishment due the prisoner. Accordingly, the innocent guards become victims of Agrippa's violence.

God has vindicated Peter. Luke continues the story and shows further proof of divine vindication in the death of Agrippa. The king goes to Caesarea to meet with a delegation from Tyre and Sidon. At that time, antagonism developed between Agrippa and the people of those two cities. Luke gives no explanation for the dispute, but it seems to have been an economic issue. The cities of Tyre and Sidon depended on the grain fields of Judea for much of their food. Apparently, Agrippa diverted grain exports from Tyre and Sidon to Caesarea, thereby diminishing their food supply.

As a matter of public policy, good relations with the king are desirable. Thus, the people of these two large cities think it best to conciliate the king, so they send a delegation to Caesarea to make peace. They secure the favor of Blastus, a servant who is in charge of the king's private quarters (v. 20). Through this trusted servant, they obtain a public audience with Agrippa.

The historian Josephus gives a more detailed account of what followed. At the time of the meeting, Agrippa is at the festival to honor the Roman emperor Claudius. He is arrayed in his royal apparel; his splendid robe glistens in the morning sun. On the second day of the festival, the people who are present apparently are happy because the grievances of those from Tyre and Sidon had been resolved. They flatter the king and address him as a god. According to Josephus, because King Agrippa accepts the acclamation as a god, he is overcome with violent pain and dies in agony a few days later.

Luke explicitly states, "An angel of the Lord struck him down," and bluntly explains, "he was eaten by worms and died" (v. 23 NIV). To be eaten by worms is a characteristic way ancient writers described a painful death resulting from divine judgment. The death of Agrippa reminds us of the deaths of Ananias and Sapphira. Like that couple, after showing disrespect for God, Agrippa is struck dead. He was not satisfied to oppose God, but he competed with Him by claiming divine honors. The fatal mistake of this arrogant tyrant is that he "did not give praise to God" (NIV). As a ruler, he is subject to the Supreme Ruler of the universe. His arrogance and abuse of power bring divine wrath.

- Describe Herod's anger (v. 19), arrogance (vv. 21-22), and ruin (v. 23).

> "We fear men so much, because we fear God so little. One fear cures another. When man's terror scares you, turn your thoughts to the wrath of God."—William Gurnall

### B. The Church Expands (v. 24)

**24 But the word of God grew and multiplied.**

Agrippa boldly executed the persecution of the church, but it did not stop the advance of the gospel. This defiant opponent of God's people died, but "the word of God continued to increase and spread" (NIV). Another great reversal occurred. The gospel thrives under persecution because more and more people heard the truth and believed.

> "The ministry of God's Word grew by leaps and bounds" (Acts 12:24 TM).

## CONCLUSION

Until the Final Judgment, the devil will continue to oppose the Church. Until that day, the Church's greatest weapon against the devil and his schemes is united, determined, persevering prayer. Evil cannot defeat God and His praying people.

## GOLDEN TEXT CHALLENGE

"THE WORD OF GOD GREW AND MULTIPLIED" (Acts 12:24).

Herod, the blasphemer and apostate Jew, died, but, says the record, the very cause which he tried to crush, continued to prosper: "the word of God grew and multiplied!" The death of the proud persecutor resulted in the greater prosperity of the Church—the Word and the Way were embraced by increasing numbers!

A similar reaction followed the earlier imprisonment of Peter and John (see Acts 6:1). When will tyrants learn that the quickest way to extend a movement is to outlaw or to persecute it?

**Daily Devotions:**
- M. Praise God for Salvation
  Exodus 15:1-11
- T. Trust God for Salvation
  Psalm 3:1-8
- W. God Defends His People
  Zephaniah 3:14-20
- T. Joy in Tribulation
  John 16:23-33
- F. Rejoice in Gospel Expansion
  Philippians 1:12-18
- S. Justice Assured
  Revelation 21:1-8

# Introduction to Summer Quarter

Psalms of lament, thanksgiving, praise, wisdom, covenant, ascent, divine justice, and the Messiah are studied in lessons 1-8 ("Different Types of Psalms").

The writer of lessons 1 and 2 is Richard Keith Whitt (B.A., M.Div., Ph.D. cand.). Reverend Whitt has earned degrees from Lee University and the Church of God Theological Seminary, and has done doctoral work at the University of Nottingham, England. An ordained bishop in the Church of God, Keith has served his denomination as a pastor for twenty-three years, district overseer for twelve years, and as a member of various boards and committees. He has taught courses for the Church of God Theological Seminary and Lee University External Studies.

Lessons 3 and 4 were compiled by Lance Colkmire (see biographical information on page 156).

Lessons 5-8 were written by Joshua Rice (see biographical information on page 156).

---

Lessons 9-13, "Practical Christianity (James)," will help Christians deal with trials, put their faith in action, tame their tongue, submit to God, and cultivate right attitudes.

The studies were written by the Reverend Dr. Jerald Daffe (B.A., M.A., D.Min.), who earned his degrees from Northwest Bible College, Wheaton College Graduate School, and Western Conservative Baptist Seminary. An ordained minister in the Church of God, Dr. Daffe has served in pastoral ministry for ten years and has been a faculty member at Northwest Bible College and Lee University for over thirty years. Dr. Daffe received the Excellence in Advising Award at Lee University. His newest book is *Crosses, Coffee, Couches, and Community*.

June 7, 2015 (Lesson 1)
# Psalms of Lament
### Psalms 4:1-8; 17:1-15; 80:1-19

**Theme:**
Different Types of Psalms

**Central Truth:**
God hears and responds to the cries of His people.

**Focus:**
Acknowledge that we can speak frankly with God and pray with confidence.

**Context:**
Three psalms crying out for divine mercy and restoration

**Golden Text:**
"Hear the right, O Lord, attend unto my cry, give ear unto my prayer, that goeth not out of feigned lips" (Ps. 17:1).

**Study Outline:**
  I. Prayer for Mercy
     (Ps. 4:1-8)
 II. Prayer for Vindication
     (Ps. 17:1-15)
III. Prayer for Restoration
     (Ps. 80:1-19)

## INTRODUCTION

The Book of Psalms (also called "the Psalter") is quoted in the New Testament more than any other Old Testament book (directly approximately 78 times and, by allusion or parallel, well over 300 times). It is a collection of psalms or poems (literally, songs sung to a stringed instrument) composed by many different authors, including David and Moses. The psalms frequently express raw emotion and heartfelt cries. The writers often ask God to wreak havoc upon their enemies, or question where God is in a time of calamity and wonder why He remains silent. Other times, the writers would break forth in exuberant praise and thanksgiving to God. It contains and speaks to the honest emotions and varied experiences Christians face along life's journey.

A person can read Psalms from beginning to end without contemplating the background, structure, or type, and still be blessed and edified. God's Word is alive. However, as most students of the Word discover, understanding the context in which the book or passage was written, considering why a particular structure was chosen when many were available, and discerning the situation, feelings, and intent of the original author can add new dimensions to the reading and make it more relevant for modern-day application. It also helps prevent quoting Scripture out of context.

There are eight basic types of psalms this unit of lessons examines: lament, thanksgiving, praise, wisdom, covenant, ascent, divine justice, and messianic. This first lesson examines three psalms of lament. A l*ament* is a frustrated cry to God about injustices that need and expect divine intervention. Psalms of lament may express the frustrations of an individual or speak corporately for a group or the nation. Scholars have classified them as "songs of disorientation" (conversely, psalms of thanksgiving are "songs of orientation"), as the writer's world has been adversely affected and life has become disturbed. These psalms usually contain a cry to God, complaint, declaration of trust in God, petition or request for help, concern for God's reputation, curse on the enemies, confidence in being heard, promise of praise, and hymn of praise or blessing. Not every psalm of lament contains every one of these elements, and the order may be rearranged; but this overview provides a basic guideline as we begin our study.

I. PRAYER FOR MERCY (Ps. 4:1-8)

A. A Confident Cry (v. 1)

¹ **Hear me when I call, O God of my righteousness: thou hast enlarged me when I was in distress; have mercy upon me, and hear my prayer.**

Many believe this psalm (and Ps. 3) may have been written during David's flight from Absalom. It was a time of great personal turmoil (see 2 Sam. 15—19).

In Psalm 4, David cries to God, "Hear me when I call" (v. 1). How many times through the centuries have believers approached God in prayer and wondered if He heard them? At times, it seems as though our prayers bounce around the room and never get past the ceiling. However, David reminds himself, and us, that God is the *source of righteousness*. This communicates three truths to us.

First, as the source of righteousness, we can be assured that God is indeed righteous. Since He is righteous, we can have the inner confidence that He is well aware of our presence in prayer and the needs we bring when we approach.

Second, it is a reminder of our covenant relationship with God. Much like a marriage, we enter into a binding relationship with God. He has our best interests in mind and works to bring about His presence, provision, peace, power, and prosperity into our lives. There are expectations for, and from, both parties in the covenant. God expects our complete surrender to and participation in the relationship. We expect Him and all He is!

Third, *righteousness* is strongly associated with the *rightness* of a cause. God does not take the abuse of His saints lightly, and vigorously works to vindicate His saints (see Ps. 17:1; 35:27; Isa. 53:11; Job 33.32). It may not happen when we think it should—but it will happen.

The simple *ACTS* acronym is utilized by many as an outline for prayer: We *adore* God for who He is (**A**doration). We *confess* our sins and offenses to Him (**C**onfession). We offer *thanks* to Him for what He has done in the past (**T**hanksgiving). These three aspects firmly remind us of who God is and what He has done for us and others in the past. It fills us with faith and confidence. Then, we can approach Him confidently and being filled with faith with our needs (**S**upplication).

Next, David declares God has moved him from a place of restriction to a place of freedom. "Distress" communicates the image of being in a narrow or tight place, being squeezed to the point that breathing is difficult. The language and grammar clearly indicate that his deliverance is due to God alone, rather than David's many skills and abilities.

He then moves back to a petition or request for God's "mercy," or favor, to be shown to him. It carries the idea of someone looking upon a poor person, being moved with compassion by their need, and responding in a way that alleviates the suffering caused by that need.

He closes the verse with a cry for God to "hear" his prayer. Prayer is an act of faith in God's ability to act in the present, but is often based on the experience of God's intervening actions in the past. If we are concerned about what God is going to do in the future, we need to remember what He has done for us in the past.

---

- In David's time of need, what encouraged him?

> "You need not cry very loud; He is nearer to us than we think."—Brother Lawrence

---

B. A Confident Response (vv. 2-5)

(Psalm 4:2-5 is not included in the printed text.)

Verse 2 gets to the heart of David's lament or complaint: people are attempting to ruin his reputation and slander his character through baseless accusations and outright lies. The danger is revealed in the Hebrew terms used for "sons of men" (humanity, v. 2). These are not the masses complaining about their king. These are people of great influence and position intentionally and actively bringing shame upon him. To emphasize his point, the writer asks the reader to pause and reflect on the words and implication ("Selah").

Yet, David professes his expected vindication—"the Lord has set apart the godly for himself; the Lord will hear when I call to him" (v. 3 NIV). This is a confession of faith in spite of the present situation. In times like this, we must look back to the times God has delivered us from adverse circumstances (or stood with us as we went through them). And we must look to Scripture to keep our minds focused on Him (Isa. 26:3). God seeks fellowship with those who love and trust Him. Faith is not faith if never tested.

In verses 4-5 of the text, we find the mature response in times of trouble. *Anger* ("stand in awe") is a natural emotion. Here, the Hebrew word used denotes intense anger that causes a person to quake. The sin is when we allow anger to control us. We refrain from sinning—"Be angry, and do not sin" (v. 4 NKJV)—by thinking the situation through rationally and privately *prior* to any response ("meditate within your heart on your bed," NKJV). For further emphasis, David admonishes us to pause and reflect on this ("Selah").

"Offer the sacrifices of righteousness" (v. 5) can be interpreted two ways: (1) offer sacrifices that are righteous (Ps. 51:19; Deut. 33:19); or (2) sacrifices should be offered by a righteous person in a righteous manner (cf. Gen. 4:5-7). However, this is really a false distinction or dichotomy. A person out of right relationship with God cannot bring sacrifices that please Him, for He looks upon the heart and motivation. He is not looking for adherence to a duty, but those who desire to learn the truth and please God. Only a righteous person can offer a righteous sacrifice.

---

1. How can a person turn God's "glory into shame" (v. 2)?
2. What should the godly person expect (v. 3)?
3. Explain the advice in verse 4.
4. What "sacrifices of righteousness" (v. 5) should we offer God?

> "If you have been mistreated, cheated, or deceived, and if your heart has been right all along, be assured that God knows this. God will eventually vindicate you."—Theodore Epp

---

### C. A Confident Confession (vv. 6-8)

**⁶ There be many that say, Who will shew us any good? Lord, lift thou up the light of thy countenance upon us. ⁷ Thou hast put gladness in my heart, more than in the time that their corn and their wine increased. ⁸ I will both lay me down in peace, and sleep: for thou, Lord, only makest me dwell in safety.**

The psalmist understands that those in the midst of trouble easily can fall prey to despair and lack of faith (v. 6). Trouble seems to be accompanied by more trouble. As a side note, it is incumbent upon those who are not in despair to encourage and pray for those who are. It is easier to have faith for someone else than it is for yourself, because you are not feeling the pains, hurts, and doubts. The time will come when they will need to do the same for you. This verse recalls Numbers 6:24-26, which reminds us that seeing the countenance or glory of God changes everything.

In Psalm 4:7, David confidently acknowledges God is present even in this time of distress. Only God can put "gladness in [the] heart." This divine action is underscored by the fact that David's faith is greater now than when things were going well (e.g., a great harvest; cf. Ps. 126:6; Isa. 9:3). It is easy to trust God when everything falls into place. It takes maturity and determination to trust Him when we are under assault.

To highlight God's ability to bring fullness of confidence and safety in difficult times, David asserts that he *will* sleep in peace (Ps. 4:8). As we all know, sleep can be difficult in troubling times (see Job 7:4). Only in the Lord is there peace and safety. Our fretting and lack of sleep change nothing, except our health, state of mind, and the condition of our faith (see Matt. 6:25-34).

---

1. What does David pray for in verse 6?
2. How did God bless David (vv. 7-8)?

> "If you know people in your church or your neighborhood that are facing adversity, I encourage you to offer a hand of friendship to them. That is what Jesus would do."—Jonathan Falwell

## II. PRAYER FOR VINDICATION (Ps. 17:1-15)

### A. Determination (vv. 1-5)

(Psalm 17:4-5 is not included in the printed text.)

**¹ Hear the right, O Lord, attend unto my cry, give ear unto my prayer, that goeth not out of feigned lips. ² Let my sentence come forth from thy presence; let thine eyes behold the things that are equal. ³ Thou hast proved mine heart; thou hast visited me in the night; thou hast tried me, and shalt find nothing; I am purposed that my mouth shall not transgress.**

David again cries out prayerfully to God in the midst of his trouble (v. 1). He asserts his integrity in two ways. First, he declares his righteousness. Second, he notes that his prayer and speech are truthful *and* upright. Speech can be truthful and still exacerbate a situation. Truth spoken without the goal of healing or reconciliation in a matter can be hurtful. Speech must be tempered with love for God and whomever we are engaging in a difficult situation. Righteousness seeks to live in harmony and covenant with God and those He places in our lives.

Verse 2 can be interpreted in two ways. First, David may be acknowledging that judgment is coming and he would rather it come from God. This seems less probable given his assertions in verse 1. Second, he is asking for God to declare him innocent so his enemies will know his integrity. God knows the actions of the body *and* intent of the heart ("things that are equal"). He notes that he has already been examined and tested by God ("proved"), even when others could not observe him, and found to live in righteousness (v. 3). Further, he declares he will continue to lead a life that does not miss God's intent for him ("transgress"). The imagery is that of knowing where the boundary is and being determined to stay away from that mark, rather than see how close he can get to the line and still be righteous.

In verse 4, David further asserts that he is aware of the nature of humanity to follow the path of wickedness and neglect of God's desires for us (see 10:5-11). However, he has chosen to obey God's instructions ("word of thy lips") and avoid the cruel ways of evil people (17:4). *Destroyer* literally means "wild beast." It is an accurate image of unrighteous ways. However, it is easy to allow those ways to encroach into our lives, even without meaning to or even being fully aware it has happened. Mindful of this, David stresses that he has faithfully followed God's well-marked path without stumbling (v. 5).

---

1. How did David describe his prayer, and why was that important (v. 1)?
2. What did David request (v. 2)?
3. Why was David confident (vv. 3-5)?

> "When we're bombarded with doubts and fears, we must take a stand and say: 'I'll never give up! God's on my side. He loves me, and He's helping me! I'm going to make it!'"—Joyce Meyer

B. Resolve (vv. 6-12)

(Psalm 17:10-12 is not included in the printed text.)
**⁶ I have called upon thee, for thou wilt hear me, O God: incline thine ear unto me, and hear my speech. ⁷ Shew thy marvellous lovingkindness, O thou that savest by thy right hand them which put their trust in thee from those that rise up against them. ⁸ Keep me as the apple of the eye, hide me under the shadow of thy wings, ⁹ From the wicked that oppress me, from my deadly enemies, who compass me about.**

Three notable aspects are addressed in this passage. First and foremost, the psalmist cries out to God because of relationship (vv. 6-7a). God hears our prayer and responds with mercy—love and kindness in action when we are in relationship with Him (see Isa. 59:2). It is an active, rather than a passive, love. It is love that responds to our needs and fears. This is all because we live in righteousness and right relationship with Him.

Second, David seeks God's protection (vv. 7b-8). In Scripture, writers use the phrase God's "right hand" as a synonym for His power. In ancient culture, being left-handed was a sign of weakness, since the majority of people were right-handed; whereas, the right hand was usually the stronger hand/arm. David certainly seeks protection from his enemies (v. 9), but also desires protection in his relationship with God (v. 8). The imagery is vivid. He asks that God guard him as He would His own pupil of the eye ("apple of the eye").

Finally, David details the nature of his enemies (vv. 9-12). They are more than just people who dislike him; they are predators, actively seeking opportunities to destroy him. They have "callous hearts, and their mouths speak with arrogance" (v. 10 NIV). David's enemies had surrounded him (v. 11) and, like a ravenous lion, were ready to pounce (vv. 11-12). When we face people who oppose us because of our stand for the gospel, Jesus said we should be both "wise" (aware) and "harmless" (innocent; Matt. 10:16).

1. How does David depict God (vv. 6-7)?
2. Describe David's predicament (vv. 9-12).

> "Holy resolution, built on fast principles, lifts up its head like a rock in the midst of the waves."—William Gurnall

C. Resolution (vv. 13-15)

(Psalm 17:13-14 is not included in the printed text.)
**¹⁵ As for me, I will behold thy face in righteousness: I shall be satisfied, when I awake, with thy likeness.**

This passage, though somewhat difficult to comprehend in the KJV, can be divided into two sections. First, verses 13-14a record the psalmist's plea for God to inflict judgment with "thy sword" upon the evildoers who "have their portion" here and now. David requests this harsh judgment so he may be vindicated and delivered. Approximately a thousand years after these writings, Jesus teaches us to turn the other cheek when evildoers afflict us (Matt. 5:39). So, how do we reconcile these two apparently contradictory approaches? We, like David, take our frustrations, hurts, and anger to God privately, which will enable us to respond like Jesus publicly.

The second section in the Psalm passage is a confident resolution that God will overflowingly fill the righteous with His treasures, so much so that it will pass to their children (v. 14b). In verse 15, this confidence in God enables David to know for certain that (1) he will see God face-to-face after this life; (2) he will be made whole in every aspect of life ("satisfied"); (3) he will live again after he dies; and (4) he will be transformed completely.

---

1. How did David ask God to intervene (vv. 13-14)?
2. Explain David's expectation (vv. 14-15).

"God uses the wicked to strengthen the resolve of the righteous."—Woodrow Kroll

---

### III. PRAYER FOR RESTORATION (Ps. 80:1-19)

A. Cry to the Shepherd (vv. 1-3)

**¹ Give ear, O Shepherd of Israel, thou that leadest Joseph like a flock; thou that dwellest between the cherubims, shine forth. ² Before Ephraim and Benjamin and Manasseh stir up thy strength, and come and save us. ³ Turn us again, O God, and cause thy face to shine; and we shall be saved.**

The psalmist draws a compelling image of the Lord God, calling Him the "Shepherd of Israel" (v. 1). The first writer of Scripture to use this imagery was Jacob, himself a shepherd, who called the Lord "the shepherd, the stone of Israel" (Gen. 49:24).

The psalmist pictures the Shepherd in His holiness and power, "enthroned between the cherubim" (80:1 NIV) on the "mercy seat" (Ex. 25:17; Heb. 9:5). From there, His light does "shine forth" (Ps. 80:1) to lead His people Israel, who are represented here by the tribes of Ephraim, Benjamin, and Manasseh (v. 2). The psalmist cries for the Shepherd to "stir up" ("awaken" NIV) His power to deliver Israel from danger and opposition. Centuries later, the Good Shepherd was asleep in a boat when a great windstorm arose on the Sea of Galilee, compelling His disciples to awaken Him, crying out, "Carest thou not that we perish?" (Mark 4:38). He did care, and He calmed the storm.

The psalmist calls on God to "turn us again" (80:3)—to restore His people, looking on them with His benevolent face—so they will be rescued.

- What did the psalmist ask of the Shepherd?

> "The true shepherd spirit . . . is loving, but he does not wink at sin. He has power over the lambs, but he is not domineering or sharp. He has cheerfulness, but not levity; freedom, but not license; solemnity, but not gloom."—Charles Spurgeon

---

B. Desperate for an Answer (vv. 4-7)

**⁴ O Lord God of hosts, how long wilt thou be angry against the prayer of thy people? ⁵ Thou feedest them with the bread of tears; and givest them tears to drink in great measure. ⁶ Thou makest us a strife unto our neighbours: and our enemies laugh among themselves. ⁷ Turn us again, O God of hosts, and cause thy face to shine; and we shall be saved.**

In verse 5, the psalmist declares the Lord has been giving His people great quantities of "the bread of tears" to drink. This is a sad contrast to Psalm 23:5, where the Shepherd prepares a joyful feast for His people to eat even in the presence of their enemies.

In 80:6, Israel's enemies are amazed by Israel's plight—a people so blessed and yet now in such distress. Their enemies mock them and fight among themselves over who can plunder the most of Israel's goods.

The psalmist desperately asks the Lord, "How long wilt thou be angry [literally, "How long will you smoke?"] against the prayer of thy people?" (v. 4). God's anger is pictured as a burning fire, and the prayers of God's people, rising with the smoke of incense (Rev. 5:8; 8:4), appear to be lost in the smoke of God's fury.

The psalmist again prays that God's face will break through the smoke to shine on His people, turn them to Himself, "and we shall be saved" (80:7).

---

1. Describe the psalmist's complaint (vv. 4-6).
2. What did the psalmist believe (v. 7)?

> "If we are whimpering, and sniveling, and begging to be spared the discipline of life that is sent to knock some smatterings of manhood into us, the answer to that prayer may never come at all. Thank God!"—A. J. Gossip

---

C. Remember the Vine (vv. 8-19)

(Psalm 80:8-13, 16-19 is not included in the printed text.)

**¹⁴ Return, we beseech thee, O God of hosts: look down from heaven, and behold, and visit this vine; ¹⁵ And the vineyard which thy right hand hath planted, and the branch that thou madest strong for thyself.**

Using a popular image for the nation of Israel (see Isa. 5:1-7; Jer. 2:21; Ez. 15:1-6; Matt. 20:1), the psalmist refers to them as a "vine"—specifically, "a vine out of Egypt" (Ps. 80:8). The Lord had transplanted His people from the "bitter" soil of Egyptian slavery (Ex. 1:14) into Canaan, a fertile land "flowing with milk and honey" (3:17).

How the new nation of Israel prospered! The Lord "prepared room for it, and caused it to take deep root, and it filled the land. The hills were covered with its shadow, and the mighty cedars with its boughs" (Ps. 80:9-10 NKJV). The land of Israel reached east to the Euphrates River and west to the Mediterranean Sea (v. 11), as God had clearly promised (Ex. 23:31; Deut. 11:24).

Just as a barrier is built around a vineyard to protect it from being trampled down, so the Shepherd had defended Israel from its enemies, allowing the land to grow and prosper. However, God had removed His protective hand—allowing passers-by and wild animals to ravage the vine's fruit (Ps. 80:12-13)—and the psalmist asks, "Why?" The answer is found in Deuteronomy 31:16-17 (and in many similar passages), where the Lord warned that Israel would "forsake Me and break My covenant. . . . Then My anger shall be aroused against them in that day, and I will forsake them, and I will hide My face from them, and they shall be devoured. And many evils and troubles shall befall them, so that they will say in that day, 'Have not these evils come upon us because our God is not among us?'" (NKJV).

Next, the psalmist pleas for the Lord to "turn again" to Israel, view the people's desperate situation, and again visit the vine He had planted with His strong hand and made strong for Himself (vv. 14-15). Without a divine visitation, God's people—who had been cut down and burned (v. 16)—were hopeless.

The psalmist repeats his plea for divine intervention in verse 17, depicting Israel as "the man of [God's] right hand." Ultimately, the Messiah becomes the fulfillment of this prayer, who, "after he had offered one sacrifice for sins for ever, sat down on the right hand of God" (Heb. 10:12).

As representative of the ravaged vine of Israel, the psalmist promises if God will give them life once more, they will not again turn their back on Him. Instead, they will "call upon [His] name" (80:18). He concludes, "Cause Your face to shine upon us, and we will be saved" (v. 19 NASB).

---

1. How had God prospered Israel, His "vine" (vv. 8-11)?
2. How had the vine suffered (vv. 12-13, 16)?
3. Describe the psalmist's plea (vv. 14-15).
4. Describe the psalmist's vow (vv. 17-18).

"Whenever the insistence is on the point that God answers prayer, we are off the track. The meaning of prayer is that we get hold of God, not of the answer."—Oswald Chambers

## CONCLUSION

By speaking honestly yet reverently to God, the psalmist set an example we should follow. God will hear and respond to our sincere cries to Him, no matter our circumstances. We should call to Him for mercy, vindication, and restoration.

## GOLDEN TEXT CHALLENGE

"HEAR THE RIGHT, O LORD, ATTEND UNTO MY CRY, GIVE EAR UNTO MY PRAYER, THAT GOETH NOT OUT OF FEIGNED LIPS" (Ps. 17:1).

David is praying genuine words issuing from a sincere heart, asking the righteous God to do what is right. We should judge our prayers according to the twofold criteria shown here: (1) Are we praying honestly and straightforwardly from our heart? (2) Are we praying in agreement with God's righteous character, asking Him to do what is right (which He always does)?

**Daily Devotions:**

M. The Lord Is Merciful
   Exodus 33:12-20
T. God Will Restore the Exiles
   Deuteronomy 30:1-10
W. Hope in the Lord
   Lamentations 3:21-26
T. Righteousness Received by Faith
   Romans 3:21-26
F. Christ's Death Shows God's Mercy
   Romans 5:6-11
S. Hope of a Transformed Body
   1 Corinthians 15:50-57

June 14, 2015 (Lesson 2)
# Psalms of Thanksgiving
Psalms 32:1-11; 116:1-19; 118:1-29

**Theme:**
Different Types of Psalms

**Central Truth:**
Thanksgiving is an appropriate response to God's goodness and mercy.

**Focus:**
Appreciate God's great love and daily express gratitude to Him.

**Context:**
David writes songs of thanks to God.

**Golden Text:**
"O give thanks unto the Lord; for he is good; because his mercy endureth for ever" (Ps. 118:1).

**Study Outline:**
I. Thankful for God's Forgiveness
   (Ps. 32:1-11)
II. Thankful for God's Compassion
   (Ps. 116:1-19)
III. Thankful for God's Enduring Mercy
   (Ps. 118:1-29)

## INTRODUCTION

In last week's lesson, we examined three psalms of *lament*—a cry or prayer to God by a person or community in distress. Today's lesson examines three psalms of thanksgiving. While the thanksgiving psalms are the opposite of lament psalms, paradoxically they are closely related. They are cries of praise or thanksgiving to God by those previously in lament, who have now been delivered out of their distress (individually or corporately).

Some make a clear distinction between *praise* and *thanksgiving*. That is, *praise* is an offering of worship given to God based on who He is (His character, qualities, and attributes). *Thanksgiving* is an offering of worship given to God for acts He has done, is doing, or shall do in the future (His actions). There are places in Scripture where that distinction may be seen (see Ps. 100:4; 147:5-7). However, it is not a hard-and-fast rule. There are places where *praise* and *thanksgiving* are used interchangeably or in parallel (see 2 Sam. 22:50; Pss. 35:18; 69:30; Heb. 13:15). Especially in thanksgiving psalms, the psalmists' primary concern was offering God worship from the depths of their heart. Language was important to them, but their focus was fulfilling the vow to praise God which they made while in the depths of their lament.

The psalms of this lesson, all attributed to David, are extremely interesting and informative. Psalm 32 was written probably after David's moral lapse with Bathsheba and his callous and fatal mistreatment of Uriah (see 2 Sam. 11;

Ps. 51). We see a man humbled because of his sin, who truly recognizes the power of forgiveness and the resulting freedom.

The circumstances leading to Psalm 116 are difficult to determine. It is clear, however, that David was thankful to be delivered from the threat of death. There are several periods in his life during which this could have been written (fleeing from Saul, Absalom, or the Philistines).

Psalm 118 has the distinction of being at the very center of the Bible. It is preceded by the shortest chapter in the Bible and followed by the longest chapter. Many believe it was written to celebrate David's formal reception of the kingship for which he had been anointed. Others believe it was written to commemorate the ark of the covenant coming into Jerusalem. Christ applied part of this psalm (vv. 22-23, 26) to Himself (Matt. 21:9, 42).

## I. THANKFUL FOR GOD'S FORGIVENESS (Ps. 32:1-11)

### A. The Transformation (vv. 1-4)

(Psalm 32:3-4 is not included in the printed text.)

**¹ Blessed is he whose transgression is forgiven, whose sin is covered. ² Blessed is the man unto whom the Lord imputeth not iniquity, and in whose spirit there is no guile.**

The psalm begins on a high note. "Blessed" carries the idea of happiness caused by walking in the way of understanding. There is a deep, satisfying confidence that results from walking with God in the path He chooses for us. A person is happy and confident when he or she has been relieved of the load that accompanies sin and rebellion ("transgression").

God's nature consists primarily of three main attributes: *love, life,* and *holiness*. Sin offends His holiness, which demands judgment of sin. His love seeks restoration. His life seeks a way to bring salvation (deliverance from death or unwholeness—death encompasses more than the cessation of physical life). The breached relationship is restored through the forgiveness of the rebellion. The Hebrew root for *forgiveness* (v. 1) conveys the idea of our sin being lifted up and taken away and having our dignity (image of God) reinstated. This is what Jesus did for us and all who sin (Matt. 11:28; Rom. 8:1-11). His holy judgment motivates us to seek salvation.

Verse 2 of the text reinforces the first verse with parallel, but slightly different, aspects. Again, the person is "blessed" whose sin is not *imputed* (an accounting term). Sin is not counted against us; however, it is not a term ignorant of the facts. One cannot say that my bank account has $1,000,000 if that is not fact. Likewise, God cannot declare us free from sin if, in fact, He has not transformed us and delivered us from and of sin.

"Iniquity" (v. 2) is something that has been bent and twisted because of perversion. Verses 3 and 4 graphically illustrate the idea: "When I kept silent, my bones grew old through my groaning all day long. For day and night Your hand was heavy upon me; my vitality was turned into the drought of summer" (NKJV). However, because David honestly and sincerely ("no guile," v. 2) has confessed his iniquity, God has forgiven him.

---

1. Who can truly call themselves "blessed" (vv. 1-2)?
2. Describe David's condition and its cause (vv. 3-4).

> "Our love for God and our appreciation of His love and forgiveness will be in proportion to the recognition of our sin and unworthiness."—Dave Hunt

### B. The Intimate Confession (v. 5)

**⁵ I acknowledge my sin unto thee, and mine iniquity have I not hid. I said, I will confess my transgressions unto the Lord; and thou forgavest the iniquity of my sin. Selah.**

While it may be easy to skip over this verse since it seems to be a restatement of the first two verses, the fact that it is bracketed between two calls to reflect ("Selah") should cause us to pause and understand the significance of what is said. The first two verses of the psalm reflect on God's activity. Here, David clarifies and emphasizes the personal facet of our involvement in the process of forgiveness. There is a deeply intimate aspect stressed in "acknowledge" and "confess" (both words translated from the same Hebrew word). It is a term used to confess sin, but it is confession based on knowledge learned from experience. Because the psalmist has suffered the full weight of his sin (due to the holy judgment), he chooses willfully to come openly and freely to God to lay bare (confess) his sin or iniquity. He refuses to conceal it from or justify it to God (unlike Adam and Eve, Gen. 3).

The imagery in the language is vivid and prophetic—an uncovered and humbled sinner comes wounded and bleeding from the effects of sin and judgment into the presence of a holy, but loving, God seeking salvation and restoration. Roughly a thousand years later, a naked and bleeding Savior carrying our sins upon Himself would come into the presence of the Father via a cross and seek salvation and restoration for us. The result is forgiveness of and deliverance from sin!

- What decision did David make, and what was the result?

### C. The Sacred Refuge (vv. 6-7)

**⁶ For this shall every one that is godly pray unto thee in a time when thou mayest be found: surely in the floods of great waters they shall not come nigh unto him. ⁷ Thou art my hiding place; thou shalt preserve me from trouble; thou shalt compass me about with songs of deliverance. Selah.**

Because of his unpretentious actions and God's merciful response, David is confident "every one" who comes with the same heart and intention will find God (v. 6). Some understand this verse to be an admonition to seek God while He can be found, as though there may be a time when He cannot be found. Certainly, there is some truth in that as we reach the end of this age. We must not presume that God will always be there when we get ready to seek Him. However, the emphasis here seems to be if we come as David did, God will protect us from being encompassed by the overwhelming and drowning effects of our twisted ways and bent spirits.

In verse 7, David emphasizes three (of many) benefits of being forgiven. First, God becomes our "hiding place." Because of forgiveness, He becomes our place of shelter that protects us from His wrath (holy judgment, Zeph. 2:3). He also becomes the covering of protection from the storms of life (Pss. 17:8-9; 31:20). Second, He guards us ("preserves") from the pressures of life ("trouble"). The imagery is that of walls pressing in from every side. God is there to watch over us and stop the walls from crushing us. Third, He encompasses us with "songs of deliverance" and victory. The Scriptures, especially the Psalms, are replete with examples and admonition for us to sing unto God (Judg. 5:3; Neh. 12:46; Pss. 47:6; 104:33; Rom. 15:9; Rev. 15:3). However, Psalm 32:7 and Zephaniah 3:17 remind us God can sing too. It also reminds us of the power of music to edify—or not.

---

- Who can sing "songs of deliverance," and in what situation?

> "Is God your refuge, your hiding place, your stronghold, your shepherd, your counselor, your friend, your redeemer, your saviour, your guide? If He is, you don't need to search any further for security."—Elisabeth Elliot

---

D. The Determined Outcome (vv. 8-11)

(Psalm 32:8-9 is not included in the printed text.)

**[10] Many sorrows shall be to the wicked: but he that trusteth in the Lord, mercy shall compass him about. [11] Be glad in the Lord, and rejoice, ye righteous: and shout for joy, all ye that are upright in heart.**

In verse 8, there is a shift in speakers from David to God himself. God promises to "instruct . . . and teach" the repentant, providing the road map we should follow. *Instruct* means to have an intelligent understanding of a matter. It involves a thorough process of considering all the outcomes of a decision or choice and then, through wisdom and common sense, making the proper decision. God promises to lead us through this process. The end result is a successful life that flows with the provision of God (see Isa. 41:20).

The etymology of *teach* carries the idea of shooting an arrow directly into the center of the target. God's teaching is often pointed, and the Holy Spirit makes sure it hits the heart of the hearer. It is designed to bring us into covenant with Him, not cause us pain. In fact, it is designed to help free us from pain—the pain of wrong decisions and resulting consequences (Pss. 25:8-10; 33:18-19).

The last phrase of 32:8—"I will guide thee with mine eye"—can be taken two ways: (1) God will observe us to see if we follow His advice or not; or (2) God will watch over and guide us as we travel through the process. Perhaps there is a third option—both.

Verse 9 may be a continuation of God's speech, or it may be David offering admonition to the reader. Either way, the instruction is the same: We should not be as animals which must be harnessed and made to go in the correct direction. God created us as free moral agents. We have the ability and will to make the conscious decision to follow Him or not. He does not constrain us against our will to obey Him. However, with the ability to choose comes the responsibility of owning the consequences of our decisions.

Making the wrong decision(s) leads to a life of sadness ("sorrows," v. 10). Those who place their confidence in God ("trusteth") shall be encompassed by God's unfailing love in action ("mercy"). Fully comprehending all this and choosing righteousness results in a heart filled with joy and a life that communicates praise (v. 11).

---

1. What does God offer (v. 8), and how must we not respond (v. 9)?
2. Who can "shout for joy," and why (vv. 10-11)?

> "What is needed for happy, effectual service is simply to put your work into the Lord's hand, and leave it there."—Hannah Whitall Smith

---

## II. THANKFUL FOR GOD'S COMPASSION (Ps. 116:1-19)

### A. Of Death and Praise (vv. 1-14)

(Psalm 116:6-14 is not included in the printed text.)

¹ I love the Lord, because he hath heard my voice and my supplications. ² Because he hath inclined his ear unto me, therefore will I call upon him as long as I live. ³ The sorrows of death compassed me, and the pains of hell gat hold upon me: I found trouble and sorrow. ⁴ Then called I upon the name of the Lord; O Lord, I beseech thee, deliver my soul. ⁵ Gracious is the Lord, and righteous; yea, our God is merciful.

David begins this psalm of thanksgiving with a declaration of "love" for the Lord (v. 1). This term is used throughout the Old Testament to describe the deep affection of God for His people (Jer. 31:3; Hos. 11:4) and even of a husband for his wife (Gen. 29:20). It is a love as strong as death itself (Song 8:6). David's love for God is motivated by God's continual intervention in his life in times of trouble (Ps. 116:1-11). As noted in the Introduction, it is difficult to ascertain whether these relate to one or several events, since we have little indication of the psalm's origin. Certainly, David felt the threat of death (vv. 3, 8) and experienced deliverance (vv. 5-9, 12). There seems to be elements of both spiritual and physical distress.

David highlights five important truths we need to embrace. First, God hears our cries and is active even when we do not see activity. Second, He is a God of salvation and deliverance. God freely chooses to look upon us with favor and compassion in our needs ("gracious," v. 5)—even if our difficulties are self-inflicted—and responds with love that intervenes ("merciful"). He does so because He is "righteous," choosing to pursue a relationship and fellowship with us, even when we are running from Him. Third, He lifts us up and gives us rest (vv. 7-9). Fourth, scattered throughout this passage is the truth that what God offers, we need to receive. So often, we feel unworthy to receive from God, but it gives Him great joy to interact with us. Finally, the proper response is to offer ourselves and all we have to God (vv. 12-14).

Since verse 14 has been so misused by charlatans to invoke guilt and fleece the flock, a brief treatment is in order (also see v. 18; 22:25). David declares that he will "pay [his] vows unto the Lord." "Pay" (*shalom*) is a covenant term that means "to perform that which brings peace and wholeness to a relationship." It is not motivated by guilt or even outside forces (someone seeking an offering or pledge). It is a declaration or act dedicated to God based on our covenant relationship with Him. While "vow" can include an offering, that is not its primary meaning. It is a promise made to God to abstain from something (e.g., food) or offer something precious ("living sacrifice," Rom. 12:1). It certainly carries the idea of sacrifice or giving something costly (whether that is a monetary or other offering, or a promise). It is a private matter determined between God and ourselves, though it may be fulfilled publicly, as David noted here.

---

1. Why did the psalmist say he loved the Lord (vv. 1-4)?
2. Describe three characteristics of God (vv. 5-6).
3. Describe a time you were "delivered . . . from death" and allowed to continue in "the land of the living" (vv. 8-9).
4. In verses 13 and 14, how does the psalmist answer his question in verse 12?

> "Your helplessness is your best prayer."—Ole Hallesby

---

B. Of Death and Presence (v. 15)

**¹⁵ Precious in the sight of the Lord is the death of his saints.**

In the midst of the threat-death-deliverance discussion, David reminds us that God does not take the death of His own lightly (see also 72:14). The root meaning of *precious* is "honor," "heavy," and "dignity." In Scripture, this word is used to describe the steadfast love of God (36:7), the thoughts of God (139:17), wisdom (Prov. 3:15), the Word of God (1 Sam. 3:1), life (26:8-11), and salvation (Isa. 43:1-4). It can also mean something "splendid" or "spectacular" (see Job 31:26). So, the death of a "saint" (those whom God loves) is costly, valuable, and worthy of esteem.

---

- What is "precious" to God, and why?

> "Death comes to the ungodly man as a penal infliction, but to the righteous as a summons to his Father's palace."—Charles Spurgeon

---

C. Of Servitude and Freedom (vv. 16-19)

**¹⁶ O Lord, truly I am thy servant; I am thy servant, and the son of thine handmaid: thou hast loosed my bonds. ¹⁷ I will offer to thee the sacrifice**

of thanksgiving, and will call upon the name of the Lord. ¹⁸ I will pay my vows unto the Lord now in the presence of all his people, ¹⁹ In the courts of the Lord's house, in the midst of thee, O Jerusalem. Praise ye the Lord.

In verse 16, David sets up an interesting paradox: he is a "servant," yet he has been "loosed" from his "bonds." *Servant* is literally one who is an indentured slave. Israelites could place themselves in servitude as payment for a debt for a period of six years or until the Year of Jubilee, whichever came first (see Ex. 21:1-27). At the end of that period, the slave could choose to remain with his master. If it was acceptable, the master took the slave and placed his ear on the doorpost and pierced the lobe with an awl, "joining" or "bonding" the servant to the home, hence the term *bondservant* (v. 6). The bondservant was treated as a family member. This is the idea behind David's paradox. He has willingly become a servant of the Lord and, as such, now has freedom.

The correct response is freely giving a "sacrifice of thanksgiving" to God (Ps. 116:17). Some see this as a literal sacrifice of unleavened cakes offered in the Tabernacle (see Lev. 7:12-15). Others, in light of Psalm 116:18's public declaration, view it as a verbal offering of praise and thanksgiving (107:22). Since the Lamb of God has been offered once for our sins (John 1:29; Heb. 9:28), we are to offer acceptable sacrifices of thanksgiving privately and publicly to Him (see Isa. 1:11-13; Rom. 6:17; Col. 2:7; Rev. 7:12), as David did (Ps. 116:18-19).

---

1. What had God freed the writer to do (v. 16)?
2. What did the psalmist long to do (vv. 17-19)?

> "A Christian is a perfectly free lord of all, subject to none. A Christian is a perfectly dutiful servant of all, subject of all, subject to all."—Martin Luther

---

## III. THANKFUL FOR GOD'S ENDURING MERCY (Ps. 118:1-29)

A. A Public Call (vv. 1-9)

(Psalm 118:8-9 is not included in the printed text.)
¹ O give thanks unto the Lord; for he is good: because his mercy endureth for ever. ² Let Israel now say, that his mercy endureth for ever. ³ Let the house of Aaron now say, that his mercy endureth for ever. ⁴ Let them now that fear the Lord say, that his mercy endureth for ever. ⁵ I called upon the Lord in distress: the Lord answered me, and set me in a large place. ⁶ The Lord is on my side; I will not fear: what can man do unto me? ⁷ The Lord taketh my part with them that help me: therefore shall I see my desire upon them that hate me.

This psalm could have been written for David's formal coronation or the entrance of the ark into Jerusalem. It is clear that it was written for a public event. The first four verses set up a call-response pattern. David sets up the initial call to the congregation to "give thanks unto the Lord" (v. 1). *Thanks* (*yadah*) is the same word used in 32:5 ("confess"), a deeply intimate word that suggests a confession from the heart based on experiential knowledge. This declaration is not based on theory, but reality—God is "good" (118:1), which means that He (1) provides for our physical needs; (2) is desirable and has our best in mind; (3) is far and beyond the riches this world can offer; (4) is morally good and can be trusted; and (5) is good in the truest sense of the word.

David proceeds to call the nation ("Israel," v. 2), the priests ("house of Aaron," v. 3), and all who are reverent ("fear the Lord," v. 4) to declare "His mercy endures forever" (NKJV), because He is good. "Mercy" (*hesed*) can also be translated as "loving-kindness" and "love." The idea is that God's love is enduring, steadfast, and active. It is not an abstract ideal, but concrete love in action and without end or limits ("forever"). He loves us in spite of ourselves, fears, and failures. He does not overlook our sins, but loves us in spite of them and has provided a way for us to be redeemed from them.

The psalmist then reflects on where God has brought him from (vv. 5-7). He was in dire straits with the walls closing in ("distress"), but God heard his cry, set him free, and brought him to a "broad place," where he was no longer pressed from every side (v. 5 NKJV; see also 2 Cor. 4:8-9). It seemed as though all humanity was against him, but God is ever present with him ("on my side," Ps. 118:6); therefore, he has no reason to "fear." The term *fear* can be understood in a couple of different ways. First, because of God's presence, the psalmist has no reason to be afraid of the persecution and affliction by others. God will come through for him. Second, the term is also used in the sense of "awe" or "reverence." David is not saying that he has become so close to God that he has lost his awe of God—as too many in Pentecostal/Charismatic circles have.

There are two extremes we must avoid. Far too many are afraid of God, rather than respecting Him. They are afraid they are unworthy or that God will harm them. Christ has made us worthy to enter the very presence of God (Heb. 4:16). However, our ability to come boldly does not mean we can come arrogantly or presumptuously. He is still God and is worthy of our trust, love, and respect (Ps. 118:8-9).

---

1. Describe God's "mercy"—His loving-kindness (vv. 1-4).
2. Explain the psalmist's confidence (vv. 5-7).
3. What is "better," and why (vv. 8-9)?

> "Let us remember the loving-kindness of the Lord and rehearse His deeds of grace. Let us open the volume of recollection, which is so richly illuminated with memories of His mercy, and we will soon be happy."—Alistair Begg

---

B. A Confident Outcome (vv. 10-18)

(Psalm 118:10-18 is not included in the printed text.)
The first section of this passage recalls the distress David suffered at the hands of others. David first identifies the nature or source of the distress (vv. 10-12b), and then makes a confident declaration of victory (vv. 12c-14). David's victory is sure, though not quite complete. He was a man of faith and optimism. Even in the darkest of times, he knew the Lord would prevail on his behalf (see 1 Sam. 30:1-6)—an excellent example to follow.

The second section continues to lift up God's intervention in David's life (vv. 15-18). There are two primary (and related) themes emphasized. First, David mentions "the right hand of the Lord" three times (vv. 15-16), which is always a reference to His power (Deut. 33:2; Ps. 89:13), though that power is manifested in many different ways. It can refer to His creative ability (Ps. 80:15; Isa. 48:13), eternal provision (Ps. 16:11), gift of land (Ps. 78:54; Isa. 54:3), victory over enemies (Ex. 15:6, 12; Pss. 21:9-10; 110:1, 5; Isa. 62:8), salvation/deliverance (Pss. 20:7; 108:6; 139:10), protection (17:7; 110:1), and care of the faithful (18:36; 63:9). Second, righteousness is the foundation for His power—God always acts righteously (48:11; 89:14-15). Here, the interaction of righteousness, salvation, power, victory, and worship come together to bring meaning and insight to the worshiper and glory to God.

---

1. Describe the psalmist's desperate situation and his hope (vv. 10-14).
2. What did the Lord accomplish by His strong hand (vv. 15-18)?

---

"If your life is an uphill slope, set your sails to catch God's power."—Woodrow Kroll

---

### C. A Joyful Conclusion (vv. 19-29)

(Psalm 118:19-27 is not included in the printed text.)
**28 Thou art my God, and I will praise thee: thou art my God, I will exalt thee. 29 O give thanks unto the Lord; for he is good: for his mercy endureth for ever.**

In reading through this psalm, one can almost envision David leading the congregation through the streets of Jerusalem to the Tabernacle. Along the way, the declarations and rejoinder of God's mercy have been made (vv. 1-4). A song of deliverance has been sung by David the worship leader (vv. 5-18). And now the congregation stands at the entrance to the Tabernacle (vv. 19-20), announces their intent, and moves into the presence of God (v. 21ff.).

Verses 22 and 23 are prophetic and messianic. Several times in the New Testament these verses are applied to Christ (see Matt. 21:42; Mark 12:10-11; Luke 20:17) to depict how He was rejected by human authorities, yet chosen of God. This should serve as great encouragement to us. Others may not see much in us, but God knows who we truly are and can become. He never rejects us (John 6:37).

The procession has now moved into the Holy Place (Ps. 118:27) and offers praises from the heart to a God who is more than worthy of the best we have to offer. His mercy endures forever!

---

1. How should we enter the house of worship (vv. 19-20)?
2. From verses 21 to 29, list eight reasons to worship the Lord.

"Praise now is one of the great duties of the redeemed. It will be their employment forever."—Albert Barnes

## CONCLUSION

During a difficult time in my life, I decided to keep a journal to chronicle my journey and record my thoughts. I forced myself to begin each day's entry with three things for which I was thankful.

In the midst of the battle, we tend to lose sight of the good things in our lives. We are not isolated, and God has not forgotten us. We need to remember the past victories and present blessings. Even in our darkest times, there is a reason to offer thanksgiving to God and remember that deliverance is just around the corner.—**Keith Whitt**

## GOLDEN TEXT CHALLENGE

"O GIVE THANKS UNTO THE LORD; FOR HE IS GOOD; BECAUSE HIS MERCY ENDURETH FOR EVER" (Ps. 118:1).

David issued this call for others to join him in thanking God because God is good and His loving-kindness never ends. More than three thousand years later, David's call still echoes from the Scriptures into the soul of all who believe in God, urging us to give thanks.

As we obey this plea to glorify God for His goodness and mercy, we will influence others to praise God with us.

**Daily Devotions:**

M. Give Offerings of Thanksgiving
   Leviticus 7:11-15
T. Thankful for God's Works
   1 Chronicles 16:8-13
W. Thankful for God's Redemptive Acts
   Psalm 75:1-10
T. Thankful for Answered Prayer
   John 11:38-44
F. Be Thankful
   Colossians 3:15-17
S. Thankful for Godly Example
   1 Thessalonians 1:2-10

June 21, 2015 (Lesson 3)
# Psalms of Praise

Psalms 33:1-22; 66:1-20; 103:1-22

**Theme:**
Different Types of Psalms

**Central Truth:**
The praise of the righteous magnifies God.

**Focus:**
Consider who God is and rejoice in what He does for us.

**Context:**
Three powerful psalms of praise

**Golden Text:**
"O bless our God, ye people, and make the voice of his praise to be heard" (Ps. 66:8).

**Study Outline:**
I. Praise God for His Sovereignty
  (Ps. 33:1-22)
II. Praise God for Answered Prayer
  (Ps. 66:1-20)
III. Praise God for His Works
  (Ps. 103:1-22)

## INTRODUCTION

In studying the life of David, we see the deep concern he had regarding the worship of the Lord. Organizing choirs and orchestra from the ranks of the Levites, he even invented new instruments of music to add to the fullness of expression in Israelite worship.

Israel and the Church, down through the centuries, have had their worship enriched by the wonderful psalms written by David. Today's lesson focuses on three of those psalms—psalms that praise God for His *sovereignty*, *answered prayer*, and His *works*.

I. PRAISE GOD FOR HIS SOVEREIGNTY (Ps. 33:1-22)

A. Instruments of Praise (vv. 1-5)

(Psalm 33:2-5 is not included in the printed text.)
**¹ Rejoice in the Lord, O ye righteous: for praise is comely for the upright.**
God made us to bring honor and glory to His name. When we turn our back on sin, choose to serve God with our whole heart, and live to glorify Him in all we think, say, and do, then our life becomes a life of praise. God imputes to us His own righteousness, and we become instruments of praise.

The psalmist, again and again, calls for praise to God, for thanksgiving, for rejoicing. He says, "Delight thyself . . . in the Lord" (37:4).

Every song of praise becomes a "new song" (33:3) when the soul is anointed afresh with the blessings of the Holy Spirit. Hymns old and new are given new meaning, new depth, and new feeling when they pour out of a heart full of praise to God.

The psalmist proceeds to give reasons why God is to be praised: "The word of the Lord holds true, and all his work endures. The Lord loves righteousness and justice, his love unfailing fills the earth" (vv. 4-5 NEB).

Adam Clarke said, "To hear the worthless inhabitants [of the earth] complain, one would think that God dispensed evil, not good. To examine the operation of His hand, everything is marked with mercy and there is no place where His goodness does not appear."

1. What is "beautiful" to God (v. 1 NKJV)?
2. How should we worship Him (vv. 2-3)?
3. Why should we worship God (vv. 4-5)?

> "The climax of God's happiness is the delight He takes in the echoes of His excellence in the praises of His people."—John Piper

B. Greatness of God's Power (vv. 6-12)

(Psalm 33:10, 12 is not included in the printed text.)

**⁶ By the word of the Lord were the heavens made: and all the host of them by the breath of his mouth. ⁷ He gathereth the waters of the sea together as an heap: he layeth up the depth in storehouses. ⁸ Let all the earth fear the Lord: let all the inhabitants of the world stand in awe of him. ⁹ For he spake, and it was done; he commanded, and it stood fast.**

**¹¹ The counsel of the Lord standeth for ever, the thoughts of his heart to all generations.**

Not only is God worthy of praise because of His *goodness*; He is worthy of praise because of His *power*. The psalmist takes us back to the beginning and points a graphic word-picture of the wonders of the Creation. He describes the universe's coming into being out of nothing as God speaks the word, with dry land appearing and continents coming into being. The boundaries of the ocean are set, and the waters are gathered into mighty oceans.

What a mighty God is our Lord! While it is impossible for our finite minds to comprehend His greatness, we still should contemplate His omnipotence. When we look at the vastness of the universe, the depth of the mighty oceans, the intricate composition of a tiny insect, the beauty of a rose—and realize all this came into being with His spoken word—our hearts should be filled with awe and wonder.

In verse 10, we are reminded there is a notable contrast between the ways of humanity and the ways of God. The ways of nations are schemes for their own selfish indulgence of advancement. People may plot and plan to work things their way, but they can only go as far as God will let them.

No matter who opposes God's plan or God's people, God can and will move to bring blessing and an inheritance to those who love and serve Him. "If God be for us, who can be against us?" (Rom. 8:31). His sovereignty will always win out, for our God is over all.

---

1. Who should be in awe of God, and why (vv. 6-9)?
2. Describe the Lord's actions to opposite kinds of nations (vv. 10-12).

> "Our God is not an impotent God with one arm; but as He is slow to anger, so is He great in power."—Abraham Wright

---

C. Greatness of God's Knowledge (vv. 13-22)

(Psalm 33:16-22 is not included in the printed text.)

**13 The Lord looketh from heaven; he beholdeth all the sons of men. 14 From the place of his habitation he looketh upon all the inhabitants of the earth. 15 He fashioneth their hearts alike; he considereth all their works.**

Since God is our Creator, He has perfect knowledge concerning us. God not only observes our actions, but He knows our hearts. "The Lord seeth not as man seeth; for man looketh on the outward appearance, but the Lord looketh on the heart" (1 Sam. 16:7).

Sometimes we get the idea we are God's special people and He doesn't care for others as He does for us. But Psalm 33:14 refutes that idea: "From his dwelling place he watches all who live on earth" (NIV).

God looks on our hearts, not with the aim of punishing or bringing judgment upon us, but with the desire to have us respond to His love. He also looks on His people with understanding, noting our needs, and giving the wisdom we need for our service to Him (v. 15). We are all objects of His love and concern, and He longs for us to commit our lives fully into His hands that He may work His perfect will in us.

God wants us to put our trust in Him. Today people do not put their trust in horses and chariots (vv. 16-17). Rather, there is a tendency to trust in money, position, material possessions, our own abilities—in anything but God. If we could only realize that all our wisdom, skill, and abilities come directly from His hand of love!

Human plans, organizations, and efforts have a vital place; but, if God is left out, we will fail. He alone is our victory (vv. 18-19). To realize that we have no power except through Christ, who lives in us and works through us, is the greatest place of victory in the Christian life.

Through long years of experience, the psalmist learned he could live a life of rejoicing because of his trust in God (v. 21). God is not glorified by our doubt and lack of faith. He wants us to live in continual confidence in Him. He wants to be our help, our shield, our Savior, our healer, and the supplier of every need (v. 20).

The focus of this psalm is on praise and thanksgiving to our sovereign God. Our worship of Him is to include adoration, commitment, and trust. God wants us not only to praise Him, but to live free from anxiety and worry, trusting our all into His loving care.

---

1. Describe God's attention to humanity (vv. 13-15).

2. To whom does God demonstrate His mercy, and how (vv. 18-19)?
3. How has God proven to be your "help" and "shield" (v. 20)?

> "I am graven on the palms of His hands. I am never out of His mind. All my knowledge of Him depends on His sustained initiative in knowing me. I know Him, because He first knew me, and continues to know me. He knows me as a friend, One who loves me; and there is no moment when His eye is off me, or His attention distracted from me, and no moment, therefore, when His care falters."—J. I. Packer

## II. PRAISE GOD FOR ANSWERED PRAYER (Ps. 66:1-20)

### A. Praise God for His Power (vv. 1-7)

(Psalm 66:6-7 is not included in the printed text.)

**¹ Make a joyful noise unto God, all ye lands: ² Sing forth the honour of his name: make his praise glorious. ³ Say unto God, How terrible art thou in thy works! Through the greatness of thy power shall thine enemies submit themselves unto thee. ⁴ All the earth shall worship thee, and shall sing unto thee; they shall sing to thy name. Selah. ⁵ Come and see the works of God: he is terrible in his doing toward the children of men.**

The psalm opens with a call to all the earth to praise the Lord. God is not Lord over Israel alone, but over all nations in all parts of the earth; therefore, people should celebrate afresh the revelation of God to their heart. The revelation centered in Israel and extended to all lands. It would have been a beautiful sight to witness the assembled Jews singing this song of praise, calling upon all the earth to "sing forth the honour of his name" (v. 2).

God should be praised for His mighty works, which elicit the subduing of all enemies to Himself. The use of the word *terrible* (vv. 3-4) does not indicate something bad, but rather that which inspires awe in the human heart ("awesome," NKJV). Even when people who do not accept God see the power of His presence on earth, they are moved to fear and awe.

In verse 5, all the world is invited to "come and see," to review the story of ancient Israel, to consider God's awe-inspiring deeds for His people. The Jews believed if the world could only comprehend what God had done for them, then the world would accept Him.

The miraculous crossing of the Red Sea always stood out to Israel as the great act of God's salvation (v. 6). That mighty event was singled out more frequently than any other as positive proof of God's power to deliver them from relentless enemies.

In verse 7, we see the wish of the psalmist for all nations to enter into the joy of the Lord. He would have the entire earth to live by the principles and laws of God. He is an unchanging God, with power and justice and love for all the world.

- Describe the types of songs we should sing to God.

> "Praise lies upon a higher plain than thanksgiving. When I give thanks, my thoughts still circle around myself to some extent. But in praise my soul ascends to self-forgetting adoration, seeing and praising only the majesty and power of God, His grace and redemption."—Ole Hallesby

---

### B. Praise God for His Deliverance (vv. 8-15)

(Psalm 66:10-15 is not included in the printed text.)

**8 O bless our God, ye people, and make the voice of his praise to be heard: 9 Which holdeth our soul in life, and suffereth not our feet to be moved.**

The nation of Israel should lift up its voice in praise to God for renewing its life when destruction and death seemed at hand. God is the restorer of life to individuals and nations that trust in Him. The Lord is always active in our preservation and deliverance from evil.

The Israelites had experienced many difficulties and were surrounded by many enemy nations, but God held their "soul in life" (v. 9) and established their feet in safety in the face of all difficulty. Israel's exposure to trouble was like a testing that would refine the nation as silver is refined (v. 10).

The terms "thou broughtest" (v. 11) and "thou hast caused" (v. 12) do not indicate God deliberately created the problems of Israel; it means here, as in many other places, that God allowed these afflictions to come upon His people. The Lord permitted difficulty for the strengthening of the nation.

In verses 13-15, the psalmist used the pronoun *I* five times. He said, "I was in trouble" (v. 14), and we get the idea that the psalmist had encountered some immense difficulty which led him to call upon the Lord. Now he assured the Lord he would go into His house with burnt offerings to fully pay the vows he had made to God when in trouble.

---

1. How had God tested His people, and what was the result (vv. 8-12)?
2. What vow did the psalmist fulfill, and how (vv. 13-15)?

> "I was delivered from the burden that had so heavily suppressed me. The spirit of mourning was taken from me, and I knew what it was to truly rejoice in God my Savior."—George Whitefield

---

### C. Praise God for Answering Prayer (vv. 16-20)

(Psalm 66:17-19 is not included in the printed text.)

**16 Come and hear, all ye that fear God, and I will declare what he hath done for my soul.**

**20 Blessed be God, which hath not turned away my prayer, nor his mercy from me.**

A manner in which God communicates from one servant to the other is by the word of testimony. Testimonies should therefore be given by all Christians, for then younger Christians can be encouraged by those more experienced in their service to the Lord. The true testimony concerns what God "hath done for my soul" (v. 16)—not trivial and self-centered expressions.

In verse 18, the psalmist asserts if he entertains iniquity in his heart, the Lord will not hear his petitions or his praise. The prayers of a sinful man are futile, and the praises of such a person are hollow sounds. Robert South said, "As long as a man regards iniquity in his heart, he cannot pray in faith; that is, he cannot build a rational confidence upon any promise that God will accept him."

In verse 19, the psalmist testifies of his innocence and honesty before the Lord. The fact that God heard his prayers is a sure sign he did not secretly regard iniquity in his heart.

The psalm concludes with a triumphant testimony that God has not turned away the prayer of the psalmist, nor has He withheld the extension of His mercy. This is prayer and praise in its finest fashion. We pray and God hears us readily; He responds with mercy and blessing, which we receive gladly.

---

- Summarize the psalmist's testimony.

---

## III. PRAISE GOD FOR HIS WORKS (Ps. 103:1-22)

### A. Worship Our Gracious God (vv. 1-5)

¹ **Bless the Lord, O my soul: and all that is within me, bless his holy name.** ² **Bless the Lord, O my soul, and forget not all his benefits.** ³ **Who forgiveth all thine iniquities; who healeth all thy diseases;** ⁴ **who redeemeth thy life from destruction; who crowneth thee with lovingkindness and tender mercies;** ⁵ **Who satisfieth thy mough with good things; so that thy youth is renewed like the eagle's.**

Contemplating the many benefits he received from God, the psalmist was caught up into a rapture of joy. He spoke to his soul and innermost being with exhortation to praise the Lord.

Not content with merely calling upon his *soul* (by which he most likely meant the seat of understanding and affection) to bless Jehovah, the psalmist also included "all that is within me" (v. 1). With this comment, he addressed his *mind* and *heart*, with all the faculties of both.

The psalmist called upon his entire being to bless Jehovah by recalling all that God had done. The Hebrew word for *benefits* (v. 2) generally means "retribution" or "reward." The bountiful benefits which God gives in accordance with His own goodness are due to His compassionate nature and not to our merit.

The first and most important benefit that came to the psalmist's mind was the reality of forgiveness from "all . . . iniquities" (v. 3). In Hebrew, the basic idea behind *forgiveth* is to do away with or negate the force of iniquity in disrupting God's relationship with humanity and to remove its influence in the active life of the person. Hence, *forgiveness* is the foundation for fellowship between God and man.

In the physical realm, a similar creative act occurs in the body, for diseases are healed. Ultimately, God redeems us from "destruction"—eternal death (v. 4).

God provides also the benefit of physical strength and health—"satisfieth thy mouth with good things" and "thy youth is renewed like the eagle's" (v. 5). Renewal of life is likened to the molting process of the eagle. Periodically, the old feathers are cast aside and the bird is able to go forth again with new vigor. Spiritual renewal, even in old age, is one of God's redemptive acts.

No wonder the psalmist exhorted his soul to bless Jehovah. His benefits were full and satisfying, and they climaxed in the crown of God's loving-kindness and tender mercies.

---

1. Where does genuine worship begin (v. 1)?
2. List various "benefits" for which we should praise God (vv. 2-5).

> "*Adoration* is the spontaneous yearning of the heart to worship, honor, magnify, and bless God."—Richard J. Foster

---

B. Celebrate God's Unfailing Mercy (vv. 6-18)

(Psalm 103:6-7, 9-12, 14-16, 18 is not included in the printed text.)

**⁸ The Lord is merciful and gracious, slow to anger, and plenteous in mercy.**

**¹³ Like as a father pitieth his children, so the Lord pitieth them that fear him.**

**¹⁷ But the mercy of the Lord is from everlasting to everlasting upon them that fear him, and his righteousness unto children's children.**

Since the faithful are always living among adverse circumstances while in this world, the psalmist reminds us it is God's ordinary work to come to the aid of His servants whenever He sees them mistreated. Indeed, this compassionate concern can be traced back to Moses and the children of Israel, which is only one instance of God's righteousness and judgment in helping those who are "oppressed" (vv. 6-7).

The God of Israel is not like pagan gods who are cold and heartless. The true God, Jehovah, possesses qualities of warmth and compassion (v. 8). God does not insist on quarreling or being angry without cause (v. 9). He will gladly set aside His judicial role whenever the sinner shows signs of repentance (v. 10). Our sins and iniquities should not mean that all hope for a new life is gone, for God is great in His mercy (v. 11). If we repent, God will cast away our transgressions "as far as the east is from the west" (v. 12).

In verse 13, the strong Father image of God is filled with tenderness of *pity*—the same basic term translated as "tender mercies" (v. 4) and "merciful" (v. 8). God understands His children and takes their weakness into consideration. The misery of our existence, which might seem to shut us out from One so infinitely perfect, is the very inducement to God to show fatherly pity toward us (v. 14; see also 78:38-39).

The psalmist reminds us that in the midst of our frail existence (103:15-16), there is one strong reason for comfort—there is a God of mercy! Jehovah is the everlasting one who raises all those who link themselves with Him to a place blessed, protected, and rewarded. Those who keep their covenant with God have the privilege of drawing on this vast store of divine help for their own needs (vv. 17-18).

---

1. List characteristics of God found in verses 6-12.
2. Describe God's fatherly nature (vv. 13-14).
3. Contrast your life with God's love (vv. 15-18).

> "God's mercy is so great that you may sooner drain the sea of its water, or deprive the sun of its light, or make space too narrow, than diminish the great mercy of God."—Charles Spurgeon

---

C. Bless the Lord (vv. 19-22)

(Psalm 103:19-21 is not included in the printed text.)

**²² Bless the Lord, all his works in all places of his dominion: bless the Lord, O my soul.**

The Lord who redeems and keeps us is the God who transcends time and space. The Lord God is the universal Almighty Sovereign, no less able than willing to fulfill His promises and execute His purposes of mercy.

Our days are as grass and as a flower of the field. We soon pass away. But God does not. Moreover, "His kingdom ruleth over all" (v. 19). All are therefore under His sovereign care.

Having finished his assertion of God's claim to universal praise, the psalmist resumed the exhortations with which he began: "Bless the Lord." His appeal, however, was no longer to his own soul but to the hosts of heaven (vv. 20-21).

The psalmist's call to the angels to join in the praise of Jehovah has its parallel only in Psalm 148. It seems to arise from the consciousness of the church (the worshiping congregation) on earth that it stands in like-minded fellowship with the angels by worshiping the Lord. After the angels and archangels, the psalmist addressed the multitude of heavenly hosts and then all creatures—wherever they may be throughout God's vast domain—that they might join in the praise to the Lord.

Then the psalmist returned once again to exhorting his own soul (103:22), ending the psalm as he began: "Bless the Lord, O my soul."

---

- Describe the ruling authority of God.

---

### CONCLUSION

The attitude of praise eliminates many undesirable traits that may creep into the life of a Christian. You cannot have your heart filled with praise and worship to God and, at the same time, be critical of your brother or sister. When your life is filled with praise, you will find that despondency disappears; unbelief is turned into faith; disapproval of others turns into compassionate love.

## GOLDEN TEXT CHALLENGE

"O BLESS OUR GOD, YE PEOPLE, AND MAKE THE VOICE OF HIS PRAISE TO BE HEARD" (Ps. 66:8).

Some scholars have observed that "*history* is philosophy teaching by example." In Psalm 66 are seen both God's special dealings with nations and with individuals. The obvious principle that emerges is simply this: Let all, both nations and individuals, submit to Jehovah, and give praise to Him.

The heart that is fervent in praise to God will seek to engage others in offering praise. The psalmist was, therefore, soliciting praises for a holy God that is worthy of praise.—***Wesleyan Bible Commentary***

**Daily Devotions:**

- M. Moses Praises the Lord
   Exodus 15:1-11
- T. Let Everything Praise the Lord
   Psalm 150:1-6
- W. Vision of Heavenly Praise
   Isaiah 6:1-7
- T. Blessed Is the King!
   Luke 19:35-40
- F. Glory to God Forever
   Romans 16:25-27
- S. Every Nation Will Worship God
   Revelation 7:9-12

June 28, 2015 (Lesson 4)

# Wisdom Psalms

**Psalms 1:1-6; 36:1-12; 127:1-5; 128:1-6**

**Theme:**
Different Types of Psalms

**Central Truth:**
Wise people order their lives according to God's Word.

**Focus:**
Perceive and choose God's plan for abundant living.

**Context:**
Selected psalms extolling biblical living

**Golden Text:**
"Blessed is every one that feareth the Lord; that walketh in his ways" (Ps. 128:1).

**Study Outline:**
I. Choose Righteousness
   (Ps. 1:1-6)
II. Avoid Sinful Living
   (Ps. 36:1-12)
III. Establish God-Centered Homes
   (Pss. 127:1-5; 128:1-6)

## INTRODUCTION

When the apostle Paul taught, "Speak to one another with psalms" (Eph. 5:19 NIV), he was referring to the collection of 150 songs and poems found in the Book of Psalms.

Christians have often turned to the Book of Psalms for encouragement and consolation. They speak forcefully to every situation of life and remind us that God does hear us, regardless of our plight. The great reformer Martin Luther considered the Psalms to be fulfilled in the person of Jesus Christ. For instance, in Psalm 1, Jesus is the man who is blessed because He did not walk, stand, or sit with those who worked against God. Jesus is the man planted by the river whose leaf never withers.

## I. CHOOSE RIGHTEOUSNESS (Ps. 1:1-6)

### A. Do Not Turn From God (v. 1)

¹ **Blessed is the man that walketh not in the counsel of the ungodly, nor standeth in the way of sinners, nor sitteth in the seat of the scornful.**

This verse describes what the righteous person does *not* do. A progression of sinfulness is shown in this one verse—from the person who is beginning to backslide all the way to the one who totally disregards God.

First, in turning away from God, an individual begins to listen to the advice of the ungodly—those who do not have the truth of God as their reference point in life. Their advice sounds good to the worldly mind, but it is contrary to the Spirit of God.

When a person begins to "walk" in this counsel, it becomes a pattern of life. Instead of allowing the Word and the Spirit of God to establish his life patterns, he begins to think like the world.

The second step in turning from God is to take the road occupied by sinners. Notice how easily one moves from listening to the advice of the ungodly to taking the road of habitual sinners—those who always miss the mark of righteousness. The *Interpreter's Bible* describes them as "professional sinners."

The third step in the downward progression is "sitting in the seat of the scornful." The *Living Bible* speaks of these people as "scoffing at the things of God." They are "the worst of the godless; they are arrogant, quarrelsome, and mischief-making foes of peace and order among men . . . mockers of goodness. Because in their own eyes they are self-sufficient, they set themselves against God" (*Interpreter's Bible*).

To sit in their seat is to take up residence among them. The progression of sin follows this pattern: listening to the wrong, standing in the path of sin, and finally, making godlessness one's home.

---

- Describe the life of someone who is not blessed.

---

> "The world is characterized by the subtle and relentless pressure it brings to bear upon us to conform to its values and practices. It creeps up on us little by little. What was once unthinkable becomes thinkable, then doable, and finally acceptable to society at large. Sin becomes respectable, and so Christians are no more than five to ten years behind the world in embracing most sinful practices."—Jerry Bridges

---

### B. Delight in Obeying God (vv. 2-3)

**² But his delight is in the law of the Lord; and in his law doth he meditate day and night. ³ And he shall be like a tree planted by the rivers of water, that bringeth forth his fruit in his season; his leaf also shall not wither; and whatsoever he doeth shall prosper.**

The blessings of the repentant person are wonderfully described in these verses. "His delight" is in God's law. In other words, he makes the law of God his occupation. This is not language just for preachers, the professionals of modern Christianity; this is the "business" of every Christian. The "law" is God's *torah*, but not in a legalistic sense. Rather, *torah* refers to the instruction, guidance, and direction that pointed "the way for the faithful Israelite and for the community of Israel" (*Interpreter's Dictionary of the Bible*).

Thus, the person who delights and meditates on the law of God is one who wants God's clear direction for his or her life. That person's prayer is "Not my will but Thine be done."

Such a person is humble in heart and is "planted" by God. Being *planted* does not refer to an accidental growing of a tree beside a river. Rather, it describes the "divine horticulturist" carefully planting us by "rivers of water," which refers to the Holy Spirit nourishing us in the Word of God.

We meditate on God's Word . . . we are fed by the Spirit of God . . . and then we bear godly fruit. Jesus said, "I am the vine, ye are the branches: He that abideth in me, and I in him, the same bringeth forth much fruit: for without me ye can do nothing" (John 15:5).

The *prosperity* of the righteous (Ps. 1:3) is best understood in terms of the redemptive work of Christ and has little or nothing to do with achieving material goals as espoused by the contemporary "prosperity gospel." It centers on the fact that Christ's mission will be fulfilled in the world for the glory of God.

- How can we benefit by meditating on the Scriptures?

> "Authority exercised with humility, and obedience accepted with delight are the very lines along which our spirits live."—C. S. Lewis

## C. Fate of the Ungodly (vv. 4-5)

**⁴ The ungodly are not so: but are like the chaff which the wind driveth away. ⁵ Therefore the ungodly shall not stand in the judgment, nor sinners in the congregation of the righteous.**

If the righteous are promised their leaf will not wither, then the ungodly stand in marked contrast as the wind will blow their efforts away. All their plans come to naught; they have no stability, no hopes for the future.

The reference to "judgment" (v. 5) does not refer only to the Day of Judgment, but also to the judging happening in the world today. While it seems the wicked prosper, ultimately the wages of sin must be paid. This judgment takes place in ways that most people do not recognize it as being divine; nonetheless, it is the judgment of God.

- What is the future of the ungodly person?

## D. Life-and-Death Patterns (v. 6)

**⁶ For the Lord knoweth the way of the righteous: but the way of the ungodly shall perish.**

The Hebrew word translated as *way* refers to "road, journey, manner, distance." It is used extensively in the Old Testament and found sixty-one times in the Psalms and sixty-seven times in Proverbs.

Notice the different verbs used in each of the two clauses. The idea of *knowing* the way of the righteous refers to God's personal knowledge of us and His care for us. That He knows our way of righteousness means He is actively involved with us.

However, that personal knowledge is absent with the ungodly. The way they walk is doomed to perish. The wicked will lose all they seek to gain by human effort.

The Bible deals with the concept of *perishing* in two ways. First, there is an unleashing of divine wrath on the ungodly in this lifetime. A second understanding of *perishing* is that of eternal damnation. The Bible clearly teaches that those who die in their sins are eternally lost. They are cut off from God forever.

---

- Are you traveling the right or the wrong way? How do you know?

> "The wicked are but as a book fairly bound which, when it is opened, is full of nothing but tragedies. So when the book of their consciences shall be once opened, there is nothing to be read but lamentations and woes."—Richard Sibbes

---

## II. AVOID SINFUL LIVING (Ps. 36:1-12)

### A. Lifestyle of the Wicked (vv. 1-4)

**¹ The transgression of the wicked saith within my heart, that there is no fear of God before his eyes. ² For he flattereth himself in his own eyes, until his iniquity be found to be hateful. ³ The words of his mouth are iniquity and deceit: he hath left off to be wise, and to do good. ⁴ He deviseth mischief upon his bed; he setteth himself in a way that is not good; he abhorreth not evil.**

When someone has no respect for God and His almighty power, there is nothing to keep that person from reaching the depths of evil. Instead of keeping God "before his eyes" (v. 1), this person "flatters himself in his own eyes" (v. 2 NKJV). "That is," observed Samuel Horsley, "he sets such a false gloss in his own eyes upon his worst actions, that he never finds out the blackness of his iniquity; which, were it perceived by him, would be hateful even to himself." Our contemporary world is filled with such people. Romans 1:28-31 describes them: "Even as they did not like to retain God in their knowledge, God gave them over to a debased mind, to do those things which are not fitting; being filled with all unrighteousness, sexual immorality, wickedness, covetousness, maliciousness; full of envy, murder, strife, deceit, evil-mindedness; they are whisperers, backbiters, haters of God, violent, proud, boasters, inventors of evil things, disobedient to parents, undiscerning, untrustworthy, unloving, unforgiving, unmerciful" (NKJV).

The wicked person described in Psalm 36 used "to be wise, and to do good" (v. 3), but he exchanged that lifestyle for "a sinful course and does not reject what is wrong" (v. 4 NIV). This man's sins are intentional—while laying awake in bed, he is plotting his next sinful acts—and his words are calculated to pervert others. This person's "conscience is deadened against evil: there is not a trace of aversion to it to be found in him, he loves it with all his soul" (*Keil and Delitzsch Commentary*).

- Describe the lifestyle of someone who does not fear God.

> "When we look at the ungodly, we are not to hate them, but to pity them, mourn over them, and pray for them. Nor have we any right to boast over them; for, by nature, and of ourselves, we are no better than they."—John Newton

B. God's Unfailing Love (vv. 5-9)

(Psalm 36:8-9 is not included in the printed text.)

**⁵ Thy mercy, O Lord, is in the heavens; and thy faithfulness reacheth unto the clouds. ⁶ Thy righteousness is like the great mountains; thy judgments are a great deep: O Lord, thou preservest man and beast. ⁷ How excellent is thy lovingkindness, O God! therefore the children of men put their trust under the shadow of thy wings.**

In these verses, the character of God is contrasted with the character of the wicked. First, God's mercy reaches to the heavens; otherwise, the wicked would be immediately destroyed. Second, even though we as God's children are living in a wicked world, God's faithfulness to us extends "to the skies" (v. 5 NIV).

God's "righteousness is like the great mountains" (v. 6)—strong, sure, unmovable. Meanwhile, His "judgments," or justice, like the ocean depths, is beyond our comprehension. Living in the middle of wickedness, we cannot grasp how God's justice will finally prevail, but His Word declares that He will one day set all things right. He cares for both "man and beast."

In verse 7, God is pictured as a loving mother bird spreading out her wings to protect her offspring. This image brings to mind Jesus' prayer in Matthew 23:37: "O Jerusalem, Jerusalem. . . ! How often I wanted to gather your children together, as a hen gathers her chicks under her wings, but you were not willing!" (NKJV).

If we will respond to God's call by drawing near to Him, He will satisfy us from His "river of delights" and "fountain of life," and His truth will light our life (Ps. 36:8-9 NIV). We will lead meaningful, purposeful, satisfying lives.

1. How are God's love, faithfulness, righteousness, and justice similar (vv. 5-6)?
2. Describe God's lack of prejudice (vv. 7-8).
3. Name two necessities God provides (v. 9).

> "God's unfailing love for us is an objective fact affirmed over and over in the Scriptures. It is true whether we believe it or not."—Jerry Bridges

## C. Fate of the Wicked (vv. 10-12)

(Psalm 36:11-12 is not included in the printed text.)

**¹⁰ O continue thy lovingkindness unto them that know thee; and thy righteousness to the upright in heart.**

David closes this psalm with a prayer. First, he asks God to continue pouring out His love on His children. We can offer such a prayer with complete assurance, for it is in perfect agreement with God's Word, which repeatedly declares God's unceasing love for His own. Even though Israel had rebelled against Him, the Lord declared, "Yes, I have loved you with an everlasting love; therefore with lovingkindness I have drawn you" (Jer. 31:3 NKJV).

Second, the psalmist asks God to show His gracious, righteous character to those whose heart is fixed on following Him (Ps. 36:10).

In verse 11, David prays for protection against the wicked people he described in this psalm's opening verses. By faith, he foresees their fate in verse 12: "The workers of iniquity have fallen: they have been cast down and are not able to rise" (NKJV).

- What does David ask of God?

## III. ESTABLISH GOD-CENTERED HOMES (Pss. 127:1-5; 128:1-6)

### A. The Home-Builder (127:1-2)

**¹ Except the Lord build the house, they labour in vain that build it: except the Lord keep the city, the watchman waketh but in vain. ² It is vain for you to rise up early, to sit up late, to eat the bread of sorrows: for so he giveth his beloved sleep.**

Three things are called *vain* in these verses: (1) building a house without the Lord's help; (2) guarding a city without the Lord's help; (3) working from dawn to dusk to provide for one's own needs while ignoring the Lord's helping hand.

The Hebrew word for *vain* means "emptiness, nothingness." Our efforts to build, protect, and provide will amount to nothing unless the Lord is our builder, protector, and provider. The positive news is that the Lord God can and will help us in these critical areas if we will lean on Him.

To "build the house" literally refers to the construction of any house. Symbolically, it can apply to the Lord's ministry within a family. Unless the Lord's presence provides the spiritual nails and mortar of a home, that family will have no lasting purpose or meaning. All its accomplishments will be in vain.

To "keep the city" was the job of the watchman staying awake and alert on the city walls or on a mountainside. If there were any signs of an invading force, his job was to sound the trumpet so the citizens could protect themselves. However, such protection would fail unless the Lord himself was watching over the city.

Similarly, human efforts to guard one's family against the never-ending onslaught of the world, the flesh, and the devil will end in failure. However, Isaiah 59:19 offers this promise to those who fear the Lord: "When the enemy comes in like a flood, the Spirit of the Lord will lift up a standard against him" (NKJV).

In ancient Israel, a *standard* was a banner that would be raised on a mountain to indicate a place of safety when an enemy was attacking. Today, in a world where evil spiritual forces are coming in like a flood, the only hope for family survival is to run to the Lord's banner.

The Lord not only protects; He also *gives sleep* (Ps. 127:2) to His children who rely on Him for provision. While we are obligated to work to provide for our families, we are not to work day and night, relying solely on our own abilities. Instead, if we will work with our hands while trusting the Lord with our heart, we can sleep at night, knowing that He promises to meet our needs.

- What do these verses teach about dependency on God?

> "A church in the house will be a good legacy, nay, it will be a good inheritance, to be left to your children after you."—Matthew Henry

B. The Gift of Children (vv. 3-5)

**³ Lo, children are an heritage of the Lord: and the fruit of the womb is his reward. ⁴ As arrows are in the hand of a mighty man; so are children of the youth. ⁵ Happy is the man that hath his quiver full of them: they shall not be ashamed, but they shall speak with the enemies in the gate.**

A high view of children is presented here. Instead of being seen as "accidents" or "burdens" or "surprises," as is too often the case in modern society, the psalmist presented the proper perspective on children—they come from the Lord.

"The word *heritage* (v. 3) suggests that children belong to God, and that He shares these precious possessions with parents," writes Roy Zuck (*Precious in His Sight*).

The word *reward* (v. 3) denotes "pleasure—something given as a tangible gift of appreciation . . . God's very personal trophy of His love" (Charles Swindoll, *Living Beyond the Daily Grind*).

While large families are often frowned upon today, verses 4 and 5 portray the presence of many children as a blessing from God. Just as arrows provide defense to an archer, so children born to a young couple can provide protection and security to the parents when they are elderly.

"The gate" (v. 5) was the place where legal disputes were heard. If a father was facing an unjust judge or false witnesses, the presence of several supportive sons might cause justice to prevail.

For us to have loyal and loving children who will bless us in our old age, we must receive them and treat them as an inheritance and reward from God.

1. How should parents view their children (v. 3)?
2. How are children like "arrows" (vv. 4-5)?

> "We know the excitement of getting a present—we love to unwrap it to see what is inside. So it is with our children; they are gifts we

unwrap for years as we discover the unique characters God has made them."—Cornelius Plantinga

---

C. Promised Rewards (128:1-4)

¹ **Blessed is every one that feareth the Lord; that walketh in his ways.** ² **For thou shalt eat the labour of thine hands: happy shalt thou be, and it shall be well with thee.** ³ **Thy wife shall be as a fruitful vine by the sides of thine house: thy children like olive plants round about thy table.** ⁴ **Behold, that thus shall the man be blessed that feareth the Lord.**

Genuine *fear* ("reverence") of the Lord is evidenced by our lifestyle. If we reverence Him, we will walk "in his ways" (v. 1).

Verses 2 and 3 contain four specific blessings God delights in giving those who lead lives of obedience to Him:

1. *"You will eat the fruit of your labor"* (NIV). God will grant employment that is sufficient to meet the needs of one's family, not allowing the provider to labor in vain. Solomon wrote, "Then I realized that it is good and proper for a man to . . . find satisfaction in his toilsome labor under the sun during the few days of life God has given him—for this is his lot" (Eccl. 5:18 NIV).

2. *"Blessings and prosperity will be yours"* (NIV). God delights both in meeting His children's basic needs and in prospering His own. It is a testimony to unbelievers when they see Christians leading holy, happy, and generous lives.

3. *"Your wife will be like a fruitful vine within your house"* (NIV). God will bless the ministry of the mother as she cares for her family. She will find deep gratification in serving at home.

4. *"Your sons will be like olive shoots around your table"* (NIV). The *Pulpit Commentary* says: "It is a common sight, in the lands where the olive grows, to see the parent tree surrounded, and, as it were, sustained, by the young olive shoots that have sprung from its roots. As they have sprung from the parent root, so they are like their parent, and they gather round, as the children do round the table at home. The godly man will be blessed in his children: their father's God will be their God; they will be as their father, and will pass on the fear of the Lord, which they first learned from him."

D. Prayer of Blessings (vv. 5-6)

⁵ **The Lord shall bless thee out of Zion: and thou shalt see the good of Jerusalem all the days of thy life.** ⁶ **Yea, thou shalt see thy children's children, and peace upon Israel.**

Zion was one of the hills of Jerusalem. Because the Jews viewed Zion as God's dwelling place on earth, they thought all blessing flowed from there.

The believer's "Zion" is Jesus Christ. It is through one's relationship with Him that a believer can expect to receive the blessings of God. "For no matter how many promises God has made, they are 'Yes' in Christ" (2 Cor. 1:20 NIV).

"The good of Jerusalem" (Ps. 128:5) meant good for the people of God. If Jerusalem was prospering, the people of Israel were prospering. Similarly, if the believer's relationship with Christ is prospering, all areas of his or her life will be blessed.

Living to see one's grandchildren is a special blessing—especially when the young are serving the God of their grandparents. There is no greater blessing than seeing our children and their children follow the Christ we love. It is the promise of Pentecost, as declared by Peter: "For the promise is unto you, and to your children, and to all that are afar off, even as many as the Lord our God shall call" (Acts 2:39).

## CONCLUSION

We should order our lives according to the Bible because it is a timeless book. Being eternal, the Bible is neither bound nor worn by time. Buildings decay, bodies become frail, and strength is exhausted, but time cannot harm God's Word in any way.

Even though the Bible was written many centuries ago, it is not outdated. Its message is for our world as much as it was for the ancient world. The Bible is for all time, every generation, every day.

## GOLDEN TEXT CHALLENGE

"BLESSED IS EVERY ONE THAT FEARETH THE LORD; THAT WALKETH IN HIS WAYS" (Ps. 128:1).

"Those who are truly happy. . . . To all saints universally: Blessed is everyone that fears the Lord, whoever he be; in every nation he that fears God and works righteousness is accepted of Him, and therefore is blessed whether he be high or low, rich or poor."—**Matthew Henry**

### Daily Devotions:

M. Seduced by Ungodly Wisdom
   Genesis 3:1-7
T. The Beginning of Wisdom
   Psalm 111:1-10
W. The Beginning of Knowledge
   Proverbs 1:1-7
T. The Wise and Foolish Builders
   Luke 6:46-49
F. Christ, the Wisdom of God
   1 Corinthians 1:18-25
S. Ask God for Wisdom
   James 1:5-8

July 5, 2015 (Lesson 5)
# Covenant Psalms
### Psalms 81:8-16; 78:1-8; 89:1-18

**Theme:**
Different Types of Psalms

**Central Truth:**
Living in fellowship with God requires obedience to Him.

**Focus:**
Clarify requirements of covenant with God and live in fellowship with Him.

**Context:**
Three psalms concerning God's covenant with His people

**Golden Text:**
"He [God] established a testimony in Jacob, and appointed a law in Israel, which he commanded our fathers, that they should make them known to their children" (Ps. 78:5).

**Study Outline:**
I. Serve God Only
   (Ps. 81:8-16)
II. Celebrate God's Faithfulness
   (Ps. 89:1-18)
III. Teach Truth to Succeeding Generations
   (Ps. 78:1-8)

## INTRODUCTION

We are accustomed to approaching the Bible in two chief sections: the Old Testament and the New Testament. These designations are not found in the biblical texts themselves. Christians have added these titles to make sense of the overall breakdown of the Scriptures. This began in the early third century AD when the church father Tertullian referred to "two testaments of the law and the gospel" in his description of the Bible. What are we to make of this title for the Holy Scriptures?

Perhaps the best way to understand the last twenty-seven books of the Bible as a "New Testament" is to consider that title alongside another frequently used one—*covenant*. This interplay is found in Jeremiah 31:31 (cited in Heb. 8:8), where God promises to "make a new covenant with the house of Israel." The Greek word for *covenant*, *diatheke*, also translates as *testament* and *will* (as in a "contractual will"). Therefore, we refer to the New Testament also as the "New Covenant."

The late Christian author Henri Nouwen notes, "The Lord did not establish a contract with His people, but a covenant" (*Creative Ministry*). God's people (from

Israel to the Church) understood themselves to be a people brought into being by God's covenant with them. This is why the constitution of the people of God changes with Jesus' death: "This cup is the new covenant in my blood, which is poured out for you" (Luke 22:20 NIV).

## I. SERVE GOD ONLY (Ps. 81:8-16)

Moses received the Ten Commandments from God on Mount Sinai after the children of Israel were freed from Egyptian bondage. The Ten Commandments were meant to function as their national constitution and spiritual manifesto. Unsurprisingly, then, the first commandment is arguably the most memorable: "You shall have no other gods before me" (Ex. 20:3 NIV). Although God is direct in this command and its subsequent prohibition of idolatry, the command is not cold or abstract. And, it certainly does not belie an indifferent God! We see this in the fact that Israel's commitment to the exclusive worship of the God of the Exodus is being celebrated in their worship songs, particularly in Psalm 81.

### A. "Hear, O Israel!" (vv. 8-10)

**⁸ Hear, O my people, and I will testify unto thee: O Israel, if thou wilt hearken unto me; ⁹ There shall no strange god be in thee; neither shalt thou worship any strange god. ¹⁰ I am the Lord thy God, which brought thee out of the land of Egypt: open thy mouth wide, and I will fill it.**

The most significant prayer in the life of the Jewish community, both ancient and contemporary, is called the *Shema*. This prayer (confession of faith) continues to be spoken aloud each day by faithful Jews (and many Christians) around the world. *Shema* is the Hebrew word for "hear" (v. 8), and this word alone has come to characterize the central commandment of the Old Testament, found in Deuteronomy 6:4ff: "Hear, O Israel: The Lord our God, the Lord is one. Love the Lord your God with all your heart and with all your soul and with all your strength" (NIV). The *Shema* was so central to the life of the nation of Israel that even Jesus agreed to its value as the greatest commandment (see Matt. 22:35-38; Mark 12:29-30). The Jewish community knows what to expect at the outset of the command to "hear!" This is what makes Psalm 81 so surprising.

The familiar command to "hear" leaves the worshiper with the expectation of *Shema*. The *Shema* represents a person's proper responsibility to love God. In this case, however, God is getting the attention of Israel. He does not want them to remember to love Him. He wants them to listen to His own testimony! He commands them to *hear* because He has something specific to tell them.

That divine testimony begins with the second of the Ten Commandments. After the first, demanding that no other gods be before Yahweh, God demands that no idol be created in Yahweh's supposed image. The temptation was great for Israel to imagine and to sculpt God as a bull, eagle, and predator, and we see the curse of idolatry enshrouding the nation at differing points of Old Testament history. Idolatry was, for example, the perpetual problem of the kings. *Why not cover all of the divine bases?* the people thought. God, however, demands exclusive worship of the mystery of His being—a mystery maintained until the revelation of Jesus Christ. The Son of God would later proclaim, "I am the way, the truth, and the life" (John 14:6).

In the Old Testament, the gods of surrounding Canaanite peoples were non-existent, or lesser (see Ps. 82:1). The apostle Paul deals with this same situation centuries later in Corinth, reminding the new Christians that "an idol is nothing at all in the world" (1 Cor. 8:4 NIV). Yet idols still matter, because they assault the exclusive covenant God has made with His people. And Paul further says "the sacrifices of pagans are offered to demons" (10:20 NIV).

In Psalm 81:10, God demands the exclusive worship of His people because of His covenant with them. This verse begins with one of the most common divine sayings in the Old Testament. It occurs particularly in the Book of Leviticus, where it justifies the stringent commandments of God. This balance is necessary; for this covenantal history God has with His people identifies the character of God as infinitely self-giving. God longs for His children to ask Him to meet their needs! Jesus said, "Which of you fathers, if your son asks for a fish, will give him a snake instead? . . . How much more will your Father in heaven give . . . ?" (Luke 11:11, 13 NIV).

- What had God prohibited (vv. 8-9), and what had He promised (v. 10)?

### One God

One of the foremost threats to early Christian teaching was Marcionism. Marcion was a heretical teacher who believed the God of the old covenant was not the same God and Father of our Lord Jesus Christ. An early church father, Tertullian, criticized the views of Marcion in his book, *Against Heresies*, contending that Marcion seeks to "separate Christ from the Creator." It is important to realize that the Old Testament does not contain a "lesser version" of God. Instead, both God and Christ are present in the old covenant, as illustrated in the Psalms.

B. Covenantal History Threatened (vv. 11-12)

**11 But my people would not hearken to my voice; and Israel would none of me. 12 So I gave them up unto their own hearts' lust: and they walked in their own counsels.**

The history of Israel's covenant with God is sketchy at best. At times, Israel maintains the covenant. Too often, however, they fall short. This is the trajectory of the entire Old Testament narrative, which is built around Israel's exile to Assyria and to Babylon. Most scholars believe the Old Testament began to attain its present form as Jewish leaders re-constructed their identity as Jews in the Exile. Because it is such a central event in the Old Testament, psalmists often built worship songs around its remembrance.

The psalmist here remembers the Psalter's opening, perhaps the most famous psalm for the ancient Hebrew people: "Blessed is the man that walketh not in the counsel of the ungodly" (1:1). Sadly, God accuses His people of breaking the words of their own songbook (81:11). They chose the counsel of the wicked over the voice of God, giving Him up.

God's response, which is common in the Old Testament, is to give the nation over to their national and personal stubborn devices (v. 12). This verse suggests that God allows humanity to make a definitive choice and to reap the consequence of that choice. We find this construction most famously in Romans 1. Faced with a sin-soaked world, God "gave them over to a depraved mind" (v. 28 NIV). We see this same motif throughout the Psalms.

- How did God cause Israel to suffer, and why (vv. 11-12)?

### C. Return to the Covenant (vv. 13-16)

(Psalm 81:14-16 is not included in the printed text.)

**13 Oh that my people had hearkened unto me, and Israel had walked in my ways!**

Although verses 11-12 walk the worshiper through Israel's dark history of disobedience and exile, despair is not the final word. There is always a divine "if," a divine yearning, in the covenant between God and His people!

While the Western view of God imagines Him to be old, emotionless, static, even indifferent—seen as an old man, bearded, with a gavel at a judge's bench—this is not the picture of the God of the Bible. Instead, God longs that His history with Israel had been different; He longs for them to take a step. He is filled with passion for His people. When they do repent and return, He promises to reverse the fate of the Exile, subdue their enemies, and satisfy His people's every need (vv. 14-16).

Psalm 81 is, then, a microcosm of the entire story of God and His people in the Old Testament. It moves from the Ten Commandments, to the Exile, to the promise of return. We can imagine the yearning of a people singing such a psalm far from home. In this psalm, the children of Israel found hope in a faraway land, remembering the God who delivered them from Egypt. Truly, He never changes.

- What did God long to do (vv. 13-16)?

> "If you think you can walk in holiness without keeping up perpetual fellowship with Christ, you have made a great mistake. If you would be holy, you must live close to Jesus."—Charles Spurgeon

## II. CELEBRATE GOD'S FAITHFULNESS (Ps. 89:1-18)

Israel's remembrance of God's faithful covenant evoked praise. This praise takes many forms in the Psalms, including clapping, shouting, dancing, and the playing of various musical instruments. In Psalm 89, the worshipers of Israel are led to sing of God's covenant love forever. Therefore, this psalm should be classified as a worshipful remembrance of Israel's history with her God.

## A. Declaration of Worship (vv. 1-2)

**¹ I will sing of the mercies of the Lord for ever: with my mouth will I make known thy faithfulness to all generations. ² For I have said, Mercy shall be built up for ever: thy faithfulness shalt thou establish in the very heavens.**

There is tremendous emphasis in the Old Testament Scripture, especially the Book of Psalms, on vocal worship. Ancient societies did not hold the modern tendency toward introspection and quietness. Activity had to be public to be considered valid. No activity could be more public than singing and vocally praising! Israel's worship reflects this culture in Psalm 89.

What will the psalmist sing about? As the text puts it, "the mercies of the Lord." This English phrase translates one of the most important words in the whole of Hebrew vocabulary. *Hesed*, often translated into English as "mercies" or "love," is difficult to capture into any other language than Hebrew. This is because in Hebrew culture, *hesed* cannot be separated from God's covenant. It is not love in the abstract or disjointed sense, but the love that is particular to the God of Israel and the relationship that He alone has established with His people. It is solely a divine quality, the covenantal love that is at the heart of God's divine nature.

Alongside God's *hesed* is His "faithfulness." The psalm acknowledges that God has been faithful, consistent, and trustworthy. How is this principally known? Once again, through God's *hesed* (v. 2), which stands firm forever. Moreover, God's covenantal love and faithfulness are not limited to the scope of earthly time and space. They have been established in the heavens. That is, God's love and faithfulness are committed to the entire span of creation throughout all eternity.

---

- Describe the psalmist's song.

> "God loves to hear your singing—so sing."—Rod Parsley

---

## B. Declaration by God (vv. 3-4)

**³ I have made a covenant with my chosen, I have sworn unto David my servant, ⁴ Thy seed will I establish for ever, and build up thy throne to all generations. Selah.**

Not only do people praise God in the Psalms, but God also speaks to His people. In this psalm, God's voice illuminates the historical characteristics of this covenant. He funnels His general love toward the specific line of David.

This passage calls us toward the knowledge of the eternal breadth of God's covenant. Biblical scholar N. T. Wright calls the covenant "the single-plan-through-Israel-for-the-world that was called into being by God as the means of addressing and solving the plight of the whole world" (*Justification: God's Plan and Paul's Vision*).

First, the covenant gave to the Hebrew people their self-identity and their means of conceptualizing their relationship with the world around them. The covenant is their community manifesto. Second, the covenant gave to the Hebrew people the mission of Abraham, to bless "all peoples on earth" (Gen. 12:3 NIV).

Third, the covenant climaxed with the Davidic monarchy, in which God and His word were nationally prioritized (albeit with a few failures). Fourth, the covenant continued through the Messiah, who came through the line of David. And so, Jesus is "the son of David" in the opening of the New Testament (Matt. 1:1).

What remarkable faith in God's eternal works is found in this psalm! The writer reminds God of His words that the Davidic covenant is everlasting. This functions as a commentary on God's proclamation in 2 Samuel 7:16: "Your house and your kingdom will endure forever before me; your throne will be established forever" (NIV). Within the theme of reminding God of His promises, the Psalms appropriate them for all peoples, then and now.

---

- Describe the covenant God made.

> "God's love is the most awesome thing about Him. It is not His justice, nor His majesty, nor even His blazing holiness, but the fact that He has made and keeps a covenant of personal commitment and love to His people."—Sinclair B. Ferguson

---

C. Declaration of Nature (vv. 5-18)

(Psalm 89:8-18 is not included in the printed text.)

**⁵ And the heavens shall praise thy wonders, O Lord: thy faithfulness also in the congregation of the saints. ⁶ For who in the heaven can be compared unto the Lord? who among the sons of the mighty can be likened unto the Lord? ⁷ God is greatly to be feared in the assembly of the saints, and to be had in reverence of all them that are about him.**

Frequently in the Psalms, God is *experienced* in nature. This should not be confused with *equating* God with nature, a view known as *pantheism*. Indeed, the Creation story of Genesis stands staunchly opposed to any such "New Age" interpretation. The biblical view is this: While God is the Creator (the agent who stands outside of His creation), the Creation is a signpost pointing the way to His divine qualities. It is this function that Psalm 89:5-13 captures so eloquently.

Not only do earthly beings praise the Lord, but so also do the heavens (vv. 5-6). We must not conceive of heaven as a place in space, connected to the afterlife alone. To "lift eyes to the heavens" in Hebrew consciousness was indeed to look up at the sky. But this was not meant to suggest that God was distant or far away. Instead, the heavens were the domain of God, constantly overlapping with the earth through Temple, Torah, and covenant. The heavenly beings of the sky—the sun, moon, clouds, winds, and stars—are declared to be harbingers of God's wonders. So then, the congregation of the holy ones joins in the praise chorus. For there is no one like the Lord in all of the heavens, not even among the heavenly beings!

In verse 7, the "assembly of the saints" can be translated "council of the holy ones" (NIV)—likely a reference to angels. Yahweh rules the council of the other sacred ones. Interestingly, this is essentially the way even Satan functions in the

Old Testament—presenting himself before God along with the holy angels (see Job 1–2). All powers are subject to the rule of the God of Israel.

When this great truth is realized—that Yahweh rules over the divine council—the psalmist lists more witnesses to God's power. Not only the heavens and the divine beings, but the seas and waves also remind us of God's rule (v. 9). The oceans declare His greatness. The fact that creation even exists, at God's founding will, reminds us of God's rule (v. 11). The existence of north and south—an order to the creation—reminds us of God's rule (v. 12). The acceptance of such a wondrous God leads to nothing less than *joy* (v. 16), *strength* (v. 17), and *security* (v. 18). The writer closes the section by declaring that the very protection, or shield, of Israel is in the hands of the Lord. They trust that He will not let them falter or fail.

---

1. Answer the questions in verses 6 and 8.
2. Describe God's power to rule (vv. 9-10).
3. What does God own, and why (v. 11)?
4. What is God's authority founded on, and what attends Him (v. 14)?
5. Describe the favor God's people enjoy (vv. 15-18).

---

III. TEACH TRUTH TO SUCCEEDING GENERATIONS (Ps. 78:1-8)

Ancient Hebrew education took various forms. At some point in their history, formal sorts of "schools" developed in which young students were professionally taught in systematic ways. After the Temple was destroyed, synagogues became institutions for both formal and informal education. We know that Pharisees taught the *Torah*—the first five books of the Bible—orally to the illiterate population of Israel, numbering in the vast majority. However, the Jews had a particular focus on the role of parents and of worship in educating the next generation. The famed *Shema* reminds parents to "impress [these commands] on your children. Talk about them when you sit at home" (Deut. 6:7 NIV). Through a lifestyle of worship, parents were instructed and expected to pass on the truth of God to succeeding generations. This is quite apparent in the worshipful Psalm 78.

A. Proverbs and Parables (vv. 1-4)

¹ **Give ear, O my people, to my law: incline your ears to the words of my mouth.** ² **I will open my mouth in a parable: I will utter dark sayings of old:** ³ **Which we have heard and known, and our fathers have told us.** ⁴ **We will not hide them from their children, shewing to the generation to come the praises of the Lord, and his strength, and his wonderful works that he hath done.**

Most psalms begin with either an exclamation of praise, a request for help, or a soulful lament. Psalm 78 surprises us with an uncommon opening, reminding us more of Solomon's proverbs than the typical psalm. After telling the readers to "give ear" (v. 1), the psalmist refers to parables and wise sayings that have been passed down from generation to generation (vv. 2-3). This leads the writer to fall in line with those fathers (v. 4). Because the truths of God's Word can be stifled only by silence, the psalmist promises to pass on the faith to the next generation. The revelation of God is made known through the teachings of Israel's fathers to their children.

- How are both hearing and telling responsibilities of God's people?

> "If you neglect to instruct [your children] in the way of holiness, will the devil neglect to instruct them in the way of wickedness? No; if you will not teach them to pray, he will [teach them] to curse, swear, and lie; if ground be uncultivated, weeds will spring."—John Flavel

### B. Hope for Future Generations (vv. 5-8)

(Psalm 78:7-8 is not included in the printed text.)

**5 For he established a testimony in Jacob, and appointed a law in Israel, which he commanded our fathers, that they should make them known to their children: 6 That the generation to come might know them, even the children which should be born; who should arise and declare them to their children.**

Israel's curriculum for passing on the faith to future generations was always built around storytelling. Jewish parents were not just teaching a doctrinal catechism to their children. They were not talking about the divine in the abstract. No, they were charged to tell their children about their particular personal and national history with this God.

What do children need to know about Israel's God? They need to know about Jacob and the patriarchs. They need to know about the giving of the Torah on Mount Sinai and how it was meant to shape the nation to be a light of justice and peace. It is only when these precepts are unleashed to reach generations to come that their ultimate power and effectiveness are seen.

1. What is God's plan for continuing the faith?
2. Does verse 8 aptly describe our world? Why or why not?

### CONCLUSION

Deuteronomy 7:9 declares the Lord as "the faithful God, keeping his covenant of love to a thousand generations" (NIV). Truly, the God revealed in the Bible is a God of covenant. He made a covenant with Noah to never again destroy creation. He made a covenant with Abraham to bless all the peoples of the earth. And He made a covenant with us, through the blood of Christ, to forever save all who call on His name.

### GOLDEN TEXT CHALLENGE

"HE [GOD] ESTABLISHED A TESTIMONY IN JACOB, AND APPOINTED A LAW IN ISRAEL, WHICH HE COMMANDED OUR FATHERS, THAT THEY SHOULD MAKE THEM KNOWN TO THEIR CHILDREN" (Ps. 78:5).

The "testimony" and the "law" of God are to be made known to each generation. *Testimony* means "witness," and probably refers to the Ten Commandments. Those ten laws were "established"—*raised up* as a witness rises to speak—as a covenant between God and His chosen people.

Even as the testimony was established, so the law was "appointed." The "law" refers to the first five books of the Old Testament (the Torah), given to show how God's covenant love was to be precisely followed in daily life.

Are we teaching our children the commands and laws of God?

## Daily Devotions:

M. God Makes Covenant With Abraham
 Genesis 15:12-18
T. Moses Reminded of God's Covenant
 Exodus 6:1-8
W. Israel Transgresses God's Covenant
 Judges 2:14-23
T. Covenant Extended to All People
 Romans 11:25-32
F. No Longer Strangers
 Ephesians 2:11-22
S. Jesus Institutes a Better Covenant
 Hebrews 8:6-10

July 12, 2015 (Lesson 6)
# Psalms of Ascent

**Psalms 121:1-8; 122:1-9; 130:1-8; 131:1-3**

**Theme:**
Different Types of Psalms

**Central Truth:**
Christians should prepare their hearts to worship God.

**Focus:**
Rehearse Israel's songs of ascent and worship God with gladness.

**Context:**
Various songs of pilgrimage

**Golden Text:**
"I was glad when they said unto me, Let us go into the house of the Lord" (Ps. 122:1).

**Study Outline:**
  I. Trust Divine Protection
     (Ps. 121:1-8)
 II. Joy Over Jerusalem
     (Ps. 122:1-9)
III. Hope in the Lord
     (Ps. 130:1-8; 131:1-3)

## INTRODUCTION

Out of the 150 worship songs that comprise the Psalter (Psalms), fifteen carry the designation, "a psalm/song of ascents." These songs of ascents are found in Psalms 120-134, and they fulfilled a very significant function in the life of the ancient Hebrew people. These psalms were part of the faithful Jews' pilgrimage to Jerusalem for the great festivals of their calendar year.

The Old Testament commitment to a weekly Sabbath was remarkably radical in its time. It is easy to take the concept of Sabbath for granted in the modern world, where "weekends" are a part of our cultural rhythm. The ancient world knew no such automatic time off from the regular workday. In fact, by the New Testament period the Jews were renowned throughout the Roman Empire for the novelty of the Sabbath. As if the weekly Sabbath were not countercultural enough, God added on much more obligatory time away from work. These were the great feasts, such as Tabernacles and Passover, that the Jews were to celebrate (see Ex. 23:14-17; 34:22-24). Some scholars suggest that observant Jews spent two to three months each year simply celebrating the festivals of God!

These festivals took place in Jerusalem, for all who could afford to travel there. We see the habit of festival attendance in the life of Jesus, first as an adolescent at Passover (Luke 2:41) and then later as an adult (John 7:10; 10:22). The Gospel of John particularly builds the story of Jesus around His attendance at various feasts. These festivals were events of national celebration, remembrance, and pride. They were the pinnacle of elevating Hebrew culture. Out of that elevation came the Psalms of Ascent.

The psalms were sung, perhaps even in order, by the pilgrims making the journey to Jerusalem. Since Jerusalem was topographically the highest city in the land, these psalms were meant to lift the spirits of the worshipers toward God and His holy city in conjunction with their physical steps. The Psalms of Ascent were a fountain of joy for worshipers gathering in Jerusalem to celebrate the goodness of God.

## I. TRUST DIVINE PROTECTION (Ps. 121:1-8)

The fact that the children of Israel existed to sing psalms was reason enough to trust God. The children of Israel had a nation, a holy city, and a temple; all these were reasons enough to trust God. After all, could there ever be a more persecuted people than the tiny Jewish nation? "The Lord did not set his affection on you and choose you because you were more numerous than other peoples, for you were the fewest of all peoples" (Deut. 7:7 NIV). Today, the Psalms of Ascent vocally celebrate the reality that even within their terrible history of captivity by Egypt, Assyria, Babylon, Persia, and Rome, God has preserved His people. He has preserved them to worship Him.

### A. A Proper Focus (vv. 1-4)

**1 I will lift up mine eyes unto the hills, from whence cometh my help. 2 My help cometh from the Lord, which made heaven and earth. 3 He will not suffer thy foot to be moved: he that keepeth thee will not slumber. 4 Behold, he that keepeth Israel shall neither slumber nor sleep.**

The Psalms of Ascent are decidedly upbeat, optimistic, and positive. This positivity, however, should not be considered in the light of modern psychology. God's people are not attempting to be positive to improve their psychological or emotional health. No, the optimism of these psalms is rooted not in the emotional state of the worshiper, but in the character of the God of Israel. Because of this fact, Psalm 121 begins by ordering that a proper focus be set on God himself.

Verse 1 does not portray the general concept of "lifting my eyes to the heavens," although this is biblical. Here, the psalmist's focus is literal. As the worshipers travel to Jerusalem, the elevation moves upward. They are climbing Palestinian hills to their top, where Jerusalem lies. So, to focus on "the hills" is to focus on the destination of the pilgrimage—Jerusalem.

This verse also plays on the centrality of Jerusalem in the life of the Israelites' faith. The Lord, the Creator of heaven and earth, is especially present at the top of Jerusalem's hill. It is this tradition, solidified in the Old Testament, that Jesus seems to change in John 4:21, 23: "A time is coming when you will worship the Father neither on this mountain nor in Jerusalem. . . . A time is coming and has now come when the true worshipers will worship the Father in spirit and truth, for they are the kind of worshipers the Father seeks" (NIV). Jesus grew up knowing and singing the Psalms of Ascent on His journeys to Jerusalem. (What a sobering thought to imagine these songs as Jesus moved toward the day of His triumphal entry!) Yet, by presenting Himself as the replacement of the Temple,

Jesus redirects the worship of the Psalms toward the "God [and] Father of our Lord Jesus Christ" (2 Cor. 1:3).

When the psalmist's focus is drawn toward the God of Jerusalem, which is also the destination of the pilgrimage, the personality and qualities of God quickly come into view.

Psalm 121:3-4 is reminiscent of its more famous counterpart in 91:11-12—a messianic prophecy that the devil quotes to Jesus in the wilderness: "You will not strike your foot against a stone" (Matt. 4:6 NIV). The same idea is here, but not in a messianic sense. Beautifully, these words apply not to the Christ, but to every common worshiper.

Besides focusing on Jerusalem as the city of God and the place of the festival, the psalmist notes that from there, God keeps all of Israel. God is not solely looking out for Jerusalem, giving Him plenty of time to sleep. He keeps the entire nation in His ever-present care.

---

1. What question does the psalmist raise, and how does he answer it (vv. 1-2 NKJV)?
2. What truth is repeated in verses 3 and 4, and why is it encouraging?

---

### Travel Song

In his book *Little Prayers and Finite Experience*, Paul Goodman captures the spirit of Ascent Psalms:

> On the high road to death
> Trudging, not eager to get
> > To that city, yet the way is
> > Still too long for my patience.
>
> Teach me a travel song,
> Master, to march along
> > As we boys used to shout
> > When I was a young scout.

The Ascent Psalms are indeed "travel songs" meant to keep us close to our Master, regardless of where the highway takes us.

---

B. God's Focus (vv. 5-8)

**⁵ The Lord is thy keeper: the Lord is thy shade upon thy right hand. ⁶ The sun shall not smite thee by day, nor the moon by night. ⁷ The Lord shall preserve thee from all evil: he shall preserve thy soul. ⁸ The Lord shall preserve thy going out and thy coming in from this time forth, and even for evermore.**

The imagery of this psalm plays on ancient Hebrew folk culture in specific ways. First, ancient Israel was a peasant agrarian culture. That is, over 80 percent of the population worked their own small plots of land as farmers. They well knew the heat of the day under the Palestinian sun during planting season.

It could sap them of their strength before the work was done. Therefore, God is their shade, their relief from the toil of their labor, and their deliverer unto the bountiful harvest.

Second, God is the protector of Israel against the sun and moon. Although this sounds strange to modern ears, fears of astrological disasters were common in the ancient world. In fact, ancient peoples often considered the sun and the moon to be deities that must be appeased. God announces He will have none of this superstition. Nothing from the natural or the spirit realms can smite His people. He is their shade from the sun; their protection during the day and night.

Finally, Psalm 121 concludes with a geographical note similarly to its introductory thoughts. The psalm celebrates the fact that God's protection is not limited to Jerusalem during the festival! Even when the festival is long gone, on their way back to their homes, God remains the same God, watchful and protective over His people. He preserves their coming and going, even forever. This truth reminds us of the promise of Jesus: "Surely I am with you always, to the very end of the age" (Matt. 28:20 NIV).

---

1. Have you found the Lord to be "your keeper" (v. 5 NKJV)? If so, how?
2. How does the Lord preserve His children (vv. 7-8)?

> "To believe that He will preserve us is, indeed, a means of preservation."—John Owen

---

## II. JOY OVER JERUSALEM (Ps. 122:1-9)

Psalm 122 marks an important step in the journey through the Psalms of Ascent. This is because it is the first such psalm to be authored by King David. David (and his son Solomon) presided over the "golden age" of Israel from his palace in Jerusalem. We should expect that he would leave behind evidence of his affection for the city that would come to be associated with his name: the "city of David." However, David's psalms of ascent are not simply anthems of nationalism, nor are they political statements. They are theological treatises, built around the worship and understanding of the God who blessed Israel and chose Jerusalem to make His name known among the nations.

### A. The Temple of the Lord (vv. 1-5)

**¹ I was glad when they said unto me, Let us go into the house of the Lord. ² Our feet shall stand within thy gates, O Jerusalem. ³ Jerusalem is builded as a city that is compact together: ⁴ Whither the tribes go up, the tribes of the Lord, unto the testimony of Israel, to give thanks unto the name of the Lord. ⁵ For there are set thrones of judgment, the thrones of the house of David.**

In Old Testament thought, Jerusalem is God's chosen city because God's temple is there. However, it is also important to remember that God chose

Jerusalem to be the "city of David" (and, therefore, of God) before the Temple was built. Yet, David's willingness to build the Temple in Jerusalem meant his name would always be synonymous with the city. He lamented, "Here I am, living in a palace of cedar, while the ark of God remains in a tent" (2 Sam. 7:2 NIV). God's response was to promise to keep the kingdom of God's people within David's lineage: "Your house and your kingdom will endure forever before me; your throne will be established forever" (v. 16 NIV).

The foreground of this psalm is the temple of God. The Temple gives to Jerusalem her meaning and her significance. Only after David expresses his longing for the Temple is Jerusalem introduced. The purpose of traveling within the gates of Jerusalem is, of course, to travel all the way to the Temple. The gates of Jerusalem are simply a step toward the greater destination of God's dwelling place.

In the same way that the gates of Jerusalem led toward the Temple, the Temple led to something of greater significance. The Temple led to God, of course, but also to His specific, biblical plan for the entire world. As N. T. Wright explains:

> The Temple was never supposed to be a retreat away from the world, a safe holy place where one might stay secure in God's presence, shut off from the wickedness outside. The Temple was an advance sign of what God intended to do with and for the whole creation. When God filled the house with His presence, that was a sign and a foretaste of His ultimate intention, which was to flood the whole world with His glory, presence, and love (*After You Believe*).

It is only when we comprehend this tremendous place of the Temple in the overall theology of the Old Testament that Psalm 122 can be viewed in balance. The point of the Temple was never the Temple! This was also the cry of the prophets: "Do not trust in deceptive words and say, 'This is the temple of the Lord, the temple of the Lord, the temple of the Lord!'" (Jer. 7:4 NIV). The point of the Temple was to be one of divine intersection with the earth, so God could make known His purposes for the whole of creation.

The point of the Temple—the point of Israel—was to bless all the peoples of the earth by way of their commitment to God. This was God's promise to Abraham, the first and ideal Jew (Gen. 12:3). The trajectory of Psalm 122 is not to laud Israel as God's prized possession, but to challenge Israel to become the example for other nations that God desires.

In verses 3-5, reference is made to the Torah's commandments to celebrate national festivals. However, Jerusalem is not simply divinely sanctioned, regardless of her actions. Instead, Israel is accountable to the judgment of God and of the righteous legacy of David. At any point in her Old Testament history, Israel must be compared to that high standard.

---

- What should make us glad, and why?

> "We need to discover all over again that worship is natural to the Christian, as it was to the godly Israelites who wrote the Psalms, and

that the habit of celebrating the greatness and graciousness of God yields an endless flow of thankfulness, joy, and zeal."—J. I. Packer

---

### B. Shalom in Jerusalem (vv. 6-9)

**6 Pray for the peace of Jerusalem: they shall prosper that love thee. 7 Peace be within thy walls, and prosperity within thy palaces. 8 For my brethren and companions' sakes, I will now say, Peace be within thee. 9 Because of the house of the Lord our God I will seek thy good.**

There are a few words in the Hebrew vocabulary that highlight the most intrinsic Old Testament values. We might call these terms Israel's linguistic and theological "headliners." Among them is *justice*, *blessed*, and *covenant love*. The latter half of Psalm 122 is built around a fourth Hebrew headliner—*peace*.

The Hebrew word translated *peace* is *shalom*. *Shalom* is so central to the Hebrew vocabulary that it is the first word of the resurrected Jesus to His disciples: "Peace be with you!" (John 20:21 NIV). Jesus' usage of the word is rooted in the Old Testament, where it plays a prominent role in the Psalms of Ascent.

We can imagine the festival worshipers ascending the hills toward Jerusalem, their prayers turning toward the city of their affection. David's prayer is not for war or dissension, but for perfect peace. He knows this peace cannot come from treaties, but only from God.

The psalm ends where it begins, with a focus on Jerusalem as the city that holds the temple of God. Jerusalem is special in Old Testament theology because of nothing else but God, pure and simple. This calls on the festive worshipers to divulge any impediment between themselves and God. The Temple's presence in Jerusalem demands admiration, worship . . . and sober accountability.

---

1. How did David pray for Jerusalem, and why?
2. How and why should we pray for Israel?

> "God is beckoning to Christian believers to come alongside the people of Israel—praying for them, blessing them, and comforting them."—Michael Utterback

---

## III. HOPE IN THE LORD (Pss. 130:1-8; 131:1-3)

Not all of the Psalms of Ascent are purely festive. Because pilgrimage was a sacred experience of worship, we should expect that some of Israel's pilgrimage songs would include introspective qualities. We meet such qualities in Psalms 130 and 131, which give us new insights into the power of these ancient songs of praise.

### A. Sin and Forgiveness (130:1-4)

**1 Out of the depths have I cried unto thee, O Lord. 2 Lord, hear my voice: let thine ears be attentive to the voice of my supplications. 3 If thou, Lord,**

shouldest mark iniquities, O Lord, who shall stand? ⁴ But there is forgiveness with thee, that thou mayest be feared.

The opening words of Psalm 130 surprise us with a new posture for the ascent psalmist. He is not praising God from the standpoint of the mountain of Jerusalem, but from the depths of the earth. Faced with the weight of the sense of his own sin, he leans into God's forgiveness. Yet, even this fact leads not to delight but to grave reverence for God's power.

In its liturgical context, we can see the manner in which such introspective songs balanced the collection of the Psalms of Ascent. After all, not every pilgrimage festival was a time of joy for the Hebrew people. God did not offer any caveats when He instituted the festivals. They were to be celebrated, regardless of the nationalistic situation, even when the Jews did not at all feel prone to celebrate. During times of threat or war, the trip to Jerusalem afforded space to ponder those sins that too often brought threat and calamity to their lives. Psalm 130 explores that very space.

---

1. For what did the psalmist long (vv. 1-2)?
2. Answer the question in verse 3.

> "To be able to look into God's face, and know with the knowledge of faith that there is nothing between the soul and Him, is to experience the fullest peace the soul can know. Whatever else pardon may be, it is above all things admission into full fellowship with God."—Charles H. Brent

---

B. Waiting and Hoping (vv. 5-8)

⁵ I wait for the Lord, my soul doth wait, and in his word do I hope. ⁶ My soul waiteth for the Lord more than they that watch for the morning: I say, more than they that watch for the morning. ⁷ Let Israel hope in the Lord: for with the Lord there is mercy, and with him is plenteous redemption. ⁸ And he shall redeem Israel from all his iniquities.

Between the space of the psalmist's pain and the answer of God lies waiting. This is all the psalmist can do in such space. Along these lines, Christian author and pastor Eugene Peterson describes the Psalms of Ascent as "songs of transition"—songs that are . . .

> Sung between the times: between the time we leave the world's environment and arrive at the Spirit's assembly; between the time we leave sin and arrive at holiness; between the time we leave home on Sunday morning and arrive in church with the company of God's people; between the time we leave the works of the law and arrive at justification by faith (*A Long Obedience in the Same Direction*, Second Edition).

It is in the waiting room of faith, the transitional space between pain and security, that the psalm gives hope. This hope is rooted not in personal circumstances, but in the character of God, who abounds in unfailing love, forgiveness, and redemption.

1. Describe a time you waited for the Lord, and the result.
2. Why should we hope in God (vv. 7-8)?

> "If the Lord Jehovah makes us wait, let us do so with our whole hearts; for blessed are all they that wait for Him. He is worth waiting for."—Charles Spurgeon

---

### C. Humility and Hope (131:1-3)

**¹ Lord, my heart is not haughty, nor mine eyes lofty: neither do I exercise myself in great matters, or in things too high for me. ² Surely I have behaved and quieted myself, as a child that is weaned of his mother: my soul is even as a weaned child. ³ Let Israel hope in the Lord from henceforth and for ever.**

The worshipers' pilgrimage to Jerusalem inspired hope, peace, and trust. In Psalm 131, we see that the journey also inspired humility. Faced with a time to reflect and to ponder the meaning of the trip, this was inevitable. The Creator of the universe had invited Israel into a covenant celebration! The realization of this awesome truth provides yet another foundation to contemplate the finite life of humanity in comparison with the eternal power of God.

Pride is, of course, the enemy of the life of faith in both the Old and New Testament. David's son, Solomon, would famously write, "Pride goeth before destruction, and an haughty spirit before a fall" (Prov. 16:18). David communicates to God that the celebration in Jerusalem is not focused on the Davidic rule, even at the pinnacle of Israel's "golden age." In fact, David refuses to concern himself with his own greatness. Instead, he acknowledges his posture before God—the posture of childlike faith. It is this faith which Jesus teaches in Matthew 18:3, "Truly I tell you, unless you change and become like little children, you will never enter the kingdom of heaven" (NIV).

This psalm is incredibly beneath the typical posture of a king. Not only is David a child before God, but he is like "a weaned child with his mother" (Ps. 131:2 NKJV). That is, David is completely dependent on God for health, for life, for sustenance, for any future. The center of his life is dependence on God. He longs for the entire nation to take such a position.

Israel's hope is in God, which demands humility before Him (v. 3). The psalmist describes this hope elsewhere in terms of wars and economies: "Some trust in chariots and some in horses, but we trust in the name of the Lord our God" (20:7 NIV).

---

1. Describe David's attitude before God and why it mattered (vv. 1-2).
2. What is unique about hoping in the Lord (v. 3)?

> "Jesus is the God whom we can approach without pride and before whom we can humble ourselves without despair."—Blaise Pascal

## CONCLUSION

The Psalms of Ascent are a treasure for the church today. They remind us that God longs to be celebrated in the hearts of true worshipers. He longs, in the words of Jesus, to be worshiped "in spirit and in truth" (John 4:23). In praying, singing, and reciting these psalms, the people of God are edified, encouraged, and awed by the reality of our loving and gracious Creator.

## GOLDEN TEXT CHALLENGE

"I WAS GLAD WHEN THEY SAID UNTO ME, LET US GO INTO THE HOUSE OF THE LORD" (Ps. 122:1).

As important as private worship is, it does not cancel the need for public worship. Rather than neglecting the church, we should gladly join with other believers in corporate worship.

We should come to the house of God with a song in our heart, and then gladly join in worshipful singing with fellow believers. After strengthening one another through "psalms and hymns and spiritual songs" (Col. 3:16), we can then better glorify God through our daily lives.

**Daily Devotions:**

M. Rejoicing Before the Lord
   2 Samuel 6:12-15
T. Approach God Reverently
   Ecclesiastes 5:1-7
W. Celebration and Declaration
   Micah 4:1-5
T. Worship in Spirit and Truth
   John 4:19-26
F. Testimony of Hope
   Acts 26:1-8
S. Saved by Hope
   Romans 8:17-24

July 19, 2015 (Lesson 7)
# Psalms of Divine Justice
### Psalms 35:1-28; 109:1-31; 140:1-13

**Theme:**
Different Types of Psalms

**Central Truth:**
We can trust God to be just in every situation.

**Focus:**
Reflect on God's just nature and depend on Him in difficult times.

**Context:**
Three psalms extolling the righteousness of God

**Golden Text:**
"I know that the Lord will maintain the cause of the afflicted, and the right of the poor" (Ps. 140:12).

**Study Outline:**
I. Appeal for Defense
   (Ps. 35:1-10, 27-28)
II. Cry for Help
   (Ps. 109:1-8, 20-31)
III. Prayer for Deliverance
   (Ps. 140:1-13)

## INTRODUCTION

The Bible does not distinguish between the terms *righteousness* and *justice*. This is true of both the Hebrew language (Old Testament) and the Greek language (New Testament). In Greek, there are no separate words for *justice* versus *righteousness*. In Hebrew, several words are available, but they are used interchangeably. Surely this challenges the way contemporary Christians are accustomed to thinking about biblical theology!

In many Christian circles, the subject of *personal righteousness* is consistently emphasized. This is especially true of Wesleyan-Pentecostal churches, with our distinctive emphasis on individual holiness. In these camps, the appearance of the term *righteousness* is immediately applied to one's personal moral decisions.

In other Christian circles, the subject of *broad social justice* is consistently emphasized. This is especially true of mainline Protestant churches, such as Presbyterians, Lutherans, Episcopalians, and some Methodists. In these groups, the appearance of the term *justice* is immediately applied to God's vision of society and its institutions.

The Bible, however, makes no distinction between these terms. It holds equally to each of them. This is a part of the supreme balance of Scripture. For those who think God is only concerned with personal morality, the majestic vision of a just society is brought to us in the Torah, especially in passages like Leviticus 19. For those who think God is only focused on the structures of society, such righteousness/justice is always the responsibility of individuals, not merely of the culture at large. This is the nature of Scripture: to correct our imbalances and false categories. Far from societal justice and personal righteousness being mutually exclusive, we find in the Bible they are the same thing! In this way, the Scriptures debunk the false theological categories of *liberal* versus *conservative*.

Nowhere is this false distinction more on display than in the Book of Psalms. For in the Psalms, God reveals Himself as a God who loves justice. He is a God with a vision for society and the individuals within it. He will not stand for anything less than this great vision.

## I. APPEAL FOR DEFENSE (Ps. 35:1-10, 27-28)

The Hebrew people possess a famous historical legacy of conquest and re-emergence. They have fallen to empires and nations, only to reemerge time and time again, regardless of the fact that no Israelite nation even existed from AD 70 until 1948 (18 centuries!). It is no wonder, then, that Hebrew culture is tremendously resilient and resolute. In fact, any society that has withstood the storms of time over a history that stretches back millennia will incorporate such resilience into its culture. This long-range view is more difficult for newer societies, such as the United States of America, which is why newer societies tend to wrestle with the question of theodicy more so than long-term societies. *Theodicy* is a term that theologians use to describe a simple question: "Why do bad things happen to good people?" Many people walk away from faith in God due to their inability to answer this question. The Psalms recognize the validity of this question. However, rather than disconnecting that question (and its answer) from the reality of God, the psalmists bring that question directly to God. It is this appeal that forms the basis of Psalm 35.

### A. Protection From Enemies (vv. 1-8)

(Psalm 35:5-8 is not included in the printed text.)

**1 Plead my cause, O Lord, with them that strive with me: fight against them that fight against me. 2 Take hold of shield and buckler, and stand up for mine help. 3 Draw out also the spear, and stop the way against them that persecute me: say unto my soul, I am thy salvation. 4 Let them be confounded and put to shame that seek after my soul: let them be turned back and brought to confusion that devise my hurt.**

Psalm 35 was written by King David, who was a worshiper, a political leader, and a mighty warrior. He was thrust into the world of ancient warfare during the battle against the Philistines when he defeated the giant Goliath. However, even before that great fight he had known altercations with dangerous animals: the lion and the bear (1 Sam. 17:34-36). By the time of Psalm 35 (whenever it was written), it can be assumed that David had a history of armed conflict. Therefore, it is not surprising to find him addressing God in military language.

We do not know if this psalm was written before or after David became king. Either way, David knew a constant and chronic state of military readiness. His life was consistently being sought by some enemy—domestic (Saul, Absalom) or foreign. Conflict was the "background noise" in David's life. David recognized that he could not fight all of his enemies. In a time period in which warfare was common, for the potential for plunder was massive, there was no way to stave off every threat. Therefore, David called on the Lord for help.

This help is both personal and national in scope. David uses personal language, asking God to help with those who "fight against me" (v. 1). However, David often stands in for the nation of Israel, which is how this psalm came to be celebrated in the worship of the nation. This is why Jesus is called the "Son of David." Here, God is portrayed as a mighty warrior, brandishing the weapons of warfare: shield, sword, spear, and javelin. What is remarkable is the amount of focus and emotional energy that is placed in God alone.

David acknowledges from the first verse that he is under imminent threat. Beginning with verse 2, however, David falls completely out of view. His vision shifts toward God, the mighty Warrior, who will remind David where his salvation lay (v. 3). This emphasis reminds us of the words to Zerubbabel in Zechariah 4:6: "'Not by might nor by power, but by My Spirit,' says the Lord of hosts" (NKJV). In Scripture, God's power always trumps the abilities of any human army, no matter how strong. This remembrance is typically rooted in the Exodus, when the most powerful empire of the day—Egypt—was no match for God's power.

In Psalm 35:4, David describes the divine fate of his enemies, should God rush to his defense. Their fate will be a shameful one, despite the pride with which they seek to attack David. This shame will not be brought on by military might alone, but by the very angel of God, twice mentioned in verses 5-6. *Angel* can also be translated "messenger," for these were beings who existed to execute the will of God. Verse 7 marks an important shift. Here we find David is not simply asking God to indiscriminately bless his efforts because he is David, the king. Instead, there is moral justification for this appeal to God's defense. In short, David has not caused this potential calamity to come upon him and his kingdom. He has been, in a sense, "minding his own business," and his enemies have laid this trip with no just cause. Therefore, David prays in verse 8 that their unjust cause might fall justly upon their own heads.

---

1. In verses 1-3, what does David ask God to do for him?
2. In verses 4-6, what does David ask regarding his enemies?
3. What does David ask regarding his enemies' plot (vv. 7-8)?

> "The Christian will be sure to make enemies. It will be one of his objects to make none; but if doing what is right and believing what is true should cause him to lose every earthly friend, he will regard it as a small loss, since his great Friend in heaven will be even more friendly and will reveal Himself to him more graciously than ever."—Alistair Begg

---

B. Complete Trust in God (vv. 9-10, 27-28)

**⁹ And my soul shall be joyful in the Lord: it shall rejoice in his salvation. ¹⁰ All my bones shall say, Lord, who is like unto thee, which deliverest the**

poor from him that is too strong for him, yea, the poor and the needy from him that spoileth him? **²⁷ Let them shout for joy, and be glad, that favour my righteous cause: yea, let them say continually, Let the Lord be magnified, which hath pleasure in the prosperity of his servant. ²⁸ And my tongue shall speak of thy righteousness and of thy praise all the day long.**

After laying his case before the Lord in verses 1-8, there is a break in the action of the psalm. David looks forward to a preferred future after God has answered his prayer. This will be a preferred future of rejoicing—not in the military might of his armies, but solely in the Lord.

God is not only David's military strategist, He is the One who brings miraculous victory. This is embedded within the story of Israel's relationship to God, experienced most notably in the Exodus from Egypt and continued in the Prophets, Gospels, and the mission of the Church.

The latter portion of Psalm 35 displays the ultimate fate of David's (thus, God's) enemies. Although they gloat over their expected victory (vv. 20-21), God is not unaware (v. 22). Instead, David calls on Him to awaken in His fierce justice. Yes, these verses seem harsh, but in them David displays his trust in God to work out David's salvation in God's own method and timing. The result will be the increased praise of God, not only in David's heart (v. 28), but for all of the people of God (v. 27). This is the benefit of such retribution—to increase the proclamation of the goodness of God.

---

1. What made David joyful, and why (vv. 9-10)?
2. To whom was David's situation a testimony, and how (vv. 27-28)?

> "This is the happy life, to rejoice in Thee, of Thee, for Thee; this it is, and there is no other."—Augustine

---

## II. CRY FOR HELP (Ps. 109:1-8, 20-31)

In Psalm 109, we encounter another appeal to God from King David for protection from his enemies. Many common themes are shared between Psalms 109 and 35. In both, David paints dramatic descriptions of his enemies, calls for their futures to be the dismal result of their malicious behavior toward him, and turns to the Lord for deliverance. In Psalm 109, however, there is a more pronounced cry for the immediate help of God. For this reason, the psalm stands out as a hymn of reckless trust in God.

### A. Description of the Wicked (vv. 1-8)

(Psalm 109:4-8 is not included in the printed text.)
**¹ Hold not thy peace, O God of my praise; ² For the mouth of the wicked and the mouth of the deceitful are opened against me: they have spoken against me with a lying tongue. ³ They compassed me about also with words of hatred; and fought against me without a cause.**

In many psalms, the true content of the poem is introduced by standard praises to God. This is not the case in Psalm 109. Instead, God is called upon as the object of the prayer, only to give way to a vivid description of the wicked who challenge King David at every side. The terse introduction to the psalm orients it toward God, but a denunciation of David's enemies ensues for the next nineteen verses.

Who are these enemies? It is not possible to say with certainty. David knew what it was to live under constant pressure and threat. What we have in verses 2-18 is what, in the ancient world, was often called a *topos*. From this word we get our English word *topic*. In the ancient world, a *topos* was a stock, standard literary device. One popular topos was the denunciation of enemies, which David employs here. His enemies are hateful (v. 3) and accusatory (v. 4). They do not return kindness for kindness, but attack David after he has done good to them (v. 5). Therefore, their fate should be justice; they should be condemned to short lives (vv. 7-8).

---

1. How had men's tongues become a weapon (vv. 1-4)?
2. What did David declare about himself (vv. 4-5)?
3. How did David ask God to intervene (vv. 6-8)?

"It is impossible for that man to despair who remembers that his Helper is omnipotent."—Jeremy Taylor

---

B. Calling on God's Compassion (vv. 20-31)

(Psalm 109:20-25, 28-29 is not included in the printed text.)
**26 Help me, O Lord my God: O save me according to thy mercy: 27 That they may know that this is thy hand; that thou, Lord, hast done it.**
**30 I will greatly praise the Lord with my mouth; yea, I will praise him among the multitude. 31 For he shall stand at the right hand of the poor, to save him from those that condemn his soul.**

Verse 20 makes no mistake about who is doing the "heavy lifting" when it comes to the judgment of David's enemies. Remember, David is a mighty warrior with soldiers at his disposal. At any moment, he can order them to enforce just retribution on his enemies. However, he does not do this. He completely trusts the Lord to provide proper repayment.

This dependence on the Lord continues in verses 21-27. David has no illusions that he, even as the anointed king of Israel, is in control. He cedes control completely to God, trusting in God's love (v. 21) and conscious of his own poverty (v. 22). Perhaps it is this very posture that Jesus calls to mind in the first words of the Sermon on the Mount: "Blessed are the poor in spirit: for theirs is the kingdom of heaven" (Matt. 5:3). After all, Jesus, the "Son of David," was certainly familiar with the psalms of David!

David continues to pour out his emptiness in Psalm 109:22-25. He is fading, fallen, scorned, even as he fasts before the Lord, a posture of humility. Finally, he breaks out in a bold request—asking God to save Him "according to [His] lovingkindness" (v. 26 NASB). The goal of David's vindication has nothing to do with his own glory or even of Israel, but with the glory of the Lord (v. 27). What is more, the gracious character of the Lord is extolled in the psalm's remaining verses. God is the antithesis of His enemies, the One who brings blessing where they bring cursing (v. 28). God will once again turn the tables on David's enemies by the force of His justice. In response to God's care for the needy, David will publicly proclaim the greatness of God (vv. 30-31).

1. Describe David's physical and emotional condition (vv. 22-25).
2. What would bring glory to God (vv. 26-29)?
3. How is God characterized in verse 31?

---

### Finding Calcutta
Mother Teresa was known globally as a champion of justice for the poor in the streets of Calcutta, India. She often met with visitors who sought to know the key to finding a similar calling. She famously and frequently exhorted such persons, regardless of their background, to "find your own Calcutta." When we are committed to God's vision for justice, we will see Calcutta all around.

---

## III. PRAYER FOR DELIVERANCE (Ps. 140:1-13)

Common themes emerge from these psalms of divine justice. These themes stem from vivid descriptions of David's enemies and bold expressions of trust in God. These two elements always go together in these particular psalms. Interestingly, David does not call for divine empowerment, but divine deliverance. That is, rather than asking for God's help to route his enemies, David asks for God to perform the work of deliverance. For this reason, these psalms stand as remarkable testimonies of radical trust in God.

### A. Defense From Violent Men (vv. 1-7)

**¹ Deliver me, O Lord, from the evil man: preserve me from the violent man; ² Which imagine mischiefs in their heart; continually are they gathered together for war. ³ They have sharpened their tongues like a serpent; adders' poison is under their lips. Selah. ⁴ Keep me, O Lord, from the hands of the wicked; preserve me from the violent man; who have purposed to overthrow my goings. ⁵ The proud have hid a snare for me, and cords; they have spread a net by the wayside; they have set gins for me. Selah. ⁶ I said unto the Lord, Thou art my God: hear the voice of my supplications, O Lord. ⁷ O God the Lord, the strength of my salvation, thou hast covered my head in the day of battle.**

Violence is not a part of the heart of God. This is sometimes lost in readings of the Old Testament that are taken out of the broader biblical context. Yes, God condones certain acts of violence in the Old Testament that are related to the purity of the nation and the continuation of His work in the world through Israel. However, the Bible is also a book of progressive revelation. As Christians, we believe the biblical message was ultimately revealed by Jesus Christ, who did not come to be violent, but to submit Himself to the horrifying violence of crucifixion.

David begins Psalm 140 with a short prayer (v. 1) followed by a description of the problem (vv. 2-3). In this psalm, men of violence are particularly singled out to be the recipients of God's justice. These violent men are determined to make war on a daily basis. Additionally, their aggressive speech feeds this addiction to violence through warfare. They want David's territory; they want his head; they want his political power. They want to make a mockery of the people of God.

David, however, knows where his help comes from. He knows his true power is not political, but theological. He will not take his focus off the justice of God. David acknowledges that he cannot keep, protect, or un-trap himself from the snares his enemies have set before him (vv. 4-5). God is his shield, his strong deliverer, and his rescuer. In the day of violence, God alone can be trusted (vv. 6-7).

---

1. List three ways David's enemies came against him (vv. 2-5).
2. How can God help us in "the day of battle" (vv. 6-7)?

> "After a hard day scrambling to find your way around in the world, it's assuring to come home to a place you know. . . . Just as your earthly house is a place of refuge, so God's house is a place of peace."—Max Lucado

---

B. Divine Retribution (vv. 8-13)

(Psalm 140:8-11 is not included in the printed text.)
**12 I know that the Lord will maintain the cause of the afflicted, and the right of the poor. 13 Surely the righteous shall give thanks unto thy name: the upright shall dwell in thy presence.**

Modern conceptions of the God of the Bible often play down His wrath. However, one cannot ignore this aspect of God's character without ignoring large swaths of Scripture. The wrath of God is a theological reality in both the Old and New Testaments. We need not shy away from it. In the Psalms, the wrath of God is often desired by godly men as a vital component of ordering a just society. This just society is the goal of God's justice. As Bible scholar N. T. Wright points out:

> Those who are called to reflect God's image through their own work must give attention to the task of working out, in a highly contested contemporary world, what that restorative justice ought to look like and how we might help bring it about. This will mean engaging with political debates and processes of various sorts, campaigning on key issues, and highlighting oppression and injustice wherever they occur. The Western world has supposed, for two hundred years and more, that splitting off questions of social justice from questions of God and faith would give us a more just society. The revolutions, totalitarianisms, and all-out wars of that period have proved us wrong. But to put God and human justice back together

again will require a sustained effort, not only by individuals but by the church as a whole, developing the corporate virtues of justice-work that will become habits of the church's heart and will appeal to the conscience of the wider world (*After You Believe: Why Christian Character Matters*).

We see this "sustained effort" toward justice pursued in the latter half of Psalm 140.

David's cry in verse 8 is a cry of justice: "Do not grant the wicked their desires, O Lord" (NIV). If the situation of society is unjust, the wicked will "exalt themselves." David knows such a world would be set against the purposes of God. Therefore, he asks for God's wrathful retribution to reorder the morality of society (vv. 9-11). It is only when sinners are revealed to be sinners that good can prevail in the world. If wicked men become "established" (v. 11), society is doomed.

Why can David expect for such retribution to be enacted? The answer is simple: David knows the character of God (v. 12). He is a student of the Scriptures and a man of praise and prayer. Therefore, his theological footing is sure. The result of God's retributive justice will be thanksgiving and stability for the "righteous" (v. 13), also translated "just ones." God's justice produces people committed to God's vision of justice.

---

1. What makes an "evil speaker" ("slanderer," NASB) dangerous (v. 11)?
2. What did David "know" about God (v. 12)?
3. How are "the upright" blessed (v. 13)?

---

"In the Bible, the wrath of God rests both on the sin (Rom. 1:18ff) and on the sinner (John 3:36)."—D. A. Carson

---

## CONCLUSION

The psalms that are dedicated to the theme of divine justice teach us much about the character of God. We find God is not lethargic or unaware of the ills of this world. Instead, He is actively engaged in bringing His justice to His people. The God who revealed Himself as the One who hears the cry of the oppressed continues His forward march into situations of hurt, injustice, and oppression, in order that He might bring ultimate healing to the pain of this world.

## GOLDEN TEXT CHALLENGE

"I KNOW THAT THE LORD WILL MAINTAIN THE CAUSE OF THE AFFLICTED, AND THE RIGHT OF THE POOR" (Ps. 140:12).

There is one institution on earth with the capacity, the presence, the credibility, the endurance, and the passion to perform the ultimate act of caring for the poor. It is the Church, the body of Christ.

The world's largest corporation is China Petro-Chemical, which boasts a labor force of 1,190,000 employees. By comparison, the Church is at least a thousand times larger. The Church is the only organization with hundreds of millions of members and the capacity to mobilize hundreds of millions of volunteers. I'm not just talking about the good people serving in soup kitchens—I'm talking about deployment of agents into every sector of society. [These are] agents aligned by one Spirit and a shared hope, drawing on immeasurable riches to achieve what cannot be done alone.—**Scott C. Todd (*Fast Living*)**

**Daily Devotions:**
- M. Jacob Prays for Deliverance
  Genesis 32:9-12
- T. Israel Cries for Vindication
  Exodus 2:23-25
- W. Justice for All
  Isaiah 56:1-8
- T. Jesus Answers Pleas for Help
  Matthew 8:1-8
- F. Jesus' Mission; Divine Justice
  Luke 4:17-21
- S. Jesus' Just Judgment
  John 5:26-30

July 26, 2015 (Lesson 8)
# Messianic Psalms
**Psalms 2:1-12; 22:1-31; 110:1-7**

**Theme:**
Different Types of Psalms

**Central Truth:**
Jesus, God's promised Messiah, is foreshadowed in the Psalms.

**Focus:**
Discover the Messiah in the Psalms and exalt His name.

**Context:**
Three psalms revealing truths about the Messiah

**Golden Text:**
"I will declare the decree: the Lord hath said unto me, Thou art my Son; this day have I begotten thee" (Ps. 2:7).

**Study Outline:**
I. The Anointed One
   (Ps. 2:1-12)
II. The Suffering Savior
   (Ps. 22:1-31)
III. The Eternal King and Priest
   (Ps. 110:1-7)

## INTRODUCTION

The power of the Psalms stretches beyond the worship liturgies of ancient Israel. In the New Testament, they point straight to Christ. In fact, Jesus made this point directly to His disciples after the Resurrection. After proving His body was real, He said, "This is what I told you while I was still with you: Everything must be fulfilled that is written about me in the Law of Moses, the Prophets, and the Psalms" (Luke 24:44 NIV). The Psalms are, then, an examination of the character and nature of the Messiah within the Old Testament.

Hundreds of Jewish texts in and around the time of Jesus give us insight into the fervor of messianic expectation among the people of God. One of these documents—what is called a Jewish *midrash*, or sermon—comments on Psalm 36 (a hymn outlining the deceit of the enemies of God). An ancient rabbi wrote:

> A man once tried to light a lamp, but every time he lit it, it went out. Finally he exclaimed, "How long shall I waste my effort on this lamp? I shall wait for the sun to shine, and then I shall have light." So it is with the Jews. When they were enslaved in Egypt, Moses emerged to redeem them, but they were enslaved again by the Babylonians. Daniel, Hananiah, Mishael, and Azariah emerged to redeem them, but they were enslaved again by the Elamites, Medes, and Persians: . . . Finally the Jews exclaimed: "We are tired of being continually enslaved and redeemed, only to be enslaved again. Let us pray for redemption not through human agency,

but through our Redeemer, the Lord of Hosts, the Holy One of Israel. Let us pray for light not from man, but from God" (cited in Allan Dwight Callahan, "The Arts of Resistance in an Age of Revolt," in *Hidden Transcripts and the Arts of Resistance: Applying the Work of James C. Scott to Jesus and Paul*, ed. Richard A. Horsley).

This commentary illustrates the manner in which ancient Jews sought to understand the coming Messiah through the prophecy of the Psalms. They looked not to a military solution, but to the salvation of God through His anointed One. We should not be surprised, then, thousands of years into the future, that the Psalms continue to testify to the power of Jesus.

## I. THE ANOINTED ONE (Ps. 2:1-12)

Psalms 47, 93, 95-97 are referred to as "enthronement psalms." They often depict the coronation of the king, but Old Testament scholar Sigmund Mowinckel reminds us they are really about the enthronement of God himself:

> The enthronement festival was the chief festival of the year, the feast of Yahweh at His personal "coming" in the hour of deepest danger and need, and with all the "salvation" and bliss which this coming includes, so that all the fundamental experiences, emotions, and ideas of religion must have met together here (*The Psalms in Israel's Worship*).

Psalm 2 is among these psalms of human and divine enthronement.

### A. Arrogance of God's Enemies (vv. 1-3)

**¹ Why do the heathen rage, and the people imagine a vain thing? ² The kings of the earth set themselves, and the rulers take counsel together, against the Lord, and against his anointed, saying, ³ Let us break their bands asunder, and cast away their cords from us.**

In this psalm, a "United Nations" scene is portrayed. However, this uniting of the nations is not bent on bettering the world or helping the nations work together. Instead, the nations have rallied to exterminate Israel and the Messiah. In so doing, they unwittingly have the arrogance to stand against Yahweh himself.

In this mock trial, the kings of the earth have assembled for suspicious dirty work. The particularity of this work is seen in the official use of God's name in verse 2. The English translation, "the Lord" (in capital letters), refers to the four Hebrew letters that represent God's name given to Moses in Exodus 3:14. It is God's most sacred name, literally devoid of vowels so it remains unpronounceable. Its best translation is simply "existence," or "I am." Christians have added vowels so we may speak God's name: *Yahweh*. The kings of the earth imagine they are playing politics—trading in land, power, and soldiers. The reality is they are toying with Yahweh, the almighty Creator of the heavens and the earth.

---

1. Answer the question in verse 1.
2. Describe the conspiracy of the nations (vv. 2-3).

---

> "Whatever failure you and I make of our lives, we do not make because God forces us to do so. In whatever way we go wrong, we do not do so because God planned that we should. We do it because of our own willfulness and wicked rebellion against God."—Clovis G. Chappell

B. Epiphany and Decree (vv. 4-12)

(Psalm 2:5, 10-11 is not included in the printed text.)

⁴ He that sitteth in the heavens shall laugh: the Lord shall have them in derision.
⁶Yet have I set my king upon my holy hill of Zion. ⁷ I will declare the decree: the Lord hath said unto me, Thou art my Son; this day have I begotten thee. ⁸ Ask of me, and I shall give thee the heathen for thine inheritance, and the uttermost parts of the earth for thy possession. ⁹ Thou shalt break them with a rod of iron; thou shalt dash them in pieces like a potter's vessel.
¹² Kiss the Son, lest he be angry, and ye perish from the way, when his wrath is kindled but a little. Blessed are all they that put their trust in him.

In the middle of the great meeting of kings, with the rulers of the world planning their military strategy against the people of the Lord, God himself suddenly shows up. Psalm 2 represents, therefore, a "mini-epiphany," an appearance of the Lord. His appearance mocks the certitude of the kings.

Arrogance is a major Old Testament theme. Listed first among the seven things God finds detestable in Proverbs 6:17-19 is a "proud look," or "haughty eyes" (NASB). In Psalm 2, Yahweh meets the arrogance of Israel's enemies with His own brand of derision. God laughs at the notion that their puny power will triumph (v. 4). They will not have the final word. They will not even have the first word. The words belong exclusively to God.

What follows is a declaration of the enthronement of David. This may seem like an odd shift, but we are reading an ancient text that comes from a time in which the stability of an entire nation was dictated by the stability of the king. In the ancient world, there was no philosophical division between religion and politics, or between the sacred and the secular. Instead, the Hebrews recognized the interconnected nature of community life. Therefore, for God to anoint and appoint David and his heirs to the throne of Israel is the ultimate antidote to the proposed chaos of the kings of the earth in the opening verses of the psalm.

This enthronement of the Davidic line (and ultimately of Jesus) is immediately apparent in the location of the throne room (v. 6). *Zion* is another term for *Jerusalem* in the Hebrew dialect. Jerusalem was also known as a "hill" due to its high position above sea level. This is where the Davidic line reigned.

In verse 7, we find enthronement language that is picked up and restated by New Testament authors. The Gospel writers use this psalm to interpret and explain the baptism of Jesus. It is echoed the loudest in the voice of God at Jesus' baptism (Matt. 3:17; Mark 1:11; Luke 3:22). It is referenced in the Father's compassionate words in Jesus' most famous parable: "My son . . . you are always with me, and everything I have is yours" (Luke 15:31 NIV). It is found in the preaching of the early apostles (Acts 13:33). And it is found in the intricate scriptural preaching of developing Christianity (Heb. 1:5; 5:5). This chorus of New Testament voices speaks to us of the tremendous significance of Psalm 2 in the life of the early church.

The purpose of God's calling His Son in Psalm 2:17 is to bequeath to Him a kingdom. Verse 8 represents the fulfillment of the ultimate promise of the Old Testament—God's massive promise to Abraham in Genesis 12:3. Since that promise, the Hebrew people had waited on the arrival of a ruler who would bring about its complete reflection. God announces that such a day has arrived in the establishment of this King over Zion. His rule will be definitive, firm, lasting, and eternal. For this reason, the nations of the earth are warned of their sobering responsibility.

When this great messianic King finally appeared on the hill of Zion, He came "gentle and riding on a donkey" (Matt. 21:5; Zech. 9:9 NIV). Humanity has been called by God to eternally trust this King.

---

1. How does God respond to rebellious nations (vv. 4-6)?
2. List three truths about the Messiah (vv. 7-9).
3. What are earthly rulers instructed to do, and why (vv. 10-12)?

> "The penalty of an evil harvest is not God's punishment; it is the consequence of defying the moral order which in love He maintains as the only environment in which maturity of fellowship and communion can be achieved."—Kirby Page

---

## II. THE SUFFERING SAVIOR (Ps. 22:1-31)

Suffering is a sacred part of life with God. Christian author Barbara Brown Taylor reminds us, "Pain is one of the fastest routes to a no-frills encounter with the Holy, and yet the majority of us do everything in our power to avoid it." She adds, "Pain makes theologians of us all" (*An Altar in the World: A Geography of Faith*). Such a theology is fleshed out in Psalm 22, a theology of pain. It is one of the wonders of the Bible that this psalm was chosen by Jesus Christ to illuminate and interpret His own pain. It still speaks to us today of a God who allows, but compassionately attends to, pain. After all, there is no healing without pain.

### A. The Crucified Christ (vv. 1-18)

(Psalm 22:3-13 is not included in the printed text.)

**1** My God, my God, why hast thou forsaken me? why art thou so far from helping me, and from the words of my roaring? **2** O my God, I cry in the daytime, but thou hearest not; and in the night season, and am not silent.
**14** I am poured out like water, and all my bones are out of joint: my heart is like wax; it is melted in the midst of my bowels. **15** My strength is dried up like a potsherd; and my tongue cleaveth to my jaws; and thou hast brought me into the dust of death. **16** For dogs have compassed me: the assembly of the wicked have inclosed me: they pierced my hands and my feet. **17** I may tell all my bones: they look and stare upon me. **18** They part my garments among them, and cast lots upon my vesture.

Jesus of Nazareth was a student of what we now call the Old Testament Scriptures. The Psalms were a centerpiece of His Bible, frequently celebrated in the worship services of both the local synagogue in Nazareth and the national temple in Jerusalem. Psalm 22 stands as a compelling reminder that Jesus was not just a Jewish leader who simply memorized the Hebrew Scriptures like other

Jewish leaders. No, He "lived into" them and "lived out of" them. They formed His identity and the primary lens through which He viewed the world. This worldview included His own suffering, which Jesus entrusted to God alone.

Such trust in God was not blind, but was often filled with lament and pathos. Nowhere is this more evident than in Psalm 22. The psalm is quoted by the crucified Jesus in the earliest written Gospel accounts (Matt. 27:46; Mark 15:34). Luke does not include it because he is writing to a Roman audience, and John's Gospel seeks to emphasize the unity of Jesus with the Father. These early accounts, however, are unapologetic about Jesus' admission of a sense of distance from God as He suffered on the cross. Some have made too much of this question from the cross, as if Jesus was disappointed that God did not immediately save Him. But Matthew 26:53 is clear that Jesus was well aware of His own power to save Himself. Instead, Jesus chose suffering.

However, choosing suffering does not make it easier. Psalm 22:3-18 depicts the intense vacillation between faith and doubt in the heart and outlook of the psalmist. He shifts in verses 3-5 to extol the trustworthiness of God. He knows God is enthroned, despite personal suffering, because of the history of the people of God. The psalmist's ancestors had put their trust in God, proving His faithfulness. Yet then, in verses 6-8, the tone shifts to the mockery of such trust by the persecutors.

This passage reminds us of the Suffering Servant of Isaiah 53, the One who bears the sins of Israel. This Suffering Servant is "despised and rejected by men" (v. 3 NKJV) just like the scourge of Psalm 22. This passage is also picked up by the Gospel writers, found in the mouths of the Jewish religious leaders who taunt Jesus: "He trusts in God. Let God rescue him now if he wants him, for he said, 'I am the Son of God'" (Matt. 27:43 NIV). Jesus feels the pain of Psalm 22 in the criticisms of the thieves, the religious leaders, and the crowds.

Verses 9-11 mark another shift in the psalm, back toward remembering to trust in God. The psalmist remembers he was born to trust God, who gave life to him. He therefore calls on God to be near. The God who gave life is the same God who takes it away. The scene does not look good. He is surrounded by enemies in verses 12-13, and the physical and social ramifications of suffering have begun to take hold.

The physical effects of suffering are dramatized in the cruel description in verses 14-18. Thirst, bruised bones, and pierced hands and feet are the cause of such brutal pain. It is almost difficult to remember we are reading the Old Testament in this passage. It is a remarkable description, a prophecy, of the crucifixion of Christ, right down to the soldiers who divide Jesus' clothing by casting lots (v. 18; see Matt. 27:35; Mark 15:24; Luke 23:34; John 19:24).

---

1. Describe David's emotional state (vv. 1-2).
2. What did David recall (vv. 3-5)?
3. How were people coming against David (vv. 6-8)?
4. How did David encourage himself (vv. 9-11)?
5. List aspects of Christ's suffering portrayed in verses 12-18.

> "How great, then, is the glory of [Christ's] self-humiliation in taking our nature that He might bring us to God! Such humiliation was not forced on Him; He freely chose to do it." —John Owen

---

B. The Rescue of God (vv. 19-31)

(Psalm 22:20-26, 29-31 is not included in the printed text.)

**$^{19}$ But be not thou far from me, O Lord: O my strength, haste thee to help me.**
**$^{27}$ All the ends of the world shall remember and turn unto the Lord: and all the kindreds of the nations shall worship before thee. $^{28}$ For the kingdom is the Lord's: and he is the governor among the nations.**

The bright hope of Psalm 22 is illuminated against its dark background. This is important because of the passage's usage in the New Testament. In the oral culture of Israel, the citation of a single Old Testament verse called to the hearer's mind the entire context of that verse. Therefore, Jesus' cry of the words of this psalm from the cross foreshadowed the psalm's hope in the rescue of God.

In the face of unimaginable suffering and the sick feeling of complete distance from God, the psalmist calls on God to remain close (v. 19). He names God as *deliverer* (v. 20) and *rescuer* (v. 21). Because of this trust in God's ultimate deliverance, the psalmist declares God's name will be praised among the community of faith (v. 22). This praise is not just personal or individual. In verse 23, it becomes a rallying cry for all who follow God—He can be praised because He has lifted up the cause of the "afflicted one" (v. 24 NIV). This is the proper context of Psalm 22 in the Crucifixion narratives of the Gospels—it tells a story of God's rescue from death and evil.

This theme of salvation expands in the final verses. Because of God's rescue, the assembly praises Him (v. 25), the poor are satisfied (v. 26), and the "ends of the earth" turn to the Lord who "rules over the nations" (vv. 27-28 NIV). These verses contain major New Testament themes. Jesus himself claimed the poor would be satisfied as a result of His kingdom (Matt. 5:3, 6). He commanded His disciples to take the gospel to "the ends of the earth" (Acts 1:8 NIV) and to preach the gospel to "all nations" (Matt. 28:19). Clearly, Jesus and the Gospel writers are reading this psalm to understand their mission!

The close of Psalm 22 emphasizes this global mission of God. It is not only a mission to all the nations, but it is a mission for future generations. A snapshot of God's eternal work is therefore found in this psalm.

---

1. Describe David's plea (vv. 19-21).
2. What did David promise to do, and why (vv. 22-25)?
3. List the prophecies of verses 26-31.

## Uncontrollably Good

In C. S. Lewis's famed allegorical novel about the gospel, *The Chronicles of Narnia*, the lion, Aslan, stands for the figure of Christ. A famous line from the book reads that Aslan "is not a safe lion," but is, instead, "good." In the Messianic Psalms, we discover the Anointed One who shakes the foundations of the world, but who is uncontrollably good.

---

## III. THE ETERNAL KING AND PRIEST (Ps. 110:1-7)

Psalm 110 represents perhaps the most important messianic psalm in the entire Canon. After all, Jesus chose to explain this psalm (and befuddle) the Pharisees with a significant teaching on His identity in Jerusalem (Matt. 22:41-46). It is also a key psalm in the argument of the writer of Hebrews (7:17, 21). Obviously, the early Christians who wrote the New Testament reflected deeply on Psalm 110. Because of this rich background, to study Psalm 110 means not only to study the Old Testament, but also the theology and practice of the New.

### A. An Everlasting Reign (vv. 1-3)

**¹ The Lord said unto my Lord, Sit thou at my right hand, until I make thine enemies thy footstool. ² The Lord shall send the rod of thy strength out of Zion: rule thou in the midst of thine enemies. ³ Thy people shall be willing in the day of thy power, in the beauties of holiness from the womb of the morning: thou hast the dew of thy youth.**

Second Samuel 7 marks a massive turn in the history of the Old Testament—a moment that stands behind the event of Psalm 110. Through David's lineage, God's rule would be established forever in Israel.

In Matthew 22:44-45, Jesus noted that David called someone else "my Lord" in Psalm 110:1, indicating that someone beyond David was in view. Such an interpretation silenced the Pharisees because it cut to the heart of 2 Samuel 7. By citing this scripture, Jesus was identifying Himself as the ruler in the line of David to whom God was eternally committed.

After Psalm 110 asserts that the house of David is overpowered by the Lord, it goes on to describe this power (vv. 2-3). God's power, greater than even King David's rule, extends from Zion all the way to the enemies of God. The picture here is one of the eternal youth of David's rule, discovered ultimately in Jesus Christ, who makes all things new.

---

- What did God the Father ("the Lord") promise to "my Lord" (God the Son)?

---

"There are no term limits on His reign. . . . There are no coups, no revolutions (at least, none that succeed). There is no threat of impeachment. He is a King who rules eternally."—Sam Storms

---

### B. A Never-Ending Priesthood (vv. 4-7)

(Psalm 110:5-7 is not included in the printed text.)
**⁴ The Lord hath sworn, and will not repent, Thou art a priest for ever after the order of Melchizedek.**

In the Old Testament, the flipside of political power was spiritual power. That is, the greatest kings operated like priests. Therefore, David is declared by God to be the most unlikely priest—the one who blesses the people of Abraham (v. 4).

The psalmist reaches backward into the annals of the history of Genesis for this obscure reference. Indeed, Melchizedek only appears here and in Genesis 14:18 in the entire Old Testament. In Genesis, this mysterious "king of Salem" blesses and is blessed by Abraham, setting a precedent for the priestly ministry of both the Levites and Jesus. Here, in Psalm 110, David is crowned not only as the king, but as the superior priest, the one that even predates the formal priesthood.

As official priest of the nation, the king can trust that God is on his side. As the one who performs the will of God, he also enforces God's wrath, judging the nations and their wicked. The apocalyptic "day of [God's] wrath" (v. 5) is here portrayed as a day of vengeance, when the earth's wrongs are put to rights (v. 6). All this was accomplished in the crucifixion of Jesus, which fulfilled the wrath of God in its entirety.

1. In His role as priest, what does Jesus Christ do (v. 4)?
2. Describe the sobering truth of verses 5-6.

"In His life, Christ is an example, showing us how to live; in His death, He is a sacrifice, satisfying for our sins; in His resurrection, a conqueror; in His ascension, a king; in His intercession, a high priest."—Martin Luther

## CONCLUSION

The Book of Psalms is an invaluable resource for understanding the work of God throughout and across biblical history. The Psalms go beyond the hymns that were sung by the people of Israel to become important New Testament texts for understanding Jesus. Nowhere is this more pronounced than in the Messianic Psalms, where the Davidic promises are fully applied to the future Messiah, Jesus Christ.

## GOLDEN TEXT CHALLENGE

"I WILL DECLARE THE DECREE: THE LORD HATH SAID UNTO ME, THOU ART MY SON; THIS DAY HAVE I BEGOTTEN THEE" (Ps. 2:7).

The second psalm is a powerful, royal psalm used in ancient Israel at the coronation of the king. In verse 7, the divine decree of the Lord is given—a decree meaning that the king was considered to be God's anointed one.

The writers of the New Testament saw this passage as being far more than a psalm to be read at the coronation of a king in Israel. They interpreted it in the light of its prophetic, messianic message. In Paul's message (Acts 13:33), he quotes from the second psalm and declares these words to be fulfilled in Jesus Christ and His resurrection from the dead. Again, in Hebrews 1:5, this psalm is quoted to demonstrate that Jesus Christ is the exalted Son of God and is superior to all prophets, all angels, and all of creation.

**Daily Devotions:**
- M. Song of the Suffering Savior
  Isaiah 53:1-12
- T. Light to the Nations
  Isaiah 60:1-7
- W. Messiah's Birth
  Luke 2:1-7
- T. Andrew Identifies the Messiah
  John 1:35-42
- F. Martha Acknowledges Jesus as Messiah
  John 11:21-27
- S. Christ, Our High Priest
  Hebrews 9:11-15

August 2, 2015 (Lesson 9)

# Encouragement for Dealing With Trials

**James 1:1-27**

**Theme:**
Practical Christianity (James)

**Central Truth:**
By God's grace, we endure and overcome trials.

**Focus:**
Remember God gives grace to endure trials and overcome through Him.

**Context:**
The Book of James was probably written from Jerusalem between AD 48 and 50.

**Golden Text:**
"Blessed is the man that endureth temptation: for when he is tried, he shall receive the crown of life, which the Lord hath promised to them that love him" (James 1:12).

**Study Outline:**
I. Persevere in Trials
   (James 1:1-12)
II. Acknowledge God's Goodness
    (James 1:13-18)
III. Hear and Obey God's Word
     (James 1:19-27)

## INTRODUCTION

"Is there anything else that could go wrong?" "If it's not one thing, it's another." Questions and comments similar to these are frequently heard when there has been a series of difficult circumstances in one's life. Financial reversals, physical problems, and spiritual battles are not unknown to us who are believers. Life in Christ is not an exemption clause to the trials of life on earth.

Trials in our lesson's scriptural setting (James 1) are not to be understood as short-term minor inconveniences. Rather, they are an external adversity resulting from being persecuted for one's faith. James opens this epistle by identifying the audience as "the twelve tribes which are scattered abroad" (v. 1). Generally, it is believed these individuals were Jewish Christians. But James' letter applied to the entire early church, which was experiencing trials because of their Christian faith and practice.

Many individuals of Jewish ancestry were scattered throughout the Roman Empire and beyond. Collectively, all of these people are referred to as the *dispersion* or *diaspora*. Some of them were believers in Christ who moved to other parts because of persecution. Others were Jews who had become believers due to missionary outreach.

The "James" indicated in verse 1 is generally believed to be the brother of Jesus. He does not pridefully display that position. Instead, he demonstrates his position in Christ as being the dominant emphasis or identity.

Prior to considering the lesson text, give special attention to the central truth: "By God's grace, we endure and overcome trials." Escape or deliverance is not always the option. But overcoming trials in spite of the difficulty can be accomplished through Christ.

## I. PERSEVERE IN TRIALS (James 1:1-12)

### A. The Work of Patience (vv. 1-4)

**¹ James, a servant of God and of the Lord Jesus Christ, to the twelve tribes which are scattered abroad, greeting. ² My brethren, count it all joy when ye fall into divers temptations; ³ Knowing this, that the trying of your faith worketh patience. ⁴ But let patience have her perfect work, that ye may be perfect and entire, wanting nothing.**

The opening verse of this epistle gets right to the point. First, James identifies himself in a spiritual relationship rather than in terms of family or position. His being the brother of Jesus and the moderator of the Jerusalem Council (Acts 15) are not the significant issues in this correspondence.

Second, James provides us with a sense of the audience. His reference to "the twelve tribes" was a common way of referring to Jews living outside of Palestine. It is not to be understood as a direct reference to the distinct tribes seen in the Old Testament. However, there is a reflection of these people still being aware of their heritage as God's chosen people, through whom all the world is to be blessed by the Messiah's coming to bring redemption.

Third, James' simple salutation is "greetings" (NKJV). It was the common short statement used in Hellenistic Greek letters. He chooses not to use the Jewish greeting of "peace" or some of the longer expressions offering grace, peace, and blessings.

As the author approaches the subject in verse 2, he uses the personal expression referring to them as "brethren." This would be inclusive of both genders. It was a common term for fellow Jews and fellow believers.

Without sharing the particulars of the trial they are facing, James immediately points them to "joy" as the best response. This is not a superficial happiness which can be easily eradicated by circumstances, but a joy which stems from their relationship with Christ. The severity of the trial is not to be a factor.

The real issue is the realization of the end result of what they are facing. Trials test the believer and produce endurance. The word translated "patience" (v. 3) is better understood as *perseverance*. *Perseverance* enables a person to steadfastly work through the situation, regardless of the immediate or long-term impact.

Verse 4 emphasizes the importance of trials or difficult circumstance in the process of personal spiritual maturity and character development. There is no way to know the strength of one's character unless put to the test. Would we rather not experience these events? Absolutely! Who wants to go through physical pain, social isolation, and financial reverses? However, when they do become part of our life, it is vital to see the value which may result.

1. According to verses 2 and 3, what should bring us "pure joy" (NIV), and why?
2. Why do Christians need perseverance (v. 4)?

> **Load Limit**
> A man was shopping in a grocery store. His young son followed closely behind, carrying a large basket. The father loaded the basket with one item after another until another customer began to feel sorry for the boy. She said, "That's a pretty heavy load for a young fellow like you, isn't it?" The boy turned to the woman and said, "Oh, don't worry. My dad knows how much I can carry." In the same way, God knows our limitations and gives to us no burden beyond what we can carry (taken from *Illustrations for Biblical Preaching*).

---

B. The Problem of Doubt (vv. 5-11)

(James 1:7-11 is not included in the printed text.)

**⁵ If any of you lack wisdom, let him ask of God, that giveth to all men liberally, and upbraideth not: and it shall be given him. ⁶ But let him ask in faith, nothing wavering. For he that wavereth is like a wave of the sea driven with the wind and tossed.**

In light of the readers' situation, wisdom to cope is absolutely necessary. At the same time, it is understandable how doubt might creep in when experiencing trials. The previous statement in verse 2 encouraged them to experience joy in the midst of trial. Wisdom would play a vital part in fostering this position.

Genuine wisdom is far beyond possessing knowledge or even learning with experience, though both are beneficial. The concept referred to here is the inner attitude of the soul which comes from God alone—without reservation or reproach against us. He desires this to be the condition of all.

Verse 6 indicates the condition for receiving this wisdom. We are to ask in complete faith without any hesitation caused by doubt. James compares doubt to a wave of the sea which does not control its own course of action. It tosses about without any consideration of itself. On a personal level, doubt does the same to us. It sucks us in and plunges us down, never stopping or providing stability.

Reflecting back to the audience's setting of trials, it helps to understand the importance of *perseverance* and *wisdom*.

In verses 7 and 8, we see *doubt* presented as *double-mindedness*. When doubt continually evidents itself, the believer cannot pray the prayer of faith and expect God's working in our life. It also permeates other areas of life, causing instability. There is the possibility of forms of unreliability also becoming evident—such as quality of work, sustained relationships, and spiritual insight.

The last three verses (9-11) remind us that wealth and social status are not the criteria for perseverance, wisdom, and faith. Joy comes from relationship with God and His working within the believer.

1. What does God promise to give "liberally" (v. 5), and why is that important?
2. What is the connection between being doubtful and "double minded" (vv. 6-8)?
3. How does James contrast the "rich" and the "low" (vv. 9-11)?

> "No matter what we are going through, no matter how long the waiting for answers, of one thing we may be sure: God is faithful."—Gloria Gaither

C. The Blessing of Enduring Trials (v. 12)

**12 Blessed is the man that endureth temptation: for when he is tried, he shall receive the crown of life, which the Lord hath promised to them that love him.**

Modern translations use the term *trial* instead of *temptation*, which is more consistent with the context. In this verse, we see the reward for enduring trials once our earthly life is completed. God promises a crown of life. The people would have been acquainted with other crowns. Royalty wore crowns signifying their position. Crowns of flowers were worn at weddings and other festivals. At Olympic Games, a crown of laurel leaves was given to the victors. The "crown of life" referred to here surely is indicative of life eternal and the rewards of heaven. There is also the honor and dignity which the persevering believer receives from the Christian community while still here on earth.

- How should we view temptation?

> "Do not grudge the hand that is molding the still too shapeless image within you. It is growing more beautiful, though you see it not, and every touch of temptation may add to its perfection."—Henry Drummond

II. ACKNOWLEDGE GOD'S GOODNESS (James 1:13-18)

A. The Source of Temptation (vv. 13-15)

**13 Let no man say when he is tempted, I am tempted of God: for God cannot be tempted with evil, neither tempteth he any man: 14 But every man is tempted, when he is drawn away of his own lust, and enticed. 15 Then when lust hath conceived, it bringeth forth sin: and sin, when it is finished, bringeth forth death.**

James now moves from the subject of *trials* to *temptations*. In the Old Testament, some of the means God used in attempting to bring rebellious Israel back into a right relationship was through drought, disease, disasters, and destructive neighbors. These were trials of considerable magnitude. However, they were not like temptations, whose purpose is to draw people away from God and into sin.

All believers should expect to be tempted. Satan repeatedly tried to tempt Jesus to sin and thus disqualify Him from His redemptive work for humankind (Matt. 4:1-11; Luke 4:1-13). Notice the timing: Jesus had just completed His forty-day fast in the desert. It points to how our adversary looks for weak times or areas of our being in which to offer temptation.

When trials come, there is the potential for temptation to occur. At that point, a believer must not fall into the trap of thinking God to be the source. James 1:13 makes the truth clear: God himself cannot be tempted by evil, and He does not tempt "any man."

Temptation can approach us in subtle whispering of suggesting this should not be happening to us as a believer . . . God must not care about us. Other times, temptation comes when we become so busy comparing our lives to believers whose situation appears so much better. That's when the "not fair" thoughts arise. James points to another source of temptation which resides within humans—our own desires.

If there wasn't the possibility to be drawn away from our lifestyle in Christ, there would be no temptation. Temptation tries to lure us away from truth and holiness. Our adversary knows the weaknesses we must overcome and offers "bait" to draw us away.

It is important to understand the breadth of temptation. The reference to *lust* (v. 14) immediately causes many to think of sexual passions that go beyond the boundaries of biblical morality. However, the scope is much broader. It could refer to the allurement of wealth, position, or popularity. Regardless of the area, the result remains the same. When temptation incubates and takes root in one's heart and mind, it is sin. Being tempted is not the sin; succumbing to it results in sin.

Sin never produces life, even though the immediate results might seem uplifting, enlightening, or exciting. However, the day of reckoning always comes. In some cases, it is much sooner than later and with far greater consequences than ever imagined. The parable of the lost son (Luke 15:11-32) demonstrates this vividly. This Jewish young man never imagined he would end up feeding pigs and nearly starving to death.

Unrepentant sin always results in spiritual death. And it may hasten one's physical death.

---

1. What can God not do, and why not (v. 13)?
2. Explain the deadly process in verses 14 and 15.

---

"Satan is too subtle, too cunning, too powerful; he watches constantly for advantages over my soul. . . . Therefore, on God alone will I rely for my keeping. I will continually look to Him."—John Owen

## B. The Source of Goodness (vv. 16-18)

**16 Do not err, my beloved brethren. 17 Every good gift and every perfect gift is from above, and cometh down from the Father of lights, with whom is no variableness, neither shadow of turning. 18 Of his own will begat he us with the word of truth, that we should be a kind of firstfruits of his creatures.**

James now makes a transition from the temptations of Satan to the goodness of God. The initial words of verse 16 are better translated as "Do not be deceived." Satan desires for us to be deceived, particularly about God. It is clearly seen when he tempted Eve in the Garden. He wanted her to believe God was not totally honest in His words (Gen. 3:3-5). James warns his fellow believers against such a trap.

God's very nature is good. He is the source of all good we enjoy (James 1:17). Nothing evil in nature comes from Him. All of His gifts are perfect. His intention is to provide the best for His children. This is seen repeatedly in His provision for Israel. Consider their deliverance from Egypt. When the plagues were poured out on the populace, the Hebrews were spared. On the journey, He miraculously provided food, water, light, and indestructible clothing. Their conquering of the more powerful peoples in the Promised Land further indicated God's intervention.

James describes God as "the Father of lights." Paul A. Cedar states:

> The phrase "Father of lights" is found only in this passage of all the New Testament. However, the reference to God as the God of light is frequent in the Scriptures, beginning with the Creation account (Gen. 1) and carrying through the Book of Revelation, which describes the New Jerusalem as needing no lamp or light of the sun (Rev. 22:5).—*The Communicator's Commentary*

God never changes. He faithfully fulfills all His promises. He is the same for all generations. His truth endures forever. The benefits of serving God are always good and repeatedly stated in Scripture:
- "The goodness of God endures continually" (Ps. 52:1 NKJV).
- "Blessed be the Lord, who daily loads us with benefits, the God of our salvation!" (68:19 NKJV).
- "Oh, that men would give thanks to the Lord for His goodness, and for His wonderful works to the children of men!" (107:8 NKJV).
- "Therefore consider the goodness and severity of God: on those who fell, severity; but toward you, goodness, if you continue in His goodness" (Rom. 11:22 NKJV).

James 1:18 says believers experience spiritual birth by the act of God through "the word of truth"—the Gospel. Believers are set free from sin and placed in right relationship with the heavenly Father, becoming "a kind of firstfruits of his creatures." The *Orthodox Study Bible* says, "In salvation we benefit not by taking on the essence or nature of God, but by taking on a new humanity consecrated to God (as with *firstfruits* in the Old Testament)."

---

1. Thank God for some of the "good" and "perfect" gifts He has given you (v. 17).

2. What is the greatest gift God has provided (v. 18)?

> "Every good gift that we have had from the cradle up has come from God. If a man just stops to think what he has to praise God for, he will find there is enough to keep him singing praises for a week."—D. L. Moody

---

## III. HEAR AND OBEY GOD'S WORD (James 1:19-27)

### A. The Path of Righteousness (vv. 19-21)

**19 Wherefore, my beloved brethren, let every man be swift to hear, slow to speak, slow to wrath: 20 For the wrath of man worketh not the righteousness of God. 21 Wherefore lay apart all filthiness and superfluity of naughtiness, and receive with meekness the engrafted word, which is able to save your souls.**

For the third time, James refers to his audience as "brethren" (v. 19). Here he includes the adjective *beloved*, or *dear*. This further identifies himself with them and their current situation. He is not writing as a leader residing in a distant location and simply giving directives. There is the sense of genuine care and desire for their following righteousness in words and actions.

Verse 19 begins with the believers' communication. He admonishes them to give attention to listening prior to their speaking. By doing so, a person can more likely absorb what is being said and then speak with a sense of wisdom and understanding. Ecclesiastes 5:3 states, "A fool's voice is known by his many words" (NKJV). In contrast is Proverbs 10:19, "He who restrains his lips is wise" (NKJV). Another quote from Proverbs furthers the need for listening and carefully choosing when to speak: "Even a fool is counted wise when he holds his peace; when he shuts his lips, he is considered perceptive" (17:28 NKJV).

Tied closely to listening and speaking is the issue of anger (James 1:20). By personality, some individuals struggle far more with anger than others. However, even the most reserved person might struggle with anger and then burst out in a regrettable manner. Unrestrained anger can result in wild accusations and word choices which not only hurt temporarily but can develop deep chasms.

Uncontrolled anger stands in complete opposition to the righteousness which should be evident in the person who is walking in the Spirit. Writing to the Galatians, Paul lists "outbursts of anger" as one of the works of the flesh that are not acceptable for anyone wanting to inherit eternal life (5:19-21 NASB).

To further emphasize the need to control one's anger, James placed it in a category of unrighteousness: "Therefore, get rid of all moral filth and the evil that is so prevalent and humbly accept the word planted in you, which can save you" (1:21 NIV). These believers already had the gospel implanted in their hearts by accepting Christ, and they were serving Him in spite of trials. Therefore, it seems these words were a reminder and encouragement to continue in righteousness. In the middle of trials, a believer might regress unless standing firmly on the principles of life in Christ.

1. When is slowness positive (vv. 19-20)?
2. Describe the exchange we need to make (v. 21).

> "Anger and bitterness are two noticeable signs of being focused on self and not trusting God's sovereignty in your life."—John C. Broger

---

B. The Pattern of Righteousness (vv. 22-26)

**²² But be ye doers of the word, and not hearers only, deceiving your own selves. ²³ For if any be a hearer of the word, and not a doer, he is like unto a man beholding his natural face in a glass: ²⁴ For he beholdeth himself, and goeth his way, and straightway forgetteth what manner of man he was. ²⁵ But whoso looketh into the perfect law of liberty, and continueth therein, he being not a forgetful hearer, but a doer of the work, this man shall be blessed in his deed. ²⁶ If any man among you seem to be religious, and bridleth not his tongue, but deceiveth his own heart, this man's religion is vain.**

Far too many churchgoers state their love for and commitment to the Scripture, but it goes no further than hearing sermons and attending Bible studies. They know the Bible's content, but fail to follow its directive and principles. This process provides no lasting spiritual benefit.

James demonstrates or likens such actions to looking at one's reflection and then promptly forgetting the image. In James' day, the source of reflection was likely a piece of burnished metal. However, the emphasis is not on how they were able to see their reflection but what they did afterward with the information. Today, too many individuals look at God's Word on Sundays, but forget about it the rest of the week.

In verse 25 we see the statement "the perfect law of liberty"—what a contrast to the concept of the old law being restrictive and binding! The law of Moses was designed to keep people from sinning. The new law, the gospel of Jesus Christ, provides freedom from the bondage of sin. In both cases, the individual receives blessings as a result of continuing in it. When we accept Christ as our personal Savior, our sins are wiped away. This new relationship doesn't merely exist or continue in a vacuum. Through God's grace, we must then demonstrate actions that reflect our commitment to Christ and His Word.

Hearing the Word has little value, if we forget it. We may have a sense of being religious because of hearing the Word but, in reality, have deceived ourselves (v. 26). In preparation for the content of chapter 3, James uses the illustration of unbridled speech indicating a lack of spirituality.

---

1. Describe the self-deception in verses 22-24.
2. How can we live in freedom (v. 25)?
3. Whose "religion is vain" (v. 26)?

> "At the day of doom men shall be judged according to their fruits. It will not be said then, Did you believe? But, Were you doers, or talkers only?"—John Bunyan

## C. The Proof of Righteousness (v. 27)

**27 Pure religion and undefiled before God and the Father is this, To visit the fatherless and widows in their affliction, and to keep himself unspotted from the world.**

In just a few words, we are given a statement of authentic spirituality. It is not intended to be a full description, but rather provides the parameters. First, genuine spirituality is evident by personal ministry to the needs of others. Repeatedly in the Old Testament, there is specific reference to the "fatherless and widows." They are to be treated with justice and not taken advantage of because of their situation (Deut. 24:17; 27:19). In Malachi's prophecy, the Lord said, "I will come near you for judgment; I will be a swift witness . . . against those who exploit wage earners and widows and orphans" (3:5 NKJV).

This care for the needy within the church can also be seen by the practice of the early church. Acts 6:1 speaks of "daily distribution" for the widows (NKJV). In 1 Timothy 5, we find the church caring for those older widows who had no family to care for them. This practice of benevolent care is presented as an ongoing aspect of ministry to be practiced by individuals and the corporate church. Regretfully, in our Western countries this responsibility has been largely left to the government.

The second test of genuine spirituality is to remain morally and spiritually "unspotted." In an attempt to reach out to needy people, there is sometimes the risk of becoming entangled in situations which could cause the compromise of one's moral standards. We must guard against this.

This final verse reminds us how easily our good can be evil spoken of, due to failing to maintain purity in words and actions. It seems that, with the aging of the "baby boomers" (those born between 1946 and 1964), this verse takes on even more significance.

- Are you practicing "pure and faultless" religion (NIV)?

> "It is not enough that we be just, that we be righteous, and walk with God in holiness; but we must also serve our generation, as David did before he fell asleep. God has a work to do; and not to help Him is to oppose Him."—John Owen

## CONCLUSION

James 1 emphasizes three aspects of Christian living: (1) While persevering in trials, it is vital to be patient, overcome doubt, and understand the blessing of difficult situations. (2) We need to recognize the goodness of God and understand temptation does not come from a holy God. (3) Righteousness comes through hearing and obeying the Word, which includes careful speech and caring for the needy.

## GOLDEN TEXT CHALLENGE

"BLESSED IS THE MAN THAT ENDURETH TEMPTATION: FOR WHEN HE IS TRIED, HE SHALL RECEIVE THE CROWN OF LIFE, WHICH THE LORD HATH PROMISED TO THEM THAT LOVE HIM" (James 1:12).

Are there times when God himself puts us through "testing"? Yes! It is never with the hope that we'll fail, but that we'll grow in faith. In those times we must trust, pray, and in spite of everything, continue to march.

"Endureth temptation" is correctly translated as "perseveres under trial" (NIV), or "endures the temptations and trials" (*Phillips*). God puts us through a lifelong process of strengthening and refinement that takes the mix of life and uses it with the goal of making us better fit for real-world living and ministry.

**Devotions:**

M. Delivered From the Enemy
   Exodus 14:13-21
T. Recognizing the Deliverer
   Psalm 66:1-9
W. God's Presence in Trials
   Isaiah 43:1-7
T. Purpose in Suffering
   Romans 5:1-5
F. More Than Conquerors
   Romans 8:31-39
S. Suffer Unashamedly
   1 Peter 4:12-19

August 9, 2015 (Lesson 10)

# Christian Faith in Action

**James 2:1-26**

**Theme:**
Practical Christianity (James)

**Central Truth:**
The Bible gives clear guidance regarding our treatment of others.

**Focus:**
Examine and practice Christian principles for our treatment of others.

**Context:**
The Book of James was probably written from Jerusalem between AD 48 and 50.

**Golden Text:**
"If ye fulfil the royal law according to the scripture, Thou shalt love thy neighbour as thyself, ye do well" (James 2:8).

**Study Outline:**
I. Avoid Discrimination
   (James 2:1-7)
II. Keep the Royal Law
   (James 2:8-13)
III. Work Your Faith
   (James 2:14-26)

## INTRODUCTION

*Discriminate*—does this word immediately bring a positive or negative connotation? An educated guess is that a majority of people lean toward the negative with thoughts of bias or prejudice. Heading the list would be *racial* or *ethnic* discrimination which can be found in countless places.

The negative side of discrimination is much broader than ethnicity and skin color. *Age* consideration arises when individuals have difficulty finding a job or are laid off so younger individuals can be hired at lower pay. There can be *religious* discrimination, which causes barriers even between believers of the same persuasion. *Geographical* discrimination occurs when presuppositions are applied to all who live in a particular community or region.

It would be terrific if becoming a believer would erase all forms of discrimination from thought or practice. However, that reality occurs only through study of the Scriptures and the convicting, regenerative work of the Holy Spirit. Prejudicial discrimination is often passed from one generation to the next. Once when I finished teaching a session about believers not succumbing to racial prejudice, some college students said to me, "We know you are right, but you have to understand our background. We'll have to work on this."

This lesson emphasizes the treatment of others based on Christian principles, rather than personal appearance or financial resources. It also causes us to take a careful look at what it means to love our neighbor. Then, finally, there is the discussion of the relationship between *faith* and *works*.

## I. AVOID DISCRIMINATION (James 2:1-7)

### A. Issue of Favoritism (vv. 1-4)

**¹ My brethren, have not the faith of our Lord Jesus Christ, the Lord of glory, with respect of persons. ² For if there come unto your assembly a man with a gold ring, in goodly apparel, and there come in also a poor man in vile raiment; ³ And ye have respect to him that weareth the gay [fine] clothing, and say unto him, Sit thou here in a good place; and say to the poor, Stand thou there, or sit here under my footstool: ⁴ Are ye not partial in yourselves, and are become judges of evil thoughts?**

Christian faith must be evident in our actions if we ever hope to reach those who have never accepted Jesus as Savior and Lord. The treatment of others is both an issue of Christian lifestyle and evangelism.

As he did in chapter 1, James refers to his readers as "brethren." He continues the personal bond while introducing another area of practical Christianity. Christian faith is of little value unless it is put into operation on a daily basis. The scenario described here could be labeled as *favoritism*, which gives it a lesser sense of wrong. But *discrimination* is still *discrimination*, regardless of what it is called.

No believer is perfect; that will occur at our final glorification. However, our faults can be effectively dealt with when we dwell within the glory of the presence of God. It is much like Isaiah's experience; when he saw the presence of God, he recognized his sin, confessed it, and received cleansing (Isa. 6:5-7).

In chapter 2, James shares a hypothetical setting to demonstrate how favoritism could enter into the believer's mind-set. He suggests that two men come into their assembly. The first man exudes prosperity by the quality of his clothing and wearing a gold ring. The second man is dressed in filthy clothing, indicating his poverty. Without hesitation, the well-dressed man is escorted to and seated in a good place. In contrast, the poor man is told to stand to the side or sit on the floor. Keep in mind, it appears these two men are represented as newcomers. Without hesitation, the partiality takes place.

In verse 4, James says if a Christian community were to act in such a manner, they are "judges with evil thoughts" (NKJV). These are "judges who reason wickedly, who, in effect, say in [their] hearts, we will espouse the cause of the rich because they can befriend us: we will neglect that of the poor, because they cannot help us" (*Adam Clarke's Commentary*).

Consider the example of Christ. He ministered equally to the wealthy, the despised, and the poor. No one who came to Him was given greater or lesser attention based on their circumstances of life.

---

- How could a church today violate this Scripture passage?

"God bestows His blessings without discrimination. The followers of Jesus are children of God, and they should manifest the family likeness by doing good to all, even to those who deserve the opposite."—F. F. Bruce

---

### B. Rich in Faith (vv. 5-7)

**5 Hearken, my beloved brethren, Hath not God chosen the poor of this world rich in faith, and heirs of the kingdom which he hath promised to them that love him? 6 But ye have despised the poor. Do not rich men oppress you, and draw you before the judgment seats? 7 Do not they blaspheme that worthy name by which ye are called?**

Continuing his pattern of address, once again James uses the term *brethren*, and adds the endearing adjective *beloved* (v. 5). He wants them to grasp an important concept in the discussion of favoritism by considering a rhetorical question.

How do we handle this question? Does it mean God specifically determines some to be poor, which enables them to then become rich in faith? If that were true, then it would seem to indicate wealthy individuals could not become people of faith. This would be totally inconsistent with what is seen in the lives of Abraham, Jacob, and Job. Instead, here we see God's granting faith to those who are of lower economic status. This follows God's selection of Israel to be His own people, although they were smaller and weaker than the people they displaced in the promised land of Canaan.

What does it mean to be "rich in faith" (v. 5)? It is not limited to a particular economic class or to a specific gender, although women often have a greater tendency to be fortresses of faith. Men's normal desire to be self-sufficient often keeps them from being ready to put their entire trust in God and develop that richness of faith. Richness of faith enables a person to stand firm in trust, even in the darkest situation. It doesn't mean everything turns out in our favor but, regardless, there is no wavering.

How does this type of faith develop? Our faith may grow as a result of being influenced by a mature believer who demonstrates faith. It also comes through studying the Bible and applying its truths to the specific settings in our life. We also build our faith in God through spending time in prayer.

In verse 6, James gets back to the problem of favoritism. Apparently overlooked was people's love for God. Focusing on appearances and possessions totally missed the fellowship of all believers, whether rich or poor.

James discusses rich people who did not love God or His people but, instead, opposed the church. These wealthy people exploited Christians, took them to court, and defamed them and the name of Jesus Christ. How ironic, then, that Christians were quick to show preference to a wealthy newcomer while pushing the poor to the side stand.

We know the early church included both wealthy and poor people. The issue here was not whether the believers had money, but how they treated others who tried to join their fellowship.

Being a college professor frequently places me in the position of being asked hard questions. After class one morning, a young man of a different skin color asked me, "Are you prejudiced?" I responded, "I don't think I am. Have I given you any reason to think that?" He smiled and then said, "No, I was just checking." It definitely provided food for thought!

- Describe the irony of the situation James describes.

---

### One Woman's Action

How one bold person can make a decisive action against discrimination was demonstrated when Rosa Parks refused to stand up and give her seat on the bus to a white passenger. She was in the designated area for black passengers one row behind the white section, but when seats for white passengers had been taken, the bus driver demanded she give up hers. Her subsequent arrest on December 1, 1955, inspired the Montgomery bus boycott which helped ignite the modern Civil Rights Movement.

---

## II. KEEP THE ROYAL LAW (James 2:8-13)

### A. Love Your Neighbor (v. 8)

**8 If ye fulfil the royal law according to the scripture, Thou shalt love thy neighbour as thyself, ye do well.**

No discussion of practical Christianity can progress far without turning to the subject of *love*. It stands as the foundational principle of our relationship with the heavenly Father. Love compelled the Father to give His Son, Jesus, as the ultimate sacrifice for the sins of humankind. Prior to His crucifixion, Jesus made *love* the standard for identifying disciples: "By this all will know that you are My disciples, if you have love for one another" (John 13:35 NKJV).

A far greater expansion of love can be found centuries earlier in the Law. In Leviticus 19:18, the Lord states, "You shall love your neighbor as yourself" (NKJV). This appears to be an ethical directive for all human conduct throughout the centuries. When being tested about the greatest commandment, Jesus lists loving one's neighbor second only to loving God (Matt. 22:35-39). Luke records the extended discussion as Jesus answers the question, "Who is my neighbor?" (see 10:25-37).

Loving one's neighbor isn't without effort and potential sacrifice. Some people are abrasive and irritating. Neighborly love may include going the extra mile to help someone in a helpless situation. Loving one's neighbor is to be the normal lifestyle of believers.

- Why do you suppose this command is called "the royal law"?

---

"Learning how to love your neighbor requires a willingness to draw on the strength of Jesus Christ as you die to self and live for Him. Living in this manner allows you to practice biblical love for others in spite of adverse circumstances or your feelings to the contrary."
—John C. Broger

### B. Breaking the Law (vv. 9-11)

**9 But if ye have respect to persons, ye commit sin, and are convinced of the law as transgressors. 10 For whosoever shall keep the whole law, and yet offend in one point, he is guilty of all. 11 For he that said, Do not commit adultery, said also, Do not kill. Now if thou commit no adultery, yet if thou kill, thou art become a transgressor of the law.**

Now James makes a strong statement about *favoritism*; it is far more than just a difference of opinion or lifestyle. *Discrimination* must be recognized for what it is—sin (v. 9)!

In verse 10, we see believers cannot pick and choose which commandments they will keep and which will be disregarded. Selective obedience never stands as an option! William Barclay describes it as follows:

> A man [person] may be in nearly all respects a good man [person]; and yet he may spoil himself by one fault. He may be moral in his action, pure in his speech, meticulous in his devotion. But he may be hard and self-righteous; rigid and unsympathetic; and, so on, his goodness is spoiled (*The Daily Study Bible Series: The Letters of James and Peter*).

It is possible for someone to feel self-righteous because of not breaking the "more serious" commandments; or, though having broken a serious law, to not feel guilty of having broken all of them. However, we all stand equally guilty before God. The weakness of being human, coupled with the temptations brought against us by the enemy of our soul, have led us to sin, and we all must repent.

- Why is it foolish to compare one sin with another sin?

> "Human legalism leads to human self-righteousness. Human self-righteousness denies the need for the saving, enabling grace of Christ. Human righteousness embraces the cruelest of Satan's lies, that a person can be righteous by keeping the law."—Paul David Tripp

### C. Mercy Over Judgment (vv. 12-13)

**12 So speak ye, and so do, as they that shall be judged by the law of liberty. 13 For he shall have judgment without mercy, that hath shewed no mercy; and mercy rejoiceth against judgment.**

Verses 12 and 13 seem to be a summary of the discussion of love and the Law, relating back to favoritism. At issue is the spirit in which an action is taken. Since the principle is to love one's neighbor as himself, the test then surrounds the spirit which dominates or motivates behavior. As believers, consideration must be given whether we approach in a legalistic, obligatory perspective or in an atmosphere of love reaching out to bless others.

Verse 13 emphasizes our being judged by the same criteria with which we judge others. How can we expect to receive mercy if we do not show it to others?

Jesus said, "Blessed are the merciful, for they shall receive mercy" (Matt. 5:7 NASB). We will encounter individuals who are difficult to love and give kindness. In ourselves, we might not be able to do it. For this reason, walking in the Spirit (Gal. 5:16) is vital. The first virtue of the fruit of the Spirit is *love* (v. 22).

---

- What will happen to "anyone who has not been merciful" (v. 13 NIV)?

> "The Gospel is good news of mercy to the undeserving. The symbol of the religion of Jesus is the cross, not the scales."—John Stott

---

## III. WORK YOUR FAITH (James 2:14-26)

### A. Faith Without Deeds (vv. 14-19)

(James 2:18-19 is not included in the printed text.)

**¹⁴ What doth it profit, my brethren, though a man say he hath faith, and have not works? can faith save him? ¹⁵ If a brother or sister be naked, and destitute of daily food, ¹⁶ And one of you say unto them, Depart in peace, be ye warmed and filled; notwithstanding ye give them not those things which are needful to the body; what doth it profit? ¹⁷ Even so faith, if it hath not works, is dead, being alone.**

Before looking at the relationship between faith and works (our deeds), let's define *faith*. We read in Hebrews 11:1: "Now faith is the substance of things hoped for, the evidence of things not seen." What does that mean to us? The rest of the chapter presents accounts of individuals that helps us see *faith* is commitment, confidence, and concentrated trust. "Commitment is the beginning aspect of faith. . . . Confidence is the enabling aspect of faith. . . . Concentrated trust is the sustaining aspect of faith" (Jerald Daffe, *In the Face of Evil You Can Find Faith*).

*Faith* is the means by which we experience salvation and are restored to a right relationship with the heavenly Father. We place our trust in Jesus and repent of our sins. It is the means by which we please God (Heb. 11:6).

In James 2, the author shows how faith plays out in daily living. He begins with a vital question: What value is there to claim being a person of faith and not show the corresponding actions or deeds? People can claim a relationship or position in Christ, but it has no value without the corresponding evidence. Actions do speak louder than words.

What does James mean by "works"? It goes far beyond helping someone who has fallen, or putting a few bucks in the Salvation Army kettle at Christmastime. Deeds that accompany faith must reflect moral character and conduct. They are to be an outer reflection of what is claimed to be present within. It is inconceivable to assume a person could have faith that brings a spiritual revolution and then lead a life inconsistent with the teachings of his or her Savior.

In verses 15 and 16, James shares a hypothetical situation to demonstrate the concept. Suppose someone within their community of believers does not have sufficient clothes or food. Would they speak words wishing the individual better times or do something tangible to meet the need? Could we be guilty of simply saying, "I'll pray for you," when we have the means to alleviate a needy believer's situation either personally or by soliciting corporate action?

James makes a very strong statement: *Faith* standing alone, unaccompanied by appropriate actions, is dead (v. 17)! The person who assumes life in Christ continues, even when there is no exterior evidences of practical Christianity, is living in a state of deception and spiritual death.

Consider an illustration from Charles Schulz's *Peanuts* cartoon. It is winter and the *Peanuts* characters are bundled up and skating on an outdoor pond. Charlie Brown has multiple coats on to protect from the cold. Unfortunately, he falls and cannot get back up off the ice, much less get upright on his skates. One by one, his friends stop by and look at him stretched out helplessly on his back, but no one offers to help. Finally, Lucy speaks up: "Be warmed, Charlie Brown." Then they all walk away.

Verse 18 provides a possibility of some believer arguing he has faith without evident actions. The response to this is how impossible it is to demonstrate faith without corresponding actions. So James declares, "I will show you my faith by my works" (NKJV). Our faith cannot remain dormant. It bursts out into specific actions that reflect the principles of Scripture and the lifestyle of our Lord. Otherwise, it becomes lifeless.

In verse 19, James leaves the human spiritual world and reflects on the demonic. The evil spirits believe there is one God. Their knowledge of God causes them to respond in fear and dread. They know who He is and His omnipotent power. However, this belief and knowledge does not result in their bowing down and serving Him. Here, we are again reminded that what we know and believe is not sufficient to claim faith and a relationship with God through Jesus Christ.

---

1. Answer the question in verse 14.
2. Answer the question in verse 16.
3. How do we demonstrate genuine faith in God (vv. 17-19)?

> "Faith and works are bound up in the same bundle. He that obeys God trusts God; and he that trusts God obeys God. He that is without faith is without works; and he that is without works is without faith."—Charles Spurgeon

---

B. Faith With Deeds (vv. 20-26)

(James 2:20-25 is not included in the printed text.)

**26 For as the body without the spirit is dead, so faith without works is dead also.**

In the final verses of this lesson, James demonstrates the role of actions/deeds in our faith. He refers to two well-known Old Testament individuals—the patriarch Abraham and the innkeeper/prostitute Rahab. Though totally different from each other, both demonstrate the relationship between faith and works. Before sharing their accounts of faith, James reiterates "faith without works is dead" (v. 20). Notice the strong form of address—"O vain man"—to anyone who could possibly consider faith without works. The word for *vain* also means "empty" or "foolish." Anyone who holds there can be faith without works is lacking spiritual insight.

Abraham's faith caused him to leave the modern ancient city area of Ur to move to a land God did not name (see Gen. 12:1-4). Abraham's maturity of faith became evident when God put him to the sternest test—sacrificing his only son, Isaac, the promised son of the covenant (22:1-19). Abraham's obedience showed the tremendous connection between faith and works.

Hebrews 11:19 indicates Abraham's faith was so strong he believed, if necessary, God would raise Isaac from the dead. Isaac was the firstborn of what was to be a great nation through his descendants, yet Abraham would have sacrificed him if God had not intervened at the last moment. Abraham's actions were proof of his total faith in God. This man of great faith was called "the friend of God" (James 2:23 NKJV; see also 2 Chron. 20:7; Isa. 41:8).

Words are cheap unless there is evidence to support them. James declared, "You see that a man is justified by works and not by faith alone" (2:24 NASB). He was not minimizing the role of faith in initial and continuing salvation. Rather, he wanted believers to understand the necessity of living in a manner consistent with faith after having come to salvation.

James' second example of Rahab (v. 25) furthers the argument of the balance between faith and works. She took the risk of hiding Joshua's two spies from the officials of Jericho (see Josh. 2). Rahab understood Israel would be successful in conquering her city. She requested safety for herself and her family when the attack occurred. Her faith can be seen by her inclusion in the faith chapter (Heb. 11:31). But, it goes even further. She marries an Israelite man and is one of four women mentioned in Christ's lineage (Matt. 1:5). This speaks loudly of the change that faith in God makes in an individual.

In James 2:26, for the third time, the author points to a dead faith without works. He says a human body is dead once the life spirit leaves. In the same manner, faith cannot be alive without works. The spiritual life that comes through the empowering of the Holy Spirit needs to be maintained. In reflecting on the lack of works, Paul A. Cedar writes: "Unfortunately, its stench of death hovers over many of our churches and over many of the lives of professing Christians. Often we have mouthed the correct confessions and mastered the orthodox theology, but our faith has been dead" (Lloyd J. Ogilvie, ed., *The Communicators' Commentary: James, 1, 2 Peter, Jude*).

---

1. How did Abraham and Rahab differ, and how were they alike (vv. 21-25)?
2. Explain the imagery in verse 26.

---

"Faith and works together grow/No separate life they never can know."—Hannah Moore

---

## CONCLUSION

This lesson has emphasized the need for believers to avoid the pitfall of discrimination that may arise from concentrating on a person's appearance and wealth. All forms of discrimination are in complete opposition to the royal law of loving one's neighbor. We also are reminded that our faith must be much more than words; it is to be demonstrated by our actions. Believers who practice discrimination and fail to love are living in a state of deception and they hurt the cause of Christ.

## GOLDEN TEXT CHALLENGE

"IF YE FULFIL THE ROYAL LAW ACCORDING TO THE SCRIPTURE, THOU SHALT LOVE THY NEIGHBOUR AS THYSELF, YE DO WELL" (James 2:8).

On a certain occasion, I had reached a point in my life when I was having trouble feeling love for several individuals I was called on to relate to on a daily basis. Over time, problems had developed because of personality clashes or disagreements. Quite frankly, I had become bitter toward several of these people, having come to feel that they had wronged me and never even acknowledged the deed. I had become negative in spirit, my inner turmoil spilling over into relationships that had nothing to do with the "problem people."

One Friday morning, a simple scriptural imperative was riveted into my spirit during my personal devotions: I must love people and act in love toward them because I love God—not because I have been treated well by them, or find it personally advantageous to "stroke" them. This simple truth was not new to me, but I had forgotten to live by it. Burdened with a series of slights, hurts, and rejections, I was allowing my negative emotions to rule me instead of allowing the Holy Spirit to produce His fruit of practical love.

If we as Christians try to love our neighbors as ourselves without first attending to our relationship with God, we will fail miserably. However, if our interactions with others are an outflow of our interaction with God in intimate devotion—as we worship and adore Him—we will know the great joy of loving others resulting from our love for God.—**Sabord Woods**

## Daily Devotions:

M. Determined to Do Right
   Ruth 1:1-10
T. Ruth Clings to Naomi
   Ruth 1:11-18
W. Boaz Shows Kindness
   Ruth 2:8-17
T. The Greatest Commandment
   Matthew 22:34-40
F. All People Are Welcome
   Luke 14:15-24
S. God Shows No Favoritism
   Acts 10:30-38

August 16, 2015 (Lesson 11)
# Tame Your Tongue
**James 3:1-18**

**Theme:**
Practical Christianity (James)

**Central Truth:**
The tongue has power to edify or destroy.

**Focus:**
Realize words can affect others for good or evil and edify others with our speech.

**Context:**
The Book of James was probably written from Jerusalem between AD 48 and 50.

**Golden Text:**
"There is that speaketh like the piercings of a sword: but the tongue of the wise is health" (Prov. 12:18).

**Study Outline:**
I. Control Your Speech
(James 3:1-5)
II. Destructive Nature of the Tongue
(James 3:6-12)
III. Speak and Live Wisely
(James 3:13-18)

## INTRODUCTION

We use the word *tongue* in a number of figures of speech. "Tongue-twister" refers to a series of words which are difficult to pronounce when placed in sequence. "It's on the tip of my tongue"—you know the name, date, person, or event but, at the moment, just can't recall it. "It was a slip of the tongue"—you made a statement which you never intended to verbalize. Maybe it was just a one-word exclamation.

The tongue is a vital part of our body. Its movement enables us to properly pronounce words. The tongue assists in the digestive process by keeping our food between the upper and lower teeth, allowing it to be properly chewed. The tongue also has a role in taste, as most of our taste buds are located in it.

Because of verbal communication, the tongue and mouth are inseparably linked. In the books of Psalms and Proverbs, the writers convey positive and negative aspects of speech. In James 3, the apostle provides extended teaching on this area of the believer's life.

One important issue is the correlation between what we say and what we do. Words are cheap, unless supported by actions. King Saul provides an example of the dichotomy which can occur. After the Lord directed him to destroy all the Amalekites and their possessions, King Agag was spared along with some of the best of the livestock. Upon meeting the prophet Samuel, Saul quickly declared he had performed the commandment of the Lord, though he had not (1 Sam. 15:13).

In studying today's lesson, careful consideration should be given to the central truth: "The tongue has power to edify or destroy." The words we speak can bring comfort, peace, joy, and direction; or, they may be the source of division, anger, abuse, and destruction.

## I. CONTROL YOUR SPEECH (James 3:1-5)

### A. Role of Teachers (vv. 1-2)

**¹ My brethren, be not many masters, knowing that we shall receive the greater condemnation. ² For in many things we offend all. If any man offend not in word, the same is a perfect man, and able also to bridle the whole body.**

Though having referred to the use of the tongue previously in chapter 1, James now does an extended presentation about controlling one's speech. Dan G. McCartney said, "Speech . . . is the vehicle for wisdom and instruction, and for blessing. But it also is capable of enormous evil, sometimes done deliberately and sometimes simply by lack of control, and is more commonly in the employ of the evil world than righteousness. Hence, it is risky to be a teacher, someone whose profession is the use of the tongue" (*Baker Exegetical Commentary on the New Testament, James*).

Teaching can be done through various means. A common way we learn from others is through demonstration. Someone shows how, and others attempt to imitate. It is a common means by which children learn from parents and other adults. However, the most widely used method of teaching is verbal communication. Those who regularly use it to convey information in a learning setting are referred to as teachers. Some hold official positions in the church and in the community. Some receive pay while others volunteer their services.

The "teachers" referred to here (v. 1 NKJV) are operating within the community of believers. Because of their knowledge and ability, teachers tend to be given a certain status within the body. Some are teachers due to being spiritually gifted for the office (Eph. 4:11). Others become teachers in the church due to their being taught by mentors and through study of the Scriptures. Spiritual maturity is also a factor.

Reviewing Jesus' ministry, we sometimes emphasize His miracles and neglect the teaching which regularly occurred. A quick review of Matthew's Gospel indicates three-fifths of the content is presented in a teaching format (see 4:23; 9:35; 15:9; 21:23; 26:55). Then, prior to ascending into heaven, Jesus gives the Great Commission, which includes evangelism to be followed with teaching (28:18-20).

In spite of the need for teaching and teachers in the Christian community, James places a major caution for consideration. Those who desire to teach place themselves in a greater position of responsibility. If they lead people astray through false doctrines and inappropriate application, they will "incur a stricter judgment" (3:1 NASB). This responsibility should not be taken lightly for either oneself or for those who will listen.

The apostle Paul also addresses some aspects of teaching. For example, there may be the pressure to teach what people want to hear rather than the truth which strikes at their attitudes and actions (2 Tim. 4:3). He also points to how some individuals who desire to be teachers are not qualified to do so because of a lack of knowledge and practice (1 Tim. 1:7). This very easily leads into being a false teacher. These words are not intended to discourage qualified people from pursuing this form of ministry in the church. However, it does place significant responsibilities on the teacher to study and to live as an example to those being taught.

At the same time, James recognizes no one is perfect. Constantly standing before people occasionally will indicate our humanity; we may stumble in our speech and say something we never intended (3:2). When that occurs, it is imperative that we apologize and correct the error.

---

1. What does James advise in verse 1?
2. Who could call himself "perfect" (v. 2)?

> "The true test of a man's spirituality is not his ability to speak, as we are apt to think, but rather his ability to bridle his tongue."—R. Kent Hughes

---

B. Bridling the Tongue (vv. 3-5)

**³ Behold, we put bits in the horses' mouths, that they may obey us; and we turn about their whole body. ⁴ Behold also the ships, which though they be so great, and are driven of fierce winds, yet are they turned about with a very small helm, whithersoever the governor listeth. ⁵ Even so the tongue is a little member, and boasteth great things. Behold, how great a matter a little fire kindleth!**

James uses three examples to demonstrate the power of verbal communication. The recipients of this letter would be aware of the power in each of the illustrations. This reminds us of the need to use practical, understandable illustrations when teaching.

The metal bit of a horse's bridle is very small, yet it controls the entire body. Horse trainers use various shaped bits to provide greater control on the animals that are more difficult to train. In the same manner, the rudder is small in comparison to the rest of the ship but, without it, stability and direction are impossible. Without the rudder, in the fiercest winds the ship easily could roll over. Yet, with the rudder, one man keeps the ship stabilized and safe for passengers and cargo. The third illustration reflects the power and destruction of a small item. A spark or small flame can quickly explode into a raging fire, consuming everything in its path. Proverbs 16:27 likens the speech of a scoundrel to "a scorching fire" (NIV).

1. How is a ship like a horse (vv. 3-4)?
2. When have you experienced the truth of verse 5?

> **A Sick Tongue**
> Wouldn't it be great if people who have difficulty controlling their verbal outbursts and statements could go to a doctor or dentist for a cure? Scrolling through a medical listing of tongue problems, you will find labels such as geographic tongue, hairy tongue, black tongue, burning tongue, and canker sores. A list of verbal tongue problems could also be developed. However, even without it, we know the Holy Spirit will help those who want to be cured of their verbal issues.

---

## II. DESTRUCTIVE NATURE OF THE TONGUE (James 3:6-12)

### A. A Fire (v. 6)

**⁶ And the tongue is a fire, a world of iniquity: so is the tongue among our members, that it defileth the whole body, and setteth on fire the course of nature; and it is set on fire of hell.**

The inflammatory nature of the tongue must not be underestimated. Ill-chosen words hurt and divide. They can contribute to conflict which initiates war with its death and destruction. In our modern world, the statements of world leaders are scrutinized for hidden meanings or signals often tied to the cultural context.

James goes a step further in describing the negative influence of the tongue. It potentially "corrupts the whole person" (NIV). This speaks of a filthiness or rotten speaking which never produces anything positive.

The unleashed tongue sweeps like a fire, eating everything in its path and leaving only ashes. It destroys life in its path and takes years to be restored, if it is even possible. The mention of *hell* here emphasizes the sinfulness which can be generated by this small member of the human body.

---

- How does the tongue affect "the whole body"?

> "O Lord, keep our hearts, keep our eyes, keep our feet, and keep our tongues."—William Tiptaft

---

### B. A Poison (vv. 7-8)

**⁷ For every kind of beasts, and of birds, and of serpents, and of things in the sea, is tamed, and hath been tamed of mankind. ⁸ But the tongue can no man tame; it is an unruly evil, full of deadly poison.**

Prior to describing the tongue as a deadly poison, James turns to the animal kingdom for a reflection on control. He divides animal life into four categories. Initially, when reviewing the species that are part of each, one may wonder who has tamed an antelope, an alligator, or a tuna. However, this train of thought misses what the author is attempting to convey. The idea being projected is *dominion*.

The full impact of what James intends comes by returning to the Creation account. At the completion of His creative work, "God blessed [humanity] and said to them, 'Be fruitful and increase in number; fill the earth and subdue it. Rule over the fish of the sea and the birds of the air and over every living creature that moves on the ground'" (Gen. 1:28 NIV). This dominion, or ruling over, includes both the domestication and hunting of the various animals.

This ability to rule over animal life is contrasted with the human inability to control the tongue. Huge, strong animals are tamed for domestic service. Even the largest fish of the ocean can be caught. But the tongue continues to be a source of untamed destruction.

In 3:8, James describes the tongue as a poison. He provides a picture of each person having poison within and being capable of thrusting its sickening and killing effect on others. In the same way we need an outside substance sent to neutralize poison, we cannot bring our tongues under control without outside intervention. Words that seemingly "slip out" are reflective of the untamed nature of this important member of the body.

---

"You may tame the wild beast . . . but you cannot arrest the progress of that cruel word which you uttered carelessly yesterday or this morning."—Frederick Robertson

---

C. A Double Response (vv. 9-12)

⁹ **Therewith bless we God, even the Father; and therewith curse we men, which are made after the similitude of God.** ¹⁰ **Out of the same mouth proceedeth blessing and cursing. My brethren, these things ought not so to be.** ¹¹ **Doth a fountain send forth at the same place sweet water and bitter?** ¹² **Can the fig tree, my brethren, bear olive berries? Either a vine, figs? So can no fountain both yield salt water and fresh.**

James uses the directive "my brethren" (vv. 10, 12) to bring special attention to the inconsistency of speech, which can easily occur from the person who has not been able to gain control of his or her tongue. Accepting Jesus as Savior doesn't immediately cause a person to have control of speech. This is where making Him Lord and walking in the Spirit makes the difference! Unless this occurs, it is possible for a person to bless God in a worship service and speak abusively to someone outside of church.

James' seemingly calm rebuke, "This should not be" (NIV), is far more potent than it appears. He follows with examples that demonstrate the inconsistency of such actions. It is impossible for a water source to provide fresh and bitter water at the same time. Neither can a fig tree bear olives, or a grapevine grow figs. In the same manner, neither can a person claim to be a believer and not take the necessary steps to take dominion (control) of one's tongue (speech).

Jesus used a similar example in Matthew 7:16-17: "Do men gather grapes from thornbushes or figs from thistles? Even so, every good tree bears good fruit, but a bad tree bears bad fruit" (NKJV). These verses, along with the statements of James, should be a major criteria for evaluating our spiritual condition. Genuine believers should use the tongue to edify rather than destroy.

---

1. Why is it so wrong to curse another person (v. 9)?
2. What cannot happen (vv. 11-12), and what should not happen (v. 10)?

> "Kind words do not cost much. Yet they accomplish much."—Blaise Pascal

---

## III. SPEAK AND LIVE WISELY (James 3:13-18)

### A. Meekness of Wisdom (v. 13)

**¹³ Who is a wise man and endued with knowledge among you? let him shew out of a good conversation his works with meekness of wisdom.**

This verse offers a number of considerations. First, *wise man* likely refers to teachers. Second, the word *knowledge* indicates expert understanding of a particular subject. This knowledge is more than just possessing information; it includes the ability to apply the information in practical ways. Facts and details are good to know; however, they have no value unless there is the ability to apply them to life situations.

Third, James draws attention to a person's *behavior* ("conversation"). He or she may have the information and ability for application, but this needs to be accompanied by a lifestyle consistent with their abilities. Wisdom must be demonstrated in words and deeds. How can anyone claim to be wise and ascend to the position of a teacher unless he or she demonstrates being a disciple of Christ?

Fourth, we see the need for the quality of *humility* ("meekness") while demonstrating faith. Humility must never be seen as low self-image or weakness; rather, it is the opposite of prideful self-promotion. When it comes to practical Christianity, wisdom cannot be forced on either believers or unbelievers. Also, any sense of prideful presentation automatically puts up a barrier which cannot be easily overcome.

The apostle Peter said, "Be clothed with humility: for God resisteth the proud, and giveth grace to the humble. Humble yourselves therefore under the mighty hand of God, that he may exalt you in due time" (1 Peter 5:5-6).

---

- Who is truly wise and understanding?

> "Not until we have become humble and teachable, standing in awe of God's holiness and sovereignty, acknowledging our own littleness, distrusting our own thoughts, and willing to have our minds turned upside down, can divine wisdom become ours."—J. I. Packer

B. Earthly Wisdom (vv. 14-16)

**14 But if ye have bitter envying and strife in your hearts, glory not, and lie not against the truth. 15 This wisdom descendeth not from above, but is earthly, sensual, devilish. 16 For where envying and strife is, there is confusion and every evil work.**

James offers a clear description of what can be expected when earthly wisdom predominates. There is no reason to expect spiritual virtues to be evident when worldliness reigns. It is sobering to see how worldly concepts can creep in and take hold of the hearts and minds of believers when competition and personal desire reign.

In verse 14, James lists four characteristics which stem from a worldly source or perspective. He begins with *bitter envy*, which can also be translated as "bitter jealousy" (NASB). This could be ambition for a particular position or for one's view of truth. When this spirit takes over, a person becomes possessed with a zeal to serve self, regardless of truth or its consequences.

The second characteristic of self-seeking is *strife*. It logically follows that division and factions will develop when a person pushes for self rather than for the good of the whole community.

Third, James lists the characteristic of *boasting*. Usually we think of boasting in terms of emphasizing or magnifying one's accomplishments. However, the boasting (or glorying) here is against what is right or truthful. This action can creep in easily when a person desperately desires to be a leader and impress people with a "new truth," which usually consists of an old heresy. This automatically leads to the fourth characteristic, *lying*. In the original language, the term translated here means "to deceive by stating a falsehood." False teachers and false prophets bring harm to believers and bring shame to the name of Christ.

Whenever these characteristics become evident, there can be no doubt of the source. They stem from the devil and reflect an unspiritual heart and mind (v. 15). As a result of their being evident within those who inappropriately desire leadership, confusion quickly reigns (v. 16). Within the atmosphere of confusion, other errors and wrongs arise. There can be no testimony of truth to unbelievers when error wrecks the community of faith. For that reason, great care must be taken when it comes to allowing individuals to teach. Their life and doctrine need to be closely evaluated. It is a matter of life and death for them and their hearers (see 1 Tim. 4:16).

---

1. What is "earthly, sensual, devilish" (vv. 14-15)?
2. What do "jealousy and selfish ambition" cause, and why (v. 16 NASB)?

> "Almost every sinful action ever committed can be traced back to a selfish motive. It is a trait we hate in other people but justify in ourselves."—Stephen Kendrick

---

C. Heavenly Wisdom (vv. 17-18)

**17 But the wisdom that is from above is first pure, then peaceable, gentle, and easy to be entreated, full of mercy and good fruits, without partiality,**

and without hypocrisy. ⁱ⁸ **And the fruit of righteousness is sown in peace of them that make peace.**

Here we see the contrast to earthly wisdom. True or genuine wisdom, which comes from above, is characterized by virtues and actions in complete opposition to what has been described in the previous three verses. Previously, James listed four characteristic of earthly wisdom. He now lists eight traits of the wisdom from God. These characteristics should flow from a person who maintains a heart for God and walks in the Spirit.

James begins with this wisdom being *pure*, or "holy." This purity does not contain ulterior motives; instead, it seeks to reflect the image of God. Immediately following is the description of being *peaceable*. While selfish ambitions are divisive, godly wisdom does not provoke unnecessary divisions and factions. This promotes both peace with God and among our fellow believers. In the Beatitudes, purity of heart precedes being a peacemaker (Matt. 5:8-9).

The next two descriptions in James 3 go hand in hand. Genuine wisdom is *gentle*, which speaks of a patient disposition; being *easily entreated* can be translated as "submissive," "reasonable," or "ready to be convinced." This trait is being ready to yield to the right, truthful choice rather than stubbornly grasping a position whether right or wrong.

The author then lists being *full of mercy and good fruits*. *Mercy* is part of God's character. It does not flow naturally from us but from His Spirit working within us and changing our human inclinations. Not only is godly wisdom merciful but also full of positive actions toward others. How different from the self-seeking earthly wisdom!

The last two of the eight—*without partiality* and *without hypocrisy*—can be paired. In chapter 2, James deals very specifically with the issue of *favoritism*, which is of earthly rather than heavenly wisdom. Honesty does not allow hypocrisy in a person's life. In a certain way, hypocrisy is a form of self-favoritism. Wisdom from above promotes truth.

Verse 18 provides a summary that applies to the entire chapter 3: "Peacemakers who show in peace raise a harvest of righteousness" (NIV). When we have peace with God, righteousness becomes evident in all our relationship and dealings.

---

- Describe godly wisdom.

---

## CONCLUSION

Taming one's tongue isn't a onetime occurrence that never needs to be duplicated. In the same manner a bit guides a horse and a rudder a ship, we need to have a constant restraint of our speech. Unleashed negative words not only are destructive within close relationships and the community of believers, but they destroy our attempts to share the gospel with unbelievers. Only as we control our tongues will wisdom from above be evident.

## GOLDEN TEXT CHALLENGE

"THERE IS THAT SPEAKETH LIKE THE PIERCINGS OF A SWORD: BUT THE TONGUE OF THE WISE IS HEALTH" (Prov. 12:18).

There are many statements in Proverbs 12 about the hurtful nature of an evil tongue. Here are a few: "The words of the wicked are, 'Lie in wait for blood'" (v. 6 NKJV); "An evil man is trapped by his sinful talk" (v. 13 NIV); "Lying lips are abomination to the Lord" (v. 22).

Verse 18 is unsurpassed for the forcefulness of the truth it expresses. It tells of the person who uses cutting, harsh words which are "like the piercing of a sword, that chatters on, not noticing or caring how he may wound the feelings of others by his inconsiderate remarks" (Ellicott).

In contrast to the one who blurts out with angry and uncontrolled words is the person who speaks with gentleness and healing. The *Moffatt* translation says, "There is healing power in thoughtful words."

**Daily Devotions:**
- M. Unjustified Complaints Anger God
  Numbers 11:1-10
- T. Rehearse God's Word
  Deuteronomy 6:3-9
- W. Fulfill Your Promises
  Deuteronomy 23:21-23
- T. Spirit-Inspired Speech
  Matthew 10:16-20
- F. Speak the Truth in Love
  Ephesians 4:11-16
- S. Speak the Gospel Boldly
  Ephesians 6:18-20

August 23, 2015 (Lesson 12)

# Do Not Live Worldly

**James 4:1-17**

**Theme:**
Practical Christianity (James)

**Central Truth:**
Worldliness alienates the Christian from friendship with God.

**Focus:**
Recognize signs of worldliness and live in Christ's righteousness.

**Context:**
The Book of James was probably written from Jerusalem between AD 48 and 50.

**Golden Text:**
"Submit yourselves therefore to God. Resist the devil, and he will flee from you" (James 4:7).

**Study Outline:**
I. Control Your Desires
   (James 4:1-6)
II. Draw Near to God
   (James 4:7-12)
III. Pursue God's Will
   (James 4:13-17)

## INTRODUCTION

*Worldliness* and *righteousness* exist on the opposite poles of lifestyle—they are completely separated from each other. No one can "straddle the fence" and have one foot in each of the two spheres. We follow one path or the other, and they vary greatly. For that reason, Jesus taught, "Enter through the narrow gate. For wide is the gate and broad is the road that leads to destruction, and many enter through it. But small is the gate and narrow the road that leads to life, and only a few find it" (Matt. 7:13-14 NIV).

*Worldliness* is commonly perceived as participating in the dregs of immoral behavior, scandalous pursuits of pleasure, and disregard for humankind. And that is true. However, *worldliness* can also be more subtle. It consists of seeking to establish one's own standards of morality and honesty and usually is influenced by the philosophies and actions of secular society. As a result, we find many people who lead "good lives" but, because of choosing separation from Jesus, are participants in worldliness.

There are many examples throughout history of individuals and groups whose desire to live apart from worldliness has driven them to a pseudo-righteousness not seen in Scripture. The Pharisees, a sect of Judaism, devised hundreds of man-made traditions so they wouldn't break the law of God. Their legalism tended to separate them from the God they wanted to serve. In the nineteenth and twentieth centuries, various holiness groups tried to separate themselves by allowing only certain hairstyles for women, following a very strict dress code, avoiding doctors and medicines, plus not participating in activities that were deemed sinful but later accepted.

Our challenge today, as it always has been, is to seek after genuine righteousness while avoiding activities that are legitimately the sins of worldliness.

## I. CONTROL YOUR DESIRES (James 4:1-6)

### A. The Desire for Pleasure (vv. 1-3)

**[1] From whence come wars and fightings among you? come they not hence, even of your lusts that war in your members? [2] Ye lust, and have not: ye kill, and desire to have, and cannot obtain: ye fight and war, yet ye have not, because ye ask not. [3] Ye ask, and receive not, because ye ask amiss, that ye may consume it upon your lusts.**

James begins this new subject area with a question: "What causes fights and quarrels among you?" (NIV). Immediately we understand there have been, and sometimes still are, situations that go beyond simply having a difference of opinion. These are deep divisions that cause brothers and sisters to have interpersonal strife. People struggle and quarrel with each other. The peace Jesus gave is not evident within or without. Instead of cultivating love for each other, which is to be the mark of discipleship, they fuss and fight.

After asking the question, James provides a straight answer: the problem lies within themselves. Their lusts or desires for pleasure are the cause for the conflict. The word for *lust* (v. 1) in the Greek language is the basis for our English word *hedonism*. It represents participating in fleshly pursuits of pleasure, especially in unrestrained sexual activities. In verse 2, the author uses a different word for *lust*. It means "to long for or to set your heart's desire on something or someone." This could be good or bad, depending on the situation. Here, it is used in the negative.

Verse 2 provides not only a sobering moment but also a shocking statement. Would a believer actually be a party to murder? This describes the ruin which may occur when a person continues to harbor envy and an ongoing drive for pleasure. It may be hidden for a long time but, in a crisis moment, explode in dimensions far beyond what could ever be imagined. There could be lying, theft, physical abuse, divorce, and other schemes in the attempt to please self.

James brings the practice of prayer into this discussion. Some of our desires possibly could be fulfilled if we were to ask for God's provision or intervention. Why not pray about the matter? If the pleasure we desire is not in opposition to God's Word, we should present it to Him in faith, believing He will do what is best for us.

In verse 3, James says we may not receive from God because we ask inappropriately, which involves a wrong reason or motive. When Christians pray, God always answers. It may be "yes," "wait," or "no." When God says "no," there are various possible reasons. Sometimes, He knows this is not the best for us or it does not fit with His will. Other times, the request is self-centered and reflects a worldly perspective, offering no glory to God and His kingdom.

1. Why do Christians sometimes fight each other (vv. 1-2)?
2. Why are some prayers never answered (v. 3)?

> "I wish that saints would cling to Christ half as earnestly as sinners cling to the devil. If we were as willing to suffer for God as some are willing to suffer for their lusts, what perseverance and zeal would be seen on all sides!"—Charles Spurgeon

---

B. Friendship With the World (v. 4)

**⁴ Ye adulterers and adulteresses, know ye not that the friendship of the world is enmity with God? whosoever therefore will be a friend of the world is the enemy of God.**

Attempting to be a Christian while participating in worldliness is spiritual adultery. In the Old Testament, God was seen as the husband of the nation of Israel (Isa. 54:5; Jer. 3:20; Hos. 9:1). In the New Testament, the Church is presented as the bride of Christ (2 Cor. 11:1- 2; Eph. 5:24-28). Our love and commitment cannot be divided. As Jesus said, we cannot serve two masters (Matt. 6:24). When a believer looks toward the world and begins to disobey God, "it is like breaking the marriage vow. It means that all sin is sin against love. . . . It means that when we win we break God's heart, as the heart of one partner in a marriage may be broken by the desertion of the other" (William Barclay, *The Letters of James and Peter*).

We have no choice but to live on the planet Earth, which serves as our world. There are no colonies on other planets to which we may escape and live in isolation. Neither do we have the option of living in a remote desert, forest, or mountain to ensure total separation. We are to live in this world but not be of it. As Jesus prayed for His disciples, this dichotomy is plainly seen: "I pray not that thou shouldest take them out of the world, but that thou shouldest keep them from the evil" (John 17:15). The only way to fulfill the Great Commission is to live as salt and light in our communities, and presenting a Christian counterculture (Matt. 5:13-16). The Word of God, rather than the world, must be the controlling factor in our beliefs and lifestyle (see 1 John 2:15).

---

- Describe "friendship with the world" (NKJV).

### Worldliness Is . . .

*Worldliness* is succumbing to the seductions of a fallen world. *Worldliness* is being concerned with worldly affairs to the neglect of spiritual needs. *Worldliness* is the state of being directed by the outward influences of the surrounding culture. Christians must reject worldliness.

C. Grace to the Humble (vv. 5-6)

**⁵ Do ye think that the scripture saith in vain, The spirit that dwelleth in us lusteth to envy? ⁶ But he giveth more grace. Wherefore he saith, God resisteth the proud, but giveth grace unto the humble.**

Verse 5 is difficult to interpret, since there is no specific scripture with this particular statement. Apparently, James is referring to a concept common in the Old Testament. Here, *jealousy* ("envy") must be interpreted as God's desire or longing for His people's undivided love. God cannot accept or tolerate a partial or divided love. Indeed, the indwelling Holy Spirit strives to promote commitment to righteousness within the believer.

As believers, we are not left to battle the temptations of worldliness on our own. God willingly offers His grace to enable the humble to overcome the temptations of the world (v. 6). It is possible to live victoriously, overcoming sin on a daily basis. In the following verses, James provides the steps for this becoming a reality. The opposite can also be seen in this verse. God *resists*, or is in opposition to, those who take pride in themselves and follow their own desires. The term *pride* reflects haughtiness or seeing oneself as being above others. It is possible to appear humble on the exterior while maintaining a prideful attitude within.

The foolishness and fateful end of pride repeatedly can be seen in the Proverbs. Not only does God hate it, but pride brings shame, contention, and destruction (8:13; 11:2; 13:10; 16:18). Why would anyone hold to pride with its fatal future when there is the opportunity to experience God's grace in humility?

- How can we receive the grace we need to live righteously?

> "It was pride that changed angels into devils; it is humility that makes men as angels."—Augustine

## II. DRAW NEAR TO GOD (James 4:7-12)

A. Submit to God (vv. 7-8)

**⁷ Submit yourselves therefore to God. Resist the devil, and he will flee from you. ⁸ Draw nigh to God, and he will draw nigh to you. Cleanse your hands, ye sinners; and purify your hearts, ye double minded.**

*Submission* is one of the three "s" words which create some struggles for many believers; the other two are *sin* and *sacrifice*. Submission provides for the lordship of Christ in our lives. We give up our desires for independence and self-sufficiency. Only when this occurs can we fully follow the will of God. It is impossible to serve God while retaining our so-called rights. Submission begins the process of our drawing near to God. It also demonstrates humility, which is opposite of the pride denounced in verse 6.

Without submission to God, the next aspect of the verse is impossible. How can anyone resist the temptations of the devil unless committed to the Master?

We are to take a bold stand against the devil and his forces. Knowing this to be a combat outside of the physical realm, it becomes vital for us to take up the armor of God (Eph. 6:10-17) and to walk in the Spirit (Gal. 5:16). Our boldness is not in the power of our words but in power of the Scriptures. Jesus demonstrated this when being tempted after His forty-day fast in the desert (Luke 4:1-13). Our boldness must also come in the form of rebuke in the name of Jesus. This applies to any rebuke of Satan or situations caused by living in a sin-struck world. Peter and John offered healing to the lame man at the Temple gate "in the name of Jesus Christ" (Acts 3:6).

Since the devil is a defeated foe and inferior to God, James indicates that resistance to the devil will result in his fleeing. That does not mean it will be immediate, but constant resisting in the name of Jesus and in the power of the Holy Spirit will bring about release from his oppression. Could it be that many believers do not experience this deliverance due to not maintaining a consistent resistance in all areas of their lives?

In tandem with resisting the devil is drawing near to God. This speaks of striving for the closest possible relationship with Him. In the Old Testament, this verb usage speaks of the priests offering sacrifices in the Temple; however, it can be applied to all of us as we come before our God to worship in the beauty of holiness. Coming to God includes having a repentant heart and hands that are producing works of righteousness. Simply going through the postures and gestures in a worship setting isn't sufficient! There must be the corresponding inner relationship with God. Otherwise, there is a double-mindedness attempting to love God and the world.

---

1. How can we resist Satan's pull (v. 7)?
2. What is the cure for being "double minded" (v. 8)?

---

> "The will of God for your life is simply that you submit yourself to Him each day and say, 'Father, Your will for today is mine. Your pleasure for today is mine. Your work for today is mine. I trust You to be God. You lead me today and I will follow.'"—Kay Arthur

---

### B. Humble Oneself (vv. 9-10)

**9 Be afflicted, and mourn, and weep: let your laughter be turned to mourning, and your joy to heaviness. 10 Humble yourselves in the sight of the Lord, and he shall lift you up.**

Drawing near to God and being a cleansed vessel in His sight takes some serious introspection. In our modern times, "repentance" too often reflects a sense of cheap grace. An easy "I'm sorry" or "Forgive me" is offered verbally without the heaviness of heart and godly sorrow, which should accompany the acknowledging of our sins against a holy, righteous God. The hollow laughter of a worldly lifestyle needs to be replaced by a heaviness of heart until being brought into a right relationship with the heavenly Father.

In verse 10, James again refers to the need for humility. Having done the necessary drawing to God and working to control desires, the resulting humility places the person in position to be lifted up in the sight of God. "Lifting up" may, in some cases, include opening new doors for personal development, service, occupation, and ministry. Both in this life and the life to come, God rewards those who faithfully serve Him.

- How does James portray the truly repentant person?

> "Many a humble soul will be amazed to find that the seed it sowed in weakness, in the dust of daily life, has blossomed into immortal flowers under the eye of the Lord."—Harriet Beecher Stowe

## C. Do Not Judge (vv. 11-12)

**11 Speak not evil one of another, brethren. He that speaketh evil of his brother, and judgeth his brother, speaketh evil of the law, and judgeth the law: but if thou judge the law, thou art not a doer of the law, but a judge. 12 There is one lawgiver, who is able to save and to destroy: who art thou that judgest another?**

The significance of James' teaching about judging can be seen by his triple use of the word *brethren/brother*. Apparently, a problem necessitated this manner of address. "Speaking evil" does not necessarily refer to false accusations. What is said might be true, but the manner in which the words are spoken and possibly even the location make it wrong. The "speaking" could refer to slander, harsh criticism, accusations, or condemnation. This type of speech should not occur within the Christian community.

Passing judgment in this manner goes against the royal law of love and the teachings of Jesus. There is only one who has the right to judge—the Lawgiver, who is God. Anytime we assume the right to judge others, we are placing ourselves in the position God alone is qualified to fulfill. Our role as believers is to obey God's law rather than using it to judge others.

- Answer the question in verse 12.

> "You may find hundreds of faultfinders among professed Christians; but all their criticism will not lead one solitary soul to Christ." —D. L. Moody

## III. PURSUE GOD'S WILL (James 4:13-17)

### A. Vapor of Life (vv. 13-14)

**13 Go to now, ye that say, To day or to morrow we will go into such a city, and continue there a year, and buy and sell, and get gain: 14 Whereas ye**

know not what shall be on the morrow. For what is your life? It is even a vapour, that appeareth for a little time, and then vanisheth away.

No matter how long a person lives, life still appears far too short. As one ages, it seems as though time passes quicker each year. However, we know there has been no change. It simply indicates the fleeting nature of our lives. In Psalm 103, David describes our life span like grass and flowers that flourish and then wither. Within a short time, it is as though they never existed (vv. 15-16). Job describes life as a "breath" of which there is no assurance (Job 7:7 NKJV).

The insecurity of life should not promote fear or inactivity! A person who constantly fears the possibility of death has difficulty living to the fullness of their potential. Taking no risk seems to be the safest response.

James 4:13 shows a different approach; it is the picture of a person making plans to travel and reside in a city for business pursuits. Projecting for the future with distinct goals is reasonable and wise. Regardless if it is a ministry, a business, or a family's finances, individuals should plan a future course of action.

In the process of planning, one reality needs to be kept in mind—no one knows what will happen tomorrow. Not only are we not knowledgeable of the future, neither are we guaranteed to live until the next day. James asked, *What is life?* He then suggests it is a mist that appears and then quickly fades away. We do not have the ability to determine how long we will live.

Consider Jesus' parable of the presumptuous rich man (Luke 12:15-21). After having a bountiful harvest far beyond the capacity of his storage barns, he makes plans to build even bigger barns. He falsely assumes that he will live into the future and enjoy this wealth. However, that very night, he unexpectedly dies.

- According to these verses, "what is your life?"

> "Between us and heaven or hell there is only life, which is the frailest thing in the world."—Blaise Pascal

B. Doing Good (vv. 15-17)

**15 For that ye ought to say, If the Lord will, we shall live, and do this, or that. 16 But now ye rejoice in your boastings: all such rejoicing is evil. 17 Therefore to him that knoweth to do good, and doeth it not, to him it is sin.**

Verse 15 seems to fit better with the previous two verses on the vapor of life. Yet, it also fits well with the concept of doing good from the perspective of both attitude and actions. How we understand God's sovereign control over our lives influences our future planning. It also determines how we see life in general. As believers, it is imperative to live and to plan within the sphere of God's will.

If we make plans for the future without considering God's intent for our life, we are being braggadocios, boastful, and presumptuous. This is applicable to all individuals, but especially for merchants looking to expand their business in other locations. God is not opposed to wealth properly gained. He does not look with disdain on the aggressive person who demonstrates skill in business matters. The issue resides in whether or not God is included in this business equation.

Proverbs 27:1 offers a vital caution: "Do not boast about tomorrow, for you do not know what a day may bring forth" (NIV). Someone advised, "Pray as though you are going to die tonight. Work as though you will live forever." Prayer will put our plans for tomorrow in the right framework.

James completes this chapter with a broad application statement. It applies to the whole idea of pursuing God's will as well as the directives in this chapter. There can be no excuse for a person who knows the truth to refuse to do what is right—case closed. "It is sin to know what you ought to do and then not do it" (4:17 NLT). Sin separates us from God; it must be repented of and restitution made where possible.

Sin should never be considered a trivial matter. We are to lead holy lives to be found acceptable in the sight of God. Allowing sins to remain will result in a steady erosion of our spiritual life. Consider the life of Solomon. Granted the gift of wisdom as a young man, he leads Israel to an epitome of glory and constructs the Temple. However, he allows his many wives to draw him away. Initially he just builds locations for them to worship their gods. Then, with time, Solomon goes and worships with them. As a result, he does not receive the long life which had been offered conditionally on his serving God (1 Kings 3:14), and a nation is soon divided (11:31).

---

1. How should we approach tomorrow (vv. 15-16)?
2. When is inaction sinful (v. 17)?

---

"Life becomes harder for us when we live for others, but it also becomes richer and happier."—Albert Schweitzer

---

## CONCLUSION

Today's lesson faces us with the challenge of being in the world but not of it. We, of necessity, live and work with people who do not share our commitment to Scripture and a lifestyle of holiness. This forces us to be careful not to inadvertently adopt their habits and views. It becomes vital for us to distinguish between the signs of worldliness and the practice of righteousness.

## GOLDEN TEXT CHALLENGE

"SUBMIT YOURSELVES THEREFORE TO GOD. RESIST THE DEVIL, AND HE WILL FLEE FROM YOU" (James 4:7).

James here used the language of warfare. A soldier submits to his commanding officer and courageously stands against the enemy. The believer is to submit to God and then to stand bravely against the devil, the enemy of his soul. If he does this, he is given the assurance that the devil will flee from him. The devil will flee even as he did from Jesus when he found that his temptations in the wilderness were of no avail.

In submitting himself to God, the believer becomes the devil's foe. The position of victory for the believer is submission to the One and resistance to the other. The devil fears only those who are completely committed to God. This fear causes the devil to flee and the believer is then free.

James has stated an amazing fact: The Christian soldier is the only warrior who is absolutely guaranteed the joy of always being in pursuit of a fleeing foe.

**Daily Devotions:**

M. Reluctance to Leave Worldly Community
   Genesis 19:15-20
T. Be Careful What You Wish For
   1 Samuel 8:10-22
W. Stand for Righteousness
   Daniel 3:12-18
T. Do Not Worry
   Matthew 6:25-34
F. God's Wrath Against Ungodliness
   Romans 1:18-25
S. Be Transformed
   Romans 12:1-3

August 30, 2015 (Lesson 13)
# Cultivate Right Attitudes
### James 5:1-20

**Theme:**
Practical Christianity (James)

**Central Truth:**
Right attitudes lead us to magnify God and treat others fairly.

**Focus:**
Identify and cultivate attitudes that glorify God.

**Context:**
The Book of James was probably written from Jerusalem between AD 48 and 50.

**Golden Text:**
"Be ye also patient; stablish your hearts: for the coming of the Lord draweth nigh" (James 5:8).

**Study Outline:**
 I. Pursue Justice
    (James 5:1-6)
 II. Be Patient in Suffering
    (James 5:7-12)
 III. Depend on God
    (James 5:13-20)

## INTRODUCTION

Becoming a believer does not automatically cause a person to cultivate and display biblical attitudes which glorify God. Yes, through regeneration we become new creations, adopted by the heavenly Father. However, this does not produce a maturity in knowing what our attitudes should be in the varied situations that arise. Our human nature and fleshly inclinations need to be brought under control.

For many of us, our personalities are such that projecting right attitudes can be a considerable challenge. Some struggle with a temperament which may flash in angry words and actions. Or, it could be stubbornness which creates problems. Others see things through a negative lens—they are the "glass half-empty" people. There are also individuals so passive that they find it hard to speak out against what is wrong.

All believers should seek to identify and cultivate attitudes that glorify God. For this to become a reality, we must intentionally strive to follow the principles of Scripture through the strength of the Holy Spirit. Right attitudes become a part of our lives as we cultivate them with God's help.

I. PURSUE JUSTICE (James 5:1-6)

A. Corruption of Riches (vv. 1-3)

**¹ Go to now, ye rich men, weep and howl for your miseries that shall come upon you. ² Your riches are corrupted, and your garments are moth-eaten. ³ Your gold and silver is cankered; and the rust of them shall be a witness against you, and shall eat your flesh as it were fire. Ye have heaped treasure together for the last days.**

James speaks to wealthy unbelievers, calling them to repentance. They are told to weep and wail because of the misery that awaits them. The directive to "weep" is the same term used when Peter "wept bitterly" in repentance after having denied Christ (Matt. 26:75). The "misery" that will come on them is the same wording Paul uses in Romans 3:16 to warn of the sorrow that awaits the unrighteous.

To emphasize the difficulty that the wealthy unrighteous face, James speaks of the destruction of their wealth (v. 2). His words are similar to what Jesus taught about selfishly storing up treasures (Matt. 6:19). James' description of gold and silver corroding is not literal, since these two metals are not subject to rust. It is better to understand this as a statement of how one's metal wealth becomes worthless, if it is only stored or hoarded and never used righteously. Besides, no one can take their wealth with them beyond the grave. Speaking of wealth being moth-eaten is a reminder of how expensive cloth was a source of wealth and trade.

Verse 3 is a personal warning of how their wealth will become a witness against them. There will be more than just the loss of their possessions; their flesh will be destroyed. This hoarding of wealth is the opposite of laying up "treasures in heaven" as encouraged by Jesus (Matt. 6:20).

- What awaits people who are ruled by greed?

> "When Jesus warns us not to store up treasures on earth, it's not just because wealth might be lost; it's because wealth will always be lost. Either it leaves us while we live, or we leave it when we die."—Randy Alcorn

B. Condemnation of Riches (vv. 4-6)

**⁴ Behold, the hire of the labourers who have reaped down your fields, which is of you kept back by fraud, crieth: and the cries of them which have reaped are entered into the ears of the Lord of sabaoth. ⁵ Ye have lived in pleasure on the earth, and been wanton; ye have nourished your hearts, as in a day of slaughter. ⁶ Ye have condemned and killed the just; and he doth not resist you.**

Wealth in itself is not in contrast to any Christian principle. One can be extremely wealthy and still be a God-fearing believer. The accounts of Abraham,

Isaac, and Jacob reflect this reality. Genesis 13:2 states, "Abram had become very wealthy in livestock and in silver and gold" (NIV). When rescuing Lot from being captured, Abraham mustered a small army of 318 trained men who had been born in his household (14:14). Isaac is described as becoming very wealthy and having so many livestock that the Philistines envied him (26:12-14). Jacob is described as being "exceedingly prosperous" with a large number of livestock and servants (30:43 NKJV).

James' declaration against riches concerns wealthy individuals who cheated their workers by withholding their wages (5:4). Apparently, they assumed no one knew about the fraud that had been taking place. However, the Lord heard the cries of their harvesters. Workers were not paid on a weekly or biweekly basis, such as we are acquainted with in our society. In Palestine, these day laborers were recipients of low pay and were to be paid at the end of each day's work. Holding back even a portion of the pay could result in hunger for them and their families.

God's law made special provisions guaranteeing proper payment. Deuteronomy 24:14-15 indicates payment was to be made prior to sunset. Failure to do so would result in laborers crying to the Lord and His declaring the employer guilty of sin. Leviticus 19:13 states that payment of daily wages was not to be delayed until the next morning.

The unjust, sinful actions of the wealthy enabled them to live in "luxury and self-indulgence" (James 5:5 NIV). In order to maintain this lifestyle, they thought nothing of accomplishing their desires on the backs of the poor. They were willing to even take other people's lives to get what they desired. No thought was given to their future accounting before the Lord. They lived only for pleasing self in the now.

---

- How had the wealthy exploited the common laborers? Where is this happening today?

> "Cruelty to the poor is . . . treachery to comrades."—G. K. Chesterton

---

II. BE PATIENT IN SUFFERING (James 5:7-12)

A. Wait Patiently (vv. 7-8)

**⁷ Be patient therefore, brethren, unto the coming of the Lord. Behold, the husbandman waiteth for the precious fruit of the earth, and hath long patience for it, until he receive the early and latter rain. ⁸ Be ye also patient; stablish your hearts: for the coming of the Lord draweth nigh.**

Oppression by the wealthy is one form of suffering found everywhere. That is to be expected from unregenerate individuals whose main purpose is serving and pleasing self. Making the situation worse is that the economically lower class find themselves in an endless cycle of poverty. When there are no other jobs available with a larger wage, there is no hope of escape. Also, when there is no one to champion the cause of the oppressed and bring about social change, it furthers the sense of hopelessness.

Once again, using the personal address of "brethren," James offered a pattern or perspective to help these suffering believers. He asked them to be patient in the middle of their suffering. This is not a statement of simply accepting their plight with an attitude of despair and helplessness. Instead, they were to keep alive their expectancy of the Lord's return. The early church existed in an attitude of expecting Jesus to return to earth in their lifetime. However, some time had passed since His ascension. James asked the believers to "be patient . . . until the Lord's coming" (v. 7 NIV).

The example of farmers waiting for the crops to grow, mature, and then ripen provides an excellent example of patience. In Israel, the "early rains," which provided the necessary moisture for planting, arrived in the fall, after mid-October. The "latter rain" came in spring, through April. This necessitated an extended period of patience. There was no way to hurry the process. In the same way a farmer waits for the harvest, believers are to faithfully await and expect the Lord's return.

- What should Christians learn from farmers?

> "The word *patience* means the willingness to stay where we are and live the situation out to the full in the belief that something hidden there will manifest itself to us."—Henri Nouwen

### B. Avoid Grumbling (v. 9)

**9 Grudge not one against another, brethren, lest ye be condemned: behold, the judge standeth before the door.**

When difficult circumstances overwhelm a group of people, even believers, it becomes so easy to blame or to grumble against one another. Hard times may compromise rational or spiritual thinking. For that reason, it is imperative that we maintain attitudes based on spiritual principles and brotherly love. Failure to do so causes sin to arise in our own hearts and then fosters unacceptable outward actions.

James reminds these believers that their unacceptable behavior is subject to God's judgment. It is not just their oppressors who will face God and answer for their sins.

> "Acrid bitterness inevitably seeps into the lives of people who harbor grudges and suppress anger, and bitterness is always a poison. It keeps your pain alive instead of letting you deal with it and get beyond it. Bitterness sentences you to relive the hurt over and over."—Lee Strobel

C. Endure Suffering (vv. 10-11)

**¹⁰ Take, my brethren, the prophets, who have spoken in the name of the Lord, for an example of suffering affliction, and of patience. ¹¹ Behold, we count them happy which endure. Ye have heard of the patience of Job, and have seen the end of the Lord; that the Lord is very pitiful, and of tender mercy.**

James now points to the need for these believers to endure their suffering. They are to demonstrate patience, understanding that difficult circumstances are not unusual for followers of the Lord. He points them to the prophets of the past who demonstrated patience in their sufferings. It is interesting that James does not indicate any prophets by name. Neither does he include a particular incident when a prophet exhibited patience in suffering. Very likely, his readers would have been knowledgeable of them.

James' statement in verse 10 also could be seen as a reminder of Jesus' words in Matthew 5:11-12: "Blessed are you when people insult you, persecute you . . . for in the same way they persecuted the prophets who were before you" (NIV).

The reference to Job (James 5:11) highlights the attitude of patience. Job lost everything—possessions, family, and health. Also, his good friends who came and mourned with him were unable to offer any helpful consolation or advice. Job refused to curse God and die, as suggested by his grief-stricken wife. Though he struggled with everything that had come his way, his faith in God remained firm.

1. Who is "happy," and why?
2. Why should we trust the Lord?

"To learn strong faith is to endure great trials. I have learned my faith by standing firm amid severe testings."—George Mueller

D. Speak Truth (v. 12)

**¹² But above all things, my brethren, swear not, neither by heaven, neither by the earth, neither by any other oath: but let your yea be yea; and your nay, nay; lest ye fall into condemnation.**

What a switch in direction with this verse! James jumps from patience to refraining from swearing. In this time period, oath-taking was common, prompting James to address this practice. His words mirror Jesus' teaching on the same issue: "Do not swear an oath at all: either by heaven, for it is God's throne; or by the earth, for it is his footstool; or by Jerusalem, for it is the city of the Great King. And do not swear by your head, for you cannot make even one hair white or black. All you need to say is simply 'Yes' or 'No'" (Matt. 5:34-37 NIV).

The real issue is *truth*. When an individual is a person of character, there is no need to attempt to have further backing for the truthfulness of one's words! They will be accepted at face value. If anyone doubts the truthfulness of your speech, no amount of oath-taking will change their opinion. Also, if a person is lying, the oath will not make it truthful. In our speech, a simple affirmation or denial should be sufficient. If a person makes a false statement in the Lord's name, he or she will be condemned.

- What can cause us to "fall under judgment" (NASB)?

> "No oath is necessary for the truthful person."—D. A. Carson

## III. DEPEND ON GOD (James 5:13-20)

### A. Prayer for Healing (vv. 13-16)

¹³ **Is any among you afflicted? let him pray. Is any merry? let him sing psalms.** ¹⁴ **Is any sick among you? let him call for the elders of the church; and let them pray over him, anointing him with oil in the name of the Lord:** ¹⁵ **And the prayer of faith shall save the sick, and the Lord shall raise him up; and if he have committed sins, they shall be forgiven him.** ¹⁶ **Confess your faults one to another, and pray one for another, that ye may be healed. The effectual fervent prayer of a righteous man availeth much.**

When is it appropriate to pray? Are there any limits to what could be considered a legitimate time and place for prayer? Will we place our trust in the Lord and express our need, regardless if it is large or small? Hearing a small child's prayer request can quickly remind us of the opportunity to pray for some of the smallest items of importance. Great care must be taken not to limit our prayers to only the big events in our lives.

Keeping in mind the context of suffering, James offers sovereign intervention as a remedy. If a believer is experiencing any type of difficulty, then prayer should be offered. This should be just as normal as singing when cheerfulness pervades. Cheerfulness is a matter of the soul that supersedes current circumstances. Paul and Silas singing in a Philippian jail at midnight is a classic demonstration. They had been physically beaten and illegally jailed, yet they sang the praises of God (Acts 16:23-25).

Here is a good point to remind us of Paul's directive about singing. Please note it is not within the atmosphere of a corporate worship service. "Sing and make music in your heart to the Lord" (Eph. 5:19 NIV). Prior to that, he includes speaking to each other using a variety of musical literature. Our ability to sing is not a factor but a matter of expressing our joy . . . even if it sounds more like noise than music.

In James 5:14, the problem of physical illness is addressed. When this occurs, the ill person is to call for the elders of the church. They are to anoint the person with oil and pray for physical recovery. The seriousness of the person's condition is evident by their being bedridden. This ministry and expectancy of healing within the body of Christ reaches back to the training of the twelve disciples. When Jesus sent out His disciples in their first training mission, He empowered them to "heal the sick, cleanse the lepers, raise the dead, cast out demons" (Matt. 10:8 NKJV).

Who are the "elders of the church"? This is not limited to individuals who have a particular position; anyone who has spiritual responsibility over other believers technically fulfills the position of *elder*. With this position comes the opportunity and responsibility to pray for the healing of those in their circle of influence.

The anointing with oil does not refer to the medicinal aspect of its usage. Here we see olive oil as symbolic of the work of the Holy Spirit.

James indicates a sense of expectancy. When prayer for healing is offered, those praying and the one being prayed for are to expect a positive result. The sick will be healed and raised from their beds of afflictions. Could it possibly be that more believers are not healed because of the lack of prayers? Could it be the lack of faith and expectancy on our part hinders healing? Remember the healing of the paralytic in Mark 2:1-5. Jesus noted the faith of the four men who carried the paralyzed man and labored to set him inside an impassably crowded house.

The latter portion of verse 15 of the text raises questions: Will our prayers bring forgiveness to another individual? If the prayers of others produce forgiveness, where does personal repentance come into the picture?

The context suggests the bedridden person was suffering as a result of unforgiven sin in his or her life. Because this person turns to God for forgiveness, physical healing can occur as the elders pray. Adam Clarke said, "It would be incongruent for God to exert His miraculous power in saving a body, the soul of which was in a state of condemnation to eternal death."

In verse 16, James writes of believers confessing their sins to other believers. Believers cannot expect God to answer their prayers when harboring unconfessed sins. But, when a believer stands in righteousness before God and offers a petition prompted and inspired by the Holy Spirit, positive results will occur.

1. What is the purpose of anointing with oil (v. 14)?
2. How are healing and forgiveness connected (v. 15)?
3. What is "powerful and effective" (v. 16 NIV), and why?

> "Christ is the Good Physician. There is no disease He cannot heal; no sin He cannot remove; no trouble He cannot help."—James H. Aughey

B. Pray for Miracles (vv. 17-18)

(James 5:17-18 is not included in the printed text.)

A *miracle* is an event which is not in accord with the natural process of events. It is in opposition to the normal laws of nature; it is a superhuman act. The Old Testament includes accounts of miracles affecting a whole nation and individuals. They range from manna on the ground six days out of every seven to feed an entire nation (Ex. 16:14-26) to a borrowed axhead floating to the top of the river into which it had fallen (2 Kings 6:5-6).

James reminds his readers that praying for the sick fits into the same framework as praying for miraculous events of all types. He uses the example of the prophet Elijah. Though human like every one of them, his powerful praying impacted the country's climate. He prayed, and a drought in which there was no dew or rain lasted for several years (1 Kings 17:1). After the Mount Carmel contest with the prophets of Baal, Elijah earnestly prayed again, and rain reappeared (18:42-45).

We know Elijah was not a superhero. He had frailties just as we do. Hearing the death threat of Jezebel, he ran for his life, but it did not negate the reality of his being able to pray!

---

- What can we learn from Elijah's example?

> **Miraculous Answer**
>
> In 1969, a major flood covered one-third of the city of Minot, North Dakota. Dikes surrounded the major buildings of Northwest Bible College, necessitating students to return home for a number of weeks until alternate facilities could be found. One married couple from Chile temporarily was living in a one-room apartment with a one-burner hot plate. When the element burned out, he simply placed his hand on the hot plate. "In the name of Jesus," he said. A miracle took place. The element was repaired and they used it for weeks to come.

---

C. Pray for Restoration (vv. 19-20)

**19 Brethren, if any of you do err from the truth, and one convert him;
20 Let him know, that he which converteth the sinner from the error of his way shall save a soul from death, and shall hide a multitude of sins.**

Praying for the restoration of individuals who have fallen into error and for the conversion of unbelievers should be normative for Christians. Spiritual restoration and spiritual transformation are a divine intervention of the Holy Spirit. We who may be used in these settings are only the instruments of God.

To stray from the truth is far more than a minor error in judgment—it is sin. Remaining in sin results in death.

Why were these last two verses used to close the epistle? Possibly, James was pointing his readers to a major area of ministry. They were surrounded by people who needed to hear the gospel of Jesus Christ. Also, some of their own may have strayed from truth and become lost in deception.

---

- How should we respond to a Christian who goes astray?

> "To convert somebody, go and take them by the hand and guide them."—Thomas Aquinas

## CONCLUSION

Right attitudes lead us to magnify God and treat others fairly. Justice, patience in suffering, and dependence on God are attitudes we need to cultivate, to the best of our ability through the empowerment of the Holy Spirit. It not only will provide a fuller life for us, but also cause a caring attitude toward sinners.

## GOLDEN TEXT CHALLENGE

"BE YE ALSO PATIENT; STABLISH YOUR HEARTS: FOR THE COMING OF THE LORD DRAWETH NIGH" (James 5:8).

*Patience* is the ability in Christ to take delays, absorb opposition, and overcome discouragements without failing either in faith or in our obedience. It is the grace to wait confidently without anxiety and without fainting. *Patience* is the triumph of faith over circumstances.

Patience must prevail against provocations. The believers to whom James wrote were oppressed by the wealthy (2:6-7). The wealthy had held back the wages of the people whom they hired and had killed the just (5:4-6). Even though the just had been praying and the answers seemed not to come, the servants of the Lord were to be patient (v. 7).

Verse 8 says we are to have patience regarding the coming of the Lord. There is no assurance that provocations and persecution will cease; they will not. But these do not delay or annul the promise of Christ's return. In fact, as the processes of cultivation tell the farmer the harvest is coming, the processes of this age tell us, "The Lord is at hand." Therefore, we are to be patient. We are to reverse the scoffing of the world and turn it into a promise, as Peter did (2 Peter 3:1-10).

"Strengthen your hearts, for the coming of the Lord is near" (James 5:8 NASB).

**Daily Devotions:**

M. Cain's Wrong Attitude
   Genesis 4:1-7
T. Abram's Right Attitude
   Genesis 13:5-9
W. Job's Reverent Attitude
   Job 1:13-22
T. A Selfless Attitude
   1 Corinthians 10:31-33
F. Take the Long View
   2 Corinthians 4:11-18
S. The Best Attitude
   Philippians 2:1-8